D

An Introduction to Functional Grammar

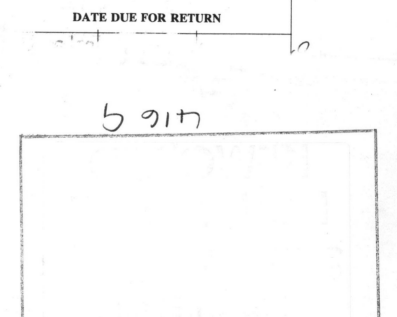

An Introduction to Functional Grammar

M.A.K. Halliday

Professor of Linguistics, the University of Sydney

Edward Arnold

First published in Great Britain 1985 by
Edward Arnold (Publishers) Ltd, 41 Bedford Square, London WC1B 3DQ

Edward Arnold (Australia) Pty Ltd, 80 Waverley Road, Caulfield East,
Victoria 3145, Australia

Edward Arnold, 300 North Charles Street, Baltimore, Maryland 21201, USA

British Library Cataloguing in Publication Data

Halliday, M.A.K.
An introduction to functional grammar.
1. English language——Grammar——1950-
I. Title
428.2 PE1112

ISBN 0-7131-6365-8

Library of Congress Catalog Card Number
84-071798

Text set in 10/11 Times Compugraphic
by Colset Private Ltd, Singapore
Printed and bound by Richard Clay (The Chaucer Press)
Limited, Bungay, Suffolk

Contents

Foreword

This book grew out of seventeen pages of class notes prepared for students in our second-year course in functional grammar and discourse analysis at the University of Sydney. Under pressure from successive groups of students, in this class and in our MA/MEd. in Applied Linguistics, it eventually attained its present size. I would like to thank all those students for their thoughtful and critical response; and also to thank the postgraduate students in the Department who have used the grammar in their own work and passed on to me their observations and suggestions.

I am extremely grateful to those colleagues who have used various drafts of the book in their teaching and provided me with challenges and comments; Joan Rothery and Clare Painter in my own department; John Collerson, of Milperra (now Macarthur) CAE; and Mark Garner, of Rusden State College (now Victoria College). I would particularly like to thank Martin Davies, of the University of Stirling, for very thoroughly working over the material and commenting on it in such detail.

It is impossible to mention more than a fraction of those whose ideas on English grammar I have drawn on over the years. But in relation to the material in these chapters I should like to acknowledge a special debt to the following: Jeffrey Ellis, Jean Ure, the late Denis Berg, Ian Catford, John Sinclair, Rodney Huddleston, Gunther Kress, Margaret Berry, Christopher Butler, Robin Fawcett, Michael Gregory, Peter Fries and Christian Matthiessen.

For encouragement and support in the preparation of the present book I owe especial gratitude to Ross Steele, President of the Applied Linguistics Association of Australia; to Richard Walker, Director of the Research and Learning Centre in Reading at Brisbane CAE; to Michael O'Toole, Head of the School of Human Communication at Murdoch University; and to Frances Christie, formerly Director of the Language Development Project at the Curriculum Development Centre, Canberra and now at the School of Education, Deakin University.

To Jim Martin I am indebted in very many ways. He has been involved throughout the work, as collaborator, as colleague and as a constant source of encouragement (and of pressure when required).

And to Ruqaiya Hasan I am indebted in all these respects and more.

What was the book to be called? I had originally referred to the expanded class notes as a 'Short Introduction to Functional Grammar'; and that was to become the title. But two objections were raised. One was that it is no longer short. I pointed out that an account of the grammar of a language in only 400 pages is no more than a thumbnail sketch and should indeed be called 'short'. But the publishers argue that it is not, on the other hand, a short book; so I have agreed to leave the word out provided that my introduction (which explains in what sense it *is* 'short') is allowed to stay as it is.

The other objection – not raised by the publishers – was that I should not be renaming 'my' grammar functional instead of systemic, when other people write grammars that they explicitly adopt the term 'functional' for. This I found difficult to accept. I am not, of course, 'renaming' anything; systemic grammar has been referred to for many years as 'systemic – functional' – there are many grammars that are functional in orientation, and systemic grammar is simply one of them. The reason the present work is not called an introduction to systemic grammar is that that is not what it is. Since it was being written specifically for those who are studying grammar for purposes of text analysis, I did not include the systemic part: that is, the system networks and realization statements, which constitute the main theoretical component (and would be central if the book was an introduction to systemic grammar). What is presented here is the functional part: that is, the interpretation of the grammatical patterns in terms of configurations of functions. These are more directly related to the analysis of text.

The title was chosen to convey this. We trust this makes the book's intention clear.

To the memory of my father

WILFRID J. HALLIDAY
(1889–1975)

who taught me to value language

Note to the Reader

The content of this book is organized in such a way that users will be able to locate grammatical features and explanation of terminology by consulting the Table of Contents, which has been designed to make the structure of the book immediately clear. It has thus been decided that an index, either of conventional grammatical terms or of the terms introduced here, would be superfluous.

Introduction

Why 'Short Introduction to Functional Grammar'?

I called this book a 'short introduction to functional grammar', and the title may need to be explained. Why 'short', why 'functional', and why 'grammar'?

It is a **short** introduction because, despite any illusion of length, it is no more than a minute fragment of an account of English grammar. Anything approaching a complete grammar would be hundreds of times this length. In fact there can be no such thing as a 'complete' account of the grammar of a language, because a language is inexhaustible. Although there can only be a finite body of text, written or spoken, in any language, the language itself — the system that lies behind the text — is of indefinite extent, so that however many distinctions we introduced into our account, up to whatever degree of fineness or 'delicacy', we would always be able to recognize some more.

It is an introduction to **functional** grammar because the conceptual framework on which it is based is a functional one rather than a formal one. It is functional in three distinct although closely related senses: in its interpretation (1) of texts, (2) of the system, and (3) of the elements of linguistic structures.

(1) It is functional in the sense that it is designed to account for how the language is **used**. Every text — that is, everything that is said or written — unfolds in some context of use; furthermore, it is the uses of language that, over tens of thousands of generations, have shaped the system. Language has evolved to satisfy human needs; and the way it is organized is functional with respect to these needs — it is not arbitrary. A functional grammar is essentially a 'natural' grammar, in the sense that everything in it can be explained, ultimately, by reference to how language is used.

(2) Following from this, the fundamental components of **meaning** in language are functional components. All languages are organized around two main kinds of meaning, the 'ideational' or reflective, and the 'interpersonal' or active. These components, called 'metafunctions' in the terminology of the present theory, are the manifestations in the linguistic system of the two very general purposes which underlie all uses of language: (i) to understand the environment (ideational), and (ii) to act on the others in it (interpersonal). Combined with these is a third metafunctional component, the 'textual', which breathes relevance into the other two.

(3) Thirdly, each **element** in a language is explained by reference to its function in the total linguistic system. In this third sense, therefore, a func-

tional grammar is one that construes all the units of a language — its clauses, phrases and so on — as organic configurations of functions. In other words, each part is interpreted as functional with respect to the whole.

It is an introduction to **grammar** because in the functional tradition in linguistics the terms used for the levels, or 'strata', of a language — the stages in the coding process from meaning to expression — are semantics, grammar, and phonology. In formal linguistics, the term 'syntax' is used to replace 'grammar'; this usage comes from the philosophy of language, where syntax is opposed to semantics (this is the context in which 'pragmatics' may come in as a third term). In the terminology of linguistics, syntax is just one part of grammar: grammar consists of syntax and vocabulary, plus — in languages which have word paradigms — also morphology. In order to make explicit the fact that syntax and vocabulary are part of the same level in the code, it is useful to refer to it comprehensively as 'lexicogrammar'; but it becomes cumbersome to use this term all the time, and the shorter term usually suffices.

There is another reason for not using the term 'syntax'. This word suggests proceeding in a particular direction, such that a language is interpreted as a system of forms, to which meanings are then attached. In the history of western linguistics, from its beginnings in ancient Greece, this was the direction that was taken: first the forms of words were studied (morphology); then in order to explain the forms of words, grammarians explored the forms of sentences (syntax); and once the forms had been established, the question was then posed: "what do these forms mean?". In a functional grammar, on the other hand, the direction is reversed. A language is interpreted as a system of meanings, accompanied by forms through which the meanings can be realized. The question is rather: "how are these meanings expressed?". This puts the forms of a language in a different perspective: as means to an end, rather than as an end in themselves. There is in fact a technical term which can be used for this kind of grammar: it has been referred to as 'synesis'. So although the book is largely about phenomena that could be called syntactic, its approach to these phenomena is that of synesis rather than that of syntax.

Scope and purpose

The theory behind the present account is known as 'systemic' theory. Systemic theory is a theory of meaning as choice, by which a language, or any other semiotic system, is interpreted as networks of interlocking options: 'either this, or that, or the other', 'either more like the one or more like the other', and so on. Applied to the description of a language, it means starting with the most general features and proceeding step by step so as to become ever more specific: 'a message is either about doing, or about thinking, or about being; if it is about doing, this is either plain action or action on something; if acting on something it is either creating or dealing with something already created', and so on; or 'a syllable is either open (ending in a vowel) or closed (ending in a consonant); if closed, the closure may be voiced or unvoiced'. Whatever is chosen in one system becomes the way in to a set of choices in another, and we go on as far as we need to, or as far as we can in the time available, or as far as we know how.

What is presented here, however, is not the systemic portion of a description of English, with the grammar represented as networks of choices, but the structural portion in which we show how the options are realized. (It is for this reason that the book is not called 'A Short Introduction to Systemic – Functional Grammar'.) This does not affect the basic orientation, which is still that of 'from general to specific', with the emphasis being on a comprehensive coverage, on breadth before depth. But it does not make explicit all the steps leading from one feature to another. The systemic portion of the grammar is currently stored in a computer.

In deciding how much ground to try to cover, I have had certain guiding principles in mind. The aim has been to construct a grammar for purposes of text analysis: one that would make it possible to say sensible and useful things about any text, spoken or written, in modern English. Within that general aim, what is included here is what I have found it possible to teach in one course. The book represents about one term's hard work in a second year undergraduate programme in linguistics (say 30 hours class time, with associated tutorials), or one year-long seminar in a Master's degree programme in applied linguistics (say 54 hours), with ongoing exercises in the analysis of texts. In our own Master's course, many of the students have been specializing in TESOL; some have been teachers of English as a mother tongue, or have had some other professional concern with language in education; while others have been interested in different applications of linguistics, such as speech pathology, artificial intelligence or language planning.

There are many different purposes for which one may want to analyse a text, including ethnographic, literary, educational, pedagogical and so on. Among the particular tasks for which this grammar has been used are: analysis of children's written compositions; analysis of teacher – pupil communication ('classroom discourse'); analysis of the language of textbooks, including textbooks being translated into other languages; comparison of different registers, or functional varieties, of English; stylistic analysis of poems and short stories; analysis of foreign learners' perceptions of how their English could be improved; and analysis of spontaneous conversation, adult – adult, child – adult, and child – child. In some cases the underlying aim has been strictly practical, in others much more of a theoretical or research nature.

In any piece of discourse analysis, there are always two possible levels of achievement to aim at. One is a contribution to the **understanding** of the text: the linguistic analysis enables one to show how, and why, the text means what it does. In the process, there are likely to be revealed multiple meanings, alternatives, ambiguities, metaphors and so on. This is the lower of the two levels; it is one that should always be attainable provided the analysis is such as to relate the text to general features of the language — provided it is based on a grammar, in other words.

The higher level of achievement is a contribution to the **evaluation** of the text: the linguistic analysis may enable one to say why the text is, or is not, an effective text for its own purposes — in what respects it succeeds and in what respects it fails, or is less successful. This goal is very much harder to attain. It assumes an interpretation not only of the environment of the text, its 'context of situation' and 'context of culture', but also of how the linguistic features of a text relate systematically to the features of its environment, including the intentions of those involved in its production.

Grammar and the text

Whatever the ultimate goal that is envisaged, the actual analysis of a text in grammatical terms is only the first step. The grammatical analysis will presumably be followed up by some further commentary or exegesis. This may be still within a general theory of language, as for example if one is studying the difference between spoken and written discourse; or it may be in terms of some conceptual structure outside of language, if for example one is setting up or testing a model of learning through verbal exploration in a science classroom, or investigating the use of language in commercial advertising, political propaganda and the like.

An example of text analysis and commentary is given in Appendix 1. This is a straightforward piece of interpretation which keeps close to the text while at the same time relating it to its context of situation and of culture. Often however the subsequent steps will take us further away from the language into more abstract semiotic realms, with different modes of discourse reinterpreting, complementing, contradicting each other as the intricacies are progressively brought to light. A text can be a highly complex phenomenon, the product of a highly complex ideational and interpersonal environment.

It is obvious that an exegetical work of this kind, whether ideological, literary, educational or anything else, is a work of interpretation. There is no way of turning it into an algorithm, of specifying a series of operations to be carried out that will end up with an objective account of the text — still less of the culture by which it was engendered. What it is important to point out, however, is that even the first step, the analysis of the text in terms of its grammar, is already a work of interpretation. An automatic parser can handle a great deal of the grammar; but there are always indeterminacies, alternative interpretations, places where one has to balance one factor against another. And in most texts there will be decisions to be taken about how far to unscramble the grammatical metaphors, as described in Chapter 10.

But whatever the final purpose or direction of the analysis, there has to be a grammar at the base. Twenty years ago, when the mainstream of linguistics was in what has been called its 'syntactic age', it was necessary to argue against grammar, pointing out that it was not the beginning and the end of all study of language and that one could go a long way towards an understanding of the nature and functions of language without any grammar at all. The authors of the original *Language in Use* materials produced for the British Schools Council showed that it was possible to produce an excellent language programme for pupils in secondary schools consisting of over a hundred units none of which contained any study of grammar.

Now however it is necessary to argue the opposite case, and to insist on the importance of grammar in linguistic analysis. If I now appear as a champion of grammar, it is not because I have changed my mind on the issue, but because the issue has changed. The current preoccupation is with discourse analysis, or 'text linguistics'; and it is sometimes assumed that this can be carried on without grammar — or even that it is somehow an alternative to grammar. But this is an illusion. A discourse analysis that is not based on grammar is not an analysis at all, but simply a running commentary on a text: either an appeal has to be made to some set of non-linguistic conventions, or to some linguistic features that are trivial enough to be accessible without a grammar, like the number of words per sentence (and even the objectivity of these is often illusory); or else the exercise remains a private one in which one explanation is as good or as bad as another.

A text is a semantic unit, not a grammatical one. But meanings are realized through wordings; and without a theory of wordings — that is, a grammar — there is no way of making explicit one's interpretation of the meaning of a text. Thus the present interest in discourse analysis is in fact providing a context within which grammar has a central place.

It is also pointing the way to the kind of grammar that is required. In order to provide insights into the meaning and effectiveness of a text, a discourse grammar needs to be functional and semantic in its orientation, with the grammatical categories explained as the realization of semantic patterns. Otherwise it will face inwards rather than outwards, characterizing the text in explicit formal terms but providing no basis on which to relate it to the non-linguistic universe of its situational and cultural environment.

'Natural' grammar

A language, then, is a system for making meanings: a semantic system, with other systems for encoding the meanings it produces. The term 'semantics' does not simply refer to the meaning of words; it is the entire system of meanings of a language, expressed by grammar as well as by vocabulary. In fact the meanings are encoded in 'wordings': grammatical sequences, or 'syntagms', consisting of items of both kinds — lexical items such as most verbs and nouns, grammatical items like *the* and *of* and *if*, as well as those of an in between type such as prepositions.

The relation between the meaning and the wording is not, however, an arbitrary one; the form of the grammar relates naturally to the meanings that are being encoded. A functional grammar is designed to bring this out; it is a study of wording, but one that interprets the wording by reference to what it means.

Wordings are purely abstract pieces of code; you cannot hear or see them. The wording is re-coded in sound or writing. At this point, the relationship is largely arbitrary, although not entirely so. Thus, what is called *rain* in English is called *pioggia* in Italian, *dozhd'* in Russian and *yŭ* in Chinese; there is nothing natural about the relation of these sounds either to any other part of the code, or to the meteorological phenomenon that lies beyond the code.

What does it mean, then, to say that grammar is 'naturally' related to meaning? To judge from the way language is built up by children, as language evolved in the human species it began without any grammar at all; it was a two-level system, with meanings coded directly into expressions (sounds and gestures). This at least is how children's 'protolanguage' is organized, the symbolic system they usually construct for themselves before starting on the mother tongue. This is then replaced, in the second year of life, by a three-level system in which meanings are first coded into wordings and these wordings then recoded into expressions. There were various reasons why this step had to be taken if the system was to expand; it opened up both the potential for dialogue, the dynamic exchange of meanings with other people, and the potential for combining different kinds of meaning in one utterance — using language both to think with and to act with at the same time.

The existing interface, that between meaning and expression, was already arbitrary, or was becoming so in the later protolinguistic stage: there is no natural connection between the meaning 'I want that, give it to me' and the sound *mamama* or *nanana* often produced by a ten-month-old as its realization. It was necessary for the system to develop this frontier of arbitrariness, otherwise communication would be restricted to the relatively small range of meanings for which natural symbols can be devised. But it was not necessary that the **new** interface, that between meaning and wording, should become arbitrary; indeed there was every reason why it should not, since such a system, by the time it got rich enough to be useful, would also have become impossible to learn. Thus the lexicogrammar is a natural symbolic system.

This motif is taken up throughout the book, though without being restated each time. What it means is that both the general kinds of grammatical pattern that have evolved in language, and the specific manifestations of each kind, bear a natural relation to the meanings they have evolved to express. When a child of nineteen months saw a complex phenomenon taking place and reported it as *man clean car* 'a man was cleaning a car', the fact that this is separated into three segments reflects the interpretation of composite experiences into their component parts; the different grammatical functions assigned to *man*, *clean*, *car*, express the different roles of these parts with respect to the whole; the distinction into word classes of verb and noun reflects the analysis of experience into goings-on, expressed as verbs, and participants in the goings-on, expressed as nouns; and so on.

The adult language has built up semantic structures which enable us to 'think about' our experience — that is, to interpret it constructively — because they are plausible; they make sense and we can act on them. And the systems of meanings have in their turn engendered lexicogrammatical structures that are likewise plausible: hence we have verbs and nouns, to match the analysis of experience into processes and participants (see Chapter 5). This is how children are able to construe a grammar: because they can make a link between the categories of the grammar and the reality that is around them and inside their heads. They can see the sense that lies behind the code.

Later on, they will learn the principle of 'grammatical metaphor' (see Chapter 10), whereby meanings may be cross-coded, phenomena represented by categories other than those that evolved to represent them (e.g. *automatic car wash*). This is a later and much more complex step in the evolution (ontogeny, and presumably also phylogeny) of the system. Grammatical metaphor is a dominant feature of adult language, and it is learnt rather late. Whereas a two-year-old can handle **general** concepts, recognizing that a red ball is a kind of ball, or a goldfish a kind of fish; and a five or six-year-old can begin to handle **abstract** concepts, like the following from a child of 5; 10:

> You mightn't think *swum* was a word, but it is. It's a made-up word. Well, every word is made up, 'cause how the earth started was a very different language, wasn't it?

— it is not until around nine or ten that a child can usually handle grammatical **metaphor**. (Hence the problems that children have with evolution when they read about dinosaurs that "some learnt to swim and some learnt to fly".)

At this point we shall incorporate into the grammar the notion of congruence. Language has evolved in such a way that our interpretation of experience (thinking with language) and our interpersonal exchanges (acting with language) are coded into semantic structures that are plausible; and with these has evolved a lexicogrammatical system that extends the plausibility principle one step further, so that even at one remove we can see (or feel; the process is an unconscious one, until linguistics begins to meddle with it) the sense that lies behind the forms. A congruent expression is one in which this direct line of form to meaning to experience is maintained intact, as it is in young children's language like *man clean car*. A metaphorical expression is one in which the line is indirect. It is neither better nor worse in itself; but it is more sophisticated, and so has to be learnt. There is no very sharp line between the congruent and the metaphorical — there rarely are any sharp lines in language, since it is an evolved system and not a designed one; but the distinction is an important one for text analysis and generation. And it is of course highly relevant, although in very complex ways, for any kind of text evaluation.

Grammar and semantics

Since the relation of grammar to semantics is in this sense natural, not arbitrary, and since both are purely abstract systems of coding, how do we know where the one ends and the other begins? The answer is we don't: there is no clear line between semantics and grammar, and a functional grammar is one that is pushed in the direction of the semantics.

How far it is pushed will depend on a number of variables. The present grammar has been able to be pushed fairly far, because of the way it is organized; in particular, because of two related characteristics: one that it uses a sparse rather than a dense model of grammatical structure (ranks, not immediate constituents; see Chapter 2), the other that it is a 'choice' grammar not a 'chain' grammar (paradigmatic not syntagmatic in its conceptual organization). Putting these two together means that there is a round of choices and operations (a 'system–structure cycle') at each rank, with clause choices realized as clause structures, realized as phrase/group choices, realized as phrase/group structures and so on; and since there is a wealth of apparatus — it is an extravagant theory, not a parsimonious one — the higher rank choices in the grammar can be essentially choices in meaning without the grammar thereby losing contact with the ground.

The last point is a critical one. The grammar needs to be explicit, if it is to go on being useful: it must be possible to generate wordings from the most abstract grammatical categories by some explicit set of intermediate steps.

This can only be tested by a computer, and it takes a very long time. There is no way in which a sketch of this kind can spell out all the steps from meaning to wording. But the requirement that this should be possible leads to an important principle, namely that all the categories employed must be clearly 'there' in the grammar of the language. They are not set up simply to label differences in meaning. In other words, we do not argue: "these two sets of examples differ in meaning; therefore they must be systematically distinct in the grammar". They may be; but if there is no lexicogrammatical reflex of the distinction they are not.

If we simply took account of differences in meaning, then any set of clauses or phrases could be classified in all kinds of different ways; there would be no way of preferring one scheme over another. The fact that this is a 'functional' grammar means that it is based on meaning; but the fact that is a 'grammar' means that it is an interpretation of linguistic forms. Every distinction that is recognized in the grammar — every set of options, or 'system' in systemic terms — makes some contribution to the form of the wording. Often it will be a very indirect one, but it will be somewhere in the picture.

The relation between the semantics and the grammar is one of realization: the wording 'realizes', or encodes, the meaning. The wording, in turn, is 'realized by' sound or writing. There is no sense in asking which determines which; the relation is a symbolic one. It is not possible to point to each symbol as an isolate and ask what it means; the meaning is encoded in the wording as an integrated whole. The choice of a particular item may mean one thing, its place in the syntagm another, its combination with something else another, and its internal organization yet another. What the grammar does is to sort out all these possible variables and assign them to their specific semantic functions.

The question might be asked: why a functional grammar, and not a functional semantics? At the present state of knowledge we cannot yet describe the semantic system of a language. We can give a semantic interpretation of a text, describe the semantic system of a fairly restricted register, and provide a general account of some of the semantic features of a language; but in one way or another semantic studies remain partial and specific. We can on the other hand describe the grammar of a language, treating the system as a whole.

The present book is intended as a resource for the interpretation of texts of a broad variety of registers in modern English; it would not be possible to write a comparably general account of English semantics. Even if one could the semantic system is so vast that a short introduction to it would be many times longer than this one. And finally, even if one produced such a work, it would not do away with the need for the grammar. The semantic description might well be made to swallow the grammar, and incorporate it as a part of itself; but the analysis of a text would still be grounded in the explanation of patterns of the wording.

Sentence and word

There is no fixed upper limit to the grammar, in terms of rank; but traditionally grammar stops at the sentence (the 'clause complex' in the present description), and there is a sense in which this does form an upper bound.

Below the sentence, the typical relationship is a constructional one, of parts into wholes. In a functional grammar this means an organic configuration of elements each having its own particular functions with respect to the whole (most elements in a grammatical structure are multifunctional). One manifestation of this structural relationship is the sequence in which the elements occur; but this is only one variable among others.

Into this constructional type of organization are introduced two minor motifs: (1) structural patterns of another kind that are more like the dynamic processes of text formation (Chapter 7), and (2) non-structural forms of organization that create cohesion — reference, ellipsis and so on (Chapter 9).

Above the sentence, the position is reversed. Here the non-constructional forms of organization take over and become the norm, while only in certain cases, particular kinds of text, are there recognizable units like the structural units lower down. And the sequence in which things occur is no longer a variable available for realizing functional relationships, like Subject before or after Finite verb; it becomes a dynamic order determined by the semantic unfolding of the discourse. Looked at from the vantagepoint of the text, a sentence is the smallest unit that cannot be displaced in sequence. Changing the order of sentences in a text is about as meaningless an operation as putting the end before the beginning.

The sentence, then, does constitute a significant border post, which is why writing systems are sensitive to it and mark it off. By and large, therefore, the chapters that follow take as their domain the traditional realm of syntax, the terrain from the sentence to the word. Grammatically, that is where the action is; and within that, the fundamental unit of organization is the clause. It should be remembered that in functional grammar (where the terminology is on the whole more consistent), a clause is the same unit whether it is functioning alone (as a simple sentence) or as part of a clause complex (a compound/complex sentence).

Sentence and word are the two grammatical units that are recognized in our folk linguistics; and this incorporates a piece of good common sense. Although when we come to explain grammar we have to recognize other structural units that are intermediate between the two — groups and phrases — these are in origin just mutations of one or the other. A phrase (in the sense in which the term is used here) is a reduced strain of clause, while a group is an enlarged strain of word. Functionally, the two come together in the middle; groups and phrases share many of the same environments.

Thus sentence and word are not so sharply set off from one another; they are no different in kind — both are units in the grammar. There is a notion that when we are speaking or writing, engaged in producing text, we are making new sentences out of old words; but this is quite misleading. It is true, of course, that words get used over again more often than sentences do; much of the time, a speaker does create new sentences — sentences that are new to him, at any rate. Rather fewer of his clauses are new; phrases and groups fewer still, and words fewest of all. But speakers create new **wordings** at all ranks; it is simply that, the larger the syntagm, the more likely it is to be original. Recently I noted *busybodyish*, *obstinacitiës*, *unselfassuredness* — forms which I doubt whether the speaker had stored ready for use.

And just as words can be new, so also sentences can be old. A good stock of the wordings we use are stored at higher rank, ranging from formulaic expressions like *the manager will see you in a minute* through *it needs to be put on a sound commercial footing* to the small change of family life like *have you remembered to take your vitamin C?* and *where's that cat?*. Proverbial sayings provide an extreme case of learnt syntagms stored at higher rank, but they are by no means unique.

It is also worth pointing out that a speaker of a language has a fairly clear idea of the probabilities attached to stored items; he 'knows' (in other words it is a property of the system) how likely a particular word or group or phrase is to occur, both in the language as a whole and in any given register of the language. The treatment of probabilities is outside the scope of the present volume; but they are an important part of the grammar and will eventually need to be taken into account in the interpretation and evaluation of texts.

System and text

The grammar, then, is at once both a grammar of the system and a grammar of the text. We follow Saussure in his understanding of the relationship between the system of language and its instantiation in acts of speaking; although not in his implied conclusion, that once the text has been used as evidence for the system it can be dispensed with — it has served its purpose. This mistake (whether due to Saussure or to his interpreters) haunted linguistics for much of the twentieth century, making it obsessed with the system at the expense of the text — and hence provoking the present swing of the pendulum in the opposite direction.

Linguists of the main European functional 'schools' — the Prague school, the French functionalists, the London school, the Copenhagen school — all, in different but related ways, regarded the text as the object of linguistics along with the system. Their view would be that one cannot really understand the one without the other. It is of little use having an elegant theory of the system if it cannot account for how the system engenders text; equally, it adds little to expatiate on a text if one cannot relate it to the system that lies behind it, since anyone understanding the text does so only because they know the system.

Discourse analysis has to be founded on a study of the system of the language. At the same time, the main reason for studying the system is to throw light on discourse — on what people say and write and listen to and read. Both system and text have to be in focus of attention. Otherwise there is no way of comparing one text with another, or with what it might itself have been but was not. And, perhaps most important of all, only by starting from the system can we see the text in its aspect as a process.

The natural tendency is to think of a text as a thing — a product. This is the form in which it is presented to us as a piece of writing; and even when we admit the category of 'spoken text' we still turn it into an object in order to be able to attend to it. We 'capture' it on tape, and then 'transcribe' it into written form. Hjelmslev, however, thought of text as process; he referred to language as system and process. It is not difficult to follow him in conceiving of text as process; the problem for text analysis is that it is much harder to represent a process than it is to represent a product.

The process/product distinction is a relevant one for linguistics because it corresponds to that between our experience of speech and our experience of writing: writing exists, whereas speech happens. A written text is presented to us as product; we attend to it as product, and become aware of its 'process' aspect as a writer but not as reader or analyst, unless we consciously focus on the activities which led to its production. Spoken language on the other hand is presented to us as process; moreover like many processes it is characterized by a continuous flow, without clear segments or boundaries, so that it appears as *text* (mass noun) rather than as *a text/texts* (count noun).

Traditionally, grammar has always been the grammar of written language; and it has always been a product grammar. Perhaps not quite always: it seems that in its earliest origins classical Greek grammar was a grammar of speech — the first attempts at syntax were tied to rhetoric, to an explanation of what it is that makes spoken discourse effective. But Aristotle took grammar out of rhetoric into logic; and since then it has been mainly a grammar of written discourse. That was how it continued to evolve in classical times; that was the foundation of medieval and renaissance syntax; and that is the received 'traditional grammar' that we are still using today. It is relatively unsuited to the spoken language, which needs a more dynamic and less constructional form of representation.

One approach to this problem would be to start from the beginning and construct a grammar that was just a grammar for speech, quite different from the existing grammars of written language. That would have the advantage of being unencumbered with product-oriented concepts and categories. But it would have three serious disadvantages: (i) that it would force an artificial polarization of speech versus writing, instead of recognizing that there are all sorts of mixed categories, such as formal speech, dramatic dialogue, subtitles, written instructions and the like, which have some of the features typical of each; (ii) that it would suggest that spoken and written language derive from different systems, a distinct 'language' lying behind each, whereas while there are systematic differences between speech and writing they are varieties of one and the same language; (iii) that it would make it extremely difficult to compare spoken and written texts, to show the influence of one mode on the other or to bring out the special properties of each in contrastive terms.

The spoken language

Perhaps the greatest single event in the history of linguistics was the invention of the tape recorder, which for the first time has captured natural conversation and made it accessible to systematic study.

Why is speech important? It is not because of any intrinsic value in spoken texts. Communities without a written language obviously have their literary and sacred texts in spoken form; when writing evolves, value tends to be transferred to the written language and speech is largely ignored; but neither mode of itself gives higher value to the text. Nor is it because speech comes first in the history of the race and of the individual; or because it is in some sense logically prior, which is in any case difficult to justify. The reason lies much deeper than this: that the potential of the system is more richly developed, and more fully revealed, in speech.

There are perhaps two main reasons for this, underlying both of which is the same general principle, that of the **unconscious** nature of spoken language. One is that spoken language responds continually to the small but subtle changes in its environment, both verbal and non-verbal, and in so doing exhibits a rich pattern of semantic, and hence also of grammatical, variation that does not get explored in writing. The context of spoken language is in a constant state of flux, and the language has to be equally mobile and alert. This puts an intense semantic pressure not only on those systems that vary the form of the message, such as those of theme and information, but also on highly-strung ones like tense and modality. The fact that grammars of English tend to be rather impoverished in their treatment of these systems is because they are much less richly exploited in the written language.

The second reason is that much of what the written language achieves lexically is achieved by the spoken language through the grammar. I have often pointed out that speech is no less complex than writing, but that the two gain their complexity in different ways. The complexity of writing lies in its density, the packing together of lexical content, but in rather simple grammatical frames. Take for example *the outlook is for continued high levels of liquidity*. As a clause this could hardly be simpler; the complexity lies in the densely-packed *continued high levels of liquidity*. We could 'translate' this into speech progressively as *liquidity will continue to be at a high level*, *the amount of cash flowing will continue to be high*, *cash is going to go on being freely available*, and so on; but this kind of meaning is typically expressed in written language and it soon becomes a fish out of water. The complexity of spoken language is more like that of a dance; it is not static and dense but mobile and intricate, like

> but you can't get the whole set done all at once because if you do you won't have any left to use at home, unless you just took the lids in and kept the boxes, in which case you wouldn't have to have had everything unpacked first; but then you couldn't be sure the designs would match, so . . .

Here much more of the meaning is expressed by grammar than by vocabulary. As a consequence, the sentence structure is highly complex, reaching degrees of complexity that are rarely attained in writing.

It is in spontaneous, operational speech that the grammatical system of a language is most fully exploited, such that its semantic frontiers expand and its potential for meaning is enhanced. This is why we have to look to spoken discourse for at least some of the evidence on which to base our theory of the language. But some linguists — or rather, perhaps, philosophers of language — have tended to take over the folk belief, typical of a written culture, according to which spoken language is disorganized and featureless, while only writing shows a wealth of structure and a purity of pattern. This is then 'demonstrated' by transcriptions in which speech is reduced to writing and made to look like a dog's dinner. Now speech was not meant to be written down, so it often looks silly, just as writing often sounds silly when it is read aloud; but the disorder and fragmentation are a feature of the way it is transcribed. Even a sympathetic transcription like that above cannot represent it adequately, because it shows none of the intonation or rhythm or variation in tempo and loudness; but it does show the way it is organized grammatically, and so enable us to analyse it as a text.

The problem is, however, that the kind of grammatical agility that is embodied in a passage like that one is not well represented by standard techniques of analysis and presentation. What is needed is a much more dynamic model of grammar in which progressive interdependencies of this kind are seen as typical rather than exceptional (see the brief discussion in Chapter 7). It should be added that no such model is being offered here, although the notion of the clause complex is intended to go a little way in that direction.

The unconsciousness of language

Lying beyond both the points raised above is the unconscious nature of spontaneous speech; and it is just in this respect that we should perhaps insist on giving priority to spoken language. There is a sense in which the nature of language itself is determined by the mode in which it is first learnt; and that is the spoken mode.

In spoken language, we perform without thinking. Talking is like walking (and developmentally the two go together; protolanguage goes with crawling, language with walking): if you think about it, you stumble (which is a metaphor we often use). This means that the categories of our language represent unconscious rather than conscious slices of meaning; and this is one of the main problems for a grammatical theory.

Suppose we think consciously about the difference between living and non-living things; and, within living things, about the difference between females and males. We will be able to draw the lines fairly clearly, but recognizing some indeterminate instances. Suppose now we want to explain to a learner of English what the meaning of *he*, *she* and *it* is. We can refer to animate and inanimate, and within animate to male and female. But when we listen to people talking English we find that the unconscious meaning of *he she* and *it* does not correspond to our conscious structuring of the world of creatures and things. We hear stretches of conversation like

> Look out! he's off the rails.
> — Oh, him. He always comes off.

referring to a truck on a child's electric train layout; or

> Don't give me the baby! I wouldn't know how to hold it.

Now it is always possible to explain particular instances, and even whole classes of instances; textbooks of English typically contain generalizations about special cases: ships and cars as *she*, for example. But these are stereotypes; they tend to be trivial, and often inaccurate: most people do not, in fact, call ships and cars *she* except in certain rather selfconscious contexts. The real meaning of the gender system in English is vastly more complex; and — this is the point — does not correspond to any of our conscious categorizations of experience. It cannot be defined, succinctly or even discursively, because the category only exists in the unconscious semantic system of the English language.

This particular category is not a very important one; it is no great matter if a foreign learner of English gets it 'wrong', and it happens to be one in which there is a lot of leeway: variation among different groups, individuals, situations and states of mind. But the principle applies across the entire system; and some of the categories are more critical. A well-known problem case for learners of English is the category of 'definite' represented by *the*, the so-called 'definite article'. The name 'definite' is an attempt to give a brief definition; there have been hundreds of discursive statements, containing many illuminating observations; but it is quite impossible to give an exhaustive account because the only way of referring to the category is by itself: *the* means 'the'. The meaning is built into our unconscious. This does not mean it cannot be learnt; but it can only be learnt in use.

This book is not a textbook of English; it is an interpretation of the English code. No attempt is made to 'teach' the categories. But an attempt is made to interpret some of them, especially the difficult and important ones like Subject (Chapter 4).

There have been so many failed attempts to define the Subject in English that grammarians have tended to give up in despair and claim that it 'has no meaning'. But it is absurd — not to mention arrogant — to assert that because you cannot define something, therefore it has no meaning. There are many categories in English grammar that I do not 'know' the meaning of — that is, to which I could give no adequate gloss which would relate them to the categories of my conscious experience. Even those of which we have some conscious understanding, however, cannot be fully defined — that is, glossed in exactly equivalent wordings. They have evolved in order to say something that cannot be said in any other way; hence, they are strictly ineffable. The best one can do is to display them at work, in paradigmatic contexts, so as to highlight the semantic distinctions they are enshrining.

There are some who find it very difficult, perhaps threatening even, to bring semantic distinctions to the level of consciousness. Such people face a problem with grammar similar to that faced by the so-called 'tone deaf' with respect to intonation. So far as I know, no-one who is tone deaf speaks his language on a monotone, or with an intonation that is in any way disordered; such people merely have trouble in bringing it to consciousness, and therefore in analysing that of their own language or learning that of a foreign one. In the same way, those who are 'grammar deaf' make all the same subtle semantic distinctions as other speakers of the language; yet they fail to recognize them when they are pointed out, and will even deny that they are possible. (I know of no quick cure for this condition. But a good dose of analysis of spontaneous speech can help.)

Theoretical approach

The theory on which this description in based, systemic theory, follows in the European functional tradition. It is largely based on Firth's system–structure theory, but derives more abstract principles from Hjelmslev and owes many ideas to the Prague school. The organizing concept is that of the 'system', which is used essentially in Firth's sense of a functional paradigm but developed into the formal construct of a 'system network'.

A system network is a theory of language as choice. It represents a language, or any part of a language, as a resource for making meaning by choosing. Each choice point in the network specifies (1) an environment, consisting of choices already made, and (2) a set of possibilities of which one is (to be) chosen; (1) and (2) taken together constitute a 'system' in this technical sense. This can be read either synoptically or dynamically: either 'if feature *a* (and *b* . . .) is present, then either *x* or *y* (or *z* . . .) is present', or 'if you have chosen feature *a* (and *b* . . .), then go on to choose either *x* or *y* (or *z* . . .)'.

This book is not an account of the theory, nor does it present system networks for the grammar of English. It presents the structures which are the output of the networks — which realize, collectively, the sets of features that are chosen. It is not a 'structural' grammar (nor a 'structuralist' grammar in the American sense): such grammars are syntagmatic, having structure as the organizing concept, and so using special devices to relate one structure to another. A systemic grammar is paradigmatic; hence there is no difference between description and agnation — describing something *consists in* relating it to everything else. Structure is an output device, the mechanism for expressing the choices that have been made.

The reason for using structural rather than systemic representations for discourse analysis is that structures are less abstract; they are so to speak 'nearer' the text. The most direct move in the analysis of a text is to give it a structural interpretation, and this is what is done here. All the structural analyses could be reinterpreted in terms of the features selected. This is not done in the chapters that follow; but as a general rule the principal systemic features are introduced as descriptive categories, and the set of alternatives shown for each.

Up to the limits of delicacy to which the analysis is taken, therefore, every feature of a text can be related to the overall system of English. As far as coverage is concerned, the analysis covers the clause, in its textual (Chapter 3), interpersonal (Chapter 4) and ideational (Chapter 5) aspects; primary classes of group and phrase (Chapter 6); and the clause complex (Chapter 7); there are also brief treatments of cohesion (Chapter 9) and grammatical metaphor (Chapter 10). In addition, as already mentioned, the description incorporates certain features of the spoken language, not only because of the importance of spoken texts but also because a framework that does not accommodate the special properties of speech is presenting an impoverished view of the system. The particular features of spoken English that are treated, also very summarily, are rhythm (Chapter 1), information focus (tonicity; Chapter 8) and key (tone; also Chapter 8). Other topics that are discussed with a concern for the rather wider range of options typically exploited in speech are theme (Chapter 3), the clause complex (Chapter 7) and modality (Chapters 4 and 10).

But there is no suggestion that the spoken language should be treated as a separate system; the intention is merely to provide a description that is adequate for both, and so ensure that speech is not left out of account. For spoken language to be fully explored, a more radical departure from the tradition of written grammars will be needed; but that lies beyond the present scope.

In general, therefore, the approach leans towards the applied rather than the pure, the rhetorical rather than the logical, the actual rather than the ideal, the functional rather than the formal, the text rather than the sentence. The emphasis is on text analysis as a mode of action, a theory of language as a means of getting things done.

Theories of language

The basic opposition, in grammars of the second half of the twentieth century, is not that between 'structuralist' and 'generative' as set out in the public debates of the 1960s. There are many variables in the way grammars are written, and any clustering of these is bound to distort the picture; but the more fundamental opposition is between those that are primarily syntagmatic in orientation (by and large the formal grammars, with their roots in logic and philosophy) and those that are primarily paradigmatic (by and large the functional ones, with their roots in rhetoric and ethnography). The former interpret a language as a list of structures, among which, as a distinct second step, regular relationships may be established (hence the introduction of transformations); they tend to emphasize universal features of language, to take grammar (which they call 'syntax') as the foundation of language (hence the grammar is arbitrary), and so to be organized around the sentence. The latter interpret a language as a network of relations, with structures coming in as the realization of these relationships; they tend to emphasize variables among different languages, to take semantics as the foundation (hence the grammar is natural), and so to be organized around the text, or discourse. There are many cross-currents, with insights borrowed from one to the other; but they are ideologically fairly different and it is often difficult to maintain a dialogue.

Fifty years after Saussure, Chomsky created a new opposition by calling his own syntagmatic, formal grammar 'generative' and claiming that as its distinguishing feature. He seems to have been unaware of, or perhaps just uninterested in, the ethnographic tradition in linguistics; his polemic was directed solely at those he was building on, referred to as 'structuralists'. By generative he meant explicit: written in a way which did not depend on the unconscious assumptions of the reader but could be operated as a formal system. His tremendous achievement was to show that this is in fact possible with a human language, as distinct from an artificial 'logical' language. But you have to pay a price: the language has to be so idealized that it bears little relation to what people actually write — and still less to what they actually say.

Following on the thrust of Chomsky's ideas, a new body of work appeared which was enormously influential and has made a permanent contribution to linguistics. There was no 'Chomsky revolution', as has been somewhat sensationally claimed; but new questions were explored, and this led to a shift of emphasis, in the United States and consequently elsewhere, from the anthropological to the philosophical standpoint. For a while this had the effect of splitting the subject into two camps and preventing any real exchange of ideas between them, but the return to a preoccupation with discourse in the 1970s did much to restore the balance. Throughout the history of western linguistics there has tended to be a polarization between these two approaches, taking of course different forms at different periods; at times they are closer together and at times further apart, with major intellectual battles being fought out between them. The roots lie partly in western thinking and partly in the nature of language itself, which is equally at home in humanities, social science, natural science, medicine and engineering, but appears very different according to where one starts.

It is easier to make a formal grammar explicit, for obvious reasons — it is based on linguistic forms. But paradigmatic functional grammars can also be 'generative', in the sense of being expressed in formal terms and used for generating or parsing by computer; examples are Sydney Lamb's relational network ('stratification') theory and Martin Kay's functional grammar. Three major contributions to artificial intelligence — Terry Winograd's *Shrdlu*, Anthony Davey's *Proteus* and William Mann's *Penman* systems — have taken systemic theory as their linguistic base. Because it is based on meaning, it is harder for a functional grammar to get off the ground in computable form; but once it is airborne it has a considerable range.

A lively and penetrating account of the currents of twentieth century linguistics can be found in Geoffrey Sampson's book *Schools of Linguistics: competition and evolution*, published in 1980. It provides a good perspective on the different approaches to the interpretation of language.

Applications

It is unlikely that any one account of a language will be appropriate for all purposes. A theory is a means of action, and there are many very different kinds of action one may want to take involving language. At the same time, one may not want a theory that is so specialized one can only do one thing with it. Some years ago one of the speakers at a conference began his paper with the words "I take it for granted that the goal of linguistics is to characterize the difference between the human brain and that of an animal". That this should be one of a hundred goals one might readily accept; but that this — or anything else — should be 'the' goal of linguistics is hard to take seriously. There are very many tasks for which linguistics is needed, and they make very different demands on the subject.

Applications of linguistics range from research applications of a theoretical nature to quite practical tasks where problems have to be solved. Some of the purposes for which linguistics is likely to be useful could be enumerated as follows:

to understand the nature and functions of language;
to understand what all languages have in common (i.e. what are the properties of language as such), and what may differ from one language to another;
to understand how languages evolve through time;
to understand how a child develops language, and how language may have evolved in the human species;]child

to understand the quality of texts: why a text means what it does, and why it is valued as it is;
to understand how language varies, according to the user, and according to the functions for which it is being used;
to understand literary and poetic texts, and the nature of verbal art;
to understand the relation between language and culture, and language and situation;
to understand many aspects of the role of language in the community and the individual: multilingualism, socialization, ideology, propaganda, &c.;
to help people learn their mother tongue: reading and writing, language in school subjects &c.;
to help people learn foreign languages;
to help train translators and interpreters;
to write reference works (dictionaries, grammars &c.) for any language;
to understand the relationship between language and the brain;
to help in the diagnosis and treatment of language pathologies arising from brain insults (tumours, accidents) or from congenital disorders such as autism, Down's syndrome;
to understand the language of the deaf (sign);
to design appliances that will aid the hard of hearing;
to design computer software that will produce and understand text, and translate between languages;
to design systems for producing and understanding speech, and converting between written and spoken text;
to assist in legal adjudications by matching samples of sound or wording;
to design more economical and efficient means for the transmission of spoken and written text;

and so on.

The test of a theory of language, in relation to any particular purpose, is: does it go? Does it facilitate the task in hand? There is usually a trade-off of breadth against depth: we need both highly specialized machines that will do just one job perfectly, and less specialized machines that will do a broad range of jobs effectively without being most efficient or economical for any one.

The account given here is biased toward breadth rather than depth. It has been used for a variety of purposes: analysis of texts, spoken and written; stylistics; computational linguistics; developmental linguistics, and study of socialization; study of functional variation in language, and the relation between language and the context of situation and of culture; and for a number of educational applications. This last is probably the broadest range of its applications; it includes experience in initial literacy, children's writing, language in secondary education, classroom discourse analysis, teaching of foreign languages, analysis of textbooks, error analysis, teaching of literature and teacher education.

The orientation is to language as social rather than as individual phenomenon, and the origin and development of the theory have aligned it with sociological rather than psychological modes of explanation. At the same time it has been used within a general cognitive framework; and some current work is exploring its possible relevance to neurolinguistics and to learning theory.

The 'code'

Stated in other terms, a grammar is an attempt to crack the code.

Each language has its own semantic code, although languages that share a common culture tend to have codes that are closely related. Whorf referred to 'Standard Average European' as the common code shared by the main European languages, which he showed to be very different from that of at least one American Indian language.

The main problem for linguistics is to give an objective account of the code. In this respect (as in many others) we are overprivileged in the English-speaking world: since more has been written about English than any other language there is little danger of its having the code of some other language foisted upon it and so getting distorted. The influence of Latin was once a distraction; but Latin was related to English, and medieval Latin, at least, shared the common European code. But by the same token, since English is so predominant there is a tendency to foist the English code on others. Modern linguistics, with its universalist ideology, has been distressingly ethnocentric, making all other languages look like imperfect copies of English.

What is the relation between the code and the culture which creates it, and which it transmits to the next generation? Linguists in the anthropological tradition had tried to establish links with meanings expressed lexically: Eskimo words for 'snow', Arabic words for 'camel' and so on. Yet vocabulary only 'reflects' culture by courtesy of its internal organization as a whole; and the assertion that 'because "camels" are important to the Arabs, "therefore" they have a lot of different words for "them" ' is as much a statement about English as about Arabic. Presumably nothing is more important than rice to the Chinese; yet Chinese has a single word for rice — and it means various other things besides. Chinese happens to be a language of a type that favours general nouns.

But what is merely comic when applied to lexis becomes seriously misleading when applied to grammar. As Whorf pointed out 50 years ago, it is naive and dangerous to take isolated grammatical phenomena and try to relate them to features of a culture. When linguists recognized this, their response was to avoid the language/culture issue altogether, thus closing the door on an important area of research. That there is a relationship between a code and the culture that engenders it is beyond question; but it is an extremely complex and abstract one.

Only the grammatical system as a whole represents the semantic code of a language. For example, it would be pointless to take one feature of the grammar of English, such as the prevalence of phrasal verbs, or the intricacies of the tense system, and try to relate it to some non-linguistic aspect of European or English-speaking culture. But it is far from nonsensical to take one such feature, put it together with a large number of other very general grammatical features — for example the clause as an item of 'news' (Chapter 3), the location of 'newsworthy' information (Chapter 8), the meaning of effective voice in material processes (Chapter 5), the tendency to nominalize (Chapter 10), and others — and derive from these a chain of reasoning, showing first the reasons **within the grammar** why phrasal verbs are favoured in English (Chapter 6), and then taking the much wider canvas of which this forms one small part and relating it to the patterns of language use in our society, the historical changes that have taken place in the last 500 years, and the ideological systems that underlie them.

Just as each text has its environment, the 'context of situation' in Malinowski's terms, so the language system has its environment, Malinowski's 'context of culture'. The context of culture determines the nature of the code. As a language is manifested through its texts, a culture is manifested through its situations; so by attending to text-in-situation a child construes the code, and by using the code to interpret text he construes the culture. Thus for the individual, the code engenders the culture; and this gives a powerful inertia to the transmission process.

To understand the code, we need an overview of the grammatical system; both in order to confront one part of it with another, and in order to interpret texts in the code. Whether the text is literature, or classroom discourse, or political or commerical propaganda, the basic grammar of the clause complex, the clause, the prepositional phrase, verbal and nominal group, and information unit, will always be involved. As already remarked, we have as yet no comprehensive semantics. But we can attempt a comprehensive view of grammar; and for any code-oriented investigation this is essential. You cannot interpret a text in its context of culture without an overall picture of the grammar through which it is encoded.

Some problems

Apart from the obvious problem of selecting what is to go in, a number of other problems arise in presenting a short sketch of a grammar. Most severe are the problem of paradigms, the problem of labels, the problem of examples, and the problem of writing about language.

(1) The problem of paradigms. Our Latin textbooks used to set out word paradigms: *mensa*, *mensa*, *mensam*, *mensae*, *mensae*, *mensā*. The purpose was to state the potential of a Latin noun. We accepted them because obviously that was how Latin was spoken: people went round chanting 'a table, oh table!, a table, of a table, to a table, by with or from a table'. No doubt they would have sounded as silly to a Roman as their English equivalent does to us.

In a functional grammar of English there is little place for word paradigms. But we may want to display paradigms of larger units such as the clause, which take up more space — like the paradigms of the duke, the aunt and the teapot in Chapter 4. They are a quick and efficient way of demonstrating a system. But there is an inherent contradiction in their use. Paradigms are by definition things that do not go together; by writing them out on the page, we turn them into syntagms, which is precisely what they are not.

Whether paradigms have a role in learning a language is highly doubtful. But they do have a role in learning linguistics, and in carrying out linguistic research. They display proportionality, which is the main heuristic technique for finding out the system of a language. Thus *mensa* is to *mensam* as *rex* is to *regem* as *pueri* is to *pueros*, **in some respect**. Similarly, *this teapot the duke gave to my aunt* is to *the duke gave my aunt this teapot* as *that I told you before* is to *I told you that before*, in some respect. What this respect is, is shown by a label.

(2) The problem of labels. To talk about proportionalities, we label them. The fact that *mensam*, *regem* and *pueros* are alike in a way that relates them consistently to *mensa*, *rex* and *pueri* is a linguistic generalization, or category; we give it a label, 'accusative', and also label the set of such categories, 'case'.

The problem is that it takes too long to present the grammar step by step in this way; so we tend to start with the labels, and it is forgotten how they were arrived at and what they are for. Thus, when we investigate the proportionality in English set out above, we find that the variation in sequence means something; 'being first' expresses a function in the clause, and we give this a label 'theme', distinguishing (in the above pairs) between 'marked theme' and 'unmarked theme'.

Such labels easily become reified, as if there exists some **thing** called the 'theme', which then has to be defined, and is defined as 'that which comes first'. But a label is no more than the name of a proportional relation, or of a term in such a relation, or of some means whereby a proportional relation is expressed.

(3) The problem of examples. Ideally every example should be a whole text; but this (apart from increasing the length) makes it hard to pick out which feature is under attention. So in order to exemplify, we either (a) select a brief extract that is understandable out of its context, (b) select a passage from a well-known text (hence *Alice in Wonderland*, which can always be consulted if the extract is not recognized), or (c) as a last resort, invent one.

But because the example has been chosen to illustrate a category, that is precisely what it does, clearly and unambiguously. However, in real life categories are not displayed in this way, and they may be very hard to identify. There is a general principle in language, that the easier a thing is to recognize, the more trivial it is likely to be; the outward sign of a semantically significant category is usually not simple or clearcut, and many factors may have to be taken into consideration in identifying it.

It would take another book to cover all intervening ground from the illustrative examples to instances in different types of discourse. Instead we give a number of short text examples, and bring in a few longer texts in which one particular feature is followed through.

(4) The problem of writing about language. There are two problems here, in fact. One is what I referred to earlier as the ineffability of linguistic categories. There is no adequate statement of the meaning of a grammatical category. Concepts like Theme and Subject and New, or the various types of process in transitivity, cannot be definitively glossed in ordinary wording. (This is not to suggest it could not be done better than I have done it.)

The other is that the whole grammatical system hangs together and it is difficult to break in at any one point without presupposing a great deal of what is still to come. With this, combined with the pressure of space, the writing tends to become very dense. (If it gets too difficult, try reading it aloud. It is amazing how much that can help.) There is always a problem when language is turned back on itself.

Possible grammars

This book is a short introduction to the functional grammar of English. It can also be read as a short introduction to functional grammar in general, using English as the language of illustration.

I remarked earlier on the tendency to ethnocentrism in modern linguistics; and there is a danger of assuming that the categories used here are valid in the description of any language. Material contained in these chapters has been used as a basis for studying a number of languages; and the researcher often begins by finding the same set of categories — because if one looks for a particular category in a language one will usually find it: early European grammarians found pluperfect subjunctives in languages the world over. Then he starts again, and asks: how would I have interpreted the grammar of this language if English had never existed? — and this time he may refuse to see anything in common at all, but in the end a balanced perspective is reached.

This is not to deny that features may be universal; but those features that are being explicitly claimed as universal are built in to the theory. An example of this is the 'metafunctional' hypothesis: it is postulated that in all languages the content systems are organized into ideational, interpersonal and textual components. This is presented as a universal feature of language. But the descriptive categories are treated as particular. So while all languages are assumed to have a 'textual' component, whereby discourse achieves a texture that relates it to its environment, it is not assumed that in any given language one of the ways of achieving texture will be by means of a thematic system (Chapter 3). Even if there is such a system, the features in it (the choices) may not be the same; and even if a feature embodies the same choice, it may not be realized in the same way. There might be a thematic system, but one which is not based on the principle of an unmarked choice for each mood; or there might be such a choice, but not realized by the order in which the elements occur. In any case, it is far from clear just how similar a pair of features in different languages should be in order to justify calling them by the same name.

I have tried throughout to keep to familar categories and to terms in general use. There are many aspects of English that need to be much more fundamentally re-examined than I have managed to achieve here; one obvious example is the circumstantial elements in the clause, which I have treated in very traditional fashion. Twentieth-century linguistics has produced an abundance of new theories, but it has tended to wrap old descriptions up inside them; what are needed now are new descriptions. Tasks have changed, ideas have changed, and languages have changed. (I have already mentioned the need for grammars of spoken language.) The old interpretations were good, but not good enough to last for all time, even when dressed up in new theoretical clothes.

The grammar is the central processing unit of a language, where meanings are accepted from different metafunctional inputs and spliced together to form integrated outputs, or wordings. Without a grammar in the system, it would be impossible to mean more than one thing at once. In order to understand how language works, therefore, we have to engage with the grammar. It is always difficult to keep grammar in focus of attention, because it is a purely abstract level of coding with no direct input – output link with the outside world. We have to get at it through the meaning or through the expression. But our understanding of the meaning system is itself very deficient; so the face of the grammar that is turned towards the semantics is hardly illuminated at all. We have little grasp of the meaning potential of the code, and are only now beginning to be able to characterize that of its subcodes, the different registers of a language.

Beyond the realm of existing human languages lies that of possible languages, those that do not exist but could do. There would be many other ways of devising a symbolic system for encoding our observations and actions. What kinds of grammar can we imagine, that would be different from those we have? This question does not seem to have been much explored, even in science fiction; but the imaginative exploration of other possible ways of meaning could throw additional light on the assumptions that are made in our own unconscious semantics. In the same way we can learn a lot by constructing the semantic system that lies behind some of the texts produced by small children; and perhaps some of those produced by computers when they are being programmed for text generation.

Meanwhile there are immediate practical and theoretical problems for which we need both to understand and to work on the languages that are in daily use around us. A functional grammar is part of the equipment we can use in trying to solve these problems.

Part I The Clause

1

Constituency

1.1 Constituency in writing

If we look at a passage of writing in English, we can see clearly that it consists of larger units made up out of smaller units. These smaller units, in their turn, are made up of units that are smaller still.

These units are what we call sentences, words and letters. A passage of written English consists of sentences, which consist of words, which consist of letters. This relationship can be diagrammed as in Figure 1-1.

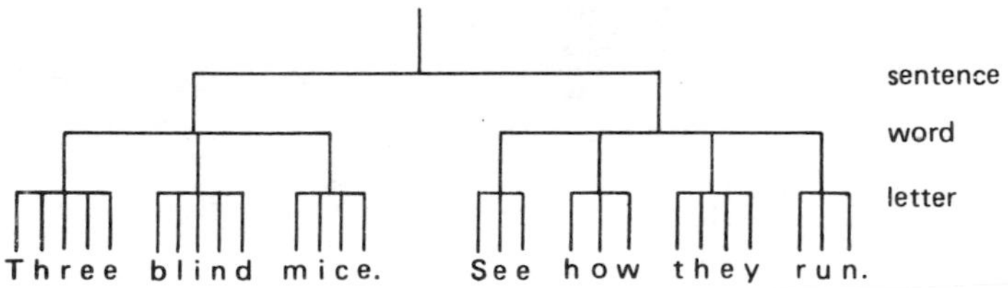

Figure 1-1 The units of written English

We are able to diagram it in this way because each unit begins where the previous one ends. Sentences follow sentences, words follow words, and letters follow letters in a simple sequence; they do not overlap, nor does anything else occur in between. The spaces that separate them — narrow spaces between letters (at least in print), wider spaces between words, and still wider spaces, with accompanying full stop, between sentences — serve to mark the units off one from another. These spaces and stops are not part of the substance of writing; they are signals showing how it is organized. We can refer to them as STRUCTURE SIGNALS.

This kind of layered part-whole relationship which occurs among the units of a written text is referred to as CONSTITUENCY. Each unit consists of one or more of the next smaller — each sentence of one or more words, each word of one or more letters. It is important to point out that the number may be **one or more**; in other words, in any given instance there may be one constituent only. Thus in Figure 1-2 the word *a* has a single constituent; it consists of only one letter:

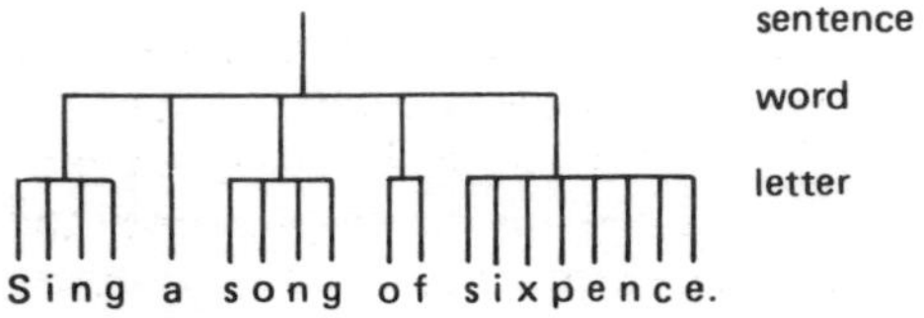

Figure 1-2 An example of single constituency

It is possible to have single constituents on successive layers, as in Figure 1-3, where *I* is a sentence consisting of one word consisting of one letter.

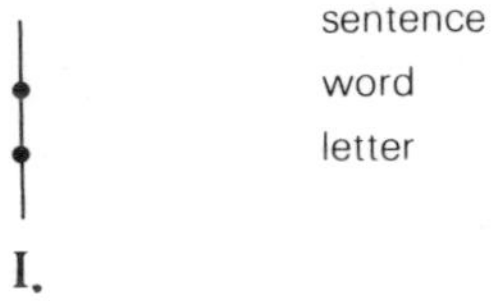

Figure 1-3 Single constituents on successive layers

Not a very common sentence, in modern English; but recognizable as the answer to "Who killed Cock Robin?"

There are other structure signals in written English besides spaces, namely the punctuation marks such as ! ? ' ' ( ) , ; : and -. The first four of these signal the meaning of a unit, or its status in the text; they are not primarily boundary signals, although they may tend to go at particular places in the structure — for example ! and ? usually occur at the end of sentences. The last four mark off some kind of sub-sentence, some unit that is intermediate between the sentence and the word. We might in fact want to build these in to our constituent hierarchy by introducing the notion of sub-sentence as shown in Figure 1-4.

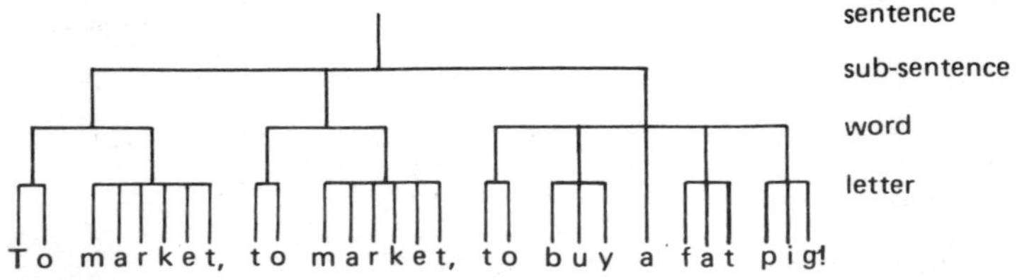

Figure 1-4 Introduction of a unit between sentence and word

There are likely to be some uncertainties at this point. We might want to recognize not just one but two layers of sub-sentence, one for units separated by a colon or semicolon and another one for units separated by a comma. We might want to insist that all sentences consist of sub-sentences, even if in any given text the majority may contain only one; or we might allow that some sentences consist of sub-sentences while others consist directly of words. We might want to build in another unit above the sentence, and say that written English consists of paragraphs and the paragraphs consist of sentences. The decisions on such matters would depend partly on the kind of writing we were interested in and partly on the kind of analysis we wanted to make, which in turn would depend on the purpose for which we were making it. There are various ways of describing orthographic constituents in English, ranging from that of sentence – word – letter, which is perhaps the simplest one that will work at all, to that of paragraph – sentence – colon unit – comma unit – word – letter, which is more complex but also accounts for more of the facts. All these would be possible representations of the CONSTITUENT STRUCTURE of a written text.

This type of analysis into constituents is often known as BRACKETING; and the constituent structure can be shown equally well by the use of brackets:

[{(To) (market) } {(to) (market) } {(to) (buy) (a) (fat) (pig) }]

Figure 1-5 Constituency shown by brackets

Whichever device we use, brackets or trees, the notation shows what goes together with what; and in what order, beginning with the units that are most closely bonded (letters bonded into words) and working up through the hierarchy of graphic units until we reach whatever is the highest one to be identified.

Note that in the discussion so far we have been concerned only with the nature of writing, without reference to the grammatical structure that lies behind it. Any stretch of written text could be analysed in this way provided it was written in alphabetic characters, with spacing and punctuation; for example, Figure 1-6. We do not need to know what it means in order to be able to analyse it in this way, since what we are describing here is its organization as a system of orthography. We can see how writing is organized into constituents just by looking at the letters and any structure signals that may be present; we do not even need to be able to recognize the letters, as might be the case in Figure 1-7.

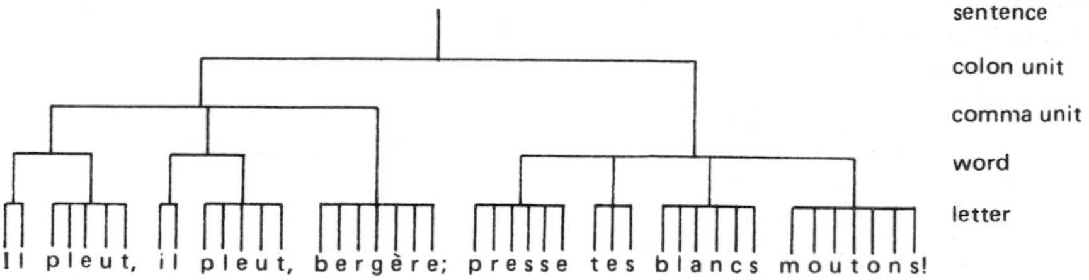

("It's raining, it's raining, shepherdess; round up your white sheep!")

Figure 1-6 Constituency in French orthography

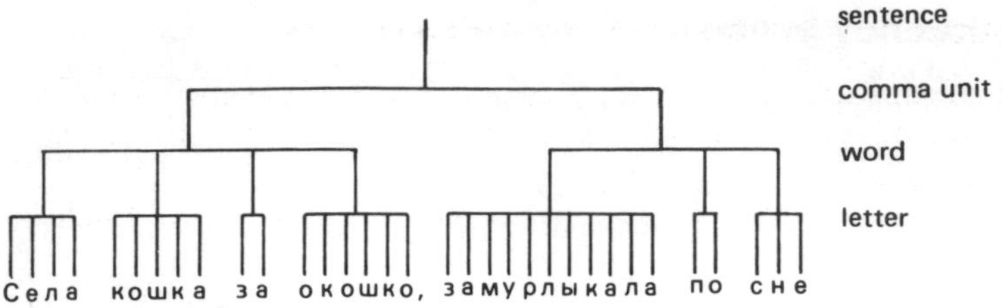

("The cat sat by the window, purring in its sleep")

Figure 1-7 Constituency in Russian orthography

Even a writing system that is not alphabetic will still display a definite constituent structure, although the units will be different from those of English or Russian. In Figure 1-8 there are characters, but no words or letters.

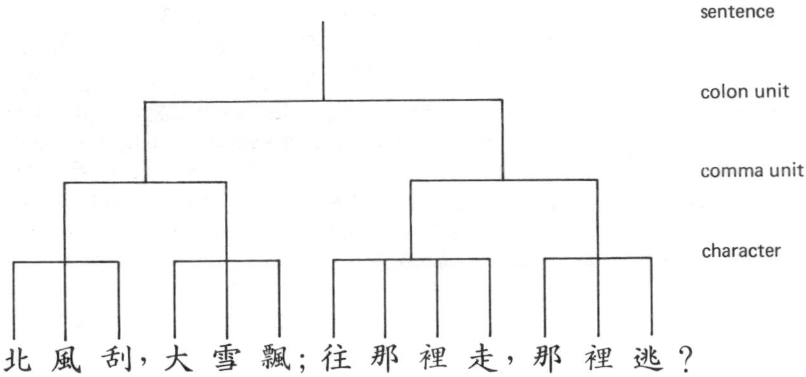

("The North Wind is blowing, snow fills the sky; where can I go, where can I fly?")

Figure 1-8 Constituency in Chinese orthography

When writing first evolved, through the gradual mapping of pictograms on to words, it took the form of simple strings of symbols. But in their early stages all writing systems developed some kind of constituent structure; and this tells us something about the nature of language itself. If discourse can be adequately represented by sequences of written symbols arranged like this in constituent hierarchies, it is reasonable to assume that language is inherently organized along something like these lines. It does not mean, of course, that this is the only form of organization in language, or even necessarily the most fundamental one; it might be merely the mode of organization that is most readily observable, or the one that is most easily adapted to another symbolic system. But it is likely that the idea of constituency will play some part in any general interpretation of the patterns of language.

We shall begin to explore the notion of constituency in grammar when we get to Chapter 2. Meanwhile in the next section we shall have a look at another example of this same general phenomenon, namely constituent structure in verse.

1.2 Constituency in verse: (1) as written

Another form of constituent structure is that which we find in verse. A poem, typically, consists of stanzas, which consist of lines, which consist of feet, which consist of syllables.

Consider as an example the following well-known fragment of English literature:

Polly put the kettle on,
Polly put the kettle on,
Polly put the kettle on,
  We'll all have tea.

Sukey take it off again,
Sukey take it off again,
Sukey take it off again,
  They've all gone away.

The version is that given by Iona and Peter Opie in *The Oxford Dictionary of Nursery Rhymes* (no. 420, p. 353).

The lines and stanzas figure in the text as graphic units; they are clearly displayed in the way the verse is set out on the page. In this instance, they are identical with the orthographic units: each line is a sub-sentence, and each stanza is a sentence. This is typical of children's verses; Mother Goose rhymes almost always can be, and usually are, printed with a comma or semicolon at the end of the line and a stop at the end of the stanza. Here is an exception, where the lines represent two parts in a dialogue:

Who comes here?
  A Grenadier.
What do you want?
  A pot of beer.
Where is your money?
  I've forgot.
  Get you gone
You drunken sot.

In this example, taken from William S. Baring-Gould and Ceil Baring-Gould, *The Annotated Mother Goose* (no. 51, p. 61), there is one stanza, consisting of eight lines; but seven sentences, each consisting of only one sub-sentence.

We will refer to the written units of the verse form as *grapho-metric* units, to distinguish them from the sentences and sub-sentences of ordinary orthography, which are constituents in the general writing system of the English language. And just as we were able to recognize two kinds of sub-sentence in writing, a colon unit as well as a comma unit, so in verse we often find another constituent intermediate between the stanza and the line, such as a couplet or quatrain; we might refer to this as a 'sub-stanza'. This gives us a rough set of typical equivalents, as shown in Table 1(1).

Table 1(1) Typical correspondences of higher graphic units

orthographic unit		grapho-metric unit
sentence	corresponds to	stanza
colon unit	"	sub-stanza
comma unit	"	line

The 'grapho-metric' units are those which belong specifically to the written representation of verse structure.

We will return to these at the end of this section; meanwhile let us consider the smaller units, the feet and the syllables. Feet and syllables are not in fact shown in the written representation of a verse form. There is nothing corresponding to the foot in writing: a foot may be one word, e.g. *Polly*; two words, e.g. *put the*; one word and part of another, e.g. *off a-*; or any other sequence of syllables containing just one strong beat. A foot is a constituent of the spoken language, not the written. Likwise the syllable is a unit of speech and not of writing, though it used to be marked off graphically by a hyphen in some children's readers, e.g. *Pol-ly put the ket-tle on*.

In linguistic terminology, foot and syllable are phonological units, not orthographic ones. Hence our account of the constituents of a poem as stanza – line – foot – syllable, if stanzas and lines are graphic units, is a mixture of constituents of two different types. We have been considering stanzas and lines as properties of verse in its written form, whereas feet and syllables belong to verse in its aspect as a phonic structure. A representation in strictly graphic terms will show stanzas consisting of lines, but with the lines then consisting of words consisting of letters. Words and letters have the same status in verse as in the everyday written language.

A grapho-metric representation of *Polly put the kettle on* would thus be exactly the same as an orthographic one, with 'stanza' and 'line' substituted for 'sentence' and 'sub-sentence'. The traditional form of written verse is simply that of ordinary spelling, and ordinary punctuation, but with a different principle for organization of the higher units. The usual constituents of written verse, in their usual relation to those of everyday writing, are shown in Table 1(2):

Table 1(2) Grapho-metric and orthographic constituents

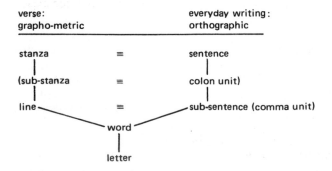

verse: grapho-metric		everyday writing: orthographic
stanza	≡	sentence
(sub-stanza	≡	colon unit)
line	≡	sub-sentence (comma unit)
	word	
	letter	

A diagram of the second half of *Who comes here?*, using the tree notation to show both orthographic and grapho-metric constituents, down to the rank of the word, is given in Figure 1-9.

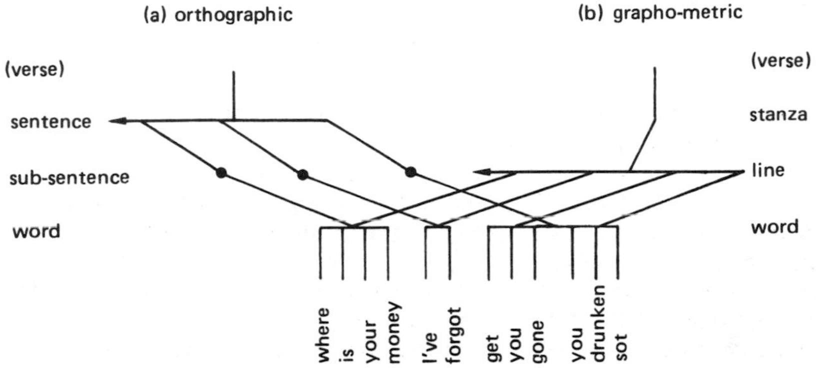

Figure 1-9 Orthographic and grapho-metric representations of part of *Who comes here?*

Let us return briefly to the higher units. In many instances, like *Polly put the kettle on*, the analysis into grapho-metric units and that into orthographic units will coincide all the way, the lower units being the same by definition and the higher ones by equivalence. The equivalence of the higher units — the fact that the stanza is often an orthographic sentence, and the line a sub-sentence — is not, of course, a coincidence. Lines and stanzas derive, in origin, from the same phonological patterns that lie behind sub-sentences and sentences, patterns of rhythm and intonation (see Section 1.3 below) — behind which, in turn, lie, further, the grammatical patterns that we shall be concerned with throughout this book. It is in children's verses that this elementary structure is most faithfully preserved — naturally, since it makes the verses both easier to understand and easier to remember. In more sophisticated verse forms, on the other hand, there is frequently a tension between the two graphic structures, with the orthographic units cutting acorss the grapho-metric ones. This sort of counterpoint becomes possible once recognized verse forms have evolved as types of linguistic structure in their own right. Here is a modern example of a sonnet, *The Bad Thing* by John Wain. Note the effect of the two simultaneous graphic constituent structures, and how the tension between them becomes a resource for meaningful variation.

The Bad Thing

Sometimes just being alone seems the bad thing.
Solitude can swell until it blocks the sun.
It hurts so much, even fear, even worrying
Over past and future, get stifled. It has won,
You think; this is the bad thing, it is here.
Then sense comes; you go to sleep, or have
Some food, write a letter or work, get something clear.
Solitude shrinks; you are not all its slave.

Then you think: the bad thing inhabits yourself.
Just being alone is nothing; not pain, not balm.
Escape, into poem, into pub, wanting a friend
Is not avoiding the bad thing. The high shelf
Where you stacked the bad thing, hoping for calm,
Broke. It rolled down. It follows you to the end.

1.3 Constituency in verse: (2) as spoken

Verse was spoken long before it was written down, and all the elements of verse structure have their basis in the spoken language.

If it is spoken aloud, a poem consists of sequences of TONE GROUPS, which consist of FEET, which consist of SYLLABLES. This pattern is not special to verse, however; it is simply the way the sound system of English is organized. These are the constituents that enter into the phonology of everyday spoken English (see Chapter 8 for further details).

But just as in the written representation of verse forms further patterns are superimposed over and above those of everyday orthography, so also there are special regularities associated with verse in its spoken mode. These regularities (1) specify the structure of the foot, by reference to the syllables of which it is made up; and (2) define two higher units, (i) the line, in terms of the number of feet, and (ii) the stanza, in terms of the number of lines.

This gives us a PHONOMETRIC structure, in which the constituents are: stanza - line - foot - syllable. Figure 1-10 gives an analysis of *Polly put the kettle on* in phonometric terms.

We now have the stanza and the line not only as graphic (grapho-metric) but also as phonic (phonometric) units. As such, they represent the higher order patterns of rhythm in the verse structure. The basic unit of RHYTHM is the foot. In *Polly put the kettle on*, four such rhythmic units (four feet) together constitute a higher rhythmic unit, which is what we call the line; and four of these units in turn together constitute a unit of higher rank still, namely a stanza. We can interpret the stanza and line, as phonic units, in terms of the architecture of the rhythm.

It was pointed out in the last section, however, that behind the (graphic) line and stanza lie phonological patterns not only of rhythm but also of INTONATION. Let us consider another example from Mother Goose:

If all the world was apple pie,
  And all the sea was ink,
And all the trees were bread and cheese,
  What should we have to drink?

If this verse is spoken naturally, one can hear very clearly that each line has its own melody — its own TONE CONTOUR, in phonological terms. We shall see in Chapter 8 that this is a characteristic of all spontaneous spoken English: it consists of an unbroken sequence of melodic units, called TONE GROUPS. Now, a line of verse typically corresponds to a tone group of natural speech; this, presumably, is how the convention of a 'line' of verse originated — in origin, it is a melodic line.

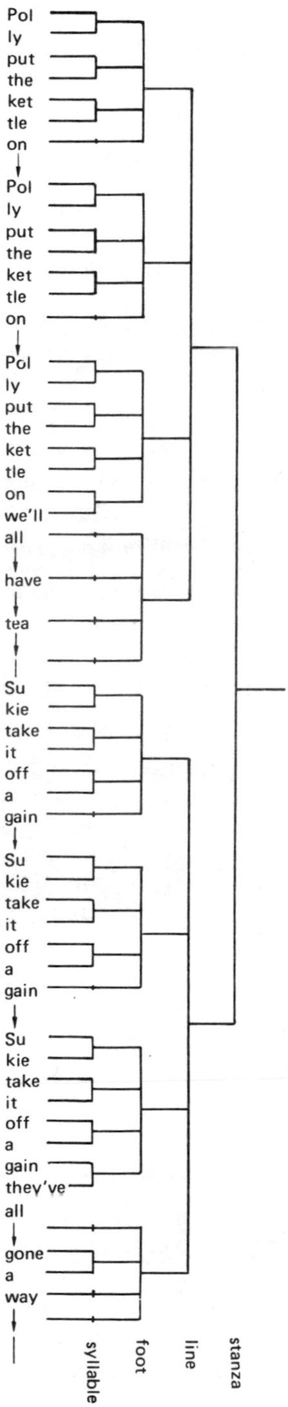

Figure 1-10 Phonometric structure of *Polly put the kettle on*

A stanza, looked at from this point of view, is a sequence of lines such that, while each one has its own tone contour, all except the last end on a rising note, the last one then ending on a falling note. The rising contour signifies that the intonation pattern is incomplete.

It is not suggested that this is how verse is always spoken aloud. Unlike rhythm, which is the basis of all verse form, intonation plays no part in determining the structure of English verse; this relationship of line to tone group (behind both of which lies the basic grammatical unit, the clause) is simply the elementary pattern, the raw material out of which verse form has evolved. But it can be seen — or rather heard, and felt — in the reciting of children's verses; and also in tum-tee-tum-tees, the jingles that are used to refer to the verse forms when teaching the rhythm to children. A tumteefication of any of the verses cited throughout these few sections will bring out clearly the melodic unity of the lines and stanzas involved.

This quality is also brought out, not surprisingly, when verse is set to music. Typically, the lines and stanzas appear on the melodic units of the musical composition, the stanza corresponding to a melody and the line to a melodic phrase. *Polly put the kettle on* consists of two stanzas, each consisting of four lines; and its musical setting consists, correspondingly, of two melodies each consisting of four melodic phrases (Figure 1-11). In this case the two melodies are different, though it is more usual for the same melody to be repeated for each stanza; but this does not affect the principle whereby the melody and the stanza correspond.

In all probability the structure of the musical composition is itself, in origin, an elaboration of the intonation and rhythm of natural spoken language.

Thus lines and stanzas, as phonometric units, have their basis in intonation. But just as the two constituent structures of written verse, that of the verse form and that of everyday written language, though deriving from the same source, can be set against each other in a meaningful counterpoint, so also the lines and stanzas of the spoken verse form interact freely in tension with the tonal patterns of the everyday spoken language, from which they too are ultimately derived.

The primary function of the lines and stanzas, as spoken units, is however a rhythmic one; as said above, they represent the organization of the verse into higher-order rhythmic units. They may also embody other regularities such as that of rhyme. In the next section we will look further into the question of rhythm, and relate the rhythmic analysis to the concept of metre.

1.4 Constituency in verse: (3) rhythm and metre

The patterns of organization of verse rhythm, taken as a whole, constitute what is known as METRE. Why then can we not refer to the constituent structure of spoken verse simply as metric structure, instead of introducing the cumbersome term 'phonometric'? The answer is: because the received tradition of English metrical analysis, which is based on the classical metrics of Latin and Greek, does not accurately account for the rhythmic properties of English verse. And it is this analysis in terms of classical metres that is known by the term 'metrics'.

By permission of Novello & Co., Ltd.

Figure 1-11 Musical setting of *Polly put the kettle on*

In order to explore the difference between the metric and the phonometric interpretations, let us return to the phonometric analysis of *Polly put the kettle on* given in Figure 1-10. This shows how the verse is organized as a passage of spoken English. There are two things to note about this analysis. (1) One is that *we'll* and *they've*, although in the written text they start new lines, in fact belong together in one foot with the previous syllable, and hence rhythmically with the preceding line (cf. the musical version). (2) The other is that we have had to allow, in two instances, for a foot consisting of silence. Each of the two stanzas ends with a silent foot.

Now it frequently happens in everyday spoken language that the rhythm of a passage is maintained across a short period of silence; and this gives rise, in verse, to the phenomenon of a SILENT BEAT. Most English verse forms have regular units of silence built into their phonometric structure; verse with no silence at all is rare, and rather monotonous to listen to. To find examples of verse without silence, where all the feet are 'filled', we usually have to turn to children's rhymes.

One rhyme in which the rhythmic movement runs on without a break is the ballad of Betty Botter. We can write this out as follows, using the slash to represent the boundary of the rhythmic (phonometric) foot, and double slash for the beginning and end of a stanza:

// Betty / Botter / bought some / butter
/ But she / said the / butter's / bitter
/ If I / put it / in my / batter
/ It will / make my / batter / bitter . . . //

One of the few examples of a recognized poem in this metre is Longfellow's *Hiawatha*.

By way of contrast, in the following verse there is a natural pause at the end of every line, taking up the time of a complete foot. This is a SILENT FOOT. This kind of rhythmic silence is represented by a caret ^.

// Little / drops of / water / ^
/ Little / grains of / sand / ^
/ Make the / mighty / ocean / ^
/ And the / pleasant / land / ^ //

The silent foot is a consequence of — in fact it is part of — the rhythmic structure of the line. A silent foot is introduced automatically whenever a line consists of an odd number of filled feet, say three or five. This is because all phonometric structures in English are binary; the feet are always in multiples of two. So if the actual number of feet to be spoken aloud is an odd number, an extra, silent foot is added to the line to even it up.

We must now look at the structure of the foot itself, to see how it is organized in terms of syllables. We have already remarked that the foot is a unit of ordinary everyday speech, where it carries the rhythmic patterns; in the same way the tone group carries the melodic patterns, those of intonation. Now in ordinary speech, just as a tone group has no definite number of feet in it, so a foot has no definite number of syllables in it. The number of syllables varies freely from one foot to the next. This used to be true also in Old English verse, where the foot had no fixed internal structure, though the line had a definite number of feet. But in mainstream English verse since Chaucer's time the foot has been internally regulated like the line; not only are there just so many feet to a line, but also just so many syllables to a foot.

Up to now we have been mainly considering one particular type of foot, that with two syllables in it like those in the *Betty Botter* rhyme. A two-syllable foot of this kind, beginning with a strong beat, is called in classical metrics a TROCHEE: it consists of a strong syllable followed by one weak one. The line *Betty Botter bought some butter* has four of these trochaic feet, and so is called a TROCHAIC TETRAMETER. In this instance the metric analysis would correspond exactly with the phonometric one based on the rhythmic patterns of spoken English. This is because each foot begins with a strong beat, and there are no feet consisting of silence.

There are two important respects, however, in which the classical metric analysis conflicts with the rhythmic structure of English verse. (1) In the first place, it does not recognize the presence of silent units. Hence a line such as *little grains of sand*, which rhythmically contains four feet, is interpreted metrically as a three-foot line, or TRIMETER, because only three feet are filled. (2) Secondly, in classical metrics, while some types of foot begin with a strong beat, others are interpreted as beginning with a weak one. Hence a contrast is made between the foot in the *Betty Botter* type of line and that in the following verse:

There was a little guinea pig,
Which, being little, was not big,
He always walked upon his feet,
And never fasted when he eat.

This verse is analysed metrically not into trochees but into IAMBS, two-syllable feet which consist of a strong syllable **preceded by** one weak one. We could represent its metric pattern as follows, using a vertical bar to stand for the metric foot (in contrast to the slash used for the rhythmic foot):

|| there was | a lit | tle gui | nea pig
| which be | ing lit | tle was | not big
| he al | ways walked | upon | his feet
| and nev | er fast | ed when | he eat ||

By way of contrast, the phonometric representation would be:

// ‸ there / was a / little / guinea / pig which
/ being / little / was not / big he
/ always / walked up/on his / feet and
/ never / fasted / when he / eat //

There is a reason for recognizing trochees and iambs as different kinds of feet: it allows the foot boundary to coincide with the boundary between lines. But rhythmically there is no justification for it. There is no difference in rhythm between trochaic and iambic metre; and if the structure of the line permits either analysis, as in a verse such as the following

If you wish to live and thrive
Let the spider walk alive

it is impossible to decide between them. What determines the overall tempo and measure of English verse — as of natural spoken English — is the rhythmic foot, not the metric foot; and the rhythmic foot, like the bar in music, always begins with a strong beat. It is no accident that the rhythmic foot also tends to correspond more closely with the division of the line into words.

Thus with a verse like the guinea-pig one, there is a significant difference between the phonometric analysis, which is based on rhythm, and the classical metric analysis. The latter was adapted to English from Latin, where it was based on the length of the syllables not their strength. Note that in English, syllable length, although it is a systematic feature of the language (cf. Chapter 8, Section 8.2 below), plays no part in verse structure.

In five-foot iambic (IAMBIC PENTAMETER) verse, both differences will appear: the metric and the phonometric analyses will show different foot boundaries, and the latter will take account of the silent beat, showing six feet to the line instead of five. Here are the two versions of the first stanza of Gray's *Elegy in a Country Churchyard*:

(a) classical metric

|| the cur | few tolls | the knell | of part | ing day
| the low | ing herd | winds slow | ly o'er | the lea
| the plow | man home | ward plods | his wear | y way
| and leaves | the world | to dark | ness and | to me ||

(b) phonometric

// ‸ the / curfew / tolls the / knell of / parting / day / ‸ the
/ lowing / herd winds / slowly / o'er the / lea / ‸ the
/ plowman / homeward / plods his / weary / way / ‸ and
/ leaves the / world to / darkness / and to / me / ‸ //

Note that here the silent beat does not take up the whole of the foot, because the sixth foot in each line also includes the weak syllable at the beginning of the subsequent line.

There are various other reasons why the phonometric analysis is more satisfactory. It relates verse rhythm to the rhythm of the spoken language, and hence gives a more accurate account of verse as spoken aloud. It correctly predicts the relative length of the syllables within the foot, which the metric analysis does not. It also allows for silence at other places than at the end of the line — wherever it would occur in a natural rendering. For example, the last line of the stanza just cited would probably be spoken as

/ leaves the / world to / darkness / ‸ and to / me / ‸ //

with a silent beat followed by two weak syllables in the fifth foot. But it is beyond our scope to pursue these points further here.

Here is a final example of phonometric analysis, this time showing variation both in the number of syllables per foot and in the number of metric feet (though not the number of rhythmic feet) per line, within the one stanza:

// swan / swam / over the / sea	1, 1, 3, 1
/ swim / swan / swim / ∧	1, 1, 1, 0
/ swan / swam / back a/gain	1, 1, 2, 1
/ well / swum / swan / ∧ //	1, 1, 1, 0

The first and third lines have four 'filled' feet, so there is no silent beat at the end. The second and fourth lines have only three, so a silent beat is added to make up the fourth. The number of syllables in each (rhythmic) foot is shown to the right; note that this variation does not alter the overall length of the foot. This analysis is given in tree notation in Figure 1-12.

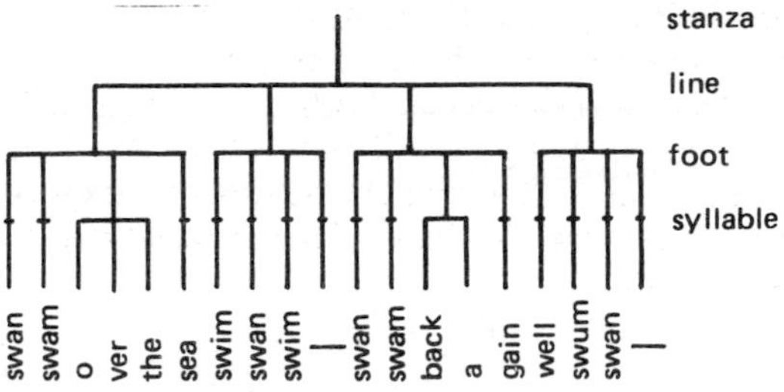

Figure 1-12 *Swan swam over the sea*

Table 1(3) gives a summary of the principal units recognized in classical metrics: the lines, with their phonometric and musical equivalents, and the various types of foot.

Table 1(3) shows that the musical structure of a line may actually differ from both the metric and the phonometric structures. This happens because there is a tradition of songs being composed with the bars in multiples of four — typically even in powers of two. Hence the iambic pentameter, the line most characteristic of English verse from Chaucer to Yeats, which as a metric unit contains five feet and rhythmically has six, when sung usually consists of eight. (These eight are often written as four bars, but if so there is always a secondary beat in the middle.) As examples, consider *Abide with*

Table 1(3) Summary of metric units, with phonometric and musical equivalents

1) Type of line	Number of 'filled' (metric) feet	Number of rhythmic feet (phonometric)	Number of bars (musical)
dimeter	2	2	2
trimeter	3	4	4
tetrameter	4	4	4
pentameter	5	6	8
hexameter	6	6	8
heptameter	7	8	8
octometer	8	8	8

2)

Type of metric foot	Number of syllables	Composition	
trochee (trochaic)	2	| ·	Strong Weak
iamb (iambic)	2	· |	Weak Strong
dactyl (dactylic)	3	| · ·	Strong Weak Weak
anapaest (-ic)	3	· · |	Weak Weak Strong
paeon(-ic) [descending]	4	| · · ·	Strong Weak Weak Weak
'' [ascending]	4	· · · |	Weak Weak Weak Strong

Example: An 'iambic pentameter' is a line consisting of five metric feet each having two syllables with the configuration Weak ^ Strong. Rhythmically it consists of six feet, one of which is silent. Musically it is typically set to an eight-bar melodic line.

me, or the various songs and hymns that are set to the Londonderry Air. No doubt the great disparity between the five feet of the idealized metric unit and the eight feet required by the melodic structure is one of the reasons why the iambic pentameter, despite its being the most highly favoured form of written verse throughout some five centuries of English poesy, is so rarely set to music — and why it hardly ever occurs in Mother Goose.

1.5 The significance of constituency

The discussion in Sections 1.2–1.4 has given some account of verse structure as a form of constituency, and shown, in the process, that a full interpretation of it involves considerably more than one simple hierarchy of constituents.

We have been able to distinguish (i) the grapho-metric structure, the way the verse is set out on the page; (ii) the phonometric structure, the way it is spoken aloud; (iii) the classical metric structure, by which the verse form is defined, and (iv), where applicable, the musical structure, the way in which it is represented in music. And all these contrast further with the natural constituents of written and spoken language: the orthographic structure, described in Section 1.1, and the phonological structure which will be sketched in Chapter 8.

As a final example of a passage of verse, Figure 1-13 shows the constituent analysis of the first two lines of *Drink to me only with thine eyes*, worked out according to principles (i)–(iv). Rhythmically, and melodically, the passage could as well be regarded as a single eight-foot line; but in the written form, and metrically, it is treated as two lines, so this version has been adopted throughout for the sake of greater consistency. Note that musically the bars are in triple time; this reflects accurately the relative length of the syllables in the majority of the rhythmic feet of the poem (not discussed here; cf. the reference in Section 1.4 above).

Of these four representations it is the second, the phonometric, which most closely approximates the way a poem is recited or read aloud. Even this is only an approximation, since the actual rendering of a piece of verse is a complex product of the tension between the phonometric structure of the verse form and the phonological system of the English language, as represented in the intonation and rhythm of everyday spontaneous conversation. The phonometric patterns come out most clearly when we say verses for children,

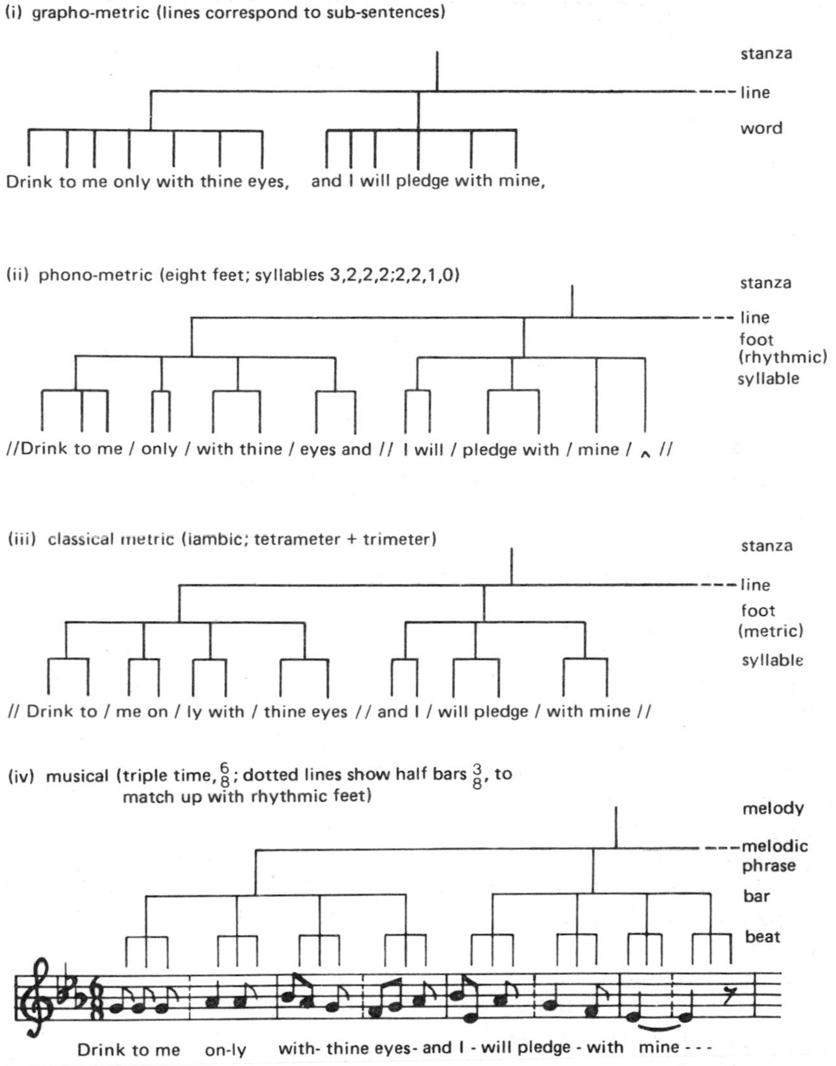

Figure 1-13 Constituents of *Drink to me only with thine eyes*

because the strict tempo rhythm of the verse is an important part of the meaning it has for a child. Later on, an English-speaking child will learn in school that is not the approved way to recite poetry. He will be asked to 'respond' to it, to say it meaningfully and with feeling; in other words, to endow it with the melody and rhythm of natural speech, together with whatever dramatic side-effects the teacher may think appropriate. But not all cultures share this convention; in some languages poetry and conversation are kept clearly apart, and no merit is gained from trying to make a poem sound like spontaneous discourse.

Our concern in this book is with grammar, and we shall not explore the phonological system of English any further at this point. For a discussion of intonation and rhythm in the context of a functional grammar see Chapter 8 below. The reasons for going into the constituent structure of writing, and of verse, by way of introduction are essentially these four:

(1) The notion of constituency is one that it is important to be able to take for granted in the discussion of grammar, and it can be demonstrated rather easily by reference to writing and to verse structure. Even if it turns out to be less simple than appears at first glance, it is still true that the basic conception of sentence - word - letter, or of a poem as made up of stanzas made up of lines made up of feet made up of syllables, serves as a useful model for the understanding of constituency in language.

(2) These structures illustrate an important fact about constituency in general: that units of different rank tend to carry patterns of different kinds. The foot, for example, is the unit of rhythm; it is the constituent which organizes the pulse or beat of the spoken language. Its function is distinct from that of other units both above and below it: from the syllable, which organizes the articulation of vowels and consonants, and the line, which — in its typical aspect as a tone group — organizes the intonation. The same principle, of the functional specialization of units of different rank, is of fundamental significance in determining grammatical structure.

(3) The fact that both writing and verse are organized into hierarchies of constituents is not accidental; it reflects a basic fact about language. If writing evolved, as it did, on a basis of layered constituency, and if poetry displays similar kinds of structure, this is because natural speech is already based on patterns of this kind — they are part of the phonological system of a language; and if such patterns are present in phonology, this in turn is because they are present in the underlying organization of linguistic form — namely in the system of the grammar.

(4) A language therefore embodies a multiplicity of constituent hierarchies, coexisting in different parts of the system. They are not unrelated: on the contrary, they are all different facets of the same phenomenon, the fact that experience itself, at least in some of its aspects, imposes a constituent-like structure on our consciousness. Constituents in speech and writing both express and symbolize this more abstract structural order. At the same time, each of these hierarchies is independent of the others, and there are infinite possibilities of matching them up in meaningful ways. They can be played with, as it were — precisely because, in the last resort, they are all on the surface of language. They are not what language really is — though they are essential mechanisms for achieving its variety of purposes.

In Chapter 2, we shall move on to a consideration of grammar, still using the notion of constituency as a mode of entry into the grammatical system. As one explores more deeply into language, constituency gradually slips into the background; and explanations begin to depend on other models of grammatical relationships. Constituent structure in language is only a mechanism for the organization and expression of meaning; and even in this respect it does not do everything, nor do the various different modes of meaning depend on it to the same degree. Nevertheless it is an important link in the chain of grammatical interpretation, and a useful point of departure from which to begin to explore.

2

Towards a functional grammar

2.1 Grammatical constituency

In analysing grammar, we can begin by applying the same notion of constituency as in Chapter 1, but using it now to represent grammatical structure. For example, Figure 2-1:

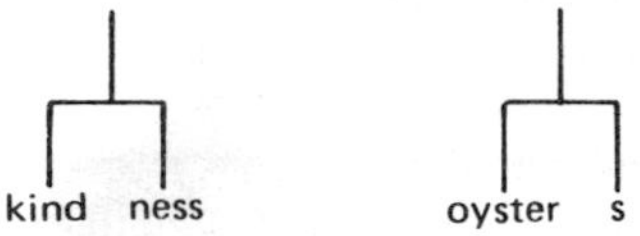

Figure 2-1 Grammatical constituent structure

This says that *kindness* consists of two parts, *kind* + *ness*; and that *oysters* likewise consists of two parts, *oyster* + *s*.

These are not the results we would have arrived at if we had been analysing these items as EXPRESSIONS in writing or speech. Considered as expressions in writing, as we were doing in Section 1.1, *kindness* is one word consisting of eight letters, and *oysters* is one word consisting of seven letters. Considered as expressions in speech, both *kindness* and *oysters* consist of two syllables; but whereas *kindness* would be analysed syllabically as *kind* + *ness*, which corresponds to its grammatical analysis, *oysters* would certainly not be analysed syllabically as *oyster* + *s*. Its syllabic composition would be *oys* + *ters*, or possibly *oy* + *sters*.

A grammatical analysis treats linguistic items not as expressions but as FORMS. To put the same thing in everyday terms: in grammar, we are exploring language not as sound or as writing but as wording. The ordinary everyday sense of the term 'wording', as in 'Could you help me with the wording of this notice?', refers to the words and structures that are used (as distinct from the pronunciation and spelling); it thus corresponds very well to GRAMMAR — which is more accurately called 'lexicogrammar': that is, it includes both structure and vocabulary. In fact the technical names for the various parts or 'levels' of language correspond quite closely to those recognized in everyday 'folk linguistic' terminology:

phonology	is the level of	sound (pronunciation)
orthography	,,	writing (punctuation and spelling)
grammar ('lexicogrammar')	,,	wording
semantics	,,	meaning

When we say that grammatically *oysters* consists of *oyster* + *s*, we mean that that is how it is put together as a piece of wording. In the same sense, *kindness* consists of *kind* + *ness*, *shining* of *shine* + *ing*, *largest* of *large* + *est*, *wheelbarrow* of *wheel* + *barrow*. There is nothing in the writing to show this structure; but we know — because we understand English — that this is how these words are built up out of smaller pieces. The smaller units are called MORPHEMES. See Table 2(1).

Table 2(1) Division of words into constituents: morphemes, syllables

Grammatical		Phonological	
morpheme	morpheme	syllable	syllable
kind	ness	kind	ness
oyster	s	oy(s)	(s)ters
shine/-	ing	shi	ning
walrus		wal	rus

Many English words consist of only one morpheme; others of two, some of three or more. We can represent these as layered constituent structures on the same principles as were applied to writing and to metrics; cf. Figure 2-2.

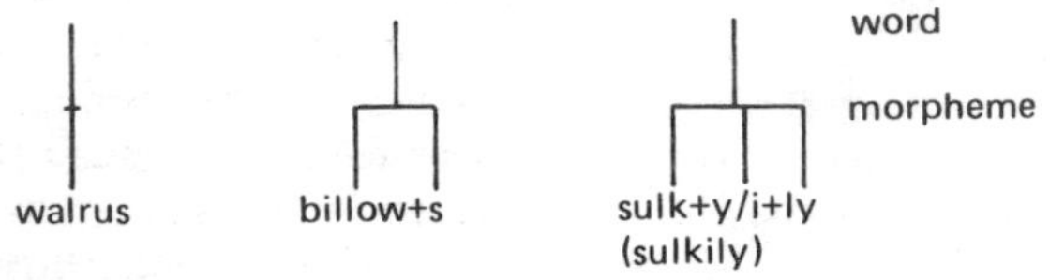

Figure 2-2 Word and morpheme

The forms separated by a slash, e.g. y/i, are regular alternatives (this morpheme is spelt y if word-final, i otherwise). Such alternatives, at any level, are known as VARIANTS.

In speaking English, we are not normally aware of the internal structure of words; no doubt that is why the constituent morphemes have never come to be marked off from one another in writing. We are somewhat more aware of how words combine into larger units; so our writing system does mark off one word from another, though not always entirely consistently. Examples of words making up larger units are given in Figure 2-3.

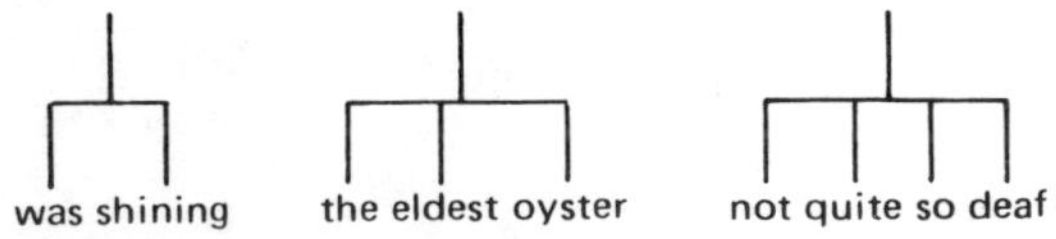

Figure 2-3 Group and word

If we call the unit next above the word a GROUP, we arrive at a constituent structure in which groups consist of words and words of morphemes, as in Figure 2-4.

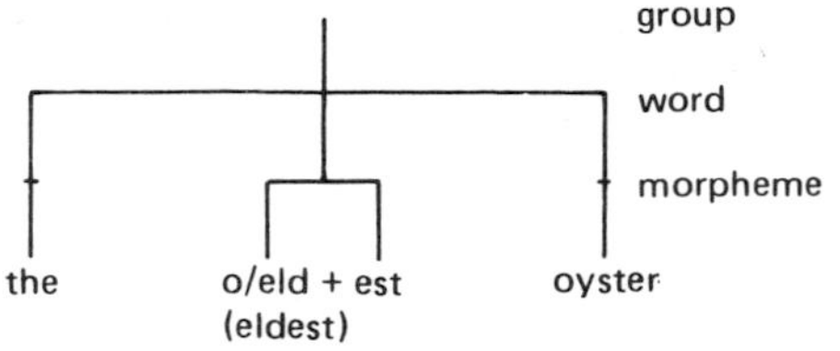

Figure 2-4 Group, word and morpheme

The group *the eldest oyster* consists of three words; two of these words, *the* and *oyster*, consist each of one morpheme, while the third, *eldest*, consists of two, *old/eld-* and *-est*. The same information is given in bracketing notation in Figure 2-5.

[{(the) } {(eld) (est) } {(oyster) }]

Figure 2-5 Group, word and morpheme: bracketing notation

In this book we shall not be concerned, except occasionally in passing, with the internal constituent structure of words; our main attention will be on the higher units, and particularly on the CLAUSE. This is because the mode of interpretation adopted here is a functional one, in which the grammatical structure is being explained by reference to the meaning; and there is a general principle in language whereby it is the larger units that function more directly in the realization of higher-level patterns. In phonology, for example, there is no direct relation between the individual vowels or consonants and anything in the grammar; these small units have no grammatical function as single elements. On the other hand the unit of intonation, the tone group, does function directly as the expression of grammatical choices. In the same way if we want to explore how semantic features are represented in the grammar we look primarily at the structure of the clause, and at what is above and around it; and only then (and only to a limited extent in the present book) do we go on to consider smaller grammatical units. Figure 2-6 gives a specimen analysis of a clause into groups and words (see Chapters 3, 4 and 5 for detailed presentation).

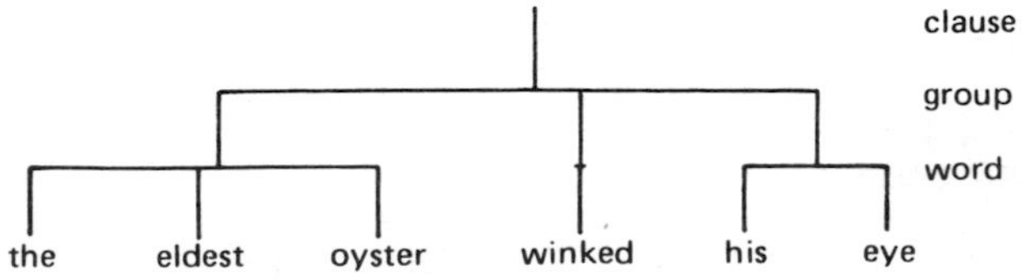

Figure 2-6 Clause, group and word

2.2 Maximal and minimal bracketing

As soon as we take account of wordings of more than minimal length and complexity, it becomes clear that constituent analysis in grammar is no longer the relatively straightforward matter that it is when we are simply looking at the orthographic structure, with its clear-cut paragraphs, sentences and words. Consider a phrase such as *seven maids with seven mops*. It consists of five words; but are they five words in a string, as in Figure 2-7 (a), or is there some more structure involved, as for example in 2-7 (b) or (c)?

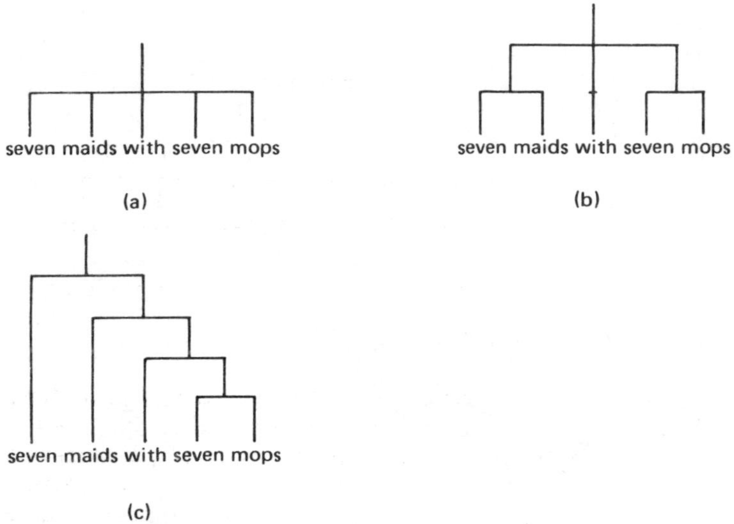

Figure 2-7 Alternative grammatical constituent analyses

These three versions, of course, by no means exhaust the possibilities. But they do demonstrate an important point: that there are two contrasting principles to choose from (though one may choose to compromise between them). One principle is: put a bracket everywhere you can. The other one is: put a bracket only where you have to. These may be referred to as maximal and minimal bracketing respectively.

Maximal bracketing means imposing the maximum amount of structure, as in Figure 2-7 (c) above. This principle is known in linguistics as IMMEDIATE CONSTITUENT ANALYSIS ('IC analysis'). Carried to its logical limit it means never allowing more than two elements in a bracket; analyses such as those in Figure 2-7 (a) and (b), where there are three or more elements bracketed together, would be rejected. The idea behind IC analysis is that there is always a logical order in which the elements of any string are combined, so that for example *the two queens* must be interpreted either as in Figure 2-8 (b) or (c) but nowise as in 2-8 (a).

A minimal bracketing approach, which may be referred to as RANKED CONSTITUENT ANALYSIS, would yield the interpretation shown in Figure 2-8 (a).

With very simple structures, the difference between the two is relatively slight, as in Figure 2-8; and cf. Figure 2-9.

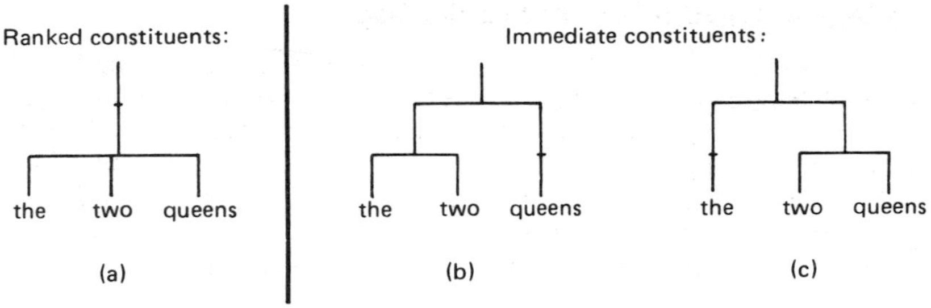

Figure 2-8 Three versions of *the two queens*

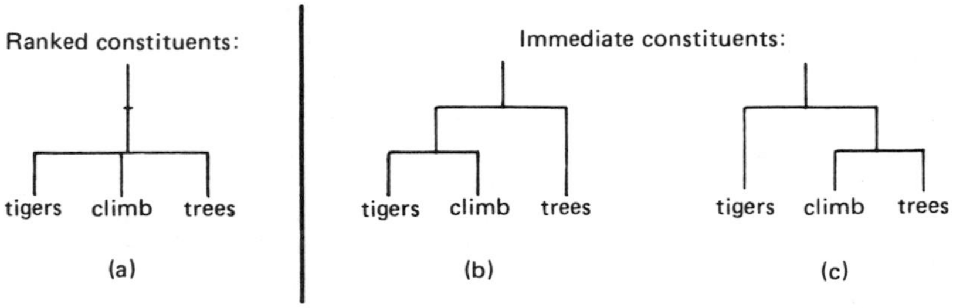

Figure 2-9 Three versions of *tigers climb trees*

Even here, as will be apparent, the different bracketings are suggestive. If we think of this clause as a piece of information, then version (b) *tigers climb* + *trees* suggests an answer to the question 'What do tigers climb?'; whereas version (c) *tigers* + *climb trees* suggests an answer to 'What do tigers do?' or perhaps to 'What climbs trees?' Version (a) *tigers* + *climb* + *trees* is more neutral; it merely suggests an answer to 'What have you to tell me?'. With longer items, the difference naturally becomes greater; compare in this regard the two versions of Figure 2-10, where the two bracketings are shown together, one above and one below the text. Here the maximal bracketing, version (b), suggests that this item (which was actually part of a longer nominal group; see Chapter 6, Section 6.2 below) has a great deal of internal structure to it.

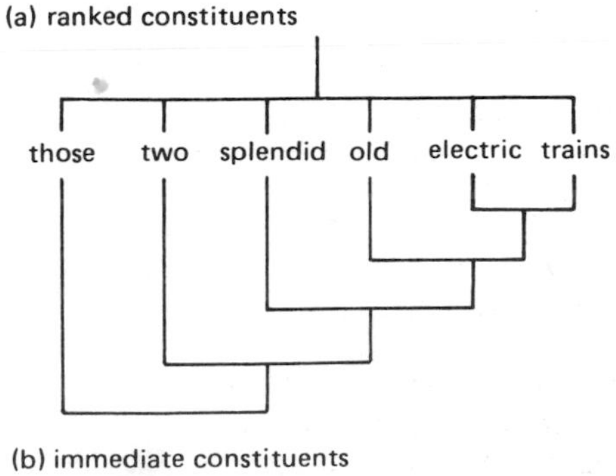

Figure 2-10 Minimal bracketing (a) and maximal bracketing (b)

If we refer to these structural representations as TREES, having BRANCHES and NODES, then maximal bracketing means more nodes, with fewer branches per node, whereas minimal bracketing means fewer nodes, but with more branches on each.

Literally interpreted, the wording 'minimal bracketing' would presumably mean no bracketing at all. It does not mean that, of course; what it means is **functional** bracketing — bracketing together only those sequences that have some function relative to a larger unit. To find out what these are is part of the task of a functional grammar; we shall be exploring this question throughout the rest of the book. But we have been able to get some idea already from the discussion in the first two sections. In the example in Figure 1-1, we would not put a bracket around the sequence of letters t - h - r, or h - r - e - e, because they do not make a word; or even around the i - n in *blind*, because they do not make a word **in this instance**. Similarly in Figure 1-10 we would not bracket together *Polly put the*, or any other sequence that did not in its context both embody a pattern of its own and serve some recognized function in the pattern of some higher unit.

In practice this means that a minimally bracketed interpretation, given a more complex example like that in Figure 2-11, would look something like version (a) in that figure; version (b) again being maximally bracketed.

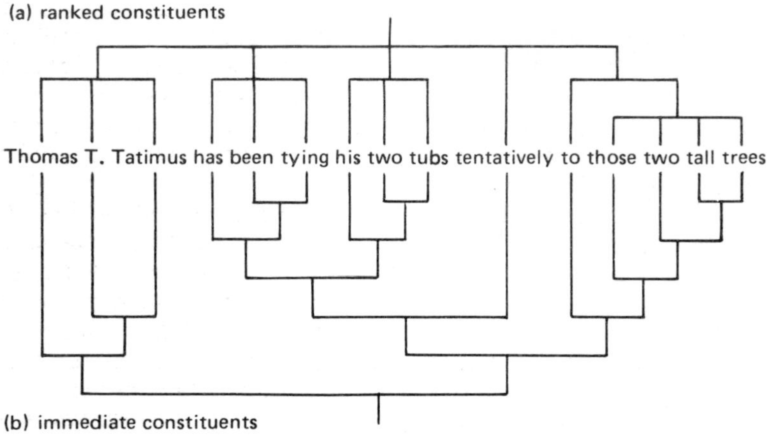
(a) ranked constituents
Thomas T. Tatimus has been tying his two tubs tentatively to those two tall trees
(b) immediate constituents

Figure 2-11 (a) minimal and (b) maximal bracketing: a more complex example

Throughout this book we shall be using minimal bracketing, since the orientation we have adopted is a functional one. The detailed principles will become explicit as the discussion proceeds. But it will be clear already that the difference between the two is a difference of kind, rather than just one of degree. If we use maximal bracketing, we are taking the concept of bracketing as a powerful explanatory device; in other words, we are attempting to explain as much of grammar as possible in terms of constituent structure. The concept of constituency is being made to do a lot of work. If we use minimal bracketing, we are relegating the concept of bracketing to a less important role, requiring the notion of constituency to take us only a limited way in the explanation of the grammar, and no further. This means, of course, that we have to bring in other concepts to take over the burden of interpretation where constituent structure is no longer relevant. The concepts in question are, in the first instance, functional ones.

In a functional grammar we carry the analysis of constituent structure up to a point that is, roughly, as far as it is taken in folk linguistic theory and in traditional school grammar. We began with the observation that, in our everyday ways of talking about writing, we have names for certain units of written language: sentence, word, and letter, if no more. But sentence and word are also used as grammatical terms; they refer to units of linguistic form, as well as to the patterns on the page. In the terms of the discussion in the preceding section, they are units of wording as well as units of writing. Sentences and words are part of the organization of language as a systematic code, the organization that lies behind the patterns formed by symbols in writing and by sounds in speech. Provided we are always aware that the terms are being used in two different senses, which may not always exactly correspond, we can retain SENTENCE and WORD as units in the grammatical constituent hierarchy; and supplement them with the three other units mentioned above, namely CLAUSE, GROUP and MORPHEME. A group is similar to a PHRASE, a term which is also quite familiar in non-technical discussions of language; we shall use both these terms, with 'group' as the more general one. The difference in meaning between them is explained in Chapter 6. The term 'clause' is still fairly technical, although it is quite widely known — more familiarly perhaps in its related sense of a clause in a contract. The term 'morpheme' is a creation of modern linguistics, as the name for the smallest unit in the grammatical constituent hierarchy.

The classroom image of grammatical structure is something like the following. Language is made up of sentences (some of which have clauses in them) consisting of words (some of which are grouped into phrases). There is no need to reject this picture; we can build on it and enrich it. A minimally bracketed constituent analysis is one which makes use of this insight, but systematizes it in a number of respects to make it more consistent and more significant. There are various ways of strengthening this conception of grammatical structure; our main strategy will be to adopt the framework of sentence, clause, group, word and morpheme as a strict hierarchy of constituents, each one being related by constituency to the next. A sentence consists of clauses, which consist of groups (or phrases), which consist of words, which consist of morphemes. Later on we shall reconsider the significance of the term 'sentence' in this hierarchy (Chapter 7).

This defines a scale of RANK for grammar, similar to the rank scales used for written language and for verse in Chapter 1. The rank scale provides the basis for a constituent analysis of the 'minimal bracketing' type. In minimal bracketing, **each node corresponds to a unit on the rank scale**; this is why we refer to it as a 'ranked' constituent analysis. The units of each rank are shown in Figure 2-12.

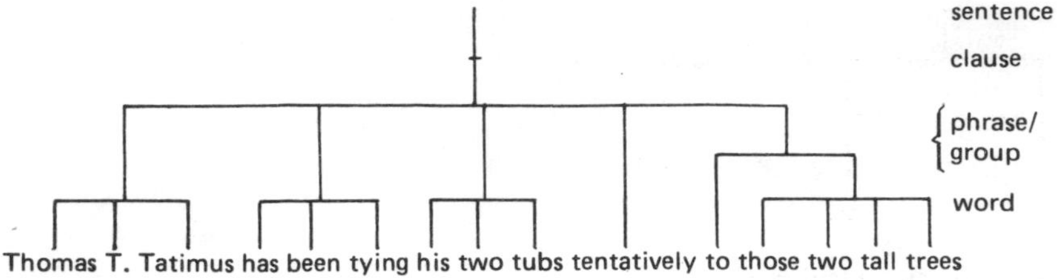

Figure 2-12 Minimal bracketing in relation to the scale of rank

We can now see more clearly the difference between the two ways of bracketing. Maximal bracketing is a statement of the **order of composition** of the constituent parts. It expresses the idea that some constructions are more closely bonded than others, to the extent that, given any grammatical structure, it is possible to specify the order in which all the pieces are put together, pair by pair. So for example in 2-9 (c) the meaning is 'to form the construction *tigers climb trees*, first put together *climb* + *trees* then put together *tigers* + *climb trees*.'

It says nothing about the function that any of the pieces have in any construction; in fact it does not imply that they have any function at all. If we refer back to Figure 2-11 (b), there we find nodes (i.e. brackets) representing sequences such as *been tying*, or *two tall trees*, or *has been tying his two tubs*; but these are strings which do not figure as structural units in the structure of this particular sentence — whether or not we might be able to construct some other sentence in which they do. This is in marked contrast to the principle of minimal bracketing, which means putting together as constituents only those sequences that actually function as structural units in the item in question.

It follows from this that, as we expressed it earlier, maximal bracketing is a way of explaining as much as possible about linguistic structure by means of the notion of constituency. Using maximal bracketing, we account for *those two tall trees* by saying: first combine *tall* and *trees*, then combine *two* with the resulting *tall trees*, then combine *those* with *two tall trees*; and it is this ORDERING by which the construction is to be explained. With minimal bracketing we are merely saying: combine *those* and *two* and *tall* and *trees*, in a single operation; the result is a group consisting of four words. This tells us very little, and so it suggests that if we are using minimal bracketing some other concept is being brought in in order to explain the grammatical structure. This is where the concept of FUNCTION is introduced. It will be necessary to say something about the particular function that each part has with respect to the structure of the whole.

2.3 Labelling

This is done by LABELLING the parts — labelling the nodes, if we want to continue with the tree metaphor. A structure is an organic whole, in which the different elements play different roles. The labelling is a way of indicating what these roles are. For example, in *tall trees*, *tall* functions as Modifier and *trees* as Head, as shown in Figure 2-13.

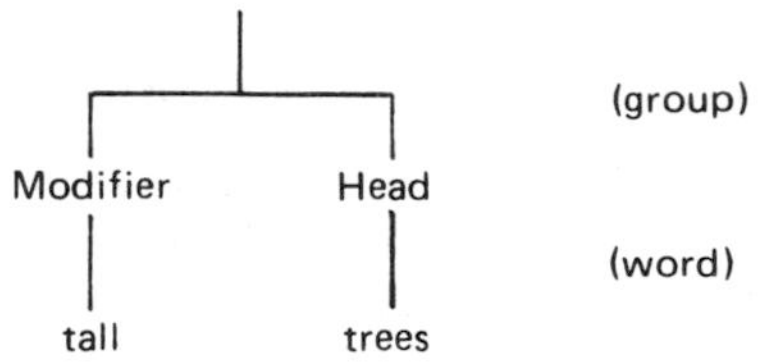

Figure 2-13 Functional labelling

The bracketing indicates that these two elements form a structure; the labelling indicates what configuration of functions that structure consists of. By associating each part with a functional label, we explain its value in relation to the whole.

Bracketing is a way of showing what goes with what: in what logical (as opposed to sequential) order the elements of a linguistic structure are combined. It says nothing about either the nature or the function of the elements themselves.

Labelling means putting names on things, and so it is a way of specifying what these elements are. The label provides some kind of a definition of the units that have been identified as parts of some larger whole.

There are in principle two significant ways of labelling a linguistic unit. One is to assign it to a class; the other is to assign a function to it. Hence there are two principles according to which we can label the constituents of a grammatical structure: (i) by CLASS, and (ii) by FUNCTION.

As pointed out at the end of the last section, the labels used in Figure 2-13 were labels expressing functions. They signify that *tall* is functioning as Modifier, and *trees* is functioning as Head, in the structure of this particular group.

Instead of using these functional labels, we would have labelled the same item in terms of classes, as in Figure 2-14.

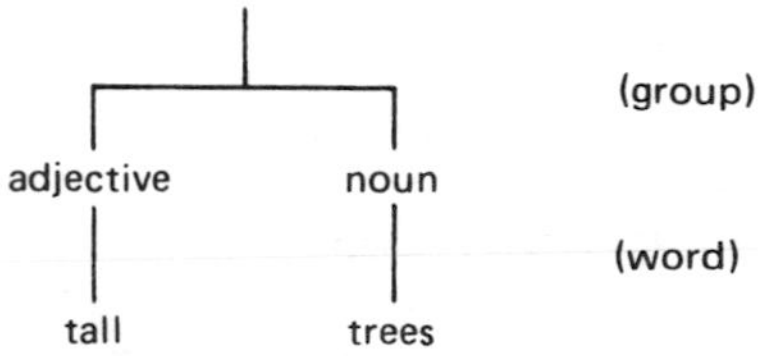

Figure 2-14 Class labelling

Whereas Modifier and Head were function labels, adjective and noun are class labels.

For the sake of consistency, throughout this book labels for classes are written entirely in lower case, while labels for Functions are written beginning with a capital letter. Since our concern here is with functional grammar, most of the labels used will be function terms. But it will be necessary to refer to classes at frequent points in the discussion.

Many of the linguistic technical terms that have become familiar in everyday use are grammatical labels of one or other of these two kinds: either class names or function names. Terms such as verb, noun, adjective, adverb, prepositional phrase, noun clause, are names of classes. Terms such as Subject, Object, Complement, Modifier, Auxiliary, are the names of functions. Wherever possible, we have made use of familiar grammatical terms — though it should always be remembered that they may have had to be redefined, in part, to fit in with the total picture. In addition, in the chapters that follow we shall be introducing a number of terms that are not so familiar; and these will be defined as we go along. Most of the new terms, again, will be labels for grammatical functions.

If all the members of a class always had one and only one function, it would not matter which sets of labels we used. We could adopt the convention of always using labels of just one kind, knowing that we could derive the other ones from them. But this is not so. To cite what is perhaps the most obvious example from everyday grammar, a member of the class 'noun' can function either as Subject or as Object, as in Figure 2-15. (Note that we shall not, in fact, be using the term OBJECT in the grammar at all. It is brought in here to provide an illustration from familiar terminology.)

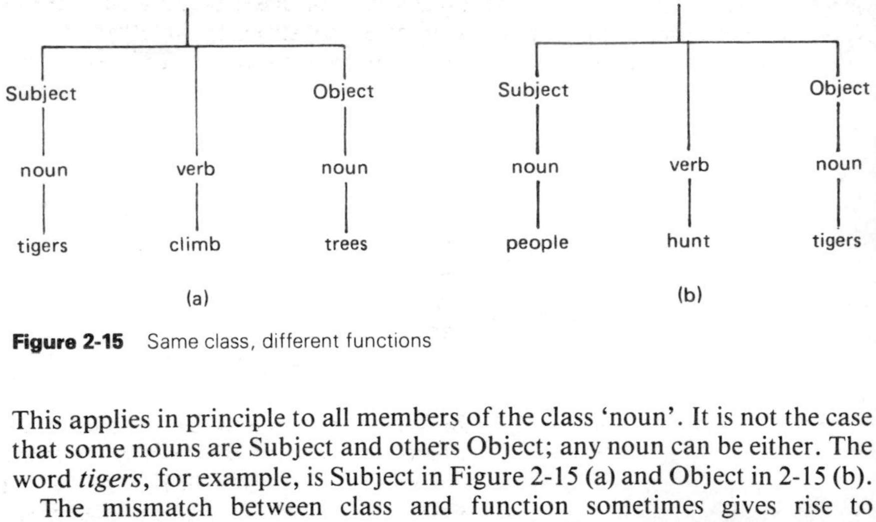

Figure 2-15 Same class, different functions

This applies in principle to all members of the class 'noun'. It is not the case that some nouns are Subject and others Object; any noun can be either. The word *tigers*, for example, is Subject in Figure 2-15 (a) and Object in 2-15 (b).

The mismatch between class and function sometimes gives rise to ambiguity. Consider for example *Mary got the first prize*: does it mean the prize that was given out earliest, or the top prize? In either case, the word *first* is a member of the **class** 'ordinal numeral', which also includes *second, third, fourth*, etc. But its **function** differs in the two cases. (i) In the sense 'prize given out earliest', *first* is functioning as a Numerative, and contrasts not only with *second, third, fourth, fifth*, etc. but also with *next* and *last*. In this sense it could be preceded by *very*, e.g. *Mary got the very first prize that was ever awarded* (*very next, very last*); it could be followed by an expression of time, e.g. *Mary got the first prize of the day*. (ii) In the sense 'top prize', *first* is functioning as a Classifier, and the set of possible items with which it is in contrast includes *second* and *third*; it hardly includes *fourth, fifth* etc., or *next* or *last*; but it does include a few others such as *consolation* and *booby*. *First* in this sense cannot be preceded by *very*; but it can be preceded by a word indicating the scope, such as *house*; or by an expression of attitude, such as *coveted* or *dreaded*. (See Chapter 6 for details.)

We cannot therefore simply decide to assign labels of the one type and then derive those of the other type from them. Just as the same class may have more than one function, so also the same function may be performed by more than one class. This too may be illustrated from the preceding example, where the function 'Classifier' is taken on either by a member of the class 'ordinal numeral' (*first prize*) or by a member of the class 'noun' (*consolation prize*).

In constituent analysis, labels are assigned to the brackets (the nodes). The principle linking the two is that wherever we put a bracket, we should be able to assign a label. This means that there is a systematic relationship between the kind of bracketing used — maximal or minimal, and the kind of labelling used — classes or functions. This can be explained as follows. Class labels are, so to speak, part of the dictionary; they indicate the potential that the word, or other item, has in the grammar of language. Function labels are an interpretation of the text; they indicate the part that the item is playing in the particular structure under consideration. Hence maximal bracketing yields a large number of nodes which can be labelled for class, because the item in question could occur as an element in some construction or other, but to which no function can be assigned in the given instance, as in Figure 2-16.

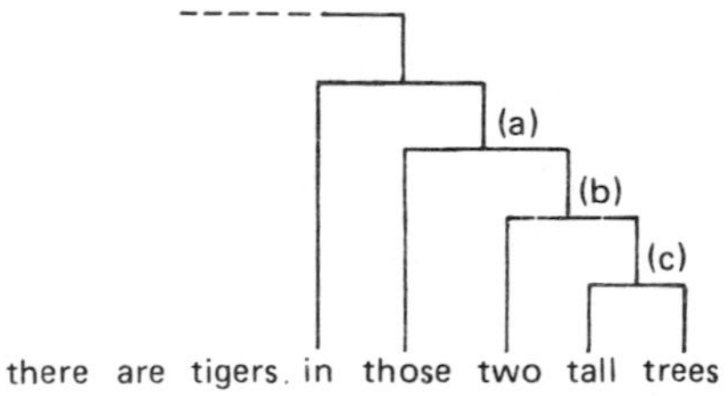

Figure 2-16 Immediate Constituents to which no function can be assigned [(b) and (c)]

The class label 'nominal group' can quite appropriately be assigned at all three nodes (a), (b) and (c): *those two tall trees*, *two tall trees*, and *tall trees* are all typical members of the class 'nominal group' in English. But (b) and (c) have no function in this particular instance; we cannot assign any function to *tall trees* when it forms part of the sequence *those two tall trees*. So function labels imply minimal bracketing, as represented in Figure 2-17, where only (a) appears as a node, while (b) and (c) do not.

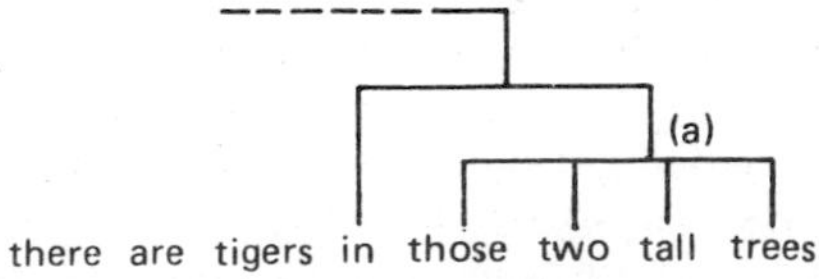

Figure 2-17 Ranked constituents

To summarize:

Maximal bracketing	is associated with	class labelling
Minimal bracketing	″ ″	function labelling

In using maximal bracketing (immediate constituent analysis), the grammarian is trying to explain as much as possible by reference to the notion of constituency; this means putting a bracket where each successive construction can be shown to occur, whether or not that item is functional in the context of the larger structure. With minimal bracketing (ranked constituent analysis), only those items are identified that have some recognizable function in the structure of a larger unit. This means that the notion of constituency is being made to carry less of the burden of interpretation. The concept of constituent structure is much weaker in a functional grammar than in a formal one.

2.4 Classes and functions

A class is a set of items that are alike in some respect. They need not be words; there are classes of group and phrase, classes of clause, and also, at the other end of the scale, classes of morpheme.

A class label indicates that what occurs at that particular node is a member of the class in question.

In the European linguistic tradition, classes were originally derived from an analysis of sentences into parts; the term 'parts of speech' is a mistranslation of the Greek *meroi logou*, Latin partes orationis, which actually meant 'parts of a sentence'. The 'parts of a sentence', which began with Plato (or before him) not as classes but as functions, were subsequently elaborated into a scheme of word classes, established on the basis of the different inflexional potential that different words had in classical Greek. The principle was as in Table 2(2).

Table 2(2) Classical definitions of word classes

Inflection for: (defines)	Word class:
number, case	noun
number, case, gender	adjective
tense, person	verb
(none)	(other words)

This could have been carried further, to take account of inflexion for voice and aspect in verbs, and for comparison in adjectives and adverbs. But the criterion of inflexion will not serve to define all relevant word classes, even in a highly inflected language such as Greek or Latin; and in languages with little or no inflexion, such as English and Chinese, other principles have to be invoked. These may be either grammatical or semantic, or some combination of the two.

There are many ways in which one word may be like another, and the resultant groupings do not always coincide; a word will typically be like one word in one respect and like a different one in another. For example, *upper* and *lower* (which may have the same function, as in *upper case* and *lower case*) both belong to the class of adjective; but *lower* is a comparative adjective, contrasting with *low*, whereas *upper* is not — we cannot say *this roof is upper than that one*. In this respect, *lower* is like *higher*; but *lower* is also a verb, whereas *higher* is not — we cannot say *that roof needs highering*. Sometimes rather clear and definite criteria do present themselves, like grammatical inflexions with fairly consistent meanings; but often they do not, and in such instances the criteria on which classes are defined tend to be rather mixed, and membership of the classes rather indeterminate, with some items clearly belonging and others whose status is doubtful.

Consider for example the class of 'noun' in English. A general definition would involve both grammatical and semantic considerations, with some of the grammatical features having an overt manifestation and others not:

(grammatical:) is either count or mass; if count, may be either singular or plural, plural usually inflected with *-s*; can be made possessive, adding -'s/-s'; can take *the* in front; can be Subject in a clause, etc.

(semantic:) expresses a person, other animate being, inanimate object or abstraction, bounded or unbounded, etc.

When we say that something is a noun, in English, we mean that it displays these characteristics, or most of them, in common with some (but not all) other words in the language.

The label 'noun' thus indicates in a general way the grammatical potential of a linguistic item; but it does not indicate what part the item is playing in any actual structure. It is part of its entry in the dictionary. In order to interpret the meaning of the item in a given instance, we use a label which specifies not the class but the function. By labelling grammatical functions we can show what part each component is playing in the overall structure, as in Figure 2-13 above. Another example is given in Figure 2-18.

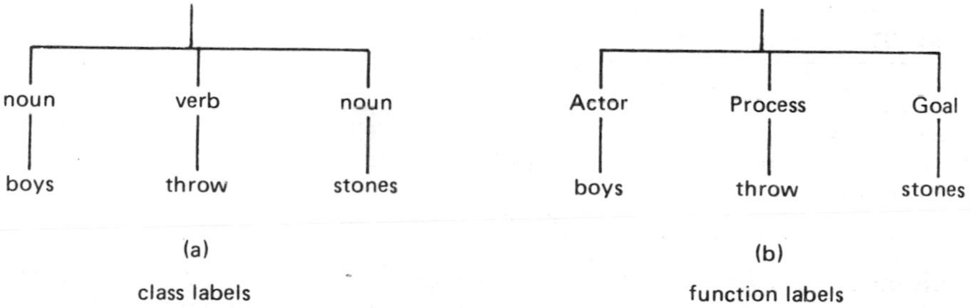

Figure 2-18 A further example of class and function labels

The label 'noun' assigns the word *boys* to a class, signifying that this word is like all other words that carry the label 'noun' in respect of its grammatical potential. The label 'Actor' describes the function of the word *boys* in *boys throw stones*. Whereas *boys* and *stones* are both assigned to the same class, that of nouns, in this particular clause they are serving different functions; so they have different functional labels, *boys* being labelled 'Actor' and *stones* 'Goal'. Cf. Figure 2-15 above.

The purpose of functional labelling is to provide a means of interpreting grammatical structure, **in such a way as to relate any given instance to the system of the language as a whole**. The labels are not assigned in random fashion to each structure as it happens to appear; they are the outcome of an interpretation of the language in terms of its systems and structures at every level. The description of a language, and the analysis of texts in the language, are not — or at least should not be — two distinct and unrelated operations; they are, rather, the two aspects of the same interpretative task, and both proceed side by side. The functional description of the language involves identifying on the one hand all the various functions that are incorporated into the grammar, and on the other hand all the different configurations by which these functions are defined — that is, all the possible structures which serve to express some meaning in the language. A STRUCTURE can be defined as any viable configuration of functions, such as that of Actor – Process – Goal in Figure 2-18 above.

It is important to note, however, that **in nearly all instances a constituent has more than one function at a time**. In *boys throw stones*, for example, we labelled *boys* 'Actor'; but the items *boys* has other functions in the clause besides this one. It is also Subject, for example. The key to a functional interpretation of grammatical structure is the principle that, in general, linguistic items are multifunctional. Most of the constituents in any construction higher than a word enter into more than one structural configuration. In the remainder of Part I we shall explore the various configurations that go to make up an English clause, and the multiple functions that constituents may have within them.

2.5 Subject, Actor, Theme

One of the concepts that is basic to the Western tradition of grammatical analysis is that of Subject. Since this is a familiar term, let us take it as the starting point for investigating the functions in an English clause.

Consider the clause

the duke gave my aunt this teapot

In accordance with the syntactic principles established by medieval grammarians, which were themselves based on the grammars of ancient Greece and Rome, each clause contains one element which can be identified as its Subject; and in this instance, the Subject would be *the duke*.

Here are some other clauses with the Subject shown in italic:

Little Miss Muffet sat on a tuffet
the lion and the unicorn were fighting for the crown
Mary had a little lamb
on Saturday night *I* lost my wife
can *you* make me a cambric shirt?
who killed Cock Robin?
where have *all the flowers* gone?

It is possible to conclude from these examples that 'Subject' is the label for a grammatical function of some kind. There seems to be something in common, as regards their status in the clause, to all the elements we have labelled in this way. But it is not so easy to say exactly what this is; and it is difficult to find in the grammatical tradition a definitive account of what the role of Subject means.

Instead, various interpretations have grown up around the Subject notion, ascribing to it a number of rather different functions. These resolve themselves into three broad definitions, which could be summarized as follows:

(i) that which is the concern of the message
(ii) that of which something is being predicated (i.e. on which rests the truth of the argument)
(iii) the doer of the action

These three definitions are obviously not synonymous; they are defining different concepts. So the question that arises is, is it possible for the category of 'Subject' to embrace all these different meanings at one and the same time?

In *the duke gave my aunt this teapot*, it is reasonable to claim that *the duke* is, in fact, the Subject in all these three senses. He is the one with whom the message is concerned; the truth or falsehood of the statement is vested in him; and he has performed the action of giving.

If all clauses were like this one in having one element serving all three functions, there would be no problem in identifying and explaining the Subject. We could use the term to refer to the sum of these three definitions, and assign the label to whichever element fulfilled all the functions in question. But this assumes that in every clause there is just one element in which all three functions are combined; and this is not the case. Many clauses contain no such element that embodies all three. For example, suppose we say

this teapot my aunt was given by the duke

— which constituent is now to be identified as the Subject?

There is no longer any one obvious answer. What has happened in this instance is that the different functions making up the traditional concept of Subject have been split up among three different constituents of the clause. The duke is still the doer of the deed; but the message is now a message concerning the teapot, and its claim for truth is vested in my aunt.

When these different functions came to be recognized by grammarians as distinct, they were at first labelled as if they were three different **kinds** of Subject. It was still implied that there was some sort of a superordinate concept covering all three, a general notion of Subject of which they were the specific varieties.

The terms that came to be used in the second half of the nineteenth century, when there was a renewal of interest in grammatical theory, were 'psychological Subject', 'grammatical Subject', and 'logical Subject'.

(i) Psychological Subject meant 'that which is the concern of the message'. It was called 'psychological' because it was what the speaker had in his mind to start with, when embarking on the production of the clause.

(ii) Grammatical Subject meant 'that of which something is predicated'. It was called 'grammatical' because at that time the construction of Subject and Predicate was thought of as a purely formal grammatical relationship; it was seen to determine various other grammatical features, such as the case of the noun or pronoun that was functioning as Subject, and its concord of person and number with the verb, but it was not thought to express any particular meaning.

(iii) Logical Subject meant 'doer of the action'. It was called 'logical' in the sense this term had had from the seventeenth century, that of 'having to do with relations between things', as opposed to 'grammatical' relations which were relations between symbols.

In the first example, all these three functions are conflated, or 'mapped' on to one another, as shown in Figure 2-19.

the duke	gave my aunt this teapot
psychological Subject grammatical Subject logical Subject	

Figure 2-19 Same item functioning as psychological, grammatical and logical Subject

In the second example, on the other hand, all three are separated (Figure 2-20).

this teapot	my aunt	was given by	the duke
psychological Subject	grammatical Subject		logical Subject

Figure 2-20 Psychological, grammatical and logical Subject realized by different items

In *this teapot my aunt was given by the duke*, the psychological subject is *this teapot*. That is to say, it is 'this teapot' that is the concern of the message — that the speaker has taken as the point of embarkation of the clause. But the grammatical subject is *my aunt*: 'my aunt' is the one of whom the statement is predicated — in respect of whom the clause is claimed to be valid, and therefore can be argued about as true or false. Only the logical Subject is still *the duke*: 'the duke' is the doer of the deed — the one who is said to have carried out the process that the clause represents.

As long as we concern ourselves only with idealized clause patterns like *John runs* or *the boy threw the ball*, we can operate with the label Subject as if it referred to a single undifferentiated concept. In clauses of this type, the functions of psychological, grammatical and logical Subject all coincide. In *the boy threw the ball*, *the boy* would still be Subject no matter which of the three definitions we were using, like *the duke* in the first of our examples above.

But as soon as we take account of natural living language, and of the kinds of variation that occur in it, in which the order of elements can vary, passives can occur as well as actives, and so on, it is no longer possible to base an analysis on the assumption that these three concepts are merely different aspects of one and the same general notion. They have to be interpreted as what they really are — three separate and distinct functions. There is no such thing as a general concept of 'Subject' of which these are different varieties. They are not three kinds of anything; they are three quite different things. In order to take account of this, we will replace the earlier labels by separate ones which relate more specifically to the functions concerned:

psychological Subject: *Theme*
grammatical Subject: *Subject*
logical Subject: *Actor*

We can now relabel Figure 2-20 as in Figure 2-21.

this teapot	my aunt	was given by	the duke
Theme	Subject		Actor

Figure 2-21 Theme, Subject and Actor

In *the duke gave my aunt this teapot*, the roles of Theme, Subject and Actor are all combined in the one element *the duke*. In *this teapot my aunt was given by the duke*, all three are separated. All the additional combinations are also possible: any two roles may be conflated, with the third kept separate. For example, if we keep *the duke* as Actor, we can have Theme = Subject with Actor separate, as in Figure 2-22(a); Subject = Actor with Theme separate, as in 2-22(b); or Theme = Actor with Subject separate, as in 2-22(c).

(a)

my aunt	was given this teapot by	the duke
Theme Subject		Actor

(b)

this teapot	the duke	gave to my aunt
Theme	Subject Actor	

(c)

by	the duke	my aunt	was given this teapot
	Theme Actor	Subject	

Figure 2-22 Different conflations of Subject, Actor and Theme

In any interpretation of the grammar of English we need to take note of all these possible forms, explaining how and why they differ. They are all, subtly but significantly, different in meaning; at the same time they are all related, and related in a systematic way. Any comparable set of clauses in English would make up a similar PARADIGM. Often, of course, there are not three distinct elements that could carry the functions of Theme, Subject and Actor, but only two, as in Figure 2-23. Note how the series of clauses in 2.23(a)–(d) forms an entirely natural sequence such as a speaker might use in a personal narrative of this kind.

(a)

I	caught the first ball
Theme Subject Actor	

(b)

I	was beaten by	the second
Theme Subject		Actor

(c)

the third	I	stopped
Theme	Subject Actor	

(d)

by	the fourth	I	was knocked out
	Theme Actor	Subject	

Figure 2-23 Narrative embodying different conflations of Subject, Actor and Theme

And often no variation at all is possible, if there is only one element that can have these functions; for example *I ran away*, where *I* is inevitably Theme, Subject and Actor. (Even here there is a possibility of thematic variation, as in *run away I did* or *the one who ran away was me*; see Chapter 3 below.) On the other hand, while explaining all these variants, we also have to explain the fact that the typical, UNMARKED form, in an English declarative (statement-type) clause, is the one in which Theme, Subject and Actor are conflated into a single element. That is the form we tend to use if there is no context leading up to it, and no positive reason for choosing anything else.

The significance of these three functional concepts is that each one corresponds to a different mode of meaning in the clause.

As a working approximation, we can define each of them as follows:

(i) The Theme is a function in the CLAUSE AS A MESSAGE. It is what the message is concerned with: the point of departure for what the speaker is going to say.

(ii) The Subject is a function in the CLAUSE AS AN EXCHANGE. It is the element that is held responsible: in which is vested the success of the clause in whatever is its particular speech function.

(iii) The Actor is a function in the CLAUSE AS A REPRESENTATION (of a process). It is the active participant in the process: the one that does the deed.

These three headings — clause as message, clause as exchange, clause as representation — refer to the three principal **kinds of meaning** that are embodied in the structure of a clause. Each of these kinds of meaning is expressed by means of certain configurations of functions. Thus Theme, Subject and Actor do not occur as isolates; each is associated with one or more other functions of the same kind, together with which it forms meaningful configurations. A meaningful configuration of functions of the same kind is what is meant by a STRUCTURE.

Thus the functional label has no significance in itself. Its significance lies in its relationship to other functions with which it is structurally associated; the total structure is what expresses, or REALIZES, the meaning intended by speaker or writer. The function Actor, for example, is defined only by its relation to other representational functions such as Process and Goal; so if in interpreting the clause *Miss Muffet ran away* we label *Miss Muffet* as Actor this is meaningful only because we also label *ran away* as Process, in this way specifying the relationship that obtains between them. Actor and Process together form a structure, one of a number of possible structures through which the clause expresses one particular kind of meaning. In similar fashion both Subject and Theme enter into configurations with other elements, forming structures which express meanings of other kinds.

In the next three chapters we shall explore these three aspects of the meaning of the English clause, using the notions of Theme, Subject and Actor as points of departure. Note that from now on the term Subject will be used only in the sense defined above, that of 'grammatical Subject' in the older terminology. It will not be used for 'psychological' or 'logical' 'Subject', for which we shall use Theme and Actor respectively. All three terms, Theme, Subject and Actor, will be further refined and explained in the chapters that follow.

3

Clause as message

3.1 Theme and Rheme

In Section 2.5 we introduced the notion of a clause as a unit in which meanings of three different kinds are combined. Three distinct structures, each expressing one kind of semantic organization, are mapped on to one another to produce a single wording.

Of the various structures which, when mapped on to each other, make up a clause, we will consider first the one which gives the clause its character as a message. This is known as THEMATIC structure.

We may assume that in all languages the clause has the character of a message: it has some form of organization giving it the status of a communicative event. But there are different ways in which this may be achieved. In English, as in many other languages, the clause is organized as a message by having a special status assigned to one part of it. One element in the clause is enunciated as the theme; this then combines with the remainder so that the two parts together constitute a message.

In some languages which have a pattern of this kind, the theme is announced by means of a particle: in Japanese, for example, there is a special postposition *-wa*, which signifies that whatever immediately precedes it is thematic. In other languages, of which English is one, the theme is indicated by position in the clause. In speaking or writing English we signal that an item has thematic status by putting it first. No other signal is necessary, although it is not unusual in spoken English for the theme to be marked off also by the intonation pattern (see below).

Following the terminology of the Prague school of linguists, we shall use the term Theme as the label for this function. (Like all other functions it will be written with an initial capital.) The Theme is the element which serves as the point of departure of the message; it is that with which the clause is concerned. The remainder of the message, the part in which the Theme is developed, is called in Prague school terminology the Rheme. As a message structure, therefore, a clause consists of a Theme accompanied by a Rheme; and the structure is expressed by the order — whatever is chosen as the Theme is put first. For examples of this Theme + Rheme structure see Figure 3-1.

the duke	has given my aunt that teapot
my aunt	has been given that teapot by the duke
that teapot	the duke has given to my aunt
Theme	Rheme

Figure 3-1 Theme – Rheme structure

In the following example, which is the first sentence of the Introduction to Roget's *Thesaurus*, the Theme is *the present Work*:

> The present Work is intended to supply, with respect to the English language, a desideratum hitherto unsupplied in any language; . . .

Some grammarians have used the terms Topic and Comment instead of Theme and Rheme. But the Topic–Comment terminology carries rather different connotations. The label 'Topic' usually refers to only one particular kind of Theme (see Section 3.5 below); and it tends to be used as a cover term for two concepts that are functionally distinct, one being that of Theme and the other being that of Given (see Chapter 8). For these reasons the terms Theme – Rheme are considered more appropriate in thc present framework.

As a general guide, the Theme can be identified as that element which comes in first position in the clause. We have already indicated that this is not how the category of Theme is **defined**. The definition is functional, as it is with all the elements in this interpretation of grammatical structure. The Theme is one element in a particular structural configuration which, taken as a whole, organizes the clause as a message; this is the configuration Theme + Rheme. A message consists of a Theme combined with a Rheme.

Within that configuration, the Theme is the starting-point for the message; it is what the clause is going to be about. So part of the meaning of any clause lies in which element is chosen as its Theme. There is a difference in meaning between *a halfpenny is the smallest English coin*, where *a halfpenny* is Theme ('I'll tell you about a halfpenny'), and *the smallest English coin is a halfpenny*, where *the smallest English coin* is Theme ('I'll tell you about the smallest English coin'). The difference may be characterized as 'thematic'; the two clauses differ in their choice of theme. By glossing them in this way, as 'I'll tell you about . . .', we can feel that they are two different messages.

First position in the clause is not what defines the Theme; it is the means whereby the function of Theme is **realized**, in the grammar of English. There is no automatic reason why the Theme function should be realized in this way; as remarked above, there are languages which have a category of Theme functionally similar to that of English but which nevertheless express it in quite a different way. But if in any given language the message is organized as a Theme – Rheme structure, and if this structure is expressed by the sequence in which the elements occur in the clause, then it seems natural that the position for the Theme should be at the beginning, rather than at the end or at some other specific point.

The Theme is not necessarily a NOMINAL GROUP, like those above. It may also be an ADVERBIAL GROUP or PREPOSITIONAL PHRASE, such as the examples in Figure 3-2.

once	I was a real turtle
very carefully	she put him back on his feet again
on Friday night	I go backwards to bed
Theme	Rheme

Figure 3-2 Themes other than nominal groups

John B. Carroll's 'Foreword' to Whorf's *Language, Thought and Reality* begins with the adverbial Theme *once in a blue moon*:

> Once in a blue moon a man comes along who grasps the relationship between events which have hitherto seemed quite separate, and gives mankind a new dimension of knowledge.

Sometimes in English the Theme is announced explicitly, by means of some expression like *as for . . .*, *with regard to . . .*, *about . . .* Usually it is only nominal Themes that are introduced by a locution of this kind. The Theme is then picked up later in the clause by the appropriate pronoun — *her*, *it* in the following examples:

> As for my aunt, the duke has given her that teapot.
> About that teapot — my aunt was given it by the duke.

This 'picking up' of the Theme by a pronoun may happen even when the Theme is not explicitly introduced, and even if the Theme is also the Subject, especially in spoken English; cf. the first example in Figure 3.3.

The Theme of a clause is frequently marked off in speech by being spoken on a separate intonation contour, or TONE GROUP as it is called; this is especially likely when the Theme is either (i) an adverbial group or prepositional phrase, or (ii) a nominal group not functioning as Subject — anything other than the most common pattern (see Section 3.3 below). But even ordinary Subject Themes are often given a tone group to themselves in everyday speech. One tone group expresses one unit of information (this is described in Chapter 8); and if a clause is organized into two information units, the boundary between the two is overwhelmingly likely to coincide with the junction of Theme and Rheme.

3.2 Simple Themes of more than one constituent

As a first step we have made two assumptions: that the Theme of a clause consists of just one element, and that element is represented by just one constituent — one nominal group, adverbial group or prepositional phrase. These two assumptions hold for the examples given so far; compare also those in Figure 3-3.

The Queen of Hearts	she made some tarts
the man in the wilderness	said to me
for want of a nail	the shoe was lost
with sobs and tears	he sorted out those of the largest size
Theme	Rheme

Figure 3-3 Further examples of Theme and Rheme

In the first sentence of the Preface to J.R. Firth's *Papers in Linguistics 1934–1951* the Theme is *the first chair of General Linguistics in this country*, which is still one single nominal group:

> The first chair of General Linguistics in this country was established in the University of London in 1944, at the School of Oriental and African Studies . . .

In each of these examples the Theme is one element, which in turn is one nominal group or one prepositional phrase.

A common variant of this elementary pattern is that in which the Theme consists of two or more elements forming a single complex element. Any element of clause structure may be represented by two or more groups or phrases forming a 'complex' (group complex or phrase complex; see Chapter 7 Additional below.) Such a 'complex' functions as a Theme in the normal way. This is illustrated in Figure 3-4.

the Walrus and the Carpenter Tom, Tom, the piper's son from house to house	were walking close at hand stole a pig and away did run I wend my way
Theme	Rheme

Figure 3-4 Group complex or phrase complex as Theme

Such Themes are still within the category of 'simple' Themes. Any group complex or phrase complex constitutes a single element within the clause; for example, two nominal groups joined by *and*, like *the Walrus and the Carpenter*, make up a nominal group complex. This is just one element in the clause, and therefore constitutes a simple Theme. The two prepositional phrases *from house to house* likewise make up a prepositional phrase complex, and this is also therefore one simple Theme. The different kinds of relationship that may be expressed in these 'complex' structures are discussed in Chapter 7 below.

The first sentence of Hjelmslev's *Prolegomena to a Theory of Language*, Whitfield's translation, has as its Theme the nominal group complex *language – human speech*, consisting of two nominal groups in apposition:

> Language — human speech — is an inexhaustible abundance of manifold treasures.

Another example of apposition in the Theme is the following, from the blurb to Hunter Davies' biography of George Stephenson:

> One hundred and fifty years ago, on 15 September 1830, the world's first passenger railway — the Liverpool to Manchester — was opened, an event which was to change the face of civilization.

Here the Theme consists of two phrases forming a phrase complex, ending at *1830*.

There is however a special thematic structure in which two or more elements within the clause are explicitly grouped together to form a single constituent of the thematic structure: typically functioning as Theme, but sometimes on the other hand as Rheme. This is a particular kind of clause, a THEMATIC EQUATIVE, which is a form of 'identifying' clause (see Chapter 5, Section 5.4 below). In a thematic equative, all the elements are organized into two constituents; these two are then linked by a relationship of identity, a kind of 'equals sign', expressed by some form of the verb *be*. Examples are given in Figure 3-5.

what (the thing) the duke gave to my aunt	was	that teapot
the one who gave my aunt that teapot	was	the duke
the one the duke gave that teapot to	was	my aunt
what the duke did with that teapot	was	give it to my aunt
how my aunt came by that teapot	was	she was given it by the duke
Theme		Rheme

Figure 3-5 Thematic equatives

Compare the first clause of the second paragraph of *Through the Looking-glass*:

The way Dinah washed her children's faces was this:

where the Theme is *the way Dinah washed her children's faces*. Strictly speaking the *was*, or other form of *be*, is outside the Theme – Rheme structure; but for the sake of simpler analysis it can be shown as part of the Rheme.

A form such as *what the duke gave to my aunt* is an instance of a structural feature known as NOMINALIZATION, whereby any element or group of elements takes on the functions of a nominal group in the clause. Any nominalization, therefore, constitutes a single element in the message structure.

In this case the nominalization serves a thematic purpose. The thematic equative pattern allows for all possible distributions of the parts of the clause into Theme and Rheme, as in Figure 3-5; and including one such as the following:

what happened was that the duke gave my aunt that teapot

where the Theme is simply *what happened*, meaning 'I want to tell you that something happened', and every component of the happening is put into the Rheme.

In the typical instance the nominalization functions as the Theme, because in a Theme – Rheme structure it is the Theme that is the prominent element. All the examples above were of this type. But — as so often happens in language — in contrast with the typical pattern there is a standing-out or MARKED alternative, exemplified by *you're the one I blame for this*, with *you* as Theme, in which the usual relationship is reversed and the nominalization becomes the Rheme. Further examples of this are given in Figure 3-6.

that	is	the one I like
this teapot	was	what the duke gave to my aunt
a loaf of bread	is	what we chiefly need
Theme		Rheme

Figure 3-6 Marked thematic equatives (nominalization as Rheme)

A thematic equative (which is sometimes called a 'pseudo-cleft sentence' in formal grammar) is simply an identifying clause with a thematic nominalization in it. Its function is to express the Theme - Rheme structure in such a way as to allow for the Theme to consist of any subset of the elements of the clause. This is the explanation for the existence of clauses of this type: they have evolved, in English, as a thematic resource, enabling the message to be structured in whatever way the speaker or writer wants.

Let us say more explicitly what this structure means. The thematic equative actually realizes two distinct semantic features, which happen to correspond to the two senses of the word *identify*. On the one hand, it identifies (specifies) what the Theme is; on the other hand, it identifies it (equates it) with the Rheme.

The second of these features adds a semantic component of exclusiveness: the meaning is 'this and this alone'. So the meaning of *what the duke gave my aunt was that teapot* is something like 'I am going to tell you about the duke's gift to my aunt: it was that teapot — and nothing else'. Contrast this with *the duke gave my aunt that teapot*, where the meaning is 'I am going to tell you something about the duke: he gave my aunt that teapot' (with no implication that he did not do other things as well).

Hence even when the Theme is not being extended beyond one element, this identifying structure still contributes something to the meaning of the message: it serves to express this feature of exclusiveness. If I say *what the duke did was give my aunt that teapot*, the nominalization *what the duke did* carries the meaning 'and that's all he did, in the context of what we are talking about'.* This is also the explanation of the marked form, that with the nominalization in the Rheme, as in *that's the one I like*. Here the Theme is simply *that*, exactly the same as in the non-nominalized equivalent *that I like*; but the thematic equative still adds something to the meaning, by signalling that the relationship is an exclusive one. Compare *a loaf of bread we need* and *a loaf of bread is what we need*. Both of these have *a loaf of bread* as Theme; but whereas the former implies 'among other things', the latter implies 'and nothing else'. Note that some very common expressions have this marked thematic equative structure, including all those beginning *that's what*, *that's why* etc.; e.g. *that's what I meant*.

Figure 3-7 gives some further examples which help to bring out the difference between a thematic equative and a clause with ordinary Theme - Rheme structure.

---

* It further indicates, by the choice of the 'pro-verb', something about the role of the duke: that he did something — he was an active participant in the process. Contrast *what happened to that teapot . . .*, where the role of the teapot is shown to have been a passive one. See Chapter 5.

(a) thematic equative
  (i) nominalization as Theme

what no-one seemed to notice	was	the writing on the wall
the thing that impresses me most	is	their enthusiasm for the job
the ones you never see	are	the smugglers
Theme	Rheme	

  (ii) nominalization as Rheme

twopence a day	was	what my master allowed me
the Walrus	is	the one I like best
Theme	Rheme	

(b) non-equative equivalents (assuming Subject as Theme; see Section 3.3 below)

no-one	seemed to notice the writing on the wall
their enthusiasm for the job	impresses me most
you	never see the smugglers
my master	allowed me twopence a day
I	like the Walrus best
Theme	Rheme

Figure 3-7 Further examples of thematic equatives

3.3 Theme and mood

What is the element that is typically chosen as Theme in an English clause? The answer to that question depends on the choice of mood.

Mood will be discussed in Chapter 4. Here we shall need to anticipate the first steps in that discussion, and introduce the primary categories of the mood system. We will restrict ourselves to independent clauses, those that can stand by themselves as a complete sentence.

Every independent clause selects for mood. Some, like *John!* and *good night!*, are MINOR clauses; they have no thematic structure and so will be left out of account. The others are MAJOR clauses. An independent MAJOR clause is either indicative or imperative in mood; if indicative, it is either declarative or interrogative; if interrogative, it is either polar interrogative ('yes/no' type) or content interrogative ('WH-' type). Examples:

indicative: declarative	Bears eat honey. Bears don't eat honey.
indicative: interrogative: yes/no	Do bears eat honey? Don't bears eat honey?
indicative: interrogative: WH-	What eats honey? What do bears eat?
imperative	Eat! Let's eat!

We will consider each of these moods in turn, from the point of view of their thematic structure.

(1) Theme in declarative clauses. In a declarative clause, the typical pattern is one in which Theme is conflated with Subject; for example, *Little Bo-peep has lost her sheep*, where *Little Bo-peep* is both Subject and Theme. All the examples in Figure 3-1 were of this kind; likewise those in 3-5 to 3-7.

We shall refer to the mapping of Theme on to Subject as the UNMARKED THEME of a declarative clause. The Subject is the element that is chosen as Theme unless there is good reason for choosing something else. Note that this adds a further explanation for the use of a thematic equative in clauses such as *you're the one I blame*, *that's what I meant*: here the Theme is Subject, and therefore unmarked, whereas in the non-identifying form *you I blame*, *that I meant*, making *you* and *that* thematic also makes them marked Themes (because not Subject), and so adds a sense of contrast which may be out of place.

In everyday conversation the item most often functioning as unmarked Theme (Subject/Theme) in a declarative clause is the first person pronoun *I*. Much of our talk consists of messages concerned with ourselves, and especially with what we think and feel. Next after that come the other personal pronouns *you*, *we*, *he*, *she*, *it*, *they*; and the impersonal pronouns *it* and *there*. Then come other nominal groups — those with common noun or proper noun as Head — and nominalizations. Providing these are functioning as Subject, then having them as Theme is still the unmarked choice.

A Theme that is something other than the Subject, in a declarative clause, we shall refer to as a MARKED THEME. The most usual form of marked Theme is an adverbial group, e.g. *today*, *suddenly*, *somewhat distractedly*, or prepositional phrase, e.g. *at night*, *in the corner*, *without much hope*, functioning as ADJUNCT in the clause. Least likely to be thematic is a COMPLEMENT, which is a nominal group that is not functioning as Subject — something that could have been a Subject but is not. For discussion of Complement and Adjunct see Chapter 4, Section 4.3 below.

The main tendencies for the selection of Theme in declarative clauses are summarized in Table 3(1).

The 'most marked' type of Theme in a declarative clause is thus a Complement: for example *nature* in *nature I loved*, *this responsibility* in *this responsibility we accept wholly*. This is a nominal element which, being nominal, has the potentiality of being Subject; which has not been selected as Subject; and which nevertheless has been made thematic. Since it could have been Subject, and therefore **unmarked** Theme, there must be very good reason for making it a thematic Complement — it is being explicitly foregrounded as the Theme of the clause. Let us look at one example, taken from the end of Bally and Sechehaye's Preface to Saussure's *Course in General Linguistics* (English translation by Wade Baskin):

> We are aware of our responsibility to our critics. We are also aware of our responsibility to the author, who probably would not have authorized the publication of these pages.
>
> This responsibility we accept wholly, and we would willingly bear it alone.

Here the Theme *this responsibility* is strongly foregrounded; it summarizes the whole burden of the preface — the special responsibility faced by scholars reconstructing from others' lecture notes the work of an outstanding colleague for publication after his death — and enunciates this as their point of departure, as what the undertaking is all about.

Sometimes even the Complement from within a prepositional phrase (see Chapter 6, Section 6.5) functions as Theme, particularly in idiomatic com-

Table 3(1) Examples of Theme in declarative clause. Theme–Rheme boundary is shown by #.

	Function*	Class	Theme example	Clause example
Unmarked Theme	Subject	nominal group: pronoun as Head	I, you, we, he, she, they, it, there	I # had a little nut-tree she # went to the baker's there # were three jovial Welshmen
	Subject	nominal group: common or proper noun as Head	a wise old owl, Mary, the King of Hearts London Bridge	a wise old owl # lived in an oak Mary # had a little lamb London Bridge # is fallen down
	Subject	nominalization	what I want	what I want # is a proper cup of coffee
Marked Theme	Adjunct	adverbial group; prepositional phrase	merrily, in spring, on Saturday night	merrily # we roll along on Saturday night # I lost my wife
	Complement	nominal group; nominalization	a bag-pudding, what they could not eat that night	a bag-pudding # the King did make what they could not eat that night # the Queen next morning fried

* Function in clause as exchange; see Chapter 4.

binations of preposition and verb: for example *that* in *that I could do without*, *two things* in *two things we need to comment on*. Perhaps the type of Complement/Theme that stands out as 'most marked', however, is a pronoun, such as *me* in *me they blame for it*. This is, as it were, the opposite end of the scale of thematic tendency from the unmarked Subject/Theme *I* with which we started.

There is one sub-category of declarative clause which has a special thematic structure, namely the exclamative. These typically have an exclamatory WH-element as Theme, as in Figure 3-8.

how cheerfully what tremendously easy questions	he seems to grin you ask
Theme	Rheme

Figure 3-8 Theme in exclamative clauses

(2) Theme in interrogative clauses. The typical function of an interrogative clause is to ask a question; and from the speaker's point of view asking a question is an indication that he wants to be told something. The fact that, in real life, people ask questions for all kinds of reasons does not call into dispute the observation that the basic meaning of a question is a request for an answer. The natural theme of a question, therefore, is 'what I want to know'.

There are two main types of question: one where what the speaker wants to know is the POLARITY 'yes or no?', e.g. *Can you keep a secret? Is John Smith within?*; the other where what the speaker wants to know is the identity of some element in the content, e.g. *Who will you send to fetch her away? Where has my little dog gone?* In both types, the word indicating what the speaker wants to know comes first.

In a yes/no question, which is a question about polarity, the element that functions as Theme is the element that embodies the expression of polarity, namely the FINITE VERB. It is the finite verb in English that expresses positive or negative: *is*, *isn't*; *do*, *don't*; *can*, *can't*; etc. So in a yes/no interrogative the finite verb is put first, before the Subject. The meaning is 'I want you to tell me whether or not'.

In a WH- question, which is a search for a missing piece of information, the element that functions as Theme is the element that requests this information, namely the WH- element. It is the WH- element that expresses the nature of the missing piece: *who*, *what*, *when*, *how* etc. So in a WH- interrogative the WH- element is put first no matter what other function it has in the mood structure of the clause, whether Subject, Adjunct or Complement. The meaning is 'I want you to tell me the person, thing, time, manner, etc.'.

Interrogative clauses, therefore, embody the thematic principle in their structural make-up. It is characteristic of an interrogative clause in English that one particular element comes first; and the reason for this is that that element, owing to the very nature of a question, has the status of a Theme. The speaker does not choose each time to put this element first; its occurrence in first position is the regular pattern by which the interrogative is expressed.

It has become part of the system of the language, and the explanation for this lies in the thematic significance that is attached to first position in the English clause. Interrogatives express questions; the natural theme of a question is 'I want to be told something'; the answer required is either a piece of information or an indication of polarity. So the realization of interrogative mood involves selecting an element that indicates the kind of answer required, and putting it at the beginning of the clause.

In a WH- interrogative, the Theme is constituted solely by the WH-element: that is, the group or phrase in which the WH- word occurs. Examples in Figure 3-9.

who how many miles with what	killed Cock Robin? to Babylon? shall I mend it?
Theme	Rheme

Figure 3-9 Theme in WH- interrogative

If the WH- word is, or is part of, a nominal group functioning as Complement in a prepositional phrase, this nominal group may function as Theme on its own, e.g. *what* in *what shall I mend it with?*, *which house* in *which house do they live in?*

In a yes/no interrogative, the Theme includes the finite verb; but it extends over the Subject as well. Finite verb plus Subject form a two-part Theme, the principle of which will be explained in Section 3.5 below. Examples in Figure 3-10.

can is should	you anybody old acquaintance	find me an acre of land? at home? be forgot?
Theme (1)	Theme (2)	Rheme

Figure 3-10 Theme is yes/no interrogative

Thus in both kinds of interrogative clause the choice of a typical 'unmarked' thematic pattern is clearly motivated, since this pattern has evolved as the means of carrying the basic message of the clause. Hence there is a strong tendency for the speaker to choose the unmarked form, and not to override it by introducing a marked Theme out in front. But marked Themes do sometimes occur in interrogatives, as illustrated in Figure 3-11.

after tea in your house	will you tell me a story? who does the cooking?
Theme	Rheme

Figure 3-11 Marked Theme in interrogative clauses

(3) Theme in imperative clauses. The basic message of an imperative clause is 'I want you to do something', or 'I want us (you and me) to do something'. Hence the unmarked Theme is *you* or *let's*, as in *you keep quiet, let's go home*. Another form of the imperative has the finite verb *do*; the function of this is to mark the clause explicitly as positive not negative, as in *do keep quiet, do let's go home*, and the Theme is *do*. In a negative imperative, where the meaning is 'I want you/us not to', the Theme is typically *don't*, as in *don't (you) argue, don't let's go home*; the latter has an alternative form *let's not go home*, with Theme *let's*.

What of the common everyday form of the 'you' imperative, which has no Subject or finite verb, as in *keep quiet, sing a song of sixpence*? Strictly speaking, these have no explicit Theme; the meaning 'I want you to', which might have been thematized, by analogy with those above, or with the interrogative, is realized simply by the form of the clause. Structurally, therefore, these imperatives may be considered as consisting of Rheme only, the thematic component of request being left implicit. However, because of the strong association of first position with thematic value in the clause, this structure has the effect of giving the verb the status of a Theme. Such clauses can thus be analysed in either of two ways; Figure 3-12 shows both possible interpretations.

('I want you to') sing	sing a song of sixpence a song of sixpence
Theme	Rheme

Figure 3-12 Theme in imperative clauses

In mood structure, the verb functions as PREDICATOR in the clause; so in the latter interpretation, as regards the functions involved, the Theme is conflated with the Predicator instead of with Subject, Adjunct or Complement. This also happens, although very infrequently, in declarative clauses; for example *forget it I never shall*, where the verb *forget* is put in first position to give it thematic status.

3.4 Other characteristic Themes

Besides those Themes we have considered so far, there are certain other elements that have special status in the thematic structure. This is because, if these elements are present at all, they tend to be, or in some cases have to be, thematic.

(1) Conjunctive and modal Adjuncts. Those that tend to be thematic, but are not obligatorily so, are Adjuncts of two kinds: conjunctive, and modal.

(i) CONJUNCTIVE ADJUNCTS are those which relate the clause to the preceding text. (They are alternatively known as 'discourse Adjuncts'.) The principal types are set out in Table 3(2); for more detail see Chapter 9, Section 9.4 below.

(ii) MODAL ADJUNCTS are those which express the speaker's judgement

Table 3(2) Conjunctive Adjuncts

	Type	Meaning	Examples
I	appositive	'i.e., e.g.'	that is, in other words, for instance
	corrective	'rather'	or rather, at least, to be precise
	dismissive	'in any case'	in any case, anyway, leaving that aside
	summative	'in short'	briefly, to sum up, in conclusion
	verifactive	'actually'	actually, in fact, as a matter of fact
II	additive	'and'	also, moreover, in addition, besides
	adversative	'but'	on the other hand, however, conversely
	variative	'instead'	instead, alternatively
III	temporal	'then'	meanwhile, before that, later on, next, soon, finally
	comparative	'likewise'	likewise, in the same way
	causal	'so'	therefore, for this reason, as a result, with this in mind
	conditional	'(if . . .) then'	in that case, under the circumstances, otherwise
	concessive	'yet'	nevertheless, despite that
	respective	'as to that'	in this respect, as far as that's concerned

Table 3(3) Modal Adjuncts

	Type	Meaning	Examples
I	probability	how likely? how obvious?	probably, possibly, certainly, perhaps, maybe, of course, surely, obviously
	usuality	how often? how typical?	usually, sometimes, always, never, for the most part, seldom, often
	opinion	I think	in my opinion, from my point of view, personally, to my mind
II	admissive	I admit	frankly, to be honest, to tell you the truth
	assertive	I assure you	honestly, really, believe me, seriously, without any doubt
	presumptive	how presumable?	evidently, apparently, no doubt, presumably
	desiderative	how desirable?	(un)fortunately, to my delight, luckily, regrettably, hopefully
	tentative	how constant?	initially, tentatively, looking back on it, provisionally
	validative	how valid?	broadly speaking, in general terms, on the whole, objectively, strictly speaking
	evaluative	how sensible?	wisely, understandably, foolishly, by mistake
	predictive	how expected?	to my surprise, as expected, amazingly, by chance

regarding the relevance of the message. The principal types are set out in Table 3(3).

It is not difficult to see why modal and conjunctive Adjuncts tend to come at the beginning of the clause: if one of them is present at all, then in a sense it is a natural theme. If the speaker includes within the message some element that expresses his own angle of judgement on the matter, it is natural for him to make this his point of departure. For example: *of course*, *perhaps*, *in my opinion*, *luckily*, *certainly*, *most of the time*, in

Of course they answer to their names?
Perhaps it doesn't understand English.

In my opinion you never think at all.
Luckily the little magic bottle had now had its full effect.
Certainly the glass was beginning to melt away.
Most of the time he doesn't know what he's doing.

Similarly if the speaker includes some element expressing the relationship to what has gone before; the Theme of the message then becomes an indication of its significance at that point in the discourse, for example: *after that*, *once upon a time*, *only*, *however*, *at any rate*, *presently*, in

After that I cut some more bread-and-butter.
Once upon a time there were three little sisters.
Only I don't exactly know what they are.
However one of the knights will show you the way.
At any rate I'd better be getting out of the wood.
Presently she began again.

(2) Conjunctions and relatives. As we have seen, conjunctive Adjuncts and modal Adjuncts tend to be given thematic status, and so typically occur in first position. But this is not obligatory; they can come elsewhere in the clause, and they may be added as an afterthought at the end.

There are other items, however, that have to be thematic; that is, they must come initially if they are present in the clause at all. These are of two kinds: conjunctions, and relatives.

(i) CONJUNCTIONS (which constitute a distinct class in the grammar) are exemplified in Table 3(4).

Table 3(4) Conjunctions

Type	Examples
co-ordinator	and, or, nor, either, neither, but, yet, so, then
subordinator	when, while, before, after, until, because, if, although, unless, since, that, whether
	even if, in case, supposing (that), assuming (that), seeing (that), given that, provided (that), in spite of the fact that, in the event that

These items are inherently thematic; in the evolution of the language they have as it were floated to the front of the clause and stayed there. The speaker does not choose each time to make *if* or *but* his Theme. He chooses the meanings 'if' or 'but', and as part of the package the words that express these meanings are assigned thematic status.

But since these items have to come first, and yet have no function as Subject, Adjunct or Complement, when one of them is present it does not take up the whole of the thematic potential of the clause. The speaker now has the choice of which element to put next; and whatever item is selected to follow will still have thematic force. So although typically it is the Subject which follows, it may alternatively be some other element, as in *if at first you don't succeed*, *but the cask of pearls no-one has ever found*. Here the only reason for putting the Adjunct *at first* or the Complement *the cask of pearls* in marked position before the Subject is to give them thematic status; and this shows that the function of Theme is still present following the *if* or the *but*.

Compare *when in any country several domestic breeds have once been established* (from Darwin's *Origin of Species*), where *in any country* is in marked thematic position.

This does not mean that there is no thematic flavour associated with the conjunction itself. Part of the Theme of any 'if' clause is precisely its conditional relationship to the clause it conditions. The theme has to be interpreted as a meaning, rather than as this or that particular item that realizes the meaning; the theme of a clause beginning with *but* is not so much the word *but* as the meaning 'contrary to the expectation just set up'. Moreover although 'marked' (non-Subject) Themes do occur after conjunctions, they are considerably rarer than they are in non-conjoined clauses, which suggests that some part of the total thematic potential in the message is as it were 'used up' when we assign a clause a particular status as co-ordinate or subordinate to another one.

Examples such as these show that more than one element in the clause may have thematic status. The interpretation of these 'multiple Themes' will be given in Section 3.5 below. Meanwhile we turn to the second class of clause-initial items.

(ii) RELATIVES are exemplified in Table 3(5).

Table 3(5) Relatives

Type	Examples
definite	which, who, that, whose, when, where (why, how)
indefinite	whatever, whichever, whoever, whosever, whenever, wherever, however

Unlike conjunctions, relatives do not form a separate word class; they are either nouns or adverbs. They function as Subject, Adjunct or Complement; either alone, or within the structure of a group, nominal or adverbial, or a phrase; e.g. *whose house*, *in which*, *with whom*, *on whose behalf*; *whichever way*, *for whatever reason*, *however badly*. A relative group or phrase of this kind functions, as a whole, as the Theme of the clause in which it occurs.

Relatives are thus like WH- interrogatives, in that they have both a function in the clause (as Subject, etc.) and a special status of their own. They are of course closely related to interrogatives; in fact the concept of 'WH- item' covers both. This in turn is part of a wider class embracing both 'WH- items' and 'TH- items', which taken together fulfil a DEICTIC or pointing out function. The general principle behind all these elements is as shown in Table 3(6).

Table 3(6) TH- and WH- items

Meaning	Class	Example
(1) I'm telling you which	TH-	[I saw] this one, them
(2) I'm not telling you which:	WH-:	
(a) I don't know	interrogative	which one, who [did you see?]
(b) I'm telling you elsewhere	relative, definite	{ [the one (thing)] which [I saw] [the one (person)] who [I saw]
(c) it doesn't matter	relative, indefinite	whichever, whoever [you saw]

3.5 Multiple Themes

In Section 3.2 we considered various instances of a Theme having more than one constituent group or phrase, like *the Walrus and the Carpenter*, or *what the duke did with that teapot*. These were still said to be 'simple Themes', since the thematic element itself was a single unit, without any further internal structure.

In the last section, 3.4, we introduced various elements that tend to, or have to, have thematic status if they occur at all: (1) conjunctive and modal Adjuncts, and (2) conjunctions and relatives. But just because their thematic status is built in, so to speak, they may not exhaust the thematic potential of the clause.

The principle at work here is as follows. If the initial element in the clause does not function as Subject or Complement or CIRCUMSTANTIAL Adjunct (this concept is defined in Chapter 5 below; it embraces all Adjuncts **other than** conjunctive and modal ones), then the Subject, Complement or Adjunct next following is still part of the Theme. This introduces the notion of a MULTIPLE THEME — where the part of the clause functioning as Theme has a further, internal structure of its own.

The internal structure of a multiple Theme is based on the functional principle that was presented in Chapter 2: the principle that a clause is the product of three simultaneous semantic processes. It is at one and the same time a representation of experience, an interactive exchange, and a message.

At this point, however, we need to introduce more general functional concepts to which we can relate these three aspects of the meaning of the clause. These are the three kinds of meaning that are embodied in human language as a whole, forming the basis of the semantic organization of all natural languages. We shall refer to these as 'metafunctions', and use for them the terms IDEATIONAL, INTERPERSONAL and TEXTUAL.

Ideational meaning is the representation of experience: our experience of the world that lies about us, and also inside us, the world of our imagination. It is meaning in the sense of 'content'. The ideational function of the **clause** is that of representing what in the broadest sense we can call 'processes': actions, events, processes of consciousness, and relations (Chapter 5).

Interpersonal meaning is meaning as a form of action: the speaker or writer doing something to the listener or reader by means of language. The interpersonal function of the **clause** is that of exchanging roles in rhetorical interaction: statements, questions, offers and commands, together with accompanying modalities (Chapter 4).

Textual meaning is relevance to the context: both the preceding (and following) text, and the context of situation. The textual function of the **clause** is that of constructing a message (this chapter).

The Theme–Rheme structure is the basic form of the organization of the clause as a message. Within this, the Theme is what the speaker selects as his point of departure, the means of development of the clause. But in the total make-up of the Theme, components from all three functions may contribute.

There is always an ideational element in the Theme. There may be, but are not necessarily, interpersonal and/or textual elements as well. The typical overall sequence of these elements is: textual ^ interpersonal ^ ideational.

(The circumflex ^ means 'followed by'.) The sequence textual ^ interpersonal may be modified, which has the effect of being 'marked'; but the ideational element is always the final one — whatever follows the first ideational element of the clause is automatically part of the Rheme.

The full range of ideational elements in the clause will be clarified in Chapter 5. In principle an ideational element is anything representing a process, a participant in a process (person, thing, institution, etc.) or a circumstance attendant on that process (time, place, manner, etc.). Such elements function in the mood structure as Predicator, Subject, Complement or Adjunct. As we saw at the end of Section 3.3, a Predicator is rarely thematic; so we usually refer simply to Subject, Complement and Adjunct in this connection. The ideational element within the Theme, then, is some entity functioning as Subject, Complement or circumstantial Adjunct; we shall refer to this as the TOPICAL THEME, since it corresponds fairly well to the element identified as 'topic' in topic–comment analysis. There is no further thematic structure within the topical Theme.

There is, on the other hand, the possibility of further structure within the textual and interpersonal components of the Theme.

(1) The textual element within the Theme may have any combination of (i) continuative, (ii) structural and (iii) conjunctive Themes, in that order. (i) CONTINUATIVES are a small set of items such as *yes*, *no*, *well*, *oh*, *now*, which signal that a new move is beginning: a response, in dialogue, or a move to the next point if the same speaker is continuing. (ii) A structural Theme is one of the obligatorily thematic elements listed in Tables 3(4) (conjunctions) and 3(5) (relatives). (iii) A conjunctive Theme is one of the conjunctive Adjuncts set out in Table 3(2).

(2) Within the interpersonal element we may have a (i) modal Theme, one of the Adjuncts shown in Table 3(3) above; (ii) the Finite verb, in a yes/no interrogative clause; and also (iii) a VOCATIVE element. The modal Adjunct precedes the Finite (if it does not, it is not thematic). The Vocative is a floating element which may come anywhere; if it is thematic, it typically marks the beginning of the interpersonal Theme, though it may follow the modal Adjunct if there is one. (This choice is determined by the information structure; see Chapter 8 below).

Table 3(7) sets out the various components that can enter into the structure

Table 3(7) Components of a multiple Theme. The arrows indicate that a WH- relative or interrogative is also a topical element.

metafunction	component of Theme
textual	continuative structural (conjunction or WH- relative) conjunctive (Adjunct)
interpersonal	vocative modal (Adjunct) finite (verb) WH- (interrogative)
ideational	topical (Subject, Complement or circumstantial Adjunct)

well	but	then	Ann	surely	wouldn't	the best idea	be to join the group
continuative	structural	conjunctive	vocative	modal	finite	topical	
textual			interpersonal				
Theme							Rheme

Figure 3-13 Maximally extended Theme

(a)

oh	soldier, soldier	won't	you	marry me
continuative	vocative	finite	topical	
textual	interpersonal			
Theme				Rheme

(b)

girls and boys	come out	to play
vocative	topical	
interpersonal		
Theme		Rheme

(alternatively, no topical Theme; *come out to play* as Rheme – cf. Figure 3-12)

(c)

on the other hand	maybe	on a week-day	it would be less crowded
conjunctive	modal	topical	
textual	interpersonal		
Theme			Rheme

(d)

so	why		worry
structural	WH-	= topical	
textual	interpersonal		
Theme			Rheme

Figure 3-14 Examples of multiple Theme

of a multiple Theme. Note that WH- elements, relative or interrogative, are rather different from the others because, besides their special WH- feature, they also function simultaneously as Subject, Complement or circumstantial Adjunct and so figure as the 'topical' element in the thematic structure.

Perhaps the most extended thematic structure we could reasonably expect to find would be something like that in Figure 3-13. Needless to say we might have to wait a long time before hearing one as complex as that. But multiple Themes of more modest dimensions are regularly found in most types of discourse. A selection of examples is given in Figure 3-14.

As will be seen from the examples in Figures 3-13 and 3-14(a), the 'yes/no' type of interrogative clause, discussed in Section 3.3, provides an example of a multiple Theme. The finite verb, as explained there, is thematic; but (for reasons given in Chapter 4 below) it is an interpersonal rather than an ideational element, and the Subject that follows it functions as the topical Theme. All clauses of this class therefore have multiple Themes.

The Theme of any clause, therefore, extends up to (and includes) the topical Theme. The topical Theme is the first element in the clause that has some function in the ideational structure (i.e. in transitivity; see Chapter 5). A simple Theme consists of this topical element only. A multiple Theme consists of this element plus one or more preceding elements; that is, it has some additional thematic material, interpersonal and/or textual. The order of these preceding elements may vary somewhat from that specified above; the sequence described there is the unmarked one, such that any departure from it adds some additional semantic feature.

It has been pointed out already that there is a close connection between thematic structure and information structure, and that if a clause is structured as two information units (realized as two tone groups), the boundary between the two nearly always coincides with that between Theme and Rheme. This is an important feature of discourse in English, and constitutes one of the strong pieces of evidence for construing the Theme in this particular way. For example,

// oh so in fact in artificial light // the colours don't show up //

3.6 Clauses as Themes

Up to now we have been considering Theme – Rheme purely as a structure within the clause, a structure whose elements are therefore constituents of the clause; and basically this is what it is. But at the same time we find thematic organization appearing in different guises throughout the system of the language, with manifestations both above the clause and below it.

Below the clause, we shall see in Chapter 6 that both the verbal group and the nominal group incorporate the thematic principle into their own structure; rather in the way that we found to be the case with interrogative clauses, where the initial position of the WH- element or the finite verb is explained on thematic grounds.

Above the clause, the same principle lies behind the organization of paragraphs in written discourse; the 'topic sentence' of a paragraph is nothing other than its Theme. The text that is analysed in the Appendix provides a

except that the topic sentence doesn't necessarily be identified / located at the beginning of a paragraph !!

clear example of a topic sentence. This is not a written text; it is taken from spontaneous conversation, and points up the fact that the same phenomenon can occur in spoken language also.

Here we shall glance briefly at a structure that is just one step above the clause, in order to take note of thematic organization in the CLAUSE COMPLEX. The clause complex is described in Chapter 7; for present purposes we need refer to only one type of complex structure, that of Head (dominant) clause plus Modifying (dependent) clauses ('hypotaxis'; see Section 7.2), as in *give that teapot away if you don't like it.*

In a clause complex of this kind the typical sequence of the parts is the one just illustrated, with the Modifying clause following the Head clause. But the reverse order is also possible, with the Modifying clause preceding; and where that order is used, the motive is thematic. If I say *if you don't like that teapot, give it away*, the effect is to thematize your imputed dislike of the teapot. We can get a feelng for this if we put together a clause complex of this kind with a related identifying clause (the thematic equative; see Section 3.2 above), as in Figure 3-15.

what the duke gives to my aunt if the duke gives anything to my aunt	will be it'll be	that teapot that teapot
Theme	Rheme	

Figure 3-15 Hypotactic clause Theme with related thematic equative

Other examples of this kind, with the comma separating Theme and Rheme, are the following:

> If ifs and ans were pots and pans, there'd be no need for tinkers.
> If winter comes, can spring be far behind?
> Where I come from, they're all mad.
> When the bough breaks, the cradle with fall.

The first of these examples comes from a time when people still talked in proverbs and there was a saying for every occasion, as happened in our great-grandmothers' day. It was the response given to a child who prevaricated, who claimed that all would have been well if . . . (*an* is an older synonym of *if*, now lost). For granny, the theme of her discourse was 'let's suppose', and this had two strands to it, one verbal 'if talk could achieve', the other non-verbal 'if things were as we fantasize them'; both neatly encapsulated by thematizing back to him the child's own *if*.

These examples pose no great problems of analysis; the point to bear in mind is that there will still be a thematic structure in each of the two constituent clauses. We can show the full pattern by representing it as in Figure 3-16. The only problem arises when there is other thematic material, as in *but honestly Mary if winter comes can spring be far behind?* Here there are two possibilities: one is to treat *but honestly Mary* as part of the Theme of the first clause, Theme_2 in Figure 3-16; the other is to treat it as part of the Theme of the clause complex, Theme_1 in Figure 3-16. Strictly speaking this depends on

if	winter	comes	can	spring	be far behind
Theme$_1$			Rheme$_1$		
structural	topical		finite	topical	
Theme$_2$		Rheme$_2$	Theme$_3$		Rheme$_3$

Figure 3-16 Theme in the clause complex

the intonation: if it is spoken as a separate tone group it is part of Theme$_1$; if not, it is part of Theme$_2$. But it does not matter very much, so long as it is shown to be thematic.

As a text example, here is the opening sentence of Franz Boas's *Introduction* to the *Handbook of American Indian languages*:

> When Columbus started on his journey to reach the Indies, sailing westward, and discovered the shores of America, he beheld a new race of men, different in type, different in culture, different in language, from any known before that time.

Here Theme$_1$ extends from the beginning down to *the shores of America*; Theme$_2$ is (structural) *when* + (topical) *Columbus*; Theme$_3$ is (topical) *he*.

There is one special circumstance that leads to the situation where something that is itself a clause functions as a Theme, and that is the phenomenon that we are calling 'grammatical metaphor' (discussed in Chapter 10). What happens here is that one type of clause is expressed metaphorically as another; or rather, to put this more accurately, a semantic configuration that would be represented congruently (non-metaphorically) by one type of clause is represented metaphorically by another.

We have actually met this phenomenon already, without describing it in these terms, in the thematic equatives discussed in Section 3.2. A clause like *what the duke gave my aunt was that teapot* is really a grammatical metaphor for *the duke gave my aunt that teapot* (in transitivity terms, it is an 'identifying' clause instead of a 'material process' clause; see Chapter 5). There is, as we saw, a reason for the choice of this metaphorical form: its function is to get the Theme – Rheme structure the way the speaker wants it. In fact, grammatically metaphorical forms are never totally synonymous with their non-metaphorical counterparts; there will always be some semantic feature or features distinguishing the two.

This class of examples illustrates grammatical metaphor of an ideational kind; the metaphorical process takes place in the ideational component. Grammatical metaphors also occur in the interpersonal component, and this too is sometimes associated with the choice of Theme. For example, in *I don't believe that pudding ever will be cooked* what the White Knight is doing is expressing the modality 'in my opinion . . . not likely' in the form of a Head clause *I don't believe*, and the thesis 'that pudding will be cooked' in the form of a dependent Modifying clause. That this is a metaphorical construction can be seen from the fact that the 'tagged' form (see Chapter 4) would be *I don't believe that pudding ever will be cooked, will it?* (not *I don't believe that pudding ever will be cooked, do I?* as it would be if the example was to be interpreted congruently). The expression *I don't believe* is functioning as an interpersonal (modal) Theme. Other examples are *I dare say you'll see her soon*, *I think I'll go and meet her*, *Do you suppose that they could get it clear?* — where similarly the tags would be *won't you?*, *shall I?* and *could they?*

The analysis is given in Figure 3-17; the literal, or congruent, interpretation is shown in version (a), the metaphorical in version (b). It is important to include both, to provide an adequate picture.

	I	don't believe	that pudding	ever will be cooked
(a)	Theme	Rheme	Theme	Rheme
(b)	interpersonal (modal)		topical	
	Theme			Rheme

Figure 3-17

For further discussion of ideational and interpersonal grammatical metaphors, see the final chapter, Chapter 10.

3.7 Predicated Themes

There is one further structural pattern that frequently contributes to the thematic organization of the clause, and that is internal predication of the form *it* + *be* + . . ., as in *it's love that makes the world go round*. Such instances are known in some formal grammars as 'cleft sentences'.

Any element having a representational function in the clause can be marked off by predication in this way. Let us go back to the duke, the aunt and the teapot — but perhaps with a slight variation: corresponding to *the queen sent my uncle that hatstand* we could have

it was the queen who sent my uncle that hatstand
it was my uncle the queen sent that hatstand to
it was that hatstand the queen sent to my uncle

To explain the function of such predications we have to anticipate the discussion in Chapter 8. It has been pointed out already that English speech progresses as an unbroken succession of melodic units called 'tone groups'; and that each tone group constitutes ('realizes') one unit of information. An information unit may be more than a clause, or less than a clause; but in the unmarked case the two are conflated — each clause is organized as one tone group, and we can take this as the norm for purposes of explanation.

The information unit serves to structure the discourse into two components, according to the status the speaker wishes the listener to accord to it as information. One part is the news: what the listener is being invited to attend to as new, or unexpected, or important. The other part is the old stuff: what is presented as being already known to the listener, that which he can take as 'given.' The 'new' is signalled by the tonic accent, a clear fall or rise (or more complex movement) in pitch.

Typically the 'new' comes at the end of the information unit, and so forms part of the Rheme of the clause, while the 'given' precedes it (and thus includes the Theme). So for example (using bold type to indicate the tonic accent):

the queen sent my uncle **that hatstand**

The accent can however come anywhere in the clause; it would be perfectly possible to make the queen the item of news, without varying anything else in the structure:

the queen sent my uncle that hatstand

Note that the 'new' element is now mapped on to the Theme.

This is a 'marked' combination, and tends therefore to be contrastive: it was the queen who sent it, not the local antique dealer. In order to make it explicit that this, and nothing else around, is the news value of this particular information unit, the speaker is likely to use the predicated form *it was the queen who* . . . . This has the effect of creating a **local** structure *it was* . . . within which the tonic accent is in its unmarked place, at the end.

Since accentuation is not marked in writing, the predication has the additional function in written English of directing the reader to interpret the information structure in the intended way. Suppose we have the sequence

John's father wanted him to give up the violin. His teacher persuaded him to continue.

In the second sentence, the natural place for the tonic accent is *continue*, which makes the effective contrast that between giving up and continuing. If we replace this with

John's father wanted him to give up the violin. It was his teacher who persuaded him to continue.

the tonic accent now falls on *teacher*; the fact that John continued is taken as given, and the contrast is between his teacher's attitude and that of his father. The thematic analysis is as in Figure 3-18.

	it	was his teacher	who	persuaded him to continue
(a)	Theme	Rheme	Theme	Rheme
(b)	Theme		Rheme	

Figure 3-18 Thematic structure of clause with predicated Theme

Version (a) shows the local, congruent thematic structure; version (b) embodies the interpretation of it as a predicated Theme.

The predicated Theme structure is frequently associated with an explicit formulation of contrast: *it was not* . . ., *it was* . . ., *who* . . . . The following example is taken from the report of the *Sydney Morning Herald*'s London correspondent on the publication of *The Holy Blood and the Holy Grail* (21 January 1982):

> And, say the authors, it was Mary Magdalen, not Mary the Mother of Jesus, who has been the real, if secret, object of Mariolatry cults down the ages.

Here the Theme is *And* . . . (*it was*) *Mary Magdalen, not Mary the Mother of Jesus,* (*who*).

Internal predication is not limited to the initial element in the clause. Here is an example of a different kind:

> Despite the limitations of Sanskrit, it was in this language that court literature still flourished.

(from Romila Thapar, *A History of India* Vol. I. Penguin Books, 1966, p. 257). Here the Theme is *despite the limitations of Sanskrit*, and the predication falls within the Rheme. Such instances are not uncommon, although it is noticeable that there is often something about them which suggests that the predicated element is to be interpreted as in some way thematic; here, for instance, the phrase *despite the limitations of Sanskrit* is a metaphorical variant of *although Sanskrit was limited* (cf. Chapter 10), which would make the remainder a separate clause with (*it was*) *in this language* as its Theme. But in default of more detailed discussion it is preferable to leave the analysis as it stands.

3.8 Theme in dependent, minor and elliptical clauses

We have not explicitly considered Theme in clauses other than independent ones, although by referring to conjunctions and relatives as structural Themes we have suggested that such clauses do display thematic structure. Figures 3-16 and 3-17 included examples of dependent clauses: *if winter comes* and *that pudding ever will be cooked*.

There is thematic structure, in fact, in all major clause types: that is, all clauses expressing mood and transitivity, whether independent or not. (Those which do not select for mood are MINOR clauses.) But, as we have seen, there is a kind of scale of thematic freedom: whereas in an independent declarative clause the speaker has a free choice of Theme — other things being equal he will map it on to the Subject, but this is merely the unmarked option — the further one moves away from this most open-ended form of the clause, the more the thematic options are restricted by structural pressures from other parts of the grammar, pressures that are themselves thematic in origin. In interrogatives and imperatives, and even more strongly in clauses that are not independent, the thematic principle has determined what it is that will be the Theme of the clause, leaving only a highly marked alternative option (as in interrogative) or else no alternative at all.

However, we have also seen that there is a compensatory principle at work whereby, if what comes first is 'fixed' (in the sense that it is the realization of some feature selected in another system), then what comes second may retain some thematic flavour. If the initial element is there as the expression not of thematic choice but of some other option in the grammar, then what follows it is also part of the Theme. We have embodied this in a general principle of interpretation whereby the Theme of a clause extends up to the first element that has some representational function in the clause (the 'topical' Theme). Hence in a dependent clause such as *if winter comes*, one part of the Theme is the *if*, expressing the nature of the clause's relation to some other clause in the neighbourhood, and the other part is *winter* which has a function both in transitivity (as Actor) and in mood (as Subject).

The significance of these patterns emerges when we come to consider the importance of clause theme in the overall development of a text. By itself the choice of Theme in each particular instance, clause by clause, may seem a fairly haphazard matter; but it is not. The choice of clause Themes plays a fundamental part in the way discourse is organized; it is this, in fact, which constitutes what is often known as the 'method of development' of the text. In this process, the main contribution comes from the thematic structure of independent clauses. But other clauses also come into the picture, and need to be taken account of in Theme – Rheme analysis. This can be seen in the text that is analysed in Section 3.9 below.

We shall not treat other types of clause in very great detail, partly because their thematic structure is less variable and partly because in any case we could not do so without making frequent reference to later chapters, to the discussion that is still to come. Here however is a summary of the thematic organization of clauses other than those that are independent, major, and explicit.

(1) Dependent clauses (Chapter 7). (i) If finite, these typically have a conjunction as structural Theme, e.g. *because*, *that*, *whether*, followed by a topical Theme; for example Figure 3-19.

[I asked] [they knew] [he left]	whether that because	pigs in spring his work	have wings the snow would melt was done
	structural	topical	
	Theme		Rheme

Figure 3-19 Theme in finite dependent clauses (with conjunctions)

If the dependent clause begins with a WH- element, on the other hand, that element constitutes the topical Theme, e.g. Figure 3-20.

[I asked] [they knew] [Caesar,]	why which side whose army	no-one was around their bread was buttered never lost a battle,
	topical	Rheme
	Theme	

Figure 3-20 Theme in finite dependent clauses (with WH- elements)

The reason for this is that the WH- element also has a function in the transitivity structure of the clause (clause as representation: Chapter 5).

(ii) If non-finite, there may be a preposition as structural Theme, which may be followed by a Subject as topical Theme; but many non-finite clauses have neither, in which case they consist of Rheme only. See Figure 3-21.

with for by	every door pigs	being locked to fly counting sheep to draw lots	[we had no choice] [they must grow wings] [she finally fell asleep] [first collect some pebbles]
structural	topical	Rheme	
Theme			

Figure 3-21 Theme in non-finite dependent clauses

(2) Embedded clauses (Chapters 6 and 7). These are clauses which function inside the structure of a nominal group, as 'defining relative' clauses, e.g. *who came to dinner*, *the dam broke*, *requiring travel permits* in *the man who came to dinner*, *the day the dam broke*, *all personnel requiring travel permits*. The thematic structure of such clauses is the same as that of dependent clauses. However, because of their down-ranking, the fact that they do not function as constituents of a sentence, their thematic contribution to the discourse is minimal, and for practical purposes can be ignored.

(3) Minor clauses (Chapter 4). These are clauses with no mood or transitivity structure, typically functioning as calls, greetings and exclamations, like *Mary!*, *Good night!*, *Well done!* They have no thematic structure either. (In this they resemble an important class of items such as titles and labels — not regarded as clauses because they have no independent speech function.)

(4) Elliptical clauses (Chapter 4). (i) Anaphoric ellipsis. Here some part of the clause is presupposed from what has gone before, for example in response to a question. The resulting forms are very varied. Some are undistinguishable from minor clauses, e.g. *Yes. No. All right. Of course.*; these have no thematic structure, because they presuppose the whole of the preceding clause. Others, which presuppose only part of the preceding clause, have their own thematic structure; the details will depend on which part is presupposed. Figure 3-22 gives some examples.

"Fire, fire!"	cried the town crier;
Rheme	'There's a fire!'

"Where? Where?"	said Goody Blair;
Theme	'Where is it?'

"Down the town,"	said Goody Brown;
Rheme	'It's down the town.'

"I	'll go see't,"	said Goody Fleet;
Theme	Rheme	(not elliptical)

"So	will	I,"	said Goody Fry.
conjunctive	finite	topical	'So will I go see it'
Theme			

Figure 3-22

(ii) Exophoric ellipsis. In this type of ellipsis the clause is not presupposing anything from what has gone before, but simply taking advantage of the rhetorical structure of the situation, specifically the roles of speaker and listener (Chapter 4, Section 4.6). Hence the Subject, and often also the finite verb, is 'understood' from the context; e.g. *Thirsty?* ('are you thirsty?'), *No idea.* ('I've no idea'), *A song!* ('let's have a song!'), *Feeling better?* ('are you feeling better?'). Such clauses have, in fact, a thematic structure; but it consists of Rheme only. The Theme is (part of) what is omitted in the ellipsis.

For the meaning of the terms 'anaphoric' and 'exophoric', see further Chapter 9 below.

3.9 Thematic interpretation of a text

Apart from a need to create his own identity « having been well and truly trained
top

and educated and, indeed, used by his father for so long, emotionally and practically » Robert felt ‖ that at twenty the last thing he wanted to do was to join a family
* text top

firm up in Newcastle, in however important a position. ‖ He must have felt ‖ that he
top text top

was being forced into a corner. ‖ This was it, for ever, a lifetime's occupation. ‖
top

And he'd better be duly grateful for ⟦what his father and his father's friends were
text top

doing for him.⟧ ‖

For all his integrity and high principles, Robert pulled a slightly fast one over his
top *

father and business partners. ‖ He did eventually get permission, « however
top top

reluctantly it was given, » from his father and partner to have leave of absence from

the Newcastle locomotive works, ‖ telling them ‖ that he'd signed a contract for only
text top

one year. ‖ It was only after his departure that they discovered ‖ that in fact he'd
top text top

signed on for three years. ‖ It was no doubt fear that he'd never get away, rather than
int top

deceit, which made him mislead them. ‖ A slight feeling of fear of his father, mixed
top

with awe, comes through in many of his letters. ‖

George finally realized ‖ that his son wanted to go off and stretch his wings in a new
top | text | top

country ‖ and there was nothing more he could do about it, no further inducements he
text | top

could offer. ‖ As it was to be only for a year, ‖ so he thought, ‖ he might as
β | text | top | top
text | top

well make the best of it, ‖ though it couldn't have come at a worse time ‖ with the
text | top | text | top

Darlington and Liverpool lines now both under way ‖ and though he had person-
text | top

ally been very hurt and saddened by his son's decision. ‖

In a letter ⟦written to Longridge⟧ on 7 June, eleven days before Robert's departure,
top

George sounds distinctly miserable, even bitter, « though trying hard to hide it, » at
*

the prospect of travelling to Liverpool in time to see Robert off. ‖ 'I am a little more
top

cheerful to night ‖ as I have quite come to a conclusion ‖ that there is nothing
text | top | text | top

for me but hard work in this world ‖ therefore I may as well be cheerful as not.' ‖
text | top

After he arrived in Liverpool and met up with Robert to bid him farewell, ‖ George
β | top
text | top

wrote to Longridge, this time on 15 June, ‖ saying ‖ what a pleasure it has been to see
int/top

Robert again. ‖ He describes the smart dinner parties ⟦that he and Robert have been
top | ⧄

to together.⟧ ‖

From Hunter Davies, *George Stevenson: the remarkable life of the founder of the railways*. Feltham, Mx: Hamlyn Paperbacks. 1980, pp. 112–13.

Notational conventions:

‖	clause boundary	[β]	clause as Theme (in clause complex)
« »	clause boundary: included clause	[text | int | top]	textual, interpersonal, topical Theme
⟦ ⟧	downranked clause (in nominal group)	*	displaced Theme
[ ]	Theme	⧄	Theme in downranked clause

Summary of thematic analysis

Paragraph 1 (*he* = Robert)	
paragraph Theme (from clause 1)	his need to create identity
displaced Theme*	Robert
clause Themes:	
dependent clause	[feeling] that + at twenty
independent clause	he
dependent ,,	[feeling] that + he
independent ,,	this [prospect]
,, ,,	and + he
Paragraph 2 (*he* = Robert)	
paragraph Theme (from clause 1)	despite his integrity and high principles
displaced Theme	Robert
clause Themes:	
independent clause	he
dependent ,,	however reluctantly
independent ,,	after his departure
dependent ,,	[discovery] that in fact + he
independent ,,	no doubt + fear that he wouldn't get away
,, ,,	a slight feeling of fear for his father
Paragraph 3 (*he* = George)	
paragraph Theme (from clause 1)	George
clause Themes:	
dependent clause	[realized] that + his son
,, ,,	and + there [was nothing]
clause complex Theme	as it was to be only for a year
clause Themes:	
dependent clause	as + it [the departure]
independent ,,	so + he
,, ,,	he
dependent ,,	though + it [the departure]
,, ,,	and + though + he
Paragraph 4 (*I* = George)	
paragraph Theme (from clause 1)	in a letter written [by George]
displaced Theme	George
clause Themes:	
independent clause	I
dependent ,,	as + I
,, ,,	[realized] that + there [was nothing]
independent ,,	therefore + I
Paragraph 5 (*he* = George)	
paragraph Theme (from clause complex)	after arriving in Liverpool and meeting Robert
clause Themes:	
dependent clause	after + he
independent ,,	George
dependent ,,	what a pleasure [seeing Robert]
independent ,,	he

Commentary:

The thematic organization of the clauses (and clause complexes, where relevant) expresses, and so reveals, the method of development of the text. In this little extract, there are five paragraphs, the first two having Robert as dominant Theme and the remaining three George. But whereas in the latter it is George himself, and his thoughts and actions, that form the paragraph Themes, in the first two it is the author's characterization of Robert — his needs and his principles; and these remain thematic throughout the paragraph. (Note that the only interpersonal Theme, apart from the interrogative *what a pleasure*, is the authorial *no doubt* qualifying Robert's fear of being restrained.) It is George who is the Theme of the book, not Robert. (George is also the Theme of the book's opening clause: *George Stephenson was born in the village of Wylam, about nine miles west of Newcastle-on-Tyne, on 9 June 1781.*)

Paragraph by paragraph, the development proceeds as follows:

(1) (apart from) Robert's need for self-identity . . . [he felt] (that) at 20 . . . this [his prospects]
(2) (despite) Robert's integrity and high principles . . . (after) his departure . . . [discovered] (that) he . . . (no doubt) his fear of restraint . . . his fear of his father
(3) George . . . [realized] (that) his son . . . (as) it [his son's departure] . . . (s) he . . . (though) it . . . (though) he
(4) George's letter . . . I [George] . . . (as) I . . . (so) I
(5) (after) George met Robert for leavetaking . . . what a pleasure . . . he [George]

First come Robert's needs and contrasting prospects; his principles and, behind his departure, his fears, including fear of his father George; then George, in relation to his son's departure; George's letter, and George himself; finally, George's meeting with Robert, and his pleasure at it. This is the thematic line, from which we know where the text is going.

The Theme provides the environment for the remainder of the message, the Rheme. In the Rhemes of the various clauses are expressed, first, the explanation of Robert's malaise, followed in the second paragraph by the details of his actions; then George's sad resignation, his attempts at cheerful acceptance, and finally his activities in Robert's company.

In the Theme–Rheme structure, it is the Theme that is the prominent element. This example shows how, by analysing the thematic structure of a text clause by clause, we can gain an insight into its texture and understand how the writer made clear to us the nature of his underlying concerns. For a further example see Appendix 1, the 'silver' text.

* A displaced Theme is a topical element which would be unmarked Theme (in the ensuing clause) if the existing marked topical Theme was reworded as a dependent clause. In the first example here, if we reworded more congruently as *Besides needing to create his own identity, Robert . . .*), then in the ensuing clause *Robert* becomes unmarked Theme.

4

Clause as exchange

4.1 The nature of dialogue

In the last chapter we set out an interpretation of the clause in its function as a message, analysing it as a two-part structure with the elements Theme and Rheme. We shall now turn to another aspect of the meaning of the clause, its meaning as an exchange.

Simultaneously with its organization as a message, the clause is also organized as an interactive event involving speaker, or writer, and audience. Let us use the term 'speaker' as a cover term for both speaker and writer. In the act of speaking, the speaker adopts for himself a particular speech role, and in so doing assigns to the listener a complementary role which he wishes him to adopt in his turn. For example, in asking a question, a speaker is taking on the role of seeker of information and requiring the listener to take on the role of supplier of the information demanded.

The most fundamental types of speech role, which lie behind all the more specific types that we may eventually be able to recognize, are just two: (i) giving, and (ii) demanding. Either the speaker is giving something to the listener (a piece of information, for example) or he is demanding something from him. Even these elementary categories already involve complex notions: giving means 'inviting to receive', and demanding means 'inviting to give'. The speaker is not only doing something himself; he is also requiring something of the listener. Typically, therefore, an 'act' of speaking is something that might more appropriately be called an 'interact': it is an exchange, in which giving implies receiving and demanding implies giving in response.

Cutting across this basic distinction between giving and demanding is another distinction, equally fundamental, that relates to the nature of the commodity being exchanged. This may be either (a) goods-&-services, or (b) information. Examples are given in Figure 4-1. If you say something to me with the aim of getting me to do something for you, such as 'kiss me!' or 'get out of my daylight!', or to give you some object, as in 'pass the salt!', the exchange commodity is strictly non-verbal: what is being demanded is an object or an action, and language is brought in to help the process along. This is an exchange of goods-&-services. But if you say something to me with the aim of getting me to tell you something, as in 'is it Tuesday?' or 'when did you last see your father?', what is being demanded is information: language is the end as well as the means, and the only answer expected is a verbal one. This is an exchange of information. Examples in Figure 4-1. These two variables, when taken together, define the four primary speech functions of OFFER, COMMAND, STATEMENT and QUESTION. These, in turn, are matched by a set

Role in exchange: \ Commodity exchanged:	(a) goods-&-services	(b) information
(i) giving	'offer' would you like this teapot?	'statement' he's giving her the teapot
(ii) demanding	'command' give me that teapot!	'question' what is he giving her?

Figure 4-1 Giving or demanding, goods-&-services or information

of desired responses: accepting an offer, carrying out a command, acknowledging a statement and answering a question. See Table 4(1).

Table 4(1) Speech functions and responses

		initiation	expected response	discretionary alternative
give	goods-&-services	offer	acceptance	rejection
demand	''	command	undertaking	refusal
give	information	statement	acknowledgment	contradiction
demand	''	question	answer	disclaimer

Of these, only the last is essentially a verbal response; the others can all be non-verbal. But typically in real-life situations all four responses are verbalized, with or without some accompanying non-verbal action. Examples:

Speaker:	Listener (becoming Speaker in his turn):
Would you like this teapot?	Yes, I would. No, I wouldn't.
Give me that teapot!	All right, I will. No, I won't.
He's giving her the teapot.	Oh, is he? Yes, he is. No, he isn't.
What is he giving her?	A teapot. I don't know; sha'n't tell you.

In moving into the role of speaker, the listener has considerable discretion. Not only can he give any one of a wide range of different responses to a question, or carry out a command in different ways; he may refuse to answer the question altogether, or to provide the goods-&-services demanded. The speaker on his part has a way of forestalling this: he can add a TAG, which is a reminder of what is expected, e.g. *will you?*, *isn't he?*, as in:

Give me that teapot, will you?
He's giving her the teapot, isn't he?

This is the function of the tag at the end of the clause. It serves to signal explicitly that a response is required, and what kind of response it is expected to be.

As long as what is being exchanged is goods-&-services, the choices open to the listener are relatively limited: accept or reject the offer, obey or refuse the command. He may hedge, of course; but that is merely a way of temporarily avoiding the choice. Now, in the life history of an individual child, the exchange of goods-&-services, with language as the means, comes much earlier than the exchange of information: infants typically begin to use linguistic symbols to make commands and offers at about the age of nine months, whereas it may be as much as nine months to a year after that before they really learn to make statements and questions, going through various intermediate steps along the way. It is quite likely that the same sequence of developments took place in the early evolution of language in the human race, although that is something we can never know for certain. It is not difficult to see why offering and requesting precede telling and asking when a child is first learning how to mean. Exchanging information is more complicated than exchanging goods-&-services, because in the former the listener is being asked not merely to listen and do something but also to act out a verbal role — to affirm or deny, or to supply a missing piece of information, as in

It's Tuesday. — Oh, is it?
Is it Tuesday? — Yes.
What day is it? — Tuesday.

What is more significant, however, is that the whole concept of exchanging information is difficult for a young child to grasp. Goods-&-services are obvious enough: I want you to take what I am holding out, or to go on carrying me, or to pick up what I have just dropped; and although I may use language as a means of getting what I want, the requirement itself is not a linguistic commodity — it is something that arises independently of language. Information, on the other hand, does not; it has no existence except in the form of language. In statements and questions, language itself is the commodity that is being exchanged; and it is by no means simple for a child to internalize the principle that language is used for the purpose of exchanging language. He has no experience of 'information' except its manifestation in words.

When language is used to exchange information, the clause takes on the form of a PROPOSITION. It becomes something that can be argued about — something that can be affirmed or denied, and also doubted, contradicted, insisted on, accepted with reservation, qualified, tempered, regretted and so on. But we cannot use the term 'proposition' to refer to all the functions of the clause as an interactive event, because this would exclude the exchange of goods-&-services, the entire range of offers and commands. Unlike statements and questions, these are not propositions; they cannot be affirmed or denied. Yet they are no less significant than statements and questions; and, as already noted, they take priority in the ontogenetic development of language.

Nevertheless there is an important reason why, when we are considering the clause as exchange, it is useful to look at propositions first. This is the fact that propositions have a clearly defined grammar. As a general rule languages do not develop special resources for offers and commands, because in these contexts language is functioning simply as a means towards achieving what are essentially non-linguistic ends. But they do develop grammatical resources for statements and questions, which not only constitute ends in themselves but also serve as a point of entry to a great variety of different rhetorical functions. So by interpreting the structure of statements and questions we can gain a general understanding of the clause in its exchange function.

We will continue to use the term 'proposition' in its usual sense to refer to a statement or question. But it will be useful to introduce a parallel term to refer to offers and commands. As it happens, these correspond more closely to the everyday sense of the word 'proposition', as in *I've got a proposition to put to you*; so we will refer to them by the related term PROPOSAL. The semantic function of a clause in the exchange of information is a proposition; the semantic function of a clause in the exchange of goods-&-services is a proposal.

4.2 The Mood element

When we come to look closely at statements and questions, and at the various responses to which these naturally give rise, we find that in English they are typically expressed by means of a particular kind of grammatical variation; variation which extends over just one part of the clause, leaving the remainder unaffected.

Consider the traditional rhyme:

He loves me.
He don't.
He'll have me.
He won't.
He would if he could.
But he can't, so he don't.

Compare this with a typical piece of information-exchanging dialogue:

The duke's given away that teapot, hasn't he?
— Oh, has he?
— Yes, he has.
— No he hasn't!
— I wish he had.
— He hasn't; but he will.
— Will he?
— He might.

What is happening in these discourses is that one particular component of the clause is being, as it were, tossed back and forth in a series of rhetorical exchanges; this component carries the argument forward. Meanwhile the remainder, here *give(n) away that teapot*, is simply left out, being taken for granted as long as the discourse continues to require it.* Similarly in the rhyme: *love(s) me* and *have me* are 'understood' from one line to the next, only a small part of the clause being used to carry the sentiments forward.

What is the component that is being bandied about in this way? It is called

* Where there is some change other than just a switch of mood or polarity, the verb substitute *do* may be used to stand in for the rest of the clause, as in *he might do*, *I wish he had done*. See Chapter 9 below.

the MOOD, and it consists of two parts: (1) the Subject, which is a nominal group, and (2) the Finite element, which is part of a verbal group. (See Chapter 6 below for detailed discussion of these two types of group.) Thus in *he might*, *he* is Subject and *might* is Finite.

The Subject, when it first appears, may be any nominal group. If it is a personal pronoun, like *he* in the rhyme, it is simply repeated each time. If it is anything else, like *the duke*, then after the first occurrence it is replaced by the personal pronoun corresponding to it. So *the duke* becomes *he*, *my aunt* becomes *she*, *the teapot* becomes *it*.

The Finite element is one of a small number of verbal operators expressing tense (e.g. *is*, *has*) or modality (e.g. *can*, *must*); these are listed in Table 4(3) below. Note, however, that in some instances the Finite element and the lexical verb are 'fused' into a single word, e.g. *loves*. This happens when the verb is in simple past or simple present (tense), active (voice), positive (polarity) and neutral (contrast): we say *gave*, not *did give*; *give(s)* not *do(es) give*. See Table 4(2).

Table 4(2) Finite elements in simple present and past tenses

tense	other categories	in body of clause	in tag
simple present	negative (polarity)	(he) doesn't love	does (he)?
	contrastive (contrast)	(he) does love	doesn't (he)?
	passive (voice)	(she) is loved	isn't (she)?
	none of above, i.e. positive, neutral, active	(he) loves ['present' + love]	doesn't (he)?
simple past	negative (polarity)	(he) didn't give	did (he)?
	contrastive (contrast)	(he) did give	didn't (he)?
	passive (voice)	(it) was given	wasn't (it)?
	none of above, i.e. positive, neutral, active	(he) gave ['past' + give]	didn't (he)?

These 'fused' tense forms are in fact the two most common forms of the English verb. When one of these occurs, the Finite *did*, *do(es)* will then make its appearance in the subsequent tags and responses, e.g. *He gave it away, didn't he? Yes, he did*. But it is already lurking in the verb as a systematic feature 'past' or 'present', and is explicit in the negative and contrastive forms.

Examples of Subject and Finite, in the body of the clause and in the tag, are given in Figure 4-2.

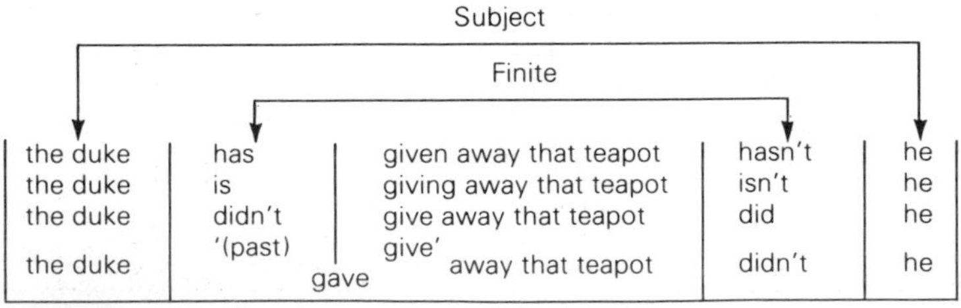

Figure 4-2 Subject and Finite

As was pointed out in Chapter 2, the term 'Subject' as we are using it corresponds to the 'grammatical Subject' of earlier terminology; but it is being reinterpreted here in functional terms. The label 'grammatical Subject' seems to imply a grammatical function whose only function is to be a grammatical function; whereas the element in question is semantic in origin, like all other elements of the clause. The Subject is not an arbitrary grammatical category; being the Subject of a clause means something.

Before saying what it means, let us first make it explicit how the Subject in English may be recognized. The Subject, in a declarative clause, is that element which is picked up by the pronoun in the tag (cf. Figure 4-2 above). So in order to locate the Subject, add a tag (if one is not already present) and see which element is taken up. For example, *that teapot was given to your aunt*: herc the tag would be *wasn't it?* — we cannot add *wasn't she?*. On the other hand with *that teapot your aunt got from the duke* the tag would be *didn't she?*; we cannot say *didn't he?* or *wasn't it?*.

This is not the definition of the Subject; it is the way of identifying it in a text. Note that the category that is identified in this way will in fact accord with the classical conception of the Subject as 'that noun or pronoun that is in person and number concord with the verb': Subjects *he*, *she*, *it* go with *has*, and *I*, *you*, *we*, *they* go with *have*. This formulation however has a rather restricted application in Modern English, because apart from the verb *be*, the only manifestation of person and number in the verb is the *-s* on the third person singular present tense. The other part of the classical definition of the Subject, 'that noun or pronoun which is in the nominative case', is even more restricted, since the only words in English which display case are *I*, *we*, *he*, *she* and *they* (and in formal language also *who*). The criterion for recognizing the Subject that we are using here — 'that nominal group that is repeated in pronoun form in the tag' — can be followed up in every declarative clause. Note that it does bring in certain things that are not traditionally regarded as Subject: not only *it* in *it's raining* but also *there* in *there's trouble in the shed*, both of which function as Subject in Modern English. Some further examples are given in Figure 4-3.

Subject and Finite are closely linked together, and combine to form one constituent which we call the Mood. (For the other function that can occur

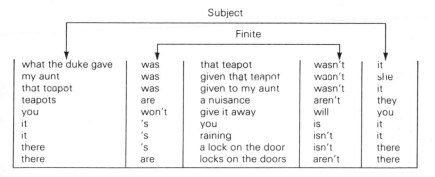

Subject

Finite

what the duke gave	was	that teapot	wasn't	it
my aunt	was	given that teapot	wasn't	she
that teapot	was	given to my aunt	wasn't	it
teapots	are	a nuisance	aren't	they
you	won't	give it away	will	you
it	's	you	is	it
it	's	raining	isn't	it
there	's	a lock on the door	isn't	there
there	are	locks on the doors	aren't	there

Figure 4-3 Subject and Finite: further examples

within the Mood, see Section 4.3 below.) The Mood is the element that realizes the selection of mood in the clause. It has sometimes been called the 'Modal' element; but the difficulty with this is that the term *modal* is ambiguous, since it corresponds both to *mood* and to *modality*.

The remainder of the clause we shall call the Residue. It has sometimes been labelled 'Proposition', but this term is also not very appropriate; partly because, as has been mentioned, the concept of proposition applies only to the exchange of information, not to the exchange of goods-&-services, and partly because, even in the exchange of information, if anything it is the Mood element that embodies the proposition rather than the remainder of the clause. We shall return to the structure of the Residue below.

The general principle behind the expression of mood in the clause is as follows. The grammatical category that is characteristically used to exchange information is the indicative; within the category of indicative, the characteristic expression of a statement is the declarative, that of a question is the interrogative; and within the category of interrogative, there is a further distinction between yes/no interrogative, for polar questions, and WH- interrogative, for content questions. (These were outlined in Chapter 3 above, Section 3.3.) These features are typically expressed as follows:

(1) The **presence** of the Mood element, consisting of Subject plus Finite, realizes the features 'indicative'.

(2) Within the indicative, what is significant is the **order** of Subject and Finite:
   (a) The order Subject before Finite realizes 'declarative';
   (b) The order Finite before Subject realizes 'yes/no interrogative';
   (c) In a 'WH- interrogative' the order is:
      (i) Subject before Finite if the WH- element is the Subject;
      (ii) Finite before Subject otherwise.

The structure is as shown in Figure 4-4.

For the analysis of WH- interrogatives, which involve a consideration of the Residue, see Section 4.4, Figures 4-10 to 4-12 below.

(a) declarative

the duke	has	given that teapot away
Subject	Finite	
Mood		Residue

(b) yes/no interrogative

has	the duke	given that teapot away
Finite	Subject	
Mood		Residue

Figure 4-4 Structure of declarative and yes/no interrogative

Why have Subject and Finite this special significance in the English clause? We need to consider each of these elements in turn, since both are semantically motivated but the contribution they bring to the clause is not the same. We will take a look at the Finite element first.

(1) The Finite element, as its name implies, has the function of making the proposition finite. That is to say, it circumscribes it; it brings the proposition down to earth, so that it is something that can be argued about. A good way to make something arguable is to give it a point of reference in the here and now; and this is what the Finite does. It relates the proposition to its context in the speech event.

This can be done in one of two ways. One is by reference to the time of speaking; the other is by reference to the judgement of the speaker. An example of the first is *was* in *an old man was crossing the road*; of the second, *can't* in *it can't be true*. In grammatical terms, the first is PRIMARY TENSE, the second is MODALITY.

(i) Primary tense means past, present or future at the moment of speaking; it is time relative to 'now'. A proposition may become arguable by having its relevance to the speech event specified in these temporal terms. (ii) Modality means the speaker's judgement of the probabilities, or the obligations, involved in what he is saying. A proposition may become arguable by being presented as likely or unlikely, desirable or undesirable — in other words, its relevance specified in modal terms. (See Section 4.5 below, and also Chapter 10.)

Finiteness is thus expressed by means of a verbal operator which is either temporal or modal. These operators are listed in Table 4(3).

Table 4(3) Finite verbal operators

Temporal operators		
past	present	future
did, was had, used to	does, is, has	will, shall, would, should
Modal operators		
low	median	high
can, may could, might	will, would, should, is to, was to	must, ought to, need, has to, had to

At the same time, there is one further semantic feature that is an essential concomitant of finiteness, and that is polarity. In order for something to be arguable, it has to be specified as being either positive or negative: either it is so, or it isn't so. Thus, as well as expressing primary tense or modality, the Finite element also realizes a polarity feature. Each of the operators listed in Table 4(3) appears in both positive and negative form: *did, didn't*; *can, can't*, etc.

Finiteness combines the specification of polarity with the specification of either temporal or modal reference to the speech event. In constitutes the verbal component in the Mood. But there has to be also a nominal component; and this is the function of the Subject.

(2) The Subject supplies the rest of what it takes to form a proposition: namely, something by reference to which the proposition can be affirmed or denied. For example, in *the duke has given away that teapot, hasn't he?*, the Finite *has* specifies reference to positive polarity and present time, while the Subject *the duke* specifies the entity in respect of which the assertion is claimed to have validity.

It is the duke, in other words, in whom is vested the success or failure of the proposition. He is the one that is, so to speak, being held responsible — responsible for the functioning of the clause as an interactive event. The speaker rests his case on *the duke* + *has*, and this is what the listener is called on to acknowledge.

It is perhaps easier to see this principle of responsibility in a proposal (a 'goods-&-services' clause), where the Subject specifies the one that is actually responsible for realizing (i.e., in this case, for carrying out) the offer or command. For example, in *I'll open the gate, shall I?* (offer) the opening depends on me; in *Stop shouting, you over there!* (command) it is for you to desist or otherwise. Hence the typical Subject of an offer is the speaker, and that of a command is the person being addressed. (Note that this is not the same thing as the Actor. The Subject in such clauses usually is the one that is also the Actor; but not necessarily so — both offers and commands can be passive, as in

> I'll be guided by your wishes, shall I?
> Get (yourself) invited to their meeting, will you?

Here the Subject is dissociated from the Actor; but the Subject still specifies the one who is responsible for the success of the proposal.) This role is clearly recognizable in the case of offers and commands; but it is the same principle that is at work in statements and questions. Here too the Subject specifies the 'responsible' element; but in a proposition this means the one on which the validity of the information is made to rest.*

Note the different Subjects in the examples in Figure 4-5.

the duke	has	given my aunt that teapot	hasn't	he (a)
my aunt	has	been given that teapot by the duke	hasn't	she (b)
that teapot	has	been given my aunt by the duke	hasn't	it (c)
Subject	Finite		Finite	Subject
Mood		Residue	Mood tag	

Figure 4-5 Variation of Subject in declarative clauses

* It is important to express it in these terms rather than in terms of true or false. The relevant concept is that of exchangeability, setting something up so that it can be caught, returned, smashed, lobbed back etc. Semantics has nothing to do with truth.

The responses would be, respectively:

(a) . . . hasn't he?	Yes, he has.	No, he hasn't.
(b) . . . hasn't she?	Yes, she has.	No, she hasn't.
(c) . . . hasn't it?	Yes, it has.	No, it hasn't.

So if we want to know why the speaker chooses this or that particular item as Subject of a proposition, there are two factors to be borne in mind. One is that, other things being equal, the same item will function both as Subject and as Theme. We saw in Chapter 3 that the unmarked Theme of a declarative clause is the Subject; so if the speaker wants to make the teapot his Theme, and to do so without the added implication of contrast that would be present if he made it a marked Theme (i.e. a Theme which is not also Subject, as in *that teapot the duke gave to my aunt*), he will choose an option with *that teapot* as Subject, namely *that teapot was given by the duke to my aunt*. Here there is an integrated choice of an item realizing two functions simultaneously: Subject in the proposition, and Theme is the message.

At the same time, however, the selection of this item as Subject has a meaning in its own right: the speaker is assigning to the teapot not only the function of starting point of the message but also that of 'resting point' of the argument. And this is brought out if we dissociate one from the other, selecting different items as Subject and as Theme. For example,

That teapot the duke gave to your aunt, didn't he?
— No he didn't. He put it up for auction.

Here the teapot is Theme ('now about that teapot:'), but the duke is Subject; it is the duke who is made to sustain the validity of the statement. Hence only *he*, not *she* or *it*, can figure in the tag and the response. In the next the teapot is still the Theme, but the Subject has now switched to the aunt:

That teapot your aunt was given by the duke, wasn't she?
— No she wasn't. She bought it at an auction.

Finally let us reverse these two roles, having the aunt as Theme and the teapot as Subject:

To your aunt that teapot came as a gift from the duke, didn't it?
— No it didn't. It was the first prize in a Christmas raffle.

Hence the Mood element has a clearly defined semantic function: it carries the burden of the clause as an interactive event. So it remains constant, as the nub of the proposition, unless some positive step is taken to change it, as in

The duke has given your aunt a new teapot, hasn't he?
(i) No, he hasn't. But (ii) { (a) the duchess has. / (b) he's going to. }

Here the proposition is first disposed of, by being rejected, in (i); this then allows for a new proposition, with change of Subject, as in (a), or change of Finite, as in (b). Each of these two constituents, the Subject and the Finite, plays its own specific and meaningful role in the propositional structure.

In the next section, we shall discuss the structure of the Residue. We shall then return to a consideration of the Mood element, with an analysis of mood in WH- interrogative, imperative, and exclamative clauses. Here meanwhile is a short text example from Alice's conversation with Humpty Dumpty:

(1)	My name	is	Alice, but —		
	Subject	Finite			
(2)	It	's	a stupid name enough		
	Subject	Finite			
(3)	What	does	it	mean?	
		Finite	Subject		
(4)	Must	a name	mean something?		
	Finite	Subject			
(5)	Of course	it	must		
		Subject	Finite		
(6)	My name	means	the shape I am		
	Subject	[present]			
		Finite			
(7)	And a good handsome shape		it	is,	too
			Subject	Finite	

The flow of the dialogue proceeds as follows:

Mood I	(1–3):	Subject — Alice's name; Finite — present tense
Mood II	(4–5):	Subject — names in general; Finite — 'high' modality
Mood III	(6):	Subject — Humpty Dumpty's name; Finite — present tense
Mood IV	(7):	Subject — Humpty Dumpty's shape; Finite — present tense

There are two non-thematic Subjects, in clauses (3) and (7), (7) having a marked Theme.

4.3 Structure of the Residue

The Residue consists of functional elements of three kinds: Predicator, Complement and Adjunct. There can be only one Predicator, one or two Complements, and an indefinite number of Adjuncts up to, in principle, about seven. An example is given in Figure 4-6.

Sister Susie	's	sewing	shirts	for soldiers
Subject	Finite	Predicator	Complement	Adjunct
Mood		Residue		

Figure 4-6 Structure of the Residue

(1) Predicator. The Predicator is present in all non-elliptical major clauses, apart from certain clauses with verbs *be* and *have* which are mentioned below. It is realized by a verbal group minus the temporal or modal operator, which as we have seen functions as Finite in the Mood element; for example, in the verbal groups *was shining*, *have been working*, *may be going to be replaced* the parts functioning as Predicator are *shining*, *been working*, *be going to be replaced*. The Predicator itself is thus non-finite; and there are non-finite clauses containing a Predicator but no Finite element, for example *eating her curds and whey* (following *Little Miss Muffet sat on a tuffet*). For the discussion of non-finite clauses, see Chapter 7 below.

The function of the Predicator is fourfold. (i) It specifies time reference **other than** reference to the time of the speech event, i.e. 'secondary' tense: past, present or future relative to the primary tense. (See Chapter 6). (ii) It specifies various other aspects and phases like seeming, trying, hoping (see Chapter 7 Additional, Section 7.A.4-6). (iii) It specifies the voice: active or passive (See Chapter 6, Section 6.3.2). (iv) It specifies the process (action, event, mental process, relation) that is predicated of the Subject. These can be exemplified from the verbal group *has been trying to be heard*, where the Predicator, *been trying to be heard*, expresses (i) a complex secondary tense, *been* + *ing*; (ii) a conative phase, *try* + *to*; (iii) passive voice, *be* + *-d*; (iv) the mental process *hear*.

There are two verbs in English which, in simple past and simple present tense, appear as Finite only, without being fused with a distinct element as Predicator. These are *be* and *have* (*have* in the sense of 'possess', not *have* in the sense of 'take'), as in Table 4(4):

Table 4(4) Simple past and present forms of *be* and *have*

	past	present
be	was, were	am, is, are
have	had	have, has

The fact that these are simple Finites, not fused forms, is shown by the negatives: the negative of *is*, *was* is *isn't*, *wasn't*, not *doesn't be*, *didn't be* as it would be if they were fusions. Similarly the negative of *has* is *hasn't* — although this varies with dialect: some speakers treat *have* like other verbs, with negative *doesn't have*, others expand it as *have* plus Predicator *got*, and others use more than one form in different contexts. In all other tenses, *be* and *have* function as Predicators in the normal way. Some examples are given in Figure 4-7.

(2) Complement. A Complement is an element within the Residue that has the potential of being Subject but is not. It is typically realized by a nominal group. So in *the duke gave my aunt that teapot* there are two Complements, *my aunt* and *that teapot*. Either of these could function as Subject in a clause related to this one.

There is one exception to this general principle: that is the attributive Complement, as in *King Alfred was a noble king*, or *its fleece was white as snow* (see Chapter 5, Section 5.4). There is no clause related to these having *a noble king* or *white as snow* as Subject. (Forms like *white as snow was its fleece* appear only as archaic literary variants; they are not systematic alternatives.)

(3) Adjunct (circumstantial). An Adjunct is an element that has not got the potential of being Subject. It is typically realized by an adverbial group or a prepositional phrase. In *my aunt was given that teapot yesterday by the duke* there are two Adjuncts: the adverbial group *yesterday* and the prepositional phrase *by the duke*.

A prepositional phrase, however, has its own internal structure, containing a Complement within it (see Chapter 6, Section 6.5 below). In *by the duke*,

(a) *be* in simple present

John	is	naughty	isn't	he
Subject	Finite	Complement	Finite	Subject
Mood		Residue	Mood tag	

(b) *be* in another tense

John	is	being	naughty
Subject	Finite	Predicator	Complement
Mood		Residue	

(c) *have* 'possess' in simple present

Mary	has	a cold	hasn't	she
Subject	Finite	Complement	Finite	Subject
Mood		Residue	Mood tag	

(d) *have* 'possess' in another tense

Mary	has	had	a cold
Subject	Finite	Predicator	Complement
Mood		Residue	

(e) *have* 'take' in simple present

Fred	has		coffee	doesn't	he
Subject	'(present) Finite	have' Predicator	Complement	Finite	Subject
Mood		Residue		Mood tag	

(f) *have* 'take' in another tense

Fred	is	having	coffee
Subject	Finite	Predicator	Complement
Mood		Residue	

Figure 4-7 Different forms of *be* and *have*

the duke is Complement with respect to the preposition *by*. So although *by the duke* is itself an Adjunct, and could not become Subject, it has as one of its constituents *the duke*, which is a Complement at another rank, and could become Subject.

In the case of *by the duke*, if *the duke* comes to function as Subject then the preposition simply disappears: *that teapot was presented by the duke*, *the duke presented that teapot*. Similarly with the Adjunct *to my aunt*; if *my aunt* becomes Subject, the *to* disappears: *that teapot was given to my aunt*, *my aunt was given that teapot*. (The principle behind this is explained in Chapter 5, Section 5.8 below.) But increasingly in Modern English the Complement to any preposition has the potential of becoming a Subject, even where the preposition has to be retained and hence to function as an Adjunct on its own. For example, in *that paper's already been written on*, *that paper* functions as Subject, leaving *on* behind as a truncated Adjunct (Figure 4-8).

The typical order of elements in the Residue is: Predicator ^ Complement(s) ^ Adjunct(s), as in *the duke gave my aunt that teapot last year for her birthday*. But, as we have noted, an Adjunct or Complement may occur

(a)

that paper	's	already	been written	on
Subject	Finite	Adjunct	Predicator	Adjunct
Mood			Residue	

(b)

somebody	's	already	written	on that paper
Subject	Finite	Adjunct	Predicator	Adjunct
Mood			Residue	

Figure 4-8 Related clauses with same item as (a) Subject (b) Complement in a prepositional phrase

thematically, either as a WH- element in interrogative or as Marked Theme in a declarative clause. This does not mean that it becomes part of the Mood element; it is still within the Residue. As a result, therefore, the Residue is split into two parts: it becomes discontinuous. In *that teapot the duke had given to my aunt last year*, where *that teapot* is a marked-thematic Complement, the Residue is *that teapot . . . given to my aunt last year*. Discontinuous constituents can be represented in the box and tree diagrams as in Figure 4-9.

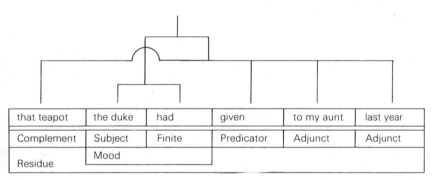

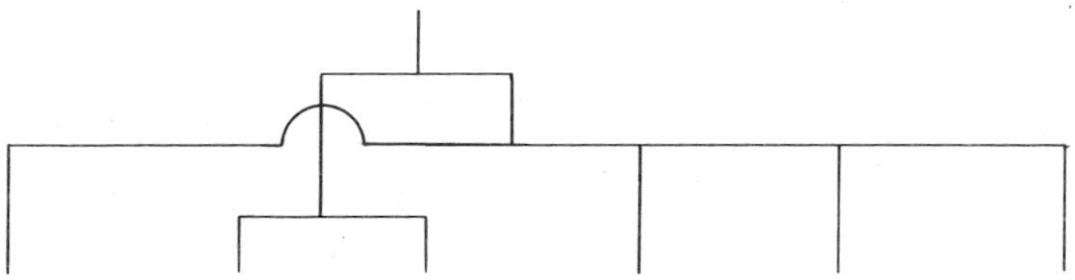

that teapot	the duke	had	given	to my aunt	last year
Complement	Subject	Finite	Predicator	Adjunct	Adjunct
Residue	Mood				

Figure 4-9 Discontinuous Residue

What has been said about Adjuncts so far relates to circumstantial Adjuncts, those that express some circumstance attendant on the process represented by the clause. In Chapter 3 we recognized two other types of Adjunct: Modal Adjunct (those with interpersonal function) and Conjunctive Adjunct (those with textual function). These now need to be discussed separately.

(4) Conjunctive Adjunct. Conjunctive Adjuncts tend to occur at points in the clause which are significant for textual organization, which means at some boundary or other: (i) clause initial, as (part of) the textual theme; (ii) clause final, as afterthought; (iii) between Theme and Rheme; (iv) between Mood and Residue. Examples:

(i) However, such men don't make good husbands.
(ii) Such men don't make good husbands, however.
(iii) Such men, however, don't make good husbands.
(iv) Such men don't, however, make good husbands.

Usually when a Conjunctive Adjunct occurs in the middle of the clause it also coincides with a boundary between two information units:

// such men / **don't** however // make good / **husbands** //

with the preceding element, here *don't*, carrying the tonic prominence (see Chapter 8 for details).

Conjunctive Adjuncts are outside the Mood–Residue organization; they have no function in the clause as exchange.

(5) Modal Adjunct. From the point of view of their place in the mood structure, Modal Adjuncts fall into two groups.

(i) Mood Adjuncts: group I in Table 3(3). These relate specifically to the meaning of the finite verbal operators, expressing probability, usuality, obligation, inclination or time. They therefore typically occur next to the Finite, either before or after it; for example *she probably hasn't arrived*, *he doesn't always hear*, *you certainly must go*, *I'd gladly help*, *she's already arrived*. There is also another set expressing intensity, e.g. *just*, *simply* as in *you simply can't tell*.

There is a great deal of minor variation among them (e.g. the time Adjunct *yet* tends to occur at the end, as in *she hasn't arrived yet*). Some of them regularly occur in thematic function, before the Subject. Wherever they turn up, they form part of the Mood element. Example in Figure 4-10:

probably	she	just	hasn't	seen	it	yet
Adjunct	Subject	Adjunct	Finite	Predicator	Complement	Adjunct
Mood				Residue		Mood

Figure 4-10 Mood Adjuncts

The principal items functioning as Mood Adjunct include the following:

(a) probability /obligation:	certainly, surely, probably, perhaps, maybe, possibly, definitely, positively
(b) usuality:	always, often, usually, regularly, typically, occasionally, seldom, rarely, ever, never, once
(c) presumption:	evidently, apparently, presumably, clearly, no doubt, obviously, of course
(d) inclination:	gladly, willingly, readily
(e) time:	yet, still, already, once, soon, just
(f) degree:	quite, almost, nearly, totally, entirely, utterly, completely, literally, absolutely, scarcely, hardly
(g) intensity:	just, simply, ever, only, really, actually

Those in (a) – (c) are typically thematic in the clause, and hence were listed in

Table 3(3). Those in (d) – (g) are not usually thematic and so did not figure in that Table.

(ii) Comment Adjuncts: group II in Table 3(3). As far as position in the clause is concerned, these are like Conjunctive Adjuncts: they tend to occur thematically, finally, between Theme and Rheme, or between Mood and Residue; and when medial, they are typically associated with a boundary between information units.

Although they are interpersonal rather than textual in function, expressing the speaker's comment on what he is saying, they are not themselves part of the proposition, and therefore fall outside the Mood–Residue structure.

Figure 4-11 gives an example with various types of Adjunct occurring in the same clause:

unfortunately	however	he	can't	usually	hear	clearly	on the telephone
Comment Adjunct	Conjunctive Adjunct	Subject	Finite	Mood Adjunct	Predicator	Adjunct	Adjunct
		Mood			Residue		

Figure 4-11 Clause with circumstantial, modal and conjunctive Adjuncts

4.4 WH- interrogative, exclamative and imperative clauses

(1) WH- interrogatives. The WH- element is a distinct element in the interpersonal structure of the clause. Its function is to specify the entity that the questioner wishes to have supplied. For reasons outlined in Chapter 3 above, it typically takes a thematic position in the clause.

The WH- element is always conflated with one or another of the three functions Subject, Complement or Adjunct. If it is conflated with the Subject, it is part of the Mood element, and the order within the Mood element must therefore be Subject ^ Finite, as shown in Figure 4-12.

who	killed		Cock Robin
Subject/WH-	'(past) Finite	kill' Predicator	Complement
Mood		Residue	

Figure 4-12 WH- element conflated with Subject

If on the other hand the WH- element is conflated with a Complement or Adjunct, it is part of the Residue; and in that case the typical interrogative ordering within the Mood element reasserts itself, and we have Finite preceding Subject, as in Figure 4-13.

(a)

whose little boy	are	you
Complement / WH-	Finite	Subject
Residue	Mood	

(b)

where	have	all the flowers	gone
Adjunct / WH-	Finite	Subject	Predicator
Residue	Mood		

Figure 4-13 WH- element conflated with (a) Complement, (b) Adjunct

What about WH- / Predicator? There is always the possibility that the missing piece the speaker wishes to have supplied may be something that is expressed in the verb — an action, event, mental process or relation — and hence functioning as Predicator. But the WH- element cannot be conflated with the Predicator; there is no verb *to what* in English, so we cannot ask *whatted he?* Questions of this kind are realized as *do* + *what* (Complement), or *what* (Subject) + *happen*; and whatever had something done to it, or happen to it, comes in as an Adjunct, in the form of a prepositional phrase, usually with the preposition *to*. An example is given in Figure 4-14.

what	have	the elephants	done	to the pier
Complement / WH-	Finite	Subject	Predicator	Adjunct
Residue	Mood			

Figure 4-14 WH- clause having question related to the process

This is one kind of Adjunct that is almost never thematic, for obvious reasons — not only would it have to override a WH- element, but it is not functioning as a circumstantial expression anyway.

(2) Exclamatives. These clauses have the WH- element *what* or *how*, in nominal or adverbial group. *what* conflates with a Complement, as in *what tremendously easy riddles you ask*; this is often an attributive Complement, as in *what a fool he is*. *how* conflates with an Adjunct, as in *how fast we're going*, *how he stares*; or with an attributive Complement, as in *how foolish he is*. In earlier English the Finite in these clauses preceded the Subject, as in *how are the mighty fallen*; but since the Finite ^ Subject sequence became specifically associated with interrogative mood, the normal order in exclamatives has become Subject ^ Finite. An example is given in Figure 4-15.

how neatly	he	spreads		his claws
Adjunct / WH-	Subject	'(present) Finite	spread' Predicator	Complement
Residue	Mood			

Figure 4-15 Exclamative clause

(3) Imperatives. Imperative clauses may have a Mood element consisting of Finite plus Subject; or one consisting of Finite only, or of Subject only; or no Mood element at all. Whether or not there is a Mood element, and whatever its structure, an imperative clause may also have a Mood tag.

More is said about imperatives in Section 4.6 below. Examples in Figure 4-16.

(a)

come	into my parlour	will	you
Predicator	Adjunct	Finite	Subject
Residue		Mood tag	

(b)

do	take	care	won't	you
Finite	Predicator	Complement	Finite	Subject
Mood	Residue		Mood tag	

(c)

let's	go	home	shall	we
Subject	Predicator	Adjunct	Finite	Subject
Mood	Residue		Mood tag	

(d)

don't	you	believe	it
Finite	Subject	Predicator	Complement
Mood		Residue	

Figure 4-16 Imperative clauses

4.5 Polarity and modality

POLARITY is the choice between positive and negative, as in *is / isn't*, *do / don't*. Typically, in English, polarity is expressed in the Finite element; each Finite verbal operator has two forms, one positive *is*, *was*, *has*, *can*, etc., the other negative *isn't*, *wasn't*, *hasn't*, *can't* (or *is not*, *cannot* . . .) etc. It was pointed out earlier (Chapter 3) that this is the reason why the Finite element is thematic in a yes/no interrogative clause: such a clause is precisely a request for information regarding polarity.

The Finite element is inherently either positive or negative; its polarity does not figure as a separate constituent. It is true that the negative is realized as a distinct morpheme *n't* or *not*; but this is an element in the structure of the verbal group, not in the structure of the clause.

However, the possibilities are not limited to a choice between yes and no. There are intermediate degrees: various kinds of indeterminacy that fall in between, like 'sometimes' or 'maybe'. These intermediate degrees, between the positive and negative poles, are known collectively as MODALITY.

But there is more than one way of getting from 'yes' to 'no'. In order to account for this, we need to refer to the distinction between propositions ('information', i.e. statements and questions) and proposals ('goods-&-services', i.e. offers and commands).

(1) Propositions. In a proposition, the meaning of the positive and negative poles is asserting and denying: positive 'it is so', negative 'it isn't so'. There are two kinds of intermediate possibilities: (i) degrees of probability: 'possibly / probably / certainly'; (ii) degrees of usuality: 'sometimes / usually / always'. The former are equivalent to 'either yes or no', i.e. maybe yes, maybe no, with different degrees of likelihood attached. The latter are equivalent to 'both yes and no', i.e. sometimes yes, sometimes no, with different degrees of oftenness attached. It is these scales of probability and usuality to which the term 'modality' strictly belongs.

Both probability and usuality can be expressed in the same three ways: (a) by a finite modal operator in the verbal group (see Table 4(3) above), e.g. *that will be John, he'll sit there all day*; (b) by a modal Adjunct of (i) probability or (ii) usuality (see Table 3(3) above), e.g. *that's probably John, he usually sits there all day*; (c) by both together, e.g. *that'll probably be John, he'll usually sit there all day*.

Note that in a statement the modality is an expression of the speaker's opinion: *that will be John* 'that's John, I think'; whereas in a question it is a request for the listener's opinion: *will that be John?* 'is that John d'you think?' Note also that even a high value modal ('certainly', 'always') is less determinate than a polar form: *that's certainly John* is less certain than *that's John*; *it always rains in summer* is less invariable than *it rains in summer*.

(2) Proposals. In a proposal, the meaning of the positive and negative poles is prescribing and proscribing: positive 'do it', negative 'don't do it'. Here also there are two kinds of intermediate possibility, in this case depending on the speech function, whether command or offer. (i) In a command, the intermediate points represent degrees of obligation: 'allowed to / supposed to / required to'; (ii) in an offer, they represent degrees of inclination: 'willing to / anxious to / determined to'. We shall refer to the scales of obligation and inclination as MODULATION, to distinguish them from modality in the sense above.

Again, both obligation and inclination can be expressed in either of two ways, though not, in this case, by both together: (a) by a finite modal operator, e.g. *you should know that, I'll help them*; (b) by an expansion of the Predicator (see Chapter 7 Additional, Section 7.A.5 below), (i) typically by a passive verb, e.g. *you're supposed to know that*, (ii) typically by an adjective, e.g. *I'm anxious to help them*.

Proposals which are clearly positive or negative, as we have seen, are goods-&-services exchanges between speaker and hearer, in which the speaker is either (i) offering to do something, e.g. *shall I go home?*, (ii)

Table 4(5) Modality and modulation

commodity exchanged	speech function		type of intermediacy		typical realization	example
information	proposition:	statement, question	modality:	probability (possible /probable /certain)	finite modal operator	they must have known
					modal Adjunct	they certainly knew
					(both the above)	they certainly must have known
				frequency (sometimes /usually /always)	finite modal operator	it must happen
					modal Adjunct	it always happens
					(both the above)	it must always happen
goods-&-services	proposal:	command	modulation:	obligation (allowed /supposed /required)	finite modal operator	you must be patient!
					passive verb Predicator	you're required to be patient!
		offer		inclination (willing /anxious /determined)	finite modal operator	I must win!
					adjective Predicator	I'm determined to win!

requesting the listener to do something, e.g. *go home!*, or (iii) suggesting that they both do something, e.g. *let's go home!* They rarely have third person Subjects, except as prayers or oaths. Modulated clauses, on the other hand, while they also occur frequently as offers, commands and suggestions (*I'll be going, you should be going, we ought to be going*), regularly implicate a third person; they are statements of obligation and inclination made by the speaker in respect of others, e.g. *John's supposed to know that, Mary will help.* In this case they function as propositions, since to the person addressed they convey information rather than goods-&-services. But they do not thereby lose their rhetorical force: if Mary is listening, she can now hardly refuse.

Table 4(5) summarizes the main categories of modality and modulation, and their typical realizations in the clause. What we have given here is a thumbnail sketch of a very rich and complex area of the grammar (which will be taken up again, in a different context, in Chapter 10). There are many further nuances within both modality and modulation, exemplified by forms such as *it must hurt* (high probability; cf. *it obviously hurts*), *must you do that?* (high inclination; cf. *you insist on doing that*). We have illustrated only from the standpoint of the positive pole; but it is equally possible to modalize negative clauses, expressing degrees of negativeness instead of degrees of positiveness so to speak: for example, *that can't be true, that certainly isn't true*; *you needn't stay, you're not expected to stay.* With the category of usuality there are special Adjuncts incorporating the negativity, such as *seldom* (*he seldom comes* 'he almost always doesn't come'), *never* (*he never comes* 'he always doesn't come'); compare, on the other scales, words such as *unlikely* ('probable + not'), *reluctant* ('almost determined + not'), *prohibited* ('required + not').

As far as the structural analysis is concerned, the finite modal operators and the modal Adjuncts have already been covered in the preceding sections. The negative word *not* occurs in two functions: either it is simply a formal or written variant of the finite negative element *n't*, in which case it is part of the Finite; or it is a distinct modal Adjunct within the Mood. In the latter case it is phonologically salient and may also be tonic, e.g.

// I will / not al/**low** it //
// we were / **not** im/pressed //

In non-finite clauses this is the only form of the negative, as in *not having been told about it, not to allow it*; here there is no Finite, but the modal Adjunct may constitute a Mood element on its own, or with the Subject if there is one, as in Figure 4-17.

for	John	not	to win
		never	having been told
	Subject	Adjunct	Predicator
	Mood		Residue

Figure 4-17 Negative modal Adjunct in non-finite clause

The expanded forms of modulation such as *expected to*, *allowed to*, *keen to*, can be interpreted structurally as complex Predicators, as shown in Figure 4-18. It is useful to label these as 'modulated', since otherwise this feature will not appear in the analysis.

John	is not	supposed to know	
Mary	is	anxious to help	them
Subject	Finite	Predicator (modulated)	Complement
Mood		Residue	

Figure 4-18 Complex (modulated) Predicators

Finally we should mention the words *yes* and *no*. These are, of course, expressions of polarity; but they are textual not interpersonal elements — they relate the polarity to what has gone before. Either they function on their own as separate elliptical clauses consisting of Adjunct only (see Chapter 9, Section 9.3 below); or they are continuatives with thematic function at the beginning of the clause, and fall outside the Mood – Residue structure. The analysis is as in Figure 4-19.

is	that	you	—	no
Finite	Subject	Complement		Adjunct
Mood		Residue		

it	's	raining	—	yes	it	usually	does
Subject	Finite	Predicator			Subject	Adjunct	Finite
Mood		Residue			Mood		

Figure 4-19 Yes and no

4.6 Absence of elements of the modal structure

We noted in Section 4.2 that a typical pattern of dialogue in English is one where the dialogue is carried forward by the Mood element in the clause. An exchange centring on the validity of an assertion — the identity of the Subject, the choice and degree of polarity — may be realized by clauses consisting of the Mood only, the Residue being established at the start and then presupposed by ellipsis, or by substitution with *do*.

Exchanges involving not the yes/no variable but the WH- variable, where just one element is under discussion, lead to a different form of ellipsis in which everything is omitted except that element. Its function in the clause is presupposed from the preceding discourse.

Examples of both kinds of ellipsis are given in Figure 4-20. The question of ellipsis is taken up again in Chapter 9.

(a) (Will you join the dance?) . . .

I	might	do
Subject	Finite	Predicator
Mood		Residue

I	won't
Subject	Finite
Mood	

(b) (Who killed Cock Robin?) . . .

I	(said the sparrow)	with my bow and arrow
Subject	·	Adjunct

Figure 4-20 (a) Substitution and ellipsis of the Residue (yes/no response) (b) Ellipsis of other presupposed elements (WH- response)

There is also a form of ellipsis of the Subject. In general, every independent clause in English requires a Subject, because without a Subject it is impossible to express the mood of the clause, at least in the usual fashion. We have already noted that the difference between declarative and yes/no interrogative is realized by the order of the elements Subject and Finite; and it is impossible to arrange two elements in order if one of them is not there. So while the *it* in *it's raining*, and the *there* in *there was a crash*, do not represent any entity participating in the process of raining or of crashing, they are needed in order to distinguish these from *is it raining*, *was there a crash*.

However, there is another feature associated with the realization of these two structures, and that is the intonation: declaratives usually go down in pitch at the end, while yes/no interrogatives typically go up (see Chapter 8 below). So it is possible to signal mood by intonation, which does not depend on the presence of a Subject; and this makes it possible for a clause to occur without one. There is in fact one condition in which clauses in English systematically occur without Subjects, one that depends on the notions of giving and demanding that were discussed at the very beginning of this chapter.

For any clause, there is one choice of Subject that is 'unmarked' — that is assumed, in the absence of evidence to the contrary. In a giving clause (offer or statement), the unmarked Subject is 'I'; while in a demanding clause (question or command), the unmarked Subject is 'you'. This means that, if a clause that on other grounds can be interpreted as offer or statement occurs without a Subject, the listener will understand the Subject 'I' — that is, Subject equals speaker, for example:

(a) Carry your bag? ('shall I . . .?')
— Would you? Thanks.

(b) Met Fred on the way here. ('I . . .')
— Did you? Where?

Whereas if it is question or command the listener will understand the Subject 'you' — that is, Subject equals listener, for example:

(c) Seen Fred? ('have you . . .?')
— No, I haven't.

(d) Play us a tune. ('Will you . . .?')
— Shall I? All right.

Notice that (d) is an ordinary imperative clause. In most accounts of English grammar the imperative is presented as if it was a special case, without any explanation. But it is not; it is simply an instance of this general principle by which a Subject is 'understood'. Being a demanding clause, its unmarked Subject is 'you'.

As these examples show, typically it is the whole of the Mood element that is left implicit in such instances: (*shall I*) *carry your bag?*, (*will you*) *play us a tune!* In an information clause, however, the Finite element may be present either because it is needed to express tense or modality, as in *might see you this evening* ('I . . .'), or because it is fused with the Predicator as in (b) above. In such instances only the Subject is 'ellipsed'.

The principle that the Subject to be supplied in a case of ellipsis is always the modally unmarked one, *I* or *you* according to the mood, can also be overridden by the context; for example in

(e) Seen Fred? ('Have you . . .?')
— No; must be away. ('He . . .')

the Subject in the response is understood as 'he (Fred)' by presupposition from the preceding question.

We remarked in 4.2 above on the relation between the semantic categories of statement, question, offer and command on the one hand and the grammatical categories of the mood system on the other. The relationship is a rather complex one. For statements and questions there is a clear pattern of congruence: typically, a statement is realized as declarative and a question as interrogative — but at the same time in both instances there are alternative realizations. For offers and commands the picture is even less determinate. A command is usually cited, in grammatical examples, as imperative, but it is just as likely to be a modulated interrogative or declarative, as in *Will you be quiet?*, *You must keep quiet!*; while for offers there is no distinct mood category at all, just a special interrogative form *shall I. . .?*, *shall we. . .?*, which again is simply one possible realization among many.* This would seem to complicate the question just raised, namely which Subject is to be understood if none is present. But in general this follows the grammar; for example, in

* It will be clear from this discussion that the imperative also could disappear as a distinct grammatical category, with *play us a tune!* interpreted as (*will you*) *play us a tune?* with ellipsis of the Mood element; cf. the tag *play us a tune, will you?* It is useful to retain it, however, because of its special categories of person and polarity.

2nd person	/go	/do/go	/you/go	/don't/go	/don't/you/go
1st person	‸let me/go	/do let me/go	‸let/me/go	‸I/won't/go	/don't let/me/go
1st & 2nd persons	‸let's/go	/do let's/go	‸let('s)/us/go	/don't let's/go; /let's not/go	/don't let('s)/us/go

Note that the *us* in *let's* is inclusive: it always includes the listener (whereas *we* in indicative is neutral in this respect).

Have an orange! (imperative 'will you'), *Like an orange?* (interrogative 'would you?'), the listener will supply 'you' as Subject and at the same time interpret the clause as an offer. There is rarely any misunderstanding, since the listener operates on the basic principle of all linguistic interaction — the principle that what the speaker says makes sense in the context in which he is saying it.

4.7 Clause as Subject

Up to this point, in our discussion of the clause as exchange, we have been illustrating the Subject with fairly simple, straightforward nominal groups: *I*, *Mary*, *this teapot*, *the man in the moon* and so on. This has been done to avoid complicating the issue with longer and more structurally complex examples.

In real discourse, obviously, there is vastly greater scope and variation in the choice of Subject in a clause. Depending on the register, we will regularly find examples such as the following (the Subject is shown by broken underlining):

(a) The scientific treatment of music had been popular ever since the days of Pythagoras, but most theorists, like the famous Greek, let their passion for numerical order override practical considerations. Thus even so outstanding a scientist as Kepler held fast, in his *De harmonice mundi* (1619), to the old astrological belief in the association between interval ratios and the structure of the universe, even of human society. The same delight in a neatly arranged system can be seen in the *Gradus ad Parnassum* (1725) of the Austrian composer Fux, . . .

(*Pelican History of Music*, Vol. II p. 246)

(b) An all-purpose calculator for business or personal use, the 8-digit display will handle lengthy calculations.

(c) A system that just keeps you warm in winter isn't a very good idea.

(d) Somehow this sort of traditional Hamlet aspect in the untraditional character he was playing didn't seem to fit together.

(e) The people who want to play with the cards that have goods trains on have to sit here.

Apart from that in (b), which is a NOMINAL GROUP COMPLEX (consisting of two nominal groups in paratactic relation; see Chapter 7 Additional, Section 7.A.1 below), each of these Subjects is a single nominal group. All of them, however, except *most theorists* in (a), contain some embedded material: either a prepositional phrase, or a clause, or both. Thus in (a) *of music*, *as Kepler*, *in a neatly arranged system* are prepositional phrases functioning as Qualifier/Postmodifier in the nominal group, and therefore form part of the

Subject of the clause; likewise the phrase *for business or personal use* in the first nominal group in (b).

The Postmodifier in the nominal group functioning as Subject in (c) is an embedded clause: *that just keeps you warm in winter*. It is a DEFINING RELATIVE CLAUSE, as described in Chapter 6, Section 6.2.2 below. This too falls within the Subject.

In (d) and (e), which are taken from spontaneous speech, the Subject nominal groups are more complex, since they contain both clauses and phrases in the Postmodifier. That in (d) has the clause *he was playing* embedded in the phrase *in the untraditional character he was playing* which in turn is embedded in the nominal group having *aspect* as its Head noun. In (e), which was spoken by a child of four, the clause *that have goods trains on* is embedded in the phrase *with the cards that have goods trains on* which is embedded in the clause *who want to play with the cards that have goods trains on*; the whole thing is a single Subject, with the noun *people* as Head.

Such items are not difficult to recognize and identify as Subjects. There is another type of embedded clause which does not figure among the examples above, and this is a clause functioning not as Postmodifier in the nominal group but as Head: in other words, functioning as if it constituted a nominal group on its own. Examples are

(f) To argue with the captain was asking for trouble.

(g) Ignoring the problem won't make it go away.

(h) That all this wealth might some day be hers had simply never occurred to her.

The analysis is as in Figure 4-21

to argue with the captain	was	asking for trouble
Subject	Finite	Complement
Mood		Residue

Figure 4-21 Embedded clause as Subject

Note that in this example the Complement is also an embedded clause.

In many instances an embedded clause functioning as Subject appears at the end of the clause in which it is embedded, with an anticipatory *it* occurring in the normal Subject position, as in *it's no use crying over spilt milk*. In such cases there will be a marked variant with the clause Subject at the beginning: *crying over spilt milk is no use*. Here are some further examples:

(j) It was fortunate for me that the captain was no naturalist.

(k) It is impossible to protect individuals against the ills of poverty, sickness and decrepitude without some recourse to the machinery of the state.

(l) Doesn't it worry you that you might get stung?

doesn't	it	worry	you	that you might get stung
Finite	Sub-	Predicator	Complement	-ject
Mood		Residue		

Figure 4-22 Embedded clause Subject with anticipatory *it*

The same pattern occurs in a clause with predicated Theme (see Chapter 3, Section 3.7 above), as in the following examples:

(m) Pensioner Cecil Burns thought he had broken the slot machine; but it was not the machine he had broken — it was the bank.

(n) It was not until fairly recently that this problem was solved

(o) The dog it was that died.

It may be helpful to show both the thematic and the modal analysis here; see Figure 4-23.

the dog	it	was	that died
Theme	Rheme		
Complement	Sub-	Finite	-ject
Residue	Mood		

Figure 4-23 Subject in Theme predication

Although the clause with predicated Theme, examples (m) – (o), is superficially similar to that with postposed clause Subject, examples (j) – (l), the two are not the same. A clause with predicated Theme has a non-predicated variant, e.g.

it was yesterday that he came: he came yesterday

One with postposed clause Subject has no such variant; the clause

it was worrying that he came

has as variant *that he came was worrying*, but not *he came worrying*, or even *he came worryingly*. This type is described in Chapter 7, Section 7.5.7, below.

4.8 Texts

Text 1: conversation between Nigel (age 4; 2) and his father

1 N. Drown a mermaid!
1 F. What?
2 N. (laughing) You can't drown a mermaid, because the mermaid goes under the water, very deep.

2 F. No, you can't drown a mermaid, a mermaid lives in the water. You can't drown a fish, either, can you?
3 N. But you can drown a deadly stonefish.
3 F. You can't – that's a fish too.
4 N. But it only goes in very shallow water, so it will drown if you make it go deep.
4 F. I don't think it will! It might get rather uncomfortable, that's all. We must go to the Shedd Aquarium again and have a look at one.
5 N. No: it wasn't in the Shedd Aquarium; it was in the Steinhart Aquarium. They haven't got one at the Shedd.
5 F. They may have.
6 N. No they haven't.
6 F. Well you don't know. We only saw a little bit of it. There's lots more that we didn't see.
7 N. I liked that fish that we saw at the Steinhart, the one that its tail wasn't like a fish. It was eating a lettuce.
7 F. Oh yes I remember. What was it called? I can't remember its name. Wasn't it funny, eating a lettuce? Actually I think it was a cabbage, wasn't it?
8 N. No – yes I think it was a cabbage. And it ate it (laughing).
8 F. It's funny that it liked cabbage. There isn't any cabbage in the sea.
9 N. I expect the people at the museum . . . the zoo . . . I mean the aquarium (laughing) gave it the cabbage.
9 F. Yes, but, I mean, why did it like cabbage? There aren't any cabbages where it usually lives, in the sea.
10 N. Yes there are cabbages – no not in the sea, but in its water.
10 F. But that is sea water, in its tank. The cabbage doesn't grow there; the aquarium people put it in.
11 N. No that's not sea . . . I mean it isn't the sea that's deep, the sea that . . . (hesitating) that's where the ships can go, far far away.
11 F. No but it's water from the sea – it's the same kind of water.

Analysis of selected clauses from the text (in terms of mood)

drown	a mermaid
Predicator Residue	Complement

what

you	can't	drown	a mermaid
Subject	Finite	Predicator	Complement
Mood		Residue	

a mermaid	lives		in the water
Subject	'present' Finite	live Predicator	Adjunct
Mood		Residue	

because	the mermaid	goes		under the water, very deep
	Subject	'present' Finite	go Predicator	Adjunct
	Mood		Residue	

you	can't	drown	a fish	either	can	you
Subject	Finite	Predicator	Complement		Finite	Subject
Mood		Residue			Mood tag	

you	can't
Subject	Finite
Mood	

that	's	a fish	too
Subject	Finite	Complement	
Mood		Residue	

but	it	only*	goes		in very shallow water
	Subject	Adjunct	'present' Finite	go Predicator	Adjunct
	Mood			Residue	

so	it	will	drown
	Subject	Finite	Predicator
	Mood		Residue

if	you	make		it	go dee
	Subject	'present' Finite	make Predi-	Complement	cator
	Mood		Residue		

oh yes	I	remember	
	Subject	'present' Finite	remember Predicator
	Mood		Residue

what	was	it	called
Complement	Finite	Subject	Predicator
Resi-	Mood		-due

wasn't	it	funny
Finite	Subject	Complement
Mood		Residue

eating	a lettuce
Predicator	Complement
Residue	

1)

actually	I	think	
Adjunct	Sub-ject	'present' Finite	think Predicator
Mood			Residue

it	was	a cabbage	wasn't	it
Subject	Finite	Comple-ment	Finite	Subject
Mood		Residue	Mood tag	

2)

actually	I think	it	was	a cabbage	wasn't	it
	Adjunct	Subject	Finite	Complement	Finite	Subject
	Mood			Residue	Mood tag	

2)

no – yes –	I think	it	was	a cabbage
	Adjunct	Subject	Finite	Complement
	Mood			Residue

* Modal (polar) Adjunct

it	's	funny	that	it	liked		cabbage*
Sub-	Finite	Complement	-ject				
		Residue		Subject	'past' Finite	like Predicator	Complement
Mood				Mood		Residue	

there	isn't	any cabbage	in the sea
Subject	Finite	Complement	Adjunct
Mood		Residue	

Summary of Subjects and Finites in the text

	No. of Occurrences	Subject	Finite	turn no.: clause no.
	(5)	you (= 'one')	can/can't	2N:1; 2F:1, 3; 3N:1; 3F:1
	(2)	mermaid	does	2N:2; 2F:2
(5)	(1)	that ('stonefish')	is	3F:2
	(1)	it (,,)	does	4N:1
	(3)	it (,,)	will/might	4N:2; 4F:1,2
	(1)	we	must	4F:3
	(2)	it ('the stonefish')	was/wasn't	SN:1,2
	(3)	they ('Shedd')	have/haven't	5N:3; 5F:1; 6N:1
	(1)	you	don't	6F:1
	(1)	we	did	6F:2
	(1)	there	is	6F:3
(3)	(1)	I ('Nigel')	did	7N:1
	(2)	I ('father')	do/can't**	7F:1
(6)	(3)	it ('that fish')	was	7N:2; 7F:2,4
	(3)	it (,,)	did	8N:2; 8F:1; 9F:1
	(2)	it ('lettuce')	was	7F:5; 8N:1
	(3)	there	is/isn't/aren't	8F:2; 9F:2; 10N:1
	(2)	aquarium people	did	9N:1; 10F:3
	(5)	that/it (the fish's water)	is/isn't	10F:1; 11N:1,2; 11F:1,2
	(1)	the cabbage	doesn't	10F:2

By looking at the mood structure, clause by clause, we can see the way the dialogue proceeds as a series of exchanges. It begins with discussion of a proposition, initiated by Nigel, that something is not possible (*you can't*), interspersed with general assertions about mermaids; these are followed by general assertions about stonefishes, which move from unmodalized (*does*) to modalized (*will, might*), and then by assertions about a particular stonefish (*was*), and about the current holdings of the Shedd Aquarium.

---

* See Chapter 6 for this 'embedding'

** same verb *remember* as Predicator

This sequence is terminated by his father, who shifts the orientation away from the third person on to themselves, with *we* and *you* as Subjects (*we must*, *you don't*). Nigel reopens the exchange, beginning with a proposition about himself and a past experience (*I [like]d*); he then reorients the past event to the third person, investing its validity in a particular fish (*it* 'that fish'). This leads on to a series of exchanges in which the dialogue centres on the fish, on its food, on presence or absence (*there is / isn't*), on the activities of the aquarium people, and on the nature of the water in which the fish was kept and fed.

We have ignored 'embedded' clauses (see Chapters 6 and 7), and also clauses functioning as modalities (*I think*, *I expect*, *I mean*; cf. Section 3.6 above), since these do not function as propositions or proposals — they play no part in the structure of the interaction. These aside, there are 43 clauses which are functioning as propositions, of which 41 are taken account of in the movement of the dialogue as described above.

Unlike the Theme, which — while it is itself a property of the clause — carries forward the development of the text as a whole, the Mood element has little significance beyond the immediate sequence of clauses in which it occurs. It tends to be the overall organization of the text that determines the choice of Theme in any particular clause, or that determines at least the general pattern of thematic choices; whereas there may be no general pattern in the choice of Subject, but only a specific propositional basis for each exchange. In this particular text, all the Themes are unmarked, which means that in every declarative clause the Theme is also the Subject. Naturally when this happens the overall sequence of Subjects will also be patterned; but the pattern displayed is first and foremost a thematic one — it depends on the status of each of the items as a Theme.

Nevertheless the ongoing selection of Subjects by a speaker or writer does give a characteristic flavour to a piece of discourse. In this particular example it is clear that initially Nigel is determining the direction of the dialogue, and that his argument has a strong orientation towards the outside world; that he starts from general propositions in the present (which being general are therefore interpreted as valid for any time) and proceeds to propositions about specific past events. This is the pattern throughout roughly the first half of the text; so much we can tell simply from looking at the Mood elements, the configurations of Subject plus Finite. In the second half, by contrast, the argumentation is much more fluid. Nigel's father raises a problem which Nigel is unable to grasp; and in the course of his attempts to elucidate it the argument switches from one Subject to another from among the various entities that figured as participants in the event in question. Here the rapid changes of orientation from one proposition to another give a rather fragmentary character to the dialogue as a whole.

Text 2: from Peter Calvocoressi: *The British Experience 1945–75*, pp. 106–7

In this text, both Subject and Theme are marked: Subject by broken underlining, Theme by solid underlining. No commentary is given.

What then were governments trying to do? There was not so very much difference between them, extremists on either side excepted – and these were ineffective. All governments accepted an obligation to contribute positively to the prosperity of both sectors. This contribution was in the nature of things essentially financial; governments provided money or facilitated credit, and with this money private and nationalized businesses would invest, modernize and grow. At the same time, and from the very earliest postwar years, governments of both colours also saw it as part of their job to intervene in economic affairs to keep wages in check, whether by bargaining with the unions or by subsidizing the cost of living or by law. Broadly speaking therefore governments were actively involved in priming industry and restraining wages. This was their economic strategy. It did not distinguish fundamentally between the private and the public sector, which were treated as parts of a single whole. There was no fixed dividing line between them.

Government intervention of this nature was inflationary. The inflation was modified so far as wage rises were restrained (or matched by higher output) but some inflation was inseparable from a policy which set out to make things happen by supplying money and credit to make them happen – the more so of course if governments were simultaneously supplying money for social services and social security benefits, the former as of right and the latter in return for contributions which did not cover the whole cost. For about twenty years inflation proceeded at around 3% a year. Then, in the early seventies, it averaged nearly 10% and was soon to shoot up much higher.

A modern democratic capitalist economy is based on inflation, and in these years the wherewithal for recovery and expansion was provided to a significant degree by government, either through fiscal policy or by direct central or local government expenditure. (Complaints that governments were impeding industry and commerce, e.g. by excessive taxation, were at bottom pleas for further inflation.) At the same time governments hoped that the private sector in particular would quickly get on its own feet, attaining a degree of profitability which would make it sturdily independent of governments; wages policies were designed to this end and when the end was not attained government, in the later years of our period, remitted taxes on business, thereby shifting the fiscal burden from companies to individuals.

These policies did not work. Unions were powerful enough to insist, if sometimes tardily, on wage rises to match or more than match the rise in the cost of living. Wage claims were increasingly geared not to price rises but to these plus anticipated further rises. Profitability remained therefore elusive, or was achieved only on paper by presenting accounts in new ways: on the hard test of how much cash there was in the bank profits were meagre. Real wage increases were also elusive. By the late sixties not only rates of profit were falling but so too was the share of wages as a proportion of the national product.

Governments were committed to inflation because they were themselves part of the system which required it. Modern capitalism thrives on expansion and credit, and without them it shrivels. Equally however it requires the right context, which is an expanding world economy: a national economy is distinct and severable from other national economies in some senses but not all. If the total economy of which it is part does not expand, then the inflation in the particular economy ceases to be fruitful and becomes malignant. Furthermore, the more the particular economy flourishes, the more dependent it is upon the total economy to which it is directing a part of its product, and the more dangerous is any pause in its alimentation – the easier it is to turn from boom to bust. Finally, any government operating within such a system becomes overwhelmingly committed to maintaining it, more especially when symptoms of collapse appear – as they did in the last decade of our period when governments felt compelled to help not only lame ducks but lame eagles too. All this was inflationary. No government could simply deflate: every government did both, aiming to deflate on balance but constantly inflating to such an extent that the compensating deflation became increasingly harsh and politically dangerous. Simply to turn off the tap would have been a double disaster, not only putting millions out of work but also ringing down the curtain once and for all on Britain's career as an industrial and trading nation. If industries were allowed to shrivel and fail they would cease producing the goods which the country exchanged for food (which it had ceased to produce for itself when it took the industrial option) and for the industrial raw materials which it did not possess within its own borders (now much reduced by loss of empire).

5

Clause as representation

5.1 Process, participant and circumstance

We now come to the third aspect of the meaning of the clause, its meaning as representation. Usually when people talk about what a word or a sentence 'means', it is this kind of meaning they have in mind — meaning in the sense of content.

In Chapter 4 we were looking at the clause from the point of view of its interpersonal function, the part it plays as a form of exchange between speaker and listener. In this chapter by contrast we shall be concerned with the clause in its ideational function, its role as a means of representing patterns of experience. A fundamental property of language is that it enables human beings to build a mental picture of reality, to make sense of their experience of what goes on around them and inside them. Here again the clause is the most significant grammatical unit, in this case because it is the clause that functions as the representation of processes.

What does it mean to say that a clause represents a process? Our most powerful conception of reality is that it consists of 'goings-on': of doing, happening, feeling, being. These goings-on are sorted out in the semantic system of the language, and expressed through the grammar of the clause. Parallel with its evolution in the function of mood, expressing the active, interpersonal aspect of meaning, the clause evolved simultaneously in another grammatical function expressing the reflective, experiential aspect of meaning. This latter is the system of TRANSITIVITY. Transitivity specifies the different types of process that are recognized in the language, and the structures by which they are expressed.

The basic semantic framework for the representation of processes is very simple. A process consists potentially of three components:

(i) the process itself;
(ii) participants in the process;
(iii) circumstances associated with the process.

These provide the frame of reference for interpreting our experience of what goes on.

Imagine that we are out in the open air and that there is movement overhead. Perceptually the phenomenon is all of a piece; but when we talk about it we analyse it as a semantic configuration — something which we express as, say, *birds are flying in the sky*. This is not the only possible way of organizing such a fragment of experience; we might have turned it into a meaning structure — 'semanticized' it, so to speak — quite differently. We might have said something like *it's winging*; after all, we say *it's raining*, without analysing that process into components, although it would be quite possible to do this also — there is in fact a dialect of Chinese which represents the phenomenon of rain as 'the sky is dropping water'. In English, there are a few processes, like raining, which are left unanalysed; but more typically the English language structures each experience as a semantic configuration on the principle illustrated above, consisting of process, participants and (optionally) circumstantial elements. So in this instance we have a process *are flying*, a participant *birds*, and a circumstantial element *in the sky*. In this interpretation of what is going on, there is doing, a doer, and a location where the doing takes place.

This tripartite interpretation of processes is what lies behind the grammatical distinction of word classes into verbs, nouns, and the rest, a pattern that in some form or other is probably universal among human languages. We can express this as in Table 5(1).

Table 5(1) Typical functions of group and phrase classes

type of element:	typically realized by:
(i) process	verbal group
(ii) participant	nominal group → used as a noun → -ness
(iii) circumstance	adverbial group or prepositional phrase → -ation → -ly

An example is given in Figure 5-1.

the lion	chased	the tourist	lazily	through the bush
participant	process	participant	circumstance	circumstance
nominal group	verbal group	nominal group	adverbial group	prepositional phrase

Figure 5-1 Clause as process, participants and circumstances

The concepts of process, participant and circumstance are semantic categories which explain in the most general way how phenomena of the real world are represented as linguistic structures. When we come to interpret the grammar of the clause, however, we do not use these concepts as they stand because they are too general to explain very much. We shall need to recognize functions which are more specific than these and which may differ according to the type of process being represented. Nevertheless they all derive from and can be related to these three general categories. In the following sections we shall explore the different types of process that are built in to the semantics of English, and the particular kinds of participant role that are systematically associated with each.

5.2 Material processes: processes of doing

In Chapter 2 we introduced the concept of ACTOR. The Actor is the 'logical Subject' of older terminology, and means the one that does the deed; for example *the mouse* in *the mouse ran up the clock*.

A 'logical' element (in this sense) is a function in transitivity structure. The traditional view of transitivity in western linguistics is as follows. (1) Every process has an Actor. (2) Some processes, but not all, also have a second participant, which we shall call a GOAL. An example is given in Figure 5-2.

(a)

the lion	sprang
Actor	Process

(b)

the lion	caught	the tourist
Actor	Process	Goal

Figure 5-2 One-participant and two-participant clauses

The implication is that in both cases the lion did something; but in (a) the doing was confined to the lion, whereas in (b) it was directed at, or extended to, the tourist. The term Goal implies 'directed at'; another term that has been used for this function is Patient, meaning one that 'suffers' or 'undergoes' the process. We will keep the familiar term Goal in the present analysis, although neither of the two really hits the mark; the relevant concept is more like that of 'one to which the process is extended'. The concept of extension is in fact the one that is embodied in the classical terminology of 'transitive' and 'intransitive', from which the term 'transitivity' is derived. According to this theory the verb *spring* is said to be intransitive ('not going through') and the verb *catch* is said to be transitive ('going through' — that is, extending to some other entity). This is an accurate interpretation of the difference between them; with the proviso that, in English at least, these concepts relate more appropriately to the clause than to the verb.

It will be noticed that the term Actor is used in the interpretation of both types of clause; and this embodies a further assumption, namely that *the lion* has the same function in both. In both cases, the lion is 'doing' something. This assumption is related to the fact that, in those Indo-European languages in which nouns are marked for case, like Greek and Latin, and modern Russian, *the lion* would be in the nominative case in both (a) and (b), whereas *the tourist* would be in an oblique case, typically the accusative; which suggests that the function of *the lion* is constant across both types. The same point can be made in relation to English; although nouns have no case, personal pronouns have, so if we replace the nouns *lion* and *tourist* by personal pronouns we would have *he sprang*, *he caught him*. This is highly suggestive; there is undoubtedly some reason for the cases to be distributed as they are. But it may not tell the whole story. For one thing, not all processes necessarily have the same grammar; and for another, even where they have there may be more than one principle at work. We shall explore the first point in Section 5.2–5.4, and the second in Section 5.8.

The assumptions that lie behind the notion of Actor are valid within certain limits. There is a large class of clauses in English which can be interpreted in this way, as consisting of a process with these particular participants — an obligatory Actor, and optionally also a Goal. This is the class that we shall refer to as a MATERIAL PROCESS.

Material processes are processes of 'doing'. They express the notion that some entity 'does' something — which may be done 'to' some other entity.

So we can ask about such processes, or 'probe' them, in this way: *What did the lion do? What did the lion do to the tourist?* Looked at from the tourist's point of view, on the other hand, the process is not one of doing but one of 'happening'; so we can also say *What happened to the tourist?* Consequently if there is a Goal of the process, as well as an Actor, the representation may come in either of two forms: either active, *the lion caught the tourist*, or passive, *the tourist was caught by the lion*. Note the analysis in Figure 5-3.

the lion	caught	the tourist
Actor	Process	Goal

the tourist	was caught by	the lion
Goal	Process	Actor

Figure 5-3 Active and passive clauses

Alternatively, the other entity may be one that is brought into being by the process, not pre-existing; as in building a house, writing a letter or starting an argument. We can thus distinguish between a 'doing to', or DISPOSITIVE type and a 'bringing about', or CREATIVE type of material process. The participant that results from the creative process is still referred to as Goal; such clauses also have active and passive options.

Material processes are not necessarily concrete, physical events; they may be abstract doings and happenings, as in Figure 5-4.

the mayor	resigned
Actor	Process

the mayor	dissolved	the committee
Actor	Process	Goal

Figure 5-4 Clauses with abstract processes

These are still treated grammatically in the language as types of action; the appropriate probes would be *What did the mayor do?*, *What did the mayor do to the committee?*

But as the process becomes more abstract, so the distinction between Actor and Goal becomes harder to draw. With a concrete process it is usually clear which role a given participant is playing: there is a sharp distinction between *the boy kicked*, where *the boy* is Actor, and *the boy was kicked*, where *the boy* is Goal. Even with concrete processes, however, we have to recognize that there are some where the Actor is involuntary, and thus in some respects like a Goal; for example *the tourist collapsed*. Despite the fact that the verb is active, this is a happening rather a doing: the probe is not *what did the tourist do?* but *what happened to the tourist?* With more abstract processes, we often find active and passive forms side by side with very little difference between them: for example *the girls' school and the boys' school combined / were combined*; *a new approach is evolving / is being evolved*. There still is some difference: if the passive form is used, we can probe for an explicit Actor — we can ask *who by?*, whereas with the active form we cannot. And this is what justifies us in still giving a different functional status to the participant in the two cases, as in Figure 5-5, where *the two schools* is Actor in the one case and Goal in the other:

the two schools	combined
Actor	Process

the two schools	were combined
Goal	Process

Figure 5-5 Active and passive in an abstract process

But this clearly exaggerates the difference, and we shall return to this point with an alternative interpretation below (Section 5.8).

Meanwhile we need to take cognizance of the fact that much of the time people are not talking about concrete processes like springing and catching, or even abstract ones like dissolving and resigning. We are talking about such momentous phenomena as what we think and feel, what Mary said to John, what is good or bad, here or there, mine or yours; these are the flesh and blood of everyday encounters. In sayings of this kind, however, the concepts of Actor and Goal do not make much sense. If I say

Mary liked that present that you brought her

it can hardly be said that Mary is an Actor and that she is 'doing something to' the present. And this is not because it is casual and colloquial; the same would be true of a majority of expressions in more highly valued modes of discourse. It would be difficult, for example, to identify an Actor in any of the following:

To be or not to be: that is the question.

We hold these truths to be self-evident.

The square on the hypotenuse of a right-angled triangle equals the sum of the squares on the other two sides.

Psychology as an empirically based study has had mixed origins in every country where it has developed.

To understand expressions such as these we need to broaden our view of what constitute 'goings-on'. It is important to recognize that there may be more than one kind of process in the grammar of a language; and that the functions assumed by the participants in any clause are determined by the type of process that is involved. For a text consisting entirely of material processes see Figure 5-6.

Jack and Jill	went	up the hill
Actor	Process: material	(circumstance)

To fetch	a pail of water
Process: material	Goal

Jack	fell down
Actor	Process: material

and	broke	his crown
	Process: material	Goal

And	Jill	came tumbling	after
	Actor	Process: material	(circumstance)

Up	Jack	got
Pro- material	Actor	-cess

and	home	he	trot
	(circumstance)	Actor	Process: material

	As fast	as	he	could caper
	(circumstance			)
			Actor	Process: material

Went	to bed
Process: material	(circumstance)

to mend	his head
Process: material	Goal

	With vinegar and brown paper
	(circumstance)

Figure 5-6 A text consisting entirely of material processes

5.3 Mental processes: processes of sensing

It might be argued that the terms Actor and Goal are just conventional labels; and that since grammatical and semantic categories are not in one-to-one correspondence, then if we use grammatical terms that are semantic in import (as nearly all grammatical terms are) we cannot expect them to be appropriate for all instances. The reasoning is quite valid; grammatical labels are very rarely appropriate for all instances of a category — they are chosen to reflect its central or 'core' signification. In this case, as it happens, the range of different clause types to which the labels Actor and Goal are readily applicable would be suspiciously few. But there is a more serious reason for questioning their relevance to the analysis of clauses such as *Mary liked that present*.

Consider the pair of clauses (i) *Mary liked the gift*, (ii) *the gift pleased Mary*. These are not synonymous; they differ in their choice of both Theme and Subject, both these roles being assigned to *Mary* in (i) and to *the gift* in (ii). But they are obviously closely related; considered from the standpoint of the present chapter, they could be representations of the same state of affairs. Yet if we apply an Actor – Process – Goal analysis we shall be saying that in (i) *Mary* is Actor and *the gift* is Goal, while in (ii) it is the other way round. This seems somewhat artificial.

Could we perhaps interpret one of these as being the passive of the other? Assuming we could find some criterion for deciding which was which, this would yield a proportion as in Figure 5-7.

Mary	liked	the gift	is to	the gift	pleased	Mary
Goal	Process	Actor	as	Actor	Process	Goal
the tourist	was caught by	the lion		the lion	caught	the tourist

Figure 5-7 Verbs *like* and *please* interpreted as active/passive pair

This says that *Mary liked the gift* is the realization of a semantic configuration that would be realized as *Mary was pleased by the gift* if such a clause existed. The drawback is, of course, that *Mary was pleased by the gift* does exist; it is a normal, and indeed very frequent, clause type in English. We can hardly explain some other clause by saying that it is doing duty as a replacement for this one. Furthermore the other clause has its own passive: *the gift was liked by Mary*, although a much less common type, undoubtedly exists also. So we cannot explain either of the active forms by saying that it is a special kind of 'passive' of the other; each one has a passive of its own. This is not an isolated instance; pairs of this kind are typical of clauses of feeling, thinking and perceiving, for example

no-one believed his story	his story convinced no-one
I hadn't noticed that	that hadn't struck me
children fear ghosts	ghosts frighten children

(For a fuller list see under point (4) below.) The contemporary language goes on creating such pairs: the slang expressions *I dig it* and *it sends me* both evolved at about the same time. Nonetheless speakers of English do not seem to feel that doublets like *believe* and *convince*, or *notice* and *strike*, semantically related though they may be, are so close that they ought to be interpreted as different forms of the same word (in the way that, for example, *go* and *went* are different forms of the same verb *go*).

It seems therefore that we should abandon the Actor – Goal trail at this point and recognize that there are clauses which are unlike material process clauses and require a different functional interpretation. Let us group together clauses of feeling, thinking and perceiving under the general heading of MENTAL PROCESS, and see whether such a category will turn out to possess other significant characteristics. Obviously clauses expressing material and mental processes are different in meaning, but that is not enough to make them constitute distinct grammatical categories; there are indefinitely many ways of drawing lines on purely semantic grounds, whereas the question we are concerned with is which of these have systematic repercussions in the grammar. Th category of 'mental process clauses' turns out to be grammatically distinct from that of material process clauses on the basis of five main criteria; these are set out in the following numbered paragraphs.

(1) In a clause of mental process, there is always one participant who is human; this is the one that 'senses' — feels, thinks or perceives, for example *Mary* in *Mary liked the gift*. More accurately, we should say human-like; the significant feature of such a participant is that of being 'endowed with consciousness'. Expressed in grammatical terms, the participant that is engaged in the mental process is one that is referred to pronominally as *he* or *she*, not as *it*.

Which particular creatures we choose to endow with consciousness when we talk about them may vary according to who we are, what we are doing or how we are feeling at the time. Pets, domestic animals and other higher mammals are often treated as conscious; the owner says of the cat *she doesn't like milk*, whereas someone who is not a cat lover, or who has been annoyed by that particular specimen, is more likely to refer to the animal as *it*. But any object, animate or not, can be treated as conscious; and since mental process clauses have this property, that only something that is being credited with consciousness can function in them as the one who feels, thinks or perceives, one only has to put something into that role in order to turn it into a conscious being, for example *the empty house was longing for the children to return*. Simply by putting *the empty house* in this grammatical environment, as something that felt a longing, we cause it to be understood as endowed with consciousness. This explains the anomalous character of clauses such as *it really likes me*, *it knows what it thinks*, where there is a tension between the *it* and the meaning of the verb. Not that such clauses are ungrammatical; far from it. But the ambiguous status of the 'sensing' participant, who on the one hand is capable of liking, knowing and thinking, and therefore is 'plus consciousness', but on the other hand is referred to as *it*, and therefore is 'minus consciousness', gives them a flavour that is somewhat humorous or quaint.

There is no trace of this pattern in material process clauses. In a material process no participant is required to be human, and the distinction between conscious and non-conscious beings simply plays no part.

(2) With regard to the other main element in a clause of mental process, namely that which is felt, thought or perceived, the position is in a sense reversed. That is to say, the set of things that can take on this role in the clause is not only not restricted to any particular semantic or grammatical category, it is actually wider than the set of possible participants in a material process. It may be not only a 'thing' but also a 'fact'.

This is not an easy concept; but it is one that is fundamental to the nature of language. In a material process, every participant is a THING: that is, it is a phenomenon of our experience, including of course our inner experience or imagination — some entity (person, creature, object, institution or abstraction), or some process (action, event, quality, state or relation). Any of these 'things' may also, of course, be the object of consciousness in a mental process; we can say *Mary liked the gift*, *Tim knows the city*, *Jane saw the stars* where *the gift*, *the city*, *the stars* are 'things' that could appear in a material process also. But we can also say

Mary was pleased that she'd got a present
Tim realized that he was in a big city
Jane saw that the stars had come out

In these examples, what is being 'sensed' is not a thing but a fact.

The typical way of expressing a fact is by means of a *that* clause, like those just cited. Often the fact that something is a fact is explicitly signalled by the words *the fact that*. . . . Here we are using the term 'fact' in a rather general sense; what is involved is actually a group of related categories which will be explored in more detail later: see Chapter 7, Section 7.5 below.

There is no way in which a fact can be a participant in a clause of material process. Grammatically speaking, facts can be sensed — seen, felt or thought; but they cannot do anything, nor can they have anything done to them. When we meet an expression such as *the fact that his father was ill upset him*, we know that *upset* is being used in the sense of a mental process; in a way that was originally metaphorical, like modern colloquial *threw him*, but is now its most usual interpretation.

(3) A third distinction between material and mental processes is that of tense. What is the basic form of the present tense in modern English? In the teaching of English as a foreign language there has been much controversy about which to teach first, the simple present *takes* or the so-called 'present continuous' (which we shall characterize as 'present in present'; see Chapter 6 below) *is taking*; and claims have been made on behalf of both. There is a reason for the controversy; in fact either one of these tenses may be the basic, unmarked form depending on the type of process expressed by the clause. In a mental process, the unmarked present tense is the SIMPLE PRESENT; we say

She likes the gift	(not *she is liking the gift*)
Do you know the city?	(not *are you knowing the city?*)
I see the stars	(not *I am seeing the stars*)

But in a material process the unmarked present tense is the PRESENT IN PRESENT; we say

They're building a house	(not *they build a house*)
Are you making the tea?	(not *do you make the tea?*)
I'm going home	(not *I go home*)

We are not saying that the other tense cannot occur; both tenses are used with both types of process. But the other one is the marked option in each case; and this means that it carries a special interpretation. The simple present with a material process is general or habitual, e.g. *they build a house for every employee*. The present in present with a mental process is a rather highly conditioned kind of inceptive aspect, as in *I feel I'm knowing the city for the first time* ('I'm getting to know'); this is somewhat difficult to contextualize, with the result that, taken out of context, it is quite likely to be understood as something else (e.g. *I'm seeing the stars* as a material process 'I'm interviewing the leading performers'). These tense patterns are set out in Table 5(2).

Table 5(2) Unmarked present tense with material and mental processes

tense: / process:	present	present in present
material	[marked] they build a house (for every employee)	[unmarked] they're building a house
mental	[unmarked] I know the city	[marked] I'm knowing the city (for the first time)

(4) The point was brought out earlier that mental processes are represented in the language as two-way processes; that is to say, we can say either *Mary liked the gift* or *the gift pleased Mary*. It is not the case that every mental process verb of the *like* type has an exact semantic equivalent of the *please* type; but it is a general feature of mental processes that they can be realized in either direction — either the senser, or the phenomenon that is being sensed, can be the Subject, still keeping the clause in the active voice. There are some verbs that do pair off fairly closely in meaning; cf. Table 5(3).

Table 5(3) Paired verbs of *like* type and *please* type

like type	please type	like type	please type
I like it	it pleases me	I forget it	it escapes me
I fear it	it frightens me	I notice it	it strikes me
I wonder at it	it amazes me	I believe it	it convinces me
I don't understand it	it puzzles me	I admire it	it impresses me
I enjoy it	it delights me	I mind it	it upsets me

On the other hand it is hard to find close parallels to *I suspect it*, *I guess it*, *I welcome it*; or to *it worries me*, *it shocks me*, *it thrills me*. These seem rather to stand on their own.

We saw in Chapter 3 and 4 that English shows a strong tendency to conflate Theme with Subject; and also a preference for Subjects that are personal pronouns. This explains one of the salient features of mental processes, that clauses of the *please* type are particularly frequent in the passive; for example

I'm worried (by the fact) that you look so tired
We were thrilled by the sound of your voice
I wasn't impressed by what I saw

There is no parallel to this bidirectionality in material process clauses. It is hard to find any convincing pairs of this kind. A possible example might be *take the train*, *the train conveys me*; but this does not seem to be an instance of any general pattern. Note that word pairs like *buy / sell*, *give / receive*, *borrow / lend* are not of this kind; they do not yield pairs of related clauses such as *I buy it / it sells me*, or *I borrow it / it lends me*.

(5) We also referred above to the fact that material processes are 'doing' processes, which can be probed, and substituted, by the verb *do*; for example

What did John do? — He ran away. What John did was run away.
What did Mary do with the gift? — She sold it.

Iental processes, on the other hand, are processes of feeling, thinking and eeing. They are not kinds of doing, and cannot be probed or substituted by 'o. We cannot say *What John did was know the answer*; or *What did Mary 'o with the gift? — She liked it.*

Taking all these five criteria into account, we can recognize a systematic istinction in English grammar between material processes and mental proesses. For the purposes of our structural analysis, the first two criteria are articularly significant because they affect the participant functions in the lause. It is clear that the participants in a mental process cannot be equated vith Actor and Goal in a material process. This is not simply a matter of findng more general labels to cover both sets of concepts. The categories themelves are quite different, and the sets of possible occupants do not match.

For the two participants in a mental process we shall use the terms SENSER nd PHENOMENON. The Senser is the conscious being that is feeling, thinking r seeing. The Phenomenon is that which is 'sensed' — felt, thought or seen.

Within the overall category of mental process, these three — feeling, hinking and seeing — then constitute the principal sub-types; we will label hem in more general terms as (1) PERCEPTION (seeing, hearing etc.), (2) FFECTION (liking, fearing etc.) and (3) COGNITION (thinking, knowing, nderstanding etc.). The grammatical basis of this subcategorization will ecome clear in Chapter 7, Section 7.5 below.

Figure 5-8 gives an example of a text with mental processes of various inds.

it	worries	me	how silent everything is
Phe-	Process: affect	Senser	-nomenon: fact

I	don't like	it
Senser	Process: affect	Phenomenon

You	needn't be scared
Senser	Process: affect

If there was anything out there	we	'd hear	it coming
	Senser	Process: perception	Phenomenon: fact

I	know
Senser	Process: cognition

I	believe	you
Senser	Process: cognition	Phenomenon

But	the quiet	puzzles	me	all the same
	Phenomenon	Process: cognition	Senser	

Listen
Process: behavioural

Can	you	feel	that throbbing
Pro- per-	Senser	-cess: -ception	Phenomenon

It	hurts	my ears
Pheno- menon	Process: affect	Senser

igure 5-8 A text illustrating mental processes

One further distinction between mental and material processes comes up a this point; this has to do with the variation in the number of participants. A we saw, material processes fall into two types, those with one participan ('intransitive') and those with two ('transitive'). With mental processes there is no such distinction into two types; all mental processes potentially involve both a Senser and a Phenomenon.

This does not mean that both must always be present in the clause. (1 There can be a Senser and no Phenomenon, as in *Jill can't see*, *Tim knows*. I reality, there is presumably something that Jill can't see — the screen perhaps, or else she has lost her eyesight and can't see anything at all; an likewise there is something that Tim knows. But what it is is not mad explicit. Most common among those with the Phenomenon implicit ar passives of the *please* type, such as *she was pleased / delighted / worried puzzled / impressed*; these come closest to being simple attributes (see Sectio 5.4 below) without the implication that any particular phenomenon is th source of the worry or delight.

(2) There can be a Phenomenon and no Senser, as in

(i) Her roguish smile can well beguile
 Her every look bewitches

(ii) He only does it to annoy
 Because he knows it teases

where the implied Senser of *beguile*, *bewitch*, *annoy* and *tease* is simp 'people'.

5.4 Relational processes: processes of being

If material processes are those of doing and mental processes those sensing, the other main category, relational processes, are those of being; fo example, *Sarah is wise*, *Tom is the leader*. The central meaning of clauses this type is that something is.

But every language accommodates, in its grammar, a number of distin ways of being, expressed as different types of relational process in the claus Those of English may be summarized as follows:

(1) intensive	'*x* is *a*'
(2) circumstantial	'*x* is at *a*'
(3) possessive	'*x* has *a*'

Each of these comes in two modes:

(i) attributive	'*a* is an attribute of *x*'
(ii) identifying	'*a* is the identity of *x*'

This gives the six types of relational process that are set out in Table 5(4).

As the Table shows, those on the right, the 'identifying' type, have as a di tinguishing feature the fact that they are reversible (*Tom is the leader / t*

Table 5(4) The principal types of relational process

type: \ mode:	(i) attributive	(ii) identifying
(1) intensive	Sarah is wise	Tom is the leader; the leader is Tom
(2) circumstantial	the fair is on a Tuesday	tomorrow is the 10th; the 10th is tomorrow
(3) possessive	Peter has a piano	the piano is Peter's; Peter's is the piano

leader is Tom), whereas those on the left, the 'attributive', are not. Some further systematic distinctions exist which are not shown in the table, but which will be brought out in the discussion below. In what follows, we first give a general note about attributive and identifying clauses, and then discuss the three 'types' separately. For the related, but distinct, category of 'existential' clauses, such as *there was a storm*, see Section 5.5 below.

In the attributive mode, an attribute is ascribed to some entity; either as a quality (intensive), as a circumstance — of time, place etc. (circumstantial) or as a possession (possessive). Structurally, this defines the two elements ATTRIBUTE and CARRIER; examples in Figure 5-9.

attribute of:			
quality (intensive)	Sarah	is / seems	wise
circumstance (circumstantial)	the queen the fair	was lasts	in the parlour all day
possession (possessive)	the piano Peter	is / belongs has	Peter's / to Peter a piano
	Carrier	Process	Attribute

Figure 5-9 Attributive clauses

In the identifying mode, one entity is used to identify another; the relationship between them is one of token and value (intensive), of phenomenon and circumstance of time, place etc. (circumstantial), or of owner and possession (possessive). (It will appear below that the concepts of 'token and value' can be generalized among all three types.) The structural functions are IDENTIFIED and IDENTIFIER, as in Figure 5-10.

identification by:			
token-value (intensive)	Tom	is / plays	the leader
circumstance (circumstantial)	tomorrow the fair	is takes up	the tenth the whole day
possession (possessive)	the piano Peter	is owns	Peter's the piano
	Identified	Process	Identifier

Figure 5-10 Identifying clauses

There are various grammatical differences between the attributive and the identifying modes, though all of them are interrelated. The fundamental difference between the two is the fact that identifying clauses are reversible, whereas attributives are not. We cannot say, corresponding to the clauses in Figure 5-8, *wise is seemed by Sarah*, *all day is lasted by the fair*, *a piano is had by Peter*. We can say, on the other hand, corresponding to those in Figure 5-9, *the leader is played by Tom*, *the whole day is taken up by the fair*, *the piano is owned by Peter*. In other words, an identifying clause has passive. An attributive clause has no passive.

It is not difficult to see the explanation for this. In attributive clauses there is only one participant, since the Attribute is not a participant; whereas in identifying clauses there are two. It is a general principle of English grammar that any participant can become a Subject. So any clause in which there are two participants will have two 'voices', active and passive, each having a different participant as Subject. A clause with only one participant, on the other hand, will have only one voice. (See the note on voice in Section 5.8 below.) This principle is obscured when the verb is *be*, because the verb *be* has no special passive form; but the clauses *the leader is Tom*, *the tenth is tomorrow*, *Peter's is the piano*, are in fact all passive clauses.

We need now to consider some further, more specific features of attributive and identifying clauses. In order to do this it will be helpful to organize the discussion under the three types of intensive, circumstantial and possessive. The paragraphs that follow take these up in turn:

(1) intensive
- (i) attributive
- (ii) identifying

(2) circumstantial
- (i) attributive
  - (a) circumstance as attribute
  - (b) circumstance as process
- (ii) identifying
  - (a) circumstance as participant
  - (b) circumstance as process

(3) possessive
- (i) attributive
  - (a) possession as participant
  - (b) possession as process
    - (one) possessor as Carrier
    - (two) possessed as Carrier
- (ii) identifying
  - (a) possession as participant
  - (b) possession as process

(1) Intensive. In the intensive type, the relationship between the two terms is one of sameness; the one 'is' the other. The problem is to specify what exactly this means.

(i) Attributive. In the case of the attributive mode, in which some qualitative attribute is assigned to a 'carrier', the meaning is '*x* is a member of the class *a*'. So *Sarah is wise* means 'Sarah is a member of the class of wise ones'; *John is a poet* 'John is a member of the class of poets'.

Verbs of attribution include *be*; *become*, *get*, *turn*, *go*, *grow*; *start out*, *turn out*, *end up*, *keep*, *stay*, *remain*; *seem*, *appear*, *look*, *sound*, *smell*, *taste*, *feel*. The Attribute is realized as a nominal group, typically (though not obligatorily) one that is indefinite; it has as Head a noun or an adjective, but not a pronoun. Attributive clauses are probed by *what?* or *how?*, e.g. *what is John?*, *how is Sarah?*. It has been mentioned that these clauses are not reversible; there are no passives, such as *wise is seemed by Sarah*. Forms like *wise is Sarah*, *a poet is John* appear only as archaic or literary variants; they are not systematic alternatives.

Figure 5-11 gives some examples of intensive attributive clauses.

the cuckoo	is	a bonny bird
it	sounds	uncommon nonsense
the baby	turned into	a pig
the glass	has got	all soft like gauze
Carrier	Process	Attribute

Figure 5-11 Intensive attributive clauses

(ii) Identifying. In the identifying mode, the meaning is '*a* serves to define the identity of *x*'. Here *a* and *x* are two distinct entities, one that is to be identified, and another that identifies it. The relationship between them, therefore, is not one of class membership, since that would not serve to identify: we may say *Sarah is wise*, but this means that there are, or may be, other wise ones besides Sarah. If we say *Sarah is the wise one*, or *Sarah is the wisest*, this does identify her; she is the only member of the class. But since these clauses are not tautologous — we are not saying 'Sarah is Sarah' — there must be some other relationship between the two halves of the equation.

What kind of a relationship is it? In the most general terms, the Identifier fixes the identity of the target element in one of two ways: either by specifying its form, how it is recognized, or by specifying its function, how it is valued. The two elements that are being related are the same in each case, but they are being looked at from opposite directions.

For example, if we are looking at a photograph and ask *Which is Tom?*, the answer is something like *Tom is the tall one*. In this case, Tom is being identified by his form; we are told how he is to be recognized. But if we are discussing the children in the family, and someone says *Tom is the clever one*, Tom is being identified by his function — in this instance, his standing or role in the group. Thus the relationship between 'Tom' and 'the tall one' is the reverse of that between 'Tom' and 'the clever one': in the former, 'Tom' is the meaning and 'the tall one' is the outward sign, while in the latter 'the clever one' is the meaning and 'Tom' is the outward sign.

So when this variable is also taken into account it defines another pair of grammatical functions, which we shall refer to as TOKEN and VALUE. In any identifying clause, one element will be the Value (meaning, referent, function, status, role) and the other will be the Token (sign, name, form, holder, occupant). These functions are then conflated with those of Identified and

Identifier; and the conflation can go either way. Either the Token or the Value can serve as the identifying element (the Identifier), as shown in Figure 5-12.

(a) active (Token/Subject)	King Louis you X	was (acted as) are (represent) shall stand for	the King of France the fairest of them all playmates ten
	Identified / Token	Process	Identifier / Value
(b) passive (Value/Subject)	my name the hardest task Hamlet	is (is called) was (was constituted by) was played by	Alice crossing the river Mr Garrick
	Identified / Value	Processs	Identifier / Token
	Subject		

Figure 5-12 Identified – Identifier and Token – Value

We can now see what constitutes the 'voice' (active or passive) in a identifying clause. If we analyse these clauses simultaneously for mood, ther will always be one element to which we can assign the Subject function. Th question then is: is Subject conflated with Token, or with Value? It is this tha determines the voice. If the Subject is the same as the Token, then the claus is active, as in *King Louis was the king of France*, or *Mr Garrick playe Hamlet*. If the Subject is the same as the Value, then the clause is passive, as i *the king of France was King Louis*, or *Hamlet was played by Mr Garrick*. It i the functions of Token and Value (and not those of Identified and Identifier that govern the selection of voice in this type of clause.

Verbs of identification include *be*, *become*; *equal*, *add up to*; *play* (*the pa of*), *act as*; *call*, *mean*, *define*; *represent*, *spell*, *express*, *form*, *give*, *con stitute*, *imply*, *stand for*, *symbolize*, *realize*, *indicate*, *signify*, *betoken*. Th Identifier is realized as a nominal group, typically (though not obligatoril one that is definite; it has as Head a noun or a pronoun, but not an adjectiv Identifying clauses are probed by *which*? or *who?*, e.g. *who was King Louis which is the hardest task?*. We have already pointed out that these clauses ar reversible; beside *you are the fairest of them all* we can have *the fairest c them all is you*, the one being the 'passive' of the other. Because the verb *b* displays no voice, clauses such as *the leader is Tom* or *my name is Alice* do n show up as passive in the verb; but as clauses they are passive, and this do tend to show up given the choice of a different verb, for example *the leader played by Tom* or *my name is called Alice*. Hence there is a proportion

Mr Garrick played Hamlet	:	Hamlet was played by Mr Garrick
	: :	
Mr Garrick was Hamlet	:	Hamlet was Mr Garrick

just as clearly as if the last one had been *Hamlet was been by Mr Garrick* — verb form that is often heard in the speech of young children, e.g. (playir hospitals) *well then the doctor won't be been by anyone!*

Up to this point, we have assumed that whatever the voice the order identity elements in the clause is constant, with Identified always precedir

Identifier. But this is not necessarily so. This is the unmarked order; but they can appear the other way round. In Figure 5-13, the probe in (2) calls for an answer in which the Subject is the Identifier; so here the Identifier comes first.

(1)

which	am	I?
Identified /Value	Process	Identifier /Token
WH/Complement	Finite	Subject
Residue	Mood	

you	are	**the frog**
Identified /Token	Process	Identifier /Value
Subject	Finite	Complement
Mood		Residue

(2)

which	is	me?
Identified /Token	Process	Identifier /Value
WH/Subject	Finite	Complement
Mood		Residue

the ugly one	is	you
Identifier /Token	Process	Identified /Value
Subject	Finite	Complement
Mood		Residue

Figure 5-13 Variable position of Identifier in identifying clauses

Notice that there is a systematic distinction between *which am I?* ('which part do I play?') with *I* as Subject, and *which is me?* ('which one depicts me?') with *which* as Subject. In the second of these the form of the personal pronoun is *me* not *I* — naturally, since here *me* is Complement, and all Complements in English are in the oblique case. The one form that could not exist is *which is I?*, with its clash between case and function. Equally anomalous is the form *it is I*, which used to be beloved of English teachers but is quite in conflict with the grammatical principles involved ('bad grammar', if you like). The 'correct' forms (that is, those consistent with the rest of the grammar) can only be *I'm it* (no longer *it am I*, since non-WH Subjects now come first; and hence more usually *I'm that one*, because tonic prominence sits uneasily on *it*); and the form that is commonly used, namely *it's me*.

How then do we know which element is the Identifier? As a general rule, this is signalled by the intonation pattern: the Identifier is the element which carries the tonic accent (see Chapter 3, Section 3.7 above). In other words, the Identifier is the element that is 'new'. This is not, in fact, true in a hundred per cent of all instances; it would involve too much detail to explain the exceptions here, but the fact that there are exceptions means that we cannot simply use the term 'New' to replace 'Identifier' — the two are distinct concepts. For practical purposes, however, we can take it that the Identifier function is realized by tonic prominence — shown in Figure 5-12, and subsequent figures, by bold type.

If we replace the verb *be*, in all the examples in Figure 5-12, with another verb of the identifying class, such as *represent*, we can see that all these examples are active in voice:

(1) Which do I represent? — You represent **the frog.**
(2) Which represents me? — **The ugly one** represents you.

This reflects the fact that Subject = Token in each case. It would be improbable for the answer to (1) to be reversed, since the Identifier is already in its unmarked place at the end. But in (2) we should be quite likely to find the answer in the passive form:

you are (are represented by) **the ugly one**

as this puts the tonic accent in final position where it typically falls. It will be useful to refer to the location of the tonic accent by reference to what it means, as information focus, or simply focus. The tonic accent in final position (strictly, on the final lexical element) is the realization of unmarked focus. Allowing unmarked information focus ('getting the tonic accent in its right place at the end') is one of the principal functions of the passive voice in English (cf. Table 5(6) below).

Intensive identifying clauses are difficult, because one and the same form may represent any one of a number of possible configurations of functions. But if we take account of meaning, wording and sound all at a time it is possible to see how the functions are bundled together and which half of the clause is which. It is surprising how seldom misunderstanding occurs in real life — because there is always a context, and this tends to rule out all but the intended interpretation. However, misunderstanding can occur with clauses of this structure; and when it does it provides an excellent insight into their nature, especially into the difficult concepts of Token and Value. Here is an example taken from a conversation between two teachers:

A. So the best students are the greatest worriers, is that it?
B. Oh, I don't think there's any virtue in worrying, is there?
A. No, I didn't mean is it because they worry that they get to be the best. I meant is it because they're the best students that they worry.

Speaker A meant 'the best students worry most', i.e. because they're good they worry, as in Figure 5-14 (a). Speaker B misinterpreted as 'the greatest worriers study best', i.e. because they worry they're good, as in Figure 5-14 (b).

	the best students	are	the greatest worriers
(a)	Identified / Token	Process: intensive	Identifier / Value
(b)	Identified / Value	Process: intensive	Identifier / Token

Figure 5-14 Ambiguity in an identifying clause

To cite one final example: it happens not infrequently in reading that, coming to an intensive identifying clause, one unconsciously predicts, on the basis of the Identified element, which way the identification will go. An article on winter sports contained a clause beginning *but the most important piece of equipment is . . .* This led to an expectation that what followed would be Token, with *the most important piece of equipment* functioning as Value; e.g. . . . *is a safety helmet*. Actually the clause was

But the most important piece of equipment is the one you can least afford.

— where the structure is not Value ^ Token but Token ^ Value. This necessitated a rapid reorientation to a different semantic perspective.

(2) Circumstantial. In the circumstantial type, the relationship between the two terms is one of time, place, manner, cause, accompaniment, matter or role. These are the circumstantial elements in the English clause, and they are discussed in more detail in Section 5.7 below.

(i) Attributive. In the attributive mode, the circumstantial element is an attribute that is being ascribed to some entity; for example *my story is about a poor shepherd boy*. These take two forms: one in which the circumstance is expressed in the form of the Attribute, as here (*about a poor shepherd boy*); the other in which the circumstance is expressed in the form of the Process, e.g. *my story concerns a poor shepherd boy.*

(a) Circumstance as attribute. Here the Attribute is a prepositional phrase and the circumstantial relation is expressed by the preposition, e.g. *about*, *in*, *like*, *with* in *my story is about a poor shepherd boy*, *Pussy's in the well*, *my love is like a red red rose*, *Fred is with the doctor*. The verb may be another verb of the attributive class, e.g. *Penelope looks like her mother*, *the prince turned into a frog*.

Note that clauses such as *on the wall is/hangs a picture*, *through all his work runs a strong vein of cynicism*, are in origin not attributive but existential. The thematically unmarked form of these clauses is that beginning with existential *there*: *there is (hangs) a picture on the wall*. The prepositional phrase then appears initially as a marked Theme; in that case the existential feature may be left inexplicit, although the *there* may still be present and will appear in any case in the tag: *on the wall (there) is a picture, isn't there?*

(b) Circumstance as process. Here the Attribute is a nominal group and the circumstance is expressed by the verb, e.g. *concerns*, *lasted*, *weighs*, *cost* in *my story concerns a poor shepherd boy*, *the fair lasted all night*, *the fish weighs five pounds*, *your ticket cost fifty dollars*. The verb expresses a circumstantial relation such as 'be + matter', 'be + extent in time', 'be + measure of weight', 'be + measure of price'. Being attributive, these are non-reversible; there are no passive equivalents such as *a poor shepherd boy is concerned by my story*, *all night was lasted by the fair*, *five pounds is weighed by the fish*, *fifty dollars was cost by your ticket*.

In (b), therefore, the Process is circumstantial; whereas in (a) it is the Attribute that is circumstantial, the Process being the same as in the intensive type. Examples in Figure 5-15.

(a)

my story	is	about a poor shepherd boy
Carrier	Process: intensive	Attribute: circumstantial

(b)

my story	concerns	a poor shepherd boy
Carrier	Process: circumstantial	Attribute

Figure 5-15 Circumstantial attributive clauses

(ii) Identifying. In the identifying mode, the circumstance takes the form of a relationship between two entities; one entity is being related to another by a feature of time or place or manner, etc. As with the circumstantial attributive, this pattern may be organized semantically in either of two ways. The relationship is expressed either (a) as a feature of the participants, as in *tomorrow is the tenth*, or (b) as a feature of the process, as in *the fair takes up the whole day*.

(a) Circumstance as participant. In this type it is the participants — Identified and Identifier — that are circumstantial elements of time, place and so on. For example, in *tomorrow is the tenth*, *tomorrow* and *the tenth* are both time elements. Similarly in *the best way to get there is by train*, both *the best way* and *by train* express manner; in *the real reason is that you're scared*, Identified and Identifier are both expressions of cause. Like other identifying clauses, these are reversible: *the tenth is tomorrow*, *by train is the best way to get there*, (*the fact*) *that you're scared is the real reason*. The relation between the participants is simply one of sameness; these clauses are in that respect like intensives, the only difference being that here the two halves of the equation — the two 'participants' — are, so to speak, circumstantial elements in disguise.

(b) Circumstance as process. In this type it is not the participants that are the expression of time, place or other circumstantial features, but the Process. In examples such as *the fair takes up the whole day*, *applause followed her act*, *a bridge crosses/spans the river*, *Fred accompanied his wife*, *the daughter resembles the mother*, the verbs *take up*, *follow*, *cross* (or *span*), *accompany*, *resemble* are so to speak 'circumstantial verbs': they encode the circumstance of time, place, accompaniment, manner etc. as a relationship between the participants. Thus *take up* means 'be + for (extent in time)'; *follow* means 'be + after (location in time)'; *cross*, *span* means 'be + across (extent in place)'; *accompany* means 'be + with'; *resemble* means 'be + like'. This means that in terms of the concept of grammatical metaphor discussed below in Chapter 10 all clauses of this type are metaphorical.

Like those in the previous paragraph, these clauses are reversible in voice. In this case, however, not only are the participants reversed but also the verb appears in the passive: *the whole day is taken up by the fair*, *her act was followed by applause*, *the river is spanned by a bridge*, *Fred's wife was accompanied by him* (or more appropriately *Jane was accompanied by her husband*), *the mother is resembled by the daughter*. There is no difficulty in recognizing these as passive clauses.

The line between the attributive and identifying modes is less clear in the circumstantial than in the intensive type of relational clause. This is natural, since it is less obvious whether an expression such as *on the mat* designates a class (that has members — the class of things that are on the mat) or an identity (the thing that is identified by being on the mat). Nevertheless there is a distinction, which we can recognize if we set up typical examples side by side:

	attributive	identifying
(a)	the cat is on the mat	the best place is on the mat on the mat is the best place
(b)	the fair lasts all day	the fair takes up the whole day the whole day is taken up by the fair

(a) active

tomorrow on the mat	is is		the tenth the best place
Identified/ Token	Process: intensive		Identifier/ Value
Subject	Finite		Complement
Mood			Residue

(a) passive

the tenth the best place	is is	tomorrow on the mat
Identified/ Value	Process: intensive	Identifier/ Token
Subject	Finite	Complement
Mood		Residue

(b) active

the fair	occupies		the whole day
Identified/ Token	Process: circum-stantial		Identifier/ Value
Subject	Finite	Pred^r^	Complement
Mood		Residue	

(b) passive

the whole day	is	occupied	by the fair
Identified/ Value	Process: circum-stantial		Identifier/ Token
Subject	Finite	Pred^r^	Adjunct
Mood		Residue	

Figure 5-16 Circumstantial identifying clauses

In the identifying mode, we can also recognize Token and Value, with exactly the same implications as in the intensive. See Figure 5-16.

(3) Possessive. In the possessive type, the relationship between the two terms is one of ownership; one entity possesses another.

(i) In the attributive mode, the possessive relationship may again be expressed either as attribute, e.g. *Peter's* in *the piano is Peter's*, or as process, e.g. *has*, *belongs to* in *Peter has a piano*, *the piano belongs to Peter*.

(a) If the relationship of possession is encoded as the Attribute, then it takes the form of a possessive nominal group, e.g. *Peter's*; the thing possessed is the Carrier and the Possessor is the Attribute. These are not, in fact, distinct from identifying clauses; the clause *the piano is Peter's* could be either attributive 'the piano is a member of the class of Peter's possessions' or identifying 'the piano is identified as belonging to Peter'. (Note that the reversed form *Peter's is the piano* can only be identifying.)

(b) If the relationship of possession is encoded as the Process, then two further possibilities arise. Either (one) the possessor is the Carrier and the possessed is the Attribute (we will call the thing possessed the 'possessed' rather than the 'possession', to avoid ambiguity; 'possession' refers to the relationship), as in *Peter has a piano*. Here piano-ownership is an attribute being ascribed to Peter. Or (two) the possessed is the Carrier and the possessor is the Attribute, as in *the piano belongs to Peter*. Here Peter-ownership is an attribute being ascribed to the piano. Neither of the two, of course, is reversible; we do not say *a piano is had by Peter*, or *Peter is belonged to by the piano*. Examples in Figure 5-17.

(a)

the piano	is	Peter's
Carrier	Process: intensive	Attribute: possession

(b) (one)

Peter	has	a piano
Carrier: possessor	Process: possession	Attribute: possessed

(two)

the piano	belongs to	Peter
Carrier: possessed	Process: possession	Attribute: possessor

Figure 5-17 Possessive attributive clauses

(ii) In the identifying mode, the possession takes the form of a relationship between two entities; and again this may be organized in two ways, with the relationship being expressed either (a) as a feature of the participants, as in *the piano is Peter's*, or (b) as a feature of the process, as in *Peter owns the piano*.

(a) Possession as participants. Here the participants embody the notion of possession, one signifying property of the possessor, e.g. *Peter's*, the other signifying the thing possessed, e.g. *the piano*. Thus in *the piano is Peter's*, both *the piano* and *Peter's* express 'that which Peter possesses', the relationship between them being simply one of identity. Note that here *the piano* is Token and *Peter's* is Value.

(b) Possession as process. Here the possession is encoded as a process, typically realized by the verb *own* as in *Peter owns the piano*. (Notice we do not normally say *Peter has the piano*, in the sense of ownership; *have* is not used as an identifying verb of possession.) The participants are possessor *Peter* and possessed *the piano*; in this case *Peter* is Token and *the piano* is Value.

In addition to possession in the usual sense of 'owning', this category includes abstract relations of containment, involvement and the like. Among the verbs commonly occurring in this function are *include*, *involve*, *contain*, *comprise*, *provide*. Some verbs of this class combine the feature of possession with other semantic features; for example *exclude* '[negative] + have', *owe* 'have on behalf of another possessor', *deserve* 'ought to have', *lack* 'need to have'. (Most verbs meaning 'come to have', on the other hand, function as material processes; for example *get*, *receive*, *acquire* — compare the tense forms in *You deserve a medal. — I'm getting one.*)

As expected, types (a) and (b) are both reversible, the latter having the verb in the passive: (a) *Peter's is the piano*, (b) *the piano is owned by Peter*. Examples in Figure 5-18.

In principle possession can be thought of as another kind of circumstantial relation, which could be embodied in some such expression as 'at Peter is a piano', 'the piano is with Peter'. Many languages typically indicate possession by circumstantials of this kind. The nearest to this in English is the verb *belong*; compare the dialectal form *is along o'me*.

The full set of relational process clauses is set out in Table 5(5).

(a) (active)

the piano	is	**Peter's**
Identified/Token: possessed	Process: intensive	Identifier/Value: possessor

(passive)

Peter's	is	**the piano**
Identified/Value: possessor	Process: intensive	Identifier/Token: possessed

(b) (active)

Peter	owns	**the piano**
Identified/Token:	Process: possession	Identifier/Value

(passive)

the piano	is owned by	**Peter**
Identified/Value	Process: possession	Identifier/Token

Figure 5-18 Possessive identifying clauses

The display in Table 5(5) includes all the categories of relational process that have been introduced into the discussion. These include (i) the relation type, as set out above: intensive / circumstantial / possessive, and their subcategories; (ii) the relation-mode: attributive / identifying; (iii) within identifying, (a) the voice: active / passive; (b) the information focus, marked / unmarked. The picture is complex, but systematic; and all these distinctions are relevant when we are analysing relational processes in the interpretation of a text. There is a great deal of rather subtle multivalence (multiple meaning) in this portion of the language system; and ambiguity can arise in both speech and writing — ambiguity which may often be exploited with positive effect.* Moreover in many registers — various kinds of scientific writing,

* For example, Tennyson's lines (in *Choric Song from The Lotus-Eaters*)

Death is the end of life. — Ah, why
 Should life all labour be?

Why should life all labour be? is clearly an attributive clause. On the other hand, *death is the end of life* is identifying. But which is Token and which is Value? If the structure is as in (a), then the sense is 'once we die, life ends (that is what death means)'; if as in (b), then 'we die when life ends (that is how death may be recognized)'.

(a)

death	is	**the end of life**
Id/Tk		Ir/Vl

(b)

death	is	**the end of life**
Id/Vl		Ir/Tk

It seems likely that both these interpretations contribute to our understanding of the text. If we then give it a marked focus, as in (c) and (d), we get two further senses with the roles recombined:

(c)

death	is	the end of life
Ir/Tk		Id/Vl

(d)

death	is	the end of life
Ir/Vl		Id/Tk

Here (c) means 'life ends when we die (that is how we know life is ended)'; (d) means 'once life ends, we die (that is what it means for life to end)'.

for example — relational processes tend to be the most frequent and perhaps the most informative of the primary clause types.

As everywhere else in the book, we have taken the analysis only up to a certain degree of 'delicacy'; many further distinctions could have been recognized. For example, it is possible to vary the information focus in the attributive mode also; we can say

Sarah seems wise **Peter** has a piano

But this does not affect the grammatical functions involved: *Sarah* and *Peter* are still Carrier, *wise* and *a piano* are still Attribute; so here the discussion of the focus has been omitted. In the identifying mode, on the other hand, the structure is partly determined by the information focus, since the focus serves as the signal of the Identifier: given

John is **the tall one** **the tall one** is John

the tall one is Identifier in both instances. So here information focus has been taken into account. This, in turn, is not the whole story; but it is as far as we can reasonably expect to go.

The distinction between attribution and identification is not quite as clear-cut as we have made it seem. Like many semantic distinctions, this one is graded; and we can approach it from either end. Let us try to bring this out, and then add a final set of examples.

In attribution, some entity is being said to have an attribute. This means that it is being assigned to a class; and the two elements that enter into this relation, the attribute and the entity that 'carries' it, thus differ in generality (the one includes the other) but are at the same level of abstraction. So for example

my brother (Carrier = member) is **tall** (Attribute = class)

'my brother belongs to the class of people who are tall'. This specifies one of his attributes; but it does not serve to identify him — there are other tall people besides. The only means of identifying something by assigning it to a class is to make that a class of one member. But if the one-member class is at the same level of abstraction as its member, we have a tautology: *my brother is my brother*. For this to constitute a definition, the two must differ in abstraction; the one-member class becomes a value to which the member is assigned as token:

my brother	is	the tallest one in the **family**
Identified / Token		Identifier / Value

Instead of describing my brother, with *is* going with *looks*, *grows*, etc., we have now defined him; *is* means 'has the status of' and goes with *equals* (as in *x equals 2*) or *represents*. The consequence of this, however, is that the relationship can be turned around; instead of using the value to identify the token, we can use the token to identify the value. We can say

my brother	is	the tallest one in the **picture**
Identified / Value		Identifier / Token

Table 5(5) I Attributive (Carrier / Subject)

(1) INTENSIVE		Sarah John	is / seems became	wise a plumber
		Carrier	Process: intensive	Attribute
(2) CIRCUMSTANTIAL	(a) Circumstance as attribute	Pussy the daughter	is is / looks	in the well like the mother
		Carrier	Process: intensive	Attribute / Circumstance
	(b) Circumstance as process	the poem the fair	concerns lasts	a fish all day
		Carrier	Process: circumstantial	Attribute
(3) POSSESSIVE	(a) Possession as attribute	the piano	is	Peter's
		Carrier/ Possessed	Process: intensive	Attribute / Possession
	(b) Possession as process — (one) Possessor as Carrier	Peter	has	a piano
		Carrier/ Possessor	Process: possession	Attribute / Possessed
	(b) Possession as process — (two) Possessed as Carrier	the piano	belongs to	Peter
		Carrier/ Possessed	Process: possession	Attribute / Possessor
		↑ Subject		

The element that is of the lower order of abstraction now becomes the Identifier; and as a result, the verb becomes passive. Instead of *my brother represents the tallest one in the family*, we have *my brother is represented by the tallest one in the picture*. Of course, in a context like this we should be likely to use *be* in both; but we can illustrate with a pair of clauses such as

his best work Identified / Token	is (represents)	the high point of the **tradition** Identifier / Value
his best work Identified / Value	is (is represented by)	the last novel he **wrote** Identifier / Token

Note how these roles are mapped on to that of Subject: the Subject is always Token in the active, and Value in the passive.

Table 5(5) II Identifying A: Active (Token / Subject)

(1) INTENSIVE		(i) unmarked focus	Sarah Mr Garrick Identified / Token	is plays Process: intensive	**the wise one** **Hamlet** Identifier / Value
		(ii) marked focus	**Sarah** **Mr Garrick** Identifier / Token	is plays Process: intensive	the wise one Hamlet Identified / Value
(2) CIRCUMSTANTIAL	(a) Circumstance as participant	(i) unmarked focus	tomorrow by train Identified / Token / Circ	is is Process: intensive	**the tenth** **the best way** Identifier / Value / Circ
		(ii) marked focus	**tomorrow** **by train** Identifier / Token / Circ	is is Process: intensive	the tenth the best way Identified / Value / Circ
	(b) Circumstance as process	(i) unmarked focus	the daughter applause Identified / Token	resembles followed Process: circumstantial	**the mother** **her act** Identifier / Value
		(ii) marked focus	**the daughter** **applause** Identifier / Token	resembles followed Process: circumstantial	the mother her act Identified / Value
(3) POSSESSIVE	(a) Possession as participant	(i) unmarked focus	the piano Id / Token / Possession	is Process: intensive	**Peter's** Ir / Value / Possession
		(ii) marked focus	**the piano** Ir / Token / Possession	is Process: intensive	Peter's Id / Value / Possession
	(b) Possession as process	(i) unmarked focus	Peter Identified / Token	owns Process: possessive	**the piano** Identifier / Value
		(ii) marked focus	**Peter** Identifier / Token	owns Process: possessive	the piano Identified / Value
			↑ Subject		

Table 5(5) II Identifying B: Passive (Value / Subject)

(1) INTENSIVE	the wise one Hamlet	is is played by	**Sarah** **Mr Garrick**
	Identified / Value	Process: intensive	Identifier / Token
	the wise one **Hamlet**	is is played by	Sarah Mr Garrick
	Identifier / Value	Process: intensive	Identified / Token
(2) CIRCUMSTANTIAL (a) Circumstance as participant	the tenth the best way	is is	**tomorrow** **by train**
	Identified Value / Circ	Process: intensive	Identifier / Token / Circ
	the tenth **the best way**	is is	tomorrow by train
	Identifier / Value / Circ	Process: intensive	Identified / Token / Circ
(2) CIRCUMSTANTIAL (b) Circumstance as process	the mother her act	is resembled by was followed by	**the daughter** **applause**
	Identified / Value	Process: circumstantial	Identifier / Token
	the mother **her act**	is resembled by was followed by	the daughter applause
	Identifier / Value	Process circumstantial	Identified / Token
(3) POSSESSIVE (a) Possession as participant	Peter's	is	**the piano**
	Id / Value / Possession	Process: intensive	Ir / Token / Possession
	Peter's	is	the piano
	Ir / Value / Possession	Process: intensive	Id / Token / Possession
(3) POSSESSIVE (b) Possession as process	the piano	is owned by	**Peter**
	Identified / Value	Process: possessive	Identifier / Token
	the piano	is owned by	Peter
	Identifier / Value	Process: possessive	Identified / Token
	↑ Subject		

Thus there are significant grammatical and semantic distinctions between identification and attribution. But at the same time they are part of a single semantic field, so that first having separated them we can bring them together again. This, in fact, is precisely what we often do as speakers of the language: we set up as Value, for identifying purposes, something that is explicitly worded in the form of membership of a class, using the expression *one of the* . . ., for example *his sister is one of the cleverest people I know*; and on the other hand we tend to interpret an Attribute not just as membership of a list but rather as being in some sense the value of the entity that carries it. So the grammatical pattern of voice and Subject assignment represents a gradation within the total field of these relational processes, along the lines set out in Table 5(6). Note how the passive works out: it is rare when associated with marked focus but frequent when its use leads to a focus that is unmarked.

Table 5(6) Attribution and identification

attribution	active (only): Subject / Carrier	that spades a drake	is are is	(a) difficult (question) all-powerful male
Identification 1: Value / Identifier	active: Subject / Token	this spades a drake	is are is/means	**the question** **trumps** **a male duck**
	passive (rare): Subject / Value	**the question** **trumps** **a male duck**	is are is / is called	this spades a drake
Identification 2: Token / Identifier	active: Subject / Token	**this** **spades** **a drake**	is are is / means	the question trumps a male duck
	passive (frequent): Subject / Value	the question trumps a male duck	is are is / is called	**this** **spades** **a drake**

5.5 Other process types; summary of process types

In the last three sections we discussed the three principal types of process found in the English clause: material, mental, relational. In addition to these very large categories we need to recognize three other, subsidiary types: behavioural, verbal and existential. Each of these is close to one of the major groupings but distinct from it in certain respects.

1. Behavioural processes. These are processes of physiological and psychological behaviour, like breathing, dreaming, smiling, coughing. Grammatically they are intermediate between material and mental processes. The Behaver is typically a conscious being, like the Senser; but the Process functions more like one of 'doing'. The usual unmarked present tense for behavioural processes in contemporary English is the present in present; but until fairly recent times it was the simple present, and we still find this functioning in its unmarked sense, as in *Why do you laugh?* alongside *Why are you laughing?* The majority of behavioural process clauses have one participant only, like the examples in Figure 5-19.

Buff the Mock Turtle I	neither laughs nor smiles sighed weep	 deeply for you
Behaver	Process	(circumstance)

Figure 5-19 Behavioural processes

This category includes, towards the 'mental' end, processes of consciousness that are being represented as forms of behaviour, like *look*, *watch*, *listen*, *think* (in the sense of 'ponder'); for example *Don't look!*, *I'm thinking*, *No one's listening*. At the other end of the scale are activities which might be classed as behavioural on semantic grounds but which, apart from the fact that the participant is typically human, are grammatically indistinguishable from intransitive material processes; for example singing or skating. These can be analysed as material. They include some where the behaviour involves two human participants, like kissing. In *Mary kissed John*, *Mary* is Actor and *John* is Goal, and the clause can be probed in the normal way for transitive material processes: *What did Mary do to John?*

2. Verbal processes. These are processes of saying, as in *What did you say? — I said it's noisy in here*. But 'saying' has to be interpreted in a rather broad sense; it covers any kind of symbolic exchange of meaning, like *the notice tells you to keep quiet*, or *my watch says it's half past ten*. The grammatical function of *you*, *I*, *the notice*, *my watch* is that of Sayer.

What about the function of *it's noisy in here*, *to keep quiet*, *it's half past ten*? In formal grammar what is said is treated as 'noun clause object of the verb *say*', meaning a down-ranked or 'embedded' clause (see Chapter 6 below). But functionally the verbalized clause is not downranked; it functions as the secondary clause in a 'clause complex' (see Chapter 7 below), being either (a) directly quoted, as in (*he said*) *'I'm hungry'*, or (b) indirectly reported, as in (*he said*) *he was hungry*. This means that such sequences consist of two clauses, as in Figure 5-20.

(a)

John	said	'I'm hungry'
Sayer	Process	2: Quoted
1: Quoting		

(b)

John	said	he was hungry
Sayer	Process	β: Reported
α: Reporting		

Figure 5-20 Verbal processes

(Only the primary clause is a verbal process, of course; the other may be a process of any kind.) For the function of *what*, in *what did you say?*, see Section 5.6 below.

It follows from what was said above about saying that, unlike mental processes, verbal processes do not require a conscious participant. The Sayer can be anything that puts out a signal, like *the notice* or *my watch*; cf. *the light* in *the light says stop*, *the guidebook* in *the guidebook tells you where everything is*. Such entities could not figure naturally as Senser in a mental process: *my watch thinks it's half past ten* is decidedly incongruous. But *my watch says it's half past ten* calls for no comment at all; a Sayer can just as readily be *it* as *he* or *she*. For this reason verbal processes might more appropriately be called 'symbolic' processes.

The verbalized clause may be either (a) a proposition, as in *(he told me) it was Tuesday*, *(she asked me) whether it was Tuesday*, *'why are you late?' (he demanded)*; or (b) a proposal, as in *(she told him) to mend his ways*, *(he promised) to go home*. The proposal may be expressed alternatively by a modulated declarative clause (see Chapter 4 above, Section 4.5): *(she told him) that he should / must mend his ways*, *(he promised her) that he would go home*. For further discussion of these see Chapter 7, Section 7.5 below.

Two other participants function regularly in a verbal process. One is the Receiver, the one to whom the verbalization is addressed. The other is a name for the verbalization itself, e.g. *a pack of lies* in *he told me a pack of lies*. This we shall call the VERBIAGE. Both are referred to in Section 5.6 below.

There is however one other type of verbal process, in which the Sayer is in a sense acting verbally on another direct participant, with verbs such as *insult*, *praise*, *slander*, *abuse*, *flatter*. This other participant will be referred to as the Target, on the model of expressions such as *the target of his abuse*. Example in Figure 5-21.

I	'm always praising	you	to my friends
Sayer	Process: verbal	Target	Recipient

Figure 5-21 Target and Recipient in a verbal process

3. Existential processes. These represent that something exists or happens, as in *there was a little guinea-pig*, *there seems to be a problem*, *has there been a phone call?* The word *there* in such clauses has no representational function; it is required because of the need for a Subject (see Chaper 4, Section 4.6 above). Phonologically it is reduced, and thus distinct from Adjunct *there* occuring in thematic position: note the contrast between *there's your father on the line* and circumstantial *there's your father*, where the latter (but not the former) contrasts with *here's* . . . .

These clauses typically have the verb *be*, or some other verb expressing existence, such as *exist*, *arise*, followed by a nominal group functioning as Existent.

The Existent may be a phenomenon of any kind, and is often, in fact, an event, as in *there was a battle*, *there followed an angry debate*. Sometimes other verbs function as Process in an existential clause, e.g. *there came a big spider*, *all around there grew a thick hedge*.

Frequently the existential clause contains a circumstantial element, as in *there was a picture on the wall*. If the circumstantial element is thematic, the word *there* may be omitted, as in *on the wall (there) was a picture*. Frequently also the existential is followed by a non-finite clause, as in *there was an old woman tossed up in a basket*, *there's someone waiting at the door*, *there's a patient to see you*; the two together form a clause complex (see Chapter 7). Structures as in Figure 5-22.

there	was	a storm
	Process	Existent: event

on the wall	there	hangs	a picture
circumstance		Process	Existent: entity

there	's	a man	at the door
	Process	Existent: entity	circumstance

there	was	an old woman	tossed up	in a basket
	Process	Existent: entity	Process: material	circumstance
α: Extended			β: Extending	

Figure 5-22

4. Summary of process types. Table 5(7) gives a summary of the types of process we have identified in the grammar of English, together with their general category meaning and the participant functions that are associated with each.

Section 5.6 and 5.7 describe the remaining participant functions, and the circumstantial functions. The total set of functions used in interpreting the clause as representation, with criteria for recognizing the various types of process, is set out at the end of the chapter, in Table 5(15).

Table 5(7) Process types, their meanings, and key participants

Process type	Category meaning	Participants

material:
  action
  event
	'doing'
	  'doing'
	  'happening'
		Actor, Goal

behavioural	'behaving'	Behaver

mental:
  perception
  affection
  cognition
	'sensing'
	  'seeing'
	  'feeling'
	  'thinking'
		Senser, Phenomenon

verbal	'saying'	Sayer, Target

relational:
  attribution
  identification
	'being'
	  'attributing'
	  'identifying'
		Token, Value
		Carrier, Attribute
		Identified, Identifier

existential	'existing'	Existent

5.6 Other participant functions

The participant functions listed in Table 5(7) are those that are directly involved in the process: the one that does, behaves, senses, says, is or exists, together with the complementary function where there is one — the one that is done to, sensed etc. Grammatically these are the elements that typically relate directly to the verb, without a preposition as intermediary.

There are other participant functions in the English clause, also specific to each particular process type. However, it is possible to group these together into two general functions common to all clauses: the Beneficiary, and the Range. These are discussed in the present section.

Beneficiary and Range are the 'oblique' or 'indirect' participants, which in earlier stages of the language typically required an oblique case and/or a preposition. Also, unlike the direct participants, they could not conflate with the Subject function in the mood system.

In Modern English the distinction between direct and indirect participants has largely disappeared. All participants can take on the Subject function; there are no cases any more; and the presence or absence of a preposition is determined on other grounds (see Section 5.8 below). But semantically the Beneficiary and the Range are not so much inherent elements in the process; they are usually (though not always) optional extras.

In the 'logical' terminology referred to in Chapter 2, where Actor is 'logical subject' and Goal is 'logical direct object', the Beneficiary is 'logical indirect object' and the Range would be 'logical cognate object'.

1. Beneficiary. The Beneficiary is the one to whom or for whom the process is said to take place. It appears in material and verbal processes, and occasionally in relational.

(a) In a material process, the Beneficiary is either Recipient or Client. The Recipient is one that goods are given to; the Client is one that services are done for. Either may appear with or without a preposition, depending on its position in the clause (*gave John the parcel*, *gave the parcel to John*); the preposition is *to* with Recipient, *for* with client. To find out if a prepositional phrase with *to* or *for* is Beneficiary or not, see if it could occur naturally without the preposition. Thus in *she sent her best wishes to John*, *to John* is Beneficiary (*she sent John her best wishes*); in *she sent her luggage to Los Angeles*, *to Los Angeles* is not Beneficiary (we do not say *she sent Los Angeles her luggage*). Clients tend to be more restricted than Recipients; in *I'm doing all this for Mary*, *for Mary* is not a Client but a type of Cause (Behalf; see Section 5.7 below). An example of a Client would be *(for) his wife* in *Fred bought a present for his wife / bought his wife a present*.

Normally the Recipient occurs only in a clause which is 'effective' (has two direct participants; see Section 5.8 below). In a material process this means one which has a Goal; the Goal represents the 'goods', as in Figure 5-23.

I	gave	my love	a ring that has no end
Actor	Process: material	Beneficiary: Recipient	Goal

Figure 5-23 Benefactive clause showing Recipient

With a Client, the 'service' may likewise be expressed through a Goal, especially a Goal of the 'created' as distinct from the 'disposed' type, one that is brought into being by the process; e.g. *a picture*, *this house* in *he painted John a picture, built Mary this house*. But it is really the process that constitutes the service; hence a Client may also appear in a 'middle' clause — one that has no Goal, but has either Process + Range, as described in sub-section (2) below, e.g. *played Mary a tune*, or else Process only, as in *play for me*. These last cannot appear without *for* (*play me*); in order to show that they are Beneficiary it is necessary to add a Range element in final position (*play for me – play a tune for me – play me a tune*).

Most typically the Beneficiary is human; especially a personal pronoun, and most commonly of all a speech role (*me, you, us*), e.g. *me* in Mae West's famous line *Peel me a grape!* But this is not necessarily so; the Beneficiary is a plant in *did you give the philodendron some water?*, and an abstract entity *loyalty* in *loyalty is owed some recognition*. Nor, of course, is the 'benefit' necessarily beneficial: *Claudius* is Beneficiary in *Locusta gave Claudius a dose of poison*.

(b) In a verbal process, the Beneficiary is the one who is being addressed; e.g. *Mary* in *John said to Mary / told Mary (a story) / asked Mary (a question) / notified Mary of the decision / imparted the news to Mary*. We shall refer to this role as the Receiver. Here the preposition is *to*, and again the prepositional phrase is associated with final position in the clause.

The Receiver is usually present in verbal process clauses where the sense is that of a causative mental process, e.g. *convince* 'make believe', *tell* 'make know', *explain* 'make understand', *show* 'make see'. Examples in Table 5(8).

Table 5(8) Receiver in verbal processes

Sayer	Process	Receiver		Gloss
she	explained	(to John)	that. . .; wh-. . .	made understand
this/she	showed	(John)	that. . .; wh-. . .	made see
this/she	told	John	that. . .; wh-. . .	made know
this/she	proved	(to John)	that. . .	made accept
this/she	convinced persuaded	John	that. . .	made believe

It may also be present with the verbs *promise, vow, undertake*: *she promised John / vowed to John that she would stay at home / to stay at home*. (Note that this is not the role of *Fred* in *he told / ordered / persuaded / wanted Fred to do it*. See Chapter 7 Additional, Section 7.A.6 below.)

(c) There are also a few relational (attributive) processes containing a Beneficiary, e.g. *him* in *she made him a good wife, it cost him a pretty penny*. We shall just refer to this as Beneficiary, without introducing a more specific term, since these hardly constitute a recognizably distinct role in the clause.

The Beneficiary regularly functions as Subject in the clause; in that case the verb is in the passive voice. Example in Figure 5-24:

were	you	asked	a lot of questions
Process:	Receiver	verbal	
Finite	Subject	Predicator	Complement
Mood		Residue	

Figure 5-24 Beneficiary as Subject

(For the function of *a lot of questions* see below on Range.)

In an attributive clause this is possible only if the clause is 'effective' (see Section 5.8 below), in which case the active form contains an Attributor, as in Figure 5-25.

(a) middle

the call	cost	me	two dollars
Carrier	Process: circumstantial	Beneficiary	Attribute

(b) effective (i) Subject = Attributor

the hotel	charged	me	two dollars	for the call
Attributor	Process: circumstantial	Beneficiary	Attribute	Carrier

(b) effective (ii) Subject = Beneficiary

I	was charged	two dollars	for the call
Beneficiary	Process: circumstantial	Attribute	Carrier

Figure 5-25 Beneficiary in an effective attributive clause

2. Range. The Range is the element that specifies the range or scope of the process. Examples are *a song* in *sing a song of sixpence*, *croquet* in *do you play croquet with the Queen today?*, *an awful blunder* in *Big Bird's made an awful blunder*. This is the meaning behind the classical category of cognate object, so-called because in the instances first examined by grammarians it was in fact cognate to the verb, as *song* is to *sing*. Cognateness is not a necessary feature; most Range elements in English are not cognate to the verb even if they are as close in meaning as, for example, *game* and *play*. But they do stand in a particular semantic relationship to the Process, as suggested by the term Range: they define its co-ordinates, so to speak.

A Range may occur in material, behavioural, mental and verbal processes.

(a) In a material process, the Range either (i) expresses the domain over which the process takes place, or (ii) expresses the process itself, either in general or in specific terms. There is not, in fact, a sharp line between these two; they really lie along a single continuum.

(i) The Range may be an entity which exists independently of the process but which indicates the domain over which the process takes place. An example is *the mountain* in *Mary climbed the mountain*. Mountains exist whether anyone climbs them or not; but *the mountain* specifies the range of Mary's climbing. Note that this is not a 'doing' relationship; you cannot say *what Mary did to the mountain was climb it*. Similarly in *John played the piano*, where *the piano* is Range; pianos also exist, independently of the act of playing them. There is a difference between playing pianos and climbing mountains — pianos exist for the purpose of being played, and would not exist otherwise. But in both these cases the Range is the domain of the process rather than another name for the process itself. When we come to *the boys were playing football*, however, although there exists an object called a football, *football* is really the name of the game; it is doubtful whether this is referring to the ball as an entity. And this leads us in to those of the second type.

(ii) The Range may be not an entity at all but rather another name for the process. Consider *John and Mary were playing tennis*, where *tennis* is Range. Tennis is clearly not an entity; there is no such thing as tennis other than the act of playing it. Likewise with *sing a song*; if we look up *song* in the dictionary we are likely to find it defined as 'act of singing', just as *game* is 'act of playing'.

Why are these processes expressed as if they were a kind of participant in the clause? In other words, why do we say *sing songs*, *play games*, rather than simply *sing*, *play*? The answer is that this structure enables us to specify further the number or kind of processes that take place. The main types of 'process Range' are as follows:

general:	they played games
specific: quantity	they played five games
specific: class	they played tennis
specific: quality	they played a good game

All these can of course be combined, as in *they played five good games of tennis*.

This pattern has given rise to a form of expression that is very common in modern English, where the process is expressed only as a Range, the verb being lexically empty. These are expressions like *have a bath*, *do a dance*, *make a mistake*, *take a look*, *give a smile*. Many of these are behavioural processes, with the Range being the word for the behaviour.

There are various reasons in English grammar why this has become a favoured construction. The main reason for its prevalence is the greater potential that is open to nouns, in contrast to verbs, for being modified in different ways: it would be hard to replace the nouns by verbs in examples such as *have a hot bath*, *do a little dance*, *made three serious mistakes*, *take another quick look*, *gave her usual welcoming smile*. The resulting nominal groups can then function as Themes and also as participants in other clause types; for example *three serious mistakes is three too many*, *her usual welcoming smile was missing that day*.

It is useful to label the Range in a material process more specifically as either 'Range: entity' or 'Range: process'. Examples of Range are given in Figure 5-26.

the dormouse	crossed	the court
Actor	Process: material	Range: entity

she	dropped	me	a curtsey
Actor	Process: material	Beneficiary: Recipient	Range: process

Figure 5-26

The Range in a material process typically occurs in 'middle' clauses, those in which there is only one direct participant — hence in which there is Actor only, no Goal. As a result it is not always easy to distinguish a Range from a Goal. Semantically a Range element is not in any very obvious sense a participant in the process; but grammatically it is treated as if it was. So the Range can become Subject of the clause, as in *five games were played before tea*. However, there are some grammatical distinctions between a Range and a Goal.

As we have already noted, the Range cannot be probed by *do to* or *do with*, whereas the Goal can. Since nothing is being 'done to' it, a Range element can never have a resultative Attribute added within the clause, as a Goal can: we can say *they trampled the field flat* meaning 'with the result that it became flat', where *the field* is Goal, but not *they crossed the field flat*, where *the field* is Range, even though the flattening may have resulted from their continued crossing of it. The Range cannot be a personal pronoun, and it cannot normally be modified by a possessive. Moreover although it can become Subject, it is more restricted than the Goal in this respect; whereas generalized Range-passives such as *this mountain has never been climbed* are quite common, Range-passives with specific Actors are rare. Thus while a Goal readily becomes Subject in clauses such as *This teapot wasn't left here by your aunt, was it?*, it is unusual to make a Range element 'modally responsible' in this way: *This mountain wasn't climbed by your aunt, was it?*, where the validity of the proposition is being asserted with respect to the mountain, sounds decidedly odd.

Finally, a Range element (other than one with an 'empty' verb like *have* or *do*) can often be realized as a prepositional phrase, and under certain conditions it has to be: *she climbed steadily up the mountain*, *he plays beautifully on the piano*, *I'm playing Mary at tennis*. (See Section 5.8 below.)

(b) In a mental process the Range is not an additional element, but provides a way of interpreting an element we have already met, so as to explain the existence of two parallel types of structure, and also the differences between them.

As we saw, mental processes are distinguished by their bi-directionality: we have both *I like it* and *it pleases me*. Of the two, it is the *please* type that is the earlier form; and these do, in certain respects, resemble 'Actor + Goal' type constructions. Like material processes, they frequently occur in the passive; and they are not too far from the concept of doing something to someone: *What does it do to you? — It pleases me*.

We shall return to this point, which is part of a wider perspective, below in Section 5.8. Suffice it to say here that the other type of mental process, that with a verb of the *like* kind, which is of more recent appearance in English, while bearing no relation at all to an Actor and Goal structure, does show some resemblances to a pattern based on the concept of Range. In a clause such as *I like it*, the element that we have called the Phenomenon, here *it*, functions rather as a specification of the domain of my liking; and is subject to the same kind of restrictions in the passive as is a material process clause with Range — the passive *it is liked* occurs rarely, and usually only in a generalized sense. Hence we may interpret the Phenomenon, in a *like* type of mental process, as a kind of Range element. Such clauses then have only one direct participant, the conscious Senser; the Phenomenon — that which 'is seen, felt or thought' — functions more as a kind of delimitation of the boundaries of the sensing process.

(c) In a verbal process, the Range is the element expressing the class, quality or quantity of what is said: *ask a silly question* is like *play a silly game*. Note how this category also relates to what we identified as the Range in a mental process, through examples like *see a sight*, *hear a noise*, *see a view*. We refer to the Range in a verbal process as the Verbiage (noting that this is not in origin a derogatory term!).

Instances of Range in a verbal process are given in Table 5(9).

Table 5(9) Range in verbal processes

Verbal process clause	Range: Verbiage
What did you say?	what
He asked a question	a question
She speaks German	German
Tell me a story	a story
Don't talk nonsense!	nonsense
He made a long speech	a long speech

5.7 Circumstantial elements

The principal types of circumstantial element in English are as follows: Extent and Location in time and space, including abstract space; Manner (means, quality and comparison); Cause (reason, purpose and behalf); Accompaniment; Matter; Role.

(1) Extent and Location. The circumstantials of Extent and Location form a four-term set as shown in Table 5(10).

Table 5(10) Circumstantials of extent and location

	Spatial	Temporal
Extent	Distance walk (for) seven miles	Duration/frequency stay (for) two hours
Location	Place work in the kitchen	Time get up at six o'clock

There is no very sharp line separating (circumstantial) expressions of Extent from (participant) expressions of Range; but there is a distinction between them: Extent is expressed in terms of some unit of measurement, like yards, laps, rounds, years, whereas Range is expressed in terms other than measure units.

The interrogative forms for Extent are *how far?*, *how long?*, *how many* [measure units]? *how many times?* The typical structure is a nominal group with quantifier, either definite, e.g. *five days*, or indefinite, e.g. *many miles*, *a long way*; this occurs either with or without preposition, the most usual preposition being *for*. The general interrogatives of Location are *where?*, *when?*. The typical structure is an adverbial group or prepositional phrase;

examples are *underneath*, *by the door*, *in Canberra*, *long ago*, *before sunset*, *on Wednesday evening*.

There are close parallels between temporal and spatial expressions, the most significant ones being the following. (i) As already indicated, both incorporate the notions of extent and location: we recognize not only extent and location in space but also extent and location in time. (ii) In both time and space, extent is measurable in standard units: we have hours and years, and we have inches and miles, and acres, or their metric equivalents (which have not yet become domesticated in the English language). (iii) In both time and space, both extent and location may be either definite or indefinite; see Table 5(11). (iv) In both spatial and temporal location, the location may be either absolute, or relative to the 'here-&-now'; and, if relative, may be either near or remote; see Table 5(12). (v) In both spatial and temporal location there is a distinction between rest and motion; and, within motion, between motion towards and motion away from, as shown in Table 5(13).

Table 5(11) Definite and indefinite extent and location

		Spatial	Temporal
Extent	Definite	five miles	five years
	Indefinite	a long way	a long time
Location	Definite	at home	at noon
	Indefinite	near	soon

Table 5(12) Absolute and relative location

			Spatial	Temporal
Location	Absolute		in Australia	in 1985
	Relative	Near	here, nearby	now, recently
		Remote	there, a long way away	then, a long time ago

Table 5(13) Rest and motion

			Spatial	Temporal
Location	Rest		in Sydney, at the airport	on Tuesday,
	Motion	towards	to Sydney	till Tuesday
		away from	from Sydney	since Tuesday

However, this spatio-temporal parallelism is far from complete; and in recent centuries the language seems to have been moving away from it. Time is unidimensional; we see it as moving, and carrying the observer along with it in the current, whereas space is three-dimensional and static, with the observer moving freely within it. This is reflected in the fact that prepositions of motion are in general not the same for time as for space: *till Tuesday*, *since*

Tuesday suggest that Tuesday comes and goes, by contrast with *to Sydney*, *from Sydney*, with Sydney staying where it is. Moreover *before* and *after* are no longer identified, as they were at an earlier stage of the language, with *in front of* and *behind*; time is no longer equated with observer-centred horizontal space, or with any one spatial dimension. The category of temporal Extent includes not only duration but also frequency (*three times*, &c.), to which there is no spatial parallel. Finally, there is a well-developed concept of abstract space, as seen in expressions such as *condemned them to poverty*, *saved them from extinction*, *my own views would be somewhere in between*, which is not paralleled in the Time function; while on the other hand there is a close semantic connection between time as a circumstantial element and time as embodied in the tense system of the verb, to which there is nothing corresponding in the Place function.

(2) Manner. The circumstantial element of Manner comprises three subcategories: Means, Quality, Comparison.

(a) Means refers to the means whereby a process takes place; it is typically expressed by a prepositional phrase with the preposition *by* or *with*. The interrogative forms are *how?* and *what with?*.

In addition to generalized expressions of means such as *by train*, *by chance*, the category includes, in principle, the concepts of both agency and instrumentality. The instrument is not a distinct category in English grammar; it is simply a kind of means. So given *the pig was beaten with the stick*, the corresponding active form is *she beat the pig with the stick*; in both, *with the stick* is a circumstantial expression of Manner.

The agent, however, although it is expressed as a prepositional phrase, typically functions as a participant in the clause; given *the pig was beaten by the stick*, the corresponding active is *the stick beat the pig* (not *she beat the pig by the stick*), where *the stick* has the function of Actor.

The line between agent and instrument is not always very sharp. In a mental process clause we may have either *she was pleased by the gift* or *she was pleased with the gift*, without any real difference in function, and either one could remain as a Manner element in the active: *he pleased her with his gift*, *he pleased her by his gift*. Nevertheless there is a significant distinction in the grammar between manner and agency, such that a passive *by* phrase, if it could not remain unchanged in the corresponding active clause, is interpreted as a participant, not as a circumstance of Manner. This reflects the fact that semantically, whereas the instrument is not usually an inherent element in the process, the agent typically is — although less clearly so when the process is expressed in the passive. For more on the concept of agency, see Section 5.8 below.

(b) Quality is typically expressed by an adverbial group, with *-ly* adverb as Head; the interrogative is *how?* or *how . . .?* plus appropriate adverb. Quality expressions characterize the process in respect of any variable that makes sense; for example *heavily* in *it was snowing heavily*, *in a calmer tone* in *Humpty Dumpty said in a calmer tone*, *too much* in *it puzzled her too much*.

(c) Comparison is typically expressed by a prepositional phrase with *like* or *unlike*, or an adverbial group of similarity or difference; for example *like an earthquake* in *it went through my head like an earthquake*. The interrogative is *what . . . like?*

Some examples of Manner circumstantials are given in Table 5(14).

Table 5(14) Examples of Manner circumstantials

	WH-form	Examples
Means	how? what with?	(mend it) with fusewire
Quality	how?	(they sat there) in complete silence
Comparison	what like?	(he signs his name) differently

(3) Cause. The circumstantial element of Cause also comprises three sub-categories: Reason, Purpose, Behalf.

(a) A circumstantial expression of Reason represents the reason for which a process takes place — what causes it. It is typically expressed by a prepositional phrase with *through* or a complex preposition such as *because of*, *as a result of*, *thanks to*; for example *for want of* in *for want of a nail the shoe was lost*. There is also one class of expressions with *of*, one of the few places where *of* functions as a full preposition (i.e. representing a minor process) as distinct from being merely a structure marker; for example *die of starvation*. The corresponding WH- forms are *why?* or *how?*.

(b) Circumstantials of Purpose represent the purpose for which an action takes place — the intention behind it. They are typically expressed by a prepositional phrase with *for* or with a complex preposition such as *in the hope of*, *for the purpose of*; for example *for lunch* in *gone for lunch*, *for the sake of* in *for the sake of peace and quiet*. The interrogative corresponding is *what for?*.

The semantic relations of reason and purpose tend to be realized as separate clauses rather than as phrases within the clause; for example *I did it to get my own back* (cf. *for (the sake of) revenge*), *because he's ardent* in *I love my love with an A because he's ardent*, *to watch them* in *she went nearer to watch them*. These 'clause complex' structures are discussed further in Chapter 7.

(c) Expressions of Behalf represent the entity, typically a person, on whose behalf or for whose sake the action is undertaken — who it is for. They are expressed by a prepositional phrase with *for* or with a complex preposition such as *for the sake of*, *on behalf of*; for example *pray for me*, *I'm writing on behalf of Aunt Jane*, *he did it for the sake of our friendship*. The usual interrogative is *who for?*

This category includes in principle the concept of the Beneficiary, the person to whom something is given or for whom something is performed. But the Beneficiary is treated in the grammar as a kind of participant: it occurs without preposition, except when in a position of prominence, and can become Subject in the passive. Hence we have to distinguish between *she gave up her job for her children* ('for the sake of': Behalf), where we could not say *she gave her children up her job*, and *she built a new house for her children* ('for the use of': Beneficiary), where we could say *she built her children a new house*. Semantically, the former is something that is not inherently a service, whereas the latter is; here the process itself has a benefactive implication, in this case because it creates a usable product. Compare the distinction introduced above between Agent and Means; and see also the immediately following section, 5.8.

Some examples of Cause circumstantials are given in Table 5(15).

Table 5(15) Examples of Cause circumstantials

	WH- form	Examples
Reason	why? how?	(they left) because of the drought
Purpose	what for?	(it's all done) with a view to promotion
Behalf	who for?	(put in a word) on my behalf

(4) Accompaniment. This element represents the meanings 'and', 'or', 'not' as circumstantials; it corresponds to the interrogatives *and who / what else?*, *but not who / what?*. It is expressed by prepositional phrases with prepositions such as *with*, *without*, *besides*, *instead of*. We can distinguish who subcategories, comitative and additive; each has a positive and a negative aspect. They are set out in Table 5(16).

Table 5(16) Examples of Accompaniment circumstantials

	WH- form	Examples
comitative, positive: accompanied by	who / what with? and who / what else?	Fred came with Tom Jane set out with her umbrella
comitative, negative: not accompanied by	but not who / what?	Fred came without Tom I came without my key
additive, positive: in addition to	and who / what else?	Fred came as well as Tom
additive, negative: as alternative to	and not who / what?	Fred came instead of Tom

Accompaniment is a form of joint participation in the process.

(a) The comitative represents the process as a single instance of a process, although one in which two entities are involved. It ranges from some cases where the two entities could be conjoined as a single element, as in *Fred and Tom set out together*, to others where they could not, like *Jane and her umbrella set out together*. Sometimes the comitative element is actually an accompanying process, as in *the Dormouse woke up with a shriek* 'woke up and shrieked simultaneously'; see Chapter 10 for the general principle involved.

(b) The additive represents the process as two instances; here both entities clearly share the same participant function, but one of them is presented circumstantially for purposes of contrast. We could say *Fred and Tom both came*; but *Fred came as well as Tom* distinguishes the two as regards their news value ('not only Tom but also Fred came'). Similarly we could say *Fred came and Tom did not*; but *Fred came instead of Tom* makes it clear which it was that was unexpected ('not Tom but Fred came').

(5) Matter. This element corresponds to the interrogative *what about?* and is expressed by prepositional phrases with prepositions such as *about*, *concerning*, *with reference to* and sometimes simply *of*; for example, *I worry about her health*, *he kept quiet on the subject of compensation for their losses*. It is particularly frequent with verbal processes, as in *they're talking about the weather*.

One way of underlining a Theme is to express it as a circumstance of Matter; e.g. *as for John, he hasn't been seen since*. Here *John* is first presented as a circumstantial element *as for John*, which makes it thematically marked and therefore prominent. Compare Chapter 3, Section 3.1 above.

(6) Role. This element corresponds to the interrogative *what as?* and represents the meaning of 'be' (attribute or identity) in the form of a circumstance; for example *as a friend* in *I come here as a friend*. The usual preposition is *as*; other complex prepositions with this function are *by way of*, *in the role/shape/guise/form of*, e.g. *they leave the place untidy by way of protest*.

We are referring to a prepositional phrase as something that expresses a 'minor process', and interpreting a preposition as a kind of mini-verb. This needs to be explained.

Typically, the prepositional phrase functions as what we have called a circumstantial element in the clause. Apart from circumstances of quality, which are mostly expressed by adverbial groups, the usual realization of a circumstance is as a prepositional phrase. A prepositional phrase contains a nominal group; but while a nominal group represents something that is potentially a participant in the process, a nominal group following a preposition is related to the process only indirectly, with the preposition acting as intermediary.

The preposition expresses the particular nature of this indirect relationship by which the nominal group is linked to the rest of the clause. This relationship is not unlike a second, minor process which is incidental to the major one for which we have used the term 'Process' as label. The preposition itself has some of the qualities of a verb; in many instances it is possible to find a non-finite verb that is similar in meaning, and thus to express the relationship in the form of a dependent clause:

(he cleaned the floor) with a mop ~ using a mop
(I'm preparing this) as my prize-winning entry ~ to be my prize-winning entry
(the police arrested him) without evidence ~ not having evidence
(she came) for a cup of tea ~ wanting a cup of tea
(grass grows) after the rain ~ following the rain

This is just an extension of the principle we have already seen at work in relational processes, whereby the circumstance may be expressed either as attribution / identity or as process:

the delay was because of a strike ~ the delay was caused by a strike

Not all prepositions have verbal equivalents in this way; with most of those expressing spatial relations, such as *in*, *on*, *under*, the only related non-finite form would be *being in*, *being on* etc. But even here the structure formed by the preposition and the following nominal group is a structure of the clausal type: the nominal group stands to the preposition in some recognizable transitivity function. We will suggest an interpretation of this in Chapter 6, Section 6.5.

Meanwhile, we have already noted one type of exception to the general principle that prepositional phrases realize circumstantial elements: namely that under certain conditions a prepositional phrase may express a participant function, as in Table 5(17).

Table 5(17) Participant functions realized by prepositional phrases

(a) *by*:	the bridge was built by the army (material: Actor) the children were frightened by a ghost (mental: Phenomenon) the calm was followed by a storm (relational: Value)
(b) *to*:	I sent a letter to my love (material: Recipient) speak roughly to your little boy (verbal: Receiver) charge it to the firm (relational: Beneficiary)
for:	she baked a pie for the children (material: Client)
(c) *on*, *in* etc.:	he plays simultaneously on three instruments (material: Range) I addressed him in fluent Russian (verbal: Verbiage)

In general this happens when the participant in question occurs at the end of the clause; with, in the case of (b) and (c), some other element between the Process and it (see next section).

There is one other type of exception to be taken into account. In certain instances an expression consisting of verbal group plus prepositional phrase may include the preposition as part of the process; for example, *look at the sky* is interpretable as process *look at* plus participant *the sky*. There is no simple diagnostic criterion for deciding these instances; but one relevant factor is the possible choice of Theme. There are various thematic structures which give an indication of how the clause is organized as representation of the process. Consider for example the following sets of clauses:

(a) I was waiting on the shore
  (i) it was on the shore that I was waiting (*not* it was the shore that I was waiting on)
  (ii) on the shore I was waiting all day (*not* the shore I was waiting on all day)
  (iii) where I was waiting was on the shore (*not* what I was waiting on was the shore)

(b) I was waiting for the boat
  (i) it was the boat that I was waiting for (*not* it was for the boat that I was waiting)
  (ii) the boat I was waiting for all day (*not* for the boat I was waiting all day)
  (iii) what I was waiting for was the boat (*not* why I was waiting was for the boat)

These suggest that (a) consists of process *wait* plus circumstance *on the shore*, while (b) consists of process *wait for* plus participant *the boat*.

However, in modern English the distinction between participants and cir-

the Dodo	pointed	to Alice	with one finger
Actor	Process: material	Location: spatial	Manner: means

the whole party	at once	crowded	round her
Actor	Location: temporal	Process: material	Location: spatial

in despair	Alice	put	her hand	in her pocket
Manner: quality	Actor	Process: material	Goal	Location: spatial

Alice	handed	the comfits	round	as prizes
Actor	Process: material	Goal	Extent: spatial	Role

the two creatures	had been jumping about	like mad things	all this time
Actor	Process: material	Manner: comparison	Extent: temporal

we	can dance	without lobsters
Behaver	Process: behavioural	Accompaniment: comitative

Figure 5-27 Clauses with circumstantial elements

cumstances is becoming increasingly blurred, and many instances will satisfy both patterns. A reasonable guide is to see whether the thematic variants of pattern (a) seem natural — particularly (i) and (ii); there will not always be an appropriate WH- form corresponding to the *where* in (iii). If they do, then the prepositional phrase can be interpreted as a circumstantial element.

Some analyses are given in Figure 5-27.

5.8 Transitivity and voice: another interpretation

In this chapter we have distinguished the types of process represented by the English clause, and the various participant functions that are associated with each. The circumstantial elements we were able to treat independently, without distinguishing them according to process type; this is because, although there are numerous restrictions on the way particular circumstantials combine with other elements, these often go with rather small classes and in any case do not affect either the structure or the meaning. Each type of process, on the other hand, is characterized by process-participant configurations where the functions are particular to that type.

For purposes of analysis we could leave it at that. But it is not the whole story; so we shall pursue the investigation one stage further, although only in a rather sketchy manner.

It is true that, from one point of view, all these types of process are different. Material, behavioural, mental, verbal, relational and existential processes each has a grammar of its own. At the same time, looked at from another point of view they are all alike. At another level of interpretation, they all have the same grammar: there is just one generalized representational structure common to every English clause.

The arguments for this interpretation are long and technical. But while, as we have seen, there is clear evidence in the grammar for distinguishing one process type from another, there is also clear evidence for saying that, in a more abstract sense, every process is structured in the same way, on the basis of just one variable. This variable relates to the source of the process: what it is that brought it about. The question at issue is: is the process brought about from within, or from outside?

This is not the same thing as the intransitive / transitive distinction. There, as we saw, the variable is one of extension. The Actor is engaged in a process; does the process extend beyond the Actor, to some other entity, or not? So *the lion chased the tourist* relates to *the lion ran*: 'the lion did some running; either the running stopped there (intransitive, *the lion ran*), or else it extended to another participant (transitive, *the lion chased the tourist*)'.

In the second interpretation, the question is again how many participants there are, one or two; but the relationship between the two possible answers is quite different. To understand it we have to restructure our thinking, rather in the way that we have to restructure our perception when looking at a figure that can be seen as either concave or convex.

Looked at from this point of view, the variable is not one of extension but one of causation. Some participant is engaged in a process; is the process brought about by that participant, or by some other entity? In this perspective, *the lion chased the tourist* relates not so much to *the lion ran* as to *the tourist ran*: 'the tourist did some running; either the running was instigated by the tourist himself (intransitive *the tourist ran*), or else by some external agency (transitive *the lion chased the tourist*)'. Note however that the terms 'transitive' and 'intransitive' are no longer appropriate here, since they imply the extension model. The pattern yielded by this second interpretation is known as the 'ergative' pattern. The clauses *the lion chased the tourist / the tourist ran* form an ERGATIVE / NON-ERGATIVE pair.

If we examine the lexicon of modern English, and look up large samples of verbs in a good dictionary, we find that many of them, including the majority of those which are in common use, carry the label 'both transitive and intransitive'. If we investigate these further, we find that where the same verb occurs with each of these two values the pairs of clauses that are formed in this way, with the given verb as Process, are not usually intransitive / transitive pairs but non-ergative / ergative ones. There are intransitive / transitive pairs, like *the tourist hunted / the tourist hunted the lion*, where *the tourist* is Actor in both. But the majority of verbs of high frequency in the language yield pairs of the other kind, like *the tourist woke / the lion woke the tourist*, where the relationship is an ergative one. If we express this structure in transitive terms, the tourist is Actor in the one and Goal in the other; yet it is the tourist that stopped sleeping, in both cases. Compare *the boat sailed / Mary sailed the boat*, *the cloth tore / the nail tore the cloth*, *Tom's eyes closed / Tom closed his eyes*, *the rice cooked / Pat cooked the rice*, *my resolve weakened / the news weakened my resolve*.

The coming of this pattern to predominance in the system of modern English is one of a number of related developments that have been taking place in the language over the past five hundred years or more, together amounting to a far-reaching and complex process of semantic change. These changes have tended, as a whole, to emphasize the textual function, in the organization of English discourse, by comparison with the experiential function; and, within the experiential function, to emphasize the cause-&-effect aspect of processes by comparison with the 'deed-&-extension' one. There is no such thing, of course, as 'completed' change in language; waves of change are passing through the system all the time. But this aspect of English — its transitivity system — is particularly unstable in the contemporary language, having been put under great pressure by the need for the language continually to adapt itself to a rapidly changing environment, and by the increasing functional demands that have been made on it ever since Chaucer's time. Let us try and give a brief sketch of the clause in its experiential function as it now appears in the contemporary language, looking at it as a way of making generalizations about processes in the real world.

Every process has associated with it one participant that is the key figure in that process; this is the one through which the process is actualized, and without which there would be no process at all. Let us call this element the MEDIUM, since it is the entity through the medium of which the process comes into existence. In the examples above, the Medium is *the boat*, *the cloth*, *his (Tom's) eyes*, *the rice*, *my resolve*. Hence in a material process the Medium is equivalent to Actor in an intransitive clause and Goal in a transitive clause. See Figure 5-28.

(a) transitive interpretation

the boat the cloth Tom's eyes the rice my resolve	sailed tore closed cooked weakened
Actor	Process

Mary the nail Tom Pat the news	sailed tore closed cooked weakened	the boat the cloth his eyes the rice my resolve
Actor	Process	Goal

(b) ergative interpretation

the boat the cloth Tom's eyes the rice my resolve	sailed tore closed cooked weakened
Medium	Process

Mary the nail Tom Pat the news	sailed tore closed cooked weakened	the boat the cloth his eyes the rice my resolve
Agent	Process	Medium

Figure 5-28 Transitive and ergative interpretations

Except in the special case of the mediopassive voice (see Figure 5-30 below), the Medium is obligatory in all processes; and it is the only element that is, other than the process itself. (For the sake of simplicity we represent meteorological processes such as *it's raining* as having no Medium; but it would be more accurate to say that here the Medium is conflated with the

Process.) The Medium is also the only element that is never introduced into the clause by means of a preposition (again with the same exception of mediopassives); it is treated as something that always participates directly in the process.

The Process and the Medium together form the nucleus of an English clause; and this nucleus then determines the range of options that are available to the rest of the clause. Thus the nucleus 'tear + cloth' represents a small semantic field which may be realized as a clause either alone or in combination with other participant or circumstantial functions. (The lexical spread of such a semantic field is very roughly that of a paragraph in *Roget's Thesaurus*.)

The most general of these further options, 'most general' because it turns up in all process types, is the ergative one whereby, in addition to the Medium, there may be another participant functioning as an external cause. This participant we will refer to as the AGENT. Either the process is represented as self-engendering, in which case there is no separate Agent; or it is represented as engendered from outside, in which case there is another participant functioning as Agent. Thus the clauses *the glass broke*, *the baby sat up*, *the boy ran* are all structured as Medium + Process. In the real world, there may well have been some external agency involved in the breaking of the glass; but in the semantics of English it is represented as having been self-caused. For that matter there may have been some external agency also in the baby's sitting up, and even in the boy's running (such as the lion referred to earlier). We may choose to put the Agent in, as in *the heat broke the glass*, *Jane sat the baby up*, *the lion chased the boy*; notice that if the passive is used, e.g. *the glass got broken*, it is always possible to ask who or what by. A large number of processes may be represented either way: either as involving Medium only, or as involving Medium plus Agent.

By using the ergative standpoint to complement the transitive one in our interpretation of English, we can match up the functions in the various process types. The table of equivalents is given as Table 5(18). In this table, the generalized ergative functions are listed first in a single column; then their equivalents in specific transitive terms are shown for each of the process types. For example, the ergative function Medium is equivalent:

in material process	to Actor (middle), Goal (effective)
in behavioural process	to Behaver
in mental process	to Senser
in verbal process	to Sayer
in attributive process	to Carrier
in identifying process	to Value
in existential process	to Existent

Thus the Medium is the nodal participant throughout: not the doer, or the causer, but the one that is critically involved, according to the particular nature of the process. The Agent is the external agency: in a material process it is the Actor, but only if there is a separate Goal; in a mental process it is the

Table 5(18) Table of transitivity functions, showing transitive and ergative equivalents (participant functions only)

	Typical preposition	Ergative function	Transitive function:						
			Material	Behavioural	Mental	Verbal	Attributive	Identifying	Existential
	PROCESS	1 Process							
PARTICIPANTS	–	2 Medium	Goal; Actor (mid.)	Behaver	Senser	Sayer	Carrier	Value	Existent
PARTICIPANTS	by	3 Agent	Actor (eff.)		Phenomenon (*'please'*)		Attributor	Token	
PARTICIPANTS	to, for	4 Beneficiary	Recipient; Client			Receiver	Beneficiary		
PARTICIPANTS	at, on &c.	5 Range	Range	Behaviour	Phenomenon (*'like'*)	Verbiage	Attribute		
CIRCUMSTANCES	for; over, across &c.	6 Extent	duration (temporal), distance (spatial)			how long? how far?			
CIRCUMSTANCES	at, in, on, from &c.	7 Location	time (temporal), place (spatial)			when? where?			
CIRCUMSTANCES	with, by, like	8 Manner	means, quality, comparison			how? what with? in what way? like what?			
CIRCUMSTANCES	through, for &c.	9 Cause	reason, purpose, behalf			why? what for? who for?			
CIRCUMSTANCES	with, besides &c.	10 Accompaniment	comitation, addition			who/what with? who/what else?			
CIRCUMSTANCES	about	11 Matter				what about?			
CIRCUMSTANCES	as	12 Role				what as?			

Phenomenon, provided the process is encoded in one direction, from phenomenon to consciousness (the *please* type) and not the other way round. There can also be an Agent in a relational process, which has not yet been referred to. In the attributive, this is a distinct function, the Attributor; e.g. *the heat* in *the heat turned the milk sour*. In the identifying, the function that is analogous to Agent is the Token, which is Subject in the active and *by*-Adjunct in the passive; e.g. *these four points* in *these four points define the critical area, the critical area is defined by these four points*. For a further discussion of the Agent, see the end of the present section below.

The other participant functions, Beneficiary and Range, we have already discussed in similar terms (Section 5.6 above). The Beneficiary is the one that stands to gain: Recipient or Client in a material process, Receiver in a verbal process and, occasionally, (called simply Beneficiary) in a relational. The Range is the scope or domain: in a material process, the scope, type, extent, quality or quantity of the process — or simply a restatement of the process itself in a nominal form; in a mental process, the Phenomenon, when encoded in the other direction, from consciousness to phenomenon (the *like* type); in a verbal process, the name of the verbalization. Thus for all the participant roles we have one functional concept that is specific to the process type, and another that is general to all processes; and the general concept derives naturally from an ergative interpretation of the grammar of the clause.

Probably all transitivity systems, in all languages, are some blend of these two semantic models of processes, the transitive and the ergative. The transitive is a linear interpretation; and since the only function that can be defined by extension in this way is that of the Goal, systems which are predominantly transitive in character tend to emphasize the distinction between participants (i.e. direct participants, Actor and Goal only) and circumstances (all other functions). But the ergative is a nuclear rather than a linear interpretation; and if this component is to the fore, there may be a whole cluster of participant-like functions in the clause: not only Agent but also Beneficiary and Range. These, seen from a transitive point of view, are circumstantial: Agent is a kind of Manner, Beneficiary a kind of Cause and Range a kind of Extent; and they can all be expressed as minor processes. But from an ergative point of view they are additional participants in the major process: the nucleus of 'Process + Medium' has an inner ring of additional participants as well as an outer ring of circumstances surrounding it.

Semantically, therefore, Agent, Beneficiary and Range have some features of participants and some of circumstances: they are mixed. And this is reflected in the fact that grammatically also they are mixed: they may enter in to the clause either directly as nominal groups (participant-like) or indirectly in prepositional phrases (circumstance-like).

But the choice of 'plus or minus preposition' with Agent, Beneficiary and Range is not just random variation; it serves a textual function. This is in fact another instance of the importance attached to the message structure in modern English. The principle is as follows. If a participant other than the Medium is in a place of prominence in the message, it tends to take a preposition; otherwise it does not. Prominence in the message means functioning either (i) as marked Theme (i.e. Theme but not Subject) or (ii) as 'late news' — that is, occurring after some other participant, or circumstance, that already follows the Process. In other words, prominence comes from occurring either earlier or later than expected in the clause; and it is this that is being reinforced by the presence of the preposition. The preposition has become a signal of special status in the message. Examples in Table 5(19).

Table 5(19) Association of prepositional phrase with textual prominence

	non-prominent	marked Theme	'late news'
Agent (her nephew)	her nephew sent her flowers	by her nephew she was sent flowers	she was sent flowers by her nephew
Beneficiary (his aunt)	he sent his aunt flowers	to his aunt he sent flowers	he sent flowers to his aunt
Range (the high jump)	John wins the high jump every time	at the high jump John wins every time	John wins every time at the high jump

The other elements in the clause are represented clearly as circumstances; they are adverbial groups or prepositional phrases. But even here there is some indeterminacy; in other words, just as those elements which are treated essentially as participants can sometimes occur with a preposition, so at least some elements which are treated essentially as circumstances can sometimes occur without one. With expressions of Extent and Location there is often no preposition, as in *they stayed two days, they left last Wednesday*. Furthermore as pointed out in Section 4.3 above, the Complement of the preposition can often emerge to function as a Subject, as in *the bed had not been slept in, she hasn't been heard from since, I always get talked to by strangers*, and an example overheard in a cinema queue *look at all these people we've been come in after by*. This pattern suggests that Complements of prepositions, despite being embedded in an element that has a circumstantial function, are still felt to be participating, even if at a distance, in the process expressed by the clause.

The same tendency away from a purely transitive type of semantic organization can be seen in the system of voice. In a transitive pattern the participants are obligatory Actor and optional Goal; if there is Actor only, the verb is intransitive and active in voice, while if both are present the verb is transitive and may be either active or passive. This is still the basis of the English system; but there is little trace of transitivity left in the verb, and voice is now more a feature of the clause.

The way the voice system works is as follows. A clause with no feature of 'agency' is neither active nor passive but MIDDLE. One with agency is non-middle, or EFFECTIVE, in voice. An effective clause is then either active or passive: active if Agent / Subject, passive if Medium / Subject. The basic system is shown in Figure 5-29.

Strictly speaking an effective clause has the feature 'agency' rather than the structural function Agent, because this may be left implicit, as in *the glass was broken*. The presence of an 'agency' feature is in fact the difference

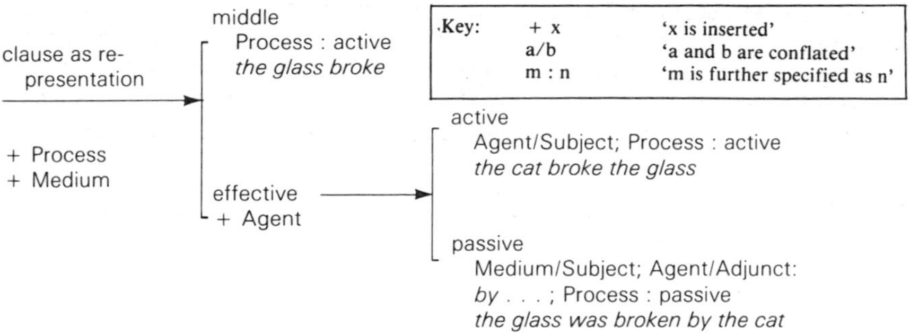

Figure 5-29 The system of voice

between a pair of clauses such as *the glass broke* and *the glass was* (or *got*) *broken* : the latter embodies the feature of agency, so that one can ask the question 'who by?', while the former allows for one participant only.

If the clause is effective, since either participant can then become Subject there is a choice between active and passive. The reasons for choosing passive are as follows: (1) to get the Medium as Subject, and therefore as unmarked Theme ('I'm telling you about the glass'); and (2) to make the Agent either (i) late news, by putting it last ('culprit: the cat'), or (ii) implicit, by leaving it out. In spoken English the great majority of passive clauses are, in fact,

(a) 'true' passive: effective; Medium / Subject, Agent: *by* . . .

(material) (mental)	the glass Mary	was was	broken upset	by the cat by the news
	Medium	Process		Agent
	Subject	Finite	Predicator	Adjunct
	Mood		Residue	

(b) Beneficiary – passive: effective; Beneficiary / Subject, Agent: *by* . . .

my aunt	was	given	this teapot	by the duke
Beneficiary	Process		Medium	Agent
Subject	Finite	Predicator	Complement	Adjunct
Mood		Residue		

(c) Range – passive: middle (i.e. medio-passive); Range / Subject; Medium: *by* . . .

(material) (mental)	songs the music	were was	sung enjoyed	by the choir by the audience
	Range	Process		Medium
	Subject	Finite	Predicator	Adjunct
	Mood		Residue	

Figure 5-30 Types of passive clause

Agent-less; *the glass was broken* is more common than *the glass was broken by the cat*. The speaker leaves the listener to locate the source.

But, as we have seen, there are other potential Subjects besides Agent and Medium. There are the other participants, the Beneficiary and the Range, either of which may be selected as Subject of the clause; the verb will then likewise be in the passive. Examples of these are given in Figure 5-30. Then there are the 'indirect' participants functioning as Complements to prepositions, some of which (as referred to above) are potential Subjects; these give various other kinds of passive such as 'Location-passive', e.g. *the bed hadn't been slept in*, 'Manner-passive', e.g. *this pen's never been written with*, and so on. Normally these are also medio-passives, i.e. they are middle not effective clauses. But passives with idiomatic phrasal verbs, such as *it's been done away with*, *she's very much looked up to*, *that prize has never been put in for*, are often 'true' passives in the sense that the prepositional phrase really represents a participant, as in the examples *look at the sky*, *wait for the boat* discussed above. Analysis in Figure 5-31.

(a) Manner-passive: middle (medio-passive); Manner / Subject; Medium: *by* . . .

the bed	hadn't	been slept	in	by anyone
Location	Process			Medium
Subject	Finite	Predicator	Adjunct	Adjunct
Mood		Residue		

(b) 'true' passive: effective; Medium / Subject; Agent: *by* . . .

it	's	been done	away	with	by the government
Medium	Process				Agent
Subject	Finite	Predicator	Adjunct	Adjunct	Adjunct
Mood		Residue			

Figure 5-31 Circumstantial passive

The introduction of the ergative interpretation of processes enables us to take one further and, in the present context, final step in the analysis of process types, one involving the feature of agency. It is often possible to add another component of agency over and above that which is embodied in the basic schemata of material, mental and relational processes.

With 'middle' clauses we find agnate pairs such as:

the bomb exploded	the police exploded the bomb	('made . . explode')
Mary believed that . .	the report convinced Mary that . .	('made . . believe')
the bananas were ripe	the sun ripened the bananas	('made . . ripe')

In transitive terms, *the bomb* remains Actor, *Mary* Senser and *the bananas* Carrier; so we have to assign other roles to the causative agent, say INITIATOR for *the police*, INDUCER for *the report* and ATTRIBUTOR for *the sun*. But in ergative terms all those in the central column are simply Agent plus Medium, since an Agent is interpreted as a causer anyway. Note that in the ergative analysis it makes no difference which structure is used; whether the clause is *the sun ripened the bananas* or *the sun made the bananas ripe, the sun* remains Agent and *the bananas* Medium, and likewise with the others. In the transitive analysis, such pairs are assigned different structural configurations; 'doing something to' the bananas is seen as different from 'making the bananas do something'.

It is also possible to have an additional feature of agency with 'effective' clauses, those which already have an Agent in them. Normally in such cases the clause has to be analytically causative in structure; for example,

(material)	the commander got the police to explode the bomb
(mental)	attention to detail made the report convince Mary
(relational)	we let the sun ripen the bananas

In each case there is a secondary Agent, and the structure is that of a discontinuous verbal group complex (see Chapter 7 Additional, Section 7.A.5 below).

Sometimes however there is a wording whereby the additional Agent can be incorporated into a simple clause; for example, in relational processes, *they made/voted Tom captain, she called the baby Ann.* Here again we would have to recognize a distinct transitive function, say that of ASSIGNER. The structure would then be as in Figure 5-32:

they she	voted called	Tom the baby	captain Ann
Assigner / $Agent_2$		Token / Agent	Value / Medium

Figure 5-32 Secondary Agent in an identifying process

These have their own passives, with secondary Agent as *by* Adjunct: *Tom was voted captain (by the club), the baby was called Ann (by her mother).*

There is another class of processes which can be interpreted in this way, as identifying processes with an additional agency feature. These involve facts, and things being turned into facts.

it is (the case) that . .	this proves that . .	('makes it the case that')
it is likely that . .	this indicates that . .	('makes it likely that')
it is certain that . .	this confirms that . .	('makes it certain that')
it seems that . .	this suggests that . .	('makes it seem that')

For a discussion of these 'caused modalities' see Chapter 7, Section 7.5.7 below. What concerns us here is the following sequence of agnate clauses, and their analysis in ergative terms (Figures 5-33, 5-34):

that	is	a fact
Token / Agent		Value / Medium

this	proves that	that	is	a fact
$Agent_2$		Token / Agent		Value / Medium

Figure 5-33 Secondary Agent with fact

that	is	a fact
Token / Agent		Value / Medium

this	proves	that	a fact
Assigner / $Agent_2$		Token / Agent	Value / Medium

this	proves	the fact
Assigner / Agent		Value / Medium

the fact	can be proved	by . .
Value / Medium		Assigner / Agent

Figure 5-34 Analysis of 'proving' – type clauses

— to which in turn we can further relate *this proves (the fact) that . .*, or simply *this proves that . .* or *this proves the fact*. Here *this* is Agent and *the fact* is Medium / Value; and these then have passives in the normal way: *that . . is proved (by . .), the fact is proved (by . .)*. Figure 5-34 shows the remaining steps in analysis:

Thus clauses of this type with *prove, show, indicate, imply, demonstrate, confirm, substantiate* (*this proves my point, the validity of his statements has not been confirmed, your comment implies a different view of things*) are identifying clauses with an additional feature of agency in them. The Value can, of course, be a fact; for example, *your comment implies that you take a different view of things*.

There is a similarity between these and some verbal processes where the same verbs may occur with personal or other Subject as Sayer; for example, *John implied / indicated / confirmed that he would help*, where John is saying something. Although in general the identifying clause of this type will have a non-personal or impersonal Subject (as Agent), the verbal process a personal Subject (as Sayer), neither of these is necessarily the case: *John proved his point* is clearly identifying, while *the timetable indicates that it's a direct flight* is verbal. In *John convinced / persuaded Mary that it was no use*, *John* is Agent / Inducer in a mental process; had this been a verbal process, with *Mary* as Receiver, it should have been possible to say *John persuaded this to Mary*, which seems unlikely. But this is an area where there is considerable overlap, and alternative interpretations are often equally justifiable.

Table 5(20) sets out the principal criteria for distinguishing the various types of process, taking account of the number and kind of participants, the voice systems, the pro-verb and the unmarked form of the present tense.* Figure 5-32 gives a small set of examples whose interpretation may not be immediately obvious, together with an analysis in both transitive and ergative terms.

---

* It also includes one other feature that was not mentioned, namely the accentuation of the verb. The verb in a relational process is typically unaccented, while that in a material process is typically accented; this explains the difference in rhythm between pairs such as the following:

// Herbert / Smith / stood for / parliament //
(material 'was a candidate for'; present *is standing for*)
// Herbert's / wife stood for / women/s / rights //
(relational 'represented'; present *stands for*)

Table 5(20) Criteria for distinguishing process types

	Material		Behavioural	Mental		Verbal	Relational:		Existential
							attributive	Identifying	
Category meaning:	doing doing, happening, doing to/with)		behaving	sensing (seeing, feeling, thinking)		saying	being (attribute)	being (identity)	being (existence)
Number of inherent participants:	1 or 2		1	2		1	1	2	1 or 0
Nature of first participant:	thing		conscious thing	conscious thing		thing	thing *or* fact	thing *or* fact	thing *or* fact
Nature of second participant:	thing			thing *or* fact				[same as 1st]	
Directionality	one way		one way	two way: *please* type *like* type		one way	one way	one way	one way
Voice:	middle *or* effective		middle	effective	middle	middle	middle	effective	middle
Type of passive:		passive		passive	medio-passive			passive	
Pro-verb:	do	do to/with	do	(do to)					
Unmarked present tense:	present in present		present in present	simple present		simple present	simple present	simple present	simple present
Accentuation of verb:	accented		accented	accented	(either)	(either)	unaccented	unaccented	unaccented

Transitivity: some text examples

lie on your back	material, middle; Manner: quality
the job takes an hour	relational: attributive, circumstantial (circumstance as Process)
it was only me	relational: identifying, intensive *it* Token, *me* Value
he's writing a book	material: effective, creative
I take your word for it	mental: cognition; *I* Senser/Medium, *your word* Phenomenon /Range
the bruises went away	material, middle
the roof blew off	material, middle; *roof* Actor/Medium
it feels soft to me	relational: attributive; *to me* modal Adjunct: comment
she felt like a prisoner	mental: affect; Manner: comparison
you were staring at me	behavioural; Place: motion to
relax your grip	behavioural; Range
measure it again	material; Frequency (Extent/Temporal)
I need your help	mental: affect; *your help* Phenomenon
the house needs some windows	relational: attributive, circumstantial (circumstance as Process)
I don't drink coffee	material; *coffee* Goal/Medium
the teapot got damaged	material, passive; *teapot* Goal/Medium
in the middle is a table	existential; Place as Theme
they asked him a lot of questions	verbal; *they* Sayer; *him* Receiver; *a lot of questions* Verbiage
answer her question	verbal; *her question* Receiver
answer the telephone	material; *the telephone* Goal
the trumpets were blown	material; *the trumpets* Range
that depends on you	relational: identifying, circumstantial (circ. as Process); Place
he lives across the road	material, middle; Place
we're getting late	relational: attributive, intensive
it's a thousand miles away	relational: attributive, intensive
I only get offered small parts	material, passive (i.e. effective, Beneficiary-passive), *I* Recipient
the instrument panel features a speedometer, . . .	relational: identifying, possessive (possession as Process); *panel* Value
silky oak is another beauty	relational: identifying, intensive; *silky oak* Token, *beauty* Value
is he qualifying as a lawyer?	material; *as a lawyer* Role
does he qualify as a lawyer?	relational: attributive, circumstantial (Role as Attribute)

our worst suspicions were confirmed	relational: identifying, intensive, agency; *suspicions* Medium/Value
one of the big ones is the DC 10	relational: identifying, intensive: Id/Vl ^ Ir/Tk
the law forbids invasion of privacy	verbal; *the law* Sayer, *invasion of privacy* Range
the elms overhung the buildings	relational: identifying, circumstantial (circ. as Process); Tk ^ Vl
I failed in both subjects	behavioural; Matter
their parents deserve a lot of credit	relational: identifying, possessive (possession as Process); Tk ^ Vl
you will develop your muscles	material; *your muscles* Goal/Medium
your muscles will develop	material; *your muscles* Actor/Medium
you will develop good breathing	material: creative; *good breathing* Goal/Medium
I'll see you back at the house	material; *I* Actor, *you* Goal; Place
the fault lay with the casings	relational: attributive, circumstantial (Matter as Attribute)
the search is continuing	material, middle; *search* Actor/Medium
this file got left behind by mistake	material, passive; *file* Goal/Medium; Manner: means
I feel rather ashamed of them	mental: affect; Attribute
he cut himself	material, effective; *he* Actor/Agent *himself* Goal/Medium
he hid himself	material, middle; *he . . . himself* Actor/Medium
don't blame me	verbal; *me* Target
we're surrounding the garden with a fence	material; *we* Actor/Agent, *the garden* Goal/Medium; Manner: means
it surrounds the place with an air of mystery	relational: attributive, circumstantial (circ. as Process); *it* Agent
they're visiting different colleges	material, middle: *colleges* Range

Note: many transitivity structures involve grammatical metaphor, as discussed in Chapter 10. It is always possible to analyse such clauses in non metaphorical terms, and this practice has been adopted with the examples above. At the same time, examples that are pointedly metaphorical have been largely avoided.

PART II Above, below and beyond the clause

6

Below the clause: groups and phrases

6.1 Groups and phrases

We have seen in Chapters 3–5 that the English clause is a composite affair, a combination of three different structures deriving from distinct functional components. These components (called 'metafunctions' in systemic theory) are the ideational (clause as representation), the interpersonal (clause as exchange) and the textual (clause as message). What this means is that the three structures serve to express three largely independent sets of semantic choice. (1) Transitivity structures express representational meaning: what the clause is about, which is typically some process, with associated participants and circumstances; (2) Mood structures express interactional meaning: what the clause is doing, as a verbal exchange between speaker/writer and audience; (3) Theme structures express the organization of the message: how the clause relates to the surrounding discourse, and to the context of situation in which it is being produced. These three sets of options together determine the structural shape of the clause.

The three functional components of meaning, ideational, interpersonal and textual, are realized throughout the grammar of a language. But whereas in the grammar of the clause each component contributes a more or less complete structure, so that a clause is made up of three distinct structures combined into one, when we look below the clause, and consider the grammar of the group, the pattern is somewhat different. Although we can still recognize the same three components, they are not represented in the form of separate whole structures, but rather as partial contributions to a single structural line. The difference between clause and group in this respect is only one of degree; but it is sufficient to enable us to analyse the structure of the group in one operation, rather that in three operations as we did with the clause.

At the same time, in interpreting group structure we have to split the ideational component into two: experiential, and logical. So far what we have been describing under the 'ideational' heading has been meaning as organization of experience; but there is also a logical aspect to it — language as the expression of certain very general logical relations — and it is this we have to introduce now. The logical component defines complex units, e.g. the CLAUSE COMPLEX discussed in the next chapter. It comes in at this point because a group is in some respects equivalent to a WORD COMPLEX — that is, a combination of words built up on the basis of a particular logical relation. This is why it is called a GROUP (= 'group of words'). It is also the reason why in the western grammatical tradition it was not recognized as a distinct structural unit: instead, simple sentences (that is, clauses, in our terms) were analysed directly into words. Such an analysis is still feasible provided we confine our attention to the sort of idealized isolated sentences that grammarians have usually dealt with, such as *Socrates runs* or *John threw the ball*; even there, however, the 'words-in-sentences' model ignores several important aspects of the meanings involved, and in the analysis of real-life discourse it leads to impossible complexity. Describing a sentence as a construction of words is rather like describing a house as a construction of bricks, without recognizing the walls and the rooms as intermediate structural units.

In this chapter we shall examine the structure of the three main classes of group: nominal group, verbal group and adverbial group; along with a brief reference to preposition and conjunction groups. The final section will be concerned with the prepositional phrase. A PHRASE is different from a group in that, whereas a group is an expansion of a word, a phrase is a contraction of a clause. Starting from opposite ends, the two achieve roughly the same status on the rank scale, as units that lie somewhere intermediate between the rank of a clause and that of a word.

6.2 Nominal group

Consider the following clause, spoken by my three-year-old son:

> Look at those two splendid old electric trains with pantographs!

Most of this clause consists of one long nominal group, *those two splendid old electric trains with pantographs*. This group contains the noun *trains* preceded and followed by various other items all of them in some way characterizing the trains in question. These occur in a certain sequence; and the sequence is largely fixed, although some variation is possible.

We can interpret the first part of this nominal group structurally as in Figure 6-1.

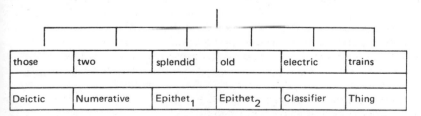

those	two	splendid	old	electric	trains
Deictic	Numerative	Epithet_1	Epithet_2	Classifier	Thing

Figure 6-1 Experiential structure of part of a nominal group

This is an experiential structure which, taken as a whole, has the function of specifying (i) a class of things, namely *trains*, and (ii) some category of membership within this class. We shall refer to the element expressing the class by the functional label Thing.

1. Experiential structure of the nominal group: from Deictic to Classifier

Membership within the class is typically expressed by one or more of the functional elements Deictic, Numerative, Epithet and Classifier. We will consider each of these in turn.

(1) *Deictic*. The Deictic element indicates whether or not some specific subset of the Thing is intended; and if so, which. It is either (i) specific or (ii) non-specific. For further discussion of these, see Chapter 9, Section 9.2 below.

(i) The specific Deictics are given in Table 6(1).

Table 6(1) Items functioning as specific Deictic

	Determinative	Interrogative
Demonstrative	this that these those the	which(ever) what(ever)
Possessive	my your our his her its their one's	whose(ver)
	[John's] [my father's] etc.	[which person's] etc.

The subset in question is specified by one of two possible DEICTIC features: either (i) demonstratively, i.e. by reference to some kind of PROXIMITY to the speaker (*this*, *these* = "near me"; *that*, *those* = "not near me"), or (ii) by possession, i.e. by reference to PERSON as defined from the standpoint of the speaker (*my*, *your*, *our*, *his*, *her*, *its*, *their* (see Figure 6-8 below); also *Mary's*, *my father's*, etc.) together with the possibility of an interrogative in both these categories (demonstrative *which?*, possessive *whose?*). All these have the function of identifying a particular subset of the 'thing' that is being referred to.

Many languages embody these two forms of deixis in the structure of the nominal group. The two are closely related, both being (as indicated by the term 'deixis') a form of orientation by reference to the speaker — or more accurately, to the 'speaker-now', the temporal–modal complex that constitutes the point of reference of the speech event. In some languages they are more systematically related to each other, the demonstrative having three terms instead of two: 'near me', 'near you' and 'not near either of us'. (Note that 'near' is not restricted to a local interpretation; the meaning is 'associated with' in some sense.) Some dialects of English have a system of this kind, the three terms being *this*, *that* and *yon*, with corresponding locative adverbs *here*, *there* and *yonder*.

There is one more item in this class, namely *the*. The word *the* is a specific, determinative Deictic of a peculiar kind: it means 'the subset in question is identifiable; but this will not tell you how to identify it — the information is somewhere around, where you can recover it'. So whereas *this train* means 'you know which train: — the one near me', and *my train* means 'you know which train: — the one I own', *the train* means simply 'you know which train'. Hence *the* is usually accompanied by some other element which supplies the information required: for example, *the long train* means 'you know which train: you can tell it by its length'. Compare *the night train*, *the train with a pantograph*, *the next train to arrive*. If there is no such information supplied, the subset in question will either be obvious from the situation, or else will have been referred to already in the discourse: for example, if you are on the platform you can say *get on the train!*, while *the train was coming nearer and nearer* might occur as a part of a narrative.

(ii) Non-specific Deictics are given in Table 6(2).

Table 6(2) Items functioning as non-specific Deictic

		singular		non-singular		unmarked
				plural	mass/ plural	
total	positive	each every		both	all	
	negative		neither (not either)			no (not any)
partial	selective	one	either			some [s ʌ m] any
	non-selective	a(n)			some [sm]	
		'one'	'two'		'not one'	(unrestricted)

These convey the sense of all, or none, or some unspecified subset; for example, *both trains have left*, *is there a train leaving soon?*, *there are some trains on the track*, *some trains are very comfortable*, *I haven't noticed any trains go by*.

It should be pointed out here that there are two different systems of NUMBER in the English nominal group, one associated with each of the two kinds of Deictics.

(i) With specific Deictics, the number system is 'non-plural/plural'; mass nouns are grouped together with singular, in a category of 'non-plural'. So *this*, *that* go with non-plural (singular or mass), *these*, *those* with plural, as in Table 6(3).

Table 6(3) Number in specific nominal groups

non-plural		plural
singular	mass	
this train	this electricity	these trains

(ii) With non-specific Deictics, the system is 'singular/non-singular'; mass nouns are grouped together with plural, in a category of 'non-singular'. So *a, an* goes with singular, weak *some* with non-singular (mass or plural), as in Table 6(4).

Table 6(4) Number in non-specific nominal groups

singular	non-singular	
	mass	plural
a train	(some) electricity	(some) trains

If there is no Deictic element, the nominal group is non-specific and, within that, non-singular.* In other words, a nominal group may have no Deictic element in its **structure**, but this does not mean it has no value in the Deictic **system** — simply that the value selected is realized by a form having no Deictic in the expression.

There may be a second Deictic element in the nominal group, one which adds further to the identification of the subset in question. We will refer to these as POST-DEICTIC, or DEICTIC_2.

The post-Deictic identifies a subset of the class of 'thing' by referring to its fame or familiarity, its status in the text, or its similarity/dissimilarity to some other designated subset. Among the words most frequently occurring as post-Deictic are:

> other, same, different, identical; complete, entire, whole; above, aforementioned; certain, customary, expected, famous, given, habitual, necessary, normal, notorious, obvious, odd, ordinary, original, particular, possible, probable, regular, respective, special, typical, usual, various, well-known

For example, *the same two trains*, *the well-known Mr John Smith*, *his usual silly self*, *a certain disquiet*.

Table 6(5) Items functioning as Numerative

	definite	indefinite
quantitative	one two three etc. [a couple of] etc. [a quarter of] etc.	few little [a bit of] etc. several [a number of] etc. many much [a lot of] etc. fewer less more [the same amount of] etc.
ordinative	first second third etc. next last	preceding subsequent etc.

* The forms *trains* and *some trains*, as in *there are (some) trains on the track*, are not in fact identical. But the distinction is a more delicate one, and for the purpose of this analysis they will be treated as variant expressions of the same category.

(2) *Numerative*. The Numerative element indicates some numerical feature of the subset: either quantity or order, either exact or inexact. The Numeratives are given in Table 6(5).

(a) The quantifying Numeratives (or 'quantitatives') specify either an exact number (cardinal numerals, e.g. *two trains*) or an inexact number (e.g. *many trains, lots of trains*).

(b) The ordering Numeratives (or 'ordinatives') specify either an exact place in order (ordinal numerals, e.g. *the second train*) or an inexact place (e.g. *a subsequent train*).

An inexact Numerative expression may be exact in the context; for example *just as many trains* ('as mentioned before'), *the next train* ('from now'). On the other hand, an exact Numerative expression may be made inexact by SUBMODIFICATION, as in *about ten trains, almost the last train*.

(3) *Epithet*. The Epithet indicates some quality of the subset, e.g. *old, long, blue, fast*. This may be an objective property of the thing itself; or it may be an expression of the speaker's subjective attitude towards it, e.g. *splendid, silly, fantastic*. There is no hard and fast line between these two; but the former are experiential in function, whereas the latter, expressing the speaker's attitude, represent an interpersonal element in the meaning of the nominal group. This distinction is reflected in the grammar in various ways.

The principal difference between the two is that experiential Epithets are potentially defining, whereas interpersonal ones are not. Take the example of *long* in *long train*. If I say *a long train*, you cannot tell which particular train I am talking about, because the Deictic *a* is non-specific; but if I say *the long train*, the specific Deictic *the* indicates that you can tell, and that the necessary information is contained in the experiential Epithet *long*. This particular train, in other words, is defined by its length, relative to some norm — perhaps some other train or trains that are present in the context. If I use an attitudinal Epithet, on the other hand, such as *mighty* in *along there came a mighty train*, this is not defining and it does not become defining even following the specific Deictic *the*. In *the mighty train came thundering down the track*, the word *mighty* does not identify this particular train by contrast with some unmighty ones.

Even in the superlative, which, with experiential Epithets, is almost always used to define (e.g. *ours was the longest train*), an attitudinal Epithet is still not defining. For example, *he said the silliest things* is normally equivalent to *he said some very silly things*. A word like *silliest* can be used to define, as in *the silliest things of all were said by the chairman*; but in that case it has an experiential function. Note that, in general, the same word may act as either experiential or interpersonal Epithet; most of the latter are adjectives of size, quality or age, e.g. *lovely, little, old*. Since expressions of attitude tend to be strung throughout the clause, rather than being associated with one particular place, there are very few words that serve only an attitudinal function.

Attitudinal Epithets tend to precede experiential ones. They may even precede Numeratives, giving them a post-Deictic flavour as in *those lovely two evenings in Bali*. They also tend to be reinforced by other words, or other features, all contributing to the same meaning: synonyms (e.g. *a horrible ugly great lump*), intensifiers, swear words, particular intonation contours, voice quality features and the like.

(4) *Classifier*. The Classifier indicates a particular subclass of the thing in question, e.g. *electric trains, passenger trains, wooden trains, toy trains*. Sometimes the same word may function either as Epithet or as Classifier, with a difference in meaning: e.g. *fast trains* may mean either 'trains that go fast' (*fast* = Epithet) or 'trains classified as expresses' (*fast* = Classifier). The line between Epithet and Classifier is not a very sharp one, but there are significant differences. Classifiers do not accept degrees of comparison or intensity — we cannot have *a more electric train* or *a very electric train*; and they tend to be organized in mutually exclusive and exhaustive sets — *a train* is either *electric, steam* or *diesel*. The range of semantic relations that may be embodied in a set of items functioning as Classifiers is very broad: it includes material, scale and scope, purpose and function, status and rank, origin, mode of operation — more or less any feature that may serve to classify a set of things into a system of smaller sets.

We have now identified the nominal group functions of Deictic, Numerative, Epithet, Classifier and Thing. The classes of word which most typically realize these functions are as follows:

Deictic	Deictic_2	Numerative	Epithet	Classifier	Thing
determiner	adjective	numeral	adjective	noun or adjective	noun

But there are other possibilities: for example, numeral occurring as Classifier, as in *first prize*, or embedded nominal group as possessive Deictic, e.g. *the day before yesterday's paper*.

These word classes — noun (= common noun), adjective, numeral and determiner — are all different kinds of NOUN; they are sub-classes of this one primary class. This larger class are sometimes referred to as 'nominals', to avoid confusion with 'noun' in its narrower, more specific sense. Other words also enter into the nominal group, namely words of the class VERB, which may function as Epithet or Classifier. Verbs function in the nominal group in one of two forms:

(i) present (active) participle, V-*ing*, e.g. *losing*, as in *a losing battle*;
(ii) past (passive, or intransitive active) participle, V-*en*, e.g. *lost*, as in *a lost cause*.

When functioning as Epithet, these forms usually have the sense of the finite tense to which they are most closely related: the present participle means 'which is (was/will be) . . . ing', the past participle means 'which has (had/will have) been . . . ed'. When functioning as Classifier, they typically have the sense of a simple present, active or passive: present (= active) 'which . . . s', past (= passive) 'which is . . . ed'.
Examples:
Verb as Epithet

(i) a galloping horse ('a horse which is galloping')
a bleeding nose ('a nose which is bleeding')

If however the verb is one which does not normally take the 'present in present' tense *be . . ing* (i.e. a verb expressing a mental or relational process), the distinction between 'which . . . s' and 'which is . . . ing' is neutralized; the next pair of examples are also Epithets:

the resulting confusion ('the confusion which results')
a knowing smile ('a smile which [suggests that the smiler] knows')

(ii) a wrecked car ('a car which has been wrecked')
a fallen idol ('an idol which has fallen')

Verb as Classifier

(i) a stopping train ('a train which stops')
a travelling salesman ('a salesman who travels')

(ii) a tied note ('a note which is tied')
spoken language ('language which is spoken')

It is natural that the more lasting attribute should tend to have a classifying function. But the present participle as Classifier does not exclude the sense of 'which is . . . ing', as in *the rising/setting sun*; and conversely, the past participle as Epithet does not always carry the meaning of 'which has been . . .', since many such forms are in fact adjectives, as in *a haunted house*, *a crowded train*. The same word may be now one, now the other: in *Would you like a boiled egg? boiled* is Classifier, 'which gets boiled', contrasting with *fried*, *poached* or *scrambled*; while in *You must drink only boiled water here*, *boiled* is Epithet 'which has been boiled'. In *He got stuck in a revolving door*, either interpretation is possible: Classifier 'of the kind which revolves', Epithet 'which was revolving' (cf. *fast trains* above). Note finally that the fact that a particular expression is a cliché does not imply that the modifying element is necessarily a Classifier — the 'permanence' is merely a feature of the wording! Thus in *a considered opinion*, *a heated argument*, *the promised land*, *a going concern*, the verbs are all Epithets: 'which has been considered', 'which has become heated' 'which has been promised', 'which is going [well]'.

Often the participle is itself further modified, as in *a fast-moving train*, *a hard-boiled egg*. The resulting compound may embody any one of a number of different experiential relations, e.g. *well-meaning*, *habit-forming*, *fund-raising*, *right-angled*, *fruit-flavoured*, *pear-shaped*, *architect-designed*, *simple-minded*, *bottle-nosed*, *iron-fisted*, *two-edged*.

2. Experiential structure of the nominal group: interpretation of ordering; the Qualifier

(1) *Ordering*. We can now follow the experiential pattern that is embodied in nominal group structure. Proceeding from left to right, we begin with the immediate context, the identification of the item in terms of the here-&-now, e.g. *those trains* 'the trains you can see over there'. Of course this identification is often in terms of the surrounding text rather than the situation, e.g. *those trains* 'the trains you've just been talking about'; but the point of reference is still the speech event. From there we go on to quantitative features: place in order, and number. These are less naturally definitive than this or

that, mine or yours, but more so than a merely qualitative attribute; and the ordinals, being the more definitive of the two, come first. An ordinal is a kind of superlative cardinal: *third* = 'three-est', i.e. identified by being at number three. Next come the qualitative features, again with superlatives preceding others: *the oldest trains* 'trains for which oldness is the identifying feature'. Often there is an intensifier, such as *very*, or an attitudinal element like *nice*, *terrible*, as a marker of the quality. Finally comes class membership; this reduces the size of the total set referred to in the noun by specifying a sub-set, e.g. *passenger train*, 'kind of train that is for carrying passengers'. We are talking here, it should be made clear, of the identifying **potential** of these elements. In any actual instance, the item in question may or may not be identifying; and this is the function of the word *the* at the beginning of the group — to signal that something that is capable of identifying is actually functioning in this way.

So there is a progression in the nominal group from the kind of element that has the greatest specifying potential to that which has the least; and this is a principle of ordering that we have already recognized in the clause. In the clause, the Theme comes first. We begin by establishing relevance: stating what it is that we are using to introduce this clause into the discourse, as 'this is what I'm on about' — typically, though by no means necessarily, something that is already 'given' in the context. In the nominal group, we begin with the Deictic: 'first I'll tell you which I mean', *your*, *these*, *any*, *a* etc. So the principle which puts the Theme first in the clause is the same as that which puts the Deictic first in the nominal group: start by relating to the speaker in the context of the speech event. From there we proceed to elements which have successively less identifying potential — which, by the same token, are increasingly permanent as attributes. By and large, the more permanent the attribute of a Thing, the less likely it is to identify it in a particular context. So we proceed with the very impermanent, quantitative characterization, which is nearest to a Deictic, e.g. *three* in *three balls*; through various qualitative features such as *new* in *new ball*; and end up with the most permanent, the assignment to a class, e.g. *tennis ball*. Within the qualitative characteristics, if more than one is specified there is again a tendency to move from the less permanent to the more permanent; e.g. *a new red ball* rather than *a red new ball*.

(2) *Qualifier*. What of the element which **follows** the Thing? The original example ended with the phrase *with pantographs*; this also is part of the nominal group, having a function we shall refer to as Qualifier.

Unlike the elements that precede the Thing, which are words (or sometimes word complexes, like *two hundred*, *very big*; see subsection 3 below), what follows the Thing is either a phrase or a clause. With only rare exceptions, all Qualifiers are EMBEDDED. What this means is that position following the Thing is reserved for those items which, in their own structure, are of a rank higher than or at least equivalent to that of the nominal group; on these grounds, therefore, they would not be expected to be constituents of a nominal group. Such constituents are said to be 'embedded', or, in earlier systemic terms, 'rankshifted'. Examples are

that has been entered   *in* the plea ⟦that has been entered⟧

being handed down	*in* the judgement ⟦being handed down⟧
before the court	*in* the matter [before the court]

Note that ⟦ ⟧ signifies an embedded clause, finite or non-finite; [ ] an embedded phrase (or group).*

Like the other, 'ranking' (i.e. non-embedded) elements of the nominal group, the Qualifier also has the function of characterizing the Thing; and again the Deictic *the* serves to signal that the characteristic in question is defining. But the characterization here is in terms of some process within which the Thing is, directly or indirectly, a participant. It may be a major process, i.e. a relative clause; or a minor process — a prepositional phrase (see Section 6.5 below). Analysis of these two is given in Figure 6-2.

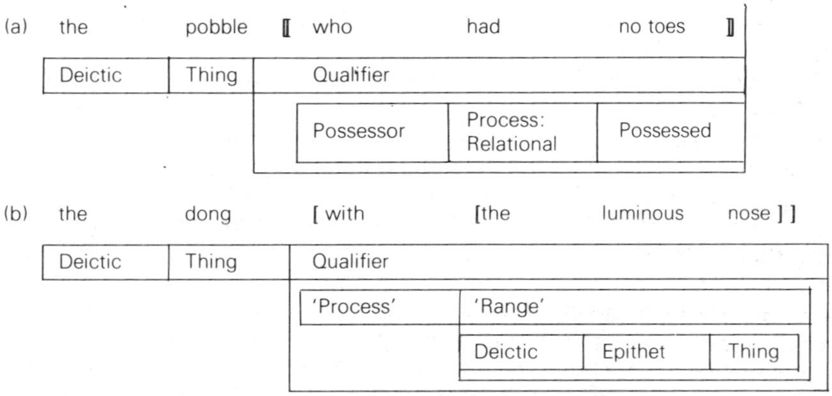

Figure 6-2 Nominal group with (a) clause and (b) phrase as Qualifier

A relative clause of this kind, as in (a) *who had no toes*, is referred to as a DEFINING RELATIVE CLAUSE. All defining relative clauses are embedded and function as Qualifier in either a nominal or an adverbial group. They contrast with NON-DEFINING RELATIVE CLAUSES, which do not function as Qualifier and are not embedded. The latter are discussed in Chapter 7, Section 7.4.1. below.

3. Experiential structure of the nominal group: the Thing

The element we are calling 'Thing' is the semantic core of the nominal group. It may be common noun, proper noun or (personal) pronoun.

The personal pronoun represents the world according to the speaker, in the context of a speech exchange. The basic distinction is into speech roles (*I*, *you*) and other roles (*he*, *she*, *it*, *they*); there is also the generalized personal pronoun (*one*). These categories are set out in Figure 6-3.

* It is important to distinguish between embedding, where the embedded item is a **constituent**, and hypotaxis, where the hypotactic item is **dependent** on another one but is not a constituent of it. This distinction is usually not made in formal grammars. See Chapter 7, Sections 7.4 and 7.5.

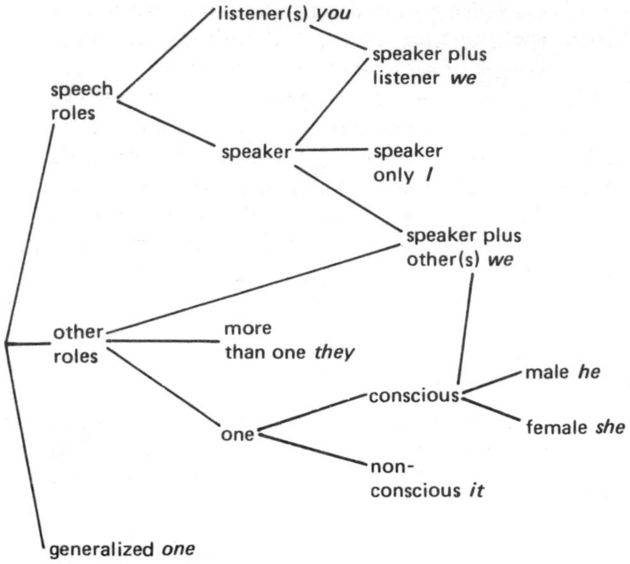

Figure 6-3 The English person categories

Proper names are names of particular persons, individually or as a group; institutions of all kinds; and places. They may consist of one word or many; those consisting of two or more words, such as *Polly Perkins*, *Ayers Rock* or *Cathay Pacific Airlines*, obviously have their own internal structure; but we shall treat all such instances simply as Thing, since it is beyond our scope here to go into the functional analysis of noun compounds.

Personal pronouns and proper names are alike in that, for both, the reference is typically unique. With pronouns, the referent is defined interpersonally, by the speech situation. With proper names it is defined experientially: there exists only one, at least in the relevant body of experience. In both cases, this means that typically there is no further specification; pronouns and proper names usually occur without any other elements of the nominal group. Sometimes they need further defining, like *you in the back row*, *Henry the Eighth* (this was how surnames started, as Qualifiers of personal names); and they may carry attitudinal Epithets, like *poor Tom* — cf. *pretty little Polly Perkins of Paddington Green*, which has both.

Common nouns, on the other hand, are precisely what their name implies, common to a class of referents; hence they are typically accompanied by a Deictic and often other elements as well. They name classes of persons, other living things, objects, collectives, and institutions; as well as, by grammatical metaphor, phenomena that would typically appear as adjectives (qualities) or as verbs (processes and relations). These metaphorical 'things' often occur without further specification, since their referents cannot be said to have members in the usual sense.

English recognizes a basic distinction of things into two semantic categories: (1) discrete, and therefore countable, realized as 'count nouns'; (2) continuous, and therefore uncountable, realized as 'mass nouns'. As pointed out above (subsection 1), mass nouns are grouped with singular count nouns if specific, e.g. *do you like this poetry/this poem*; and with plural count nouns if non-specific, e.g. *I've written some poetry/some poems*.

Typically what the distinction means is not that a mass noun is something that cannot be enumerated, but that if it is enumerated it is by kinds rather than by units; for example, *I've got a new polish here* 'a new kind of polish'.

Otherwise, if a 'mass' noun is to be itemized, it has to be measured out: *an acre of ground, a can of beer*. (The simple form *a beer* is then used with the presumption of a standard measure.) More will be said about these measure expressions below, after discussion of the logical structure of the nominal group.

4. A note on interpersonal and textual contributions

We noted at the beginning of the chapter that in analysing group structure it is not necessary to set up three distinct 'lines' corresponding to the experiential, interpersonal and textual metafunctions. A single structural representation will suffice.

We have been able to express this in experiential terms, because it is a general principle of linguistic structure that it is the experiential meaning that most clearly defines constituents. Interpersonal meanings tend to be scattered prosodically throughout the unit; while textual meanings tend to be realized by the order in which things occur, and especially by placing of boundaries. These are very general tendencies, worked out differently in every language but clearly discernible in all. In Part I we saw this pattern in the clause, and it will become clearer by the end of Part II. The textual meaning of the clause is expressed by what is put first (the Theme); by what is phonologically prominent (and tends to be put last — the New, signalled by information focus); and by conjunctions and relatives which if present must occur in initial position. Thus it forms a wave-like pattern of periodicity that is set up by peaks of prominence and boundary markers. The interpersonal meanings are expressed by the intonation contour; by the 'Mood' block, which may be repeated as a tag at the end; and by expressions of modality which may recur throughout the clause. The pattern here is prosodic, 'field'-like rather than wave-like. To complete the triad, first proposed by Pike, of 'language as particle, wave and field', the kind of meaning that is expressed in a particle-like manner is the experiential; it is this that gives us our sense of the building blocks of language. Since we are using particle theory (constituency) as the foundation of the present analysis — it tends to be conceptually and operationally simpler than models of wave or field — it is natural to represent the structure of the nominal group, in which the functional components are (in English) rather clearly defined, in straightforwardly experiential terms.

We shall say little more about the other components, beyond recognizing their presence in what has already been discussed. (1) Interpersonal meanings are embodied (a) in the person system, both as pronoun (person as Thing, e.g. *she, you*) and as possessive (person as Deictic, e.g. *her, your*); (b) in the attitudinal type of Epithet, e.g. *splendid* in our earlier example; (c) in the connotative meanings of lexical items functioning in the group, and (d) in prosodic features such as swear-words and voice quality. Textual meaning i embodied throughout the entire structure, since it determines the order ir which the elements are arranged, as well as patterns of information structur as in the clause (note for example that the unmarked focus in a nominal grou is on the word that comes last, not the word that functions as Thing: o *pantographs*, not on *trains*).

Figure 6-4 shows the structure of this example, as interpreted so far:

those	two	splendid	old	electric	trains	with pantographs	
Deictic	Numerative	Epithet		Classifier	Thing	Qualifier	
		Attitude	Quality				
						'Process'	'Range'
							Thing

Figure 6-4 Nominal group, showing multivariate structure

5. Logical structure of the nominal group

We now need to consider the structure of the nominal group from a differen and complementary, point of view; seeing it as a logical structure. This do not mean interpreting it in terms of formal logic; it means seeing how it repr sents the generalized logical–semantic relations that are encoded in natur language. These will be discussed in greater detail in Chapter 7; for the pu poses of the nominal group we need to take account of just one such relatio ship, that of subcategorization: '*a* is a subset of *x*'. This has usually bee referred to in the grammar of the nominal group as MODIFICATION, so we wi retain this more familiar term here.

Let us first consider the same example, but this time starting with the mo general term, *trains*. Moving to the left, we get: (which trains? —) *electr trains*; (which electric trains? —) *old electric trains*; (which old electr trains? —) *splendid old electric trains*; and so on. Calling *trains* the Head, w can represent this as in Figure 6-5, using the letters of the Greek alphabet

those	two	splendid	old	electric	trains
				Modifier	Head
←					
ζ	ϵ	δ	γ	β	α

Figure 6-5 Head and Modifier

The basis of the subcategorization of course shifts as we move to the lef 'what type of . . .?' 'what quality of . . .?', 'how many . . .?' and on — this is the principle underlying the experiential structure. Here ho ever we are not concerned with the differences but with the similarities: wi the general relationship that runs throughout the pre-Head modification the nominal group, whatever the experiential function of the individu elements. Figure 6-6 gives another example:

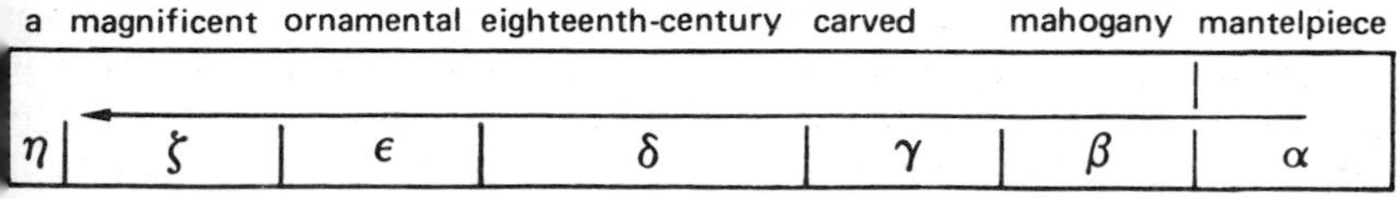

Figure 6-6 Modification: a further example

Within this logical structure there may be 'sub-modification': that is, internal bracketing as in *a rather more impressive figure* (Figure 6-7).

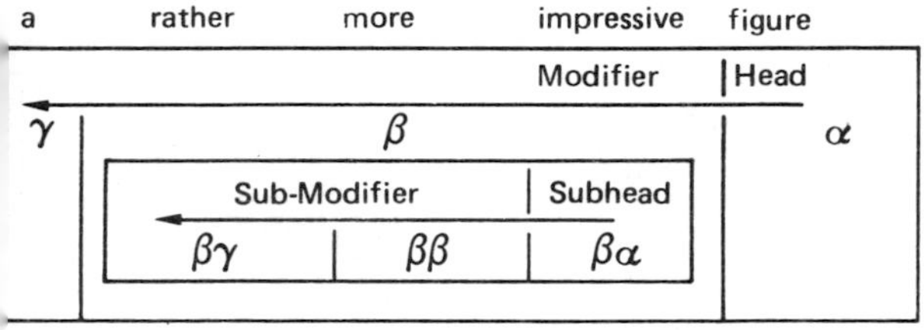

Figure 6-7 Submodification

Sub-modification may have the effect of disturbing the natural ordering of elements in the group; this accounts for additional items occurring before the Deictic, as in *almost the last buttercup*, *such a bright moon*, and also for displaced elements as in *not so very difficult a task*.

The same phenomenon of internal bracketing is also found in examples such as *apple green pyjamas*, *second-hand car salesman*, *full time appointment*, all of which are $\beta\beta$ ^ $\beta\alpha$ ^ α. Formally this is identical with submodification, although it is usually not referred to as such, the term being kept for grammatical rather than lexical expansion. As usual there are borderline cases, e.g. *dark/deep* or *light/pale* with colour words (is *deep red* more like *very red* or more like *blood red*?). But as long as the structural representation is clear it is really unnecessary to introduce a distinct term.

The element following the Head is also a modifying element; we can distinguish the two positions by using the terms Premodifier and Postmodifier. The distinction is not a functional one, but depends, as noted above, on the rank of the modifying item; compare *a weatherboard shack by the roadside* with *a roadside shack made out of weatherboard*.* Sometimes it is possible to assign a single overall order of modification to both pre-Head and post-Head items: in *old electric trains with pantographs*, for example, we might recognize a sequence δ ^ β ^ α ^ γ, since trains with pantographs are a subset of electric trains (but not of old electric trains). If the pantographs could go into the Premodifier, we would presumably have *those two splendid old pantographed electric trains*. We should beware, however, of assuming that the taxonomic order of modification always corresponds to something in the extra-linguistic universe; it may do, or it may not. The more valid test is the

* Note that these two are not synonymous. But they differ in information structure (textual meaning), not in their logical or experiential meaning.

second one, that of rewording with everything in the Premodifier and seeing what the likely order would be; but it is not always possible to do this in a natural, and therefore a reliable way. A simpler alternative, therefore, is to treat these as two distinct chains of modification, one Pre- and one Post-, each dependent on the Head but neither bracketed inside the other, as in Figure 6-8.

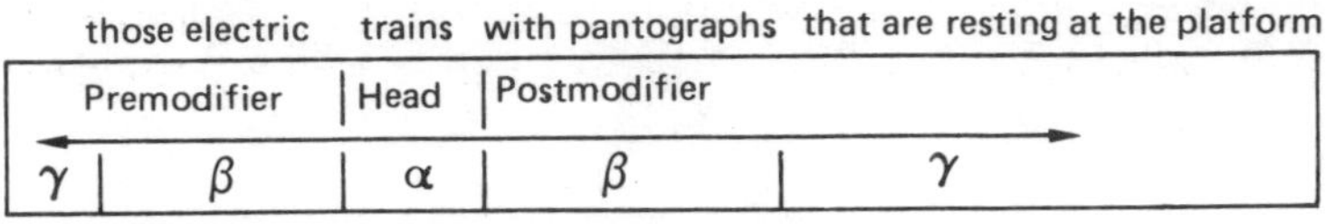

Figure 6-8 Premodifier and Postmodifier

This has to be distinguished, of course, from *those electric trains with pantographs that are resting on the wires*, where *that are resting on the wires* modifies *pantographs* not *trains* (Figure 6-9).

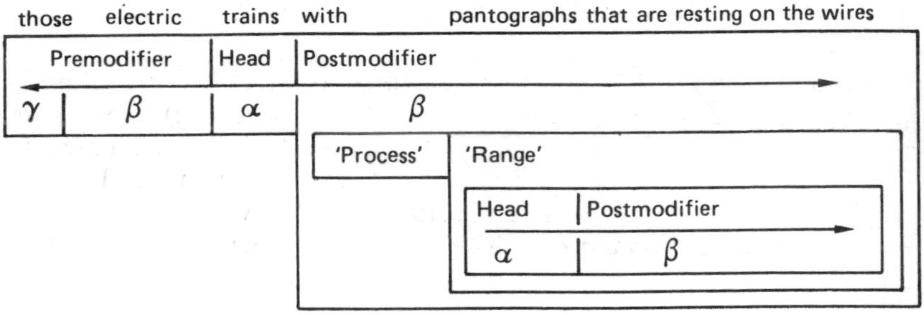

Figure 6-9 Further embedding within Postmodifier

What the logical analysis does is to bring out the recursive aspect of th modifying relation, showing the nominal group as a regressive bracketing This is the property that generates long strings of nouns such as are found i headlines and the names of parts of machines, e.g.

investment trust cash management account
jobs plan grant bid
weigh shaft lever balance weight
live steam injector feed water valve

(see Appendix 2). We refer to this as a UNIVARIATE structure, a structur generated by the recurrence of the same function: α is modified by β, which i modified by γ, which is . . . . The type of structure exemplified by Deictic + Numerative + Epithet + Classifier + Thing + Qualifier we call MULTIVARIATE structure: a constellation of elements each having a distinc function with respect to the whole. It is not that one is right and the othe wrong; but that in order to get an adequate account of the nominal group and a concept of what is meant by a 'group' as the grammatical resource fo epresenting *things*, we need to interpret it from both these points of view at nce.

. Head and Thing

Ve have assumed so far that the Head of the univariate structure is also lways the Thing, in the multivariate structure. But this is not so. There is lways a Head in the nominal group (unless it is 'branched', like *one brown* in *ne blue eye and one brown*); but there may be no Thing. It is quite normal to ave Numerative or Deictic as Head, as in Figure 6-10:

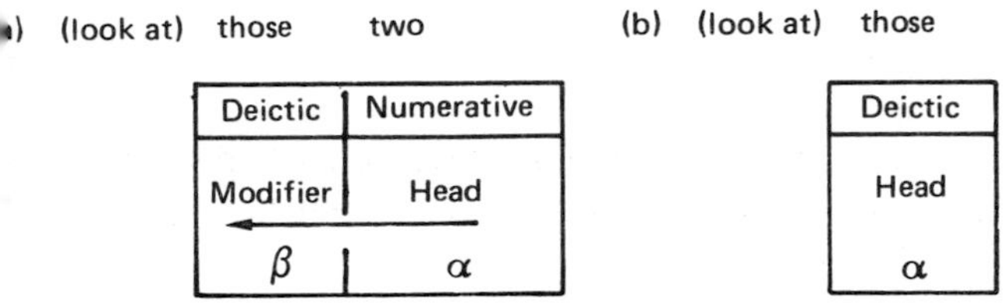

igure 6-10 Nominal groups with (a) Numerative, (b) Deictic as Head

pithets and Classifiers do not normally function as Head. The exception is he superlative, which in other ways also (e.g. place in sequence) resembles a Jumerative of the ordering kind rather than an Epithet: for example *(he vants) the smallest*. With other Epithets, and with Classifiers, if the Thing is ot made explicit it is realized as a substitute *one/ones*; for example *(he vants) a small one/a wooden one*. The substitute is then both Head and hing, as in Figure 6-11:

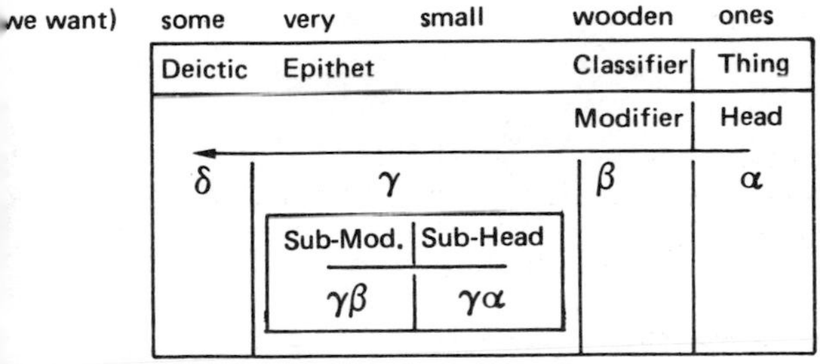

igure 6-11 Nominal group with substitute *one*

There is one very common type of nominal group where Head and Thing lo not coincide, namely those involving a measure of something. These measure' nominals include collectives, e.g. *a pack of cards*; partitives, e.g. *a lice of bread*; and quantitatives, e.g. *a yard of cloth*.

In the logical structure, the measure word (*pack*, *slice*, *yard*) is Head, with he *of* phrase as Postmodifier. The Thing, however, is not the measure word out the thing being measured: here *cards*, *bread*, *cloth*. The measure expresion functions as a complex Numerative, as in Figure 6-12:

a	pack	of	cards
Numerative			Thing
Modifier	Head	Postmodifier	
β	α	β	

Figure 6-12 Nominal group with measure expression

In the experiential structure, therefore, it is the Numerative that is embeddec and since it is embedded, it comes to the front and may be followed by a full structured nominal even beginning with a Deictic, as in *a cup of that goo strong tea*. This is the same pattern that we get with *three of those enormou spiders*, where the Numerative is made the Head of the logical structur Analysis in Figure 6-13:

	three		of	those	enormous	spiders
another	two	cups	of	that	good strong	tea
Pre-Numerative				Deictic	Epithet	Thing
Deictic	Numer-ative	Measure (Thing)				

Figure 6-13 Internal structure of the measure expression (or other embedded Numerative

It often happens that the Epithet is transferred to the Head, as in *a stro cup of tea*, although clearly it is the tea that is strong, not the cup. It is part the rather ambivalent nature of this structure, in which Head and Thing a separated, that causes this to happen; but it also arises because in ma instances the Epithet could apply equally well to either, as in *a cloud of thi smoke, a thick cloud of smoke*, which provides the model for *a strong cup tea*. (Classifiers, on the other hand, do not get transferred; we do not say *brown slice of bread*.) Sometimes the Epithet belongs more naturally with t Numerative, as in *a large cup of tea*; but even here one can never have Epithet that characterizes the item in question in any way other than in function as a Numerative — one cannot say *a blue cup of tea* to mean 'a cu of tea in a blue cup'. Finally, it is not unusual to have an Epithet in both po tions, as in *a thick layer of powdery snow*.

In some ways similar to the 'measure' type are nominal groups expressin 'facet' of a thing: *the back of the house, my side of the bed, the north face the Eiger*. The facet word (*back, side, face*) is the Head; it would be possib to interpret these also as Thing (i.e. Head = Thing), but they could be co sidered as embedded Deictics, with the faceted noun (*house, bed, Eiger*) Thing. The argument for separating Head and Thing is less clear here th with the measure Numeratives; but it is supported by the fact that fac expressions often function as complex prepositions, e.g. *in front of, by t side of*. This gives the analysis in Figure 6-14 (see also the section on prepo tional phrases, 6.5 below).

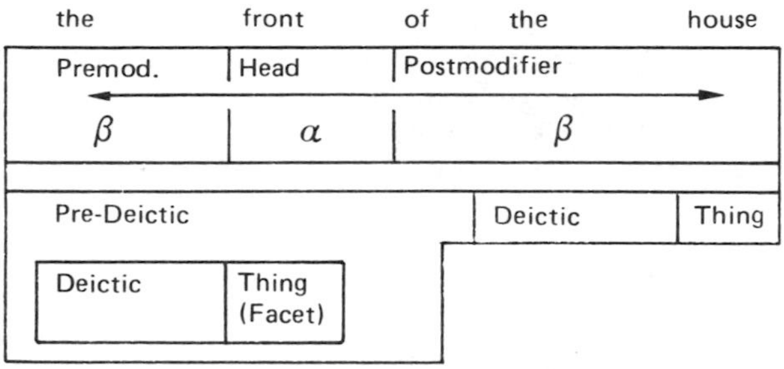

Figure 6-14 Nominal group with facet expression

6.3 Verbal group

The verbal group is the constituent that functions as Finite plus Predicator (or as Predicator alone if there is no Finite element) in the mood structure (clause as exchange); and as Process in the transitivity structure (clause as representation). In the clause

someone's been eating my porridge

the verbal group is *has been eating*.

A verbal group is the expansion of a verb, in the same way that a nominal group is the expansion of a noun; and it consists of a sequence of words of the primary class of verb. If we consider *has been eating* just as a word sequence, it contains a 'lexical verb' *eat*, which comes last; a finite verb *has*, which comes first; and an auxiliary verb *been* which comes in between. No other ordering of these three components is possible.

As with the nominal group, we can express this both as an experiential and as a logical structure, although the relation between the two will turn out to be rather different. Because there is very much less lexical material in the verbal group — only one lexical item, in fact — the experiential structure is extremely simple; and most of the semantic load is carried by the logical structure, including the tense system.

1. Experiential structure of the verbal group

The experiential structure of the finite verbal group is Finite plus Event, with optional Auxiliary (one or more). They range from short, one-word verbal groups, such as *ate*, where the Finite is fused with the Event and there is no Auxiliary, to long strings like *couldn't have been going to be being eaten* (Figure 6-15):

(a)

ate
Finite/Event

(b)

couldn't	have	been	going to	be	being	eaten
Finite	$Auxiliary_1$	$Auxiliary_2$	$Auxiliary_3$	$Auxiliary_4$	$Auxiliary_5$	Event

Figure 6-15 Experiential structure of the verbal group

The most striking feature of this is its parallelism with the nominal group. The verbal group begins with the Finite, which is the verbal equivalent of the Deictic, relating the process to the 'speaker-now'; the Finite does so by tense or modality (cf. Chapter 4 above) whereas the Deictic does so by person or proximity, but each of these provides the orientation of the group. The verbal group ends with the Event, which is the verbal equivalent of the Thing; the former expresses a process, which may be event, action, act of consciousness or relation, whereas the latter expresses an entity of some kind, but both represent the core of the lexical meaning.

This is not, of course, a coincidence. Both verbal and nominal group begin with the element that 'fixes' the group in relation to the speech exchange; and both end with the element that specifies the representational content — the difference being that, since things are more highly organized than events, there are additional lexical elements in the nominal but none in the verbal group. And it is not difficult to explain why the structures should be this way round. Initial position is thematic; and the natural theme of a process or participant is its relation to the here-and-now. Final position is informative; and the newsworthy component of a process or participant is what it is all about. So the structure of groups recapitulates, in the **fixed** ordering of their elements, the meaning that is incorporated as **choice** in the message structure of the clause.

Just as with the nominal group, therefore, there is no call to give a separate analysis corresponding to each of the three semantic components experiential, interpersonal, textual. The textual meaning is embodied in the ordering of the elements. The interpersonal meaning resides in the deictic features associated with finiteness — primary tense or modality — together with any attitudinal colouring that may be present in the lexical verb. And further systematic distinctions of both kinds may be realized by intonation and rhythm: contrast the neutral *he hasn't been working*

// ‸ he / hasn't been / **working** //

with a variant such as *he has not BEEN working*

// ‸ he has / not / **been** / working //

which has 'marked negative (polarity)' and 'contrastive past (tense)', as in Figure 6-16:

has	not	**been**	working
Finite present	Polarity: negative: marked	Auxiliary: past: contrastive	Event

Figure 6-16 Verbal group with marked polarity and contrastive tense

However, the structural labelling of the words that make up the verbal group is of limited value, not only because the meaning can be fully represented in terms of grammatical features (of tense, voice, polarity and modality), but also because it is the logical structure that embodies the single most important semantic feature of the English verb, its recursive tense system, and the elements of the logical structure are not the individual words but rather more complex elements. These are described in the next sub-section.

2. Logical structure of the verbal group

The verbal group is also structured logically, but in a way that is quite different from, and has no parallel in, the nominal group. The logical structure of the verbal group realizes the system of tense.

Consider the verbal group *has been eating*. This actually makes three separate tense choices: (1) present, expressed by the *-s* in *has* (i.e. by the fact that the first verb is in the present form); (2) past, expressed by the verb *have* plus the *-en* in *been* (i.e. plus the fact that the next verb is in the past/passive participle form V-*en*); (3) present, expressed by the verb *be* plus the *-ing* in *eating* (i.e. plus the fact that the next verb is in the present/active participle form V-*ing*). The complete tense can be built up as in Figure 6-17.

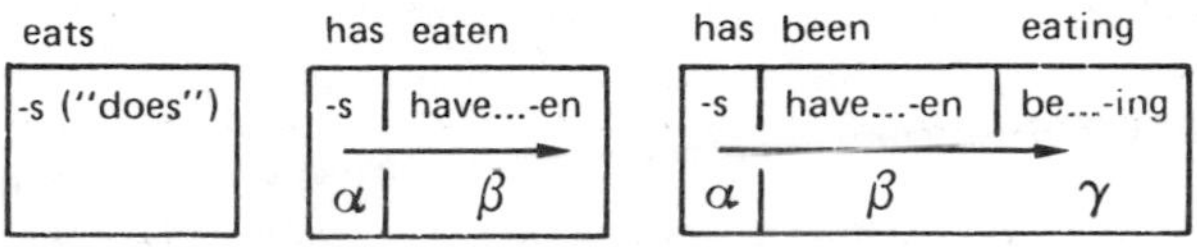

Figure 6-17 'Present in past in present' tense

Thus tense in English is a recursive system. The primary tense is that functioning as Head, shown as α. This is the Deictic tense: past, present or future relative to the speech event. The modifying elements, at β and beyond, are secondary tenses; they express past, present or future relative to the time selected in the previous tense. Realizations are as shown in Table 6(6).

Table 6(6) Realization of primary and secondary tenses

	primary	secondary
past	V-*ed* (simple past tense) as in *was/were, took, walked*	*have* + V-*en* as in *have been, have taken, have walked*
present	V-*s* (simple present tense) as in *is/are, takes, walks*	*be* + V-*ing* as in *be being, be taking, be walking*
future*	*will* + V (infinitive) as in *will be, will take, will walk*	*be going to* + V (infinitive) as in *be going to be*, be *going to take, be going to walk*

In naming the tenses, it is best to work backwards, beginning with the deepest and using the preposition *in* to express the serial modification. Thus the tense in Figure 6-18 is 'present in past in future in past'.

was	going to	have	been	working
[past]	be going to...[inf.]	have...-en		be...-ing
α–	β+	γ–		$\delta\emptyset$
past:	future:	past:		present
	"present	in past	in future	in past'

Figure 6-18 Naming of tenses

It is useful to have a notation also for the tenses themselves; we use – for 'past', + for 'future' and ∅ (zero) for 'present'.

Clearly it is possible to represent every instance of a verbal group by a structural analysis showing the Auxiliaries, in a way that is parallel to what is done for the nominal group. However, the elements of the verbal group are purely grammatical (that is, the options they represent are closed — past/present/future, positive/negative, active/passive — not open-ended); so it is simpler just to use a logical notation. The tense of the verbal group in Figure 6-23 could be shown as $\alpha - \wedge \beta + \wedge \gamma - \wedge \delta\emptyset$, or simply as $- \; + \; - \; \emptyset$. There are no general symbols for polarity and voice, but these can be shown by abbreviations: pos./neg., act./pass.; with perhaps only neg. and pass. needing to be marked.

The expression of polarity is tied to that of finiteness, as has already been explained. The expression of voice is an extension of that of tense. The active has no explicit marker; the passive is expressed by *be* or *get* plus V-*en* (past/passive participle), appearing as an additional modifying element at the end. The passive thus functions like an extra secondary tense; and it displays a distinctive combination of presentness (*be*) and pastness (V-*en*) suggesting 'to be in a present condition resulting from a past event' e.g. *are joined* (*the two halves of the city are joined by a bridge*). For this reason there is no very clear line between passives and attributes having passive form. Examples of the passive are given in Figure 6-19.

is	eaten
[present]	be...-en
$\alpha\emptyset$	β
present	passive

has	been	eaten
[present]	have...-en	be...-en
$\alpha\emptyset$	β-	γ
past	in present	passive

has	been	being	eaten
[present]	have...-en	be...ing	be...-en
$\alpha\emptyset$	β-	$\gamma\emptyset$	δ
present	in past	in present	passive

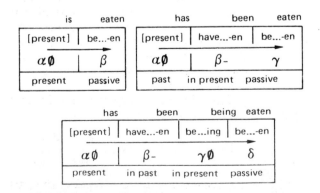

Figure 6-19 Passive verbal groups

For most of the known history of English the number of passive tenses has, as far as we can tell, lagged behind the number of the active ones. But since the system opened up in the way it has done the passives have caught up, and now every active tense has its passive counterpart, formed in this manner as an extension of the logical structure. The longest tense form I have noted down was in fact a passive:

it'll	've been	going to	've been	being	tested
$\alpha+$	$\beta-$	$\gamma+$	$\delta-$	$\epsilon\emptyset$	ζ

This is 'passive: present in past in future in past in future'.

Since the tense system is recursive, there should be no longest possible tense. However in practice there are certain restrictions which limit the total set of those that occur. These restrictions, or 'stop rules', are as follows:

(i) Apart from α, future occurs only once.
(ii) Apart from α, present occurs only once, and always at the deepest level
(iii) Apart from α, the same tense does not occur twice consecutively.

That is: following (i), we do not hear *she is going to have been about to do it*; following (ii), we do not hear *he has been having done it*; following (iii), we do not hear *they will have had done it*. These three restrictions limit the total number of finite tenses to thirty-six. These 36 finite tenses are shown in Table 6(7).

3. Finite, sequent and non-finite tense systems

There are in fact three systems of tense in English:

System I:	finite	36 tenses
System II:	sequent	24 tenses
System III:	non-finite/modalized	12 tenses

The finite system, System I, is the one displayed to the left of Table 6(7). The way it works can be illustrated by building up clauses with associated time expressions. Table 6(8) shows a four-degree tense *she's been going to have known* built up from one end and then demolished from the other; each form is accompanied by an appropriate time Adjunct. It will be noted that the order of time Adjuncts is the reverse of that of the tenses; there is what is known as 'mirror concord' between them, invariable except that the one corresponding to the primary tense can be picked out and made thematic, e.g. *by now she's known for some time*, *for a while she was going to have known already by tonight*. The clause chosen is one of mental process, so as to be able to be built up naturally from the simple present.

System II is that which is available following a past projection (see Chapter 7) such as *they said*. Note the following equivalences:

She arrived yesterday. She has arrived just now. She had arrived before that.	} They said she had arrived	(yesterday. (just then. (before that.

What happens here is that in the environment of a 'past' feature, the past element in three of the System II tenses is neutralized; past, past in present

Table 6(7)

TENSE			Non-finite, and finite modal, tenses (12): read as far as β		Finite non-modal tenses (36): read as far as α		
ε	δ	γ	β			α	
						past	1
			(none)	I		present	2
						future	3
						past	4
			past	II	in	present	5
						future	6
						past	7
			present	III	in	present	8
						future	9
						past	10
			future	IV	in	present	11
						future	12
						past	13
		past	in future	V	in	present	14
						future	15
						past	16
		present	in past	VI	in	present	17
						future	18
						past	19
		present	in future	VII	in	present	20
						future	21
						past	22
		future	in past	VIII	in	present	23
						future	24
						past	25
	past	in future	in past	IX	in	present	26
						future	27
						past	28
	present	in past	in future	X	in	present	29
						future	30
						past	31
	present	in future	in past	XI	in	present	32
						future	33
						past	34
present	in past	in future	in past	XII	in	present	35
						future	36

Finite non-modal tense		Non-finite, and finite modal tenses: (perfective, imperfective; modal)
1 took / did take 2 take(s) / do(es) take 3 will take	I	to take, taking; can take
4 had taken 5 has taken 6 will have taken	II	to have, having; can have + taken
7 was taking 8 is taking 9 will be taking	III	to be, being; can be + taking
10 was going to take 11 is going to take 12 will be going to take	IV	to be, being; can be + going/about to take
13 was going to have taken 14 is going to have taken 15 will be going to have taken	V	to be, being; can be + going to have taken
16 had been taking 17 has been taking 18 will have been taking	VI	to have, having; can have + been taking
19 was going to be taking 20 is going to be taking 21 will be going to be taking	VII	to be, being; can be + going to be taking
22 had been going to take 23 has been going to take 24 will have been going to take	VIII	to have, having; can have + been going to take
25 had been going to have taken 26 has been going to have taken 27 will have been going to be taken	IX	to have, having; can have + been going to have taken
28 was going to have been taking 29 is going to have been taking 30 will be going to have been taking	X	to be, being; can be + going to have been taking
31 had been going to be taking 32 has been going to be taking 33 will have been going to be taking	XI	to have, having; can have + been going to be taking
34 had been going to have been taking 35 has been going to have been taking 36 will have been going to have been taking	XII	to have, having; can have + been going to have been taking

Tense form		Temporal Adjuncts	
she knows	αØ	now	Ø
she's known	αØ β-	for a while now	- Ø
she's been going to know	αØ β- γ+	by tonight for a while now	+ - Ø
she's been going to've known	αØ β- γ+ δ-	already by tonight for a while now	- + - Ø
she was going to've known	α- β+ γ-	already by tonight for a while	- + -
she'll 've known	α+ β-	already by tonight	- +
she knew	α-	already	-

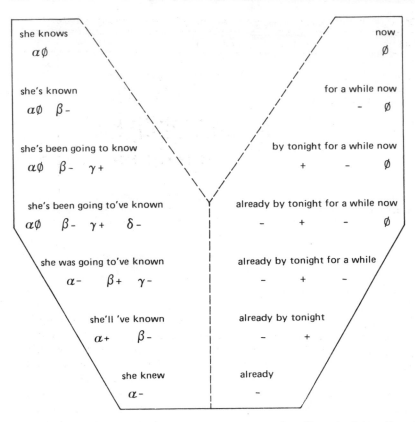

Table 6(8) Building up a complex tense form from the left and from the right, with associated temporal Adjuncts showing mirror concord

and past in past are all represented as past in past. Since there are six such triads, System II has 2 × 6 = 12 fewer tenses than System I.

System III is the tense system available in non-finite and in modalized forms. Here a further neutralization takes place, i.e. **both** that in System II **and** a parallel one in the future. Table 6(9) shows the effect of both these steps. By step (1), *arrived*, *has arrived* and *had arrived* are all represented by the one form *have arrived*. (This appears as *have arrived* following a modal Finite, and as *to have arrived* [perfective] or *having arrived* [imperfective] when non-finite.) This is the same neutralization as that which produced System II, the only difference being that the System II form is a finite one, *had arrived*. By step (2), *will arrive*, *is going to arrive* and *will be going to arrive* are all represented by the one form *be going to arrive*, or *be about to arrive* (the two are synonymous as far as tense is concerned), these again having modalized, perfective and imperfective variants.

What happens here is that (i) past, past in present and past in past are all represented by past; (ii) future, future in present and future in future are all represented by future. There are twelve such triads; total number of tenses is 36 − (2 × 12) = 12.

Table 6(9) Derivation of System III by the neutralization of certain contrasts in System I

System I	System III
	(a) non-finite
(1) She arrived yesterday	Having arrived yesterday, she . . .
She has arrived just now	" just now, she . . .
She had arrived before that	" before that, she . . .
	(b) modalized
	She must have arrivedyesterday
	" just now
	" before that
	(a) non-finite
(2) She will arrive tomorrow	Being about to arrive tomorrow
She is going to arrive just now	" just now
She will be going to arrive after that	" after that
	(b) modalized
	She must be going to arrive tomorrow
	" just now
	" after that

The difference between this and System II is that in System III the effect is simply to eliminate the choice of primary tense. System I minus the 'α' tense gives System III. The non-finite or modalized verbal group has no deictic tense element: non-finites because they have no deictic at all (that is what non-finite implies: not anchored in the here-&-now); modalized because, while they have a deictic element (being finite), their deixis takes the form of modality and not tense. Strictly speaking, the first secondary tense of the non-finite should be labelled α, since that becomes the Head element; but it seems simpler and clearer to retain the association of α with finiteness and show non-finites as beginning with β.

Here is an example of a clause complex consisting of two clauses each of whose verbs has selected a System III tense:

(a) non-finite

to have been going to be spending all that time preparing the class . . .
$\beta-$ $\gamma+$ $\delta\emptyset$

(b) modalized

. . . she must have been about to be being inspected
α^{mod} $\beta-$ $\gamma+$ $\delta\emptyset$ ϵ^{pass}

The tenses of System III are shown in the right-hand column of Table 6(7). Note that, to save duplication, the labelling of tenses for both systems is shown on the left. The class I form of System III is tenseless: that is *taking*, *to take*; *must* (or other modal) + *take*.

It is possible, obviously, to think of this set of tenses as a list and to represent them all as experiential structures. But this would fail to bring out the meaning, which is based on **serial** tense choices: e.g. future (*will do*) → past in relation to that future (*will have done*) → present in relation to that past in relation to that future *will have been doing*, and so on. Also it would suggest a clear-cut distinction between tenses that exist and others that don't, whereas the system varies for different speakers; moreover it is tending to expand all the time, although it has probably just about reached its limits. What has happened is that relative time — before, at or after a defined time reference — has come to be interpreted, in the semantics of English, as a kind of logical relation; a way of subcategorizing events similar to the subcategorizing of things, except that the latter is multidimensional (and hence lexicalized) whereas the former is based on a single semantic dimension and can therefore be expressed entirely by grammatical means.

4. Phrasal verbs

The class of word functioning as Event in the verbal group structure is the verb. We can refer to this more specifically as the 'lexical verb' to distinguish it from the finites and auxiliaries.*

PHRASAL VERBS are lexical verbs which consist of more than just the verb word itself. They are of two kinds, plus a third which is a combination of the other two:

(i) verb + adverb, e.g. *look out* 'unearth, retrieve'
(ii) verb + preposition, e.g. *look for* 'seek'
(iii) verb + adverb + preposition, e.g. *look out for* 'watch for presence of'

Examples:

(i) Could you look out a good recipe for me?
— Yes I'll look one out in a moment.

(ii) I'm looking for a needle; could you help me find one?
— Yes I'll look for one in a moment.

(iii) Look out for snakes; there are lots around here.
— Yes I'll look out for them.

Expressions of this kind are lexical items; *look out*, *look for* and *look out for* belong as separate entries in a thesaurus or dictionary. They are thus tending more and more to function as grammatical constituents; but this tendency is far from complete, and grammatically they are rather unstable.

Experientially, a phrasal verb is a single Process, rather than Process plus circumstantial element. This can be seen from their assignment to process types. For example, the verb *see* represents a mental process, and so has

---

* A major point of difference between the verbal group and the nominal group is that the Event (unlike the Thing) is not the point of departure for the recursive modifying relationship. Hence it does not figure as an element in the notation. It could be argued that a phrasal verb represents an expansion of the Event, giving something like

come along up out from under
α β γ δ ϵ ζ

(or, more seriously, the adverbial part of it, as far as the word *out*). But we have not explored this line of approach here.

simple present as its unmarked present tense, as in *do you see that sign?* (not *are you seeing that sign?*). But *see off* is material, and so has present in present: *are you seeing your brother off?* (not *do you see your brother off?* which can only be habitual). The transitivity analysis is therefore as in Figure 6-20.

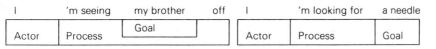

I	'm seeing	my brother	off
Actor	Process	Goal	

I	'm looking for	a needle
Actor	Process	Goal

Figure 6-20 Transitivity analysis of phrasal verbs

The same pattern is reflected in the thematic variation. If the prepositional phrase *for a needle* was a circumstantial element it should be able to be thematized; but we do not say *for that I'll look*; the more likely form is *that I'll look for*. Similarly with the adverbial ones: *see off* is a single process, so whereas we would say *there I'll see John* (= *I'll see John there* but with *there* instead of *I* as Theme), there is no form *off I'll see John* thematically related to *I'll see John off*.

The grammar enables us to explain why phrasal verbs have evolved to the extent that they have done in modern English. The leading edge is formed by those of type (i), the adverbial ones, which are particularly widely spread. Typically these have non-phrasal, one word synonyms, or near-synonyms; yet the phrasal form tends to be preferred, and is strongly favoured in the spoken language. Why is this?

Suppose we have a two-participant clause, active in voice, in which the main item of news is the Goal. The Goal comes at the end, and this is where the prominence — the information focus — typically falls. We can express the process either phrasally or non-phrasally — there is nothing very much to choose between the two:

they cancelled **the meeting** they called off **the meeting**

Suppose however that I want the focus of information to be the Process rather than the Goal. At this point a significant difference arises. If I say

they **cancelled** the meeting

the result is that the information focus is now non-final; this is a marked, strongly foregrounded option, and therefore carries additional overtones of contrast, contradiction or unexpectedness. I may not want these overtones; but the only way I can avoid them is to leave the focus unmarked — i.e. at the end. This means that the Process, not the Goal, must come last. In Chinese, which has a similar word order and information structure, there is a special construction, the *bǎ* construction, for achieving this; but in English it is impossible — I cannot say *they the meeting cancelled* — unless the Process is split into two parts. This therefore is what happens, with a phrasal verb: it splits the Process into two parts, one functioning as Predicator and the other as Adjunct, with the Adjunct coming in its normal place at the end:

they called the meeting **off**

This also explains something that is often presented as an arbitrary rule of English, but is in fact anything but arbitrary: that if the Goal is a pronoun it almost always occurs within the phrasal verb (*they called it off* rather than *they called off it*). This is part of the same story; a pronoun is hardly ever newsworthy, since it refers to something that has gone before, so if the Goal is a pronoun it is virtually certain that the Process will be under focus. (But not quite; the pronoun may be contrastive, and if so it **can** come finally, e.g. *they rang up me, but apparently nobody else.*)

Figure 6-21 gives the analysis of a clause with a phrasal verb of the adverbial type (i) in it, in terms of (a) transitivity and (b) mood:

	they	called		the meeting	off
(a)	Actor/ Agent	Process: material		Goal/Medium	
(b)	Subject	'past' Finite	*'call'* Predicator	Complement	Adjunct
	Mood		Residue		

Figure 6-21 Phrasal verb in transitivity and mood structure

Similarly with the prepositional type (ii): in *I'm looking for a needle*, the mood constituents are *looking* Predicator, *for a needle* Adjunct, and this accounts for the ordering relative to other Adjuncts, e.g. *I've looked everywhere for a needle.* The third type include some where both adverb and preposition are (or may be) part of the Process, e.g. *look out for, put up with, put in for*; and others where only the adverb is within the Process, e.g. *let in for, put up to*, as in *he let me in for it, he put me up to it*. Analyses as in Figure 6-22.

MELisshit Don't do MEL next year it's even shittier, ask any 2nd year student!!!

(a)

he	put		in	for the job
Actor	Process			Goal
Subject	'past' Finite	*put* Predicator	Adjunct	Adjunct

(b)

they	put		him	up	to the job
Actor	Process		Goal		Location
Subject	'past' Finite	*put* Predicator	Complement	Adjunct	Adjunct

Figure 6-22 Further examples of phrasal verbs

There will often be doubt about whether these complex lexical items can be interpreted grammatically as a single Process or not. In such cases it is important to consider the transitivity of the clause as a whole, to see whether it ppears to be structured as process plus participant or process plus circum-tance. Whichever analysis gives the more coherent overall picture is the one hat is to be preferred.

.4 Adverbial group, conjunction group, preposition group

. Adverbial group

'he adverbial group has an adverb as Head, which may or may not be accom-anied by modifying elements. Premodifiers are grammatical items like *not* nd *rather* and *so*; there is no lexical premodification in the adverbial group. Vhat there is is therefore more like what we have called 'submodification' in he nominal group, with submodifiers relating to an adjective as their Sub-Iead.

We can represent the adverbial group as a logical structure as in Figure -23.

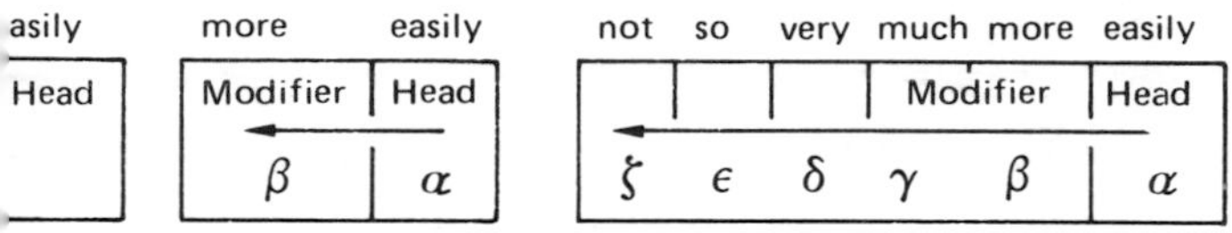

igure 6-23 Premodification in the adverbial group

Postmodification is of one type only, namely comparison. As in the ominal group, postmodifiers are embedded; they may be (a) embedded lauses, or (b) embedded prepositional phrases. Examples:

(a) much more easily ⟦than you would have expected⟧
as grimly ⟦as if his life depended on it⟧
too quickly ⟦for us to see what was happening⟧
not long enough ⟦to find my way around⟧
(b) as early [as two o'clock]
faster [than fifteen knots]

'here are also the type favoured in grammar tests, such as *John runs faster han Jim*, where the embedded element is said to be a clause with the Finite nd Residue presupposed by ellipsis: 'than Jim runs'. It appears however that hese are now embedded prepositional phrases, since the normal form of a ersonal pronoun following *than* or *as* is oblique/absolute rather than ominative: *John runs faster than me* (not *than I*). The same applies in the ominal group when the Head is an adjective: *John isn't as tall as me*.

This is the only instance of embedding other than in a nominal group. All ther embedding in English is a form of nominalization, where a group, hrase or clause comes to function as part of, or in place of (i.e. as the whole f), a nominal group. See further Chapter 7, Sections 7-4 and 7-5 below.

Strictly speaking the domain of these comparative Postmodifiers is not the Iead of the group but an item within the Premodifier: *as*, *more*, *less*, *too* (the exception is *-er* comparatives like *faster*). This could be shown as in Figure 6-24 (a); cf. the nominal group, where given *a better man than I am* we could show *than I am* as dependent on *better* rather than on *man*.* But this is not really necessary: structure is not the appropriate concept for interpreting semantic domain, and the locus of comparison may in any case be part of the Head (the *-er* in *faster, readilier*) or even part of the Postmodifier (the exceptional form *enough*, which follows the Head). It seems unnecessary to represent pairs such as *too fast (for me) to follow, slowly enough (for me) to follow*, or *as fast as I could count, faster than I could count*, as having different structures. They can be analysed as in Figure 6-24(b).

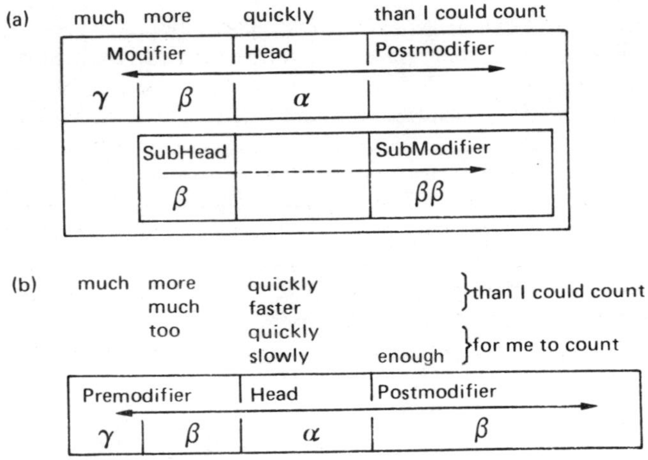

Figure 6-24 Adverbial groups with embedded Postmodifiers

2. Conjunction group

Within the 'primary' word class of adverbials, there is another class beside adverbs, namely conjunctions.

Conjunctions also form word groups by modification, for example *even if just as, not until, if only*. These can be represented in the same way, as β ^ α structures (or α ^ β in the case of *if only*). Note however that many conjunctive expressions have evolved from more complex structures, e.g. *as soon as in case, by the time, nevertheless, insofar as*. These can be treated as single elements without further analysis. They are themselves, of course, subject to modification, e.g. *just in case, almost as soon as*.

3. Preposition group

Prepositions are not a sub-class of adverbials; functionally they are related to verbs. But they form groups by modification, in the same way as conjunc

* Cf. *the brightest star in the sky*, where *in the sky* would modify *brightest*.

tions; e.g. *right behind, not without, all along, way off* as in *right behind the door, not without some misgivings, all along the beach, way off the mark.*

Again there are more complex forms, such as *in front of, for the sake of,* which can be left unanalysed. These are also subject to modification, as in *just for the sake of, immediately in front of.* It is important to make a distinction between a PREPOSITION GROUP, such as *right behind* or *immediately in front of,* which is a Modifier–Head structure expanded from and functionally equivalent to a preposition, and a PREPOSITIONAL PHRASE, which is not an expansion of anything but a clause-like structure in which the Process/Predicator function is performed by a preposition and not by a verb. Prepositional phrases are discussed in the final sub-section of this chapter (6.5).

Complex prepositions such as *in front (of), for the sake (of),* have evolved from prepositional phrases, with *front, sake* as 'Complement'. Many expressions are indeterminate between the two, for example *by the side of, as an alternative to, on the grounds of*; expressions like these are on the way to becoming prepositions but have not quite got there. In general however there is a difference; those which have become prepositions typically occur without a Deictic preceding the noun (*in front of,* not *in the front of*), and the noun occurs in the singular only (*in front of,* not *in fronts of*). In some instances duplex forms occur: *beside* has become a full preposition, but because it is often used in an abstract or metaphorical sense a modern version of the original complex form *by the side of* has reappeared along with it, and this in its turn is now starting to follow the same route towards prepositional status.

6.5 Prepositional phrase

A prepositional phrase consists of a preposition plus a nominal group, for example *on the burning deck.*

We have explained a preposition as a minor verb. On the interpersonal dimension it functions as a minor Predicator having a nominal group as its Complement; and, as we saw above in Sections 4.3 and 5.8, this is felt to be essentially no different from the Complement of a 'full' Predicator — prepositional Complements increasingly tend to have the same potential for becoming Subject, as in *this floor shouldn't be walked on for a few days.* No doubt one reason for this tendency has been the lexical unity of phrasal verbs, referred to in Section 6.3; because *look up to* is a single lexical item, with a one word near-synonym *admire,* it is natural to parallel *people have always looked up to her* with *she's always been looked up to.*

Thus the internal structure of *across the lake* is like that of *crossing the lake,* with a non-finite verb as Predicator. In some instances there is a non-finite verb that is more or less interchangeable with the preposition, e.g. *near / adjoining* (*the house*), *without / not wearing* (*a hat*), *about / concerning* (*the trial*). There is in fact an area of overlap between prepositional phrases and non-finite clauses; some instances can be interpreted as either, and some non-finite verb forms can be classified as prepositions, e.g. *regarding, considering, including.* In principle, a non-finite clause implies a potential Subject, whereas a prepositional phrase does not; but the prevalence of so-called 'hanging participles' shows that this constraint is not always taken very seriously (e.g. *it's cold not wearing a hat*). More significant is the fact that **non-finite clauses are clauses**; that is, they can be expanded to include other elements of clause structure, whereas prepositional phrases cannot. One can say either *he left the city in his wife's car* or *he left the city taking his wife's car*; but only the latter can be expanded to *he left the city taking his wife's car quietly out of the driveway*.

Likewise on the experiential dimension the preposition functions as a minor Process. The nominal group corresponds in function to one or other of the participants Range, Goal or Attribute, though without any very clear distinction among them. We shall interpret it in all cases as a Range. But the constituency is the same whether we represent the prepositional phrase experientially, as in Figure 6-25 (a), or interpersonally, as in 6-25 (b).

(a)

the boy	stood	on	the burning deck
Actor	Process: material	Place	
		'Process'	'Range'

(b)

the boy	stood		on	the burning deck
Subject	(past) Finite	'stand' Predicator	Adjunct	
Mood		Residue		
			'Predicator'	'Complement'

Figure 6-25 Representation of the prepositional phrase

But note that prepositional phrases are phrases, not groups; they have no logical structure as Head and Modifier, and cannot be reduced to a single element. In this respect, they are clause-like rather than group-like; hence when we interpret the preposition as 'minor Predicator' and 'minor Process' we are interpreting the prepositional phrase as a kind of 'minor clause' — which is what it is.

As regards its own function, a prepositional phrase occurs either (i) as Adjunct in a clause, or (ii) as Qualifier in a nominal group, for example *on the radio* in (i) *I heard good news on the radio*, (ii) *the news on the radio was good*. As Adjunct, it may also occur initially, as marked Theme; e.g. *on the radio I heard good news*. The exception is prepositional phrases with *of*, which normally occur only in function (ii); the reason is that *of* is not a true preposition, but rather a structure marker in the nominal group (as *to* is in the verbal group). Hence *of* -phrases do not occur as clause elements, except those with Matter function, in the sense of 'about', as in *Of Julius Caesar it is said that he was ambitious*.

6.6 Summary of word classes

Figure 6-26 shows the classes of word that we can recognize as functioning in English groups and phrases. These are the 'parts of speech' of a functional grammar.

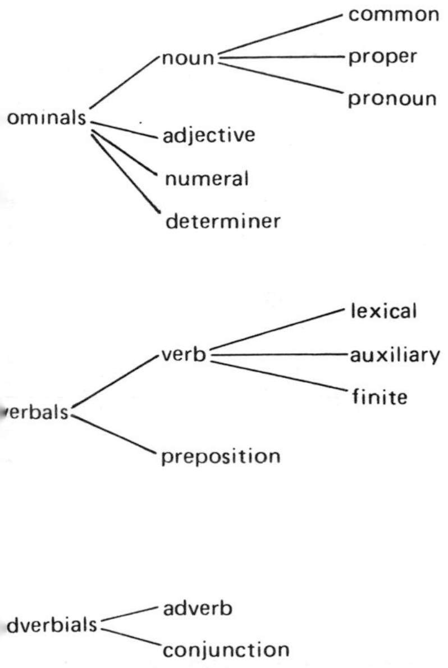

Figure 6-26 Summary of word classes

7

Above the clause: the clause complex

7.1 'Clause complex' and 'sentence'

We said in Chapter 6 that a group — verbal group, adverbial group, nomina group — could be interpreted as a WORD COMPLEX: that is to say, a Heac word together with other words that modify it. This is why the term GROUP came to be used. It meant 'group of words', or 'word group'; and it suggest how the group no doubt evolved, by expansion outwards from the word.*

However, because of the very diverse ways in which phenomena can be subcategorized, groups developed their own multivariate constituent struc tures, with functional configurations such as the Deictic + Numerative + Epithet + Classifier + Thing of the nominal group in English. Treating th group simply as a 'word complex' does not account for all these variou aspects of its meaning. It is for this reason that we recognize the group as distinct rank in the grammar.

In the same way, a sentence can be interpreted as a CLAUSE COMPLEX: Head clause together with other clauses that modify it. There is the same kin of relationship between sentence and clause as there is between group an word: the sentence has evolved by expansion outwards from the clause. S when we represent sentences in the grammar, the same question arises: doe the notion of 'clause complex' allow us to account for all aspects of the mean ing of the sentence? Or should a sentence also be interpreted as a multivariat constituent structure, with its own range of functional configurations?

The picture here is somewhat different. We certainly cannot account for a of sentence structure simply in terms of Head + Modifier; there ar numerous kinds of modifying, and also other similar relationships. At th same time there is nothing like the structure of the nominal group referred t above, where the elements are (i) distinct in function, (ii) realized by distinc classes, and (iii) more or less fixed in sequence. A configuration of such kind **has** to be represented as a multivariate structure. In a sentence, on th other hand, the tendency is much more for any clause to have the potenti for functioning with any value in a multi-clausal complex. In other words, th relation among the clauses in a sentence is generally more like that of a strin of nouns such as *railway ticket office staff*, which could be explained as (univariate) word complex, than that of *these two old railway engines*, whic could not.

* It is important to maintain the terminological distinction between GROUP and PHRASE, which lost if a nominal group is referred to as a 'noun phrase'. Although group and phrase are bo of intermediate rank as constituents, they have arrived there from different ends: a group i bloated word, whereas a phrase is a shrunken clause.

We shall assume, therefore, that the notion of 'clause complex' enables us to account in full for the functional organization of sentences. A sentence will be defined, in fact, as a clause complex. The clause complex will be the only grammatical unit which we shall recognize above the clause. Hence there will be no need to bring in the term 'sentence' as a distinct grammatical category. We can use it simply to refer to the orthographic unit that is contained between full stops. This will avoid ambiguity: a sentence is a constituent of writing, while a clause complex is a constituent of grammar.

We shall interpret the relations between clauses in terms of the 'logical' component of the linguistic system: the functional–semantic relations that make up the logic of natural language. There are two dimensions in the interpretation. One is the system of interdependency, or 'tactic' system, parataxis and hypotaxis, which is general to all complexes — word, group, phrase and clause alike. The other is the logico-semantic system of expansion and projection, which is specifically an inter-clausal relation — or rather, a relation between processes, usually (but not always) expressed in the grammar as a complex of clauses. These two together will provide the functional framework for describing the clause complex. The unit that is arrived at in this way is that which lies behind the concept of 'sentence' as this has evolved, over the centuries, in the written language. Hence in the analysis of a written text each sentence can be treated as one clause complex, with the 'simple' (one clause) sentence as the limiting case. With a spoken text, we will be able to use the grammar to define and delimit clause complexes, in a way that keeps them as close as possible to the sentences of written English.

7.2 Types of relationship between clauses

Consider the following example:

It won't be surprising if people complain if they don't punish him if he's guilty

This contains four clauses; each one other than the first modifies the one preceding it. We can represent this in Figure 7-1.

it won't be surprising	if people complain	if they don't punish him	if he's guilty
Head	Modifier →		
α	β	γ	δ

Figure 7-1 Progressive modification

Usually the pattern is less regular than this; there are dependent clauses branching out at different places, and the clauses are not all of the same kind. A more typical example would be:

I don't mind if you leave as soon as you've finished as long as you're back when I need you.

Here there is a variation in the clause relationships: 'H if M', 'H as soon as M', 'H as long as M', 'H when M'. And the structure is no longer a simple dependency chain, with each clause dependent on the one preceding; the first three clauses form one block, and the last two form another which is dependent on it. This is shown in Figure 7-2.

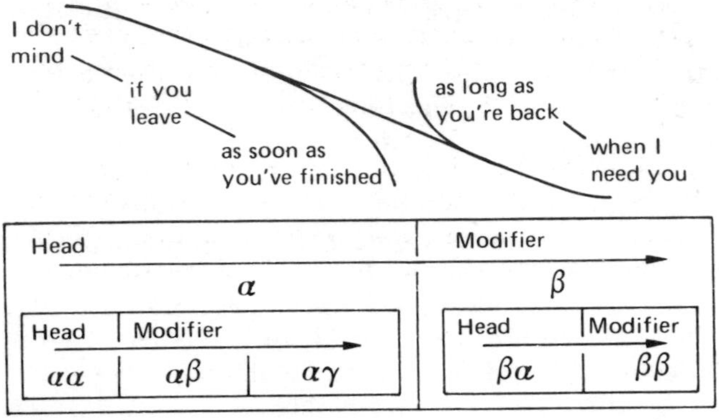

Figure 7-2 Modification with nesting (internal bracketing)

It follows from this that the order of the two blocks could be reversed; we could have

> As long as you're back when I need you I don't mind if you leave as soon as you've finished.

Figure 7-3 shows the analysis of this second version.

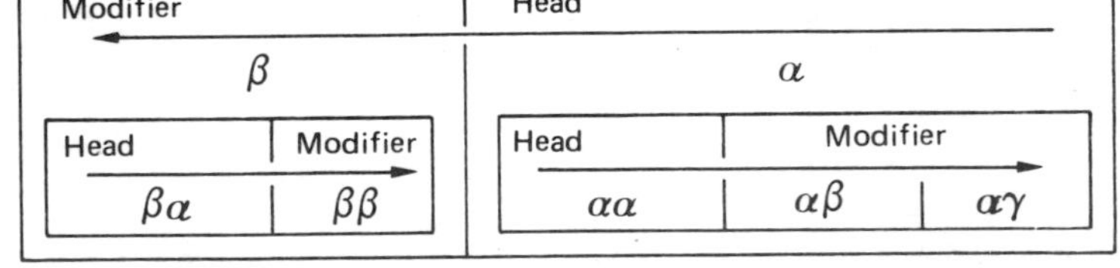

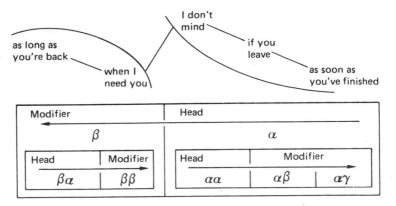

Figure 7-3 Modification with internal regressive bracketing

As a first step, therefore, we can interpret the relationship between these clauses as one of modification, the same concept that was used to explain one aspect of the relationship between the words in a verbal or nominal group. We have had to take account of the possibility of internal bracketing, or

NESTING; but that too is a general property which we have already found in group structure. The question that arises at this point is: in what other ways does the concept of modification need to be refined and enriched in order to account for relationships within the clause complex?

The concept needs to be extended, we shall suggest, along two separate vectors, by introducing two distinct sets of alternatives: (i) the type of interdependency, or 'taxis'; (ii) the logico-semantic relation. We shall summarize these in the present section, and then go on to examine each in greater detail.

(i) Type of interdependency. The relation of modifying, whereby one element 'modifies' another, is not the only relationship that may obtain between the members of a complex.

Where one element modifies another, the status of the two is unequal; the modifying element is dependent on the modified. But two elements may be joined together on an equal footing, neither being dependent on the other.

The general term for the modifying relation is HYPOTAXIS. Hypotaxis is the relation between a dependent element and its dominant, the element on which it is dependent.* Contrasting with this is PARATAXIS, which is the relation between two like elements of equal status, one initiating and the other continuing.

All 'logical' structures in language are either (a) paratactic or (b) hypotactic. The clause complex involves relationships of both kinds.

Hypotactic structures will be represented by the Greek letter notation already used for modification in the structure of the group. For paratactic structures we shall use a numerical notation 1 2 3 . . ., with nesting indicated in the usual way: 11 12 2 31 32 means the same as 1(1 2) 2 3(1 2).

A typical clause complex is a mixture of paratactic and hypotactic sequences, either of which may be nested inside the other; for example

I would	if I could,	but I can't
1 α	1 β	2

There is a paratactic relationship between *I would if I could* and *but I can't*, shown as 1 2; and a hypotactic relationship between *I would* and *if I could*, shown as α β.

We will refer to the members of a pair of related clauses, in paratactic or hypotactic relation, as PRIMARY and SECONDARY. The primary is the initiating clause in a paratactic structure, and the dominant clause in a hypotactic; the secondary is the continuing clause in a paratactic structure and the dependent clause in a hypotactic. This is set out in Table 7(1):

Table 7(1) Primary and secondary clauses

	primary	secondary
parataxis	1 (initiating)	2 (continuing)
hypotaxis	α (dominant)	β (dependent)

* An earlier name for the higher term in the dependency relation, that on which something is dependent, was TERMINANT. The problem with this turns out to be that it is too readily misinterpreted as 'coming last in sequence'. The dependency relation, however, is neutral as regards the sequence in which the elements occur.

For most purposes we shall be able to refer to 'primary' and 'secondary' clauses and avoid using the more specific terms.

(ii) Logico-semantic relation. There is a wide range of different logico-semantic relations any of which may hold between a primary and a secondary member of a clause complex. But it is possible to group these into a small number of general types, based on the two fundamental relationships of (1) EXPANSION and (2) PROJECTION.

(1) Expansion: the secondary clause expands the primary clause, by (a) elaborating it, (b) extending it or (c) enhancing it.
(2) Projection: the secondary clause is projected through the primary clause, which instates it as (a) a locution or (b) an idea.

If we return to the examples given above, in Figures 7-1–7-3, these were all of the same type of interdependency (hypotaxis) and same logico-semantic relation (expansion: enhancement).

An example of a projecting complex (projection: locution) would be

John reported that Mary had told him that Fred had said the day would be fine.

The analysis of this is given in Figure 7-4:

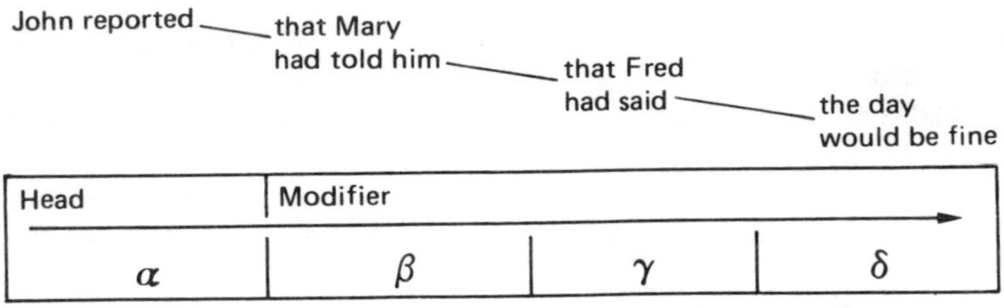

Figure 7-4 Clause complex of the 'projection' type

Within the general categories of expansion and projection, we recognize first of all a small number of subtypes: three of expansion, and two of projection. The names of these, with suggested notation, are as follows:

(1) Expansion:
- (a) elaboration = ('equals')
- (b) extension + ('is added to')
- (c) enhancement × ('is multiplied by')

(2) Projection:
- (a) locution “ (double quotes)
- (b) idea ‘ (single quotes)

These symbols combine with those for parataxis and hypotaxis:

$=2 \quad =\beta \quad +2 \quad +\beta \quad \times 2 \quad \times\beta$ “2 “β ‘2 ‘β

Below is a brief definition of each of these categories, with examples:

(1a) Elaboration: 'i.e.' — one clause expands another by elaborating on it (or some portion of it): restating in other words, specifying in greater detail, commenting, or exemplifying.

(1b)	Extension: 'and'	one clause expands another by extending beyond it: adding some new element, giving an exception to it, or offering an alternative.
(1c)	Enhancement: 'so, yet, then'	one clause expands another by embellishing around it: qualifying it with some circumstantial feature of time, place, cause or condition.
(2a)	Locution: 'says'	one clause is projected through another, which presents it as a locution, a construction of wording.
(2b)	Idea: 'thinks'	one clause is projected through another, which presents it as an idea, a construction of meaning.

Examples are given in Table 7(2):

Table 7(2) Basic types of clause complex

		(i) paratactic	(ii) hypotactic
(2) Projection	(a) elaboration	John didn't wait; 1 he ran away. $=2$	John ran away, α which surprised everyone $=\beta$
	(b) extension	John ran away, 1 and Fred stayed behind. $+2$	John ran away, α whereas Fred stayed behind. $+\beta$
	(c) enhancement	John was scared, 1 so he ran away. $\times 2$	John ran away, α because he was scared $\times\beta$
(1) Expansion	(a) locution	John said: 1 "I'm running away" "2	John said α he was running away. "β
	(b) idea	John thought to himself. 1 "I'll run away" '2	John thought α he would run away. 'β

In hypotaxis, the two clauses, primary and secondary, can occur in either order: either $\alpha \wedge \beta$ or $\beta \wedge \alpha$. But it is always the secondary clause that is dependent, that does the expanding or gets projected. Examples of the $\beta \wedge \alpha$ sequence are:

While Fred stayed behind,	John ran away	$+\beta \wedge \alpha$
Because he was scared,	John ran away	$\times\beta \wedge \alpha$
That John had run away	no-one believed	'$\beta \wedge \alpha$
β	α	

The logical symbol is always attached to the symbol for the dependent clause.

In parataxis, only the order $1 \wedge 2$ is possible — because the question of which is the primary clause in a paratactic relation is simply a matter of which comes first.

In a paratactic expansion, therefore, it is always the secondary clause that does the expanding; if we say

John ran away; he didn't wait 1 ^ =2
1 2

the structure is still 1 ^ =2.

With a paratactic projection, on the other hand, it is possible for the primary clause to be the projected one, as in

"I'm running away," said John "1 ^2
1 2

This is because projection is inherently a directional (asymmetric) relation.

Parataxis and hypotaxis are discussed in more detail in the next section (7.3). Following that we take up the more specific categories of expansion and projection.

7.3 Types of interdependency: parataxis and hypotaxis

Parataxis and hypotaxis are general relationships which are not restricted to the rank of the clause. They define complexes at any rank: clause complex, group or phrase complex, word complex. There is a further note on group and phrase complexes in the final section of this chapter.

Parataxis is the linking of elements of equal status. Both the initiating and the continuing element are free, in the sense that each could stand as a functioning whole.

Hypotaxis is the binding of elements of unequal status. The dominant element is free, but the dependent element is not.

Parataxis and hypotaxis define a kind of structure that we have called 'univariate', to distinguish it from the multivariate structures that we find everywhere else. A multivariate structure is a configuration of different functional relationships, like Theme – Rheme, or Actor – Process – Beneficiary – Goal. Note that, although it is the functions that are labelled, the structure actually consists of the relationships among them. A univariate structure is an iteration of the same functional relationship: for example 'and' as in *Bill Brewer, Jan Stewer, Peter Gurney, Peter Davy, Dan'l Whiddon, Harry Hawk, Old Uncle Tom Cobbley and all*; 'equals' as in *Tom, Tom, the piper's son* (Tom = Tom = the piper's son); 'is a subset of' as in *new-fashioned three-cornered cambric country-cut handkerchief* (what kind of handkerchief? — country-cut; what kind of country-cut handkerchief? — cambric, . . .); and so on.

In principle, the paratactic relation is logically (i) symmetrical and (ii) transitive. This can be exemplified with the 'and' relation.

(i) 'salt and pepper' implies 'pepper and salt', so the relationship is symmetrical; (ii) 'salt and pepper', 'pepper and mustard' together imply 'salt and mustard', so the relationship is transitive.

The hypotactic relation is logically (i) non-symmetrical and (ii) non-transitive. For example, 'when': (i) 'I breathe when I sleep' does not imply 'I sleep when I breathe'; (ii) 'I fret when I have to drive slowly' and 'I have to drive slowly when it's been raining' together do not imply 'I fret when it's been raining'.

This basic pattern may be modified by the nature of the logico-semantic relationship; for example, 'quote' as a paratactic relation is obviously not symmetrical: 'John says, quote: it's raining' cannot be reworded as 'it's raining, quote: John says'. But whenever it is logically possible, a given semantic relationship will be symmetrical and transitive in combination with parataxis but not in combination with hypotaxis. For example, the 'and' relation with hypotaxis is expressed by structures such as *besides* plus non-finite clause; and it is clear that *besides undergoing the operation he also had to pay for it* does not imply *besides having to pay for the operation he also underwent it*. Conversely, if 'when' is expressed paratactically, it will be by such expressions as *at the same time*; and *I sleep, and at the same time I breathe* does imply *I breathe, and at the same time I sleep*. Even with projection the difference appears; for example hypotactic *John said that Mary said that it was Tuesday* does not imply *John said that it was Tuesday*, because the projected clause is being treated as what John meant; whereas *John said: "Mary said: "It's Tuesday"."* does imply *John said: "It's Tuesday"*. because here the projection refers to what John said and in reporting Mary John did in fact speak those words. (This is not casuistry; it is related to the fundamental semantic properties of the two kinds of projection. See Section 7.5 below.)

Dependent clauses may be finite or non-finite. Other clauses in the clause complex are finite. Paratactically related clauses that are nested within a dependency are of course dependent for this purpose; for example,

She set to work very carefully,
α
nibbling first at one and then at the other,
$=\beta\ 1$
and growing sometimes taller and sometimes shorter,
$\beta+2$
until she had brought herself down to her usual height.
$\times\gamma$

In parataxis there is no dependence of either element on the other; so there is no ordering other than that which is represented by the sequence. This is why we use the numerical notation:

pepper	and salt		salt,	pepper and	mustard
1	2		1	2	3

The only modification is that which arises through internal bracketing or NESTING, as in

soup	or salad;	meat,	chicken	or fish;	and cheese	or dessert
11	12	21	22	23	31	32

These are word complexes, but the same principles apply to paratactic clause complexes, as in

John came into the room and sat down, Lucy stood in the doorway, and Fred waited outside

where the structure is 11 12 2 3.

In a hypotactic structure the elements are ordered in dependence, and this ordering is largely independent of the sequence. Hence we can have various sequences: dependent clause (i) following dominant, (ii) preceding dominant, (iii) enclosed in or (iv) enclosing dominant:

You never can tell till you try.	α ^ β
If wishes were horses, beggars would ride.	β ^ α
Picture, if you can, a winkle.	α « β »
He might, he said, finish it himself.	β « α »

Hypotactic structures may also involve nesting, as illustrated in Figures 7-2 and 7-3 above. Sometimes there are two possible interpretations, as with *she took her umbrella in case it rained when she was leaving*:

	She took her umbrella	in case it rained	when she was leaving
(a)	α	β	γ
(b)	$\alpha\alpha$	$\alpha\beta$	β

In (a) it rained when she was leaving, or at least that was what she was anticipating; in (b), she took her umbrella when she was leaving. So in (b) there is internal bracketing of the first two clauses.

Typically, hypotactic and paratactic structures combine in the same clause complex. Here is a more complicated example taken from spontaneous discourse; it was spoken by a girl aged nine:

> Our teacher says that if your neighbour has a new baby and you don't know whether it's a he or a she, if you call it 'it' well then the neighbour will be very offended.

The 'dependency structure', showing hypotactic ordering, is as in Figure 7-5.

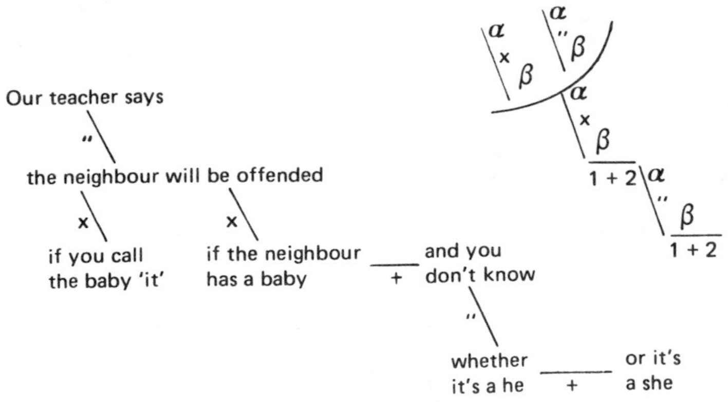

Figure 7-5 Hypotaxis and parataxis combined

The constituency structure is shown in Figure 7-6:

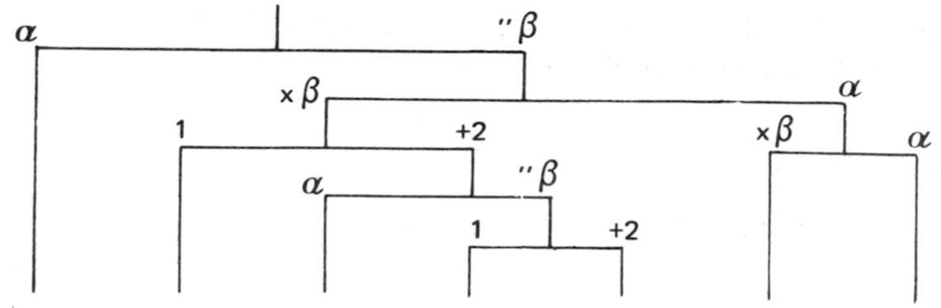

Figure 7-6 Constituent structure of preceding example

This can be represented as at the foot of the tree:

$\alpha \wedge \beta\beta 1 \wedge \beta\beta 2\alpha \wedge \beta\beta 2\beta 1 \wedge \beta\beta 2\beta 2 \wedge \beta\alpha\beta \wedge \beta\alpha\alpha$

or, using brackets (and showing type of interdependency), as:

$\alpha \wedge$ "$\beta\ (\times\beta\ (1 \wedge +2\ (\alpha \wedge$ "$\beta\ (1 \wedge +2)))) \wedge \alpha\ (\times\beta \wedge \alpha))$

The notation that is used here expresses both constituency and dependency at the same time: constituency by bracketing (using either brackets or repeated symbols), dependency by the letters of the Greek alphabet. A diagrammatic form of representation is illustrated in Figure 7-7:

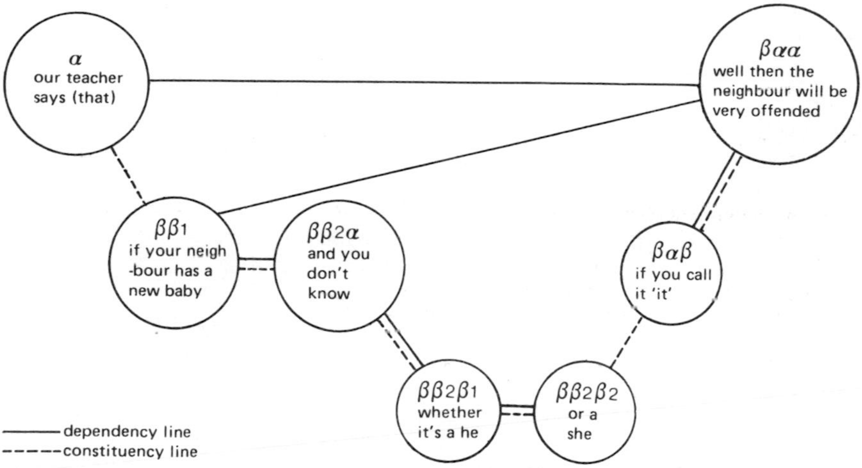

Figure 7-7 Alternative diagram for a clause complex

There is a reason for exploring these different types of notation. The clause complex is of particular interest in spoken language, because it represents the dynamic potential of the system — the ability to 'choreograph' very long and intricate patterns of semantic movement while maintaining a continuous flow of discourse that is coherent without being constructional. This kind of flow is very uncharacteristic of written language. Since grammatical theory evolved as the study of written language, it is good at synoptic-type 'product' representations, with constituency as the organizing concept, but bad at dynamic-type 'process' representations, which is what are needed for the interpretation of speech. A ball-and-chain picture of this kind is a small experiment in choreographic notation — something which unfortunately cannot be pursued further here.

Parataxis and hypotaxis are the two basic forms taken by logical relations in natural language. The terms in a logico-semantic relation are ordered by them as either equal (paratactic) or unequal (hypotactic).

The logico-semantic relations themselves, in the English clause complex, are the five listed in Section 7.2: 'i.e.', 'and', 'so . . .', 'says' and 'thinks'. These are, of course, generalized glosses designed to suggest the core meaning of the category; they should not be taken as definitions. We shall see later (Chapter 7 Additional) that they are not limited to the clause complex, but represent basic semantic motifs that run throughout the language as a whole.

These relations, which (when combined with parataxis and hypotaxis) constitute the 'logical' component of a natural language, are not reducible to elementary logical relations of a non-linguistic kind. As an example, consider the relation of 'and' in its paratactic environment. It was remarked above that 'pepper and salt' implies 'salt and pepper'; but this is not to say that the wordings *pepper and salt* and *salt and pepper* are synonymous — they are clearly not. There is a clear priority accorded to the one that comes first, as is shown by the fact that we do not say *butter and bread*; or rather we do say *butter and bread* — as a way of censuring someone who we consider has spread the butter too thickly: *that's not bread and butter, it's butter and bread!* Thus although each implies the other, they are not identical in meaning, because while parataxis is a symmetrical relationship, expansion is not. In a hypotactic environment even the implication does not hold, because hypotaxis itself is not symmetrical; thus there is a considerable semantic distance between the examples cited earlier (*besides undergoing the operation he also had to pay for it / besides having to pay for the operation he also underwent it*), despite the fact that one of the semantic features which this structure realizes is still that of 'and'.

It is important to interpret these 'logical' relationships in their own terms as part of the semantics of a language, and not to expect them to fit exactly into non-linguistic logical categories — although since the latter were derived from natural language in the first place there will obviously be a close relationship between the two.

7.4 Elaborating, extending, enhancing: three kinds of expansion

In Section 7.2 we introduced the notion of expansion: given a clause, in its multiple function as process, exchange and message, then this may enter into construction with another clause which is an expansion of it, the two together forming a clause complex.

It was suggested that there are essentially three ways of expanding a clause: elaborating it, extending it and enhancing it. For those who like similes (others should ignore the comparison), these could be compared with three ways of enriching a building: (i) elaborating its existing structure; (ii) extending it by addition or replacement; (iii) enhancing its environment.

1. Elaboration

In ELABORATION, one clause elaborates on the meaning of another by further specifying or describing it. The secondary clause does not introduce a new element into the picture but rather provides a further characterization of one that is already there, restating it, clarifying it, refining it, or adding a descriptive attribute or comment. The thing that is elaborated may be the primary clause as a whole, or it may be just some part of it — one or more of its constituents.

(1) Paratactic (notation 1 = 2). The combination of elaboration with parataxis yields three types, the first two of which could be regarded as APPOSITION between clauses:

(i)	exposition 'in other words'	P i.e. Q
(ii)	exemplification 'for example'	P e.g. Q
(iii)	clarification 'to be precise'	P viz. Q

(i) Exposition. Here the secondary clause restates the thesis of the primary clause in different words, to present it from another point of view, or perhaps just to reinforce the message; for example

> That clock doesn't go; it's not working.
> She wasn't a show dog; I didn't buy her as a show dog.
> Each argument was fatal to the other: both could not be true.

The relationship may be made explicit by conjunctive expressions such as *or (rather), in other words* or *that is to say*; or, in writing, *i.e.*

(ii) Exemplification. Here the secondary clause develops the thesis of the primary clause by becoming more specific about it, often citing an actual example; for example

> We used to have races — we used to have relays.
> Your face is the same as everybody else has — the two eyes so, nose in the middle, mouth under.

Here the explicit conjunctives are *for example*, *for instance*, *in particular*; or, in writing, *e.g.*

(iii) Clarification. In this case the secondary clause clarifies the thesis of the primary clause, backing it up with some form of explanation or explanatory comment.

> Alice could only look puzzled: she was thinking of the pudding.
> They weren't show animals; we just had them as pets.
> He never said anything to her; in fact his last remark was evidently addressed to a tree.

I wasn't surprised — it was what I had expected.

Expressions such as *in fact*, *actually*, *indeed*, *at least* are common in this type; the nearest written abbreviation is again *i.e.*, or sometimes *viz.*

The conjunctives are not structural markers of the paratactic relationship; they are cohesive rather than structural (see Chapter 9 below). Very often the two clauses are simply juxtaposed. This often makes it difficult to decide, in spoken language, whether they form a clause complex or not; but if the rhythm and intonation are maintained, and the semantic relationship of elaboration is clearly present, this can be taken as a criterion for treating them as such. In written language the apposition may be signalled by a special punctuation mark, the colon; but this is a fairly recent innovation, never very consistently used, and the lack of any clear structure signal is no doubt the reason why the abbreviations *i.e.*, *e.g.* and *viz.* were first introduced and continue to be used.

(2) Hypotactic (notation $\alpha = \beta$). The combination of elaboration with hypotaxis gives the category of NON-DEFINING RELATIVE CLAUSE (also called 'non-restrictive', 'descriptive'). This functions as a kind of descriptive gloss to the primary clause, as in

They decided to cancel the show, which upset everybody alike.

These dependent clauses may be either finite or non-finite. We will consider these two in turn.

(i) Finite. If the secondary clause is finite, it has the same form as a defining relative clause of the WH- type (see Chapter 6, Section 6.2.2 above). It differs from a defining relative clause, however, in two ways: there is a distinction in the meaning, and there is a corresponding distinction in the expression, both in speech and in writing.

As far as the meaning is concerned, these clauses do not define subsets, in the way that a defining relative clause does. In *the only plan which might have succeeded* the defining clause *which might have succeeded* specifies a particular subset of the general class of plans. A non-defining relative clause, on the other hand, adds a further characterization of something that is taken to be already fully specific. This 'something', therefore, is not necessarily just a noun; the domain of a non-defining relative may be a whole clause, as in the example above, or any of its constituents. It is helpful to treat them under three headings, although these are not sub-types, simply convenient groupings:

(a) Clauses with *which* whose domain is either the whole of the primary clause or some part of it that is more than a nominal group; e.g.

If I ever did fall off — which there's no chance of . . .
From then on we started winning prizes, which turned out to be very easy

meaning 'there is no chance of my falling off', 'winning prizes turned out to be easy'. Here the sequence is always $\alpha\,\hat{}\, = \beta$.

(b) Clauses with *which* (occasionally *that*), *who* or *whose* whose domain is a nominal group; e.g.

She was hard at work on the white kitten, which was lying quite still.

This meant allowing the Commission to raise charges on these lines to the point where they would pay for themselves — which charges would probably be more than the traffic could bear anyway.

When the nominal group is non-final in the primary clause, the secondary clause is often enclosed, so as to follow immediately after it, as in

Inflation, which was necessary for the system, became also lethal.

Parliament, whose historic role was to make laws, vote taxes and redress grievances, allowed the redress of industrial grievances to be mooted and contested elsewhere.

The mouse, who seemed to be a person of authority among them, called out.

Here the structure is α « = β »; the angle brackets denote enclosure, doubled as always where the delimited element is a clause.

(c) Clauses with *when* or *where*, having as domain some expression of time or place, e.g.

The first few days are a time for adjustment, when the kitten needs all the love and attention you can give it.

Have you been to Wensleydale, where the cheese comes from?

The meaning is 'which is when . . .,' 'which is where . . .'. Those with *where* often refer to abstract space, as in

Now consider the opposite situation, where the velocity decreases.

In this group also the secondary clause may be enclosed, as in

In winter, when the fields are white,
I sing this song for your delight.

As far as their expression is concerned, non-defining relative clauses are clearly signalled both in speech and in writing. In written English, a non-defining relative clause is marked off by punctuation — usually commas, but sometimes by being introduced with a dash; whereas a defining relative clause is not separated by punctuation from its antecedent. This in turn reflects the fact that in spoken English, whereas a defining relative clause enters into a single tone group together with its antecedent, a non-defining relative forms a separate tone group. Furthermore, the primary and secondary clauses are linked by TONE CONCORD: that is to say, they are spoken on the same tone. For example, in *if I ever did fall off — which there's no chance of*, the tone would probably be tone 4, falling-rising:

//4 if I / ever / **did** fall / off //4 ‸ which there's / no / **chance** of //

while in *have you been to Wensleydale, where the cheese comes from?*

//2 have you / been to / **Wensley**/dale where the //2 **cheese** / comes from //

both clauses would have tone 2, rising.* More specifically, the secondary clause is in tone concord with that part of the primary clause that constitutes its domain. Thus where the secondary clause is enclosed, a typical sequence would be 4 – 4 – 1, as in

//4 ‸ in/**flation** //4 ‸ which was / necessary for the **system** // 1 ‸ became / also / **lethal** //

Here the concord is between the secondary clause and its antecedent *inflation*, both of which have tone 4; this tone suggests that they are non-final, and the sequence is then completed with a tone 1. Whichever tone is used, however, it will be the same in both parts; the tone selected for the (relevant portion of the) primary clause is repeated in the secondary clause. This tone concord is the principal signal of the apposition relationship in English, and applies also to paratactic clause complexes of exposition and exemplification referred to above.

There is one group of non-defining relative clauses which strictly speaking would belong with extension rather then elaboration; for example,

She told it to the baker's wife, who told it to the cook.

Here the *who* stands for 'and she' and the clause is semantically an additive. Compare also (where the sense is 'and in that case'):

It might be hungry, in which case it would be very likely to eat her up.

Note that such instances are not characterized by tone concord. Also extending rather than elaborating are possessives with *whose* or its variants (*of whom/which*), which do not further characterize the noun that constitutes their domain but add a new one related to it by possession; contrast elaborating *come and meet Mary, whose birthday we're celebrating* ('the girl whose . . .') with extending *the shop was taken over by an Indian, whose family came out to join him*. But for most purposes these and all other non-defining relatives can be treated as elaborating clauses.

(ii) Non-finite. Here the same semantic relationship obtains as with the finites, and again the domain may be one nominal group or some larger segment of the primary clause, up to the whole clause. For example:

I worked for a local firm at that time, selling office equipment.

It's my own invention — to keep clothes and sandwiches in.

The hairy coat holds a layer of air close to the skin, insulating the body against changes in the outside temperature.

There was a real fire there, blazing away just as brightly.

These also contrast with defining clauses, as in *I needed something to keep sandwiches in*, *she met some people just leaving the building*, where *to keep sandwiches in*, *just leaving the building* are embedded as Postmodifier, and

* In British English this would be likely to be the 'sharp fall-rise' variant, tone *2*, signalling *Wensleydale* as New (see Chapter 8 below).

do not form a separate tone group — there is no tonic on *something*, *people*. Again the non-defining clause does form a separate tone group, usually with tone concord; and again there is the corresponding distinction in the punctuation.

As is usual with non-finite clauses, the meaning is less specific; both the domain and the semantic relationship to it are left relatively inexplicit. There is no WH- form, as there is with the finites; nor is there usually any preposition acting conjunctively, as there typically is with non-finite clauses of extension and enhancement such as *besides* or *on* in *besides selling office equipment*, *on leaving the building*. There may be an explicit Subject in the dependent clause, as in

John went off by himself, the rest of us staying behind.

It's a much bigger house, for the children to have their own rooms.

But in most instances the Subject is left implicit, to be presupposed from the primary clause; and it is often difficult to identify it exactly — e.g. is it the hairy coat which insulates the body, or is it the holding of a layer of air close to the skin? The question is really irrelevant; it is precisely the function of the non-finite to make it unnecessary to decide.

2. Extension

In EXTENSION, one clause extends the meaning of another by adding something new to it. What is added may be just an addition, or a replacement, or an alternative. The principal categories are as set out in Table 7(3).

Table 7(3) Categories of extension

Category	Meaning
(i) addition	
'and', additive: positive	X and Y
'nor', additive: negative	not X and not Y
'but', adversative	X and conversely Y
(ii) variation	
'instead', replacive	not X but Y
'except', subtractive	X but not all X
'or', alternative	X or Y

(1) Paratactic (notation 1 +2). The combination of extension with parataxis yields what is known as CO-ORDINATION between clauses. It is typically expressed by *and*, *nor*, *or*, *but*.

(i) Addition. Here one process is simply adjoined to another; there is no implication of any causal or temporal relationship between them. For example,

I breed the poultry, and my husband looks after the garden.
I said you *looked* like an egg, sir; and some eggs are very pretty, you know.

The referents of the two processes may be related in the world of experience; if they share the same semiotic plane then they must be, at the very least by simultaneity or succession, but this is not represented as a semantic feature. An example of an adversative would be:

We liked that breed of dog, but we felt we weren't in a position to own one at the time.*

Paratactic additions are often accompanied by cohesive expressions such as *too, in addition, also, moreover, on the other hand.*

(ii) Variation. Here one clause is presented as being in total or partial replacement of another:

Don't stand there chattering to yourself like that, but tell me your name and your business.

They did a good job, only they were so slow about it.

I would have let you know, only I couldn't find your phone number.

The meaning is 'instead of' or 'except for'. Note that the *but* here is not adversative, and so is not replaceable by *yet*; nor is it concessive — it does not correspond to hypotactic *although* (see subsection 3 below). Cohesive expressions used with total replacement include *instead, on the contrary.*

In the alternative type one clause is offered as alternative to another:

Either you go ahead and take the plunge or you wait till you think you can afford it, which you never will.

The associated cohesive conjunctions include *conversely, alternatively, on the other hand.*

(2) Hypotactic (notation $\alpha = \beta$). The combination of extension with hypotaxis also embraces addition, replacement and alternation, but with the extending clause dependent. The dependent clause may be finite or non-finite.

(i) Finite. Hypotactic clauses of addition are introduced by the conjunctions *whereas, while,* as in

While his disappearance was proof that he hadn't wanted her, the five hundred pounds he had spent on the ring was indication that he had wanted something else.

Broad Chalke (Wilts), with a population of a mere 560, has a doctor and surgery in the village, whereas many places with over twice that number are sometimes lucky even to have a weekly surgery held by a visiting doctor.

The executioner, the King and the Queen were all talking at once, while all the rest were quite silent.

There is no clear line between the additive and the adversative; these clauses sometimes have an adversative component, sometimes not.

There is no finite form for replacement. For subtraction the finite clause is introduced by *except that, but (for the fact) that*; e.g.

---

* Note that *but* contains the semantic feature 'and', so we do not say *and but*. For the same reason we do not say *although . . . but*, because that would be a mixture of hypotaxis and parataxis; whereas *although . . . yet* is quite normal — there is no 'and' in *yet*.

He kept on pretty well, except that he had a habit of now and then falling off sideways.

Finite clauses with *whereas*, *while*, *except that*, if they follow the primary clause, have a strongly paratactic flavour (cf. on *because*, *though* in subsection 3 below). The line between parataxis and hypotaxis is not very sharp; as a working rule, if the extending clause could precede (thereby becoming thematic in the clause complex), the relationship is hypotactic. An example where the extending clause could not precede is

He pretended to know all about it — whereas in fact he had no idea of what was happening.

This would be interpreted as paratactic. In such instances the conjunction is always unaccented.

The hypotactic form of the alternative relation is *if . . . not*. For example,

If you haven't lost it, then it's in that cupboard

'either you've lost it, or else it's in that cupboard'. These can be recognized because it does not matter which of the alternatives is treated as the negative condition; we could just as well say *if it's not in that cupboard then you've lost it*.

(ii) Non-finite. The non-finite form of extension is an imperfective clause which is often, though not always, introduced by a preposition functioning conjunctively, such as *besides*, *instead of*. If there is no conjunctive preposition, the form is identical with an elaborating one. Examples of addition:

(a) (additive)

Besides missing the wedding she had to spend the whole week in hospital.

We used to go away at the weekend, taking all our gear with us.

So she wandered on, talking to herself as she went.

Note that, when the sequence is $\beta \wedge \alpha$, a non-finite clause without preposition is usually enhancing rather than extending; this can be established by adding a conjunctive preposition such as *on* (temporal), *by* (manner), *with* (causal), e.g. *(on) leaving the ramparts you come to a fortified tower*, *(by) helping others you also help yourself*, *(with) leaving it so late we missed the best bargains*. (See subsection 4 below.)

(b) (adversative)

Maintain adequate forward momentum, without letting the wheels spin.

Hardly knowing what she did, she picked up a little bit of stick and held it out to the puppy.

The players all played at once, without waiting for turns.

With a non-finite clause of variation, there is always a conjunctive preposition; for example

(replacive)
Instead of just working for a living you could be sitting on your backside all day.
(subtractive)
You won't get rid of it, other than giving it away.

Table 7(4) gives a summary of the markers of extension:

Table 7(4) Principal markers of extending clauses

	Paratactic	Hypotactic	
		finite	non-finite
(i) addition			
'and', positive	(both . . .) and; not only . . . but also	while, whereas	besides, apart from, as well as
'nor', negative	(neither . . .) nor	—	—
'but', adversative	(and) yet; but	while, whereas	without
(ii) variation			
'instead', replacive	but not; not . . . but	—	instead of, rather than
'except', subtractive	only, but, except	except that	except for, other than
(iii) alternation			
'or', alternative	(either . . .) or (else)	if . . . not (. . . then)	—

3. Enhancement

In ENHANCEMENT one clause enhances the meaning of another by qualifying it in one of a number of possible ways: by reference to time, place, manner, cause or condition.

The principal categories are set out in Table 7(5).

Table 7(5) Principal types of enhancement

Category	Meaning
(i) temporal	
same time	A meanwhile B
different time: later	A subsequently B
different time: earlier	A previously B
(ii) spatial	
same place	C there D
(iii) manner	
means	N is via/by means of M
comparison	N is like M
(iv) causal-conditional	
cause: reason	because P so result Q
cause: purpose	because intention Q so action P
condition: positive	if P then Q
condition: negative	if not P then Q
condition: concessive	if P then contrary to expectation Q

(1) Paratactic (notation 1 ×2). The combination of enhancement with parataxis yields what is also a kind of co-ordination but with a circumstantial feature incorporated into it. It is typically expressed (a) by the conjunctions *then*, *so*, *for*, *but*, *yet*, *still*; (b) by a conjunction group with *and*: *and then*, *and there*, *and thus*, *and so*, *and yet*; or (c) by *and* in combination with a conjunctive (that is, a conjunctive expression that is not structural but cohesive) such as *at that time*, *soon afterwards*, *till then*, *in that case*, *in that way*. Note also that some conjunctives, such as *meanwhile*, *otherwise*, *therefore*, *however*, *nevertheless*, are extending their use in modern spoken English so as to become structural conjunctions; in this function they are unaccented (spoken without salience). Some examples are given below.

(i) temporal
same time

It's the Cheshire Cat: now I shall have somebody to talk to.

later time

The three soldiers wandered about for a minute of two, and then quietly marched off after the others.

She floated gently down without ever touching the stairs with her feet; then she floated on through the hall.

(ii) spatial
same place

Alice looked up, and there stood the Queen in front of them.

(iii) manner
means

Keep on subtracting the difference, and in that way you will arrive at the correct figure.

comparison

She likes the simple life, and so does he.

(iv) causal–conditional
cause: reason/purpose
(a) cause ^ effect

Alice didn't want to begin another argument, so she said nothing.

(b) effect ^ cause

Alice was standing with her hands ready, for she was any moment expecting him to fall.

condition: positive

the ends of his mouth might meet behind, and then I don't know what would happen to his head.

condition: negative

I like to follow up one line at a time, otherwise there's a muddle.

condition: concessive
(a) concession ^ consequence

It looked good-natured; still it had *very* long claws and a great many teeth.

(b) consequence ^ concession

Evidently Humpty Dumpty was very angry, though he said nothing for a minute or two.

A typical sequence of paratactic clauses of this kind, each marked with a specific 'enhancing' conjunction, is the following:

I had to write this play for Mrs Grundie but I got it wrong so I had to re-write it all again and then she got really interested in it.

Here the structure is clearly $1\ \times 2\ \times 3\ \times 4$.

Frequently however a sequence of paratactic clauses which have to be interpreted as being in some circumstantial relation to each other, especially a temporal sequence, is marked simply by *and*, without any further conjunctive expression; e.g. *I got the interest and started showing and I got another dog and started breeding* . . . It could be argued that these are 'enhancement' by time, since the events described take place in a time sequence. However, the speaker could have used *then* (and had done, in fact, in the immediately preceding discourse: *so I bought one as a pet, and then it progressed from there*). For most purposes therefore it seems preferable to analyse such instances as extending, treating 'and' as in some sense the unmarked form of the expansion type.

Certain conjunctions that are normally hypotactic ('subordinating con-unctions'), especially *when*, *till*, *because* and *though*, often occur in what eems closer to a paratactic function; e.g. *For a minute or two she stood look-ng at the house, and wondering what to do next, when suddenly a footman in very came running out of the wood.* We return to these following the discus-ion of hypotaxis below.

Typical markers of paratactic categories are given in the following table, 'able 7(6).

Note that the conjunctives such as *afterwards*, *nevertheless*, *in that way* are imply examples of a large class of expressions that can co-occur with *and* in is context (see Chapter 9 below).

able 7(6) Principal markers of paratactic enhancement

(i) temporal	
same time	(and) meanwhile; (when)
different time: later	(and) then; and + afterwards:
different time: earlier	and/but + before that/first
(ii) spatial	
same place	and there
(iii) manner	
means	and + in that way; (and) thus
comparison: positive	and + similarly; (and) so, thus
iv) causal–conditional	
cause ^ effect	(and) so; and + therefore
effect ^ cause	for; (because)
condition: positive	(and) then; and + in that case
condition: negative	or else; (or) otherwise
concession ^ consequence	but; (and) yet, still; but + nevertheless
consequence ^ concession	(though) *

There are thus three distinct meanings of *but*: (i) adversative, as in *they're pretty, but I can't grow them* ('on the other hand'); (ii) replacive, as in *don't drown them, but give them just enough* ('instead'); (iii) concessive, as in *I can't grow them, but I keep trying* ('nevertheless'). Only the last embodies a logical opposition between the two terms.

(2) Hypotactic (notation $\alpha \times \beta$). The combination of enhancement with ypotaxis gives what are known in traditional formal grammar as 'adverbial auses'. As with parataxis, these are clauses of time, place, manner, cause, ondition and concession. They may be finite or non-finite.

The finite ones are introduced by a hypotactic conjunction ('subordinating onjunction'). The non-finite are introduced either (a) by a preposition such s *on*, *with*, *by* functioning conjunctively — note that sometimes the same ord is both conjunction and conjunctive preposition, e.g. *before*, *after*; or) by one of a subset of the hypotactic conjunctions — there are a few of ese, such as *when*, which can function also with a non-finite clause. The ost usual of these conjunctions and conjunctive prepositions are listed gether in a single table, Table 7(7).

Table 7(7) Principal markers of hypotactic enhancing clauses

	Finite	Non-finite	
	conjunction	conjunction	preposition
(i) temporal			
same time: extent	as, while	while	in (the course/process of)
same time: point	when, as soon as, the moment	when	on
same time; spread	whenever, every time		
different time: later	after, since	since	after
different time; earlier	before, until/till	until	before
(ii) spatial			
same place: extent	as far as		
same place: point	where		
same place: spread	wherever, everywhere		
(iii) manner			
means			by (means of)
comparison	as, as if, like, the way	like	
(iv) causal-conditional			
cause: reason	because, as, since, in case, seeing that, considering		with, through, by, at, as a result of, because of, in case of,
cause: purpose	in order that, so that		(in order/so as) to; for (the sake of), with the aim of, for fear of
condition: positive	if, provided that, as long as	if	in the event of
condition: negative	unless	unless	but for, without
condition: concessive	even if, although	even if, although	despite, in spite of, without

(i) Finite. The following are some examples of hypotactic enhancing clauses which are finite:

He lives there while he's on the job
He grinned almost from ear to ear, as he leant forwards
When she had come close to it, she saw that it was Humpty Dumpty himself.
As soon as she had recovered her breath a little, she called out to the White King.
Whenever the horse stopped, he fell off in front.
We've hardly seen him since he got his new bike.
She did not venture to go near the house till she had brought herself down to nine inches high.
As far as I can tell nothing has changed.
Blisters formed wherever the spray had touched the skin.
He talks about it just as if it was a game.
It wasn't at all like conversation, as he never said anything to her.
I carry it upside down, so that the rain can't get in
I carry it upside down in case the rain gets in.
I shouldn't know you again if we *did* meet.
That's the last one, unless you've got some hidden away somewhere.
The way things are going we'll all be out of a job.

With a finite clause, the conjunction serves to express both the dependency (the hypotactic status) and the circumstantial relationship. As well as simple conjunctions such as *because*, *when*, *if*, and conjunction groups like *as if*, *even if*, *soon after*, *so that*, there are three kinds of complex conjunction, one derived from verbs, one from nouns and the third from adverbs.

(a) Verbal conjunctions are derived from the imperative or from the present/active or past/passive participle + (optionally) *that*: *provided (that)*, *seeing (that/how)*, *suppose/supposing (that)*, *granted (that)*, *say (that)*. In origin these are projections; their function as expanding conjunction reflects the semantic overlap between expansion and projection in the realm of 'irrealis' (see subsection 4 below): 'let us say/think that . . .' = 'if . . .', as in *say they can't mend it, shall I just throw it away*?

(b) Nominal conjunctions include *in case*, *in the event that*, *to the extent that*, and *the* + various nouns of time or manner, e.g. *the day*, *the moment*, *the way*. These last have evolved from prepositional phrases with the enhancing clause embedded in them, e.g. *on the day when we arrived*; but they now function to introduce hypotactic clauses just like other conjunctions, e.g. *their daughter was born the day we arrived*, *the way they're working now the job'll be finished in a week*.

(c) Adverbial conjunctions are *as/so long as*, *as/so far as*, *(as) much as*, e.g. *as long as you're here . . .*, *as far as I know . . .*, *much as I'd like to . . .* (compare non-finite *as well as*, which is extending not enhancing). In origin these express limitation, a particular point up to which a certain circumstance is valid.

(ii) Non-finite. Some examples of non-finite enhancing clauses:

They must be crazy, throwing all that good stuff away.
Being somewhat irritated by the whole procedure he induced a fit of coughing and left.
To claim your rebate simply fill in the voucher and post it to us.

Turn off the lights before leaving.
While pondering which way to go I completely lost my bearings.
Despite adequate notice being given there were still many applicants disappointed.
You won't get away without the work being completed.

A non-finite dependent clause frequently presupposes its subject from the dominant clause. But if instead it has an explicit Subject of its own, this Subject appears in oblique (e.g. *him*) or possessive (e.g. *his*) form:

(In order) for him to be away everyone works harder [perfective].
With him/his being away everyone works harder [imperfective].

Where possible (i.e. in the imperfective) formal etiquette prescribes the possessive, which reflects the earlier status of these non-finite clauses as embedded; but the current form is the 'oblique' case (distinct from 'nominative' only in the words *him her me us them*), showing that these clauses are now not embedded but dependent.

If the dependent clause is non-finite, the circumstantial relationship is made explicit by the conjunction or conjunctive preposition. The conjunctions are a subset of those occurring in finite clauses, and their meaning is essentially the same. The prepositions tend to be somewhat less specific, e.g. *in turning the corner*, *on thinking it over*, *with you being away*, *without John knowing*; and the meaning of the clause introduced by a preposition may vary according to the sense of the primary clause:

Without having been there I can't say what happened
(cause: reason 'because I wasn't there')

Without having been there I know all that happened
(condition: adversative 'although I wasn't there')

Without having been there I rather like the place
(indeterminate)

Nevertheless it is usually possible to assign these clauses to the categories of time, manner and cause, and to match the prepositions up in a general way with the conjunctions, as in Table 7(7) above. In one instance the conjunctive prepositions incorporate a further distinction that is not made by the corresponding conjunction: compare

With leaving out two questions she failed the exam.
By leaving out two questions she (was able to concentrate on what she knew best and so) passed the exam.

Both of these correspond to the finite *because she left out two questions*; but whereas the first expresses an unintended consequence, the second expresses an intended one.

4. Expansion clauses that are not explicitly marked for any logical-semantic relation

Two kinds of problem arise in analysis, one with finite the other with non-finite clauses.

A finite clause is in principle independent; it becomes dependent only if ntroduced by a binding (hypotactic) conjunction. If it is joined in a clause omplex, its natural status is paratactic. In this case its logical-semantic relaionship to its neighbour is in principle shown by a linking (paratactic) onjunction.

Frequently however two or more finite clauses with no conjunction in them re nonetheless related by expansion; and this is recognized in writing by their eing punctuated as one sentence. Typically in such instances the relation is ne of elaboration as described above. But in both spoken and written nglish we find unconjoined sequences which seem to be functioning as lause complexes, yet which do not seem to be restricted to the elaborating ype. Here is an example from spontaneous speech, with the clauses related y expansion marked off by commas:

> At the last meeting somebody almost got drowned, he was practising rescuing somebody, no-one had really shown how to do it, he had to be dragged out by some of the older lads, nobody really thought it was that bad, they just thought he'd got cramp or something.

gnoring the projections, there are six clauses, of which only the first and the ast pairs seem to be linked by elaboration. There are two ways of approachng this situation. One is to say 'wherever I could recognize a relation of xtension or enchancement, as shown by the possibility of inserting a conunction without changing the logical-semantic relation, I will do so'; this vould suggest re-wording along the lines of:

||| At the last meeting somebody almost got drowned; || he was practising rescuing
1 $=2$
somebody, || 'but' no-one had really shown how to do it, || 'so' he had to be
$+3\alpha$ $3'\beta$
dragged out by some of the older lads. ||| Nobody really thought it was that
x4 1α $1'\beta$
bad; || they just thought he'd got cramp or something |||
$=2\alpha$ $2'\beta$

The alternative is to say 'if the speaker had wanted to relate these by extension r enhancement he could have done so; he didn't, so I will treat them as emantically unrelated, whatever the sequence of the events to which they efer'. This would give

||| At the last meeting somebody almost got drowned; || he was practising rescuing
1 $=2$
somebody. ||| No-one had really shown how to do it. ||| He had to be dragged out
1 $1'\beta$
by some of the older lads. ||| Nobody really thought it was that bad; || they just
$1'\alpha$ $1'\beta$
thought he'd got cramp or something |||
$=2\alpha$ $2'\beta$

This latter principle is the same as that invoked with reference to the interpreation of *and* in subsection 3 above.

A non-finite clause, on the other hand, is by its nature dependent, simply by virtue of being non-finite. It typically occurs, therefore, without any other explicit marker of its dependent status. Hence when a non-finite clause occurs without a conjunction, there is no doubt about its hypotactic relation in a clause complex; but there may be no indication of its logical-semantic function. Here therefore the same question arises, with examples such as

Alice walked on in silence, puzzling over the idea.

And they trotted off, Alice repeating to herself the words of the old song.

He scrambled back into the saddle, keeping hold of Alice's hair with one hand.

Unlike the finites, however, these cannot be assigned unmarkedly to just one category; they may be elaborating or extending, and even enhancing, given the appropriate context. The best solution here is to find the nearest finite form. If this is a non-defining relative clause, the non-finite is elaborating. If it is a co-ordinate clause, the non-finite is extending. If it is an enhancing clause, the non-finite is enhancing and could probably be introduced by a conjunctive preposition. For example:

He left the house, closing the door behind him.
and closed the door . . . [extending]

I worked for a local firm, selling office equipment
; I sold . . . ('I was doing some work, which was . . .') [elaborating]

Not wanting to offend, Mary kept quiet.
Because she did not want . . . [enhancing]

Having said goodbye, John went home.
After he had said . . . [enhancing]

Some precipitation is expected, falling as snow over high ground.
which will fall . . . [elaborating]

The Sonora road was opened by Mexican explorers, supplanting the Anza trail.
and supplanted . . . [extending]

Instances such as those quoted earlier, e.g. *Alice walked on in silence, puzzling over the idea*, illustrate an area of overlap between extension and enhancement; they can be interpreted as 'while'-type temporals (same time extent), but unless the simultaneous time factor is foregrounded, as it is perhaps in the last one (*he scrambled back into the saddle, 'while' keeping hold of Alice's hair with one hand*), they are probably best treated as straightforward 'and'-type additives.

Finally we should note the distinction between the two aspects of the non-finite clause, imperfective and perfective. The imperfective represents the real, or actual, mode of non-finiteness ('realis'), while the perfective represents the unreal, or potential, mode ('irrealis'). So for example

Reaching the monument, continue straight ahead. (imperfective)
To reach the monument, continue straight ahead. (perfective)

Historically the imperfective combined with the preposition 'at, in' (*a-*

doing), and meant 'act in progress'; hence real, actual, present, ongoing, steady state or (dependent) proposition. The perfective combined — and still does — with the preposition 'to', and meant 'goal to be attained'; hence unreal, potential, future, starting and stopping, change of state or (dependent) proposal (for further discussion see Chapter 7 Additional below.) As a hypotactic clause of expansion, therefore, the perfective expresses purpose, and *to* can function on its own as a conjunctive preposition. All other non-finite expansions are imperfective.

5. Embedded expansions

In Chapter 6 we discussed embedding, the 'rank shift' by which a clause or phrase comes to function within the structure of a group, like *who came to dinner* in *the man who came to dinner*. We represent embedded clauses as ⟦ ⟧, embedded phrases as [ ]:

the man ⟦ who came to dinner ⟧ / ⟦ coming to dinner ⟧
the man [in the iron mask]

The characteristic function of an embedded element is as Postmodifier in a nominal group, as in the above examples. Other functions are: as Head of a nominal group (i.e. as a nominalization), e.g. *that you're sorry* in *that you're sorry isn't enough*; and as a Postmodifier in an adverbial group, e.g. *as you can* in *as quickly as you can*. These are summarized in Table 7(8). All embedding falls into one or other of these major categories; there are no further types. It should be remembered that the category of nominal group includes those having adjective (Epithet) as Head, e.g. *so big that we couldn't carry it*, where ⟦ *that we couldn't carry it* ⟧ is embedded.

It is important to distinguish between embedding on the one hand and the 'tactic' relations of parataxis and hypotaxis on the other. Whereas parataxis and hypotaxis are relations BETWEEN clauses (or other ranking elements; see Section 7.6 below), embedding is not. Embedding is a mechanism whereby a clause or phrase comes to function as a constituent WITHIN the structure of a group, which itself is a constituent of a clause. Hence there is no direct relationship between an embedded clause and the clause within which it is embedded; the relationship of an embedded clause to the 'outer' clause is an indirect one, with a group as intermediary. The embedded clause functions in the structure of the group, and the group functions in the structure of the clause.*

As always, the fact that the two categories are clearly distinct in principle does not mean that every instance can be definitively assigned to one or the other on some fixed and easily identifiable criterion. The vast majority of instances are clear; but there are anomalous and borderline cases which are

* Where the embedded element functions as Head, we may leave out the intermediate (nominal group) step in the analysis and represent the embedded clause or phrase as functioning directly in the structure of the outer clause, as Subject or whatever. This is a notational simplification; it does not affect the status of the embedded element as a nominalization. Note that this still does not make it resemble hypotaxis; in hypotaxis one clause is dependent on another, but in no sense is it a constituent part of it.

Table 7(8) Types of embedding (rank shift)

	In nominal group	In adverbial group
As Postmodifier clause:		
finite	the house ⟦ that Jack built ⟧	sooner ⟦ than we had expected ⟧
non-finite	the house ⟦ being built by Jack ⟧	sooner ⟦ than expected ⟧
phrase	the house [by the bridge]	sooner [than the rest of us]
As Head clause:		
finite	⟦ what Jack built ⟧	
non-finite	⟦ for Jack to build a house ⟧	
phrase	[by the bridge]	

bound to cause difficulty. We shall attempt to describe and illustrate the categories as explicitly as possible in what follows.

Like clauses in a paratactic or hypotactic relation, an embedded element may also be either an expansion or a projection. Embedded projections are discussed in Section 7.5, subsection 5 below. Here we are concerned with expansions. All the examples cited above were examples of expansion.

The meaning of a embedded clause, or phrase, that is functioning as an expansion is essentially to define, delimit or specify. Thus the characteristic embedded expansion is the 'defining relative clause' (also called 'restrictive'), like *that Jack built* in *the house that Jack built*. It function is to specify which member or members of the class designated by the Head noun, in this instance *house*, is or are being referred to. Similarly in the following examples *that ever were invented* defines *poems*, and *(who is) taking the pictures* defines *girl.*

(this is) the house	⟦that Jack built⟧
(I can explain) all the poems	⟦that ever were invented⟧
(do you know) the girl	⟦ (who is) taking the pictures ⟧

Figure 7-8 shows the analysis of a clause containing a nominal group containing an embedded clause. (The analysis is given in terms of Mood; the embedding could, of course, equally well be incorporated into an analysis in terms of transitivity.)

Within embedded clauses, the distinction that appeared in parataxis and hypotaxis, among the three categories of elaborating, extending and enhancing, is of very much less relevance. However, since the range of semantic relations is roughly equivalent, and since there are subcategories that need to be distinguished, it may be found helpful if we continue to refer to the same framework.

(i) Elaborating. The typical defining relative clause, introduced by *who*, *which*, *that*, or in its so-called 'contact clause' form without any relative marker (e.g. *he told* in *the tales he told*), is elaborating in sense. The relative element in the embedded clause restates the nominal antecedent; thus in

the man ⟦ who came to dinner ⟧ stayed for a month

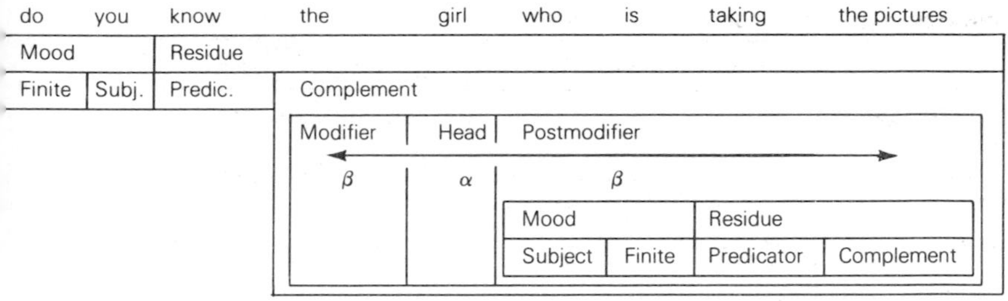

Figure 7-8 Analysis of a clause containing a nominal group with embedded clause as Postmodifier

the man who came to dinner and the man who stayed for a month are the same man. This is the same principle by which non-defining relatives are also elaborating in function; cf. subsection 1 above. The defining ones however do not form a separate tone group, because there is only one piece of information here, not two — *who came to dinner* is not news, but simply part of the characterization of that particular participant.

These clauses may be non-finite, as in *a voice* ⟦*choking with passion*⟧; note again the difference between imperfective and perfective, as in the following set:

(imperfective)
- (a) active — the person taking pictures — ('who is/was taking')
- (b) passive — the pictures taken by Mary — ('which were/are taken') (according to the tense of the outer clause)

(perfective)
- (a) active — the (best) person to take pictures — ('who ought to take'); the (best) pictures to take — ('which someone ought to take')
- (b) passive — the pictures to be taken — ('which are/were to be taken')

Glosses in parenthesis suggest the nearest equivalent finite form.

Note that in examples such as *the first person who came in*, *the best person to do the job*, the embedded clause strictly has as its domain not the Head noun *person* but a modifying element; the meaning is 'the first-who-came-in person', 'the best-to-do-the-job person'. Compare *a hard act to follow, the longest bridge ever built*. We can express this relationship structurally as in Figure 7-9:

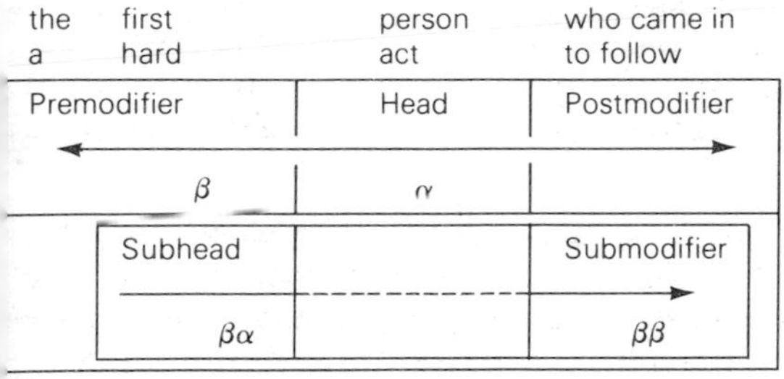
the
first
person
who came in
a
hard
act
to follow
Premodifier
Head
Postmodifier
β
α
Subhead
Submodifier
βα
ββ

Figure 7-9 Embedding on a Premodifier

But as already pointed out (Chapter 6, Section 6.4.1 above) constituency is not a very appropriate form for representing semantic domain, and for most purposes it suffices to show the clause simply as embedded in the nominal group: *a hard act* ⟦ *to follow* ⟧. More such examples will be found under 'enhancing' below.*

Although a non-finite embedded clause with a preposition is generally circumstantial in meaning, and hence enhancing, there is one other type (in addition to the perfectives with *to*, already noted) that is elaborating; namely those with *of* where the relation is appositive, e.g. *the job of cleaning the barracks* where the job consists in cleaning the barracks. Some of these are uncertain, e.g. *the advantage of shopping early, the trouble with asking directions* where shopping early, asking directions could be either elaborating (appositive) 'which consists in' or enhancing (circumstantial) 'which results from'.

In all the examples which have been discussed so far, the embedded clause functions as Postmodifier. It was pointed out in Chapter 6 that there are structures in which the Head is fused with the relative element in the embedded clause: this happens with *what*, meaning 'that which', and with *whoever, whatever, whichever* meaning 'anyone who, anything that/which', as in *what we want* 'the thing + that we want', *whoever gets there first* 'anyone / the one + who gets there first'. The effect of this fusion is that the embedded clause comes to function as Head, although it may be helpful to represent it separately in the analysis (Figure 7-10).

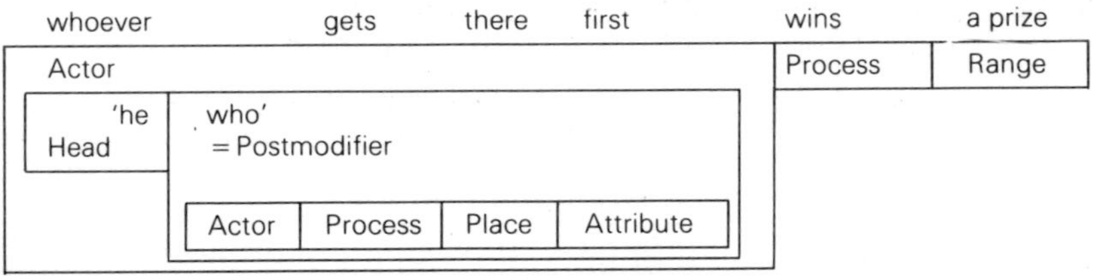

Figure 7-10 Elaborating embedded clause (finite) as Head

For a further type of embedded clause functioning as Head see subsection 6 below.

(ii) Extending. There are no embedded clauses corresponding to the paratactic and hypotactic categories of addition, replacement and alternation (and, or, instead, except).

The only sense of extension which produces embedded clauses is that of possession, introduced by *whose* or *of which*:

* Note the distinction between *a better person to do that would be Mary*, where ⟦to do that⟧ is embedded on the Premodifier *better*, and *you'd have to be a better person to do that* where *to do that* is a hypotactic × β clause of purpose 'in order to (be able to) do that' (i.e. 'only if you were a better person could you do that').

the people + ⟦ whose house we rented ⟧
that song + ⟦ I can never remember the words of ⟧

The category of possessive in the non-defining relative clauses was referred to in subsection 2 above; these are the equivalent in the 'defining' type.

(iii) Enhancing. Here the relation between the embedded clause and the Head noun is a circumstantial one of time, place, manner, cause or condition. This may happen in two ways, giving two sub-types: (a) those where the circumstantial sense is in the Head noun, (b) those where it is in the embedded Postmodifying clause.

(a) Here the Head noun is one of a class which expresses a circumstantial relation, e.g. *time*, *place*, *way*, *reason*, *purpose*. Such nouns are inherently 'enhancing' in sense; the specific semantic feature may or may not be picked up in the following conjunction: *the time when* . . . or *the time (that)* . . ., *the reason why* . . . or *the reason (that)* . . ., etc. The embedded clause may be finite or non-finite. Examples of finite are:

the reason ⟦ why I like her ⟧ (is she doesn't have favourites)
(that must have been) the first occasion ⟦ when professionals took part ⟧
the only other place ⟦ I would want to live ⟧ (is New Zealand)

Note the different analyses of the following:

||| the time you phoned || I was in the bath |||
$\times\beta$ α
'when you phoned': hypotactic clause complex

||| the time =⟦ I like best ⟧ is the hour before dawn |||
'the time which I like best': elaborating embedded clause

||| the time ×⟦ you should leave ⟧ is when they start yawning |||
'the time when you should leave': enhancing embedded clause

Examples of non-finite embedded clauses:

(there is) no reason ⟦ to expect anything different ⟧
the purpose ⟦ of keeping bees ⟧ (is to increase the honey supply)
the best way ⟦ to find out ⟧ is to ask

As usual the imperfective is associated with the actual (e.g. *the time of planting*) and the perfective with the virtual (e.g. *the time to plant*) — obligation, purpose, prediction, hypothesis and so on. But this may be overridden by the lexical meaning of the Head noun, e.g. *purpose* (*the purpose of* . . . *ing*); and the combination of *for* + imperfective also expresses purpose, in the sense of destiny (*the best time for* . . . *ing*).

The typical context for nominal groups of this kind is in circumstantial relational processes where the circumstantial meaning of time, place, etc. is encoded as a participant (cf. Chapter 5, Section 5.4; see especially Table 5(5), II/2(a)). In an identifying clause the other participant in the Token – Value relation is often another enhancing clause, also embedded, but as Head not Postmodifier. An example is given in Figure 7-11.

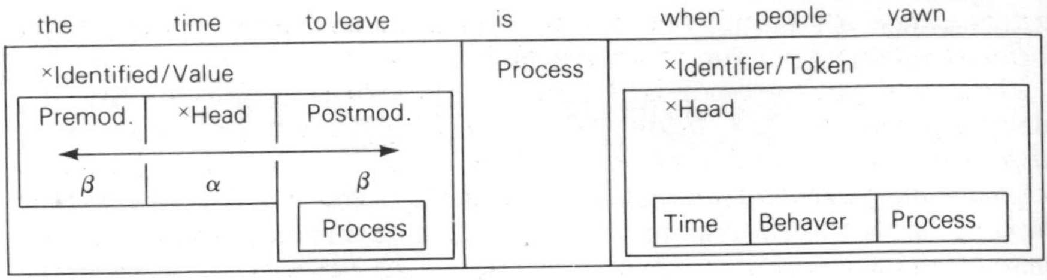

Figure 7-11 Circumstantial identifying clause with embedded enhancing clauses

(b) In this subtype the enhancing function is not in the Head but in the Postmodifier; it is the embedded clause that expresses the circumstantial relation. For example, *the house* × ⟦ *where she lived/in which she lived / (which/that) she lived in* ⟧.

These are again a kind of defining relative clause, one in which the relative element is a circumstance not a participant. If the clause is finite, the relative is a WH- prepositional phrase — that is, a prepositional phrase with WH- Complement (e.g. *in which*) or one of its variants *which . . . in*, *that . . . in*, *. . . in*.

(you're) the one × ⟦ I've always done the most for ⟧
(the Council were expected to make available) the funds × ⟦ without which no new hospital services could be provided ⟧
(she couldn't find) anyone × ⟦ she could give the message to ⟧

Sometimes *where* or *when* can be used in this function, e.g. *the house where (in which) she lives*, *the meeting when (at which) the whole committee resigned.**

It is possible to have a pair of semantically related nominal groups in one of which the Postmodifier is elaborating and in the other of which it is enhancing, e.g.

the money = ⟦ we got for the car ⟧
the money × ⟦ we sold the car for ⟧

— the first corresponding to *we got $5,000 for the car*, the second to *we sold the car for $5,000*. This simply follows from the difference in transitivity between these two non-embedded clauses.

If the clause is non-finite, there are in fact two distinct types. One corresponds to the finites, having a WH- prepositional phrase (or one of its variants) as relative; the most common are 'destiny' clauses with *to* or *for*, e.g. *a cause* × ⟦ *for which to fight/to fight for* ⟧, *a glass* × ⟦ *for drinking out of* ⟧, *someone* × ⟦ *to give the message to* ⟧, *nothing* × ⟦ *to write home about* ⟧,** but ordinary imperfectives also occur: *new solutions* × ⟦ *now being*

* Alternatively these could be interpreted as type (a) with *house*, *meeting* as, by extension, nouns of place and time. But if they were it should be possible to use a *that* or a contact relative clause and say *the house she lived*, *the meeting that the committee resigned*. The fact that these are not possible suggests that nouns like *house*, *meeting* are not (yet) nouns of the place, time class (contrast *the first occasion that professionals took part*).

** Since a possessor can also be realized as an *of* phrase, this leads to the well-known ambiguity *experimented with*]]. Only the 'destiny' type allow an explicit Subject, with *for*: *a new pen* × [[*for you to write with*]].

The second type corresponds to the hypotactic enhancing clauses with conjunctive preposition, e.g. *death* × [[*by drowning*]], *his anger* × [[*at being suspected of complicity*]], *the trouble* × [[*with everyone having a say*]], *a pain* × [[*like having a red-hot needle stuck into you*]], *your help* × [[*in cooking the dinner*]]. In general the noun functioning as Head is the name of a process, so these often have close hypotactic parellels; e.g. *he was angry* × ||β *at being suspected*, *if you help me* × ||β *in cooking the dinner*, *it's difficult* × ||β *with everyone having a say*.

There is actually a finite equivalent, found in examples such as *the applause* × [[*when she finished singing*]], *the scar* × [[*where the bullet entered*]], *the difference* × [[*since I started taking Brandex*]]. These are compressed variants of an elaborating embedded clause with an enhancing clause dependent on it:

the applause × [[which erupted × ||β when she finished singing]]
the scar = [[which has formed × ||β where the bullet entered]]

The non-finites are in fact of the same kind: *the trouble with everyone having a say* could be reworded as *the trouble* = [[*which arises* × ||β *with everyone having a say*]]. But there is no need to show either finite or non-finite examples as other than just embedded enhancing clauses.

Like elaborating clauses, enhancing clauses may have some premodifying element as their strict semantic domain, e.g.

comparison:
(she felt) more tired × [[than she'd ever felt before]]
(I'm) as certain of it × [[as if his name were written all over his face]]

result:
(Alice was) too much puzzled × [[to say anything]]
(they were in) such a cloud of dust × [[that at first Alice could not make out which was which]]
(it was) not big enough × [[to go over his head]]
(he was) so angry × [[that he could hardly speak]]

The embedded clauses relate to *more*, *as*; *too much*, *such*, *not . . . enough* and so. Again, however, there is no need to represent this relationship as a structural one.

5. Acts

There is one further function of embedded clauses which is related to expansion in that, although there is no Head noun (so the embedded clause itself functions as 'Head'), the embedded clause is the nominalization of a process. For example, [[*threatening people*]] *will get you nowhere*.

Such a clause is the name of an action, event or other phenomenon; let us call it an 'act'. An 'act' clause may also occur as Postmodifier to a Head noun

of expressions such as *the visiting of relatives*: going to visit relatives, or having relatives come to visit? Cf. the note on non-finite enhancements in subsection 3 above.

of the appropriate class, e.g. *the act* =⟦ *of threatening people* ⟧. Hence it is reasonable to treat these as elaborations. Other examples:

||| 1 =⟦ Having a wrong view ⟧ is of course deplorable + ||2 but =⟦ α attacking other people × ||β for having views ⟧ is more deplorable |||

It was careless of him =⟦ to put another man's helmet on ⟧

=⟦ Worrying over what happened ⟧ won't change anything

These examples show typical contexts for such nominalizations: relational processes, especially attributive ones where the attribute is an evaluative term, and a restricted range of material processes. There is one other common environment, namely mental processes of perception. Examples:

I heard =⟦ the water lapping on the crag ⟧
We were watching =⟦ the catch being brought in ⟧ and you could see =⟦ the boats turn × || as they rounded the headland ⟧

Here what is being seen or heard is again some action or event; the clause is typically imperfective, but sometimes perfective (without *to*) to highlight the end state as distinct from the process:

imperfective:
I saw the boats turning / (passive) being turned

perfective:
I saw the boats turn / (passive) turned

If the embedded clause is used as Postmodifier the Head noun is usually one of sight or sound: *I heard the noise of . . ., I had a view of . . .* etc.; in this case the clause is always imperfective.

We have now reached a point where we can relate these clauses to their close relatives that lie just beyond the bounds of expansion, on different frontiers.

(1) Process nominal groups: *the turning of the boats*. Here the process has been nominalized at the word rank, with *turning* as noun; cf. *the departing/departure of the boats*. The structure is that of a nominal group with prepositional phrase with *of* as Postmodifier; the Complement of the *of* phrase corresponds to what would be the Complement if the process was realized as a clause. Examples:

| The building [of [the bridge]] | presented a problem.
Devaluation is taken to be | a humiliation [akin to [the defacing [of [statues [of [national heroes]]]]]] |

Where there would be an explicit Subject, if the process was realized as a clause, what corresponds to this is the 'possessor' of the process, as in *his handling of the situation, nobody's peeling of potatoes is as careful as mine*.*

* If the relative functions as means (instrument), where the usual preposition is *with*, there may in fact be no preposition, the sense of instrument being derived from the 'destiny' sense of the clause as a whole: e.g. *Alice had no more breath* × ⟦*for talking*⟧, i.e. 'for talking with', 'with which to talk'. Contrast the elaborating type *no more water* =⟦*for drinking*⟧, where there is no circumstantial sense (and therefore no preposition could occur).

(2) Facts: *we saw that the boats had been turned*. Facts are a kind of projection, and are discussed in Section 7.5 below. It is with embedded clauses of this kind, especially in the context of seeing and hearing, that the line between projection and expansion is hardest to draw.

If I say *I can see the boats turning*, this is an event. A process 'the boats are turning' is being treated as a single complex phenomenon — a 'macrophenomenon'. If I say *I can see that the boats are turning*, this is a fact. The process 'the boats are turning' is being treated as the projection or idea of a phenomenon — a 'metaphenomenon', something not just bigger but of a different order of reality. So we can say *I can see that the boats have been turned* (fact) but not *I can see the boats having been turned* — not, at least, with = ⟦ *the boats having been turned* ⟧ as embedded process, only in the sense of *the boats* + ⟦ *having (*= which have) *been turned* ⟧. This is natural, because you cannot see a past event. You can see the state of affairs resulting from that past event; but the past event itself can only be treated as a projection, a 'fact'. In the present, both are possible; but the meaning is significantly, even if at this point very slightly, different. If the 'seeing' is understanding, or what is seen is a report in writing, then again the relationship must be one of projection.

Metaphenomena — projections — can be associated only with certain types of process, essentially saying, thinking, and liking, plus in certain circumstances being; the details are given in Section 7.5 below. Macrophenomena — expansions — can enter into material processes. Thus you can say = ⟦ *crushing him like that* ⟧ *broke his bones*. But you cannot say *it broke his bones that you crushed him like that*, because finite *that* ('indirect') clauses can only be projections, not expansions. (You can on the other hand say *it broke his heart that you crushed him like that*, because heart-breaking, unlike bone-breaking, is a mental process.) Complication arises because the names of metaphenomena, nouns such as *belief* and *fact*, can sometimes enter into material processes where the metaphenomena by themselves cannot. For example, although we cannot say *it destroyed his life that the experiment had failed*, we can say *the knowledge that the experiment had failed destroyed his life* — not the idea as such, but his knowledge of it, was the destroyer. We might even say *the fact that the experiment had failed destroyed his life*, with *fact* standing not for a metaphenomenon but for a phenomenon, a 'state of affairs'. In other words the names of projections can function as participants in processes other than those of consciousness, because they can label events or states of affairs; and this is another aspect of the rather shaded area that lies on the borderline of expansion and projection.

7.5 Reports, ideas and facts: three kinds of projection

In Section 7.2 we introduced the notion of projection, the logical-semantic relationship whereby a clause comes to function not as a direct representation of (non-linguistic) experience but as a representation of a (linguistic) representation. It was pointed out that projection combines with the same set of interdependencies that have been shown to occur with expansion: parataxis, hypotaxis and embedding. Thus in the following examples *(that) Caesar was ambitious* is a 'projected' clause:

"Caesar was ambitious," says Brutus	(paratactic)
Brutus says that Caesar was ambitious	(hypotactic)
Brutus' assertion that Caesar was ambitious	(embedded)

In this section we will explore more systematically the different types of projection that occur in English.

1. Quoting ('direct speech'): verbal process, parataxis

The simplest form of projection is 'direct' (quoted) speech, as in

> She keeps saying to us "I stay up till twelve o'clock every night".

The projecting clause is a verbal process, one of saying, and the projected clause represents that which is said.

Here the 'tactic' relationship, the type of dependency, is parataxis; the two parts have equal status. In written English, the projection is signalled by quotation marks ('inverted commas'; for the significance of double and single quotation marks see below). In spoken English, the projecting clause is phonologically less prominent than the projected: if it comes first, it is often proclitic (non-salient and pre-rhythmic: see Chapter 1, Section 1.2 above), while if it follows all or part of the projected, instead of occupying a separate tone group it appears as a 'tail', a post-tonic appendage that continues the pitch movement of the preceding projected material; for example

(a) Brutus said: "Caesar was ambitious". 1 ^ "2
(b) "Caesar was ambitious," said Brutus. "1 ^ 2
(c) "Caesar," said Brutus, "was ambitious". "1 « 2 »
(d) "Was Caesar ambitious?" asked Mark Anthony. "1 ^ 2

Typically, in (a) *Brutus said* will be proclitic; in (b), *said Brutus* will fall, continuing the falling tone (tone 1) on *ambitious*; in (c) it will rise, continuing the falling-rising tone (tone 4) on *Caesar*; in (d) *asked Mark Anthony* will rise, continuing the rise (tone 2) or fall-rise (tone *2*) on *ambitious*.

The reason for this is that the main function of the projecting clause is simply to show that the other one is projected: someone said it. There is nothing in the wording of a paratactic projected clause to show that it is projected; it could occur alone, as a direct observation. In written English it is signalled prosodically, by punctuation; and if the quoted matter extends to a new paragraph the quotation marks are usually repeated, as a reminder. The parallel to this, in spoken English, is the repetition of the projecting clause, as in the following example:

> My brother, he used to show dogs, and he said to me, he said, "Look," he said, "I really think you've got something here," he said. "Why don't you take it to a show?" And I said "Oh, yea. Right-oh."

Without this kind of repetition, the fact that a passage of discourse is projected may easily be lost sight of.* In written English typically only the first clause complex will be explicitly accompanied by a projecting clause. Note that the analysis accurately reflects the paratactic pattern, showing projection where it occurs in the structure but not where it is simply presumed by cohesion; cf. the following example:

||| Thomas could just see out of the hole, || but he couldn't move |||
1 ×2

||| "Oh dear," « he said, » "I am a silly engine." |||
"1 « 2 »

||| "And a very naughty one too," || said a voice behind him. ||| "I saw you." |||
"1 2 1

||| "Please get me out; || I won't be naughty again." |||
1 +2

||| "I'm not so sure," || replied the Fat Controller. ||| 'We can't lift you out with a crane, || the ground's not firm enough." |||
"1 2 1 ×2

Since the amount and type of explicit projection is a significant discourse variable it is important to show exactly where and in what form it occurs.

What is the nature of the projected clause? The projected clause here stands for a 'wording': that is, the phenomenon it represents is a lexicogrammatical one. Take for example *"I'm not so sure," replied the Fat Controller.* While the projecting clause *replied the Fat Controller* represents an ordinary phenomenon of experience, the projected clause *I'm not so sure* represents a second-order phenomenon, something that is itself a representation. We will refer to this as a 'metaphenomenon'. If we want to argue, the issue is not 'is he, or is he not, so sure?' — that is a separate question;** it is 'did he, or did he not, say these words?' The total structure, therefore, is that of a paratactic clause complex in which the logical–semantic relationship is one of projection; the projecting clause is a verbal process, and the projected clause has the status of a wording.

Verbs used in quoting clauses include

(1) *say*, the general member of this class;
(2) verbs specific to (a) statements and (b) questions, e.g. (a) *tell* (+Receiver), *remark*, *observe*, *point out*, *report*, *announce*; (b) *ask*, *demand*, *inquire*, *query*;
(3) verbs combining 'say' with some circumstantial element, e.g. *reply* ('say in response'), *explain* ('say in explanation'), *protest* ('say with reservation'), *continue* ('go on saying'), *interrupt* ('say out of turn'), *warn* ('say: undesirable consequences');

Some speakers introduce a special voice quality into their quoted speech, which could in principle serve as an ongoing prosodic marker and obviate the need for repeating the 'saying' clause — although the acoustic effect probably depends mainly on the initial change of tamber, and if so it will tend to diminish as the quoted speech continues.

* In order to argue this we should have to turn it into a first order phenomenon: *and is he*?

(4) verbs having connotations of various kinds, e.g. *insist* ('say emphatically'), *complain* ('say irritably'), *cry, shout* ('say loudly'), *boast* ('say proudly'), *murmur* ('say sotto voce'), *stammer* ('say with embarrassment').

A very wide range of different verbs can be pressed into service under this last heading, verbs which are not verbs of saying at all but serve, especially in fictional narrative, to suggest attitudes, emotions or expressive gestures that accompanied the act of speaking, for example *sob*, *snort*, *twinkle*, *beam*, *venture*, *breathe*; e.g.

> "It is a great thing, discretion," mused Poirot.

Here the implication is that Poirot is trying to give the impression of thinking aloud, while making sure the listener 'overhears'.

2. Reporting ('indirect speech'): mental process, hypotaxis

Talking is not the only way of using language; we also use language to think. Hence a process of thinking also serves to project; for example,

> Dr Singleman always believed that his patient would recover.

Here again there is a phenomenon, *Dr Singleman always believed*, and a metaphenomenon *his patient would recover*. The difference between this and the examples given above is that here (i) the projecting clause is a mental process, more specifically one of cognition; and (ii) the projected clause is not a wording but a meaning.

Something that is projected as a meaning is still a phenomenon of language — it is what was referred to above as a 'metaphenomenon'; but it is presented at a different level — semantic, not lexicogrammatical. When something is projected as a meaning it has already been 'processed' by the linguistic system; but processed only once, not twice as in the case of a wording. So for example the phenomenon of water falling out of the sky may be coded as a meaning, by a mental process of cognition, in *(she thought) it was raining*; but when the same phenomenon is represented by a verbal process, as in *(she said:) "it's raining"*, it is the **meaning** 'it is raining' that has been recoded to become a wording. A wording is, as it were, twice cooked. This is symbolized in an interesting way by the punctuation system of English, which uses both single and double quotation marks; in principle, single quotation marks stand for a meaning and double quotation marks stand for a wording. We are unconsciously aware that when something has the status of a wording it lies not at one but at two removes from experience; it has undergone two steps in the realization process. This symbolism has been adopted in our present notation, in which ' stands for a projected meaning and " for a projected wording:

||| Dr Singleman believed	|| his patient would recover |||
α	'β

When something is projected as a meaning, we are not representing 'the very words', because there are no words. If we want to argue about whether or not the doctor held this opinion, we have no observed event as a point of reference. Hence in combination with the tactic system the basic pattern for projecting meanings is not parataxis, which treats the projection as a free-standing event, but hypotaxis, which makes it dependent on the mental process. In other words, the typical pattern for representing a 'thinking' is the hypotactic one.

As pointed out earlier, the hypotactic relationship implies a different perspective. If we contrast the following pair of examples:

(a) Mary said: "I will come back here to-morrow".
(b) Mary thought she would go back there the next day.

then in (a) the standpoint in the projected clause is that of the Sayer, Mary; she is the point of reference for the deixis, which thus preserves the form of the lexicogrammatical event, using *I*, *here*, *come*, *tomorrow*. In (b) on the other hand the standpoint in the projected clause is simply that of the speaker of the projecting one; so Mary is 'she', Mary's present location is 'there', a move towards that location is 'going', and the day referred to as that immediately following the saying is not the speaker's tomorrow but simply 'the next day'. Furthermore, since the saying clause has past time the projected clause carries over the feature of temporal remoteness: hence *would*, not *will*. Hypotactic projection preserves the deictic orientation of the projecting clause, which is that of the speaker; whereas in paratactic projection the deixis shifts and takes on the orientation of the Sayer.

So far, therefore, we have the pattern in Table 7(9):

Table 7(9) Basic types of projection

type of projecting process: \ taxis:	paratactic 1 2	hypotactic $\alpha\beta$
verbal "	projection of wording 1 "2	
mental '		projection of meaning α 'β

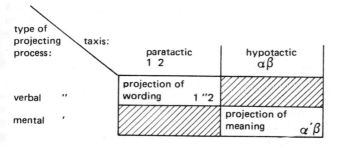

This is the basic pattern of projection. But, by the familiar semogenic process of recombination of associated variables (more simply known as filling up the holes), other forms have come to exist alongside.

3. Reporting speech, quoting thought

It is possible to 'report' a saying by representing it as a meaning. This is the 'reported speech', or 'indirect speech', of traditional western grammars; for example, *the noble Brutus hath told you Caesar was ambitious* (Figure 7-12).

Brutus	hath	told	you	Caesar	was	ambitious
α →						"β
Mood		Residue		Mood		Residue
Subject	Finite	Predicator	Complement	Subject	Finite	Complement
Sayer	Process: verbal		Receiver	Carrier	Process: relational	Attribute

Figure 7-12 Reported speech

In this instance, Brutus had indeed said those very words:

> *Brutus*: As Caesar loved me, I weep for him; as he was fortunate, I rejoice at it; as he was valiant, I honour him: but, as he was ambitious, I slew him. [. . .]
>
> *Mark Anthony*: The noble Brutus
> Hath told you Caesar was ambitious.
> If it were so, it was a grievous fault.

But the principle behind this hypotactic representation of a verbal event is that it is not, in fact, being presented as true to the wording; the speaker is reporting the gist of what was said, and the wording may be quite different from the original, as in the following (where A is a shopkeeper, B an elderly, hard-of-hearing customer and C is her grandson):

A. It doesn't work; it's broken. You'll have to get it repaired.
B. What does he say?
C. He says it needs mending.

This is not to suggest, of course, that when a speaker uses the paratactic, 'direct' form he is always repeating the exact words; far from it. But the idealized function of the paratactic structure is to represent the wording; whereas with hypotaxis the idealized function is to represent the sense, or gist.

Verbs used in reporting statements and questions are largely the same as those used in quoting, with two main variations. One is that many semantically complex verbs for rhetorical acts are used only in reporting, not in quoting; e.g. *insinuate*, *imply*, *remind*, *hypothesize*, *deny*, *make out*, *claim*, *pretend*, *maintain*. The other is that verbs that are not intrinsically saying verbs are generally not used to report, even though they may be used to quote in narrative contexts. We are unlikely to find, corresponding to the example at the end of the previous subsection, *Poirot mused that discretion was a great thing*.

This combination of a verbal process with 'reporting', although we are treating it as logically subsequent to quoting, being arrived at by analogy with the reporting of a mental process, is the normal way of representing what people say, in most registers of English today. The opposite combination, that of a mental process with 'quoting', is also found although considerably more restricted. Here a thought is represented as if it was a wording, for example

I saw an ad in the paper for dachshunds, and I thought "I'll just inquire" — not intending to buy one, of course.

||| I thought || "I'll just inquire" |||
1 '2

The implication is 'I said to myself . . .'; and this expression is often used, recognizing the fact that one can think in words. Only certain mental process verbs are regularly used to quote in this way, such as *think*, *wonder*, *reflect*, *surmise*.

We can now revise Table 7(9) as Table 7(10). First, however, in order to do so, let us establish the following terms:

paratactic projection:	quote
hypotactic projection:	report
what is projected verbally:	locution
what is projected mentally:	idea

Table 7(10) Four types of projection complex

Type of projecting process: / Taxis:	Quote paratactic 1 2	Report hypotactic α β
Locution " verbal	Wording 1 "2 She said, "I can"	Wording represented as meaning α "β She said she could
Idea ' mental	Meaning represented as wording 1 '2 She thought, "I can"	Meaning α 'β She thought she could

Quoting and reporting are not simply formal variants; they differ in meaning. The difference between them derives from the general semantic distinction between parataxis and hypotaxis, as it applies in the particular context of projecting. In quoting, the projected element has independent status; it is thus more immediate and lifelike, and this effect is enhanced by the orientation of the deixis, which is that of drama not that of narrative. Quoting is particularly associated with certain narrative registers, fictional and personal; it is used not only for sayings but also for thoughts, including third person thoughts projected by an omniscient narrator, as in

"And that's the jury-box," thought Alice.

Reporting, on the other hand, presents the projected element as dependent. It still makes a choice of mood; but in a form which precludes it from functioning as a move in an exchange. And the speaker makes no claim to be abiding by the wording.

Traditional school exercises of the kind 'turn into direct/indirect speech' suggest that the two always fully match. This is true lexicogrammatically, in that it is always possible to find an equivalent — although not always a unique one: given *Mary said she had seen it*, the quoted equivalent might be *I have seen it*, *I had seen it* or *I saw it*, or *she* (someone else) *has seen it*, etc. (cf. Chapter 6, Section 6.3 above). But it is not true as a general statement about usage. Semantically the two do not exactly match, and there are many instances where it does not make sense to replace one by the other. Note for example *Alice thought that that was the jury-box*, where we should have to change *Alice thought* to something like *Alice said to herself* in order to avoid the sense of 'held the opinion' which is the natural interpretation of a verb of thinking when it is projecting by hypotaxis.

There are different ways of referring back to what is quoted and what is reported. Typically a reference item, usually *that*, is used to pick up a quoted passage, while a substitute, *so / not*, is used with a report. For example,

She said, "I can't do it." — Did she really say that?
She said she couldn't do it. — Did she really say so?

(For the difference between reference and substitution see Chapter 9 below.) This is because the act of quoting implies a prior referent, some actual occasion that can then be referred back to, whereas in reporting there is nothing but the reported text. This explains the difference in meaning between *I don't believe that* 'I do not accept that assertion as valid' and *I don't believe so* 'in my opinion such is not the case'. Compare:

The sky is about to fall.	(i)	— Who said that?
	(ii)	— Who said so?

It is clear that both *that* and *so* stand for something that is projected, as shown by the verb *said*. In (i) this projected element is being treated as a quote: 'who produced that verbal act?' — hence we can ask *who said that?* if we want to identify a speaker from among a crowd, like a teacher finding out who was talking in class. In (ii), on the other hand, the expression *the sky is about to fall* is being treated not as anybody's verbal act but as a text; the meaning is 'who affirmed that that was the case?', with the implication that the contrary is conceivable.

In verbal processes, therefore, *he said that* simply attests his production of the wording, whereas *he said so* raises the issue of whether what he said is in fact the case. With mental processes the picture is more complex, since the reference form tends to be associated with certainty and the substitute with uncertainty; the principle is actually the same, but operating in a different environment (cf. the different senses of *thought* in quoting and reporting, referred to above). Substitution does not refer; it simply harks back. It has the general semantic property of implying, and so excluding, possible alternatives; cf. the nominal substitute *one* as in *a big one*, meaning 'there are also small ones, and I don't mean those'. This is why *so*, which is a clause substitute, has the general sense of 'non-real', by contrast with what is 'real'; besides (i) projection, where it signifies what is asserted or postulated, it is used in two other contexts: (ii) hypothetical, as opposed to actual, and (iii) possible, as opposed to certain. Hence:

(i)	*I think so*	but	*I know* [*that*]	not	*I know so*
(ii)	*if so*	"	*because of that*	"	*because so*
(iii)	*perhaps so*	"	*certainly*	"	*certainly so*

See Chapter 9 for further discussion.

4. Projecting offers and commands

So far we have considered just the projection of propositions: that is, statements and questions. We must now turn to the projection of clauses of the 'goods-&-services' kind, offers and commands, to which we gave the general name 'proposals'.

Offers and commands, and also suggestions which are simply the combination of the two (offer 'I'll do it,' command 'you do it', suggestion 'let's do it'), can be projected paratactically (quoted) in the same way as propositions, by means of a verbal process clause having a quoting function. For example (using an exclamation mark as an optional notational variant),

> If we're talking when she's writing up on the board, all of a sudden she'll turn round and go "will you be quiet!"

> ||| she'll go || will you be quiet |||
> 1 "2!

Here the verb *go* is the quoting verb.

As with propositions, there is an extensive set of verbs used for quoting proposals, especially in narrative fiction:

(1) the general verb *say*;
(2) verbs specific to offers and commands, e.g. *suggest*, *offer*, *call*, *order*, *request*, *tell*, *propose*, *decide*;
(3) verbs embodying some circumstantial or other semantic feature(s) such as *threaten* (offer: undesirable), *vow* (offer: sacred), *urge* (command: persuasive), *plead* (command: desperate), *warn* (command: avoid undesirable consequences), *promise* (offer: desirable), agree (offer in response);
(4) verbs involving some additional connotation (largely identical with those used to quote propositions), e.g. *blare*, *thunder* ('order imperiously'), *moan* ('plead whiningly'), *yell* ('order vociferously'), *fuss* ('order officiously'), as in:

> "Steady old boy, steady" soothed his Driver
> "Collar that Dormouse," the Queen shrieked out
> "1! 2

These are the 'direct commands' of traditional grammar, to which we would need to add 'direct offers (and suggestions)'; in other words, all proposals projected as 'direct speech'. Like propositions, proposals can also be reported: projected hypotactically as 'indirect speech' — indirect commands, etc. But the parallel between quoting and reporting is not so close as with propositions, because reported proposals merge gradually into causatives without any very clear line in between. Thus not only are there many verbs used in quoting which are not used in reporting — again the complex ones: we would not write *his Driver soothed him to be steady* or *soothed that he should keep steady* — but also there are many verbs used to report that are not used to quote, verbs expressing a wide variety of rhetorical processes such as *persuade*, *forbid*, *undertake*, *encourage*, *recommend*.

With propositions, the reported clause is finite.* With proposals, it may be finite or non-finite. The non-finites are typically perfective, e.g. *I told you to mind your head*, though a few verbs take imperfective projections, e.g. *she suggested talking it over*. The finites are declarative, usually modulated with *should, ought to, must, has to, is to, might, could, would*, e.g. *I told you you had to mind your head, she suggested they might talk it over*.

How do we decide where to draw the line between these and causatives such as *she got him to talk it over*? As a first step, if there is a quoted equivalent with the same verb, the structure is clearly a projection; e.g. the form

||| he threatened || to blow up the city |||
α "β!

could be paralleled by *"I'll blow up the city!" he threatened*. Typically if a proposal is projected it may not actually eventuate; hence we can say without contradiction *he threatened to blow up the city, but didn't*, or *the Queen ordered the executioner to cut off Alice's head, but he didn't* — whereas it is self-contradictory to say *the Queen got the executioner to cut off Alice's head but he didn't*.

More generally, we can assume that any verb denoting a speech act can in principle be used to project. Hence a verbal process with a non-finite dependent clause can normally be interpreted as a projection; and if the non-finite dependent clause could be replaced by a finite one with modulation this makes it more certain, since it rules out purpose clauses:

||| he promised || to make her happy |||
||| he promised || he would make her happy |||
α "β

as distinct from *he promised, (in order) to make her happy*, which is an expansion with structure α ^ $\times\beta$. Causatives are excluded because they are not verbal processes; they also usually do not have finite equivalents — we do not say *I'll make that you should regret this!*

It might seem that offers and commands could be projected only verbally; there would be no equivalent, with proposals, to the projection of a proposition by a mental process. We do not think something to happen. But we do **wish** it to happen; and this is just as much a form of projection. Proposals are projected by mental processes; but in this context there is an important distinction between propositions and proposals, deriving from their fundamental nature as different forms of semiotic exchange. Whereas propositions, which are exchanges of information, are projected mentally by processes of cognition — thinking, knowing, understanding, wondering, etc. — proposals, which are exchanges of goods-&-services, are projected mentally by affective processes of reaction: wishing, liking, hoping, fearing and so on. For example:

* Except for certain projected ideas, which may take a non-finite form on the model of the Latin 'accusative + infinitive', e.g.

||| I understood || them to have accepted |||
||| he doesn't believe || you to be serious |||
α 'β

Mary hopes	to go to Sweden next year
I wish	they would keep quiet
the keeper wanted	the children to stay away from the cage
I don't like	you to go too near
α	'β!

Thus while propositions are thought, proposals are hoped. As with those that are projected verbally, so with those that are projected mentally the exact limits are fuzzy; they merge with causatives and with various aspectual categories. The relevant criteria are similar to those set up for propositions, except that we cannot realistically test for quoting, since mental proposals are rarely quoted.* For reporting, however, if the process in the dominant clause is one of affect, and the dependent clause is a future declarative, or could be replaced by a future declarative, then the structure can be interpreted as a projection; for example *we hope you will not forget*. In the next section we shall suggest an alternative interpretation for those where the dependent clause is non-finite and its Subject is presupposed from the dominant clause, e.g. *he wanted to go home* (where it is difficult to find a closely equivalent finite form); but there will always be a certain amount of arbitrariness about where the line is drawn.

Notice therefore that there is a proportion such that

she wanted him to go	(mental)	proposal
is to she told him to go	(verbal)	
as		
she knew he was going	(mental)	proposition
is to she said he was going	(verbal)	

We can now expand Table 7(10) into 7(11):

Table 7(11) Projection of propositions and proposals

Type of projecting process; projected speech function \ Taxis:		Quote paratactic 1 2	Report hypotactic α β
Locution verbal		Wording 1 "2	Wording represented as meaning α "β
	Proposition	He said "I can"	He said he could
	Proposal	She told him "Do"	She told him to do
Idea Mental		Meaning represented as wording 1 '2	Meaning α 'β
	Proposition	He thought "I can"	He thought he could
	Proposal	She willed him "Do"	She wanted him to do

* Note that *"I wish he'd go away," thought Mary* is a quoted proposition incorporating a reported proposal, not a quoted proposal, which would be *"Let him go away!" wished Mary*. As with mental propositions, the notion behind quoting is generally that of 'saying to oneself', or saying silently to a deity as in prayer.

5. Free indirect speech

As we have seen, a reported proposition typically takes on a set of related features collectively known as 'indirect speech'. What happens is that all deictic elements are shifted away from reference to the speech situation: personals away from first and second person (speaker and listener) to third, and demonstratives away from near (here-&-now) to remote. A part of this effect is the 'sequence of tenses': if the verb in the reporting clause has past as its primary tense (see Chapter 6, Section 6.3), then typically each verb in the reporting clause has its finite element in the corresponding System II ('sequent') form:

Primary tense		*Modality*	
Non-sequent	Sequent	Non-sequent	Sequent
am / is / are	was / were	can / could	could
have / has	had	may / might	might
do / does (&c.)	did (&c.)	will / would	would
shall / will	should / would	should	should
was / were	had been	ought to	ought to
did (&c.)	had done (&c.)	must / has to	had to

In other words, an additional 'past' feature is introduced at the Finite element in the mood structure. The use of the sequent form is not obligatory; it is less likely in a clause stating a general proposition, for example. But overall it is the unmarked choice in the environment in question.

If the reported clause is interrogative it typically shifts into the declarative; the declarative is the unmarked mood, and is used in all clauses that do not select for mood independently, including all dependent clauses. A yes/no interrogative becomes declarative, introduced by *if* or *whether*; a WH- interrogative becomes declarative with the WH- element remaining at the front.

With the imperative the relationship is less clear. We noted in Chapter 4 that the imperative is a somewhat indeterminate category, having some features of a finite and some features of a non-finite clause. Similarly the category of reported imperative ('indirect command') is not very clearly defined. But non-finite clauses with *to*, following a verb such as *tell* or *order*, can be interpreted as reported proposals. They likewise display the properties of 'indirect speech', although without sequence of tenses, since the verb does not select for tense. E.g.

"I know this trick of yours."	She said she knew that trick of his.
"Can you come tomorrow?"	He asked if she could come the next day.
"Why isn't John here?"	She wondered why John wasn't there.
"Help yourselves."	He told them to help themselves.
"We must leave to-night."	She said they had to leave that night.

There is another mode of projection which is sometimes described as 'intermediate between direct and indirect speech,' namely 'free indirect speech':*

* 'Free indirect speech' encompasses a range of different feature combinations; it is a projection 'space' rather then a single invariant pattern. The account given here represents it as an idealized form.

Table 7(12) Direct, free indirect and indirect speech

Type of projecting process:	Speech function:		Orientation: Quote — Taxis: Paratactic "1 2	Report — 1 2	Report — Hypotactic α β
LOCUTION Verbal"			Wording "1 2	Wording represented as meaning (except intonation)	Wording represented as meaning α "β
	Proposition	statement	"I can", he said	He could, he said	He said he could
		question	"Are you sure?" asked Fred	Was she sure, Fred asked	Fred asked if she was sure
	Proposal		"Wait here," she told him	Wait there, she told him	She told him to wait there
IDEA mental'			Meaning represented as wording '1 2	Meaning (intonation represented as wording)	Meaning α 'β
	Proposition	statement	"I can," he thought	He could, he thought	He thought he could
		question	"Am I dreaming?" wondered Jill	Was she dreaming, Jill wondered	Jill wondered if she was dreaming
	Proposal		"Wait here," she willed him	Wait there, she willed him	She wanted him to wait there
			"direct"	"free indirect"	"indirect"

Quoted ('direct')	"Am I dreaming?" Jill wondered.
'Free indirect'	Was she dreaming, Jill wondered.
Reported ('indirect')	Jill wondered if she was dreaming

Strictly speaking it is not so much intermediate as anomalous: it has some of the features of each of the other two types. The structure is paratactic, so the projected clause has the form of an independent clause retaining the mood of the quoted form; but it is a report and not a quote, so time and person reference are shifted — *was she* not *am I*. This is another example of the semogenic principle whereby the system fills up a slot it has created for itself. Our Table now looks like 7(12).

As the table shows, free indirect speech can be projected both verbally and mentally, and includes both propositions and proposals — everything, in fact, that can be both quoted and reported.

The intonation pattern of free indirect speech is still further anomalous, since it follows that of quoting and not that of reporting: the projected clause takes the intonation that it would have had if quoted (that is, identical with its unprojected form), and the projecting clause follows it as a 'tail'. This is because the projected clause still has the status of an independent speech act.

It is possible to introduce a special notation for free indirect speech if this is desirable for purposes of analysis, writing $\overset{,,}{\smile}$ and $\overset{,}{\smile}$.

6. Embedded locutions and ideas

Like the three types of expansion, both locutions and ideas can be embedded. Besides entering into paratactic and hypotactic clause complexes, they can be 'rank-shifted' to function as Qualifiers within a nominal group, as in *the assertion that Caesar was ambitious* (Figure 7-13).

Such instances are still projections; but here the projecting element is the noun that is functioning as Thing, in this case *assertion*.

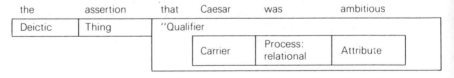

the	assertion	that	Caesar	was	ambitious
Deictic	Thing	"Qualifier			
			Carrier	Process: relational	Attribute

| the assertion "[[that Caesar was ambitious]] |

Figure 7-13 Nominal group with embedded projection

Nouns that project belong to clearly defined classes, verbal process nouns (locutions) and mental process nouns (ideas); they correspond rather closely, and in many instances are derived from, the verbs used in the projecting clause, especially the reporting ones (cf. above, 2 and 3). Some of the principal nouns of projection are the following:

(I) Propositions

(a) stating: projected clause either (i) finite, *that* + indirect indicative, or (ii) non-finite, *of* + imperfective

(1) locutions

statement; *report*, *news*, *rumour*, *claim*, *assertion*, *argument*, *insistence*, *proposition*, *assurance*, *intimation*

(2) ideas

thought, *belief*, *knowledge*, *feeling*, *notion*, *suspicion*, *sense*, *idea*, *expectation*, *view*, *opinion*, *prediction*, *assumption*, *conviction*, *discovery*

(b) questioning: projected clause either (i) finite, *if/whether* or WH- + indirect indicative, or (ii) non-finite, *whether* or WH- + *to* + perfective

(1) locutions

question; *query*, *inquiry*; *argument*, *dispute*

(2) ideas

doubt, *problem*, *question*, *issue*, *uncertainty*

(II) Proposals

(a) offering (incl. suggesting): projected clause either (1) non-finite, *to* + perfective or *of* + imperfective, or (ii) finite, future indirect indicative

(1) locutions

offer, *suggestion*, *proposal*, *threat*, *promise*

(2) ideas

intention, *desire*, *hope*, *inclination*, *decision*, *resolve*

(b) commanding: projected clause either (i) non-finite, *to* + perfective, or (ii) finite, modulated or future indirect indicative

(1) locutions

order; *command*, *instruction*, *demand*, *request*, *plea*

(2) ideas

wish, *desire*, *hope*, *fear*

Examples:

Ia1 the assertion "⟦. that such an effort is necessary to salvation ⟧
2 the belief '⟦. that other holders of sterling were about to sell ⟧
b1 the argument "⟦? whether inflation was caused by government action or by private action ⟧
2 the question '⟦? how long the social contract could survive ⟧
IIa1 the threat "⟦! that offenders would be punished by law ⟧
2 the government's intent '⟦! to protect real wages ⟧
b1 the decree "⟦! that all tax concessions should be abolished ⟧
2 the hope '⟦! of getting money of this kind as a gift ⟧

In all such instances the noun is the name of a locution or an idea, and the clause that it projects serves to define it in exactly the same way that a 'restrictive' relative clause defines the noun that is expanded by it. Hence any noun that belongs to a projecting class may be defined (restricted) in either of these two ways, either by projection (e.g. *the thought that she might one day be a queen*) or by expansion (e.g. *the thought that came into her mind*). This leads to ambiguities such as *the report that he was submitting*, referred to in Section 7.5.8 below.

Where the projected clause is non-finite the Subject can be presupposed from the primary clause provided it is the participant that is actually doing

Table 7(13) Paratactic, hypotactic and embedded projections

Type of projecting process: / rank:	Orientation: / Speech function:	Clause complex			Nominal group
		Quote	Report		
		Taxis: Paratactic 1 2		Hypotactic α β	Embedded ⟦ ⟧
Locution Verbal "		1 "2	1 "2	α "β	"⟦
	Proposition	The nurse asked "Does it hurt?"	The nurse asked did it hurt?	The nurse asked if it hurt	the nurse's question whether it hurt
	Proposal	The nurse said "Don't worry!"	The nurse said not to worry	The nurse told him not to worry	the nurse's injunction not to worry
Idea mental '		'1 2	'1 2	α 'β	'⟦
	Proposition	"I shall fail," he thought	He would fail, he feared	He was afraid he would fail	his fear that he would fail
	Proposal	"You will succeed," she resolved	He would succeed, she resolved	She determined that he would succeed	her determination for him to succeed
		"direct"	"free direct"	"indirect"	"indirect qualifying"

the projecting — Senser or (more rarely) Sayer. So *the thought of being a queen (encouraged her), her desire to be a queen . . ., her assertion of being a queen . . .*, where 'she' is doing the thinking, etc.; but *the news of her being a queen* (proclaimed by someone else), *the thought of her being a queen* (in someone else's mind), and so on. These correspond to the non-finite forms with hypotaxis referred to in subsection 4 above: *she wanted to be a queen, they wanted her to be a queen*. In the finite forms, of course, the Subject is always made explicit.

Table 7(13) is the current version of our table, somewhat reduced so as to save space.

7. Facts

Thus verbal processes, and mental : cognitive processes, project in the indicative mode (propositions), while verbal processes, and mental : affective processes, project in the imperative mode (proposals). The projecting environment may be a verbal or mental process clause, or a nominal group with a verbal or mental process noun (locution or idea) as its Head.

There is one other type of projection, one which involves neither mental nor verbal process but comes as it were ready packaged in projected form. We refer to this type as a FACT.

Consider *That Caesar was dead was obvious to all*. Here *that Caesar was dead* is certainly a projection; but there is no process of saying or thinking which projects it. Its status is simply that of a fact; and it can indeed function as Qualifier to the noun *fact*, e.g. *the fact that Caesar was dead was obvious to all*.

In either case, it is embedded. Because there is no projecting process involved, to which it could be paratactically or hypotactically related, a fact can appear only in embedded form: either as Qualifier to a 'fact' noun, or as a nominalization on its own (Figure 7-14).

that Caesar was dead	was	obvious	to all
Carrier/Subject "[[	Process: relational	Attribute	Receiver

Figure 7-14 Attributive clause with projected fact

It is not that a fact is projected out of the air, so to speak, but that there is no participant doing the projecting; no Sayer or Senser is involved. A fact is projected impersonally, either by a relational process ('it is the case that . . .') or by an impersonal mental or verbal process; and this projection may be made explicit, as in

it is / may be / is not (the case) that . . .
it happens (to be the case) that . . .
it seems / is thought (to be the case) that . . .
it is said (to be the case) that . . .
it has been shown / can be proved (to be the case) that. . .

Here the *it* is not a participant in the projecting process but is simply a Subject placeholder (cf. *the fact is that* . . .); hence the fact clause can occupy its position at the front: *that Caesar was ambitious is certainly the case / is widely held / is generally believed*, etc. By contrast we do not normally say *that Caesar was ambitious was thought / said by Brutus* — at least not in a reporting context, only in the special sense of 'these lines were spoken by . . .'; and this is because, as we have seen, where there is a personal projecting process, mental or verbal, the clause that is projected by it is not embedded but hypotactic.

Other than with impersonals such as *it is said, it seems*, the typical environment for a fact is a relational process, e.g. (attributive) *it is a pity / obvious / significant that Caesar was ambitious*, (identifying) *the reason why Caesar was killed is that he was ambitious*, etc. Here the fact is an embedded clause standing as a nominalization on its own, functioning as the realization of an element in the relational process clause (Carrier or Identifier/Token, in these examples.)* Since it is embedded, it can always be turned into a Qualifier by the addition of a noun of the 'fact' class, e.g. *the fact that Caesar was ambitious*.

There are four sub-classes of fact noun: (1) cases, (2) chances, (3) proofs and (4) needs. The last is discussed lower down.

(1) 'cases' (nouns of simple fact), e.g. *fact, case, point, rule, principle, accident, lesson, grounds*

(2) 'chances' (nouns of modality), e.g. *chance, possibility, likelihood, probability, certainty, offchance, impossibility*

(3) 'proofs' (nouns of indication), e.g. *proof, indication, implication, confirmation, demonstration, evidence, disproof*

The first relate to ordinary non-modalized propositions 'it is (the case) that . . .'; the second to modalized propositions 'it may be (the case) that . . .'; and the third relate to propositions with indications, which are equivalent to caused modalities, 'this proves / implies (i.e. makes it certain / probable) that . . .'.

There is no mental process corresponding to fact or chance, no implication of a conscious participant that is doing the projecting. A fact, as already pointed out, is an impersonal projection. However, it is possible for a fact to enter into a mental process without being projected by it. In this case it functions as a Phenomenon within the mental process clause. Note the following pair (Figure 7-15):

---

* Strictly speaking the embedded 'fact' clause functions as Head of a nominal group which in turn functions as an element in the ranking clause. But since it takes up the whole of that nominal group we can just as well leave out that stage in the structural analysis and show it as directly embedded into the clause, as in Figure 7-14 above.

||| Mark Anthony | thought || that Caesar was dead |||

α		'β
Senser	Processı	

||| Mark Anthony | regretted '⟦ (the fact) that Caesar was dead ⟧ |||

Senser	Process	Phenomenon: fact

gure 7-15 Mental process with (a) idea, (b) fact

ı (a) the clause *that Caesar was dead* is projected as an 'idea' by *Mark nthony thought*. It is therefore a separate, hypotactic clause; and hence (i) it ınnot be preceded by *the fact*; (ii) it cannot be replaced by *Caesar's death*; ii) it can bc quoted: *"Caesar is dead," thought Mark Anthony*. In (b), owever, the clause *that Caesar was dead*, although it is a projection, is not rojected by *Mark Anthony regretted*, which is a clause of affect not of ɔgnition. It is not an idea but a fact; hence it is embedded, and hence (i) it can ɛ preceded by a 'fact' noun; (ii) it can be replaced by a nominal group *'aesar's death*; (iii) it cannot readily be quoted: *Mark Anthony regretted, Caesar is dead"* is very forced. The form *Mark Anthony feared that Caesar as dead* is an example of a type that allows both interpretations, and hence is nbiguous: as idea (hypotactic), 'he thought (and wished otherwise)', or as ıct (embedded), 'he was afraid because'.

The same two possibilities occur with mental processes of the 'please' type Chapter 5), e.g.

(a) ||| it strikes me || that there's no-one here |||
α 'β

(b) ||| it worrics me '⟦ that there's no-one here ⟧ |||

he first means 'in my opinion there's no-one here', with *there's no-one ere* as an idea. The second means 'there's no-one here, and that worries ıe', with *there's no-one here* as a fact. The two are very distinct in speech, ıanks to the intonation pattern (see below); the different analyses are given ı Figure 7-16.

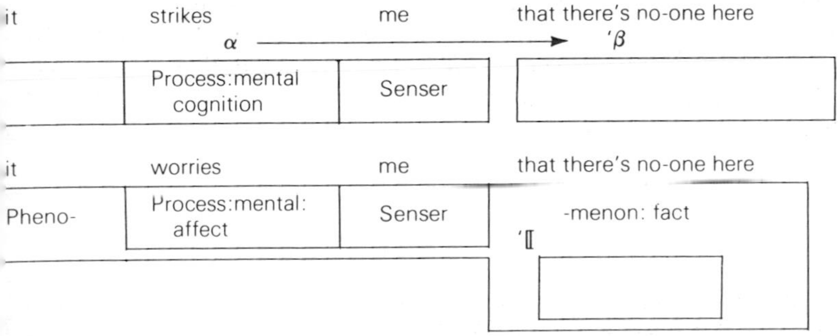

igure 7.16

Table 7(14) Summary of principal types of projection

Type of process doing the projecting (quotes & reports only):		Rank: / Orientation: / Speech function	Clause complex: Quote — Taxis: Paratactic	Report — 1 2	Hypotactic
Locution " (Projected wording)	Verbal	Proposition	"1. 2 "It is so," he said	"1. 2 It was so, he said	α He said that was so
		Proposal	"1! 2 "Do so!" he told them	"1! 2 They should do so, he told them	α He told ther do so
Idea ' (Projected meaning)	Mental	Proposition	'1. 2 "it is so," she knew	'1. 2 It was so, she knew	α She knew tl was so
		Proposal	'1! 2 "Do so!", she said to herself	'1! 2 She would do so, she decided	α She decided she wou so
			"direct"	"free indirect"	"indirec

The difference in structure is clear from the intonation pattern. That of (a corresponds to *I rather think there's no-one here*, with falling tonic (tone on *here* and perhaps a separate falling-rising tonic (tone 4) on *strikes/think* that of (b) corresponds to *it worries me, the emptiness of the place*, a com pound tone group with tone 1 on *worries* and tone 3 on *here/emptines.* showing clearly that *that there's no-one here* is functioning as a postpose Subject. Again, *it strikes me* is a cognitive process, and so can project an ide whereas *it worries me* is affective and cannot.

But even with some cognitive and verbal processes, a projected eleme may occur which is **not projected by that process**; for example (cognitive) *h accepted (the fact) that he had been wrong*, (verbal) *he admitted (the fac that he had been wrong, her looks conveyed (the fact) that she was angr* And there will also be 'borderline cases', instances where the line is hard t draw.

Finally, as may be expected an embedded projection may belong to th class of proposals rather than propositions, as in *the requirement that sho should be worn, the need to maintain good relations*. This defines the fourt category of 'fact' nouns referred to earlier:

Nominal group		
	Fact	
:mbedded [[ ]] :	as Postmodifier	As Head
"[[. is assertion that it was so	→ the saying that it is so	→ (it is said) that it is so
"[[! is order to them to do so	→ the stipulation to do so	→ (it is stipulated) to do so
'[[er knowledge that it was so	→ the fact that it is so	→ that it is so
'[[! er decision to do so	→ the need to do so	→ to do so
"indirect qualifying"	"impersonal qualifying"	"impersonal"

same as on left

(4) 'needs' (nouns of modulation): e.g. *requirement*, *need*, *rule*, *obligation*, *necessity*, *onus*, *expectation*, *duty*

These again have no corresponding mental process verbs; they differ from nouns like *order* (the name of a verbal process) and *insistence* (the name of a mental process) in the same way that *fact* differs from *thought* and *statement* — they do not imply a Sayer or a Senser. Like a proposition, a proposal may either be embedded as Qualifier to one of these nouns, as in the examples above, or may function on its own as a nominalization e.g. *it was the rule that shoes had to be worn*; and we can construct similar pairs, for example

(a) ||| he insisted || that they had to wait in line |||
α 'β!

(b) ||| he resented (the rule) '[[! that they had to wait in line]] |||

where in (a) it is the clause *he insisted* that does the projecting, while in (b) the projected clause is embedded. Here too there is an impersonal form of expression, *it is required/expected that you wait in line*; these are the imperative (proposal) equivalents of *it is said/thought that . . .* with propositions.

They have an important function as 'objective modulations' whereby the speaker disclaims responsibility for making the rules (see Chapter 10 below).

What kind of projection is a fact? It is still a meaning, a semantic abstraction, not some third type differing both from meanings and from wordings (indeed there is no third level to which it could belong). But it is not a meaning created in anybody's consciousness, nor is it emitted by any signal source; it is simply got up so as to function as a participant in some other process — typically a relational process, but sometimes also a mental or a verbal one. Not, however, in a material process; facts cannot do things, or have things done to them (for apparent exceptions to this principle see subsection 7.4.b above).

Let us now expand our projection table once more, to take account of quotes, reports and facts, both as meanings and as wordings (Table 7(14)).

8. Summary of projection

Jill says something; this is a verbal event. To represent it, I use a verbal process *Jill said*, plus a quote of her verbal act "*It's raining*". The two have equal status (paratactic), because both are wordings. That is to say, both my locution *Jill said* and Jill's locution *it's raining* are lexicogrammatical phenomena.

Fred thinks something; this is a mental event. To represent it, I use a mental process *Fred thought*, plus a report of his mental act *(that) it had stopped*. The two have unequal status (hypotactic), because one is a wording while the other is a meaning. That is to say, my locution *Fred thought* is a lexicogrammatical phenomenon, but Fred's idea 'that it had stopped' is a semantic one.

Thus parataxis is naturally associated with verbal projections and hypotaxis with mental ones. But, as we have seen, the pattern can be inverted. I can choose to report a verbal act, presenting a locution as a meaning; and I can choose to quote a mental act, presenting an idea as a wording. If we report speech, we do not commit ourselves to 'the very words': if I say *Henry said he liked your baking*, you would not quarrel with this even if you had overheard Henry expressing his views and know that what he had actually said was *That was a beautiful cake*.

Both verbal and mental acts have names, such as *statement*, *query*, *belief*, *doubt*; and these also serve to project, with the projected clause embedded as Postmodifier: *the belief that the sky might fall on their heads*. There is a point of overlap between these and embedded expansions of the elaborating type (relative clauses): both may be introduced by *that*, and this produces ambiguities such as *the report that he had submitted disturbed everyone*:

(a) the report = ⟦ that he had submitted ⟧
'the document which he had drafted'

(b) the report "⟦ that he had submitted ⟧
'to hear that he had yielded'

Parallel to projected information (propositions) is the projection of goods-&-services (proposals) which likewise may be paratactic, hypotactic r embedded as Qualifier to a noun; and again the phenomenon may be erbal (locution, projected by the processes *offer*, *command*, *suggest/ uggestion*, etc.) or mental (idea, projected by *intend/intention*, *wish*, *hope*, c.). The difference in the mental processes is that propositions are projected y cognitive processes whereas proposals are projected by affective ones.

However, it is possible for an idea to be associated with a mental process hile not being projected by it, as in *they rejoiced that their team had won*. /hen one clause projects another, the two always form a clause complex; but ere, where *that their team had won* comes ready made as a projection, rather ian being turned into one by the process of rejoicing, the idea is embedded nd the whole forms a single clause. This happens particularly when a proosition is an object of affect: when the fact that . . . is a source of pleasure, ispleasure, fear or some other emotion.

Such projections may be embedded as they stand, as nominalizations — quivalent to functioning as Head. But frequently they occur as Postmodifier) a noun of the 'fact' class, e.g. *the fact that their team had won*. Fact nouns clude 'cases', 'chances' and 'proofs', related to propositions; and 'needs', lated to proposals. We refer to these projections, therefore, as facts. /hereas any clause that is projected by another process, verbal or mental, is ther a quote (paratactic) or a report (hypotactic, or embedded if the process a noun), any clause that has the status 'projected' but without any projectg process is a fact and is embedded, either as a nominalization or as Postodifier to a 'fact' noun. This includes some of those functioning in mental rocesses, as mentioned above, and all projections functioning in relational rocesses (since a relational process cannot project). It also includes mpersonal' projections such as *it is said* . . ., *it is believed* . . ., *it seems* . . ., here the 'process' is not really a process at all, but simply a way of turning a ict into a clause.

Facts are in a sense intermediate between 'metaphenomena' (quotes and ports) and first-order phenomena, or 'things'. All these orders of henomena — quotes, reports, facts and things — enter into structural relaonships in the grammar. But whereas quotes and reports typically enter into ause complexes — that is, they keep their status as clauses, except when ualifying a projecting noun — facts are 'objectified' and enter as constiients into the structure of other clauses, for example

(he accepted) that he had made a mistake
(he regretted) having made a mistake
that he had made a mistake (distressed him)
(it was) that he had made a mistake (that most distressed him)
the fact that he had made a mistake (was his main concern)
the fact of his having made a mistake (he quite accepted)
(he regretted) his mistake

fact thus functions as a participant, with certain roles in certain process pes. It cannot function everywhere, as we have seen (cf. Table 5(20) bove) — a fact cannot do things, nor can you do things to it; but you can iink or talk about facts, and assign attributes or identities to them. A form f expression that is very frequent in spontaneous discourse is that in Figure -17:

Table 7(15) Principles of projection

	Phenomenon [not projected]	Metaphenomenon [projected]		Status
		Idea [projected meaning]	Locution [projected wording]	
Thing [non-embedded constituent in process of any kind]	the sky; fall			constituent of independent clause
Act [(embedded) constituent in material or mental process]	(they heard) the sky falling			embedded clause
Fact [(embedded) constituent in relational process]		(the likelihood was) that the sky would fall.	→	embedded clause
Report [dependent on] mental process		(they believed) that the sky would fall	→	hypotactic clause
Quote [independently related to] verbal process		←	"the sky will fall" (they said)	paratactic clause (independent)

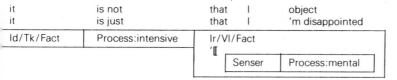

it	is not	that	I	object
it	is just	that	I	'm disappointed
Id/Tk/Fact	Process:intensive	Ir/Vl/Fact '[[		
			Senser	Process:mental

Figure 7-17 'It's not that . . ., it's that . . .'

It is important to stress that quotes, reports and facts are categories of the language, not of the real world. There is no implication that a fact is something which is true. Anything that can be meant in the language can have the status of a fact. What distinguishes ideas and locutions from other elements in the language is that their referents are linguistic phenomena: an idea represents a semantic phenomenon, a locution represents a lexicogrammatical one. Of the two, the semantic phenomenon: is closer to the 'real world', the world of non-linguistic experience. A locution, as we put it earlier, has been processed twice over: 'first' represented semantically and 'then' re-coded as a wording — with the consequence that it can now be an exact replica of the phenomenon it is representing, in other words a quote. An idea has been processed only once, as meaning. A fact is a kind of idea; one that has been so fully 'semanticized' that is no longer explicitly projected, but is already wrapped and packaged to take its place in linguistic structure. It is thus able to participate in processes, although only those of a non-material kind.

Thus there is a natural relationship among the types of phenomena, the processes they enter into, and the grammatical structures. Things enter directly without projection, into material processes. Facts enter into relational processes; indirectly (being projections) but still as constituents (since the process is not what projects them). Reports are associated with mental processes; not as constituents (the process is what determines their status as projections, so they can hardly be participants in it), but dependently (since they are not direct representations of any event). Quotes are associated with verbal processes; again not as constituents (for the same reason), but independently (since they are direct representations of verbal events). Then, by the most fundamental of all semogenic processes, the associated factors evolve into independent variables and recombine in different ways. In this way the meaning potential of the system is constantly renewing and enlarging itself. See Table 7(15).

7 Additional

Group and phrase complexes

Now that we have described 'complexes' of the clause, we can return briefly to a consideration of complex structures involving groups and phrases.

Groups and phrases form complexes in the same way that clauses do, by parataxis or hypotaxis. Only elements having the same function can be linked in this way. Typically this will mean members of the same class: verbal group with verbal group, nominal group with nominal group and so on. But it also includes other combinations, especially: adverbial group with prepositional phrase, since these share many of the same circumstantial functions in the clause; and nominal group with prepositional phrase, as Attribute (e.g. *plain or with cream*).

1. Parataxis: groups and phrases

Groups and phrases can be linked paratactically by apposition and by co-ordination. As with paratactic clauses the former are elaborating in function, the latter extending. Instances of the enhancing type are less common, since the meanings are too specific to be readily expressed as a relationship between units smaller than clauses; but they do occur.

(i) Elaborating. As with clauses, appositional group or phrase complexes are characterized by tone concord, signalling the semantic relationship of elaboration. Examples:

verbal group:
(Unfortunately she) got killed, got run over, (by one of those heavy lorries).

nominal group:
(Bankers have reason to like dear money rather than cheap money because) depositors — the people who provide the money — (do).

adverbial group/prepositional phrase:
(I couldn't have done it) alone, without help.

It is important to distinguish between an elaborating group and an embedded group occurring as Qualifier: e.g. (elaborating) *his latest book, 'The Jaws of Life'*, (embedded) *his book 'The Jaws of Life'*. The former is related to a non-defining relative, it means '*his latest book — which is The Jaws of Life*', and is marked by tone concord

//4 ‸ his / latest / **book** the //4 jaws of / **life** was a //1 ghastly suc/**cess** //

The latter is related to a defining relative clause; it means 'this particular book of his (he has written others)' and has no tonic on *book*.

Note that *or* in the sense of an alternative name for something is elaborating not extending; e.g. *Eric, or Little by Little*.

(ii) Extending. Here the semantic relationship is one of 'and, or, nor, but, but not', as in the following examples:

verbal group:
(I) neither like nor dislike (it).

nominal group:
(a) All the King's horses and all the King's men (couldn't put Humpty Dumpty together again).
(b) Either you or your head (must be off, and that in about half no time).

adverbial group/prepositional phrase:
Swiftly and without a moment's hesitation (he leapt into the fray).

A number of common expressions like *slowly but surely*, *last but not least*, *by hook or by crook* belong to this pattern.

(iii) Enhancing. As noted above, enhancing relationships are essentially between processes as a whole, and only rarely can they be interpreted as holding between particular elements of a process. Some examples:

verbal group:
(He) tried, but failed, (to extract the poison).

nominal group:
All those on board, and hence all the crew, (must have known that something was amiss).

adverbial group/prepositional phrase:
(She took it) calmly enough, although not without some persuasion.

Again there are some cliché-like instances, e.g. (*he's been here*) *thirty-five years if a day*.

As with paratactic clauses, a paratactic group or phrase complex is not limited to two members. For example: (elaborating) *that old theatre, the Empire, the one they demolished last year*; (extending) *(you've been listening) at doors — and behind trees — and down chimneys*. This includes the possibility of nesting (see Section 7.2 above).

We are not in general going below the rank of the group. But note that paratactic relationships are also found within group structures, as relationships between words, as in *three or four (days)*, *bigger and better (bananas)*, *(he) either will or won't (object)*, *(a) firm but gentle (voice)*. Figure 7-18 gives

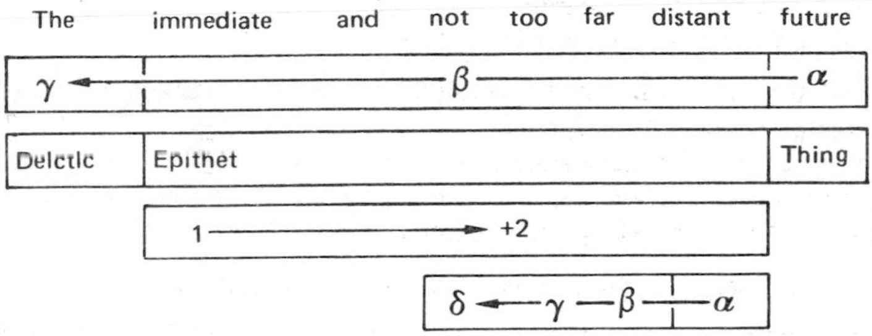

Figure 7-18 Nominal group with word complexes

an example of a nominal group incorporating both a paratactic and a hypotactic word complex; the structure is:

Deictic / γ ^ Epithet / β 1 ^ β 2 δ ^ β 2 γ ^ β 2 β ^ β 2 α ^ Thing / α

2. Hypotaxis: nominal group

(i) Elaboration. We saw in Chapter 6 that a nominal group can have as Postmodifier not only an embedded clause ('defining relative' clause) but also an embedded prepositional phrase, as in *the man* = [*in the moon*].

There is the same contrast between embedding and hypotaxis with a phrase as there is with a clause. Parallel to

(a) || (this is) my new house, = ||β which Jack built ||
(b) || (this is) the house = [[that Jack built]] ||

we have

(c) (have you seen) | my new hat, = |β with the feather in |
(d) (have you seen) | my hat = [with the feather in] |

The secondary element in (c) is a descriptive phrase, 'note that it has a feather in it', not a defining one as in (d).

(ii) Extending. In exactly the same way, a nominal group may be extended hypotactically by a prepositional phrase:

(he bit a large piece out of) | his teacup + |β instead of the bread-and-butter |
| the incoming government + |β unlike its predecessor | (was not troubled by any such scruples)

3. Hypotaxis: adverbial group/prepositional phrase

(i) Elaborating. This is the relationship that is found in sequences such as:

(I shall sit here) | from now = |β until Tuesday |
(the rope stretched) | from one corner = |β to the other |

Note the difference between these, which have two prepositional phrases in hypotactic relation, and phrases with *between*, which consist of one prepositional phrase with two paratactic nominal groups as Complement:

(he stood) between [the door + |2 and the window]

It may be helpful to diagram these, as Figure 7-19.

(ii) Extending. The hypotactic extension of adverbial groups/prepositional phrases is essentially the same as that for nominal groups, with *as well as*, *instead of*, *rather than*, etc.:

(I want to talk to them) | face to face + |β rather than on the telephone |
(why can't they arrive) | on time + |β instead of two hours late |

(iii) Enhancing. With prepositional phrases and adverbial groups of place and time there is also a hypotactic relation of enhancement, with the special semantic feature of 'narrowing', as in *tomorrow before lunch*. Here is a possible sequence:

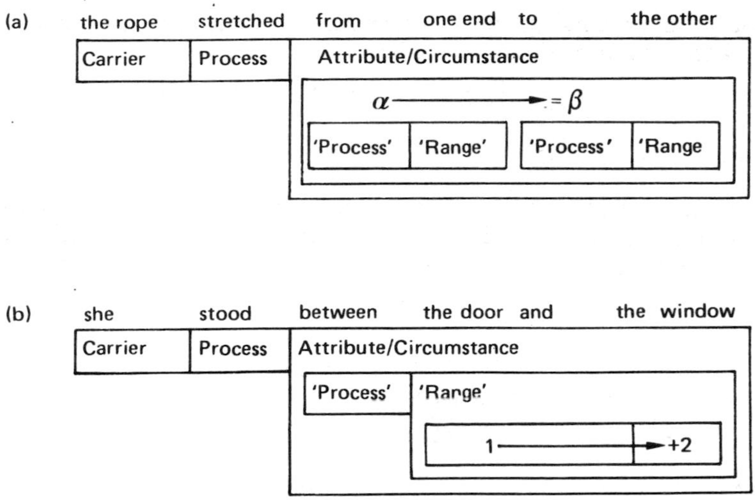

Figure 7-19 · (a) Two hypotactic (elaborating) prepositional phrases, (b) one prepositional phrase with paratactic nominal group as Complement.

(it's) | upstairs × |β to the left of the landing × |γ in the main bedroom × |δ against the far wall × |ε in the small cupboard × |ζ in the top drawer × |η at the back right hand corner |

Perversely, however, English tends to go the other way, and this employs embedding not hypotaxis (hence many of the prepositions could be replaced by *of*):

(it's) [at [the back right-hand corner [in/of [the top drawer [in/of [the small cupboard [against [the far wall [in/of [the main bedroom [to the left of [the landing [upstairs]]]]]]]]]]]]

The address on the outside of an envelope forms a similar sequence.

This 'narrowing' relationship is in fact the same as that found in the nominal group, where the 'logical' structure of the Premodifier is a hypotactic sequence of words. This also goes 'in reverse', hence the ordering . . . $\gamma\beta\alpha$; but it is hypotactic not embedded:

ζ those ε two δ splendid γ old β electric α trains

This brings us round by another route to the analysis given in Chapter 6.

4. Hypotaxis: verbal group, expansion (1) general

In a hypotactic verbal group complex, e.g. *tried to do*, the sequence is always $\alpha \wedge \beta$. The primary group may be finite or non-finite; it is the primary group that carries the mood of the clause, e.g. *she tried to do it*, *what was she trying to do*, *having tried to do it* etc. The secondary group is always non-finite, this being the realization of its dependent status. It may be perfective, with or without *to*, e.g. *(to) do*; or imperfective, e.g. *doing*. The other non-finite form, the 'past/passive participle', e.g. *done*, usually stands for the perfective, as in *I want it (to be) done, consider it (to have been) done*; but in itself it is neutral, and in other contexts it neutralizes the distinction, e.g. *I saw it (be/being) done.*

The difference in meaning between perfective and imperfective was discussed above (Section 7.4, subsection 4). The general principle is that the perfective is 'unreal' and the imperfective is 'real'; they may be opposed in any one of a number of contrasts, as future to present, appearance to reality, starting off to going on, goal to means, intention to action, or proposal to proposition; and sometimes the difference between them is minimal. The pairs of examples in the following table, Table 7(16), will give some feeling for the distinction:

Table 7(16) Perfective and imperfective in the secondary verbal group

	Perfective	Imperfective	
	'irrealis' (*to-*) *do*	(*a-*, i.e. 'at, in') *doing* 'realis'	
Appearance	seems to know	[no special form]	Reality
Appearance leading to realization	turns out to know	turns out knowing	Realization following appearance
Initial state	starts to win	ends up winning	Final state
Activating	begins to work	keeps working	Maintaining
Goal	try to relax	try relaxing	Means
Intention	decides to write	gets down to writing	Action
Proposal	would like to paint	likes painting	Proposition
Attempt leading to success	managed to open	succeeded in opening	Success following attempt

There are numerous types of hypotactic relation, which could be approached in various different ways. It turns out, however, that they correspond fairly systematically to the different patterns in the clause complex: expansion (elaboration, extension, enhancement) and projection (locution, idea); so we will interpret them along these lines. The present subsection deals with those related by expansion.

(1) Elaborating a process: phase. Here the verb in the primary group is of the 'intensive: attributive' class (Chapter 5, Section 5); and the semantic relation between the two is one of PHASE. The basic notion is 'be (intensive) + do', using 'do' to stand for any process.

The specific categories are shown in Table 7(17).

The two dimensions of phase are time-phase and reality-phase. The reality-phase, or realization, system is based on the contrast between 'apparent' (*seems to be*) and 'realized' (*turns out to be*); both are perfective, the first being unreal, the second unreal emerging into real. There is a variant of the 'realized' which is imperfective, e.g. *she turns out knowing all about it*; this is looking at it from the 'real' end, as reality emerging from appearance. We can also relate the passive to this general meaning.

The time-phase system has split into two. The original opposition *is doing / is to do* (meaning, in modern terms, 'keeps doing' and 'will do') has disappeared, since both have turned into grammatical categories of the verbal group (see Chapter 6, Section 6.3 above). The former has evolved into tense,

Table 7(17) Phase

Category: Meaning	System	Term	Aspect	Examples
[be	time-phase → tense	present in	imperf.	is doing]
[be	time-phase → tense (→ modality	future in required to)	perf.	is to do]
keep	time-phase	durative	imperf.	keeps (on) / goes on doing
start	time-phase	inceptive	imperf. / perf.	starts / begins doing / to do; gets doing; stops doing, ceases doing / to do
[be	reality-phase → voice	passive	neutral	is done]
seem	reality-phase	apparent	perf.	seems / appears to do
prove	reality-phase	realized	perf.	proves / turns out to do

defined along the dimension of future / present / past. Thus the *be . . . ing* form, as in *he is doing*, which was originally two verbal groups like modern *keeps doing*, is now the secondary present tense form within the one group, meaning 'present in . . .'; e.g. *is doing* 'present in present', *was doing* 'present in past', *will have been doing* 'present in past in future', *was going to be doing* 'present in future in past' etc. In a similar way the *be to . . .* form, as in *he is to do*, turned into a secondary future; but here there has been a further change: *is to* has now turned into a modal form, and its function as secondary tense has been taken over by *is going to*.

The other part of the time-phase system, that has remained as a category of phase, is that of 'inception': 'durative' going on, contrasting with 'inceptive/conclusive', starting and stopping. Of these, the 'go on' term takes the imperfective; starting and stopping take either, with little difference in meaning — except that *stop* requires imperfective; *stop* + perfective gives a hypotactic clause complex of purpose, as in

||| she stopped × ||β to think |||

At the deepest level time-phase and reality-phase are the same thing: both are concerned with the stages of becoming. A process is something that emerges out of imagination into reality, like the rising of the sun. Before dawn, the sun shines only in the future, or only in the imagination — as future turns into present, imagination turns into reality. The two categories of phase are related to modality and tense; but whereas modality and tense are interpreted as subcategorizations of one process (they are grammatical variants within one verbal group), phase is interpreted as a hypotactic relation between two processes: a general one of becoming, that is then elaborated by the specific action, event, mental process or relation that is being phased in or out. Examples (cf. Figure 7-20):

(the egg) | seemed = |β to get | (further and further away)
(Alice) | began = |β nibbling | (at the mushroom)
(the call) | turned out = |β to have been | (a false alarm)

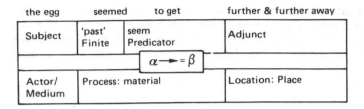

the egg	seemed	to get	further & further away
Subject	'past' Finite	seem Predicator	Adjunct
	$\alpha \rightarrow = \beta$		
Actor/ Medium	Process: material		Location: Place

Figure 7-20 Hypotactic verbal group complex:phase

(2) Extending a process: conation. Here the basic notion is that of 'have (possession) + do'; in other words, success. The semantic relation between the primary and the secondary verb is one of CONATION: trying, and succeeding. This too has provided the resources for another tense form and another modality (Table 7(18)):

Table 7(18) Conation

Category: Meaning	System	Term	Aspect of β-verb	Examples
[have	→ tense	past in	neutral	has done]
[have	→ modality	required to	perf.	has to do]
try	conation	conative	perf.	try to/and do, attempt to do; avoid/(can't) help doing
succeed	conation	reussive	imperf./ perf.	succeed in doing; manage/get to do; fail (in) doing/to do
[can	→ modality	be able to	perf.	can do]
can	potentiality	be able to	perf.	be(un)able/(not) know how to do
learn	potentiality	become able to	perf./ imperf.	learn to do; practise doing

Again, there are two dimensions: there is the potential, and the actual. The potential means having, or alternatively not having, the ability to succeed. The actual means trying, or not trying; and succeeding, or not succeeding. The form with *have* has evolved like the forms with *be* above. Originally two verbal groups, it is now either (i) + *done*, a secondary tense form 'past in', e.g. *has done* 'past in present', *will have done* 'past in future', *was going to have done* 'past in future in past' and so on; or (ii) + *to do*, a modal form (of the 'modulation' type; see Chapter 10, Section 10.8 below), e.g. *has to do* 'must do'. In other words, 'possessing' a process, if combined with past/passive, means past (success); if combined with 'unreal', it means (future) obligation.

The other form that has turned into a finite element within the verbal group is the potential form *can*, in the sense of 'have the ability to'; it is cognate with *know*, so 'know how to'. This is now also a modal form, again of the modulation type — in this case not obligation but inclination/ability.

Of the remainder of this type, most take the perfective form of the secondary verbal group, as in *try to do*. The imperfective occurs only (i) with the negative terms *avoid*, and (with *in*) *fail*; *avoid doing*, *fail in doing*; and (ii) with succeed (again with *in*). The difference between *manage to do* and *succeed in doing* is slight; the former implies attempt leading to success, the latter success following attempt. For *try* + imperfective, e.g. *try counting sheep*, see the next subsection.

Once again these forms are related to tense and modality, the hypotactic verbal group complex being intermediate between the simple verbal group, as in *has done*, *has to do*, and the clause complex as in, say, *by trying hard Alice reached the key*. Examples (and cf. Figure 7-21):

(Alice) | tried + | β to reach | (the key)
(one of the jurors) | didn't know how + | β to spell | (stupid)
(she) | managed + | β to shake | (him out of his helmet)

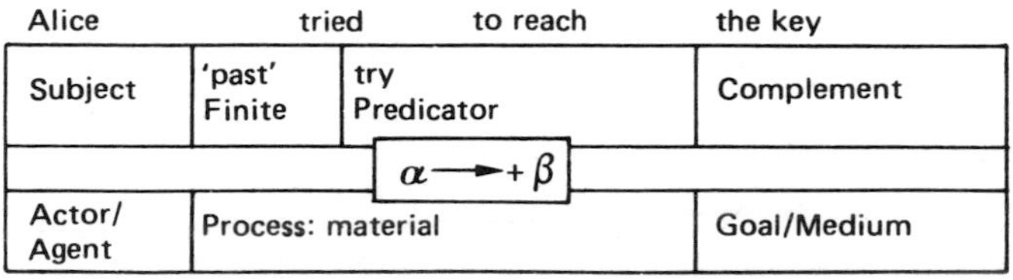

Figure 7-21 Hypotactic verbal group complex:conation

(3) Enhancing a process: modulation. Here the basic notion is that of 'be (circumstantial) + do', e.g. *help to do* 'do being-with (someone)'. As with all instances of enhancement, there are a number of different kinds; the principal ones are set out in Table 7(19).

Here the primary verb is again not a separate process; but this time it is a circumstantial element in the process expressed by the secondary verb. If

Table 7(19) Modulation

Category	Aspect	Example
Time	imperf. perf.	begin by, end up (by) doing 'do first, last' tend to do 'do typically'
Manner:quality	imperf. perf. perf. perf. perf.	insist on doing 'do perversely' hasten to do 'do quickly' venture to do 'do tentatively' hesitate to do 'do reluctantly' regret to do 'do sadly'
Cause:reason	perf. perf.	happen to do 'do by chance' remember/forget to do 'do / not do according to intention'
Cause:purpose	imperf.	try doing 'do as means to end'
Accompaniment	perf./ imperf.	help (to) do/(in, with) doing 'do together with someone'

Alice	ventured	to interrupt	him
Mood		Residue	
Subject	'past' Finite	venture Predicator	Complement
		α ⟶ ×β	
Actor/ Agent	Process: material		Goal/Medium

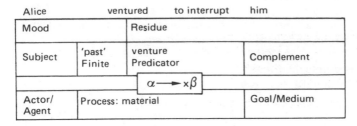

Figure 7-22 Hypotactic verbal group complex:modulation

Alice ventured to ask something, this means she did ask it; but she did so tentatively. (The doubtful one here is *hesitate*, which perhaps belongs with the 'projection' type as a mental process.) Probably all of these would turn out to be metaphorical in the terms described in Chapter 10 (Sections 10.4–10.6). Examples (analysis in Figure 7-22):

(here Alice) | ventured × |β to interrupt | him
(I) | happened × |β to look up |
(they all) | helped × |β sort | (the pieces out)

5. Hypotaxis: verbal group, expansion (2): passives and causatives

A clause containing a verbal group complex is still a single clause, and represents a single process. It has only one transitivity and voice structure.*

If it is a paratactic complex, this process consists to two happenings — two actions, events or whatever. If the verbal group complex is hypotactic, on the other hand, there is only one happening. Thus in a paratactic complex each verbal group has a definite voice, although the voice must be the same in each case; but in a hypotactic complex only the group that expresses the happening, the secondary group, actually embodies a feature of voice. The primary group is active in form, but there is no choice involved. (The exception to this is when the clause is causative; see (2) below.)

The different types of hypotactic complex have different potentialities as regards passive and causative. These will be discussed in turn.

(1) Passive

If the secondary verbal group is passive, the meaning of the categories of phase is unaffected; but there is an effect on the interpretation of conative forms.

(i) Elaborating : phase. Here the transitivity functions remain the same whether the clause is passive or active; there is an exact proportion *ants are biting me* : *I'm getting bitten by ants* :: *ants keep biting me* : *I keep getting bitten by ants*:

(ants) | keep = |β biting | (me)
(I) | keep = |β getting bitten | (by ants)

* Where there is a shift in transitivity, as in *you'll either kill someone else or get killed yourself*, the structure is that of a clause complex.

Compare:

no-one seems to have mended the lights yet
  the lights don't seem to have been mended yet

when will they start printing the book?
  when will the book start being printed?

See Figure 7-23 for the analysis in mood and transitivity.

(a)

ants	keep	biting	me
Mood		Residue	
Subject	'present' Finite	keep Predicator	Complement
		$\alpha \rightarrow =\beta$	
Actor/ Agent	Process: material		Goal/Medium

(b)

I	keep	getting bitten	by ants
Mood		Residue	
Subject	'present' Finite	keep Predicator	Adjunct
		$\alpha \rightarrow =\beta$	
Goal/ Medium	Process: material		Actor/Agent

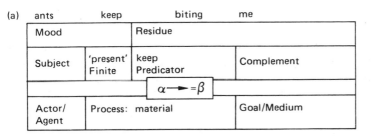

Figure 7-23 Active/passive with phase

(ii) Extending: conation. Here the relation of passive to active is different, because a conative verb, although not constituting a separate happening, does in fact represent a behavioural process, and it retains its behavioural sense when the clause is passive. Thus an elaborating active/passive pair such as *people started to accept her/she started to be accepted* is not paralleled by the corresponding extending pair

(people) | tried + | β to accept | (her)
  (she) | tried + | β to be accepted |

(see analysis in Figure 7-24). The extending complex is a two-part process, in which the Subject fills a dual participant role: Behaver (in the conative component) plus Actor, or some other role, in the happening itself.*

* Note the incongruence of the form *people failed to accept her*, meaning 'people did not accept her despite her efforts'. Here *failed to* is functioning as a simple negative, such that there is a proportion
  she was not accepted: people did not accept her : :
  she failed to be accepted: people failed to accept her
Compare examples such as *I sent them a letter but it failed to arrive*. These should perhaps be interpreted as a form of enhancement, meaning 'it arrived negatively'!

(a)

people	tried	to accept	her
Mood		Residue	
Subject	'past' Finite	try Predicator	Complement
	$\alpha \rightarrow +\beta$		
Behaver Actor/Agent	Process: material		Goal/Medium

(b)

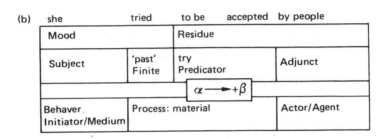

she	tried	to be accepted	by people
Mood		Residue	
Subject	'past' Finite	try Predicator	Adjunct
	$\alpha \rightarrow +\beta$		
Behaver Initiator/Medium	Process: material		Actor/Agent

Figure 7-24 Active/passive with conation

For the same reason, Adjuncts in the clause may relate semantically to the conative component like *hard*, *quickly* in *she tried hard to write well*, *she quickly learnt to tell them apart*. There is no need in the analysis to tie these structurally to the primary verbal group; but it is useful to specify their function, by labelling them as 'conative Adjunct'.

(iii) Enhancing: modulation. Many of the 'enhancing' verbal group complexes are simply inappropriate in the passive; they characterize an approach or attitude to the process, and this is likely to apply to an Actor but not to a Goal — it does not make much sense to say *she hastened to be reassured*, or *your word ventures to be doubted*. Others, such as *happen* and *tend*, are impersonal and so are indifferent to the selection of voice; e.g. *the house happened to have been built facing the wrong way*. Since they are all metaphorical, in the sense that the verbal group is representing a circumstance and not some aspect of a process, the functional analysis provides only a partial interpretation; to get the full picture we would need to take account of the congruent form (see Chapter 10), e.g. *by chance the house had been built facing the wrong way*. There would be no change of role in the passive (Figure 7-25).

(a)

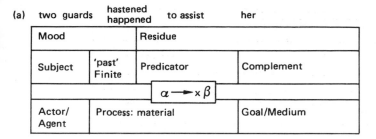

two guards	hastened happened	to assist	her
Mood		Residue	
Subject	'past' Finite	Predicator	Complement
	$\alpha \rightarrow \times\beta$		
Actor/ Agent	Process: material		Goal/Medium

(b)

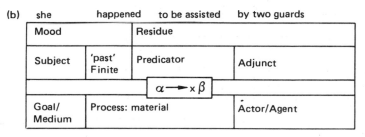

she	happened	to be assisted	by two guards
Mood		Residue	
Subject	'past' Finite	Predicator	Adjunct
	$\alpha \rightarrow \times\beta$		
Goal/ Medium	Process: material		Actor/Agent

Figure 7-25 Active/passive with modulation

(2) Causative

We saw in Chapter 5 that there is a causative element in the structure of the English clause. For example, *John rolled the ball* can be interpreted either as 'John (Actor) did something to the ball (Goal)' or as 'John (Agent) caused the ball (Medium) to do something'.

We can always express this agency analytically, by saying *John made the ball roll*. In the ergative analysis this looks the same as *John rolled the ball*; but in the transitive it does not, and this enables us to interpret the difference between them: in *John rolled the ball*, he acted directly on it, whereas in *John made the ball roll* he may have done so by leverage, psychokinesis or some other indirect force (Figure 7-26).

	John	rolled	the ball
transitive: ergative:	Actor Agent		Goal Medium

John	made	the ball	roll
Initiator Agent		Actor Medium	

Figure 7-26 Interpretation of causative form

As always, it is the combination of the two analyses, the transitive and the ergative, that gives the essential insight.

In the transitive analysis we introduced the notion of an Initiator, a participant who brings about the action performed by the Actor. This function appears in the explicit causative structure with the verb *make*. We can then, of course, extend the agency further: *Mary made John roll the ball*, as in Figure 7-27.

	Mary	made	John	roll	the ball
transitive:	Initiator		Actor		Goal
ergative:	Agent		Agent		Medium

Figure 7-27 A three-participant causative

Note that in the ergative analysis the function of Agent recurs, allowing for indefinite expansion along the lines of *Fred made Mary make John . . .*

But there is still only one process, that of rolling; so we can still represent it as two verbal groups in hypotactic relationship. In this instance, however, they are discontinuous (see Figure 7-28):

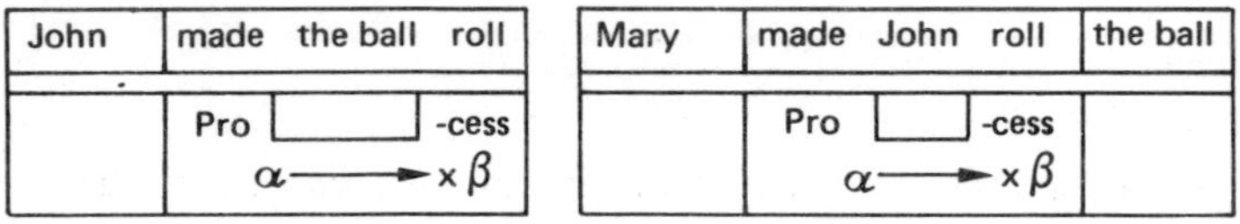

Figure 7-28 Hypotactic verbal group complex:causative

Causatives with *make*, *get/have* and *let* are of the enhancing type. But there are causative forms of all the three types.

(i) Elaborating: phase.

(a) Reality-phase. It would be possible to recognize causative forms of reality-phase, as follows:

(1) apparent: John seems to be responsible
(caus.) Mary considers John to be responsible
(2) realized: John turns out to be responsible
(caus.) that proves John to be responsible

But *consider* and *prove* are better treated as, respectively, mental and verbal processes, with the proposition/process being projected; cf. *it seems/turns out that John is responsible*.

(b) Time-phase. Here the same verbs also function causatively:

(1) durative: the ball kept rolling
(caus.) John kept the ball rolling
(2) inceptive: the ball started/stopped rolling
(caus.) John started/stopped the ball rolling

Note that these then have passives: *the ball was kept/started/stopped (from) rolling (by John)*.

(ii) Extending: conation.

(a) Conation. There is no causative form of the conative — that is, no word meaning 'make . . . try'; this can of course be expressed analytically, for example

(she) | made | (him) × |β try + |β to eat | (it)

The causative of the reussive has *help*, and perhaps *enable*:

reussive: John managed to open the lock
(caus.) Mary helped John to open the lock

(b) Potentiality. Here there are causative forms as follows:

(1)	potential:	the patient can see clearly
	(caus.)	this enables the patient to see clearly
(2)	achieval:	John learnt to fly
	(caus.)	Mary taught John to fly

Again, these causatives have passives: *the patient is enabled to see clearly*, *John was taught to fly by Mary*.

(iii) Enhancing: modulation. Only one or two modulations have causative equivalents; e.g.

John remembered to do it
(caus.) Mary reminded John to do it

However, there is a special set that exist only as causatives, where the meaning is simply that of agency: *make*, *force*, *let*, *allow* etc. These admit of three degrees of modulation:

(high:)	this made (forced, required) them (to) accept our terms
(median:)	this had (got, obliged) them (to) accept our terms*
(low:)	this let (allowed, permitted) them (to) accept our terms

The concept of agency is inherently a circumstantial one. We have already seen that the Agent, which from one point of view is a participant in the clause (*John did it*), is from another point of view a kind of Manner (*it was done by John*). It is thus not surprising that the causative Agent enters into this kind of hypotactic structure, with the agency expressed as a process through verbs like *force* and *allow*.

Furthermore, causatives have passives; so we can have

(high:)	they were made/forced/required to accept
(median:)	they were got/obliged to accept
(low:)	they were allowed/permitted to accept

and this enables us to interpret modulation as it occurs within the verbal group:

(high:)	they are required to accept	they must accept
(median:)	they are obliged to accept	they should accept
(low:)	they are allowed to accept	they may accept

* Also imperfective: *got them working*, *had him begging for mercy*.

Verbal modulation with *must*, etc., is now a kind of modality (see Chapter 10); it is semantically related to those passive causative modulations which have the circumstantial senses of 'do under compulsion/from obligation/ with permission'. What links this semantically to modality in the other sense, that of probability, is that both represent a judgement on the part of the speaker: just as in *that may be John* the *may* expresses the speaker's judgement of likelihood ('I consider it possible'), so in *John may go* the *may* expresses the speaker's judgement of obligation ('I give permission'). Analyses in Figure 7-29.

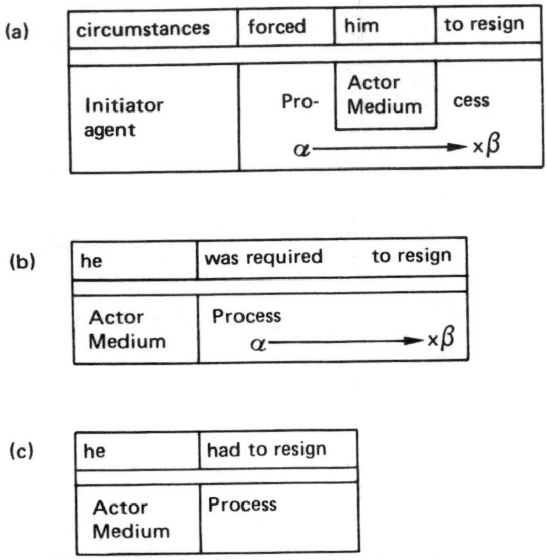

Figure 7-29 Modulation (a) as causative verbal group complex with Agent
(b) as verbal group complex
(c) as modality (finite element of verbal group)

6. Hypotaxis: verbal group, projection

We pointed out in the previous subsection that a hypotactic verbal group complex of the 'expansion' type represented a single happening. Thus, there is only one time reference; if the reference is to to-morrow, then the tense of the primary group will be future:

(i)	phase:	he'll start to do it tomorrow	(not: he starts)
(ii)	conation:	he'll try to do it tomorrow	(not: he tries)
(iii)	modulation:	he'll help to do it tomorrow	(not: he helps)

An expression such as *want to do* looks at first sight very similar to these; but whereas we can say *he'll want to do it to-morrow*, it is also quite normal to say *he wants to do it tomorrow*. The wanting and the doing have distinct time references. We can even say *yesterday I wanted to do it tomorrow* — but not *yesterday I started to do it tomorrow*.

The relation between *want* and *to do* is one of projection. A projection of *do it*, as in *wants to do it*, is a meaning, and thus does not imply 'does it' — whereas an expansion, such as *tries to do it* or *starts to do it*, does imply 'does it', even though the doing may be partial or unsuccessful.

We saw in Section 4 of this chapter that a mental process of affect projects an exchange of the goods-&-services type, i.e. a proposal. If the Subject of the projection is the same as that of the mental process clause, the proposal is an offer, as in *she wants to do it*; if the two are different, then the proposal is a command, as in *she wants you to do it*. In the first type, the Subject is not repeated, but is carried over from the affective clause. (It can then be made explicit by a reflexive, as in *she wants to do it herself*.)

All such projections could be treated as clause complexes, as in Figure 7-30.

||| she wants '||β! to do it |||

||| she wants '||β! him to do it |||

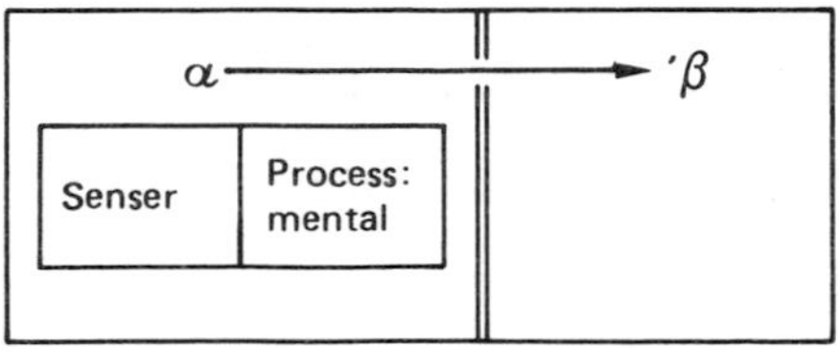

Figure 7-30 Projecting clause complex with *want*

However, there are some respects in which they resemble verbal group complexes. (1) The projected element, a (typically perfective) non-finite, has — like the expansion types — given birth to what are now tenses of the verb, the two future forms *will* and *be going to*. (2) The WH- probe is *what does she want to do?*, rather than simply *what does she want?*; compare *what is she trying to do?* not *what is she trying?*. (3) The command forms — those with change of Subject — resemble some of the causative expansions; compare the following pairs, including the passives:

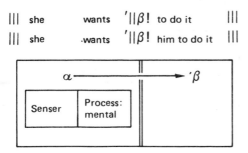

she wants him to do it	she causes him / gets him to do it
he is wanted to do it	he is caused / got to do it
she wants it (to be) done	she causes it to be done / gets it done

It is in this area that expansion and projection come to meet and overlap. Causing something to be done means that it is done, with 'external agency' as a circumstantial feature. Wanting something to be done means that it is envisaged, or projected, but may or may not happen: its status is that of a metaphenomenon, not a phenomenon. But the line between the two is narrow. In general, if the relationship can be expressed by a finite *that* clause, as in *she wished that he would come*, then in principle it is a projection; but in this respect too there is a 'grey' area: *she wanted that he should come* is possible, but uncommon, whereas *she allowed that he should come* is uncommon, but possible.*

Despite the borderline cases, projection is, as we have pointed out, a different kind of relationship from expansion. It is always, in fact, a relationship **between** processes — between a mental or verbal process on the one hand, and another process (of any kind) that is mentalized or verbalized (projected) by it. Nevertheless it is not inappropriate on grammatical grounds to treat some projections as verbal group complexes, on the analogy of the types of expansion to which they are somewhat similar in meaning. Figure 7-31 gives some analyses for purposes of comparison. Examples under (a) are analysed (i) as verbal group complex, (ii) as clause complex. Those under (b), with *that* clause, are analysed only as clause complex, since here the alternative does not arise.

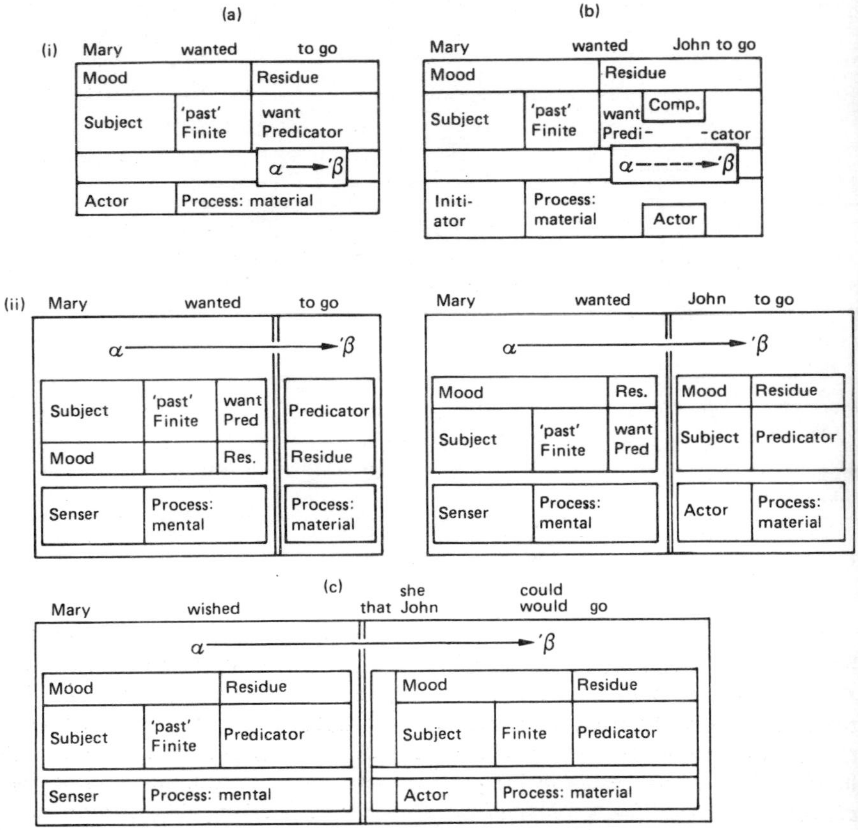

Figure 7-31 Projecting verbal group / clause complexes: (a) *Mary wanted to go* (i) as verbal group complex [preferred], (ii) as clause complex;
(b) *Mary wanted John to go* (i) as verbal group complex, (ii) [preferred] as clause complex;
(c) *Mary wished that she could / John would go* as clause complex

* Note also that *want to*, which is particularly frequent in dialogue with first and second person Subject, *I* or *you*, is then often phonologically reduced, with *wanna*, like *gonna*, *gotta* etc.

Table 7(20) Some types of projection in the hypotactic verbal group

	Category: Meaning	System	Term	Aspect of β-verb	Examples
	[will	desideration → tense	future	perf.	will do
	[going to	intention → tense	future in (secondary)	perf.	is going to do
	want	desideration	desiderative	perf.	want/wish/desire/long to would like/prefer to do would rather do would hate to do
Proposal: idea			(neg.) (negative)	imperf.	like/enjoy doing mind/hate/can't stand doing
	intend	intention	resolving	perf.	mean/plan/intend to do decide/resolve/ make up mind to do
			considering	imperf.	intend/consider doing
	expect	expectation	expectative	perf.	hope/expect/aspire to do
	need	need	needing	perf.	need/require to do
	fear	fear	fearing	perf.	fear/be afraid/be scared to do
	ask	demand	demanding	perf.	ask/demand/request to do
	consent	consent	consenting (negative)	perf.	agree/consent to do refuse/decline to do
Proposal: locution	promise	promise	promising	perf.	promise/vow/ undertake to do
			threatening	perf.	threaten to do
Proposition: idea	pretend	pretence	pretending	perfective	pretend to do
Proposition: locution	claim	claim	claiming	perf.	claim to do

To go into all the types of projection that cluster around this area would be beyond our present scope. Table 7(20) lists some of the more common types. All of them **could** be analysed as clause complexes; but there is a case for treating some of them as complexes of the verbal group — perhaps just those that are proposals, are perfective in aspect, and have the same Subject in both halves. This would exclude (1) propositions, like *pretend* and *claim* (*she claims to be infallible* = *she claims that she is infallible*); (2) imperfectives, e.g. *she doesn't like/mind John leaving so early*; and (3) 'causatives', e.g. *I didn't mean/expect you to notice*, and all 'indirect commands' such as *who asked you to comment*? It would also exclude those where the projecting process is itself causative, like *tempt* ('make want'), *decide* in *she tempted John to stay, what decided them to change their plans?* All these would be interpreted as projecting clause complexes along the lines discussed in Section 7.5.

Clause complex analysis: text 1 [Alice in Wonderland]

||| 'Well, be off, then!' || said the Pigeon in a sulky tone, || as it settled down again
''1! 2α $2\ {}^{\times}\beta$

into its nest. ||| Alice crouched down among the trees || as well as she could, || for
α ${}^{\times}\beta\ 1$

her neck kept getting entangled among the branches || and every now and then she
$\beta\ {}^{\times}2\ 1$ $\beta\ 2\ {}^{+}2\ 1$

had to stop || and untwist it. ||| After a while she remembered || that she still held the
$\beta\ 2\ 2\ {}^{+}2$ $1\ \alpha$

pieces of mushroom in her hands, || and she set to work very carefully || nibbling first
$1\ '\beta$ $2\ \alpha$

at one and then at the other, || and growing sometimes taller and sometimes shorter,
$2\ {}^{=}\beta\ \alpha\ 1$ $2\ \beta\ \alpha\ {}^{+}2$

|| until she had succeeded in bringing herself down to her usual height. |||
$2\ \beta\ {}^{\times}\beta$

Clause complex analysis: text 2 [child, age 7, and parent]

||| How do you see || what happened long ago || before you were born? |||
α $'\beta?\ \alpha$ $\beta\ {}^{\times}\beta$

You read about it in books?

||| No ||| use a microscope || to look back |||
α ${}^{\times}\beta$

How do you that?

||| Well || if you're in a car || or you're in an observation coach || you look back || and
$1\ {}^{\times}\beta\ 1$ $1\ \beta\ {}^{+}2$ $1\ \alpha\ 1$

then you see || what happened before || but you need a microscope || to see || what
$1\ \alpha\ {}^{\times}2\ \alpha$ $1\ \alpha\ 2\ \alpha\ '\beta?$ ${}^{+}2\ \alpha\ \alpha$ $2\ \alpha\ {}^{\times}\beta\ \alpha$

happened long ago || because it's very far away |||
$2\ \alpha\ '\beta?$ $2\ {}^{\times}\beta$

Clause complex analysis: text 3 [monologue]

||| But while you're being kept waiting || while there's this long delay || and people
${}^{\times}\beta\ 1$ $\beta\ {}^{=}2\ 1$

wearing uniforms stride up and down || looking || as if they have some serious
$\beta\ 2\ {}^{+}2\ \alpha$ $\beta\ 2\ 2\ {}^{+}\beta\ \alpha$ $\beta\ 2\ 2\ '\beta\ {}^{\times}\beta$

business to attend to || you don't realize || that you're being kept waiting delib-
$\beta\ 2\ 2\ \beta\ {}^{\times}\beta$ $\alpha\ \alpha$ $\alpha\ '\beta\ \alpha$

erately || so that the people you're going to be employed by can observe you ||
$\alpha\ \beta\ \alpha\ {}^{\times}\beta$

so as to see || how you behave || when you feel under stress || or start to
$\alpha\ \beta\ \alpha\ {}^{\times}\gamma\ \alpha$ $\alpha\ \beta\ \alpha\ \gamma\ '\beta?\ \alpha$ $\alpha\ \beta\ \alpha\ \gamma\ \beta\ {}^{\times}\beta\ 1$

lose confidence in yourself |||
$\alpha\ \beta\ \alpha\ \gamma\ \beta\ \beta\ {}^{+}2$

8

Beside the clause: intonation and rhythm

8.1 Introductory: foot and tone group

We introduced the notion of constituency in the first chapter by referring to constituents that were not grammatical but formed structures of other kinds: graphic, phonic and metric. Every language displays constituent structures at a number of levels simultaneously.

In this chapter we take up another aspect of phonological constituency, namely the organization into higher units, the foot and the tone group. These higher rank constituents are not simply metric units; they are part of the English language system. All natural discourse in spoken English is made up of an unbroken succession of tone groups, and these in turn are made up of rhythm groups or 'feet'; and these units function in the expression of meaning. The same thing is true in many languages, perhaps all, though English is a language in which a relatively heavy semantic load is carried by rhythm and intonation.

The chapter will be divided into three main sections: Rhythm, Tonicity, and Tone. (1) Rhythm: taking the syllable for granted, we shall discuss the structure of the unit next above the syllable, the FOOT; this will link up with the brief observations on metrics in the first chapter. (2) Tonicity: we shall then discuss the construction of feet into TONE GROUPS, showing how the tone group serves to organize discourse into INFORMATION UNITS, with each information unit comprising the functions of Given and New. (3) Tone: finally we shall consider the system of TONE, its resources and meanings, and show how the selection of tone realizes (i) systems of KEY, relating to the mood system discussed in Chapter 4, and (ii) certain logical sequences, relating to the system of interdependency or 'taxis' discussed in Chapter 7.

8.2 Rhythm

Natural speech in all language is highly rhythmic; it tends to have a regular beat. But it may be rhythmic in different ways, depending on the language.

There is a broad division into two kinds of rhythm in language, although some languages fit more clearly into one kind or the other while some languages are more a mixture of the two. (i) Syllabic rhythm, or SYLLABLE-TIMING: in this type of rhythm the tempo depends on the syllable (or on a sub-syllabic unit the mora), so that all syllables tend to be of roughly the same length. Languages fitting clearly into this type are usually those of fairly simple syllable structure, like Japanese and French. (ii) Pedalian rhythm, or FOOT-TIMING (commonly called stress-timing): in this type of rhythm the tempo depends on the foot (a unit consisting of one or more syllables), so that all feet tend to be of roughly the same length — which means of course, that the syllables must vary in length, since a foot may consist of varying numbers of syllables. If a foot with, say, four syllables is of about the same duration as a foot with one syllable, then each of the four must obviously be shorter than the one. English is a language that is markedly of this second type. It is very clearly foot-timed rather than syllable-timed.

Sometimes the beat will be completely regular, or as regular as we can make it; for example in verse written for children, like

	James /	James /	said to his /	mother /	"Mother," he /	said, said /	he
syllables:	1	1	3	2	3	2	1

Here each foot takes up exactly the same amount of time, whether it has three syllables, two syllables or one. Similarly in counting:

	. . . twenty/seven twenty/	eight twenty/	nine /	thirty thirty/one	thirty/two . . .
syllables:	4	3	1	4	3

The feet are marked off with slashes; the syllable immediately following the slash is the SALIENT syllable, the one carrying the beat or ICTUS in classical prosody.

In natural speech, the tempo is not as regular as in counting or in children's rhymes. Nevertheless there is a strong tendency in English for the salient syllables to occur at regular intervals; speakers of English like their feet to be all roughly the same length. It should be emphasized that, like all the other generalizations made in this book, this is a statement about what actually happens, subconsciously, in natural speech; it is not a 'rule' of popular or school grammar to be assiduously followed — or rebelled against with a flourish of independence. The tendency towards a regular beat is much more marked in casual, spontaneous speech than in self-conscious monitored speech such as lecturing or reading aloud; it is also, apparently, more marked in British and Australian than in American or Canadian speech. Surprisingly little instrumental analysis has yet been done on this; but the provisional finding is that, on the average, in spontaneous conversation carried on at a constant speed, a two-syllable foot will be about one fifth as long again as a one-syllable foot (i.e., slightly longer, but nothing like twice as long); a three-syllable foot will be longer again by a little bit less than a fifth; and so on. The proportion would work out something like the following:

no. of syllables in foot:	1	2	3	4
relative duration of feet:	1	1.2	1.4	1.6

This regularity is based on the 'descending' foot: that is, a foot with the beat at the beginning. Theoretically, one could just as well analyse a stretch of discourse into 'ascending' feet, with the beat at the end; but for English this will not work, because it is impossible to predict the relative duration of syllables that way. Moreover it does not correspond to the physiological facts. English is spoken in a succession of pulses with diminishing air pressure on each:

/James / James / said to his / mother, / "Mother," he / said, said / he

Here again it contrasts with French, where not only does the pulse correspond to the syllable (not the foot), but also each pulse is characterized by increasing (not decreasing) air pressure.

The principle of the descending foot also makes it possible to predict the relative duration of the syllables **within** the foot, where there is more than one. This would take us beyond our present scope; the details will be found in David Abercrombie, "Syllable quantity and enclitics in English". But it can be clearly heard that the two-syllable foot is not simply divided into two equal parts; in the example above, the sixth foot *said, said* is long + short, whereas the fourth foot *mother* is short + long:

— ∪	∪ —
said, said	mother

All these features are characteristic of informal discourse, showing that the descending foot is a systematic element in English phonological structure.

The beat at the beginning of the foot may be silent; we show this silent beat with a caret ^. This is a common feature of verse rhythms; but again it is also characteristic of spontaneous speech, which can tolerate up to two complete 'silent feet' without the rhythm being lost. The rhythm is maintained sub-vocally in the speaker's — and also in the listener's — consciousness. This rhythmic silence could be found in an instance such as the following:

Is he coming back this afternoon?
Apparently he is, yes; although I don't really know why.

/ ^ap/parently he / is / yes / ^ / ^ although I / don't really / know / why /

It does not take very long to be able to recognize the rhythm of English speech, provided one has access to recordings of fairly rapid spontaneous dialogue in which there are sustained 'turns' by the speakers. The main difficulty comes from passages which could equally well be analysed as (say) three long feet or six short ones, such as

/ put them′ back / just′ where you / found′ them /

It does not really matter which is preferred; here, since a pronoun such as *them* in an ordinary non-contrastive context is unlikely to be salient, the analysis into three feet is probably correct — a more emphatic delivery, with shorter feet, would have come out as

/ put them / back / just / where you / found them /

But in general the rhythm will be that which fits in with the tempo of the surrounding discourse.

8.3 Tonicity

The foot, then, is one of the units of English phonological structure. Each foot consists of a whole number of syllables, which may be one or more than one, up to about six or seven as a maximum.

The foot is the rhythmic unit of the language. Above the foot there is one higher constituent, which is the melodic unit of the language. This is generally referred to as the TONE GROUP (less commonly 'tone unit'). Melody as a linguistic feature is called INTONATION; so the tone group is the unit of intonation.

Each tone group consists of a whole number of feet, one or more than one; the maximum in natural speech is around ten or a dozen.

There is an important difference between the tone group and the foot as regards their function in the expression of meaning in English. The foot is not itself the realization of any semantic unit. This is not to say that variation in rhythm never by itself carries contrast in meaning; there are instances where it does, e.g., *tell me when he comes*, *the question which he discussed*:

/ tell me / when he / comes / 'inform me of the time of his arrival'	hypotactic projection
/ tell me when he / comes / 'inform me at the time of his arrival'	hypotactic expansion
/ ‸ the / question / which he dis/cussed / 'the question: "which did he discuss?" '	embedded projection
/ ‸ the / question which he dis/cussed / 'the question that was discussed by him'	embedded expansion

Such contrasts are based on grammatical accent: interrogatives are accented, and hence embody a salient syllable, whereas relatives and conjunctives are not. But there is no higher level unit that is typically realized as one foot. In this respect the foot is like the syllable; it is a phonological constituent, but does not represent a constituent of any other kind.

The tone group on the other hand is not only a phonological constituent; it also functions as the realization of something else, namely a quantum or unit of information in the discourse. Spoken discourse takes the form of a sequence of INFORMATION UNITS, one following the other in unbroken succession with no pause or discontinuity between them.

We mark the boundary of the tone group by a double slash // :

// ‸ ap/parently he / is // yes // ‸ / ‸ although I / don't really / know / why //

8.4 Nature of the information unit

An information unit does not correspond exactly to any unit in the clause grammar. The nearest grammatical unit is in the fact the clause; and we can regard this as the unmarked or 'default' condition: other things being equal, one information unit will be coextensive with one clause. But other things are often not equal. Thus a single clause may be mapped into two or more information units; or a single information unit into two or more clauses. Furthermore the boundaries may overlap, with one information unit covering, say, one clause and half of the next. So the information unit has to be set up as a constituent in its own right. At the same time, its relationship to the grammatical constituents is by no means random, and instances of overlapping boundaries are clearly 'marked'; so the two constituent structures, the grammatical and the informational, are closely interconnected.

The information unit is what its name implies: a unit of information. Information, as this term is being used here, is a process of interaction between what is already known or predictable and what is new or unpredictable. This is different from the mathematical concept of information, which is the measure of unpredictability. It is the interplay of new and not new that generates information in the linguistic sense. Hence the information unit is a structure made up of two functions, the New and the Given.

In the idealized form each information unit consists of a Given element accompanied by a New element. But there are two conditions of departure from this principle. One is that discourse has to start somewhere, so there can be discourse-initiating units consisting of a New element only. The other is that by its nature the Given is likely to be 'phoric' — referring to something already present in the verbal or non-verbal context; and one way of achieving phoricity is through ellipsis, a grammatical form in which certain features are not realized in the structure (see Chapter 9 below). Structurally, therefore, we shall say that an information unit consists of an obligatory New element plus an optional Given.

The way this structure is realized is essentially 'natural' (non-arbitrary), in two respects: (i) the New is marked by prominence; (ii) the Given typically precedes the New. We will look at these two features in turn.

(i) Each information unit is realized as a pitch contour, or TONE, which may be falling, rising or mixed (falling-rising, rising-falling) (for the details of the tones see Section 7 of this chapter, below). This pitch contour extends over the whole tone group. Within the tone group, one foot (and in particular its first syllable) carries the main pitch movement: the main fall, or rise, or the change of direction. This feature is known as TONIC PROMINENCE, and the element having this prominence is the TONIC element (tonic foot, tonic syllable). We indicate tonic prominence by a form of graphic prominence: bold type for print, wavy underlining for manuscript and typescript. The element having this prominence is said to be carrying INFORMATION FOCUS.

(ii) The tonic foot defines the culmination of what is New: it marks where the New element ends. In the typical instance, this will be the last functional element of clause structure in the information unit. As this implies, the typical sequence of informational elements is thus Given followed by New. But whereas the end of the New element is marked by tonic prominence, there is nothing to mark where it begins; so there is indeterminacy in the structure. If we take an instance out of context, we can tell that it culminates with the New; but we cannot tell on phonological grounds whether there is a Given element first, or where the boundary between Given and New would be. (This is not always true; see below.) For example, in Figure 8.1

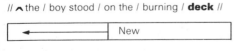

// ^ the / boy stood / on the / burning / **deck** //

Figure 8-1 Unit with New element only

we know that *on the burning deck* is New, because that is the element on which the prominence falls; but we cannot tell whether the New extends also to *stood* and *the boy*.

In real life we do not usually meet with text out of context, so there is other evidence for interpreting the information structure. Here is an example (from the 'silver' text; see Appendix 1):

In this job, Anne, we're working with silver. Now silver needs to have love.

The second clause was spoken as follows:

// ^ now / silver / needs to have / **love** //

Taken by itself, the second clause is also undecidable; all we know is that at least *love* is New. But given the preceding clause, we know that *silver* was in fact Given; the New element starts at *needs*:

// ^ now / silver / needs to have / **love** //

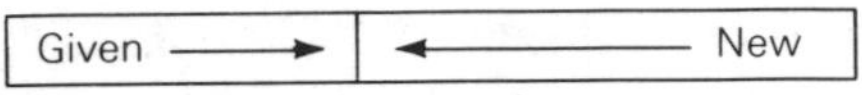

Figure 8-2 Unit with Given and New elements

(As remarked above, it is not quite true to say that there are no phonological indices of the Given–New structure before the tonic prominence; this is one of the functions of variation in rhythm. Compare the two following versions:

(a) I'll tell you about silver. It needs to have love.

// ^ it / needs to have / **love** //

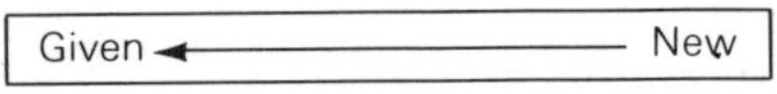

(b) I'll tell you what silver needs to have. It needs to have love.

// ^ it needs to have / **love** //

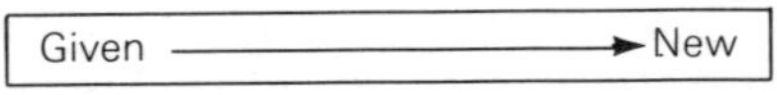

Figure 8-3 Rhythmic indications of information structure

In (a), *needs* is salient, which indicates that it is the beginning of the New; whereas in (b) it is part of the initial proclitic foot, reflecting the fact that in this instance it is Given, being mentioned in the preceding clause. But not all Given elements are characterized by this absence of salience.)

The unmarked position for the New is at the end of the information unit. But it is possible to have Given material following the New; and any accented matter that follows the tonic foot is thereby signalled as being Given. For example:

You say "Madam, isn't that beautiful?" If you suggest it's beautiful, they see it as beautiful.

// ^ if / you sug/**gest** it's / beautiful // they / **see** it as / beautiful //

Figure 8-4 Marked information structure

Iere *suggest* and *see* are New; *you* and *they* are also New, not because they ave not been mentioned before but because they are contrastive (in this case vith each other). But 'it + be beautiful' is Given. The fact that the two occurrences of *beautiful* are both post-tonic makes explicit the fact that they refer ack to the question "*Isn't that beautiful?*" in the preceding sentence. This is n instance of MARKED INFORMATION FOCUS.

.5 Meaning of Given and New

Ve can now see more clearly what the terms Given and New actually mean. 'he significant variable is: information that is presented by the speaker as ecoverable (Given) or not recoverable (New) to the listener. What is treated s recoverable may be so because it has been mentioned before; but that is not he only possibility. It may be something that is in the situation, like *I* and *ou*; or in the air, so to speak; or something that is not around at all but that he speaker wants to present as Given for rhetorical purposes. The meaning : this is not news. Likewise, what is treated as non-recoverable may be something that has not been mentioned; but it may be something unexpected, hether previously mentioned or not. The meaning is: attend to this; this is ews. One form of 'newness' that is frequent in dialogue is contrastive mphasis such as that on *you* and *I* in the following:

// **you** can / go if you / like // **I'm** not / going //

There are a number of elements in language that are inherently 'given' in he sense that they are not interpretable except by reference to some previous nention or some feature of the situation: anaphoric elements (those that efer to things mentioned before) and deictic elements (those that are interreted by reference to the 'here-&-now' of the discourse). Typically these ems do not carry information focus; if they do, they are contrastive. So hen we say that, for any information unit, the unmarked structure is that vith the focus on the final element, this excludes any items that are inherently iven. So for example in *How'd you go at that interview today?* the nmarked form, and the one actually used by the speaker, was

// how'd you / go at that / **interview** to/day //

ith *today*, which is a deictic element, occurring as a post-tonic item.

Here is a little text from a five-year-old child showing clearly his mastery of he information structure:

Child: Shall I tell you why the North Star stays stíll?
Parent: Yès, dò.
Child: Because thǎt's where the màgnet is, and it gets attràcted by the eàrth. But the ǒther stars dǒn't. so thěy move aròund.

// shall I / tell you / why the / North / Star / stays / **still** //
// **yes** // **do** //
// ‸ because / **that's** // where the / **magnet** / is // ‸ and it gets at/**tracted** by the
// **earth** // ‸ but the / **other** / stars // **don't** // ‸ so / **they** // move a/**round** //

The child begins with an offer of information in which everything is fresh; the focus is in its unmarked place, at the end. The offer is accepted, and he continues with the explanation. The pattern is now as in Table 8(1):

Table 8(1) Given and New elements in the 'North Star' text

	Given		New	
1	because		that's	contrastive
2	where		the magnet	fresh
3	and	it	gets attracted	"
4			by the earth	"
5	but		the other	contrastive
6	stars		don't	"
7	so		they	"
8			move around	fresh

(Note in relation to the discussion in the next chapter, Chapter 9, that all th Given items, and also the New items that are contrastive, are also cohesive i the discourse.) In the explanation, each of the four clauses is structured int two information units; the focus is (i) on items containing new (fresh information (*the magnet*, *gets attracted*, *by the earth*); and (ii) on contrastiv items (*that* (=the North Star), *the other* (stars, i.e., not the North Star), *don'* (get attracted), *they* (again by contrast to the North Star) *move around* (*mov around* also contrasts with *stays still*). Note in connection with Section 7 o this chapter that all fresh items are tone 1 and all contrastive items tone 4. Th Given items are the anaphoric reference item *it*; the word *stars* (post-toni following *other*), and the conjunctives *because . . . and . . . but . . . so* (hark ing back to *why* in the first turn.)

8.6 Given + New and Theme + Rheme

There is a close semantic relationship between information structure an thematic structure (thematic structure was discussed in Chapter 3). Othe things being equal, a speaker will choose the Theme from within what Given and locate the focus, the climax of the New, somewhere within th Rheme.

But although they are related, Given + New and Theme + Rheme are n the same thing. The Theme is what I, the speaker, choose to take as my poi of departure. The Given is what you, the listener, already know about or ha accessible to you. Theme + Rheme is speaker-oriented, while Given + Ne is listener-oriented.

But both are, of course, speaker-selected. It is the speaker who assigns bo structures, mapping one on to the other to give a composite texture to t discourse and thereby relate it to its environment. At any point of the di course process, there will have been built up a rich verbal and non-verb environment for whatever is to follow; the speaker's choices are made again the background of what has been said and what has happened before. T environment will often create local conditions which override the globa unmarked pattern of Theme within Given, New within Rheme.

Within any given scenario, or set of contextual conditions, the speaker can exploit the potential that the situation defines, using thematic and information structure to produce an astonishing variety of rhetorical effects. He can play with the system, so to speak. A very frequent type of linguistic game-playing is the use of these two systems to achieve complex manoeuvres of putting the other down, making him feel guilty and the like. Since these strategies usually have a lengthy history of interaction behind them, it is hard to exemplify in a short space; but here is a little conversation overheard on a commuter train:

Are you coming báck into circulation?
— I didn't know I was òut.
— I haven't sěen you for ages.

// ^ are / you coming / **back** into / circu/lation //
// ^ I / didn't / know I was / **out** //
// ^ I / haven't / **seen** you for / ages //

Here is the analysis in thematic and informational terms:

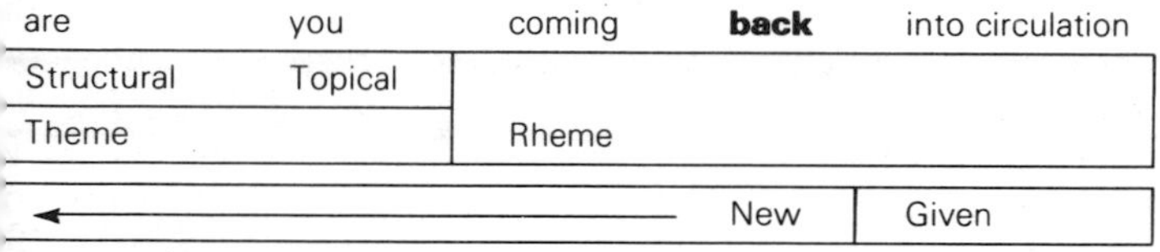

Figure 8-5 Theme and information (1)

Speaker 1 initiates the dialogue: (i) Theme *are you* 'I want to know something about you; give an account of yourself — yes or no?'; (ii) *into circulation* treated as Given, 'that's the norm', with the New made up of contrastive *back* 'but you've been away' plus fresh *are you coming* 'so I need an explanation'.

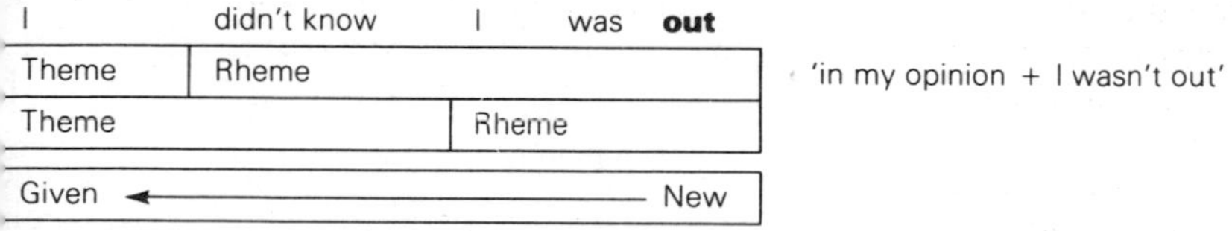

I
didn't know
I
was
out
Theme
Rheme
Theme
Rheme
Given
New
'in my opinion + I wasn't out'

Figure 8-6 Theme and information (2)

Speaker 2 recognizes the attack and defends himself with mild irony:
(i) Theme 'from my angle', with *I didn't know* as interpersonal metaphor for 'in my estimation' plus negative (see Chapter 10 below);
(ii) Information: New = contrastive *out* (contrasting with *back*) and extending back over everything except perhaps the initial *I*; 'as I see it, I was not away, so you are wrong.'

Speaker 1 returns to the attack in a vein which a fiction writer might label 'accusingly': (i) Theme *I*, i.e., 'I stick to my perspective (the only one that

I	haven't	**seen**	you	for ages
Theme	Rheme			
←		New	Given	

Figure 8-7 Theme and information (3)

counts)'; (ii) Information: New = contrastive *seen* (and hence the clause element *haven't seen*) 'so you **were** out of circulation'; *for ages* treated as Given by reference back to *into circulation* with implication of regularity over a long period. The overall message is: 'you weren't where I was, to be kept tabs on; so it's your fault'. It is not hard to make a character sketch of the two speakers on the basis of this little bit of dialogue. Note that because something is not phonologically prominent this does not mean it is not important to the message!

The intonation and rhythm shown here are as they were on the occasion observed. One can think of many variants in the textual semantics. Speaker 1, for example, might have put another focus on *I* in the last line:

// **I** haven't // **seen** you for / ages //

thus making his own selfcentredness a little more explicit. It is a useful exercise to take a passage of spontaneous dialogue and vary the texture of Theme + Rheme and Given + New noting the effect. One sees very clearly how this interplay of thematic and information structure carries the rhetorical gist of the clause.

Let us give one more example of marked and unmarked information structure, showing how what is marked in one environment may be unmarked in another. We referred in Chapter 3 to the systems of nominalization in the English clause, systems whose function is to distribute the elements of the clause into alternative patterns of Theme and Rheme. There are two main types: THEME IDENTIFICATION, as in *what Little Miss Muffet sat on was a tuffet*, or *the one who sat on a tuffet was Little Miss Muffet*; and THEME PREDICATION, as in *it was Little Miss Muffet who sat on a tuffet*, *it was a tuffet that Little Miss Muffet sat on*. Now, it was said above that the unmarked locus of information focus is at the end of the clause (on the final lexical element, to be exact); and this is generally true. But under the special conditions of theme predication, there is a reversal of marking; here, the unmarked information focus is located on the Theme. For example:

Table 8(2) Marked and unmarked information focus combined with unpredicated and predicated theme

	Unmarked		Marked	
Non-nominalized	you Theme Given	were to **blame** Rheme New (focus)	**you** Theme New	were to blame Rheme Given
Nominalized (predicated Theme)	it's **you** Theme New	who were to blame Rheme Given	it's you Theme Given	who were to **blame** Rheme New (focus)

it is precisely the function of this system to align Theme + Rheme with Given + New in such a way that the focus falls on the Theme; this makes the Theme New and the Rheme Given. But this, in turn, is the unmarked condition, so that once again there will be a marked variant in contrast with it. We could construct a context for the marked variant as follows:

What utter confusion!
— Yeah. But I'm not going to complain to anyone.
— I should hope not. It's you who were to **blame**.

8.7 Tone

Besides being the domain of the organization of the information process into Given and New, through the location of the information focus, the constituent that we call the 'information unit' has another function, an interpersonal as distinct from a textual one. It is the domain of the choice of TONE.

The choice of 'tone' realizes the semantic values of KEY, which are related to the system of Mood (Chapter 4). Strictly speaking 'key' is outside the scope of the present volume, for precisely this reason: it is not expressed structurally, but prosodically, by the TONE CONTOUR, the melodic movement of the tone group. But it may be helpful to give a brief outline.

Tones 1 and 2. The English tone system is based on an opposition between falling and rising pitch, in which falling pitch conveys certainty and rising pitch uncertainty. The falling / rising opposition is the most fundamental one there is, and it probably plays some part in the system of every language, though with vast differences among different languages in its scope and value in the system. In English, where it plays a very important part indeed, the meaning relates rather specifically to POLARITY, the positive / negative opposition. Thus, falling pitch means 'polarity known', while rising pitch means 'polarity unknown'.

Hence in the most straightforward instance the unmarked realization of a statement is falling tone, TONE 1; that of a yes-no question is a rising tone, TONE 2; while that of a WH- question is again tone 1. The reason the WH-question has tone 1 is that, although it is a question, what is in question is not the polarity but the identity of some particular participant or circumstance.

The system then extends outward from the simple opposition of falling and rising, in two directions: (i) by neutralization (neither falling nor rising), and (ii) by combination (both falling and rising).

Tone 3. The falling / rising opposition may be neutralized, giving a level tone which as it were opts out of the choice. This is TONE 3.

The term 'level' expresses its value in the system, as neither fall nor rise. Phonetically, in fact, it is very hard to find one that is absolutely level; of the many thousands of instances that I have observed in the study of intonation, almost every one has had a slight rising pitch. The realization of this tone actually varies from a rise that is quite distinct and merges phonetically with tone 2, to one that is so slight that it can be heard only when the speech is stretched. Hence this tone is usually referred to as 'low rising'.

The basic meaning of tone 3 is 'not (yet) decided whether known or unknown'; and it has a number of specific functions all of which amount to its being dependent on something else — provisional, tentative, afterthought and so on.

Tones 4 and 5. These are combinations of falling and rising, on a single tone contour; their meanings are predictable from this.

TONE 4, falling-rising, means 'seems certain, but turns out not to be'. It is associated with reservations and conditions, having a general sense of 'there's a "but" about it'.

TONE 5, rising-falling, means 'seems uncertain, but turns out to be certain'. It is used on strong, especially contradicting, assertions, and merges into a high variety of tone 1. It often carries an implication of 'you ought to know that'.

Both these complex tones, 4 and 5, therefore begin as one simple tone and then as it were cancel this out by the other. They are now totally fused, and do not feel to speakers of the language like compound tones (these also exist; see below). But their meanings clearly derive from their component elements and no doubt this is how they evolved.

It is possible to state the general tendency in English regarding the relative frequency of the tones. In normal conversational English, tone 1 is the most frequent, followed by tone 4; then there is a gap, after which comes tone 3 then another gap, then tones 2 and 5, in that order. Tone 2 is, naturally, more common in dialogue than in narrative. In more formal speech, and in loud reading, tone 3 increases in frequency, being used as a device for breaking up unmanageably long chunks into smaller information units. Tone 5 is particularly characteristic of children's speech.

Compound tones. Since tone 3 is used for information that is contingent, it frequently occurs tacked on to the end of another tone, so closely bonded with it that the combination constitutes a single tone group. This happens particularly (i) with clause-final adjuncts, and (ii) with other clause-final elements that are as it were semi-New — previously mentioned but still newsworthy. Here is an example of each kind (constructed):

(i) // 13 ‸ you / can't get / **ìn** with/out a / **tīcket** //

(ii) How d'you get on with the people next door?
— //13 ‸ I / hardly / **knòw** the / new / **neīghbours** they //4 **sěem** / very friendly //

These are treated as compound tone groups not because the two tone contours flow into one another without interruption — the same is true of any succession of tone groups — but because in such instances no pre-tonic options are available with the tone 3 (see below for tonic and pretonic). Hence the interpretation as a single tone group, TONE 13 ('one three', not 'thirteen'). The other compound tone that occurs is TONE 53 ('five three'). There is no 'two three' or 'four three', because tones 2 and 4 already end on a rise. The addition of a final rise is therefore not phonologically distinctive with these tones.

The following conversation exemplifies the tones of English. The participants are the manageress of the silverware department in a large department store, and a new salesgirl, Anne, who has just started work in the store. The manageress is initiating Anne into the art of selling silver. This text is analysed in detail in Appendix 1.

//4 ‸in / **thǐs** job / Anne we're //1 working with / **sìlver** / ‸//1 ‸now / silver / needs to have / **lòve** / ‸ (//1 **yeà** //) //3 you / **know** the //4 people that / **bŭy** silver //1 **lòve** it //

//1 **yeà** //I guess they / **wòuld** //

//1 **yeà** //1 mm / well / **nàturally** I / mean to / say that it's //13 got a / lovely / **gleàm** a/about it you / **knōw** // 3 ‸and / if they come / **īn** they're //1 usually / people who / love / beautiful / **thìngs** //1 ‸so / you / have to be / beautiful / **wìth** it you / know // 1 ‸and you / **sèll** it with / beauty //

//1 **ùm** //

//1 ‸you /‸I'm / **sùre** you know / how to do //4 **thǎt** / ‸/ ‸//1 oh but you / **mùst** //1 let's hear /‸ / let's hear / ‸ / **lòok** / ‸ you say //1 **màdam** //5 isn't / that / **beâutiful** //4 ‸if / you sug/**gěst** it's / beautiful //1 they / **sèe** it as / beautiful //

8.8 Tonic and pretonic

The (phonological) structure of the tone group is

(P ^) T

i.e., obligatory Tonic, optionally preceded by Pretonic. There is no separate post-tonic element.

Each element T, P consists of at least one complete foot. If there is no complete foot before the 'tonic foot' (the foot carrying tonic prominence), then that tone group consists of Tonic only; any weak syllables preceding the tonic foot are proclitic to what follows. Of the following examples, (i a) and (i b) consist of Tonic only; whereas (ii) consists of Pretonic + Tonic:

(i a) //1 **Jenny's** / coming to / see us //
(i b) //1 ‸my / **daughter's** / coming to / see us //
(ii) //1 ‸to/morrow my / **daughter's** / coming to / see us //

The principle behind this is simply this: that the Pretonic contour carries further choices in meaning, more delicate distinctions with the general meaning that is carried by the contour of the Tonic — but only a complete foot, one with a salient syllable in it, can embody an intonation choice. In (i b), although *my* precedes the tonic foot, it is proclitic, and hence non-salient, and so makes no selection in the tone system; whereas in (ii) the words *tomorrow my* include a complete foot, with salience on *tomorrow*, which therefore makes a systematic choice in the pretonic system.

We shall not discuss the pretonic systems here; for a detailed account see my *Intonation and Grammar in British English*. A brief reference was made earlier (8.2) to the function of the pretonic segment in the information (Given + New) structure.

The following two sections describe in outline some of the principal meanings that are expressed by the tonic contours.

8.9 Key

In a declarative clause, the unmarked tone is tone 1 (falling); this expresses a statement without other concomitant features. Other tones convey a statement with certain additional semantic features, as follows:

tone 2: statement + contradiction, protest
// 2 that / can't be / **true** // ('don't try to tell me!')
// 2 ‸ it / didn't / **hurt** you // ('so don't make a fuss')

tone 3: statement + modality: possible, unimportant
// 3 that / could be / **true** ('possibly; so what?')
// 3 ‸ it / doesn't / **matter** //

tone 4: statement + reservation
// 4 that / could be / **true** // ('I concede — though it seems unlikely')
// 4 ‸ you / might have / **told** me // ('at least I could expect that')

tone 5: statement + assertion
// 5 that's / really / **true** // ('believe me!')
// 5 ‸ I've / always / **told** you // ('so you shouldn't be surprised')

In a WH- interrogative, the unmarked tone is again tone 1:

// 1 what does he / **want** //

Tone 2 expresses the question more tentatively:

// 2 what does he / **want** // ('may I ask?')

But with the tonic on the WH- element, tone 2 is an echo question:

// 2 **what** does he / want // ('remind me — I've forgotten', 'I didn't hear')

In a yes/no interrogative, on the other hand, the unmarked tone is tone 2:

// 2 ‸ has she / **finished** //

Tone 1 expresses the question more peremptorily:

// 1 has she / **finished** // ('that's what I want to know — she should have done')

Other tones are less common with interrogative clauses.

In an imperative clause, there are two unmarked tones, tone 1 for 'command', tone 3 for 'invitation':

// 1 go a/**way** //	// 1 tell me / what you / **saw** //
// 3 take your / **time** //	// 3 have a nice / **day** //

With negatives, however, tone 3 is often used even in the sense of 'command' (i.e., prohibition), tone 1 being rather peremptory in the negative:

// 3 don't go a/**way** //	// 1 don't go a/**way** // ('or else!')

In the 'marked positive' imperative with *do*, the unmarked tone is tone 13, with the fall on *do*:

// 13 **do** look / where you're / **going** //

The other tone that occurs commonly with imperatives is tone 4, having the sense of 'at least':

// 4 give me / **time** //

Minor clauses have varied tones depending on their function. Greetings tend to have tone 1 or tone 3, exclamations tone 5; calls (vocatives) have every possible tone in the language, with noticeable differences in meaning. Many set phrases have one particular tone associated with them, for example:

// 5 far / **from** it // // 5 **certainly** // // 4 **hardly** //
// 3 your / **turn** // // 1 good / **evening** // // 3 good / **night** //

8.10 Tone as expression of relationship in a unit complex

In addition to its function in the expression of key, the system of melodic contours (the 'tone system') also expresses certain logical relations between successive information units in a discourse. These two meanings are not as different as they might seem. Whereas 'key' is the meaning of the tone in its paradigmatic environment, i.e., in association with other, non-tonal choices (those of mood), what we are describing now is the meaning of the tone in its syntagmatic environment, i.e., in succession with other tone choices. Again we will mention only some of the more general features, treating just two of the sub-systems involved.

(1) TONE CONCORD: sequences of two or more instances of the same tone. Tone concord is the phonological realization of apposition between groups (paratactic elaboration; see Chapter 7 Additional, Section 7.A.1). For example,

// 1 where's my / green **hàt** the // 1 one with / two little / **feàthers** //
// 2 have you / seen my / green / **hát** the // 2 one with / two little / **féathers** //
// 4 ‸if you / see my / green / **hǎt** the // 4 one with / two little / **feǎthers** // 1 let me / **knòw** //

In each case *the one with two little feathers* echoes exactly the tone of *my green hat*, to which it is in apposition. The same principle extends to the non-defining relative clause, which is the hypotactic equivalent of this; the above examples could be replaced by *my green hat, which I had on yesterday*, and the same tone concord feature would function as the realization of it (see Chapter 7, Section 7.4.1).

(2) TONE SEQUENCES: tone sequences 1-1, 3-1 and 4-1. A sequence of two semantically related clauses may be related in the grammar (a) cohesively, (b) paratactically, (c) hypotactically. Here is a typical set of examples:

// 1 ‸she / packed her / **bàgs** // 1 then she / left / **hòme** //
// 3 ‸she / packed her / **bāgs** and // 1 left / **hòme** //
// 4 ‸as / soon as she'd / packed her / **bǎgs** she // 1 left / **hòme** //

The tone sequences 1-1, 3-1 and 4-1 are the unmarked realizations of these three grammatical relationships, respectively.

However, as is very typical of such associations of grammatical and phonological variants, the tonal and structural features may be combined in any of the possible ways. Here, as we have represented things, there are nine possibilities; and each has its own particular nuance. If for example the speaker says

// 4 ‸ she / packed her / **bǎgs** // 1 then she / left / **hòme** //

a tension is set up between the lexicogrammatical pattern, which treats the two parts as cohesive but not structurally related, and the prosodic pattern, which treats the first clause as not only incomplete but dependent on the second for its interpretation. We get the opposite effect in

// 1 ‸ as / soon as she'd / packed her / **bàgs** she // 1 left / **hòme** //

In writing, the unmarked sequences typically come out as follows:

She packed her bags. Then she left home.	(1-1)
She packed her bags, and left home.	(3-1)
As soon as she'd packed her bags she left home.	(4-1)

The effect of the marked combinations can be represented like this:

She packed her bags then she left home.	(4-1)
As soon as she'd packed her bags. She left home.	(1-1)

The problem is, of course, that because these are marked forms the writing system has no clear way of indicating them. At best, it can signal that something unusual is afoot, and leave it to the reader to discern what that something is.

The outline of intonation and rhythm given in this chapter is designed to meet the requirements of text interpretation up to a level that is compatible with the delicacy reached in the rest of the book — which is what might be called a thumbnail sketch. The notation, showing intonational and rhythmic structure, tonic prominence, and tone, represents what has to be accounted for in a functional grammar in order to make explicit the contributions made by these features to the overall meaning of a text.

9

Around the clause: cohesion and discourse

9.1 The concept of cohesion

In two of the foregoing chapters we have been concerned with the textual organization of the clause. In Chapter 4 we described the thematic structure, based on the functions of Theme and Rheme; and in the last chapter we described the information structure, based on the functions of Given and New.

Both theme and information are realized as configurations of structural functions, though with two important differences between them. Theme is a system of the clause; and it is realized by the sequence in which the elements of the clause are ordered — Theme comes first. Information is not a system of the clause: it has its own domain, the information unit, which typically corresponds to a clause but not necessarily so; and it has its own realization in the form of tonic prominence — which typically comes at the end of the information unit, but again not necessarily so. It is these differences that make it possible for thematic and informational patterns to be combined in so many varying ways. Theoretically, there is no reason why Given and New should not also have been organized as a system of the clause and realized by the sequence of the elements — like Theme and Rheme, only based on final instead of initial position, with the New always coming last. Notice, however, that this arrangement would have greatly curtailed the potential of these two systems in the language, since they would have been combinable in only one way, with the Theme always selected from within the Given, and the New always selected from within the Rheme. As it is, Theme + Rheme and Given + New are **typically** combined in this way, but at the same time they are independent of each other: it is possible for the same element to be both Theme and New, and this is a meaningful choice. In other words, theme and information are related by the 'good reason' principle: other things being equal, the information unit is also a clause, hence a thematic unit; the New follows the Given, and thus the focus of information, which is the culmination of the New, also forms the culmination of the Rheme.

Theme and information together constitute the internal resources for structuring the clause as a message — for giving it a particular status in relation to the surrounding discourse. But in order that a sequence of clauses, or clause complexes, should constitute a text, it is necessary to do more than give an appropriate internal structure to each. It is necessary also to make explicit the external relationship between one clause or clause complex and another, and to do so in a way which is not dependent on grammatical structure.

We have described the pattern of structural relationships between clauses (Chapter 7); these are what produce clause complexes. A clause complex corresponds closely to a SENTENCE of written English; in fact it is the existence of the clause complex in the grammar which leads to the evolution of the sentence in the writing system. But the clause complex has certain inbuilt limitations, from the point of view of its contribution to the texture of a discourse. The things that are put together in it have to be clauses; and they have to occur next to one another in the text. These are inherent in the nature of grammatical structure.

As we saw, a very wide range of semantic relationships is encoded through the clause complex. But in order to construct discourse we need to be able to establish additional relations within the text that are not subject to these limitations; relations that may involve elements of any extent, both smaller and larger than clauses, from single words to lengthy passages of text; and that may hold across gaps of any extent, both within the clause and beyond it, without regard to the nature of whatever intervenes. This cannot be achieved by grammatical structure; it depends on a resource of a rather different kind. These non-structural resources for discourse are what are referred to by the term COHESION.

There are four ways by which cohesion is created in English: by reference, ellipsis, conjunction, and lexical organization. We can illustrate all of these from the following text.

Little Boy Blue, come blow your horn!
The sheep's in the meadow, the cow's in the corn.
Where is the boy that looks after the sheep?
He's under the haycock, fast asleep.
Will you go wake him? No, not I!
For if I do, he'll be sure to cry.

The use of *he . . . him . . . he* to refer back to 'the boy that looks after the sheep' is an instance of reference. The forms *no not I* and *if I do* exemplify ellipsis; they have to be interpreted as *no I* (*will*) *not* (*wake him*) and *if I* (*wake him*). The word *for* expresses a conjunctive relationship between 'I will not' and 'if I do he will cry'. The word *sheep* in line three reiterates *sheep* in line two; *cow* relates to *sheep*, *corn* to *meadow*, and *wake* and *asleep*; these are all examples of lexical cohesion. We will first summarize these, and then devote a section to each in turn.

(1) REFERENCE. A participant or circumstantial element introduced at one place in the text can be taken as a reference point for something that follows. In the simplest case this means that the same thing comes in again, like *the boy who looks after the sheep . . . he . . . him . . . he* above. But it may also mean that it serves as a basis for comparison, like *Henry . . . someone else* in *Henry can't play today. We'll have to find someone else*, where *someone else* means 'someone other than Henry'.

(2) ELLIPSIS. A clause, or a part of a clause, or a part (usually including the lexical element) of a verbal or nominal group, may be presupposed at a subsequent place in the text by the device of positive omission — that is, by saying nothing, where something is required to make up the sense. Either the structure is simply left unfilled, as in *not I* for *I will not wake him*, which is ellipsis

properly so called; or else a placeholding element is inserted to signal the gap, like the *do* in *for if I do*, which is referred to as SUBSTITUTION.

(3) CONJUNCTION. A clause or clause complex, or some longer stretch of text, may be related to what follows it by one or other of a specific set of semantic relations. These relations are basically of the same kind as those which obtain between clauses in an expanded clause complex, as described in Chapter 7 under the headings of elaboration, extension and enhancement. The most general categories are those of apposition and clarification, addition and variation, and the temporal and causal-conditional: 'namely; and, or, yet; then; so, then'.

(4) LEXICAL COHESION. Continuity may be established in a text by the choice of words. This may take the form of word repetition; or the choice of a word that is related in some way to a previous one — either semantically, such that the two are in the broadest sense synonymous, or collocationally, such that the two have a more than ordinary tendency to co-occur. Lexical cohesion may be maintained over long passages by the presence of keywords, words having special significance for the meaning of the particular text.

These resources collectively meet the text-forming requirements referred to earlier. They make it possible to link items of any size, whether below or above the clause; and to link items at any distance, whether structurally related or not. Note, however, that they meet these requirements in different ways. Reference is a relationship between things, or facts; it may be established at varying distances, and although it usually serves to relate single elements that have a function within the clause (processes, participants, circumstances), it can give to any passage of text the status of a fact, and so turn it into a clause participant. For example *that* in the following passage:

> "I'm just one hundred and one, five months and a day."
> "I can't believe *that*!" said Alice.

Ellipsis (including substitution) is a relationship involving a particular form of wording, either a clause or some smaller item; it is usually confined to closely contiguous passages, and is particularly characteristic of question + answer or similar 'adjacency pairs' in dialogue. For example, *so* in Alice's reply:

> ". . . if you've seen them so often, of course you know what they're like?"
> "I believe so," Alice replied thoughtfully.

Conjunctive relations typically involve contiguous elements up to the size of paragraphs, or their equivalent in spoken language; conjunction (in this sense) is a way of setting up the logical relations that characterize clause complexes in the absence of the structural relationships by which such complexes are defined. For example *then* in the Gnat's answer:

> "Supposing it couldn't find any?" she suggested.
> "Then it would die, of course."

Finally reiteration and collocation are relations between lexical elements: most typically between single lexical items, either words or larger units, e.g.

locomotive (word), *steam engine* (group), *in steam* (phrase), *steam up*, *get up steam* ('phrases' in the dictionary sense); but also involving wordings having more than one lexical item in them, such as *maintaining an express locomotive at full steam*. Lexical ties are independent of structure and may span long passages of intervening discourse; for example

> [the little] voice was drowned by a shrill scream from the engine

where *engine* was separated from the latest previous occurrence of a related lexical item (*railway journey*) by thirty-six intervening clauses.

Many instances of cohesion involve two or three ties of different kinds occurring in combination with one another. For example:

> "You don't know much," said the Duchess; "and that's a fact."
> Alice did not at all like the tone of this remark, and thought it would be as well to introduce some other subject of conversation.

where the nominal group *this remark* consists of a reference item *this* and a lexical item *remark*, both related cohesively to what precedes. Similarly in *some other subject of conversation*, both *other* and *subject* relate cohesively to the preceding discussion, which was about whether or not cats could grin. Typically any clause complex in connected discourse will have from one up to about half a dozen cohesive ties with what has gone before it, as well as perhaps some purely internal ones like the *that* by which the Duchess refers back to the first part of her own remark.

Cohesion is, of course, a process, because discourse itself is a process. Text is something that happens, in the form of talking or writing, listening or reading. When we analyse it, we analyse the product of this process; and the term 'text' is usually taken as referring to the product — especially the product in its written form, since this is most clearly perceptible as an object (though now that we have tape recorders it has become easier for people to conceive of spoken language also as text). So it is natural to talk about cohesion as a relation between entities, in the same way that we talk about grammatical structure, for example the structure of the clause. In the last resort, of course, a clause (or any other linguistic unit) is also a happening; but since a clause has a tight formal structure we do not seriously misrepresent it when we look at it as a static configuration. The organization of text is semantic rather than formal, and (at least as far as cohesion is concerned; we are not going into questions of register structure in this book) much looser than that of grammatical units. We shall represent cohesive relations simply by additions to the structural notation. But it is important to be able to think of text dynamically, as an ongoing process of meaning; and of textual cohesion as an aspect of this process, whereby the flow of meaning is channelled along the speaker's purposive courses instead of spilling out aimlessly in every possible direction.

9.2 Reference

(1) It seems quite likely that reference first evolved as an 'exophoric' relation: that is, as a means of linking 'outwards' to some person or object in the environment. So, for example, the concept of 'he' probably originated as 'that man over there'.

In other words we may postulate an imaginary stage in the evolution of language when the basic referential category of PERSON was DEICTIC in the strict sense, 'to be interpreted by reference to the situation here and now'. Thus 'I' was 'the one speaking': 'you', 'the one(s) spoken to'; 'he, she, it, they' were the third party, 'the other(s) in the situation'.

The first and second persons 'I' and 'you' naturally retain this deictic sense; their meaning is defined in the act of speaking. The third person forms *he she it they* can be used deictically; but more often than not, in all languages as we know them, such items are *anaphoric*: that is, they point not 'outwards' to the environment but 'backwards' to the preceding text. The following is a typical example:

Peter, Peter, pumpkin eater,
Had a wife and couldn't keep her.
He put her in a pumpkin shell
And there he kept her very well.

Here *he* and *her* are anaphoric, 'pointing' respectively to Peter and to his wife.

An anaphoric relationship of this kind creates what we are calling cohesion. Presented with one of these words, the listener has to look elsewhere for its interpretation; and if he has to look back to something that has been said before, this has the effect of linking the two passages into a coherent unity. They become part of a single text.

The quality of texture depends partly on cohesion and partly on structure. If the pronoun and its referent are within the same clause complex, this is already one text by virtue of the structural relationship between the clauses; the cohesion merely adds a further dimension to the texture. If on the other hand there is no structural relationship, the cohesion becomes the sole linking feature, and hence critical to the creation of text. The cohesive relationship itself is not affected by considerations of structure; *Peter . . . he* form an identical pattern whether they are within the same clause complex or not. But they carry a greater load in the discourse if they are not.

It is not the words and structures, the lexicogrammatical features as such, that make a text. A text is the product of ongoing semantic relationships. If 'Peter' runs through the narrative structure of the discourse, then whether he is mentioned by name or by 'pro-name' or not at all he will provide a source of coherence. Whatever requires the listener or reader to store and retrieve what has gone before has this effect. But the third person forms *he him his* are the main resources, since they are both anaphoric and explicit. We can leave Peter out altogether; but this is possible only under certain structural conditions, as in *Peter . . . had a wife and (he) couldn't keep her*. This is anaphoric, but not explicit. Or we can go on calling him *Peter*, which is explicit, but not anaphoric: since it does not require you to retrieve him from elsewhere, if we go on calling him *Peter* every time you will begin to wonder whether we are still talking about the same guy. To keep him in the picture, we need to use PERSONAL reference items.

(2) The second type of reference item is the DEMONSTRATIVE, *this / that, these / those*. Demonstratives may also be either exophoric or anaphoric; in

origin they were probably the same as third person forms, but they retain a stronger deictic flavour than the personals, and have evolved certain distinct anaphoric functions of their own.

The basic sense of 'this' and 'that' is one of proximity; *this* refers to something as being 'near', *that* refers to something as being 'not near'. The 'that' term tends to be more inclusive, though the two are more evenly balanced in English than their equivalents in some other languages. Proximity is typically from the point of view of the speaker, so *this* means 'near me'. In some languages, there is a close correspondence of demonstratives and personals, such that there are three demonstratives rather than two, and (while they almost always have third person referents) the direction of reference is near me ('this'), near you ('that') and not near either of us ('yon'). This pattern was once widespread in English and can still be found in some rural varieties of Northern English and Scots. In modern standard English *yon* no longer exists, although we still sometimes find the word *yonder* from the related series *here*, *there* and *yonder*; but another development has taken place in the meantime.

Given just two demonstratives, 'this' and 'that', it is usual for 'that' to be more inclusive; it tends to become the unmarked member of the pair. This happened in English; and in the process a new demonstrative evolved which took over and extended the 'unmarked' feature of 'that' — leaving *this* and *that* once more fairly evenly matched. This is the so-called 'definite article' *the*. The word *the* is still really a demonstrative, although a demonstrative of a rather particular kind.

Consider the following examples:

(a) The sun was shining on the sea.
(b) This is the house that Jack built.
(c) Algy met a bear. The bear was bulgy. The bulge was Algy.

In (a) we know which 'sun' and which 'sea' are being referred to even if we are not standing on the beach with the sun above our heads; there is only one sun, and for practical purposes only one sea. There may be other seas in different parts of the globe, and even other suns in the heavens; but they are irrelevant. In (b) we know which 'house' is being referred to, because we are told — it is the one built by Jack; and notice that the information comes **after** the occurrence of the *the*. In (c) we know which bear — the one that Algy met; and we know which bulge — the one displayed by the bear; but in this case the information had already been given **before** the *the* occurred. Only in (c), therefore, is *the* anaphoric.

Like the personals, and the other demonstratives, *the* has a specifying function; it signals 'you know which one(s) I mean'. But there is an important difference. The other items not only signal that the identity is known, or knowable; they state explicitly how the identity is to be established. So

my house = 'you know which: the one belonging to me'
this house = 'you know which: the one near me'

but

the house = 'you know which — the information is there somewhere if you look for it'

In other words, *the* merely announces that the identity is specific; it does not specify it. The information is available elsewhere. It may be in the preceding text (anaphoric), like (c) above; in the following text (CATAPHORIC), like (b); or in the air, so to speak, like (a). Type (a) are self-specifying; there is only one — or at least only one that makes sense in the context, as in *Have you fed the cat?* (HOMOPHORIC).

Thus *the* is an unmarked demonstrative, while *this* and *that* are both 'marked' terms — neither includes the other. Their basic deictic senses are 'near' and 'remote' from the point of view of the speaker. But they are also used to refer within the text. The 'near' term *this* typically refers either anaphorically, to something that has been mentioned immediately before, or by the speaker, or is in some way or other being treated as 'near', as in (a) below; or cataphorically to something that is to come, as in (b):

(a) "You may look in front of you, and on both sides, if you like," said the Sheep; "but you can't look *all* round you — unless you've got eyes at the back of your head."
But these, as it happens, Alice had *not* got.

(b) "The great art of riding, as I was saying, is — to keep your balance. Like this, you know — "
He let go the bridle, and stretched out both his arms to show Alice what he meant.

(Example (b) is EXOPHORIC in the immediate context, but cataphoric in the text.) The singular *this* is also used to refer in the same way to extended passages of text, as in (c):

(c) "Come back!" the Caterpillar called after her. "I've something important to say!"
This sounded promising, certainly: Alice turned and came back again.

The 'remote' term *that* refers anaphorically to something that has been mentioned by the previous speaker, now the listener, as in (d), or is being treated as more remote or from the listener's point of view, as in (e):

(d) "But he's coming very slowly — and what curious attitudes he goes into!"
. . .
"Not at all," said the King. "He's an Anglo-Saxon Messenger — and those are Anglo-Saxon attitudes."

(e) "I'll put you through into Looking-glass House. How would you like *that*?"

Again, the singular *that* often refers back to an extended passage of text, as in (f):

(f) "If that's all you know about it, you may stand down," continued the King.

where *that* refers to the whole of the preceding interrogation taking up two pages of the story. Note that the reference item *it* is similarly used for text reference, as in (g):

(g) "So here's a question for you. How old did you say you were?"
Alice made a short calculation, and said "Seven years and six months."
"Wrong!" Humpty Dumpty exclaimed triumphantly. "You never said a word like it."

The locative demonstratives *here* and *there* are also used as reference items; *here* may be cataphoric, as in (g) above, or anaphoric and 'near' as in (h); *there* is anaphoric without the sense of 'near', as in (j):

(h) "I think you ought to tell me who *you* are, first."
"Why?" said the Caterpillar.
Here was another puzzling question; . . .

(j) "Suppose he never commits the crime?" said Alice.
"That would be all the better, wouldn't it?" the Queen said, . . .
Alice felt there was no denying *that*. "Of course it would be all the better," she said: "but it wouldn't be all the better his being punished."
"You're wrong *there*, at any rate," said the Queen.

The temporal demonstratives *now* and *then* also function as cohesive items, but conjunctively rather than referentially (see Section 9.5 below).

(3) There is a third type of reference that contributes to textual cohesion, i.e. COMPARATIVE reference. Whereas personals and demonstratives, when used anaphorically, set up a relation of co-reference, whereby the same entity is referred to over again, comparatives set up a relation of contrast. In comparative reference, the reference item still signals 'you know which'; not because the same entity is being referred to over again but rather because there is a frame of reference — something by reference to which what I am now talking about is the same or different, like or unlike, equal or unequal, more or less.

Any expression such as *the same*, *another*, *similar*, *different*, *as big*, *bigger*, *less big*, and related adverbs such as *likewise*, *differently*, *equally*, presumes some standard of reference in the preceding text. For example, *such*, *another*, *more* in (a), (b) and (c):

(a) "Why did you call him tortoise, if he wasn't one?" Alice asked.
"We called him Tortoise because he taught us," said the Mock Turtle angrily: "really you are very dull!"
"You ought to be ashamed of yourself for asking such a simple question," added the Gryphon.

(b) "At the end of two yards," she said, putting in a peg to mark the distance, "I shall give you your directions — have another biscuit?"

(c) "I like the Walrus best," said Alice: "because, you see see, he was a *little* sorry for the poor oysters."
"He ate more than the Carpenter, though," said Tweedledee.

Like personals and demonstratives, comparative reference items can also be used cataphorically, within the nominal group; for example *much more smoothly than a live horse*, where the reference point for the *more* lies in what follows.

Table 9(1) summarizes the principal categories of reference item in English.

Table 9(1)

(1) *Personals*		Head		Deictic
Class \ Function		Determinative	Possessive	
Singular	Masculine	he / him	his	his
	Feminine	she / her	hers	her
	Neuter	it	[its]	its
Plural		they / them	theirs	their

(2) *Demonstratives* Class \ Function		Head	Deictic	Adjunct
Specific	Near	this / these	this / these	here (now)
	Remote	that / those	that / those	there (then)
Non-specific		it	the	

(3) *Comparatives* Class \ Function		Deictic / Numerative	Epithet	Adjunct / Submodifier
General	Identity	same, equal, identical &c.		identically, (just) as &c.
	Similarity	similar, additional &c.	such	so, likewise, similarly &c.
	Difference	other, different &c.		otherwise, else, differently &c.
Particular		more, fewer, less, further &c.; so, as &c. + numeral	bigger &c.; so, as, more less &c. + adjective	better &c.; so, as, more, less &c. + adverb

As has already been made clear, there is no structural relationship between the reference item and its referent. In order to mark the cohesive relationship in the text, we can devise some form of notation such as that shown in Figure 9-1 (see p. 296).

9.3 Ellipsis and substitution

Reference is a relationship in meaning. When a reference item is used anaphorically, it sets up a semantic relationship with something in the

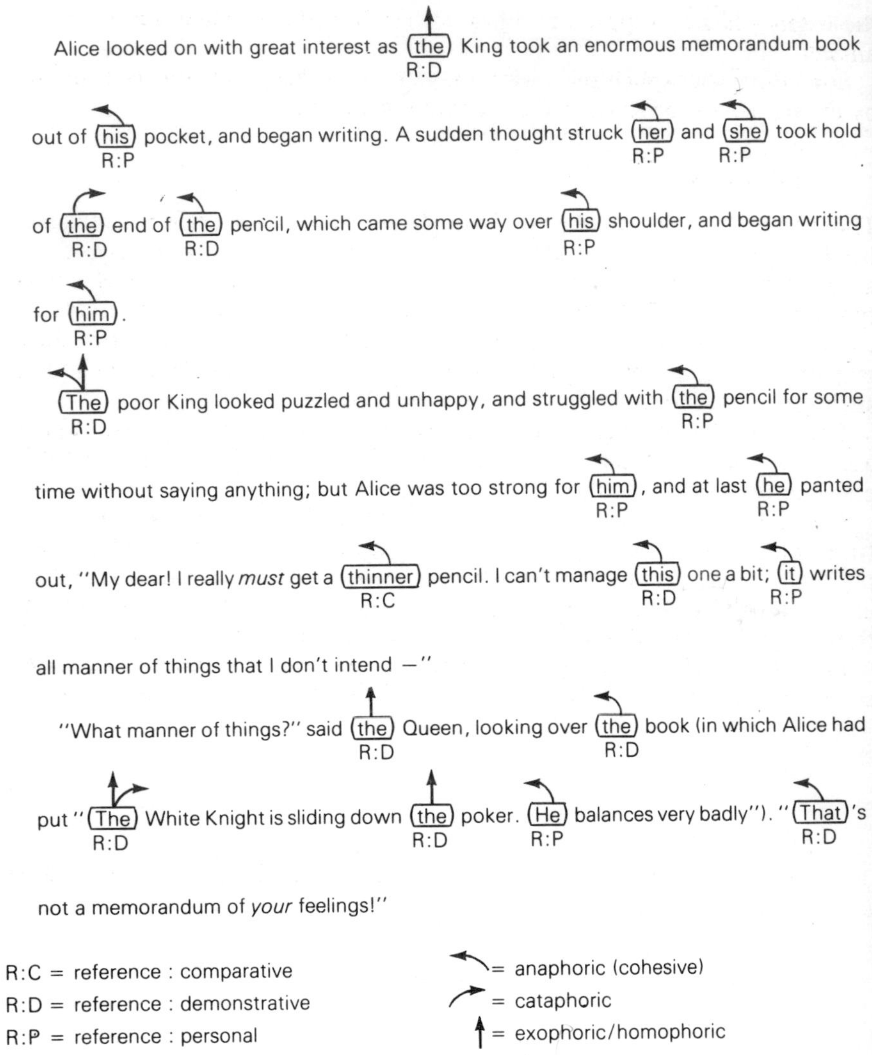

Alice looked on with great interest as the King took an enormous memorandum book
R:D
out of his pocket, and began writing. A sudden thought struck her and she took hold
R:P R:P R:P
of the end of the pencil, which came some way over his shoulder, and began writing
R:D R:D R:P
for him.
R:P
The poor King looked puzzled and unhappy, and struggled with the pencil for some
R:D R:P
time without saying anything; but Alice was too strong for him, and at last he panted
R:P R:P
out, "My dear! I really *must* get a thinner pencil. I can't manage this one a bit; it writes
R:C R:D R:P
all manner of things that I don't intend —"
"What manner of things?" said the Queen, looking over the book (in which Alice had
R:D R:D
put "The White Knight is sliding down the poker. He balances very badly"). "That's
R:D R:D R:P R:D
not a memorandum of *your* feelings!"
R:C = reference : comparative
R:D = reference : demonstrative
R:P = reference : personal
= anaphoric (cohesive)
= cataphoric
= exophoric/homophoric

Figure 9-1 Text analysed for reference

preceding text; and this enables the reference item to be interpreted, as either identical with the referent or in some way contrasting with it.

Another form of anaphoric cohesion in the text is achieved by ellipsis, where we presuppose something by means of what is left out. Like all cohesive agencies, ellipsis contributes to the semantic structure of the discourse. But unlike reference, which is itself a semantic relation, ellipsis sets up a relationship that is not semantic but lexicogrammatical — a relationship in the wording rather than directly in the meaning. For example, in

> Why didn't you lead a spade?
> — I hadn't got any.

the listener has to supply the word *spades* in order to make sense of the answer.

Sometimes an explicit indication may be given that something is omitted, by the use of a substitute form; for example *one* in

I've lost my voice.
— Get a new one.

The substitute serves as a place-holding device, showing where something has been omitted and what its grammatical function would be; thus *one* functions as Head in the nominal group and replaces the Thing (with which the Head is typically conflated). Ellipsis and substitution are variants of the same type of cohesive relation. There are some grammatical environments in which only ellipsis is possible, some in which only substitution is possible, and some, such as *I preferred the other [one]*, which allow for either.

There are three main contexts for ellipsis and substitution in English. These are (1) the clause, (2) the verbal group and (3) the nominal group. We shall consider each of these in turn.

(1) The clause. Ellipsis in the clause is related to mood, and has been illustrated already in Chapter 4. Specifically, it is related to the question–answer process in dialogue; and this determines that there are two kinds: (a) yes / no ellipsis, and (b) WH- ellipsis. Each of these also allows for substitution, though not in all contexts. We will consider the yes / no type first.

(a) yes / no ellipsis: (i) the whole clause. In a yes / no question-answer sequence the answer may involve ellipsis of the whole clause, e.g.

Can you row?
— Yes. [I can row]

Is that all?
— No. [that is not all]

The first clause in such a pair is not necessarily a question; it may have any speech function, e.g.

Have another biscuit?
— No, thank you. [I won't have another biscuit]

You're growing too.
— Yes [I'm growing too], but I grow at a reasonable pace.

Corresponding in meaning to *yes* and *no* are the clause substitutes *so* and *not*. (Etymologically the word *yes* contains the substitute *so*; it is a fusion of (earlier forms of) *aye* and *so*.) In certain contexts these substitute forms are used: (i) following *if* — *if so*, *if not*; (ii) as a reported clause — *he said so*, *he said not*; (iii) in the context of modality — *perhaps so*, *perhaps not*. Examples (and cf. Chapter 7, Section 7.5.3 above):

"*Are* you to get in at all? That's the first question, you know." It was, no doubt; only Alice did not like to be told so.

Does your watch tell you what year it is?
— Of course not. [Of course my watch does not tell me . . .]

I dare say you never even spoke to Time!
— Perhaps not. [Perhaps I never even spoke to Time]

If you've seen them so often, of course you know what they're like.
— I believe so. [I believe I know what they're like]

If I like being that person, I'll come up; if not [if I don't like being that person], I'll stay down here till I'm somebody else.

But they should be five times as *cold*, by the same rule —
— Just so. [They *are* five times as cold]

The general principle is that a substitute is required if the clause is **projected**, as a report; with modality ('perhaps') and hypothesis ('if') being treated as kinds of projection, along the lines of:

he said so -- I thought so — I think so — it may be so — perhaps so — let us say so — if so

In addition, the substitute *not* is used when the answer is qualified by a negative in some way:

I shouldn't be hungry for it, you know.
— Not at first [you wouldn't be hungry for it at first], but . . .

where a positive clause is simply presupposed by ellipsis:

Would you like to see a little of it?
— Very much indeed. [I should very much indeed like to see a little of it]

(a) Yes / no ellipsis: (ii) part of the clause. As an alternative to the ellipsis of the whole clause, there may be ellipsis of just one part of it, the Residue. For example:

Must a name mean something?
— Of course it must. [mean something]

I can't believe that.
— Can't you? [believe that]

"The horror of that moment," the King went on, "I shall never, *never* forget!"
"You will [forget the horror of that moment], though," the Queen said, "if you don't make a memorandum of it."

Take pen and ink and write it down.
— I will [take pen and ink and write it down], if I can remember it so long.

Hold your tongue!
— I won't! [hold my tongue]

With a declarative response, if there is a change of Subject only, we may have substitute *so*, *nor* in initial position (= 'and so', 'and not') followed by the Mood element.

Of course you know your A B C ?
— To be sure I do. [know my A B C]
— So do I. [know my A B C]

I haven't the slightest idea.
— Nor have I. [the slightest idea]

The order is Finite ^ Subject (to get the Subject under unmarked focus). If the Subject is unchanged, so that the focus is on the Finite, the order is Subject ^ Finite:

> I want to be a Queen.
> — So you will [be a Queen], when you've crossed the next brook.

The negative has various forms:

> They've never replied.
> — So they haven't / Nor they have / Neither they have [replied]

Not infrequently, the Residue is substituted by the verbal substitute *do*, as in:

> They say an apple a day keeps the doctor away.
> — It should do [keep the doctor away], if you aim it straight.

If the focus is on the Residue (and hence falls on *do*), the substitute form is *do so*:

> Alice very obediently got up, and carried the dish round, and the cake divided itself into three pieces as she did so. [as she carried the dish round]

(b) WH- ellipsis: (i) the whole clause. In a WH- sequence the entire clause is usually omitted except for the WH- element itself, or the item that is the response to the WH- element:

> I think you ought to tell me who you are, first.
> — Why? [ought I to tell you who I am]

> It writes all manner of things I don't intend.
> — What manner of things? [does it write]

> What did they draw?
> — Treacle. [they drew treacle]

> They're at it again.
> — Who? [who are at it again?]
> — The lion and the unicorn, of course. [are at it again]

The substitute *not* may appear in a WH- negative, as in *Don't look now. — Why not?* Substitution is less likely in the positive, except in the expressions *how so?*, *why so?*

(b) WH- ellipsis: (ii) part of the clause. Sometimes in a WH- clause, or its response, the Mood element is left in and only the Residue is ellipsed. For example, with WH- Subject:

> They're at it again.
> — Who are? [at it again]

> Who can untie this knot?
> — I can. [untie that knot]

Similarly if the WH- element is part of the Residue:

> Don't look now.
> — Why shouldn't I? [look now]

Thus clausal ellipsis and substitution occurs typically in a dialogue sequence where in a response turn everything is omitted except the information-bearing element. This may be:

(a) in a yes / no type environment:
  (i) polarity only: *yes no so not*
  (ii) mood: *will you? I will* etc.
  (iii) mood + polarity: *so do I nor do I so he was* etc.

(b) in a WH- type environment:
  (i) WH- only: *who? where? John over there* etc.
  (ii) WH- + polarity: *why not? not me* etc.
  (iii) WH- + mood: *why didn't they? I could tomorrow* etc.

A clause consisting of Mood only, such as *I will*, could equally occur in either environment; typically, in a yes / no environment, the focus would be on *will*, which bears the polarity ('Will you . . . ?' — *I* ***will***.), whereas in a WH-environment, the focus would be on *I*, which carries the information ('Who will . . . ?' — ***I*** *will*.).

The elliptical or substitute clause requires the listener to 'supply the missing words'; and since they are to be supplied from what has gone before, the effect is cohesive. It is always possible to 'reconstitute' the ellipsed item so that it becomes fully explicit. Since ellipsis is a lexicogrammatical resource, what is taken over is the exact wording, subject only to the reversal of speaker–listener deixis (*I* for *you* and so on), and change of mood where appropriate.

(2) The verbal group. Since the verbal group consists of Finite plus Predicator, it follows automatically that any clausal ellipsis in which the Mood element is present but the Residue omitted will involve ellipsis within the verbal group. There is no need to repeat the discussion of this phenomenon.

Substitution in the verbal group is by means of the verb *do*, which can substitute for any verb provided it is active not passive, except *be* or, in some contexts, *have*. The verb *do* will appear in the appropriate non-finite form (*do, doing, done*). Examples:

Does it hurt?
— Not any more. It was doing last night.

Have the children gone to sleep?
— I think they must have done.

As we have seen, this *do* typically substitutes for the whole of the Residue (or, what amounts to the same thing, when the verb is substituted by *do*, the rest of the Residue is ellipsed).

Since there are no demonstrative verbs — we cannot say *he thatted, he whatted?* — this need is met by combining the verb substitute *do* with demonstratives *that, what*. For example:

A shower of little pebbles came in at the window, and some of them hit her in the face.
"You'd better not do that again!"

The next thing is, to get into that beautiful garden — how is that to be done, I wonder?

I shall sit here, on and off, for days and days.
— But what am *I* to do?

The form *do not* functions as a single reference item. (For the difference between reference and ellipsis–substitution, see the note at the end of the present section.)

(3) The nominal group. Ellipsis within the nominal group was referred to in Chapter 6, where it was shown that an element other than the Thing could function as Head; for example *any* in

Have some wine.
— I don't see any wine.
— There isn't any.

There is a nominal substitute *one*, plural *ones*, which functions as Head; it can substitute for any count noun (that is, any noun that is selecting for number, singular or plural); for example,

That's a joke. I wish you had made it.
— Why do you wish I had made it? It's a very bad one. [a very bad joke]

This here ought to have been a *red* rose-tree, and we put a white one [a white rose-tree] in by mistake.

Like *do* in the verbal group, the nominal substitute *one* is derived by extension from an item in the structure of the full, non-elliptical group — in this case the indefinite numeral *one*, via its function as Head in a group which is elliptical as in

I vote the young lady tells us a story.
— I'm afraid I don't know one.

The parallel development is as shown in Table 9(2):

Table 9(2)

	As Modifier	As elliptical Head	As substitute Head
Verbal *do*	he does know does he know he doesn't know	perhaps he does surely he doesn't	he may do he never has done
Nominal *one*	one green bottle a green bottle	there was one there wasn't one	a green one ten green ones

In some instances the nominal substitute fuses with a Modifier, as in *yours*, *mine*, *none* in the following:

Take off your hat.
— It isn't mine. [my hat]
— Stolen!
— I keep them to sell. I've none [no hats] of my own.

These can be analysed as elliptical, the elements *my*, *your*, *no* etc. having a special form when functioning as Head.

We remarked earlier that ellipsis–substitution is a relationship at the lexicogrammatical level: one of 'go back and retrieve the missing words'. Hence the missing words must be grammatically appropriate; and they can be inserted in place. This is not the case with reference, where, since the relationship is a semantic one, there is no grammatical constraint (the class of the reference item need not match that of what it presupposes), and one cannot normally insert the presupposed element. Reference, for the same reason, can reach back a long way in the text and extend over a long passage, whereas ellipsis - substitution is largely limited to the immediately preceding clause.

But the most important distinction, which again follows from the different nature of the two types of relationship, is that in ellipsis - substitution the typical meaning is not one of co-reference. There is always some significant difference between the second instance and the first (between presupposing item and presupposed). If we want to refer to the same thing, we use reference; if we want to refer to a different thing, we use ellipsis - substitution: *Where's your hat? — I can't find it. — Take this (one).* Each can take on the other meaning, but only by making it explicit: *another hat* (reference, but different), *the same one* (substitution, but not different). Thus reference signals 'the same member' (unless marked as different by the use of comparison); ellipsis - substitution signals 'another member of the same class' (unless marked as identical by *same*, etc.). The difference is most clear-cut in the nominal group, since nouns, especially count nouns, tend to have clearly defined referents; it is much less clear-cut in the verbal group or the clause.

Within the nominal group, 'another member' means a new modification of the Thing; Deictic (*this one*, *another one*, *mine*), Numerative (*three*, *the first (one)*), or Epithet (*the biggest (one)*, *a big one*). In the verbal group, it means a new specification of polarity, tense or modality through the Finite element (*did*, *might (do)*, *hasn't (done)*); and there is a slight tendency for ellipsis to be associated with change of polarity and substitution with change of modality. This tendency is more clearly marked with the clause, where ellipsis adds certainty (yes or no, or a missing identity), whereas substitution adds uncertainty (if, maybe, or someone said so); this is why, in a clause where everything is ellipsed except the modality, it is quite usual to use a substitute (*possibly so*, *perhaps so*) **unless** the modality is one of certainty — here we say *certainly* (elliptical), but not *certainly so*.

Figure 9-2 is a short text marked for ellipsis and substitution. For the sake of the exposition, the ellipsed items have been shown at the side, although this is not a necessary part of the analysis.

9.4 Conjunction

We saw in Chapter 7 that the fundamental logical-semantic relations of expansion and projection take many different forms in combination with other features. An example is given, in Appendix 3, of the causal relation expressed in a variety of grammatical guises. Most of the encodings presented there are structural: the causal relation is realized in the structure of a clause, or of a hypotactic clause complex. Examples are also given, however, of non-structural relations, where cause and effect are in different sentences but the relationship is still made explicit; for example

> She didn't know the rules. Consequently she died.
> She died. For she didn't know the rules.

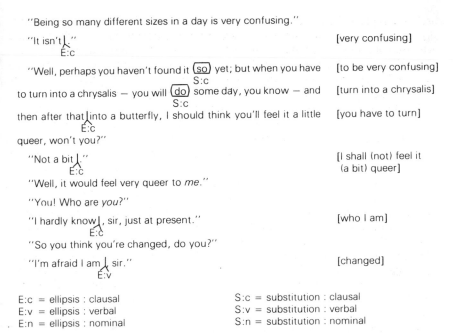

"Being so many different sizes in a day is very confusing."	
"It isn't ⅄." (E:c)	[very confusing]
"Well, perhaps you haven't found it (so) (S:c) yet; but when you have	[to be very confusing]
to turn into a chrysalis – you will (do) (S:c) some day, you know – and	[turn into a chrysalis]
then after that ⅄ (E:c) into a butterfly, I should think you'll feel it a little	[you have to turn]
queer, won't you?"	
"Not a bit ⅄." (E:c)	[I shall (not) feel it (a bit) queer]
"Well, it would feel very queer to *me*."	
"You! Who are *you*?"	
"I hardly know ⅄ (E:c), sir, just at present."	[who I am]
"So you think you're changed, do you?"	
"I'm afraid I am ⅄ (E:v) sir."	[changed]

E:c = ellipsis : clausal
E:v = ellipsis : verbal
E:n = ellipsis : nominal

S:c = substitution : clausal
S:v = substitution : verbal
S:n = substitution : nominal

Figure 9-2 Text analysed for ellipsis and substitution

Here the relationship of cause constitutes a cohesive bond between the two clauses; and it is expressed by the words *consequently* and *for*.

This type of cohesion is known as conjunction. A range of possible meanings within the domains of elaboration, extension and enhancement is expressed by the choice of a conjunctive Adjunct (an adverbial group or prepositional phrase), or of one of a small set of conjunctions *and or nor but yet so then*, typically (and in the case of the conjunctions obligatorily) in thematic position at the beginning of the clause.

(1) Elaboration. There are two categories of elaborative relation, (a) apposition and (b) clarification. We will consider the appositive type first.

(a) apposition. In this type of elaboration some element is re-presented, or restated, either (i) by exposition, the 'i.e.' relation, or (ii) by example, the 'e.g.' relation. Typical conjunctive expressions of these two kinds are as follows:

(i) expository:	in other words, that is (to say), I mean (to say), to put it another way
(ii) exemplifying:	for example, for instance, thus, to illustrate

(b) clarification. Here the elaborated element is not simply restated but reinstated, summarized, made more precise or in some other way clarified for purposes of the discourse:

(i) corrective:	or rather, at least, to be more precise
(ii) distractive:	by the way, incidentally

(iii) dismissive: in any case, anyway, leaving that aside
(iv) particularizing: in particular, more especially
(v) resumptive: as I was saying, to resume, to get back to the point
(vi) summative: in short, to sum up, in conclusion, briefly
(vii) verifactive: actually, as a matter of fact, in fact

(2) Extension. Extension involves either addition or variation. Addition is either positive 'and', negative 'nor' or adversative 'but'; but since the adversative relation plays a particularly important part in discourse it is best taken as a separate heading on its own. Variation includes replacive 'instead', subtractive 'except' and alternative 'or' types.

(a) addition

(i) positive: and, also, moreover, in addition
(ii) negative: nor

(b) adversative: but, yet, on the other hand, however

(c) variation

(i) replacive: on the contrary, instead
(ii) subtractive: apart from that, except for that
(iii) alternative: alternatively

(3) Enhancement. The various types of enhancement that create cohesion are (a) spatio-temporal, (b) manner, (c) causal-conditional and (d) matter. Each of these will be briefly discussed and exemplified.

(a) spatio-temporal. Place reference may be used conjunctively within a text, with *here* and *there*, spatial adverbs such as *behind* and *nearby*, and expressions containing a place noun or adverb plus reference item, e.g. *in the same place*, *anywhere else*. Here spatial relations are being used as text-creating cohesive devices.

Note however that most apparently spatial cohesion is in terms of metaphorical space; for example *there* in *there you're wrong*; cf. expressions like *on those grounds*, *on that point*. These are actually expressions of Matter. Many conjunctive expressions of the enhancing kind are also in origin spatial metaphors; e.g. *in the first place*, *on the other hand* (*hand* involves a double metaphor: 'part of the body' — 'side' [*on my right hand*] — 'side of an argument').

Temporal conjunction covers a very great variety of different relations, the most general categories being as follows:

(i) simple
[a] following: then, next, afterwards [including correlatives first . . . then]
[b] simultaneous: just then, at the same time
[c] preceding: before that, hitherto, previously
[d] conclusive: in the end, finally

(ii) complex
[e] immediate: at once, thereupon, straightaway

[f] interrupted: soon, after a while
[g] repetitive: next time, on another occasion
[h] specific: next day, an hour later, that morning
[j] durative: meanwhile, all that time
[k] terminal: until then, up to that point
[l] punctiliar: at this moment

Those that are called 'complex' are the simple ones with some other semantic feature or features present at the same time.

Many temporal conjunctives have an 'internal' as well as an 'external' interpretation; that is, the time they refer to is the temporal unfolding of the discourse itself, not the temporal sequence of the processes referred to. In terms of the functional components of semantics, it is interpersonal not experiential time. Parallel to the 'simple' categories above we can recognize:

(iii) simple internal
[m] following: next, secondly ('my next point is') [incl. correlatives first . . . next]
[n] simultaneous: at this point, here, now
[o] preceding: hitherto, up to now
[p] conclusive: lastly, last of all, finally

These shade in to temporal metaphors of an enhancing kind such as *meanwhile, at the same time* (*meanwhile let us not forget that . . . , at the same time it must be admitted that . . .*).

(b) comparative. Manner conjunctives create cohesion (i) by comparison, (ii) by reference to means. Comparison may be (a) positive ('is like'), or (b) negative ('is unlike'):

(i) comparison
[a] positive: likewise, similarly
[b] negative: in a different way

Expressions of means are not often conjunctive; those that are are usually also comparative, e.g. *in the same manner*.

(c) causal-conditional. In many types of discourse the relation of cause figures very prominently as a cohesive agent. Some cause expressions are general, others relate more specifically to result, reason or purpose:

(i) general: so, then, therefore, consequently, hence, because of that; for

(ii) specific
[a] result: in consequence, as a result
[b] reason: on account of this, for that reason
[c] purpose: for that purpose, with this in view

Conditionals subdivide into (i) positive, (ii) negative and (iii) concessive.

(i) positive: then, in that case, in that event, under the circumstances
(ii) negative: otherwise, if not

Table 9(3) Synoptic summary of expansion

type of expansion		functional relationship with which expansion is combined	COHESION between clause complexes (non-structural)	INTERDEPENDENCY between clauses in a clause complex: paratactic	hypotactic	
(+) ELABORATION	opposition	expository exemplificatory	In other words For example	that is	which, who NON-DEFINING RELATIVE CLAUSE	[non-finite clause
	clarification	{ various types	Or rather, Anyway, Actually &c.	at least		
(=) EXTENSION	addition	positive negative adversative	Also Neither However	and nor but	while whereas	besides without
	variation	replacive subtractive alternative	On the contrary Otherwise Alternatively	 only or	 except that if not . . . then	instead of other than
(×) ENHANCEMENT	spatio-temporal: place	extent point(s)	 There	 there	as far as where(ver)	
	spatio-temporal: time	extent point(s) prior subsequent { various complex types	Throughout Simultaneously Previously Next Finally, At once, Meanwhile &c.	 now then	while when(ever) before, until after, since as soon as &c.	while, in when, on before, unti after, since
	manner	means quality comparison	Thus Likewise	 so	 as, as if	by like, as if
	causal-conditional: cause	reason result purpose insurance	Therefore Consequently To that end	so, for thus	because in order that in case	with, by as a result (so as) to, in case of
	causal-conditional: condition	positive negative concessive	In that case Otherwise Nevertheless	then otherwise though	if, as long as unless although	if, in event without despite*
	matter	respective	In that respect			
class of item { that is being related: / by which relationship is realized			clause(complex): prepositional phrase or adverb	independent clause: conjunction	finite or non-finite dependent clause: conjunction, preposition, or relative (noun)	

EMBEDDING of clause as Modifier in nominal group	CIRCUMSTANTIATION in clause (as process)	PHASE, CONATION &c. in verbal group complex (TENSE, VOICE in verbal group)		ATTRIBUTION or IDENTIFICATION as relational process in clause
which, who; [non-finite clause] that DEFINING RELATIVE CLAUSE	as ROLE	PASSIVE VOICE is $[v^n]$	PHASE (a) TIME start, keep (b) REALITY seem, turn out	INTENSIVE 'is' (=)
whose, of which DEFINING RELATIVE CLAUSE (POSSESSIVE)	with, including without ACCOMPANIMENT instead of except (for)	PAST TENSE has $[v^n]$ OBLIGATION has to $[v^o]$	CONATION & POTENTIALITY try; succeed; can; learn	POSSESSIVE 'has' (+)
DEFINING RELATIVE CLAUSE (CIRCUMSTANTIAL) (a) CIRCUMSTANCE AS HEAD place (where/that) time (when/that) reason (why/that) &c. (b) CIRCUMSTANCE AS MODIFIER [HEAD noun] where/at which when/on which for which about which &c.	for at, in PLACE for at, on before after during &c. TIME by, with [adverb] like MANNER because of for in case of CAUSE in the event of in default of despite about MATTER	PRESENT TENSE is (at) $[v^{ŋ}]$ EXPECTATION is to $[v^o]$	MODULATION (a) TIME begin by (b) MANNER venture, hesitate (c) CAUSE happen, remember	CIRCUMSTANTIAL 'is at' (a) CIRCUMSTANCE AS PROCESS occupies, follows, causes concerns &c. (b) CIRCUMSTANCE AS PARTICIPANT is at, in, on, before, like, because of, about &c. (×)
finite or non-finite rankshifted clause: relative (noun, adverb, or prepositional phrase)	prepositional phrase: preposition	verbal group: auxiliary	verbal group complex: verb	nominal group: verb or preposition

(iii) concessive: yet, still, though, despite this, however, even so, all the same, neverthcless

(d) respective. Here cohesion is established by reference to the 'matter' that has gone before. As noted earlier, many expressions of matter are spatial metaphors, involving words like *point*, *ground*, *field*; and these become conjunctive when coupled with reference items. Typical expressions are:

(i) positive: here, there, as to that, in that respect
(ii) negative: in other respects, elsewhere

It is clear that a number of these different types of conjunctive relation overlap with one another. The conjunctive relation of 'matter' is very close to some of those of the elaborative kind, and the concessive ('despite X, nevertheless Y') overlaps with the adversative ('X and, conversely, Y'). Such pairs are characterized by differences of emphasis, and some instances can be assigned to one member or the other; but others can not, and may be interpreted either way. The categories given here are those which have been found most useful in the interpretation of texts, and their schematization is such as to relate to other parts of the system of the language. Table 9(3) sets out the conjunctive relations so as to show how they match up semantically with parataxis and hypotaxis in the clause complex.

Secondly the whole phenomenon of conjunction shades into that of reference. Many conjunctives have reference items embedded in them, typically *that* or *this*: *in that case*, *despite this*, *from there on*, etc. etc. In such cases the conjunctive relation can be taken as the predominant one, because it embodies more meaning — more semantic features; any instance which can be assigned to a conjunctive category can be interpreted as such and the reference item ignored.

One question that arises in the interpretation of a text is what to do about conjunction that is implicit. It often happens, especially with temporal and causal sequences, that the semantic relationship is clearly felt to be present but is unexpressed; for example

> George Stephenson died on 12 August 1848 . . . He was buried at Holy Trinity, Chesterfield.

where there is obviously a temporal relationship between the two parts; cf. the following where the relation is one of cause:

> Hudson decided next to establish himself in London. He bought what was then considered to be the largest private house in London, Albert House, ...

It is clear that texture is achieved through conjunctive relations of this kind and there is no reason not to take account of it. On the other hand, the attempt to include it in the analysis leads to a great deal of indeterminacy, both as regards whether a conjunctive relation is present or not and as regards which particular kind of relationship it is. Consider the extract:

> Around 1823, certain normally staid and sensible firms in the city of London got themselves very worked up about the possibilities of great fortunes to be made in South America. The idea was admittedly very exciting. Everybody

knew the old stories, even if many of them were legendary, about the Inca gold mines, about the Spanish conquistadores and the undreamt of mineral wealth which they had found. These mines had been worked by hand, without machines, and long since left abandoned. Think what can now be done, suggested some bright speculator, using all our new and marvellous steam engines!

This is a highly cohesive passage; but it is difficult to say what implicit conjunctive relationship would hold between pairs of adjacent sentences, or between each sentence and anything that precedes it.

It is perhaps as well, therefore, to be cautious in assigning implicit conjunction in the interpretation of a text. It is likely that there will always be other forms of cohesion present, and that these are the main source of our intuition that there is a pattern of conjunctive relationships as well. Moreover the present or absence of explicit conjunction is one of the principal variables in English discourse, both as between genres and as between texts in the same genre; this variation is obscured if we assume conjunction where it is not expressed. It is important therefore to note those instances where conjunction is being recognized that is implicit; and to characterize the text also without it, to see how much we still feel is being left unaccounted for.

Figure 9-3 gives an example of a text showing conjunctive relations. The headings that may be found useful for most purposes of analysis are the general ones of appositive, clarificative; additive, adversative, variative; temporal, comparative, causal, conditional, concessive, respective.

"Heat is only the motion of the atoms I told you about."

"(Then) what is *cold*?"
C:cond

"Cold is only absence of heat."

"(Then) if anything is cold it means that its atoms are not moving."
C:cond

"Only in the most extreme case. There are different degrees of cold. Ø A piece of ice is cold
C:ap

compared with warm water. (But) the atoms of a piece of ice are moving — they are moving
C:conc

quite fast, (as a matter of fact). (But) they are not moving as fast as the atoms of warm water.
C:ap C:conc

(So that) compared with the water, the ice is cold. (But) even the water would seem cold, if
C:c C:ad

compared with a red-hot poker. (Now) I'll tell you an experiment you ought to try one day."
C:temp

C:ad = additive	C:caus = causal	C:cond = conditional
C:ap = appositive	C:conc = concessive	C:temp = temporal
Ø = implicit conjunction		

Figure 9-3 Text analysed for conjunction

9.5 Lexical cohesion

The remaining type of pattern by which a speaker or writer creates cohesion in discourse is his choice of lexical items.

Lexical cohesion comes about through the selection of items that are related in some way to those that have gone before.

(1) Repetition. The most direct form of lexical cohesion is the repetition of a lexical item; e.g. *bear* in

> Algy met a bear. The bear was bulgy.

Here the second occurrence of *bear* harks back to the first.

In this instance, there is also the reference item *the*, signalling that the listener knows which bear is intended; and since there is nothing else to satisfy the *the*, we conclude that it is the same bear. But this referential link is not necessary to lexical cohesion; if we had *Algy met a bear. Bears are bulgy*, where *bears* means 'all bears', there would still be lexical cohesion of *bears* with *bear*. In this case, however, there would be only one tie; whereas in the example cited first there are two, one referential (*the*) and one lexical (*bear*).

As the last example shows, in order for a lexical item to be recognized as repeated it need not be in the same morphological shape. For example, *dine*, *dining*, *diner*, *dinner* are all the same item, and an occurrence of any one constitutes a repetition of any of the others. Inflexional variants always belong together as one item; derivational variants usually do, when they are based on a living derivational process, although these are less predictable. (For example, *rational* and *rationalize* are probably still the same lexical item, though the relationship between them has become rather tenuous; but neither now goes with *ration* — *rational* is closer to *reason*, though not close enough to be considered the same item.)

In Landor's line

> I strove with none, for none was worth my strife

there is a strongly felt cohesion between *strife* and *strove*, suggesting that *strive*, *strove* and *strife* are one and the same lexical item.

(2) Synonymy. In the second place, lexical cohesion results from the choice of a lexical item that is in some sense synonymous with a preceding one; for example *sound* with *noise*, *cavalry* with *horses* in

> He was just wondering which road to take when he was startled by a noise from behind him. It was the noise of trotting horses. . . . He dismounted and led his horse as quickly as he could along the right-hand road. The sound of the cavalry grew rapidly nearer . . .

Here again the cohesion need not depend on identity of reference. But once we depart from straightforward repetition, and take account of cohesion between **related** items, it is useful to distinguish whether the reference is identical or not, because slightly different patterns appear.

(a) with identity of reference. Here the range of potentially cohesive items includes synonyms of the same or some higher level of generality: synonyms in the narrower sense, and *superordinates*. For example, in

> Four-&-twenty blackbirds, baked in a pie.
> When the pie was opened, the birds began to sing.

we have one instance of repetition (*pie . . . pie*) and one of synonyms (*blackbirds . . . birds*). *birds*, however, is at a higher level of generality than *blackbirds*; it is a superordinate term. In fact we might have (disregarding the scansion, of course) any of the following sequences:

four-&-twenty blackbirds . . .	the blackbirds began to sing
,,	the birds began to sing
,,	the creatures began to sing
,,	they began to sing

the reference item *they* being simply the most general of all. Compare *python . . . snake* in the verse quoted in Appendix 3 below (*. . . who bought a Python from a man . . . the Snake is living yet*); and *pig . . . creature* in the following passage from *Alice*:

> This time there could be no mistake about it; it was neither more nor less than a pig, and she felt that it would be quite absurd for her to carry it any further. So she set the little creature down, and . . .

Such instances are typically accompanied by the reference item *the*. This interaction between lexical cohesion and reference (*the pig . . . the creature . . . it*) is the principal means for tracking a participant through the discourse.

Related to these are examples such as the following, where there is still identity of reference, although not to a participant, and the synonym may not be in the same word class (*cheered . . . applause*; *cried . . . tears*):

> Everyone cheered. The leader acknowledged the applause.

> I wish I hadn't cried so much! I shall be punished for it, I suppose, by being drowned in my own tears!

(b) without necessary identity of reference. The occurrence of a synonym even where there is no particular referential relation is still cohesive; for example

> There was a man of Thessaly
>   And he was wondrous wise.
> He jumped into a hawthorn bush
>   And scratched out both his eyes.
> And when he saw his eyes were out
>   With all his might and main
> He jumped into a quickset hedge
>   And scratched them in again.

where the quickset hedge is not the same entity as the hawthorn bush but there is still cohesion between the synonyms *hedge* and *bush*.

In this type of cohesion we find other semantic relationships, particular variants of synonymy: hyponymy (specific – general) and meronymy (part – whole). Given a lexical set consisting of either hyponyms, where *x y* and *z* are all 'kinds of' *a*, or meronyms, where *p q* and *r* are all 'parts of' *b*, as in Figure 9-4: the occurrence of any pair of items within the set will be cohesive; for example

> Elfrida had a beautiful little glass scent-bottle. She had used up all the scent long ago; but she often used to take the little stopper out . . .

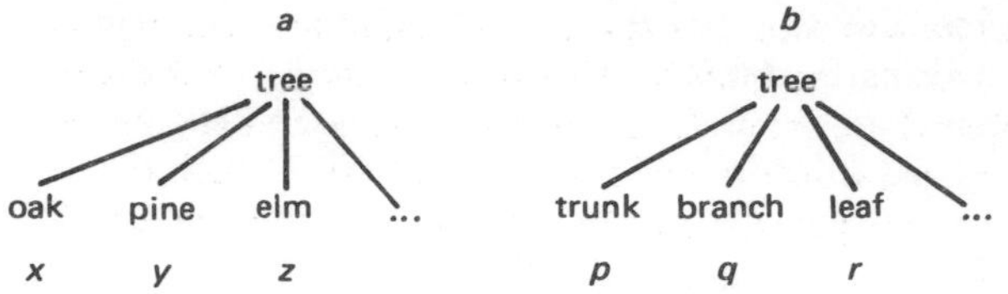

Figure 9-4

> She knelt down and looked along the passage into the loveliest garden you ever saw. How she longed to get out of that dark hall, and wander about among those beds of bright flowers and those cool fountains, . . .

where *stopper* is a meronym of *bottle*, and *flowers* and *fountains* are co-meronyms of *garden*. Examples of hyponymy:

> Then they began to meet vegetation — prickly cactus-like plants and coarse grass . . .

> The chessmen were walking about, two and two!
> "Here are the Red King and the Red Queen," Alice said . . .

where *plants* and *grass* are co-hyponyms of *vegetation*, and *Red King* and *Red Queen* are co-hyponyms of *chessmen*. There is no very clear line between meronymy and hyponymy, especially with abstract terms; and a given set of items may be co-hyponyms of one term but co-meronyms of another — for example *chair*, *table*, *bed* are 'kinds' (hyponyms) of *furniture*, but 'parts' (meronyms) of *furnishings*; *forward*, *half-back*, *back* are 'kinds' of *players* but 'parts' of a *team*, and so on. But since either relationship is a source of lexical cohesion it is not necessary to insist on deciding between them.

Finally a special case of synonymy is its opposite, antonymy. Lexical items which are opposite in meaning, namely *antonyms*, also function with cohesive effect in a text. For example, *woke* and *asleep* in

> He fell asleep. What woke him was a loud crash.

(3) Collocation. At the same time there are other instances of lexical cohesion which do not depend on any general semantic relationship of the types just discussed, but rather on a particular association between the items in question — a tendency to co-occur. This 'co-occurrence tendency' is known as *collocation*. For example,

> A little fat man of Bombay
> Was smoking one very hot day.
> But a bird called a snipe
> Flew away with his pipe,
> Which vexed the fat man of Bombay.

There is a strong collocational bond between *smoke* and *pipe*, which makes the occurrence of *pipe* in line 4 cohesive.

Clearly there is a semantic basis to a collocation of this kind; a pipe is something you smoke, and the words *pipe* and *smoke* are typically related as Range to Process in a behavioural process clause. Hence *pipe* here will be nterpreted as 'the pipe that he was smoking at the time'. But the relationship s at the same time a direct association between the words; if *pipe* is in the text hen *smoke* may well be somewhere around, at least with considerably greater robability than if we just pulled words out of a hat on the basis of their overall frequency in the language. We get ready for it, so to speak; and hence if it loes occur it is strongly cohesive.

As a matter of fact, even where there is a relation of synonymy between exical items, their cohesive effect tends to depend more on collocation, a imple tendency to co-occur. Of course if both relationships are present they einforce each other; but if a pair of synonyms are not regular collocates their ohesive effect is fairly weak, whereas words which are closely associated but vithout any systematic semantic relationship are nevertheless likely to have a oticeably cohesive effect. This is because collocation is one of the factors on vhich we build our expectations of what is to come next.

So for example there is a strong collocational bond between *cold* and *ice*, out not nearly so strong between *cold* and *snow*, though it would make just as good sense; *snow* is more likely to conjure up *white*. We collocate *friends* and *elations*, and also *friends* and *neighbours*; but not very often *relations* and *neighbours*, although *family* and *neighbourhood* seem to be associated. The xtreme cases of such collocational patterns are to be found in fixed phrases nd cliches, like *flesh and blood*, *stretch of the imagination*; but these ctually contribute little to cohesion, since they are so closely bound together hat they behave almost like single lexical items.

Notice finally that collocations are often fairly specifically associated with one or another particular register, or functional variety of the language. This s true, of course, of individual lexical items, many of which we regard as 'technical' because they appear exclusively, or almost exclusively, in one kind of text. But it is also noteworthy that perfectly ordinary lexical items often appear in different collocations according to the text variety. For example *hunting*, in a story of the English aristocracy, will call up *quarry* and *hounds* (or, at another level, *shooting* and *fishing*); in an anthropological text, words like *gathering*, *agricultural* and *pastoral*; as well as, in other contexts, *bargain*, *souvenir*, *fortune* and suchlike.

Figure 9-5 is an example of a text marked for lexical cohesion, using the categories of repetition, synonymy and collocation.

9.6 The creation of texture

We have identified the following features as those which combine to make up the 'textual' component in the grammar of English:

(A) structural
  1 thematic structure: Theme & Rheme (Chapter 3)
  2 information structure and focus: Given & New (Chapter 8)

(B) cohesive (Chapter 9)
  1 reference
  2 ellipsis and substitution
  3 conjunction
  4 lexical cohesion

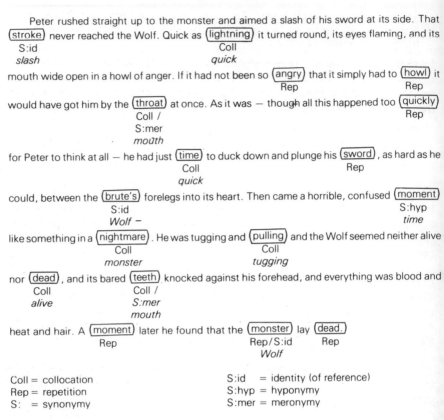

Peter rushed straight up to the monster and aimed a slash of his sword at its side. That
[stroke] never reached the Wolf. Quick as [lightning] it turned round, its eyes flaming, and its
stroke: S:id *slash*; lightning: Coll *quick*

mouth wide open in a howl of anger. If it had not been so [angry] that it simply had to [howl] it
angry: Rep; howl: Rep

would have got him by the [throat] at once. As it was — though all this happened too [quickly]
throat: Coll / S:mer *mouth*; quickly: Rep

for Peter to think at all — he had just [time] to duck down and plunge his [sword], as hard as he
time: Coll *quick*; sword: Rep

could, between the [brute's] forelegs into its heart. Then came a horrible, confused [moment]
brute's: S:id *Wolf* –; moment: S:hyp *time*

like something in a [nightmare]. He was tugging and [pulling] and the Wolf seemed neither alive
nightmare: Coll *monster*; pulling: Coll *tugging*

nor [dead], and its bared [teeth] knocked against his forehead, and everything was blood and
dead: Coll *alive*; teeth: Coll / *S:mer* *mouth*

heat and hair. A [moment] later he found that the [monster] lay [dead.]
moment: Rep; monster: Rep/S:id *Wolf*; dead: Rep

Coll = collocation
Rep = repetition
S: = synonymy
S:id = identity (of reference)
S:hyp = hyponymy
S:mer = meronymy

Figure 9-5 Text analysed for lexical cohesion

These are the resources that give 'texture' to a piece of discourse, without which it would not be discourse. In order to do this, these resources are deployed in certain ways; ways which vary considerably according to the register of the text, but about which it is possible to make some general observations as well.

We do not ordinarily meet with language that is not textured. What we call 'nonsense' is something we disagree with; but it is perfectly adequate as discourse — otherwise there would be nothing with which to disagree. (We have the notion of 'incoherent', but this usually refers to the slurred speech of the temporarily deranged.) People go to great lengths to interpret as text anything that is said or written, and are ready to assume any kind of displacement — some error in production, or in their own understanding — rather than admit that they are being faced with 'non-text'. Like everything else we have been investigating, this is an unconscious process; we are not aware of making such adjustments when we listen or read. But it is sometimes brought to consciousness by marginal instances which one has to work hard at decoding: strange children, foreign learners, faulty translations and the like.

One way to see how these resources work is to deconstruct a text, destroying its textual patterns one by one. Here is the North Star text (see Chapter 8, Section 8.5) after surgery:

The magnet is at the North Star. The earth attracts the North Star. The earth does not attract the stars which are not the North Star. The stars which are not the North Star move around.

In this case we simply removed the cohesion and selected the unmarked options in the various textual systems. If instead we were to select an option at random (as distinct from the unmarked option), we might end up with something like the following version of the 'silver' text (see Appendix 1):

With silver we, Anne, are dealing in this job. What needs to have love is silver. Silver is loved by the people that buy silver. It is silver that silver has a lovely gleam about. The people who love beautiful things are usually people if people come in.

This is, of course, an artificial exercise, set up for purposes of highlighting the textual component of meaning. In real life the different 'metafunctions' are so closely interwoven into the fabric of discourse that it is difficult to conceive of one being disturbed while the others remain unaffected — although certain aphasic conditions may approximate to such a pattern.

In the remainder of this section we attempt a brief summary of the part played by the features listed above in the creation of text. We will group them under four headings: (1) theme and focus; (2) lexical cohesion and reference; (3) ellipsis and substitution; (4) conjunction; with a note on text structure at the end. For research on which this discussion is based see these items in the Bibliography: Berry (1981), Fries (1981), Hasan (1983), Martin (1983).

(1) Theme and focus. These are the manifestations in English of what the Prague linguists of the 1930s, who were the first to explore this area of grammar systematically, called 'functional sentence perspective (FSP)'.

(a) The choice of Theme. The choice of Theme, clause by clause, is what carries forward the development of the text as a whole. This point was made in Chapter 3 and is illustrated by the texts examined there and in Appendix 1.

The patterning of clause Themes throughout a text tends to differ from one register to another. In narrative and expository texts it is quite likely for the same participant (whose 'sameness' is expressed lexicoreferentially; see (2) below) to remain as topical Theme for a certain stretch of discourse: either a protagonist in the tale, if it is narrative, or that which is being expounded, in an expository context. In texts with a more stepwise structure, involving sequences of instructions or logical argument, one is more likely to find the Theme of one clause selected from within the Rheme of the clause preceding; and there are likely to be conjunctive Themes. In dialogue, there may be alternation of Themes, especially between *I* and *you* representing speaker and listener; and Finite and WH- Themes, in interrogative clauses.

(b) The choice of focus. The choice of information focus, by contrast, expresses the main point of the information unit, what it is that the speaker is presenting as news; the pattern of focus throughout the text likewise expresses the main point of the discourse. In speech, the focus is realized by tonic prominence; it typically falls on the final lexical element, in the clause or in whatever unit is matched with the information unit, although it can be 'marked' and put anywhere. In writing, the principle is that (i) the information unit is a clause, unless some other unit is clearly designated by the punctuation; and (ii) the focus falls at the end of the unit, unless some positive signal to the contrary is given, either by lexical cohesion (no focus on repeated word) or by grammatical structure (predication: *it is . . . that . . .*).

(c) The combination of Theme and focus. Since the unmarked place of focus is at the end of the information unit, and since the unmarked information structure is 'one information unit one clause', this gives a kind of diminuendo – crescendo movement to the typical clause of English: the downward movement from initial, thematic prominence being caught up in the upward movement towards final, informational prominence, as shown in Figure 9-6. Note how this gives to each message (Chapter 3) the character of a move in an exchange (Chapter 4).

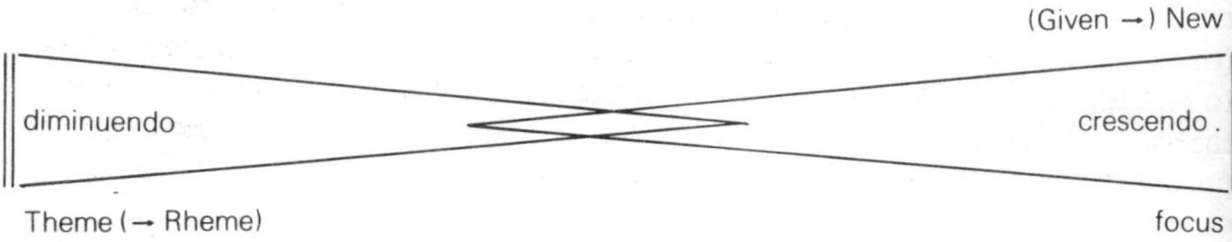

Figure 9-6 From speaker to listener: the wave-like effect of thematic and focal prominence

The two kinds of prominence are complementary. The Theme, as pointed out in Chapter 8, is speaker-oriented prominence; it is 'what I am talking about'. The New, which culminates in the focus, is listener-oriented prominence: it is 'what I am asking you to attend to'. As the clause moves away from the first peak, it moves towards the second; and this imparts a small-scale periodic or wave-like movement to the discourse. Larger-scale periodicity may then be superimposed on this, for example by a similar overall pattern in the paragraph.

(2) Lexical cohesion and reference. An important characteristic of many varieties of text is the referential chain, produced by a combination of lexical cohesion (repetition and synonymy) and reference. A typical chain from a narrative might be:

A little boy called John . . . John . . . he . . . the lad . . . him . . .

These are sometimes called 'participant chains'; but they are not restricted to participants in the sense of persons — they may be objects, institutions, abstractions, passages of text: anything that can have a participant role in a transitivity structure. Similar chains, though less frequent and less extensive, can be formed with circumstantial elements, and even with the process itself, e.g. *run away . . . do that . . . do it . . . get away . . . escape altogether.*

What gives the text its coherence, however, is not simply the presence of such chains but their interaction one with another. If the tokens (individual occurrences) in one chain relate to the tokens in another chain by some grammatically definable relationship (most typically, perhaps, a relationship in transitivity, because that is where the most highly structured configurations are found), this is strongly cohesive; for example Process *drown* + Medium *fish . . . deadly stonefish . . . it* in text 1 in Chapter 4, Section 4.8 above. Typically such interlocking chains overlap, one taking over from another, like *drown* + *mermaid* → *drown* + *fish* → *fish* + *eat* in the same text; and this is one of the sources of the dynamic flow of discourse.

Like other text-forming patterns, these referential chains and their interlocking chain complexes vary in kind and extent from one register to another. They have been most studied in narrative, but they feature in other types of text besides.

(3) Ellipsis and substitution. If reference, and referential chains, are more typical of narrative, ellipsis and substitution are more characteristically found in dialogue, where the typical sequence is based on pairs, or triads, or longer structures, that are related not so much by ideational as by interpersonal meaning: request → assent, question → answer → acknowledgment, statement → challenge → justification → qualified acceptance, and so on. In sequences of this kind the dynamic comes from the constant shifting in the role relationships among the interactants; and this means that, rather than (or, at least, in addition to) the persistence of identical referents there is likely to be the sort of 'same but different' semantic relation that is typically maintained by ellipsis or substitution: the same process but different polarity or modality, the same class of entity but different member, different deixis or so on.

Typically this kind of cohesion is also accompanied by cohesion among lexical items; this may perhaps depend, relatively, more on collocation and less on structural semantic relations like synonymy, the cohesive force of collocation being much more localized. In the same way the textual 'reach' of ellipsis and substitution is considerably shorter than that of reference. On the whole, types of cohesion with a more local effect, ellipsis / substitution and collocation, tend to be associated with dialogue; those with a more global effect, reference and synonymy, with monologue; although these are no more than very general tendencies.

(4) Conjunction. The difference between conjunction and the other text-forming resources is that conjunctive relations are essentially relations between messages or between larger complexes that are themselves constructed out of messages. As has been shown, the logical-semantic relationships that are coded in the form of conjunction are also manifested in many other ways (see also Appendix 3 below).

As a cohesive resource conjunction works in two ways, once again corresponding to the distinction between the ideational and the interpersonal 'metafunctions'.

(a) External (ideational) conjunction. This sets up a relationship between processes. A simple pattern of this kind is that of a sequence of events shown as following one another in time, e.g. *first* [this happened], *next* [that happened], *finally* [the other happened]. All the conjunctive relations set out in Section 9.4 above may function in this way.

(b) Internal (interpersonal) conjunction. This sets up a relationship between propositions or proposals; for example *first* [I say this], *next* [I say that], *finally* [I say the other]. Here the semantic relations are between the steps in an argument, not between phenomena of experience.

Not all conjunctive categories have an 'internal' interpretation; and in some cases, particularly elaboration and certain types of extension, it is often hard to tell the internal and the external apart. Despite these indeterminate instances, the distinction is a valid one, and important to the creation of texture. Different registers vary both in their overall use of conjunction and in their orientation to that of an internal or external kind.

The line between conjunction and paratactic expansion is a fuzzy one; many instances could be interpreted as either. This is reflected in the fact that, in writing, it is often possible to write either . . . . *So* . . . (which we should interpret as conjunction) or . . . , *so* . . . (which we should interpret as parataxis), with little difference in meaning. But this kind of overdetermination is found throughout the linguistic system, and particularly in the grammar of very general and fundamental semantic relations such as those of expansion and projection.

(5) Text structure. With the clause complex, described in Chapter 7, we reached the upper limits of grammatical structure. The sentence, evolving as a unit of written language, embodies the unconscious awareness of that upper limit.

This does not mean that there are no lexicogrammatical **relations** obtaining over larger domains; as we have been seeing in this chapter, the semantic relations of coreference, synonymy, expansion and so on are manifested in lexicogrammatical items and patterns just as systematically as the semantics of processes or speech functions. But whereas the latter are realized through grammatical **structures**, the former are not, or not necessarily. There is no structural relationship between, say, two occurrences of a lexical item, or between *John* and *he* — the members of such pairs are not linked in any constructional pattern. It is this non-structural relationship to which we give the name of cohesion.

Is there then no structure above the clause complex? There is; but not grammatical structure. A text has structure, but it is semantic structure not grammatical. Just as a syllable has a phonological structure, and a clause has a grammatical structure, a text has a semantic structure; but while the concept of structure is the same, the level at which it is 'coded' is different. So a text does not consist of clause complexes. It consists of elements of its own, which vary from one register to another: narrative, transactional, expository, . . . each has its own elements and configurations — but which are, or whose own smaller constituents are, realized as clauses or clause complexes in the same way that, say, morphemes, which are the smallest constituents in the grammar, are realized as syllables or syllable complexes.

For a text to be coherent, it must be cohesive; but it must be more besides. It must deploy the resources of cohesion in ways that are motivated by the register of which it is an instance; it must be semantically appropriate, with lexicogrammatical realizations to match (i.e. it must make sense); and it must have structure. But to say this is not in any way to imply that it must be homogeneous, univocal or 'flat'. Discourse is a multidimensional process; 'a text', which is the product of that process, not only embodies the same kind of polyphonic structuring as is found in the grammar (for example in the structure of the clause, as message, exchange and representation), but also, since it is functioning at a higher level of the code, as the realization of semiotic orders 'above' the language, may contain in itself all the inconsistencies, contradictions and conflicts that can exist within and between such higher-order semiotic systems. Because it has this potential, a text is not a mere reflection of what lies beyond; it is an active partner in the reality-making and reality-changing processes.

10

Beyond the clause: metaphorical modes of expression

10.1 Rhetorical transference

Among the 'figures of speech' recognized in rhetorical theory are a number of related figures having to do with verbal transference of various kinds. The general term for these is METAPHOR.

The term 'metaphor' is also used in a more specific sense to refer to just one kind, in contrast to METONYMY; and sometimes a third term is introduced, namely SYNECDOCHE. All three involve a 'non-literal' use of words.

Treating the three as distinct, we can define them as follows:

(1) Metaphor. A word is used for something **resembling** that which it usually refers to; for example, *flood . . . poured in*, *oozes*, *stem the tide* in

A flood of protests poured in following the announcement [a large quantity . . . came in]
He oozes geniality [displays all over]
The government still hopes to stem the tide of inflation [resist the force of]

Most instances involve transfer from a concrete to an abstract sense, and one large class of these is from material to mental process, as in *it escapes me*, *I haven't grasped it*, *I don't follow*.* If the fact of resemblance is explicitly signalled, by a word such as *like*, as in *protests came in like a flood*, this is considered to be not metaphor but simile.

(2) Metonymy. A word is used for something **related to** that which it usually refers to; for example, *eye*, *skirt*, *breathe* in

Keep your eye on the ball [gaze]
He's always chasing skirts [girls]
It won't happen while I still breathe [live]

Body parts are favourite sources of metonymy, and many such expressions have been incorporated into the language, with words like *hand*, *heart*, *head* as in *have a hand in*, *bare one's heart*, *keep your head*. The nature of the relationship is very varied, but is often something like cause, or source, or instrument.

---

* Most abstract vocabulary was in fact concrete in origin, but this is obscured for speakers of English because abstract terms are typically borrowed from Latin or Greek and we are no longer aware of their original concrete senses: e.g. *despise*, Latin *dēspicere*, from *dē* 'down' and *specere* 'to look'. We become aware of it when the same thing happens with native words, e.g. *look down on*.

(3) Synecdoche. A word is used for some larger whole of which that which it refers to is a part; for example, *strings*, *roof*, *bite* in

At this point the strings take over [stringed instruments]
They all live under one roof [in one house]
Let's go and have a bite [have a meal]

These are generally thought of as lexical, or lexicosemantic, processes, with synedoche being based on meronymy, and metaphor and metonymy on kinds of synonymic relationship. Alternatively, we can interpret them grammatically, in terms of the relational processes discussed in Chapter 5. Then:

Metaphor derives from the intensive ('is') type of relational process:

a large quantity	is	a flood
to resist the force	is	to stem the tide
to discharge all over	is	to ooze

the one being Token, the other Value. Metonymy derives from the circumstantial ('is at') type:

the gaze	is from	the eye
feelings	are in	the heart
living	is by	breathing

(In simile, resemblance is treated as a circumstantial relationship of comparison 'is like'.) Synecdoche derives from the possessive ('has') type; in the special sense that a whole 'has' its parts:

violins	have	strings
a house	has	a roof
a meal	consists of	bites

Thus metaphor, metonymy and synecdoche are forms of lexical variation stemming from the three fundamental semantic relationships of elaboration, extension and enhancement as described in Chapter 7.

Metaphor is usually described as variation in the use of words: a word is said to be used with a transferred meaning. Here however we are looking at it from the other end, asking not "how is this word used?" but "how is this meaning expressed?" A meaning may be realized by a selection of words that is different from that which is in some sense typical or unmarked. From this end, metaphor is variation in the expression of meanings.

Once we look at it this way, however, we recognize that lexical selection is just one aspect of lexicogrammatical selection, or 'wording'; and that metaphorical variation is lexicogrammatical rather than simply lexical. Many metaphors can be located in lexical expressions, like those above; but even with these there is often grammatical variation accompanying them. There is no way to represent *he oozes geniality* in a literal form simply by replacing the word *oozes* with another lexical item. Similarly for *protests flooded in*: we should have to say *protests came in in large quantities*, or *protests were received in large quantities*; or even *very many people protested*. There is a strong grammatical element in rhetorical transference; and once we have recognized this we find that there is also such a thing as grammatical metaphor, where the variation is essentially in the grammatical forms although often entailing some lexical variation as well.

10.2 Grammatical metaphor

If something is said to be metaphorical, there must also be something that is not; and the assumption is that to any metaphorical expression corresponds another, or perhaps more than one, that is 'literal' — or, as we shall prefer to call it, CONGRUENT. In other words, for any given semantic configuration there is (at least) one congruent realization in the lexicogrammar. There may then be others that are in some respect transferred, or METAPHORICAL.

This is not to say that the congruent realization is better, or that it is more frequent, or even that it functions as a norm; there are many instances where a metaphorical representation has become the norm, and this is in fact a natural process of linguistic change. Nor is it to suggest that a set of variants of this kind will be totally synonymous; the selection of metaphor is itself a meaningful choice, and the particular metaphor selected adds further semantic features. But they will be systematically related in meaning, and therefore synonymous in certain respects.

Metaphorical modes of expression are characteristic of all adult discourse. There is a great deal of variation among different registers in the degree and kind of metaphor that is encountered; but none will be found entirely without it. The only examples of discourse without metaphor that we normally meet with are in young children's speech, and in traditional children's rhymes and songs that seem to survive for that very reason: that they lack grammatical metaphors. Otherwise, any text of more than minimal length is almost certain to present us with instances where some metaphorical element needs to be taken into account.

There are two main types of grammatical metaphor in the clause: metaphors of mood (including modality), and metaphors of transitivity. In the terms of our model of semantic functions, these are, respectively, interpersonal metaphors and ideational metaphors. We shall say something about each of these in turn.

10.3 Ideational metaphors

In Chapter 5 we suggested a framework for interpreting the clause in its ideational function, as the representation of a process. There were three steps involved:

(i) selection of process type: material, mental, relational, with their various intermediate and secondary types; realized as

(ii) configuration of transitivity functions: Actor, Goal, Senser, Manner etc. representing the process, its participants, and any circumstantial elements; realized in turn as

(iii) sequence of group/phrase classes: verbal group, nominal group, adverbial group, prepositional phrase, and their various sub-classes.

When we use such a framework, as a way of getting from the meaning to the wording, we make the assumption that there are typical ways of saying things: that there is a systematic relationship among steps (i), (ii) and (iii) such that for any selection in meaning there will be a natural sequence of steps leading towards its realization. For example, if I want to talk about what Mary saw, I will represent this (i) as a mental process of perception, having (ii) a structure of Process + Senser + Phenomenon, this being (iii) realized as nominal group (conscious being) + verbal group (perception) + nominal group (any thing or fact); e.g. *Mary saw something wonderful.*

There is an important sense in which this assumption is true. We do not know whether language evolved initially along these lines, beginning with congruent modes of representation and gradually elaborating them — we only start thinking of these as 'congruent', of course, when incongruent ones develop alongside them. It is entirely possible that metaphor has been inherent in the nature of language from the very beginning. But, either way, we are able to recognize the congruent forms for what they are. Part of knowing a language is to know what is the most typical 'unmarked' way of saying a thing. At the same time, we also recognize that there are these other possibilities, where the unmarked mode has been departed from and the speaker or writer has chosen to encode things differently.

1. Metaphors of transitivity

So, for example, instead of *Mary saw something wonderful*, I may choose to say *Mary came upon a wonderful sight*, where the process has been represented as a material process *came upon* and the perception has been turned into a 'participant' *a sight*. Or I may say *a wonderful sight met Mary's eyes*, with the process of perception split up into Actor *a sight*, material Process *meet* and Goal *eyes*; and Mary represented simply as the possessor of the eyes. These are all plausible representations of one and the same non-linguistic 'state of affairs'. They are not synonymous; the different encodings all contribute something to the total meaning. But they are potentially co-representational, and in that respect form a set of metaphoric variants of an ideational kind.

As another example, if I am reporting the success of a mountaineering expedition, instead of writing *they arrived at the summit on the fifth day* I may choose an expression such as *the fifth day saw them at the summit*. Here the time 'the fifth day' has been dressed up to look as if it was a participant, an onlooker 'seeing' the climbers when they arrived.

Here is a rather absurd example invented to illustrate the kinds of grammatical variation that can arise. Among the social events in the local paper we might find it reported that *the guests' supper of icecream was followed by a gentle swim*. We might 'unscramble' this as *in the evening the guests ate icecream and then swam gently*. The reworded version is not noticeably better or worse; but it is obviously different. The two versions are analysed in Figure 10-1:

(1) Congruent mode

	in the evening	the guests	ate	ice cream	and	then	swam	gently
Function	circumstance: Time	participant: Actor	process: Material	participant: Goal		circumstance: Time	process: Material	circumstance: Manner
Class	prepositional phrase	nominal group	verbal group	nominal group		adverbial group	verbal group	adverbial group

(2) Metaphorical mode

	the guests'	supper of	ice cream	was followed by	a	gentle	swim
Function	participant:	Identified		process: Relational (Circumstantial: Time/Identifying)	participant:		Identifier
Class	nominal group			verbal group	nominal group		
Function (in group)	Modifier/ Deictic: Possessive	Head/Thing	Modifier/ Qualifier: Appositive			Modifier/ Epithet	Head/Thing

Figure 10-1 Congruent and metaphorical wordings compared

In the second version:

(i) the process of 'eating' and the circumstance 'in the evening' have been fused into the noun *supper* functioning as Head/Thing in a nominal group functioning as Identifier;

(ii) the participants 'the guests' and 'ice cream' have been embedded as (a) Modifier/Deictic: Possessive and (b) Modifier/Qualifier: Appositive in this nominal group;

(iii) the process of 'swimming' has been encoded as a noun *swim* functioning as Head/Thing in a nominal group functioning as Identified;

(iv) the circumstance 'gently' has been encoded as a Modifier/Epithet within this nominal group; and

(v) the circumstance 'then' has been encoded as a verbal group *was followed by*, functioning as a Relational process of the Circumstantial/Identifying type.

Although these are all in origin metaphorical, in the sense in which we are using the term, each one taken by itself is entirely natural: we would say *we had supper there*, rather than *we ate there in the evening*; circumstances are often encoded as processes like *following* — cf. Chapter 5, Section 5.4; and *a gentle swim* seems as predictable linguistically after an ice cream supper as it does in the real world. Yet the whole effect is rather unnatural — about as unnatural as the fully congruent form.

It seems that, in most types of discourse, both spoken and written, we tend to operate somewhere in between these two extremes. Something which is totally congruent is likely to sound a bit flat; whereas the totally incongruent often seems artificial and contrived.

2. The representation of metaphorical forms

How do we represent 'incongruent' modes of expression in the analysis? In principle, we can treat metaphorical expressions in either of two ways, either (1) taking them at their face value, or (2) interpreting them in their congruent form. For example, given *the fifth day saw them at the summit* we can analyse either as in Figure 10-2, or as in Figure 10-3.

the fifth day	saw	them	at the summit
Senser	Mental: Perception	Phenomenon	Place

Figure 10-2 Analysis of metaphorical form

they	arrived	at the summit	on the fifth day
Actor	Material	Place	Time

Figure 10-3 Analysis of congruent rewording

Neither of these two is satisfactory by itself. The first ignores the fact that *the fifth day saw them* is decidedly incongruent; it is not an ordinary mental process clause like *Mary saw something*, and *a day* is not a conscious being. The second ignores the fact that this is not what the speaker, or writer, said. He did not, in fact, say *they arrived at the summit on the fifth day*, which he could quite well have chosen to do if he had wanted.

It is possible to combine the two into a single representation, as in Figure 10-4:

'on the fifth day'		'they'	'at the summit'	'arrived'
circumstance Time		participant Actor	circumstance Place	process Material
the fifth day	saw	them	at the summit	
participant Senser	process Mental: Perception	participant Phenomenon	circumstance Place	

Figure 10-4 The two analyses combined

The technique here is to match the elements vertically as closely as possible, for three reasons: (i) to bring out contrasts in grammatical function; (ii) to show where there is also lexical metaphor; and (iii) to suggest reasons for the choice of a metaphorical form. Here, for example, we can see that (i) *the fifth day* is congruently a circumstance of Time, metaphorically a Senser; (ii) *saw* may be a lexical metaphor, since it does not appear in the congruent version; and (iii) one reason for choosing the metaphorical mode might be to make the time element an unmarked Theme — there is no other way of doing this. It is not necessary, of course, to write in the the words 'process, participant, circumstance' since they are clearly implied by the description of the functions; if we do so, it is simply in order to bring out more explicitly one particular aspect of the metaphor. Using the same technique, but this time omitting these general labels, we could represent the clause of Figure 10-1 in a single diagram as in Figure 10-5.

'the guests'	'ate	in the evening'	'ice cream'	'and	then'	'gently'		'swam'
Actor	Material	Time	Goal		Time	Manner		Material
the guests'	supper	of	ice cream	was followed	by	a	gentle	swim
Identified				Relational: (Circ.: Time/Identifying)		Identifier		
nominal group				verbal group		nominal group		
Modifier/ Deictic: Possessive	Head/ Thing		Modifier/ Qualifier: Appositive				Modifier/ Epithet	Head/ Thing

Figure 10-5 Combined analysis of Figure 10-1

There is no very clear line to be drawn between what is congruent and what is incongruent. Much of the history of every language is a history of demetaphorizing: of expressions which began as metaphors gradually losing their metaphorical character. Again this is most obvious with lexical metaphors: no-one now thinks of *source* as a metaphor, in *the source of the trouble*; or *dream* in *I wouldn't dream of telling him*; or *barrier* in *there is no barrier to our mutual understanding*. But there are similar instances also in grammar.

We referred in Chapter 5, Section 5.6.2 to the set of expressions like *have a bath, do a dance, make a mistake*, where the verb simply expresses the fact that **some** process takes place, and carries the verbal categories of tense, polarity and so on, while the process itself is coded as a nominal group functioning as Range. This entire set of expressions is really incongruent. So is another class of expressions not previously mentioned, that exemplified by *she has brown eyes, he has a broken wrist*, where the congruent forms would be *her eyes are brown, his wrist is broken*. It is possible to represent these as metaphorical in the usual way, as in Figure 10-6. Other instances of this general class are *she enjoys excellent health, he writes good books* ('the books he writes are good', or 'he writes books, which are good'), *we sell bargains* 'the things we sell are cheap'.

'they'		'danced'	'in Hungarian style'	
Behaver nominal group		Behavioural verbal group	Manner: comparison prepositional phrase	
they	did	a	Hungarian	dance
Actor nominal group	Material verbal group	Range nominal group		
			Modifier / Classifier	Head / Thing

'her eyes'	'are'		'brown'
Carrier	Relational (Intensive/Attributive)		Attribute
she	has	brown	eyes
Carrier	Relational (Possessive / Attributive)	Attribute	
nominal group	verbal group	nominal group	
		Modifier / Epithet	Head / Thing

Figure 10-6 Two domesticated transitivity metaphors

But these 'metaphors' have become part of the system of English; they are now the unmarked form of encoding for these particular types of process. For most purposes it is unlikely that one will need to take account of their metaphorical character in the analysis of a particular text. Yet the congruent forms do exist in the language, so that there is a sense in which the use of an incongruent form does represent a choice, even if it is now the unmarked choice for expressing the process in question. Setting the analysis out in this way gives a reminder of the reasons why the pattern has evolved as it has: in (a), *dance* can be qualified or quantified and still appear under unmarked focus; while in (b) *she* can function as Subject and unmarked Theme.

In some instances we may be able to establish a chain of metaphorical interpretations leading from the clause under scrutiny to something we might consider to be its congruent form. There is an example of this in the Appendix below (step 2, and Figure A-3): *now silver needs to have love*. As it stands this is a relational: possessive process with *silver* as Carrier and *love* as Attribute. A metaphorical interpretation might embody the following steps: (1) 'silver needs to receive love', material process with *silver* as Actor, *love* as Goal; (ii) 'silver needs to be given love', material process with *silver* as Benefciary, *love* as Goal; (iii) 'silver needs to be loved', mental process with *silver* as Phenomenon and implicit feature of consciousness 'by people'. For most purposes it is enough to set out just the two outer representations, although at times it is of interest to trace the full metaphorical kinship.

Here are some further examples to suggest something of the diversity of ideational metaphors. In each case (a) is the metaphorical form as found in the text, (b) is a suggested congruent version. In many instances a number of moves have been made simultaneously, and intermediate versions could be derived.

(a) I haven't had the benefit of your experience.
(b) Unfortunately I haven't experienced as much as you.

(a) He has a comfortable income.
(b) His income is large enough for him to be able to live comfortably.

(a) Two pupils used their access to the school's computer to probe its secrets.
(b) Two pupils were able to reach the school's computer and managed in this way to probe its secrets.

(a) Advances in technology are speeding up the writing of business programs.
(b) Because technology is getting better people can write business programs faster.

(a) Forward journeys must start on the date stamped on the ticket.
(b) A traveller is allowed to set out only on one date, namely that shown by the stamp on his ticket.

(a) These difficulties necessitated the allocation of one extra packer.
(b) Because these tasks were difficult they needed to allocate one extra packer.

(a) To add alcohol impairment to the problem of inexperience is an invitation to disaster.
(b) If someone who has not had much experience is also impaired by alcohol something disastrous may happen.

(a) The tracks offer a range of walks of varying length.
(b) One can walk along different tracks, some shorter some longer.

Let us follow one more of these through step by step (Figure 10-7):

advances in technology		are speeding up	the writing of business programs	
Actor nominal group		Process:material verbal group	Goal nominal group	
Thing	Qualifier: Place (abstract)		Thing	Qualifier: Medium

advances in technology	are making	the writing of business programs	faster
Attributor/Agent	Process: attributive	Carrier/Medium	Attribute

advances in technology	are enabling	people	to write	business programs	faster
Initiator	Process: α causative	Actor	Process: β material	Goal	Manner: quality

because	technology	is advancing	people	are (becoming) able to write	business programs	faster
	×β ←		α			
	Actor	Process: material	Actor	Process:material/ modulation	Goal	Manner: quality

because	technology	is getting	better	people	are able to write	business programs	faster
	×β ←			α			
	Carrier	Process: attributive	Attribute	Actor	Process: material/ modulation	Goal	Manner: quality

Figure 10-7 Step by step analysis of a transitivity metaphor

3. Metaphor in spoken and written language

We have rejected any idea that metaphoric wording is inherently either 'a good thing' or 'a bad thing', although this is not to deny that the extent and kind of ideational metaphor in a text is likely to have some bearing on its impact, in the context in which it occurs.

The factor that counts for most in determining the extent of metaphor in the grammar of a text is whether that text is spoken or written; speech and writing are rather different in their patterns of metaphoric usage. This is because speech and writing differ in the kind of complexity that they typically display.

It might be assumed that metaphor, even if not inherently good or bad, is at least inherently complex, and that the least metaphorical wording will always be the one that is maximally simple. The often professed ideal of 'plain, simple English' would seem to imply something that is in general what we are calling congruent. But the concept of 'plain and simple' is itself very far from being plain and simple; anything approaching technical language, for example, tends to become noticeably more complex if one 'simplifies' it by removing the metaphors. As a test of this, try constructing a congruent variant of the clause *braking distance increases more rapidly at high speeds*.

The explanation is, of course, that there is more than one kind of simplicity and complexity. There are no doubt many kinds; but two in particular concern us here, one typically associated with writing and the other with speech. The complexity of written language is a lexical complexity; written language attains a high lexical density (that is, it has a greater number of lexical items per clause, and the lexical items have a higher information content), often accompanied by a relatively simple grammatical structure. The complexity of spoken language is a grammatical complexity; spoken language constructs complex dependency structures (that is, elaborate edifices of parataxis and hypotaxis, out of both clauses and phrases), often accompanied by a relatively simple choice of words. Metaphorical 'complexity' is typically that of written language.

Consider the following sentence, from a book on railways written for children:

> In bridging river valleys, the early engineers built many notable masonry viaducts of numerous arches.

The clause complex and transitivity analysis is given in Figure 10-8.

in	bridging	river valleys	the early engineers	built	many notable masonry viaducts of numerous arches
$^{\times}\beta$ ←			α		
	Process: material	Goal	Actor	Process: material	Goal

Figure 10-8 An example of high lexical density

As a grammatical structure at the rank of clause and clause complex, this is extremely simple. Let us now reword it in a form more typical of the spoken language.

In a comparable context (see *The Horizon Book of Railways*, pp. 74–5), a natural spoken version, still retaining the same lexical items, might run somewhat as follows:

> In the early days when engineers had to make a bridge across a valley and the valley had a river flowing through it, they often built viaducts, which were constructed of masonry and had numerous arches in them; and many of these viaducts became notable.

Here the structure of the clause complex is

$$1\,\alpha\,\beta\,1 \wedge 1\,\alpha\,\beta\,2 \wedge 1\,\alpha\,\alpha \wedge 1\,\beta\,1 \wedge 1\,\beta\,2 \wedge 2$$

where (a) there are more structurally related clauses, and (b) the clauses are on the whole more complex in transitivity structure than in the original. (This is obviously not the only possible rewording; but it is not one that has been carried to an extreme — my first attempt had nine clauses in it.)

On the other hand, the lexical density in the spoken version is very low — as it must be, since the ideational content is the same in both, and it has now been distributed across six clauses instead of two. The lexical density in the orginal version is high; and this leads to heavily loaded nominal groups such as that in Figure 10-9.

many	notable	masonry	viaducts	of	numerous	arches
Numerative	Epithet	Classifier	Thing	Qualifier		
				'Pred'	'Complement'	
					Numerative	Thing

Figure 10-9 A dense nominal group

In the spoken version the same information is spread over three clauses in a total of nineteen words.

If we want to characterize the difference between the complexity of spoken language and that of written language, we could say (using another metaphor for the purpose) that the complexity of written language is crystalline, while that of spoken language is choreographic. In written discourse the ideational content is tightly packed, in structural patterns that are basically simple in form; in spoken discourse it is loosely strung out, in dynamic patterns that are highly intricate in movement. Needless to say, the validity of any such observation about the difference between speech and writing is like that of a generalization such as that men are taller than women: both of them are tendencies, to which not all instances conform. But this does not destroy their general validity.

By no means all instances of high lexical density involve metaphor. The example just analysed is not, in fact, highly metaphorical in character: we may accept *early engineers*, and even *bridging river valleys*, as congruent, leaving only *built notable viaducts* as something that can be explained only through some kind of transference. But a great deal of lexical condensation does involve metaphor, and this is why the complexity of written language is closely associated with metaphorical processes in the grammar. The examples given at the end of the preceding section bring this out; here is one further example:

> The argument to the contrary is basically an appeal to the lack of synonymy in mental language.

This as it stands is an identifying clause with structure Id/Vl ^ Ir/Tk. We could reword it as

> In order to argue that [this] is not so [he] simply points out that there are no synonyms in mental language.

The second version approximates more closely to natural speech; and this effect has been achieved by removing the grammatical metaphors.

How far does one go in this direction in the course of textual analysis?

There is no universally valid answer to this question, suited to all occasions; it will depend on what the analysis is for, and what one is trying to achieve by it. A general guide would be: unscramble as far as is needed. If we return to the examples given at the beginning, a clause such as *the fifth day saw them at the summit* needs explaining because of the tension in the grammar between *day* as Subject and *saw* as active Predicator; in many instances, however, it is only when we come to interpret in semantic terms that we become aware of metaphorical effects — and some of these may turn out to reside in forms that can now be regarded as fully coded in the language, exactly as happens with lexical metaphors. But the more we raise questions about register-type variation in language, the more we find ourselves having to take account of metaphorical processes in the grammar, because (as we have seen to be the case with speech and writing) different functional varieties of language differ mainly in their patterns of wording, and the extent and kind of metaphor employed is one of the significant dimensions of variation.

10.4 Interpersonal metaphors

The grammar also accommodates metaphors of an interpersonal kind, in the expression of mood and modality. An example of metaphor in modality was given in Chapter 3 (see Figure 3-17): *I don't believe that pudding ever will be cooked*, where it was pointed out that *I don't believe* is functioning as an expression of modality, as can be shown by the tag, which would be *will it?*, not *do I?*. The example was brought in at that point in order to explain the thematic structure; let us now represent this same clause in a way that brings out the metaphoric element in its modal structure (Figure 10-10):

<table>
<tr><td colspan="3">'probably'</td><td>'that pudding</td><td>never</td><td>will</td><td>be cooked'</td></tr>
<tr><td colspan="3">Modality: probability</td><td>Subject</td><td>Modality: frequency</td><td>Finite</td><td>Predicator</td></tr>
<tr><td colspan="6">Mood</td><td>Residue</td></tr>
<tr><td>I</td><td>don't</td><td>believe</td><td>that pudding</td><td>ever</td><td>will</td><td>be cooked</td></tr>
<tr><td colspan="7">α ——→ 'β</td></tr>
<tr><td>Subject</td><td>Finite</td><td>Predicator</td><td>Subject</td><td>Modality</td><td>Finite</td><td>Predicator</td></tr>
<tr><td colspan="2">Mood</td><td>Residue</td><td>Mood</td><td></td><td></td><td>Residue</td></tr>
</table>

Figure 10-10 An interpersonal metaphor

1. Metaphors of modality

This is an example of a very common type of interpersonal metaphor, based on the semantic relationship of projection. In this type the speaker's opinion regarding the probability that his observation is valid is coded not as a modal element within the clause, which would be its congruent realization, but as a separate, projecting clause in a hypotactic clause complex. To the congruent form *it probably is so* corresponds the metaphorical variant *I think it is so*, with *I think* as the primary or 'alpha' clause.

The reason for regarding this as a metaphorical variant is that the proposition is not, in fact, 'I think'; the proposition is 'it is so'. This is shown clearly by the tag; if we tag the clause *I think it's going to rain* we get

I think it's going to rain, isn't it?

not *I think it's going to rain, don't I?* In other words the clause is a variant of *it's probably going to rain (isn't it?)* and not a first person equivalent of *John thinks it's going to rain*, which does represent the proposition 'John thinks' (tag *doesn't he?*).

There is in fact a wide range of variants for the expression of modality in the clause, and some of these take the form of a clause complex. If we limit ourselves first to the meaning of 'probability', the principal categories are as shown in Table 10(1):

Table 10(1) Expressions of probability

Category	Type of realization	Example
(1) Subjective		
(a) explicit	I think, I'm certain	I think Mary knows
(b) implicit	will, must	Mary'll know
(2) Objective		
(a) implicit	probably, certainly	Mary probably knows
(b) explicit	it's likely, it's certain	it's likely Mary knows

What happens is that, in order to state **explicitly** that the probability is subjective, or alternatively, at the other end, to claim **explicitly** that the probability is objective, the speaker projects the proposition as a 'fact' and encodes the subjectivity (*I think*), or the objectivity (*it is likely*), in a projecting clause. (There are other forms intermediate between the explicit and implicit: subjective *in my opinion*, objective *in all probability*, where the modality is expressed as a prepositional phrase, which is a kind of halfway house between clausal and non-clausal status.)

Suppose now that Mary doesn't know, or at least we don't think she knows. There are now two possibilities in each of the 'explicit' forms:

(1) Subjective
    I think Mary doesn't know / I don't think Mary knows
(2) Objective
    it's likely Mary doesn't know / it isn't likely Mary knows

Here another metaphorical process has taken place: the transfer of the polarity feature into the primary clause (*I don't think, it isn't likely*). On the face of it, these are nonsensical: it is not the thinking that is being negated, nor can there be any such thing as a negative probability. But non-thought and negative probabilities cause no great problems in the semantics of natural language. Since the modality is being dressed up as a proposition, it is natural for it to take over the burden of yes or no.

Figure 10-11 gives the analysis of two of these examples.

'probably'	'Mary		knows'
Modality	Subject	'present' Finite	know Predicator
Mood			Residue

it	seems		likely	that	Mary		knows
α →					'β		
Subject	'present' Finite	seem Predicator	Complement		Subject	'present' Finite	know Predicator
Mood		Residue			Mood		Residue

	'Mary	won't	know'
	Subject	Finite/Modality /Polarity	Predicator
	Mood		Residue
'in my opinion'	'Mary	doesn't	know'
Modality	Subject	Finite/Polarity	Predicator
Mood			Residue

I	don't	think	Mary		knows
α →			'β		
Subject	Finite/ Polarity	Predicator	Subject	'present' Finite	know Predicator
Mood		Residue	Mood		Residue

Figure 10-11 Analysis of probability expressions

2. A further account of modality and modulation

It is not always possible to say exactly what is and what is not a metaphorical representation of a modality. But speakers have indefinitely many ways of expressing their opinions — or rather, perhaps, of dissimulating the fact that they *are* expressing their opinions; for example

it is obvious that . . .
everyone admits that . . .
it stands to reason that . . .
it would be foolish to deny that . . .
the conclusion can hardly be avoided that . . .
no sane person would pretend that . . . not . . .
commonsense determines that . . .
all authorities on the subject are agreed that . . .
you can't seriously doubt that . . .

and a thousand and one others, all of which mean 'I believe'.

The reason this area of the semantic system is so highly elaborated metaphorically is to be found in the nature of modality itself. A very brief account of modality was given in Chapter 4, Section 4.5; we can now give a somewhat more systematic description of the principal features of the modality system.

Modality refers to the area of meaning that lies between yes and no — the intermediate ground between positive and negative polerity. What this implies more specifically will depend on the underlying speech function of the clause. (1) If the clause is an 'information' clause (a proposition, congruently realized as indicative), this means either (i) 'either yes or no', i.e. 'maybe'; or (ii) 'both yes and no', i.e. 'sometimes'; in other words, either probability or usuality. (2) If the clause is a 'goods-&-services' clause (a proposal, which has no real congruent form in the grammar, but by default we can characterize it as imperative), it means either (i) 'is wanted to', related to a command, or (ii) 'wants to', related to an offer; in other words, either obligation or inclination. We refer to type (1) as MODALIZATION and to type (2) as MODULATION; this gives a system as in Figure 10-12.

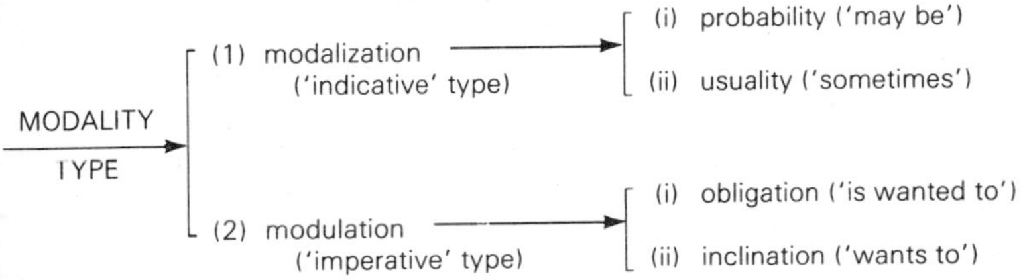

Figure 10-12 System of types of modality

The four types are set out in diagrammatic form in Figure 10-13.

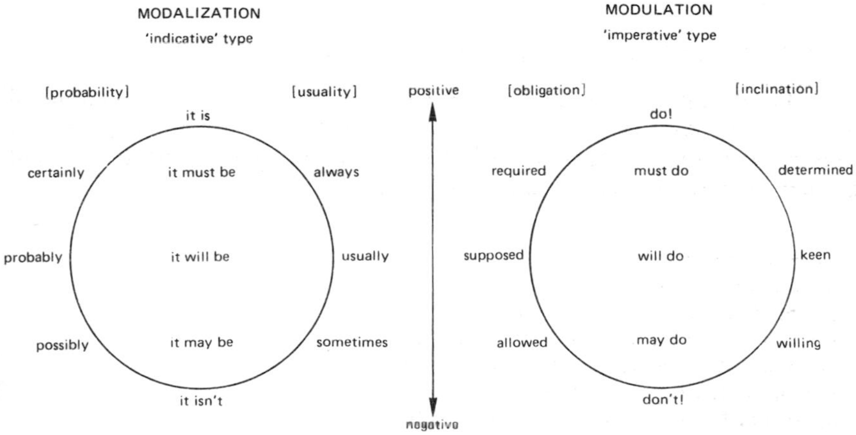

Figure 10-13 Diagram showing relation of modality to polarity and mood

In philosophical semantics modalization is referred to as 'epistemic' modality and modulation as 'deontic' modality. Here is an example of each:

1. i	Mary will probably know	[probability]
1.ii	It will usually work	[usuality]
2. i	Fred should tell them	[obligation]
2.ii	John will take you home	[inclination]

As is brought out by these examples, the modal auxiliaries can occur in all four types. Not every one in the full list of modal auxiliaries (*can*, *could*, *may*, *might*; *shall*, *should*, *will*, *would*; *must*, *need*, *ought to*, *is to*, *has to*) can express all four — their use is more restricted in the categories of usuality and inclination than in the other two. But as a class they extend over these senses; and since the general function of the modal auxiliaries is to express degrees of polarity, this gives an idea of how all these four scales are semantically related. At the same time, each one of the four types can be expressed in other ways besides.

The basic distinction that determines how the modality will be expressed is the distinction between subjective and objective modality discussed in the preceding section. Let us refer to this as the 'orientation'; there are then four possible orientations, as shown in Figure 10-14:

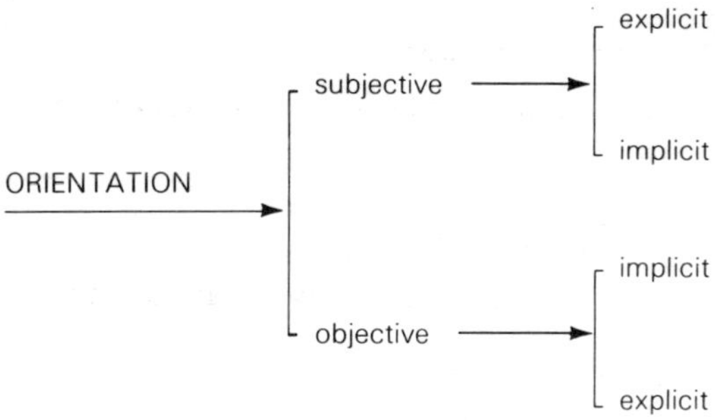

Figure 10-14 System of orientations in modality

Table 10(2) 'Type' and 'orientation': examples

	Subjective: explicit	Subjective: implicit	Objective: implicit	Objective: explicit
Modality: probability	I think [in my opinion] Mary knows	Mary'll know	Mary probably knows [in all probability]	it's likely that Mary knows [Mary is likely to]
Modality: usuality		Fred'll sit quite quiet	Fred usually sits quite quiet	it's usual for Fred to sit quite quiet
Modulation: obligation	I want John to go	John should go	John's supposed to go	it's expected that John goes
Modulation: inclination	(I undertake for Jane to help)	Jane'll help	Jane's keen to help	it's a pleasure for Jane to help

These combine freely with the type of modality, except that there are no systematic forms for making the subjective orientation explicit in the case of usuality ('I recognize it as usual that . . .') and inclination ('I offer on behalf of') — there are limits to the speaker's overt intrusion. Examples are given in Table 10(2).

The third variable in modality is the value that is set on the modal judgement: high, median or low. These values are summarized in Table 10(3):

Table 10(3) Three 'values' of modality

	Probability	Usuality	Obligation	Inclination
High	certain	always	required	determined
Median	probable	usually	supposed	keen
Low	possible	sometimes	allowed	willing

The median value is that for which the negative is freely transferable between the proposition and the modality:

it's likely Mary doesn't know/it isn't likely Mary knows
Fred usually doesn't stay/Fred doesn't usually stay
John's supposed not to go/John isn't supposed to go
Jane's not keen to be seen/Jane's keen not to be seen

With the outer values, if the negative is transferred the value switches from high to low, or from low to high:

{ it's certain Mary doesn't know/it isn't possible Mary knows
it's possible Mary doesn't know/it isn't certain Mary knows }

{ Fred always doesn't stay (never stays)/Fred doesn't sometimes stay (doesn't ever stay)
Fred sometimes doesn't stay/Fred doesn't always stay }

{ John's required not to go/John isn't allowed to go
John's allowed not to go/John isn't required to go }

{ Jane's determined not to be seen/Jane isn't willing to be seen
Jane's willing not to be seen/Jane isn't determined to be seen }

The system of values is therefore as in Figure 10-15:

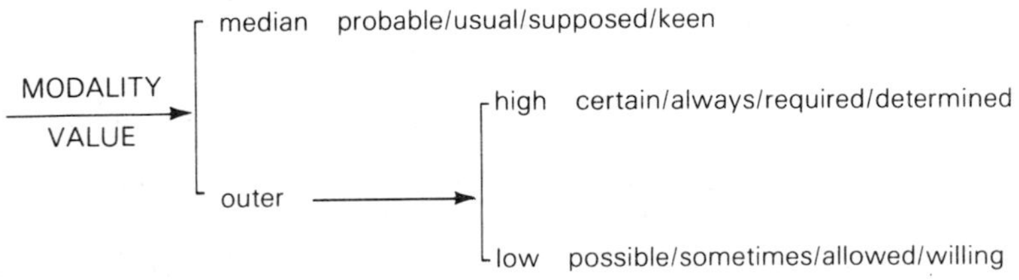

Figure 10-15 System of values in modality

These are set out in diagrammatic form, showing values for probability and obligation with both positive and negative propositions, in Figure 10-16.

Probability: proposition positive	Probability: proposition negative	Value	Obligation: proposal positive	Obligation: proposal negative
that is John	that isn't John		say!	don't say!
that must be John that certainly is John	that can't be John that certainly isn't John it isn't possible that's John	high	you must say you're required to say	you mustn't say you're required not to say you're not allowed to say
that will be John that probably is John	that won't be John that probably isn't John it isn't probable that's John	median	you should say you're supposed to say	you shouldn't say you're supposed not to say you're not supposed to say
that may be John that possibly is John	that may not be John that possibly isn't John it isn't certain that's John	low	you can say you're allowed to say	you needn't say you're allowed not to say you're not required to say
that isn't John	that is John		don't say!	say!

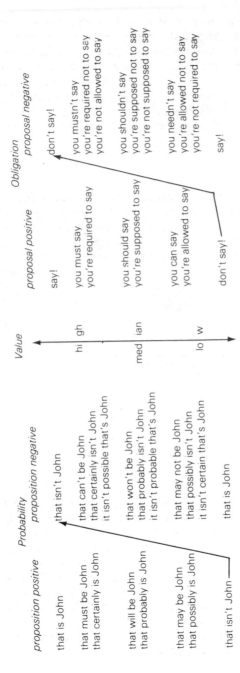

Figure 10-16 Probability and obligation with positive and negative propositions and proposals

If we ignore the gaps, this gives a set of 4 × 4 × 3 = 48 categories of modality. These are, of course, only the broad outlines; the actual number of semantic distinctions that can be recognized as systematic within the modality system runs well into the thousands. There are other variables that are not given here; and there are more delicate distinctions to be made within those that are. For example, we have recognized only the three values high, median and low, and therefore taken no cognizance of the semantic distinctions that are realized by the different modal verbs within each of these sets:

high:	must ought to need has to is to
median:	will would shall should
low:	may might can could

To go further would be inconsistent with the overall depth of detail, or degree of 'delicacy', which we have tried to achieve in this thumbnail sketch of English. But it is useful to be able to characterize instances of modality in a text in terms of their type, orientation and value as outlined here. We can adopt for this purpose a notation that is simple and transparent:

type:	prob / usu / obl / incl
orientation:	s:ex / s:im / o:im / o:ex
value:	high / med / low

as exemplified in Figure 10-17:

must	you	make	all that noise
Finite / Modal : incl / s : im / high	Subject	Predicator	Complement
Mood		Residue	

Figure 10-17 Analysis of modalized clause

There is one further semantic category which, although strictly not a kind of modality (since it is not an intermediate degree of polarity), is closely related to it, and uses some of the same means of expression; namely potentiality, as in *John can do it* 'it is possible for John to do it' — he has the ability, or there is nothing standing in his way. Since grammatically this belongs with modality, we can treat it as a further distinct type, symbolized 'pot'; and recognize subjective orientation (implicit only), realized as *can*, and objective orientation, with the implicit realized as *is able to* and the explicit realized as *it is possible (for . . .)*.

The difference in meaning between the subjective and the objective types can be seen from the effect of the tag. Compare:

he couldn't have meant it, could he?
surely he didn't mean it, did he?

In the first, the speaker wants the listener to confirm his estimate of the probabilities: 'I think it unlikely; do you share my opinion?'. In the second, he wants the listener to provide the answer: 'I think it unlikely, but is it in fact the case?'. It is possible to switch from a subjectively modalized clause to a non-modalized tag, as in

> What do you reckon would be good for a five-year-old kid?
> — She'll like fairy tales, does she?

Here the salesperson's reply means 'I think it likely she likes fairy tales; is that the case?' — whereas *she'll like fairy tales, will she?* would have meant 'do you agree that it is likely?'. The speaker is assuming, in other words, that the customer knows the preferences of the child; there would be no point in simply exchanging opinions on the subject.

The explicitly subjective and explicitly objective forms of modality are all strictly speaking metaphorical, since all of them represent the modality as being the substantive proposition. Modality represents the speaker's angle, either on the validity of the assertion or on the rights and wrongs of the proposal; in its congruent form, it is an adjunct to a proposition rather than a proposition in its own right. Speakers being what we are, however, we like to give prominence to our own point of view; and the most effective way of doing that is to dress it up as if it was this that constituted the assertion ('explicit' *I think . . .*) — with the further possibility of making it appear as if it was not our point of view at all ('explicit objective' *it's likely that . . .*). The examples at the beginning of this section show some of the highly elaborated forms that such an enterprise can take.

The importance of modal features in the grammar of interpersonal exchanges lies in an apparent paradox on which the entire system rests — the fact that we only say we are certain when we are not. If unconsciously I consider it certain that Mary has left, I say, simply, *Mary's left*. If I add a high value probability, of whatever orientation, such as *Mary's certainly left*, *I'm certain Mary's left*, *Mary must have left*, etc., this means that I am admitting an element of doubt — which I may then try to conceal by objectifying the expression of certainty. Hence whereas the subjective metaphors, which state clearly 'this is how I see it', take on all values (*I'm sure*, *I think*, *I don't believe*, *I doubt*, etc.) most of the objectifying metaphors express a 'high' value probability or obligation — that is, they are different ways of claiming objective certainty or necessity for something that is in fact a matter of opinion. Most of the 'games people play' in the daily round of interpersonal skirmishing involve metaphors of this objectifying kind. Figure 10-18 gives a further example; containing both an interpersonal metaphor and one of an ideational kind.

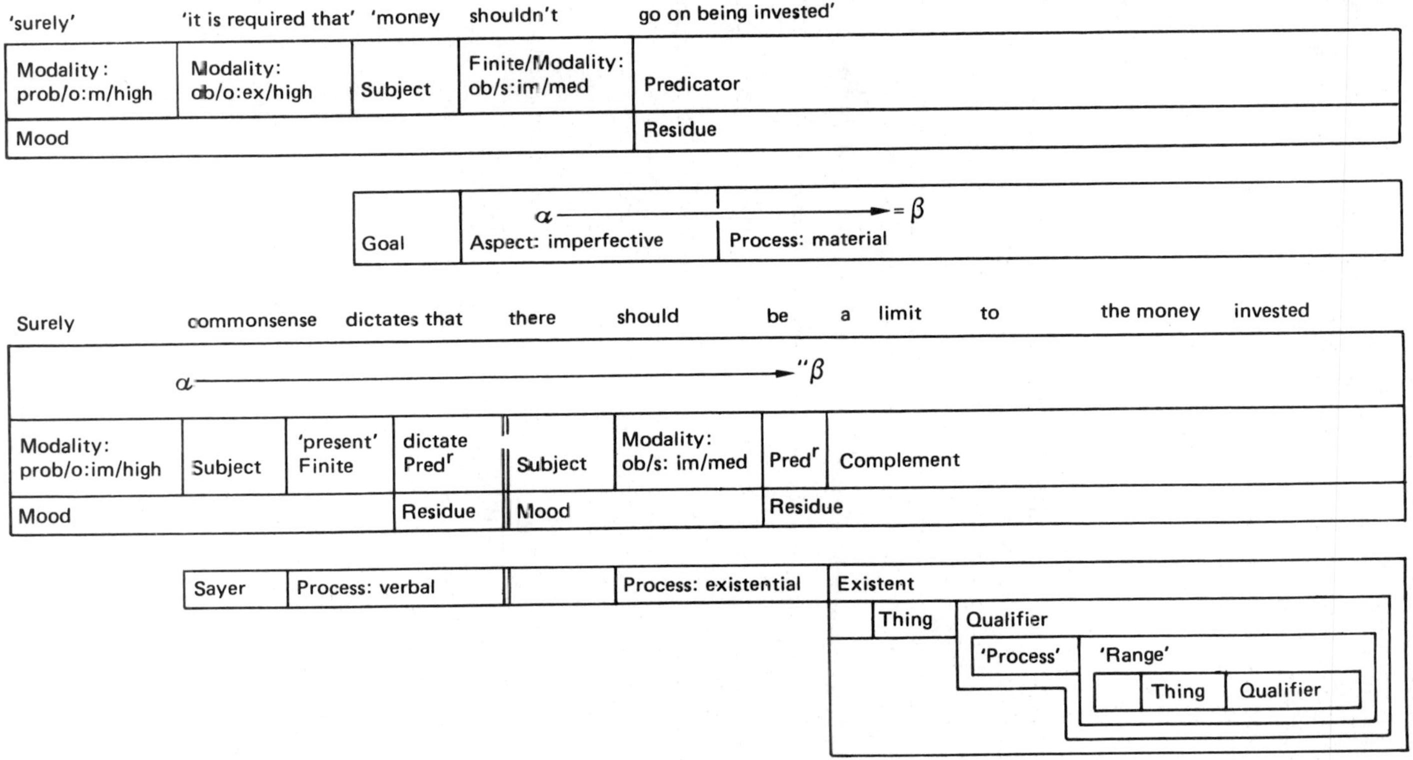

Figure 10-18 Example with modal and transitivity metaphors

3. Metaphors of mood

The other main type of interpersonal metaphor is that associated with mood. Mood expresses the speech function; and as we saw in Chapter 4 the underlying pattern of organization here is the exchange system — giving or demanding information or goods-&-services, which determines the four basic speech functions of statement, question, offer and command.

Obviously this is just the bare bones of the system. There is a vast range of rhetorical modes in every language; in English we can recognize offering, promising, threatening, vowing, undertaking, ordering, requesting, entreating, urging, persuading, commanding, instructing, encouraging, recommending, advising, prohibiting, dissuading, discouraging, warning, bribing, intimidating, blackmailing, shaming, cajoling, nagging, hinting, praising, reproving, blaming, flattering, parrying, hedging, complaining, insulting, boasting, claiming, stating, predicting, hoping, fearing, preaching, arguing, contradicting, submitting, insisting, asserting, denying, accusing, teasing, implying, disclosing, acknowledging, assenting, querying, disputing, accepting, doubting, responding, disclaiming, consenting, refusing, proclaiming, assuring and reassuring — to name only a few. These are not simply a list; they are systematically interrelated, and each one represents a particular complex of semantic features, each feature being one out of a contrasting set exactly as are those involved in modality. So, for example, 'threat' is 'give' (as opposed to 'demand') 'goods-&-services' (as opposed to 'information') 'oriented to addressee' (as opposed to 'oriented to speaker' or 'neutral') and 'undesirable' (as opposed to 'desirable'), e.g. *I'll shoot the pianist!*, reported as *he threatened to shoot the pianist*. If we substitute 'desirable', keeping the rest constant, we get 'promise'; if we substitute 'oriented to speaker' then instead of 'desirable/undesirable' we get 'sacred' ('vow') versus 'profane' ('undertaking'); and so on. Taken by itself, however, the clause *I'll shoot the pianist!* could represent any one of these (*he threatened/promised/vowed/undertook to shoot the pianist*); these speech functions all contain the feature combination 'give + goods-&-services', i.e. 'offer', and the wording of the clause specifies no more than that.

In other words, all these rhetorical categories can be recognized by speakers of the language, and have names which are used to represent them, both as 'things' (noun *a threat* 'act of threatening') and as processes (verb *to threaten*). The verbs express verbal (symbolic) processes and most of them, therefore, can project some act of speaking as a report or as a quote, e.g. *he threatened to shoot/that he would shoot the pianist*; *"I'll shoot the pianist," he threatened*. But the speech act itself carries no explicit signal of being an instance of this or that specific category. It selects for mood, realizing the basic speech functions of offer, command, statement or question as described in Chapter 4; note that here already there is the possibility of metaphorical transference, since these are only the congruent patterns. Beyond that, however, its specific rhetorical function is made manifest by any or all of a variety of other factors, which are actually of five different kinds:

(1) Paradigmatically associated (that is, simultaneous) lexicogrammatical features; for example 'key', realized by the selection of tone (see Chapter 8); lexical connotations; e.g.

// 1+ 3 ^ I'll / **shoot** that / bastard of a / **pianist** //

where '1 + ' means the wide variety of tone 1, falling from high to low, meaning 'key: strong'.

(2) Syntagmatically associated (that is, preceding or following) lexicogrammatical features; for example expansion by a conditional clause, e.g.

I'll shoot the pianist if he doesn't play in time.

Note that some verbs can be used 'performatively'; that is, as CONSTITUTING the rhetorical act they name: *I (hereby) promise to . . .*, *Do you undertake to . . .?* The verb *threaten* cannot; but *promise* can, so *promise* may stand in metaphorically for *threaten*, as in:

I promise you I'll shoot the pianist.

(3) Paralinguistic and behavioural features such as voice quality, facial expression and gesture. (4) Features of the context of situation: what is going on, who are taking part, and what the speech acts are designed to achieve. (5) Features of the context of culture: other things being equal, it is generally regarded as undersirable to shoot pianists even if their playing is not quite up to standard.

The lexicogrammatical resources of mood, therefore, and the associated patterns of modality and key, carry a very considerable semantic load, as the expression of interpersonal rhetoric. Not surprisingly, these categories lend themselves to a rich variety of metaphorical devices; and it is by no means easy to decide what are metaphorical and what are congruent forms. Some common speech-functional formulae are clearly metaphorical in origin, for example (i) *I wouldn't . . . if I was you*: command, congruently *don't . . .!* functioning as warning, (ii) *I've a good mind to . . .*: modalized offer, congruently *maybe I'll . . .*, typically functioning as threat; (iii) *she'd better . . .*: modulated command, congruently *she should . . .*, typically functioning as advice. Some words, such as *mind*, seem particularly to lend themselves to this kind of transference: cf. *would you mind . . .?*, *mind you!*, *I don't mind . . .* (including *I don't mind if I do*, positive response to offer of drink in environment pub) and so on.

Metaphors of this kind have been extensively studied in speech act theory, originally under the heading of 'perlocutionary' acts. From a linguistic point of view they are not a separate phenomenon, but another aspect of the general phenomenon of metaphor, like the ideational metaphors discussed in the first part of the chapter. They can be represented in the same way, by postulating some congruent form and then analysing the two in relation to each other. Some examples are given in Figure 10-19.

(a)

'tentatively	is	the position	still	available?'
Interpersonal Adjunct	Finite	Subject	Adjunct	Complement
Mood				Residue

	I	was	wondering	if	the position	is	still	available
Logical:	α → 'β							
Inter-personal:	Subject	Finite	Predicator		Subject	Finite	Adjunct	Complement
	Mood		Residue		Mood			Residue

(b)

	'if	you		move	I	'll	shoot'
Logical:	×β → α						
Inter-personal:		Subject	'do Finite	move' Predicator	Subject	Finite	Predicator
		Mood		Residue	Mood		Residue

	don't	move	or	I	'll	shoot
Logical	1 → +2					
Inter-personal:	Finite	Predicator		Subject	Finite	Predicator
	Mood	Residue		Mood		Residue

(c)

'you	shouldn't	say	such a thing'
Subject	Finite	Predicator	Complement
Mood		Residue	

how	could	you	say	such a thing
WH/Adjunct	Finite	Subject	Predicator	Complement
Residue	Mood			

(d)

'the evidence	is	(the fact) that	they	cheated	before'
Subject	Finite	Complement: clause	Subject	'did Finite / cheat' Predicator	Adjunct
Mood		Residue	Mood	Residue	

look		at	the way	they	cheated	before
'do Finite	look' Predicator	Adjunct				
		'Predicator'	Complement: clause	as above		
Mood	Residue					

Figure 10-19 Further examples of interpersonal metaphors

Note that the last of these examples, Figure 10-19 (d), embodies both interpersonal and ideational metaphor; it is interpreted here as a statement realized in the imperative, but this also involves interpreting it as an identifying clause 'the evidence is . . .', related to 'look at the way . . .' via 'consider (the fact) . . .'. Depending on the context, it might be functioning congruently as a request; in that case only the ideational metaphor need be recognized, with *consider the fact that they cheated before* taken as the congruent form.

The concept of grammatical metaphor, itself perhaps a metaphorical extension of the term from its rhetorical sense as a figure of speech, enables us to bring together a number of features of discourse which at first sight look rather different from each other. But when we recognize the different kinds of meaning that come together in the lexicogrammar, and especially the basic distinction between ideational and interpersonal meaning, we can see that what look like two different sets of phenomena are really instances of the same phenomenon arising in these two different contexts. In all the instances that we are treating as grammatical metaphor, some aspect of the structural configuration of the clause, whether in its ideational function or in its interpersonal function or in both, is in some way different from that which would be arrived at by the shortest route — it is not, or was not originally, the most straightforward coding of the meanings selected. This feature is not to be interpreted as something negative or deviant; it is partly in order to avoid any such connotations that we have used the term 'metaphorical' rather than 'incongruent'. But it is something that needs to be accounted for in an adequate interpretation of a text.

How far we go in pursuing metaphorical forms of discourse in any given instance will depend on what we are trying to achieve. In the most general terms, the purpose of analysing a text is to explain the impact that it makes: why it means what it does, and why it gives the particular impression that it does. But within this general goal we may have various kinds and degrees of interest in exploring this or that specific instance; sometimes a note to the effect that the expression is metaphorical is all that is needed, whereas at other times we may want to trace a whole series of intermediate steps linking the clause to a postulated 'most congruent' form. These are not to be thought of as a 'history' of the clause; as we have seen, in some areas the metaphorical form has become the typical, coded form of expression in the language, and even where it has not, there is no way of tracking the process whereby a speaker or writer has arrived at a particular mode of expression in the discourse. What the metaphorical interpretation does is to suggest how an instance in the text may be referred to the system of the language as a whole. It is therefore an important link in the total chain of explanations whereby we relate the text to the system. A text is meaningful because it is an actualization of the potential that constitutes the linguistic system; it is for this reason that the study of discourse ('text linguistics') cannot properly be separated from the study of the grammar that lies behind it.

Appendix 1

The 'silver' text: analysis and interpretation

In the following account, the text is first described in a sequence of seven 'steps', representing the segments into which it divides itself naturally on linguistic grounds. The text is the 'silver' text already cited in Chapter 8; and only the manageress's turns are discussed in detail, because it is her conversation, and the other speaker, Anne, confines herself to qualified acknowledgments. The seven steps of the manageress' speech are indicated in Figure A-1.

Step 1 | // 4 ^ in / **thǐs** job / Anne we're // I working with // **sìlver** //

Step 2 | // 1 ^ now / silver / needs to have / **lòve** // [// 1 **yeà** //]
// 3 you / **knōw** ^ the // 4 people that / **bǔy** silver // 1 **lòve** it //

// 1 **yèa** // I guess they / **wòuld** //

Step 3 | // 1 **yèa** // 1 mm / ^ well / **nàturally** I / mean to / say that it's // 13 got a / lovely / **gleàm** a/bout it you / **knōw** // 3 ^ and / if they come / **īn** they're // 1 usually / people who / love / beautiful / **thìngs** //

Step 4 | // 1 ^ so / you / have to be / beautiful / **wìth** it you / know //
1 ^ and you / **sèll** it with / beauty //

// 1 **ùm** //

Step 5 | // 1 ^ you / ^ I'm / **sùre** you know / how to do // 4 **thǎt** // ^
// 1 oh but you / **mùst** //

Step 6 | // 1 let's hear / ^ / let's hear / ^ / **lòok** / ^ you say // 1 **màdam** //
5 isn't / that / **beâutiful** //

step 7 | // 4 ^ if / you sug/**gěst** it's beautiful // 1 they / **sèe** it as / beautiful //

Figure A-1 The 'Silver' text

Following the step by step analysis is a general interpretation based on each of the various linguistic features taken as a whole; thematic structure, types of process and so on. In a final short note the text is considered in relation to its context of situation.

[Step 1] Clause 1:

In this job, Anne, we're working with silver.

Theme. The Theme is *in this job*: 'I'm going to tell you about the job that has to be done'. It is a marked Theme, since, while the clause is declarative, it is not the Subject; hence it is foregrounded, and this helps the listener to recognize it as thematic not only for this clause but for the whole of the succeeding exchange. The message is then completed with a description of what the job is. The vocative *Anne* marks the boundary between Theme and Rheme.

Information. The Theme-Rheme boundary is also marked by the division into tone groups. The manageress organizes the clause into two units of information, one for the Theme and one for the Rheme; this is the typical distribution when there are two information units in the clause, and it is a pattern that is particularly associated with marked Themes. The first information unit has the Deictic element *this* as Focus, referring exophorically to the context of situation, the silverware department in which the exchange takes place; since *this* is non-final in the unit, it is a marked focus, and hence not only is it itself shown to be New but the following item *job* is at the same time shown to be Given, signalling the taken-for-grantedness of the fact that Anne is there to do a job – a fact which is an essential datum for the whole exchange.

The second information unit has *silver* as Focus, this time unmarked; the New element is the whole of *(are) working with silver*, signalled by the salience (rhythmic prominence) of *working* which opens the pretonic section of a new tone group. Anne knows perfectly well, of course, that they are working with silver; but this is what she is being called upon to attend to.

Cohesion. There is no cohesion with what went before, as far as we can tell; but there is cohesion with the situation by means of the exophoric deictic *this* and the lexical items *job* and *silver*.

Mood. The clause is a declarative, functioning congruently as a statement; the Subject is *we*, and this includes Anne, the vocative serving to define the meaning of *we* as 'you and I'.

Whereas imperative 'we' (in *let's*) is always inclusive, in the indicative English makes no distinction between inclusive and non-inclusive 'we' (including or not necessarily including the listener), so one way of suggesting an inclusive interpretation is by tying the *we* to a Vocative. The manageress is reducing the distance between Anne and herself by bringing Anne on the inside: 'we're in this together', reinforced by the assignment of *we* to the Subject role, as the element held responsible for the validity of the assertion — the tag would be *aren't we?*

Key. The first information unit has the contrastive tone 4 (falling-rising), meaning 'whatever may be the case with other jobs, here . . .'. The second unit has the unmarked statement tone, tone 1 (falling); it is used here in its typical sense of giving information — where 'information' means, as already remarked, something to which the listener is being invited to pay attention; there is no suggestion that Anne is not already fully aware of what is being imparted to her.

Transitivity. On the face of it this is a material process clause, with *we* as Actor/Medium, *in this job* as Location/Spatial and *with silver* as Manner: Means, or perhaps even Accompaniment — the former suggests 'handling', the second 'doing a job in association with'. We might want to consider whether the clause is a grammatical metaphor for another type of process whose congruent form would be

we	are concerned with	silver
Identified	Process:relational: circumstance:matter	Identifier

with the identifying sense of 'what concerns us is silver'. What makes this interpretation less likely, perhaps, is the present in present tense *are working*; this is the unmarked present for a material process, but in a relational process the unmarked present form is the simple present tense and we might have expected rather *we work with silver*, with *work* non-salient:

// ‸ we work with / silver //

The first clause stands as the explicit point of departure for the passage as a whole. Not only does its Theme provide the context for all that follows, but the entire clause serves to enunciate the source and likely direction of the text. Analysis in Figure A-2.

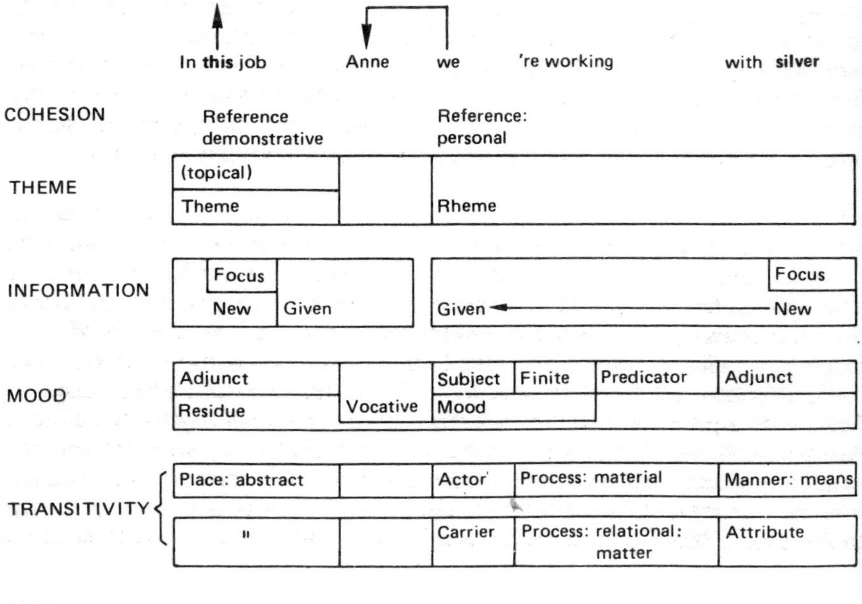

Figure A-2 Step 1 (clause 1)

[Step 2] Clauses 2–3:

> Now silver needs to have love. [Yea]
> You know — the people that buy silver love it.

Theme. Clause 2 has a two-part Theme: continuative *now* meaning 'relevant information coming' and topical *silver* meaning 'I'm going to tell you about silver'. This is switched in Clause 3 to *the people that buy silver* — the customers. Both topical Themes are unmarked, since they function also as Subject. The rhematic element in the two clauses introduces the item *love*: silver needs love, customers love silver.

Information. The first clause has an information structure that is unmarked in every respect: one tone group to the clause, with Focus at the end. The Given is the topical Theme *silver*, with *needs to have love* as the New. In the second clause the distribution is marked (two information units to the clause); as usual in such instances, the transition from one to the other marks the boundary between Theme and Rheme.

The first of the two has marked tonicity: focus on *buy*, showing *silver* to be Given. The item *silver* is thus Given throughout Step 2, despite its change of position in the sequence of elements in the clause. In the second the tonicity is unmarked, with Focus on *love* which is the only lexical item in the information unit.

Cohesion. There are two ties with the preceding step, continuative *now* (conjunction) and lexical item *silver* (repetition). Clause 3 contains both *silver* and *love* as repetitions linking it with Clause 2. There is also the reference item *it* referring back to *silver* within the same Clause.

Mood. The two clauses are both declarative, and express statements; the manageress is giving information. The *now* suggests that she sees this as something not merely to be attended to but perhaps even unknown, or at least representing an angle that Anne might not have thought of. The Subject is, first, *silver* and then *the people that buy silver*; both of which, as we saw, are also Theme — in other words the complex status of 'point of departure/validity carrier' shifts from the silver to the customers who buy it.

Transitivity. In the experiential component the picture is more complex. *Silver needs to have love* is presented as a relational process of possession, the Process being *have*, the Carrier (Possessor) *silver* and the Attribute (Possessed) *love*. This could then be interpreted as a metaphorical representation of a meaning that would be congruently expressed as *silver needs to be given love*; silver may need to have love, but this does not mean that it goes out and gets it. Some external agency is involved (the passive represents the feature of agency, whether or not there is an item explicitly functioning as Agent), with silver being the Beneficiary. This still leaves 'love' represented as a commodity, a participant in the transmission process; which suggests that we might take a further analytical step and set up a congruent form *needs to be loved*. This interprets love as a Process; and it will be a mental not a material process, in which the other participant involved must be as good as human ('+ consciousness').

Then comes *you know*, which means 'explanatory comment coming'; and the explanatory comment is *the people that buy silver love it.* Here the speaker has moved over explicitly to a mental process clause with *love* as the Process, as in our suggested interpretation of the preceding clause: 'people love silver'. Which people? — this is indicated by an embedded clause of elaboration (a defining relative clause): '(those) that buy it'. But what is the relationship between the buying and the loving? This is not a congruent clause comparable to *the people that buy silver polish it*; rather it appears to be a metaphorical variant of an identifying clause 'those that buy silver = those that love silver'. But which is the cause and which is the effect? Is it 'if a person buys silver, then he will love it', as in

those who buy silver	are	those who love silver
Id/Tk	(realize)	Ir/Vl

or is it 'if a person loves silver, then he will buy it', as in

those who buy silver	are	those who love silver	
Id/Vl	(are realized by)	Ir/Tk	?

Perhaps the second is slightly more likely; but the clause *the people that buy silver love it* is in fact ambiguous as regards which is logically prior, the buying or the loving, and derives its effect in this passage (where it is being offered in explanation of *silver needs to have love*) precisely from this ambiguity. See Figures A-3 and A-4.

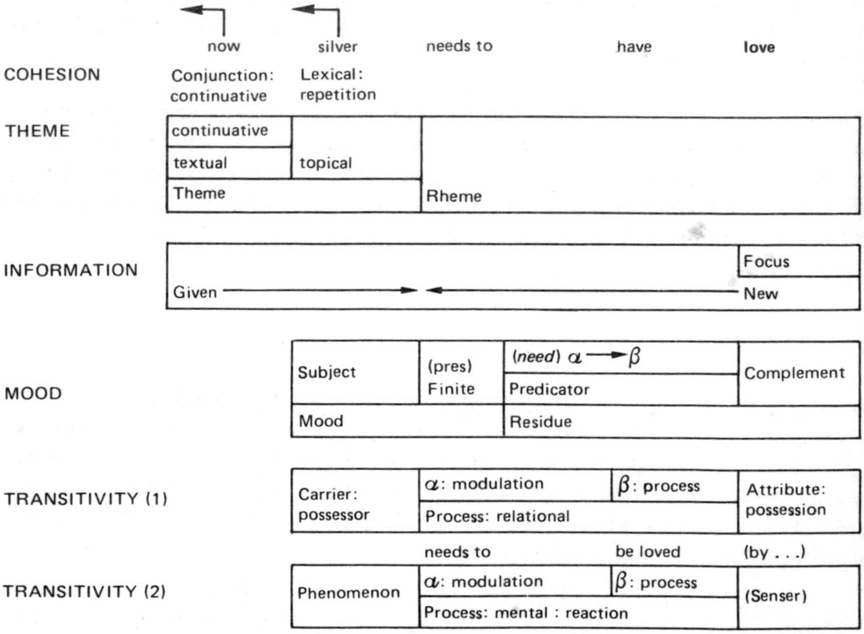

Figure A-3 Step 2 (clause 2)

	the people that **buy**	silver		**love**	it
COHESION		Lexical: repetition		Lexical: repetition	Reference: personal
THEME	Theme (topical)			Rheme	
INFORMATION		Focus		Focus	
	←	New	Given	New	Given
MOOD	Subject		(pres) Finite	*(love)* Predicator	Complement
	Mood			Residue	
TRANSITIVITY (1)	Senser		Process: mental: reaction		Phenomenon

	the people that buy silver	are	the people that love it
TRANSITIVITY (2)	Identified/Value	Process: relational: intensive	Identifier/Token

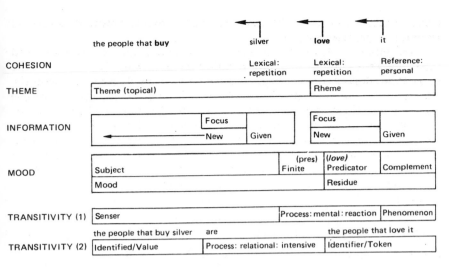

Figure A-4 Step 2 (clause 3)

[Step 3] Clauses 4–6:

> [Yea — guess they would]
> Yes, mm — well naturally, I mean to say that it's got a lovely gleam about it, you know; and if they come in, they're usually people who love beautiful things.

Anne responds rather doubtfully, perhaps a little bemused by this approach, and puzzled as to how to interpret it. The manageress responds to her doubts by adding a further piece of explanation.

Theme. She feels that this needs some initial buildup, so she inaugurates it with a complex multiple Theme *well* + *naturally* + *I*. But this, in turn, introduces a clause *I mean to say* which is a metaphorical variant of an apposition; the meaning is 'I will restate it in another way'. Effectively therefore the whole of *well naturally I mean to say that it* becomes thematic:

> well: 'since you query it, I'll respond to your doubt.'
> naturally: 'I consider it self-evident'
> I mean to say that: 'to put it another way'
> it: 'silver'

The remainder, *has got a lovely gleam about it*, is then the Rheme.

The next clause *if they come in* is a β-clause in a hypotactic clause complex, and so is thematic as a whole. It is again incongruent, a way of saying 'those who come in . . .' (see below on transitivity). Thus Step 3 has the same thematic pattern as Step 2 on which it is elaborating: first 'silver', then 'the customers':

Step 2:	cl. 2	silver	cl. 3	the people that buy silver
Step 3:	cl. 4	it [silver]	cll. 5-6	if they come in, they [=those who come in]

love and *beauty* remain in the Rheme, as before.

Information. The manageress assigns a separate tone group to the modal Adjunct *naturally*, giving prominence to her contention that Anne should have thought of this for herself. Apart from this, the distribution of information is unmarked, with one information unit per clause. The Focus is also unmarked, falling on the final element other than anything which is anaphoric: *gleam* [*about it*], *come in*, *beautiful things*. Like the thematic structure, the information structure is also parallel to Step 2:

Step 2:	cl. 2	love	cll. 3	[the people that] buy . . . love
Step 3:	cl. 4	lovely gleam	cll. 4-5	[if they] come in . . . [love] beautiful things

Cohesion. In Step 3 there are two referential chains, one of 'silver' the other 'the customers': 1) [*silver*] . . . *it* . . . *it*; 2) [*the people that buy silver*] . . . *they* . . . *they*. Each of these relates by cohesion to Step 2.

There is also the lexical chain [*love*] . . . *lovely* [*gleam*] . . . *love* . . . *beautiful* [*things*], also cohesive into Step 2. The lexical sequence is *love* . . . *love* . . . *lovely* . . . *love* . . *beautiful*, and it is continued in Step 4 as *beautiful* . . . *beauty*. The hinge word here is *lovely*, which ensures that love and beauty form a single lexicosemantic set here and not two. *Lovely* has the two senses of 'lovable' and 'beautiful', and has served in English ever since Elizabethan times to make explicit the link between these two semantic fields; the manageress uses it in just this way, to form a chain of motifs from 'people love silver', through 'people love beauty' and 'silver is beautiful', to 'you must be beautiful too'.

Mood and modality. The clauses are again declaratives, functioning congruently as statements, with Subject = Theme, the Subjects again being *it* ('silver') and *they* ('the customers'). Here however the statements are accompanied by modalities: *naturally* ('they love silver'), *usually* ('they are people who love beautiful things').

Transitivity. Clause 4 *it's got a lovely gleam about it* is also, like clause 2, a possessive, and might be regarded as a metaphorical variant of *it gleams lovelily* ('lovably/beautifully'). There is no adverbial form of *lovely*, so the only way of introducing this word is as Epithet or Attribute; the manageress selects the possessive *it has a gleam*, with *lovely* as Epithet of *gleam*. The relationship of *it has a gleam* to *it gleams* is a metaphorical one; but the form *it has a gleam* is now so much a part of the regular system of English that it does not really function any longer as a marked metaphorical alternative. If anything, *it gleams* is probably now the marked variant.

Clauses 5 and 6 make up a hypotactic clause complex of the enhancing, conditional type; but the condition is implicational not logical. The form *if they come in they (are people who) love beautiful things* is an implicational conditional, one where the meaning is 'if . . ., then it can be deduced that (then that is because) . . .'. The corresponding logical conditional, where the meaning is 'if . . ., then it follows that . . .', would be *if they (are people who) love beautiful things, they come in.* Note that it would be very difficult to get in the 'usually' in the latter form. The alpha-clause, *they are usually people who love beautiful things*, is attributive, with *they* as Carrier and *people who love beautiful things* as Attribute. It could be argued that the hypotactic complex is a metaphorical variant of a single clause *those who come in are usually people who love beautiful things*; compare in this respect clause 3 above, *the people that buy silver love it*. Here however there is no ambiguity; the only interpretation is 'people (who) come in (do so) mostly because they love beautiful things'. See Figures A-5 and A-6.

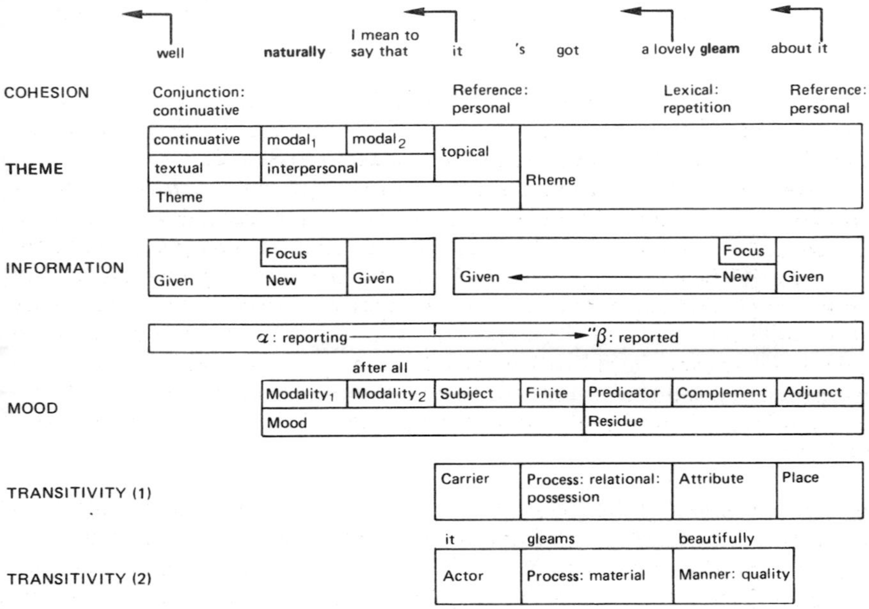

Figure A-5 Step 3 (clause 4)

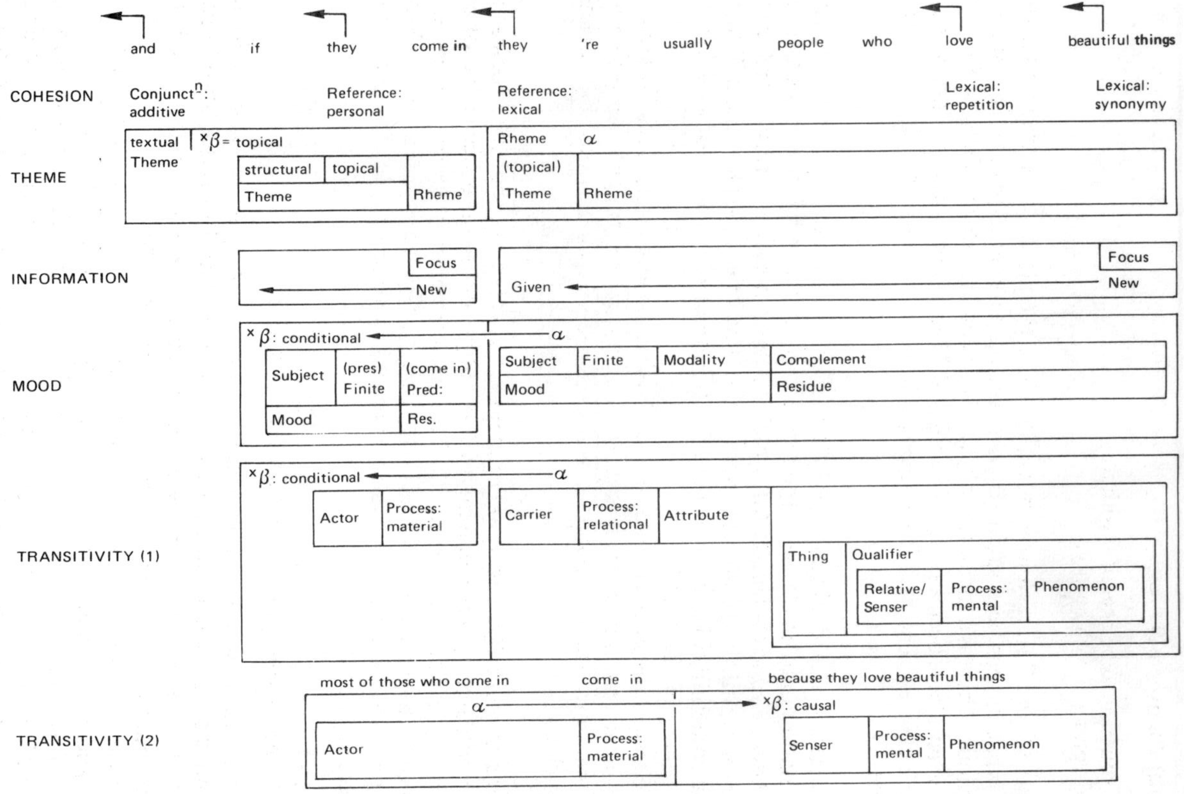
and if they come in they 're usually people who love beautiful things
COHESION
Conjunctⁿ: additive
Reference: personal
Reference: lexical
Lexical: repetition
Lexical: synonymy
THEME
textual Theme
×β = topical
structural
topical
Theme
Rheme
Rheme
α
(topical) Theme
Rheme
INFORMATION
Focus
New
Given
Focus
New
MOOD
×β: conditional
α
Subject
(pres) Finite
(come in) Pred:
Mood
Res.
Subject
Finite
Modality
Complement
Mood
Residue
TRANSITIVITY (1)
×β: conditional
α
Actor
Process: material
Carrier
Process: relational
Attribute
Thing
Qualifier
Relative/ Senser
Process: mental
Phenomenon
most of those who come in
come in
because they love beautiful things
TRANSITIVITY (2)
α
×β: causal
Actor
Process: material
Senser
Process: mental
Phenomenon

Figure A-6 Step 3 (clauses 5–6)

[Step 4] Clauses 7–8

> So you have to be beautiful with it;
> and you sell it with beauty.

Theme. Clause 7 starts a new move, in which the manageress draws a lesson from what she has been saying before, showing its consequences for Anne's behaviour. There is a thematic conjunctive *so* making this explicit: 'it follows from what I have been saying'. The topical Theme now shifts to *you*, 'Anne', in both clauses. The motifs of silver, selling and beauty are all now in the Rheme.

Information. The distribution of information is unmarked; each clause is one information unit. In clause 7, the Focus is on *with*, with *it* 'silver' as Given; *you*, *have (to)* and *(be) beautiful*, which all embody salience, form a pre-tonic to the tone group and constitute part of the New. We could gloss the information as something like 'we have been talking about silver; now you and it must have beauty in common'.

In clause 8 the Focus is on *sell*; and everything else in the clause is Given: non-salient *you*, post-tonic *it* and *with beauty*. This highlights *sell* (the only time this word occurs in the text) as the unique information-bearing element in the clause.

Mood and modality. The mood of clause 7 is declarative; but the Predicator *be* is modulated by *have to*, a high value obligation, so the effect is that of an imperative 'be beautiful with it'. This interpretation is borne out by the salience of the *you*. Typically, Subject *you* is non-salient in indicative, salient in imperative (because in the unmarked case a second person imperative is Subjectless); contrast

> // 4 ‸ if you / listen / **cărefully** . . . (indicative)
> // 1 ‸ now / you / listen / **càrefully** // (imperative)

There is an alternative interpretation: the salience of the *you* could be explained as indicative but contrastive, 'silver is beautiful and so should *you* be'. But since both meanings are clearly present, both the contrast and the command, there is no need to decide between the two.

Clause 8 is also declarative, but without modulation; this time the *you* is non-salient, and again two factors coincide to determine it this way — it is now not contrastive, but in fact Given from the preceding clause; and the declarative, being unmodulated, does not function as realization of a command. At the same time, it is simple present *you sell*, not present in present *you are selling*, and therefore, since the clause is a material process, habitual; and a habitual present in such a context also has the force of an injunction: 'this is the way things are'. The *you* in such cases may in fact be the generalized pronoun *you*, informal equivalent of *one*: 'one sells it with beauty'. (There is also a true imperative with non-salient *you*, as in *you take the third turning on the left*; once again the force would be the same).

Thus the manageress is now moving into the regulative mode; she is the boss, and she is giving Anne her orders, telling her what to do. Anne has now, for the first time, become the Subject; and the Subject in a command is the one designated by the speaker as 'modally responsible', responsible for carrying it out. The meaning is: this is your job.

Transitivity. Clause 7 is a relational attributive process with *you* 'Anne' as Carrier and *beautiful* as Attribute, modulated by the obligation *have to*. Note that, despite the fact that *beautiful* is an inherent not a behavioural quality, there is nothing untoward about the instruction 'be beautiful'; the clause is congruent, not metaphorical. The element *with it* is a circumstantial of Accompaniment; the sense is 'you as well as silver together'.

Clause 8 is likewise congruent: material process *sell*, with Actor and Goal. Here the circumstantial element *with beauty* is presumably one of Manner, subcategory Means: beauty is the means by which silver is (to be) sold. But there is perhaps also an echo of the sense of accompaniment from the preceding clause: 'you and beauty join in the selling of silver'. See Figures A-7 and A-8.

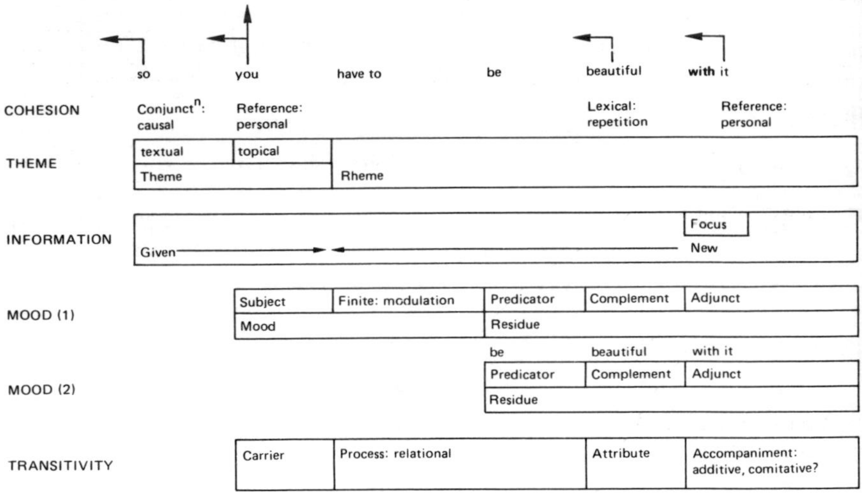

Figure A-7 Step 4 (clause 7)

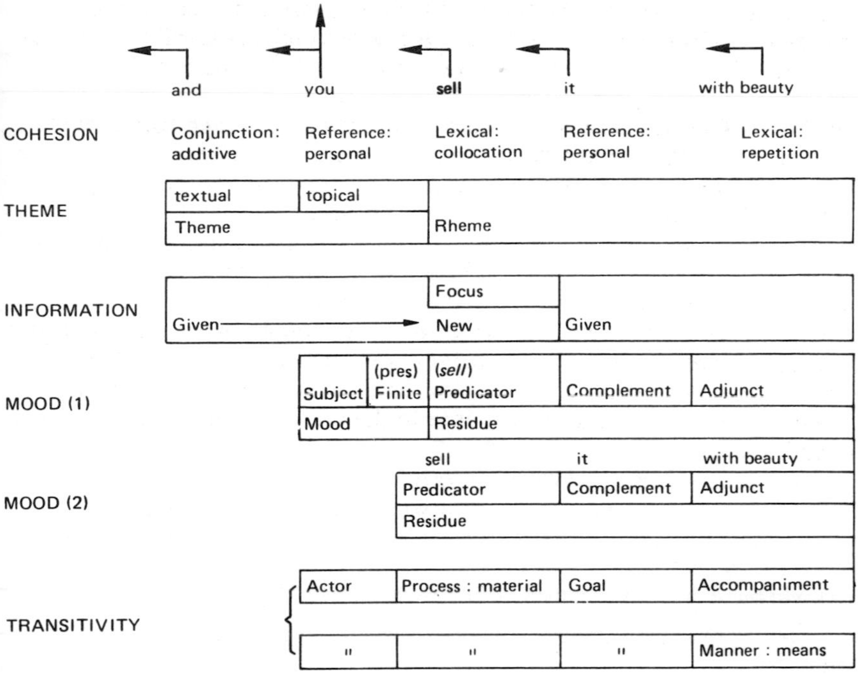

Figure A-8 Step 4 (clause 8)

[Step 5] Clauses 9–10:

> [Um]
> You — I'm sure you know how to do that.
> Oh but you must!

Clause complex. The wording *I'm sure you know how to do that* forms a hypotactic clause complex of structure α ^ β, the relationship being one of projection in each case. However, it contains two grammatical metaphors. One is interpersonal: *I'm sure* as expression of modality 'surely'. The other is ideational: *know how to* as expression of modulation 'are able to'. Both of these are referred to below.

Theme. If taken as congruent, the Themes of the respective clauses would be *I*, *you* and *how*. But if we treat it as a metaphorical variant of a congruent form *surely you can do that*, we interpret the thematic structure as: interpersonal Theme *I'm sure*, topical Theme *you*. As Anne continues to look doubtful despite this reassurance, the manageress goes on *oh but you must*, which has a multiple Theme consisting of continuative *oh* ('I take in what you mean and am surprised by it'), conjunctive *but* ('contrary to your protestation'), topical *you*. Thus Anne is again topical Theme of both parts.

Information. Clause 9 is split into two units of information, with *I'm sure* as a separate information point — Anne is asked to take note of the manageress's assurance. The second Focus is *do that*, which has the contrastive tone 4 implying 'at least — even though you may not be an expert in silver'. In clause 10 the tonic is in its unmarked place at the end; the ellipsis brings the finite *must* into final position, so the effect is to get the Focus on the modal auxiliary (the meaning of which is discussed below).

Cohesion. There is the reference form *do that*, which does duty for a non-existent reference verb *to that* and is anaphoric to *sell it with beauty*, perhaps including also *be beautiful with it*. And there is ellipsis of the Residue in *oh but you must*. The ellipsis, however, leaves an ambiguity: would the full form be *oh but you must know how to do that*, or *oh but you must do that*?

Mood and modality. It was said above that the clause contained an interpersonal metaphor *I'm sure*. We can tell that this is a metaphorical expression of modality if we add a tag. The tagged form of the clause would be *I'm sure you know how to do that, don't you*?, showing that the Subject is *you* and *I'm sure* is a thematic modal. Otherwise, the tagged form would be *I'm sure you know how to do that, aren't I?*

As will be seen from the discussion of modality in Chapter 10, the form *I'm sure* is an explicit subjective form (that is, one where the speaker makes it explicit that the clause is an expression of his judgment, using *I*) of the high value probability ('more than likely') of which the non-metaphorical expression is either *surely* or *certainly*. A modality of this kind is the speaker's assessment of the probability that his observation is valid. Now, if the speaker has no doubt, he says simply 'it is so'. If he adds a probability, this means that he is not sure; and this is true even if he adds a high value probability 'it is certainly so'. Hence the apparent paradox that we say something is certain only when it isn't. If we hear a knock on the door, then *that's certainly Mary*, or *that must be Mary*, is less certain than *that's Mary*. And *surely that's Mary* is even less certain than that.

This explains the semantic drift to which such expressions are extremely prone. In Elizabethan English *surely* meant what *certainly* does today, but in the intervening period it gradually moved further away from 'it is so', to the extent that it now means something like 'I gather it isn't so, though I find it hard to believe'. Its place was then taken by *certainly* — which is now moving in a similar direction, for example *it certainly can't go on raining like this all week!* The explicit subjective forms *I'm sure*, *I'm certain* are not quite so clearly distinct from one another as *surely* and *certainly*; so we cannot be quite sure (or certain) which is the more appropriate gloss on the manageress' remark.

Coming to *oh but you must*, we have to add another dimension to the meaning of modality. On the one hand, *must* expresses high value probability: it is the implicit subjective equivalent of *certainly*. So *you must know how to do that* is equivalent to *you certainly know how to do that*. (It is also equivalent to *you surely know how to do that*, because *must* has drifted along with *surely*; but in that sense it has the tone of a 'surely' clause, namely a rising terminal tone 2 or 4, whereas here it has the tone of a 'certainly' clause, with falling terminal, tone 1 or 5). On the other hand, the modal auxiliaries express another semantic system, that of modulation; and there are two kinds of modulation, passive (obligation) and active (inclination or ability). So an expression such as *she must be very helpful* means either 'she certainly is helpful' (probability) or 'she is required to be helpful' (obligation). Hence another possible interpretation of *oh but you must* is as ellipsis for *oh but you must do that*, i.e. 'you are required to do that'. It is impossible to rule out either of these interpretations here; both meanings are sensible, and it seems in fact that both should be understood. The manageress is as it were slipping imperceptibly from certainty (as reassurance) to necessity (as injunction) — from 'I know you can' to 'you've got to'.

Transitivity. Modulation is an ideational as much as an interpersonal system; and clause 9 has to be understood as an active modulation. The wording *know how to* is a lexicogrammatical metaphor for 'can' in the sense of ability, 'be able to'; *you know how to do that* is a variant of *you are able to do that, you can do that*.

This sense of *know how* as active modulation 'are able to' in clause 9 is what seems to lead up to the interpretation of *must* as passive modulation 'are required to' in clause 10. A parallel example would be something like *I'm sure you can win. — Well . . . — Oh but you must!* ('you've got to win'). See Figures A-9 and A-10.

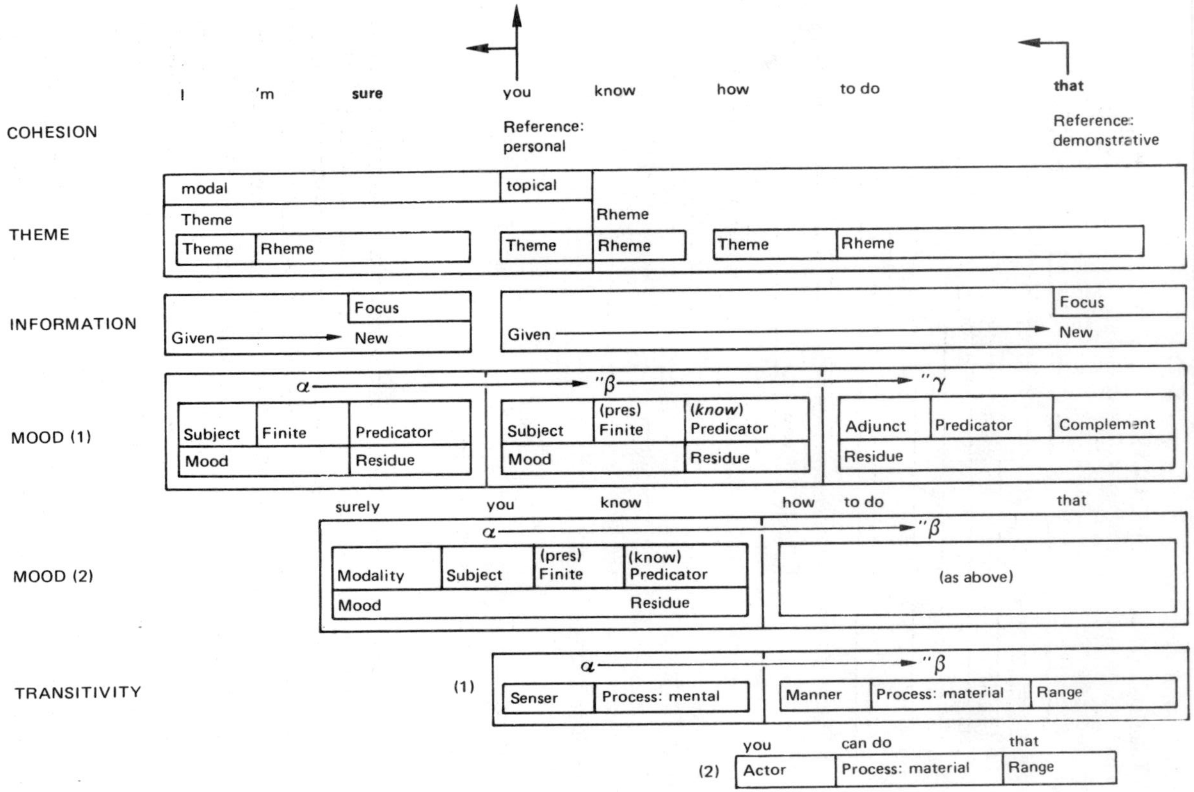

Figure A-9 Step 5 (clause 9)

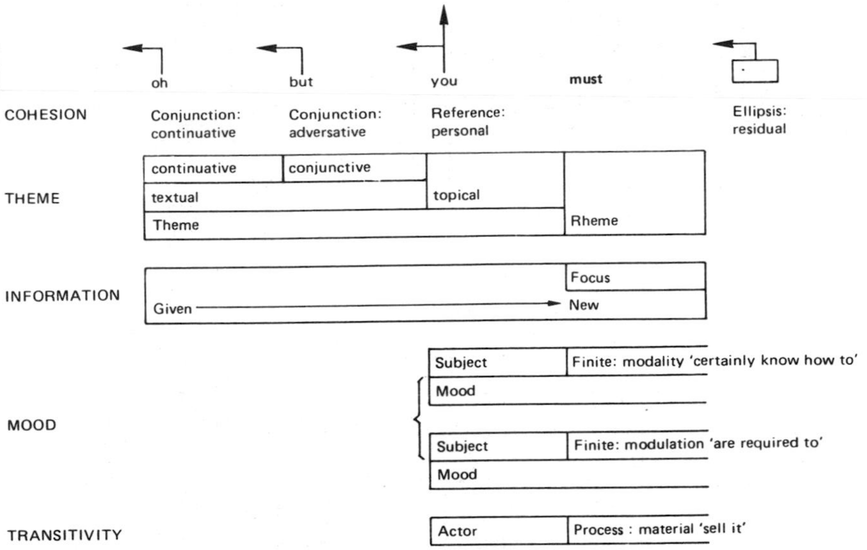

Figure A-10 Step 5 (clause 10)

[Step 6] Clauses 11–12:

> Let's hear — let's hear — look: you say
> "Madam! Isn't that beautiful!"

Theme. The manageress now decides to rehearse Anne in salespersonship, and begins *let's hear*, with thematic *let's*, as a friendly way of saying 'I want you to try saying for me . . .'. However, she senses that Anne needs more than just encouragement; she needs a model she can aspire to, some clearer idea of what is expected of her. So the manageress changes her tack, signalling this by the word *look*, and proceeds to give a demonstration. Clause 11 then takes the simple form *you say*, with thematic *you*; this is non-salient, so we cannot differentiate as between 'Anne' and impersonal 'one'.

Clause 12 is the demonstration, and it has a complex three-part Theme: interpersonal (1), vocative *madam*; interpersonal (2), finite *isn't*; topical, exophoric *that*. This is the weakest kind of topical Theme, the Subject following the Finite in a yes/no interrogative; but it still has some thematic status, since the various markers of the Theme – Rheme boundary come after such a Subject and not before it. So whereas Anne has been the Theme for all the other clauses following the *so* in clause 7, in the demonstration addressed to an imaginary customer it is once again the silver that takes this role.

Information. The wordings *let's hear . . . let's hear* are both arrested proclitics (pre-rhythmic elements) which are abandoned before turning into information units. The word *look* gets a tone group to itself, the tonic serving to draw Anne's attention to the demonstration that is to follow: 'now watch this!'. *you say* is again proclitic, and announces the dramatized quote that is to follow. This has two tone groups, one the attention-calling vocative *madam*, the other the whole of *isn't that beautiful* with unmarked focus on *beautiful*.

Cohesion. The reference item *that* is exophoric, accompanied by a gesture towards the silver. The word *beautiful* picks up again the lexical motif of *beauty* from clause 8.

Mood. The initial inclusive imperative *let's hear* is followed by exclusive imperative *look*; while this form often simply introduces a new step in a proposal or in an argument, here it can be interpreted both in this way and literally in the sense of 'watch!'. *you say* is a declarative functioning as command (cf. what was said on clause 8 in Step 4 above). The clause *isn't that beautiful* has the low variety of tone 5 that is characteristic of exclamations, especially where they are encoded as yes/no interrogatives; the sense is 'I invite you to share my wonder at its beauty'.

Transitivity. *isn't that beautiful* is an attributive relational clause with *that* 'silverware' as Carrier and *beautiful* as Attribute. It is entirely congruent. See Figure A-11.

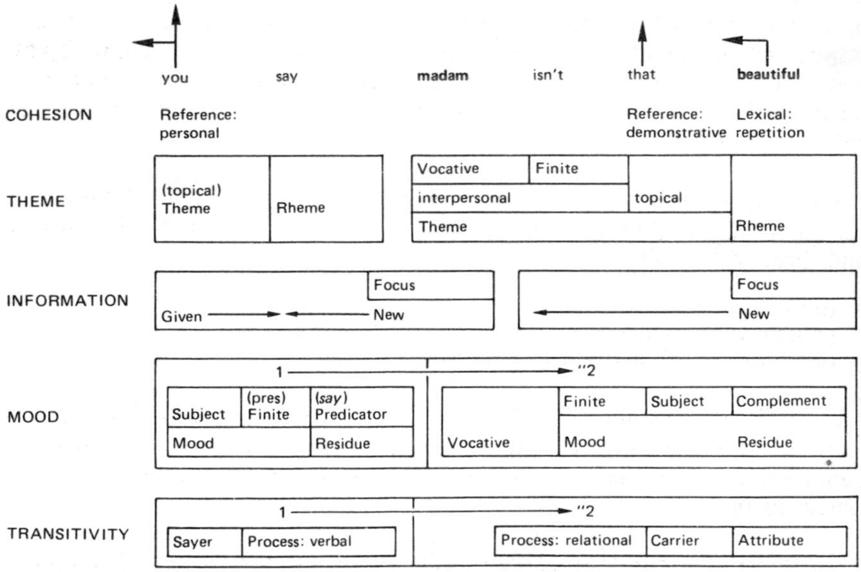

Figure A-11 Step 6 (clauses 11–12)

[Step 7] Clauses 13–14

If you suggest it's beautiful.
they see it as beautiful.

Clause complex. Clauses 13–14 form a hypotactic clause complex of structure $\beta \wedge \alpha$; the relationship is one of exhancement, specifically conditional. Clause 13 is itself a clause complex of structure $\alpha \wedge \beta$, the beta clause being projected. The overall structure is thus

$^{\times}\beta\alpha \wedge \beta``\beta \wedge \alpha$

Theme. In the outer complex, since the order is $\beta \wedge \alpha$, the whole of the beta clause is thematic: *if you suggest it's beautiful.* Within this, the first clause has a multiple Theme consisting of structural *if*, topical *you* 'Anne'; the second has topical Theme *it* 'silver'. The alpha clause has topical Theme *they* 'the customers'. This brings the customers back as the final Theme, in the progression Anne – silver – customers: if Anne (Theme 1) does her job, which is to assert that silver (Theme 2) is beautiful, then the customers (Theme 3) will see it as beautiful, and hence, by implication, buy it. As always, *beautiful* appears in the Rheme.

Information. There are two information units, in which *beautiful* appears as post-tonic, and hence Given on both occasions. The Focus is marked, in both instances being located on the Process: *you + suggest*, *they + see*, with *you* and *they* both salient, signalling the confrontation between them. The tone sequence is $4 \wedge 1$. the typical form for $\beta \wedge \alpha$ clause complexes of the enhancing type.

Cohesion. This follows the pattern that has become established throughout the passage, with 'silver' and 'the customers' carried forward referentially and 'beauty' lexically:

(silver . . .) it . . . it
(customers . . .) they
(beautiful . . .) beautiful . . . beautiful

Mood. The clauses are all declarative. Two of them are secondary (hypotactic) clauses: one projected, as 'report' following *suggest*; one enhancing, a conditional of the logical kind. The primary clause is a statement in congruent form.

Transitivity. The conditional clause consists of a verbal process plus report; the reported clause is attributive, '(that) silver is beautiful'. The primary clause also expresses the attributive relationship 'silver is beautiful', but it has two possible interpretations. In one interpretation it is metaphorical for a mental process plus projection, 'they understand that it is beautiful'; in the other it is congruent with a 'mentally caused' attribute, 'they consider it beautiful'. The difference between the two is that in the first interpretation the beauty is in the silver, whereas in the second it is in the eye of the beholder. But there is no clear sense of ambiguity about it; as often in such instances,

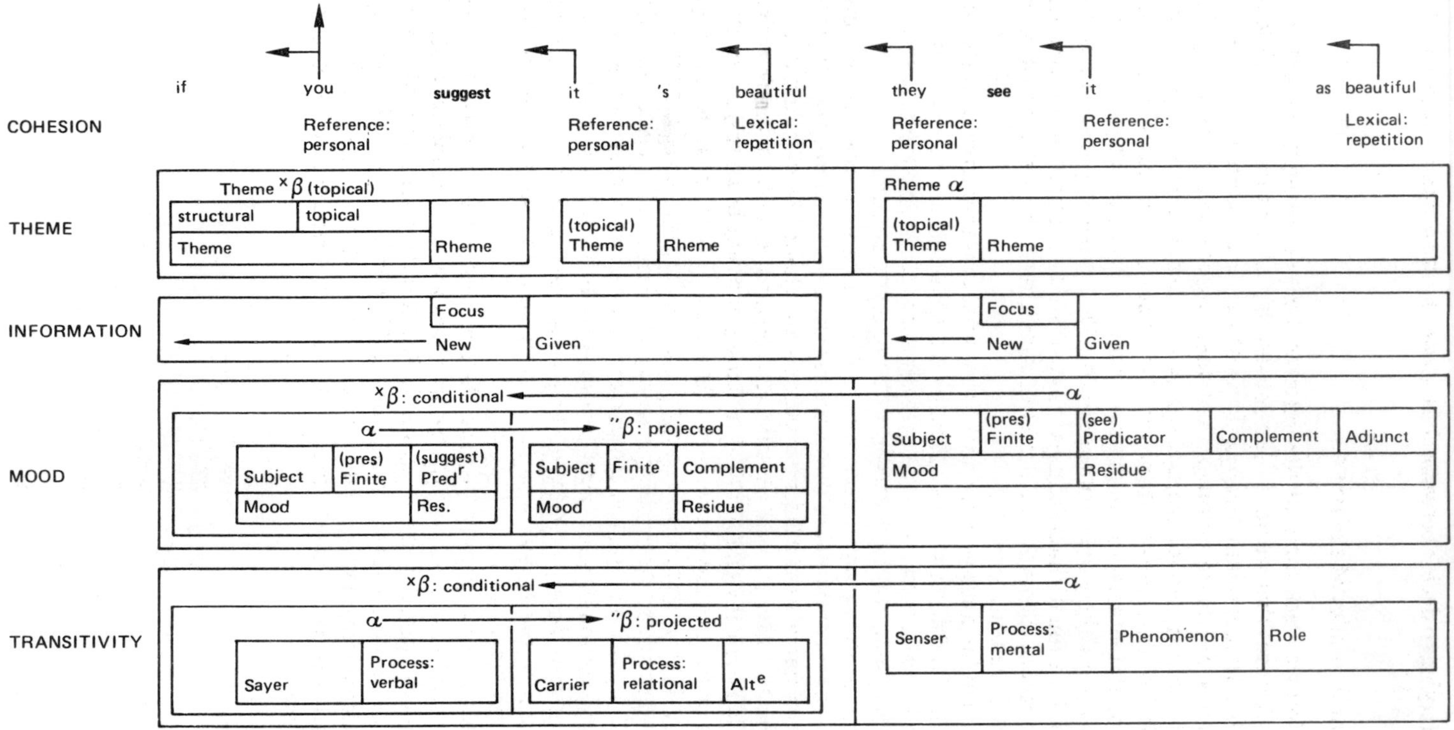

Figure A-12 Step 7 (clauses 13–14)

rather than trying to decide between the two we should probably accept both. See Figure A-12.

General characteristics of the text

In this section we trace some of the patterns that run through the text as a whole. The features that we have been considering are features that we identify through a lexicogrammatical analysis of the text, clause by clause, or clause complex by clause complex. But their significance in carrying the meaning of the text derives from the way they are woven throughout the whole fabric, both as separate strands and, even more, in interaction one with another. Not all features, of course, may turn out to be equally important; but there is always likely to be some patterning in the development and combination of ideational, interpersonal and textual meanings — aspects of transitivity, mood, theme and information, and cohesion — that constitutes the essence of the text.

In the present instance we may note certain patterns that emerge under all these headings, and especially two pairs of intersecting patterns: one textual, the intersection of cohesive chains with thematic structure; the other ideational-interpersonal, the intersection of mood and transitivity.

(1) Cohesion, theme and information. All texts display cohesive chains made up of some combination of lexical repetition and reference; a typical example from narrative would be a participant chain like *a little boy . . . John . . . he . . . him . . . he*. A 'chained' element may be a single entity within the clause, in any grammatical function; or it may be a complex entity, either thing or fact, of any extent up to the whole of the preceding text, e.g. [extended text] . . . *this argument . . . it . . . it*. In the silver text there are four cohesive chains: silver, Anne, love / beauty and buy / sell / customers. Of these, the first two represent simple entities; the third is also treated as a simple entity, although with considerable grammatical variation (*love* as noun, *love* as verb, *beauty, beautiful* etc.); while the fourth is first worded as a complex entity *the people that buy silver*, and then summed up in the reference item *they*.

These chains are interwoven through the text, around the motifs of 'silver is lovely (= lovable and beautiful)', 'people love beauty', 'people love silver' and 'you (must) bring out silver's beauty'. But the effectiveness of this interchaining depends on the textual structure, and in particular on the organization of the clauses into Theme and Rheme. Table A(1) shows the distribution of the occurences of 'chained' items in the message structure of each constituent clause.

Table A(1) Thematic distribution of lexicoreferential chains

	Theme:					Rheme:	
	Non-topical Themes		Chained topical Themes				
1	in this job				Anne	silver	
2		now	silver				love (n)
3			silver	people that buy		it	love (vb)
4	naturally	well	it			it	lovely [gleam]
5				they			
6				they			love beautiful [things]
7		so			you	[with] it	beautiful
8		and			you	it	[with] beauty
9	I'm sure				you		
10		oh but			you		
11					you		
12			that				beautiful
13	if				you	it	beautiful
14				they		it	beautiful

From this display we can see clearly what has been called the 'method of development' of the text. The whole of the first clause is thematic in the discourse: it is the 'topic sentence' of the 'paragraph', to use the terminology of composition theory. But it has its own Theme, a marked Theme *in this job*; and that goes on to function as the theme of the whole passage.

The job is concerned with silver; and in the next clause, introduced by the thematic continuative *now*, silver is transferred into the Theme. This is a temporary measure; it soon passes back into the Rheme, where it remains for the rest of the time — except for the dramatic interlude in clause 12 where Anne is being shown how to sell silver, and silver becomes the topic in an interpolated exclamation. Its thematic function in Step 2 (clauses 2 and 3) is to serve as a bridge to 'the customers', referred to as *the people that buy silver*; the customers now take over the development, though because of Anne's halfhearted response the manageress repeats the move, by way of explanation, in Step 3 (clauses 4–6). Hence there is a seesaw effect:

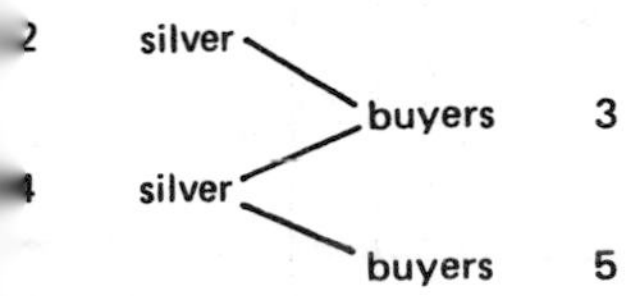

before the customers' thematic role is fulfilled.

Step 4, introduced by the thematic conjunctive *so*, begins the second part of the text, in which the consequences for Anne's behaviour are spelt out: 'so this is what you have to do'. Anne therefore now becomes the Theme, and, again with the exception of the manageress' dramatic interlude, takes over the development up to the final step. Finally, in clause 14, the Theme once again becomes *they*. The customers are brought back as the culminating Theme of the passage, since it is the nature of their response, after all, to which the discourse is ultimately directed.

Thus the thematic progression is: job – silver – customers – Anne – customers. Silver starts in the Rheme, becomes momentarily thematic, then settles down again in the Rheme. The customers and Anne occur throughout only as Theme. Love and beauty, on the other hand, occur only in the Rheme; they never enter into the line of development of the text. If we then consider the type of cohesion by which these entities are chained, we find that love and beauty are always referred to lexically — no less than ten times in this short passage; Anne and the customers, after the first occurrence, always referentially; while silver is mixed: it occurs three times lexically, thereafter always as *it*. The interplay of the cohesive forms with Theme and Rheme is shown in Table A(2):

Table A(2) Thematic status and cohesive type of chained elements (first occurrence omitted)

	Thematic status	Cohesive type
Anne	Theme	referential
customers	Theme	referential
love / beauty	Rheme	lexical
silver	Theme	lexical
	Rheme	referential

The first three are predictable enough, and are related to the fact that both the thematic structure and the information focus are largely unmarked throughout: the topical Theme is therefore mainly both Subject and Given, and we expect to find a pronoun in such a function complex. With silver, however, the position is reversed: it is referred to pronominally in the Rheme but lexically when functioning as Theme. The three lexical occurrences in quick succession, of which the second and third are foregrounded because they are in contexts where one would expect a pronoun, mark 'silver' out as occupying the centre of the stage. Its status once established, it is then displaced by the human participants and removed from prominence, becoming not only non-thematic but also non-focal, the most taken-for-granted position in the clause.

Thematic prominence is speaker-oriented: it expresses 'what I am on about' The manageress' concerns are exactly displayed by the 'thematic progression' referred to above. By contrast, informational prominence is listener-oriented: it expresses 'what's news to you' — or rather, since it is still assigned by the speaker, 'what I want you to attend to'. When we come to consider the status of love and beauty, we find they are marked by listener-oriented prominence, being New in no less than seven out of their ten occurrences, and focal in five of these. Since, obviously, only one out of the ten occurrences was a first occurrence, this is a very high proportion to be given the status of New, and it explains the impact of the love and beauty motif: it is this that the manageress wants to impress on Anne as the point of most significance. This is what she has to act on, in order to get the job done. Only three times is beauty reduced to a Given status, and this always in the context of a Process that is under focus as being Anne's task: once in ***sell** it with beauty*, and subsequently in the final two clauses which show how beauty is to be exploited: *if you **suggest** it's beautiful, they **see** it as beautiful*.

Some of the other items under focus are modalities, by which the manageress represents her point of view on the ongoing situation, switching the focus of attention from the ideational content to the interpersonal force. This in turn relates to the complementary patterns that emerge in the development of transitivity and mood; and these will be considered in the next section.

(2) Transitivity and mood. In steps 1–3, the manageress is describing the background to the job; and she uses transitivity patterns that are highly metaphorical. Silver is presented not only as something beautiful, and therefore an object of love, but also as something needing to be loved; and the customers are the lovers — lovers of beauty, therefore of beautiful things,

therefore of silver. Lexically there is play on the meaning of *lovely* ('lovable', 'beautiful') and also on the meaning of *silver* ('metal', 'ware'). This in turn is achieved through play on grammatical meaning; there are grammatical metaphors not only in the expression of 'needs to be loved' but also in the complex and ambiguous causal relation between the buying of silver and the loving of it — do they buy it because they love it, or do they love it because they buy it?

In steps 4–7, the discourse shifts to the task itself and Anne's role in carrying it out. As the manageress gets down to brass tacks she moves away from ideational metaphors. The first two clauses are perhaps transitional, as the point of the first part becomes clear: *so you have to be beautiful with it, and you sell it with beauty* — although even these clauses, while perhaps vague as regards the exact nature of the circumstantials with *with*, are not really metaphorical. For the remainder of the passage the transitivity structures are entirely 'straight' — typical, congruent expressions of the ideational semantic content.

When we come to look at the mood, the position is almost exactly reversed. Mood expresses the interpersonal force, and again there is a shift at step 4, where the manageress moves on from description of the background; but the movement this time goes the other way, from congruent to metaphorical. Steps 1–3 form a sequence of declarative clauses, all functioning congruently as statements. The manageress is setting the scene, and the expressions of mood are unambiguous and unmetaphorical: 'this is how things are'. There is no suggestion that any of it is a matter of opinion, so the clauses are also unmodalized — that is, until Anne begins to look dubious, when the manageress brings up reinforcements in the form of the modal *naturally*, meaning 'of course; you can see it for yourself'.

In steps 4–7 the pattern changes. At this point the manageress moves into the instructional mode: 'so this is what has to be done, in order to carry out the task'. The interpersonal structures now become more varied, and some are metaphorical. The declarative is used twice as a command, once with modulation, *you have to be beautiful with it*, and once without, *you sell it with beauty*. There is an exclamatory yes/no interrogative *isn't that beautiful!*; and there is a modality expressed as an attribute of the speaker *I'm sure*, followed up by another modality *oh but you must* which is elliptical and ambiguous, meaning (i) 'it is certain that you can do it' and (ii) 'it is necessary that you should do it'. It is not now the content that is being embellished; it is the force, the interactive element in the discourse. The manageress is giving Anne orders; but she is dressing them up as speech acts of other kinds. And this reflects the ambiguity of the role relationship between them. The relationship of manageress to new salesgirl embodies the three components of senior to junior, expert to novice, and teacher to apprentice; to which by virtue of her personality the manageress adds another, that of mother to daughter. These can be seen not only in the mood and modality but also in other interpersonal features such as the tendency to include Anne and herself within one wording: *Anne, we . . .*; *let's . . . .* This is kept up right to the end, when the final clause complex, while expressed as a conditional declarative, embodies the injunction 'what you must do is suggest to them that it's beautiful'; provided you do that, the appropriate result will follow.

Table A(3) Ideational and interpersonal metaphor

Steps: \ Component:	transitivity	mood
1–3	metaphorical	congruent
4–7	congruent	metaphorical

Thus the ideational and interpersonal meanings show a complementary movement between the metaphorical and the non-metaphorical, as shown in Table A(3). This reflects the organization of the discourse around the two tasks of exposition and injunction, the one following the other. The exposition (explanatory description) is characterized by metaphorical expression of the content and congruent expression of the force: the nature of the process is disguised, the nature of the speech act is not. The injunction, on the other hand, is characterized by congruent expression of the content and metaphorical expression of the force: the nature of the process is not disguised, but the nature of the speech act is. And this underlines the importance of metaphor in ordinary discourse, since in each case it is brought in to help with that component that is critical to the move in question — ideational in the first part, and interpersonal in the second.

Here finally is a representation of the context of situation of this text, the 'contextual configuration' of field, tenor and mode. Field refers to the nature of the social action: what it is the interactants are about. Tenor refers to the statuses and role relationships: who is taking part in the interaction. Mode refers to the rhetorical channel and function of the discourse: what part the text is playing. These could be summarized as follows.

(1) Field. (a) General. Retail selling in department store: silver department. Task: selling silverware. (b) Specific. Instruction of new member. Task: teaching how to sell silverware. Means of achievement: [premise 1] virtues of silver, [premise 2] customers' appreciation thereof, [action] encouragement of this appreciation.
(2) Tenor. Manageress and new salesgirl; a complex status relationship embodying (a) senior–junior, (b) expert–novice, (c) teacher–apprentice; with a fourth, personal relationship at a metaphorical level, (d) mother–daughter.
(3) Mode. Natural, spontaneous speech. One-sided dialogue (monologue with acknowledgments). Part 1, expository: exposition – doubt – explanation. Part 2, exhortatory: injunction – doubt – illustration and reassurance.

The structure of the text, by which this configuration is realized, could be set out as in Table A(4).

Table A(4) Structure of the text

Step	Clauses		
	1	Initiation: announcement of task 'the job is . . .'	
	2–3	Enunciation of conditions on achievement 'silver is . . .; customers . . .'	exposition: indicative mode (information)
		Anne unconvinced 'I doubt whether it is so (maybe it is)'	exposition: indicative mode (information)
	4–6	Explanation of conditions 'because silver is . . ., customers . . .'	exposition: indicative mode (information)
	7–8	Prescription of required behaviour 'so this is what you have to do'	injunction: imperative mode (goods-&-services)
		Anne unconvinced 'I doubt whether I can do (maybe I can)'	injunction: imperative mode (goods-&-services)
	9–10	Reassurance and reassertion 'you can, and you have to'	injunction: imperative mode (goods-&-services)
	11–12	Demonstration of required behaviour 'here's how'	injunction: imperative mode (goods-&-services)
	13–14	Conclusion: prediction of fulfilment 'do that and you'll succeed'	

An analysis of this kind has two aims, one being a higher variant of the other. The first aim is to show why the text means what it does. The second aim, more difficult of attainment, is to show why it is valued as it is — why it is effective, or not effective, in relation to its purpose, or as a specimen of its kind.

It is impossible to achieve the second aim without the first: evaluation rests on interpretation.

Some texts are consciously and carefully planned, executed and polished. Others, like the present one, are spontaneous and unselfconscious. A text of either kind may succeed or fail, in relation to its various functions; most discourse falls somewhere in between the rhetorical ideal and the total flop. But it is a mistake to think that success depends on conscious planning, or that spontaneous discourse is formless and unstructured. It is clear that the present text is very highly organized in relation to the task in hand. Whether Anne in fact sold any silverware we do not know; but the linguistic interpretation of her first encounter with the job suggests that she probably got off to a good start.

Appendix 2

A note on the grammar of little texts

It was pointed out in the Introduction that, at the present state of our knowledge about language, we cannot yet write 'the semantics of English'; we can describe only the semantics of this or that particular register, or of a particular body of text. We can on the other hand make an attempt at 'the grammar of English'. A grammatical description can never be complete; but as far as it goes it can be comprehensive, covering all functional varieties of the language.

This is possible because, for the most part, grammar is not specialized according to language use; a grammar is a grammar for all texts. Different registers select and foreground different options within the grammar, but do not normally have a special grammar of their own. This is not to imply that different registers necessarily have a specialized semantic system, or that there can never be a comprehensive semantic description covering all functional varieties; only to point out that linguistics has not yet reached the stage where it can provide one.

At the same time, even grammar is only more or less the same for all varieties; some registers do have fairly distinct grammars. It is obviously not possible to take much account of this in a short introduction; some indication of the sort of variation that may occur has been given in the discussion of metaphor, showing that grammatical metaphor is particularly a feature of the written mode. But the distinction of spoken and written, while it is a fundamental one, is still at a very general level.

There is one more specialized group of texts that deserves a mention here because these texts are often of interest in their own right, and that is the ones that might be called 'little' texts. There are certain texts which the context of situation determines have to be short, like telegrams and newspaper headlines; and, since they have to achieve quite a lot in that very limited space, they tend to have their own grammar for doing so, which differs in certain respects from the grammar of other registers of English not constrained by such limitations.

Examples include not only headlines and telegrams but also titles, product labels, certain kinds of instructions (some recipes, for example), signboards and lecture notes. The last may in fact be very long; but they tend to have the properties of short texts because they are highly condensed.

A first approximation to the grammar of little texts might be to say that they retain all the lexical words and leave out all the grammatical ones; this is the standard description of 'telegraphese', including the so-called 'telegraphic speech' of young children's speech in the transition from protolanguage to mother tongue, like *more meat!*, *light green*, *man clean car*. But while there is something in this, it is obviously not the whole story. Of course, not all little texts are alike; the label is a cover term for a number of more or less distinct varieties each of which has special features of its own. But we can observe certain general tendencies based on recognizable principles, and some of these are outlined below. Like every other topic in this book, each one could be the subject of an entire treatise on its own.

1. Nominals without deixis. Both nominal groups and verbal groups tend to shed those elements of structure that serve to link them with the here-&-now. Thus nominal groups occur without determiners; for example,

BANDIT THREATENS TO KILL MAN
TAKE KEY FROM LOCK
CRAMBO HITS BULLSEYE AS CAR OF YEAR

As for the first, if we were to 'translate' it into general English we should probably write *a bandit threatens to kill a man*. But we cannot simply equate these two one with the other, because there is no overall equivalence of function. If we were reporting this sensational event as a piece of news we would probably break it up into various quanta of information, beginning perhaps with an existential *there was this bandit . . .*

The second and third demand specific deictics: *take the key from the lock*, *hits the bullseye as the car of the year*. None of these however depends for its interpretation on any preceding text. The key and the lock are both there in view; *the bullseye* in this expression is homophoric (self-defining), *the year* is exophoric to the current year and *the car* is cataphoric to the defining Qualifier *of the year*. There are other environments in which *the* cannot be omitted: certain fixed expressions (cf. *whatever the weather* in the example below), and cases where it is necessary for making the uniqueness explicit, such as *the lotion for all skins*, where leaving out the *the* would destroy the message that being for all skins is a feature that uniquely defines this particular lotion.

2. Verbals without deixis. In similar fashion, verbal groups occur without the Finite element:

CABINET SEARCHING FOR A WAY OUT
LAWYERS TO STAND FIRM ON FEE RISE
PUBLIC CONFIDENCE SHAKEN

Here the primary, deictic tense is omitted, the effect being that the verbal group becomes non-finite. The reworded forms would presumably be *the cabinet are searching for a way out*, *the lawyers are to stand firm . . .*, *public confidence has been shaken*. Note that the second of these, *lawyers to stand firm*, represents, in non-finite form, the old future form *are to*, more usually now *are going to*.

We pointed out in Chapter 6, Section 6.3.3, that the use of System III of the verbal group neutralizes certain distinctions: for example, we cannot in fact tell whether to equate the second with *lawyers are (going) to stand firm* or with *lawyers will stand firm*. The third one might be either *confidence has been shaken* or *confidence was shaken*. It may be part of the meaning to avoid selecting in these systems, which in the general grammar would be obligatory in an independent clause; cf. the point made about the use of non-finite forms in dependent clauses, in Chapter 7, Section 7.4.4.

3. Mood. (i) A clause element which is obligatory in the general grammar may be omitted in a little text. This may be because the feature it realizes can readily be supplied, or because the reference is intended to apply to all cases, or to cases that are clearly defined. For example,

USE SPOOL AS IS FOR THESE MACHINES
SPIN DRYER WANTED, WILL PICK UP SAME DAY
WHATEVER THE WEATHER BRIMSHADE PROTECTS

In the first there is a Finite but no Subject; the meaning is clearly 'as it (the spool) is'; likewise in the second, 'the advertiser will pick it up'. In the second and third there is no Complement. The former presupposes *spin dryer* from the previous clause; note that although formally it appears as ellipsis, functionally this corresponds to reference in the general grammar (there is no ellipsis of a Complement alone). With the latter the sense is 'protects you and your property', or 'protects everything that needs protecting'. Perhaps the most common of all omission is that of Finite (/ Predicator) *be* in attributive clauses, e.g.

MARKET BUOYANT
CORRECT WEIGHT GUARANTEED
TURNER UNFIT TO PLAY

Here the principle is: supply the unmarked verb for the clause in question.

(ii) In some cases the clause simply evades the choice of mood; the writer is not making any specific selection. Here it is impossible to assign to a particular class of mood; or rather, it would be possible, but to do so would be to impute a specific meaning that is not demonstrably present. This is particularly common in titles, for example

TINTERN ABBEY REVISITED
DESTINATION PEKING
FACTS FROM FIGURES

These are clearly clause-like because they have a transitivity structure: Range – Process; Identified – Identifier; Medium – Location. But they have no speech function. In this respect they resemble 'absolute' nominal groups (see below, 4); but they differ from absolute nominals in that the examples above have a Theme – Rheme structure; the first element in each case (*Tintern Abbey*, *destination*, *facts*) is thematic, which is no doubt a reason for selecting a pattern of this kind. A type that has appeared more recently is one that has become common in road signs, for example

END FREEWAY CONDITIONS

This looks like an imperative, but it is not. Since it is no shorter than its general equivalent *freeway conditions end*, presumably the form is chosen for textual reasons, to get the thematic and informational prominence distributed in the most appropriate way.

(iii) In a third type, there is a selection of mood, but one that does not follow the patterns of the general grammar. For example,

MOTHER WILL MIND CHILD IN GOOD HOME

This is an offer; it means 'I (the advertiser) will'. But since the identity of the offerer is not recoverable from the context, she has to specify the relevant semantic features; in this case, that she belongs to the class of 'women who have and are currently caring for children'. In the general grammar such a clause would be likely to be interpreted as a statement, comparable to *one of the mothers will look after the children for the day*. (Such forms do occur as modulation: inclination, but in the third person; e.g. *Mother will look after the children for us — won't you, Mother?*)

(iv) Other variants include finiteless modulations such as

THIS WARRANTY TO BE RETURNED WITHIN THIRTY DAYS

where the *is* is omitted following the principle of no verbal deixis as in 2, above. Unlike *lawyers to stand firm*, however, the present example is a proposal, not a proposition. Not surprisingly, in view of their instability in the general grammar, it is proposals that receive the more distinctive treatment in little texts. Here is an example from a telegram:

ESSENTIAL ADVISE AVAILABILITY SEPTEMBER MISSION

'tell us whether you can get away on a job next September'.

4. Unattached nominals. Many little texts consist of just a nominal group in ABSOLUTE function, announcing simply that 'this is a / the . . . ' or 'there is / must be . . .'. Examples of these are product names, public announcements, headings, nameplates, street and building signs; for instance,

NEW RAIL LINK	*NO DECISION YET*
QUALITY TOMATOES	*DENTAL SURGERY*
A CHRISTMAS WISH	*CITY VIA HARBOUR BRIDGE*

One important class of such nominals is those that constitute instructions. Since a nominal group has no mood potential, it might seem difficult for it to function as an instruction; but there are grammatical means for ensuring that it does so. One that works for prohibitions is by adding an appropriate negative Deictic, sometimes also making the Thing a verbal noun:

NO THROUGH ROAD	*NO WAITING*

Positive nominals can however be equally effective as prohibitions, e.g. *shavers only* ('no other appliances must be plugged in'), *bus zone* ('so don't park!'), *flammable* ('don't strike a light!'), *private property* ('so keep off!'), *dead slow* ('don't drive fast!'). And some are positive injunctions, such as *litter* ('put it here!'), *interstate bookings* ('apply here for a ticket'), *way in*.

What is striking about these nominals is the amount of information, including of course interpersonal 'information' such as praise or denigration, that gets packed into them. It is here perhaps that little texts display the greatest grammatical ingenuity. We have noted at various places the tendency of English to package as much matter as possible into the nominal group; and also that there are good reasons for doing this — only nominals entertain all possible thematic variation. But there is no independent Theme - Rheme structure **within** a nominal group; so when the nominal group stands alone the aim is to communicate effectively without the unnecessary trappings — unnecessary in the context, that is — that accumulate with anything that is encoded as a clause: Process — Medium construct, explicit Subject and so on.

We end this sketch with a few observations about the special features of little texts consisting of absolute nominal groups.

(i) Clause-like Premodifiers allow some clausal relations to be incorporated while still not requiring all the features of a clause:

THE EASY-TO-SERVE SNACK CRACKER BISCUITS
THE ANCÒL WIN A FAMILY HOLIDAY COMPETITION
SAME DAY EMERGENCY PLUMBING SERVICE

(ii) Long strings of Classifiers were already referred to (Chapter 6, Section 6.2.5) as being characteristic of names of machine parts as well as of newspaper headlines; they occur in other functions besides:

SECURITY DOOR CHAIN GUARD
POKER MACHINE LOBBY INTERESTS
SLIDE VALVE TAIL ROD GLAND
OIL WINDFALL PROFITS TAX BILL
THIS MAGNIFICENT EXECUTIVE DOUBLE BRICK HOME

They may extend to even greater lengths:

5-PIECE FAMILY SIZE MIRROR POLISH FINISH STAINLESS STEEL TEA SET
UNEXPIRED SEASON TICKET DEPOSIT FACILITIES WITHDRAWAL CANCELLATION ORDER

(iii) We also find in these little texts collocations, especially of Classifier and Thing, that would be difficult and often ambiguous in the general grammar. For example, *tree policy*, in *tree policy switch*, would be unlikely elsewhere, even though it is obvious what it means; likewise *swim death*, *problem stains*, *control brief*. Others are impenetrable without the context; for example *bone worry* — the complete heading was *bone worry in space*, but even this is slightly opaque until one reads on and finds that 'astronauts' bones weaken and fail to grow properly in space', so in addition to our other anxieties we now have what an even more ingenious sub-editor might have diagnosed as a *space bone worry*.

Such examples are lexically innovative, but they do not run counter to any grammatical principles of the general grammar. In some instances, however, we would need to modify our description of the grammar; for example,

LIFT ROO QUOTA CALL
POLICE DRINK TEST TABLES REVIEW
GREEK SONG'S GET WINS AQUEDUCT DASH

Not all these texts of course are equally little; and some are little appendages to longer texts. Nevertheless they display interesting features in common which derive from their very specialized functions and are in some way related to the constraint in length. Then there are other kinds of text, not so little as these but also with clearly delimited boundaries, which also display particularities in their grammar: jokes, graffiti, short verses such as limericks, crossword clues, verses on greetings cards, potted biographies, public notices and so on. They are all part of the English language, and their grammar is part of the grammar of English, likewise capable of interpretation in functional terms.

Appendix 3

Variations on a causal theme

The logical-semantic relations of expansion and projection, and their subcategories, form the basis of the English clause complex. But at the same time they are very general relations that recur throughout the semantic system of the language and are manifested in various other environments in the lexicogrammar.

As an example, we find them directly represented in the transitivity system. The general category of expansion is what lies behind the 'relational' process type: in a relational process, one element is an expansion of another. More significantly, the subcategories of relational processes are analogous to those of the expanded clause complex:

(1) intensive	processes	('be')	are	elaborating
(2) possessive	,,	('have')	,,	extending
(3) circumstantial	,,	('be at')	,,	enhancing

1. Elaboration. If the 'elaborating' relationship is encoded as a relationship between processes, we get an appositive clause complex, paratactic or hypotactic; for example,

(a) paratactic $1 = 2$

Mary missed the party; she stayed at home.

(b) hypotactic $\alpha = \beta$

Mary missed the party, which was a pity ('Mary's missing the party')
Mary missed the party, which she regretted ('missing the party')
Mary missed the party, which everybody enjoyed ('the party')

The domain of the elaboration shifts with the shift from parataxis, where it is the whole clause, to hypotaxis, where it may be the whole clause or some part of it down to a single participant. In each case the same relationship of elaboration can be encoded as a process in its own right — that is, as a relationship between things, including of course complex things or 'macro-phenomena':

to stay at home	was	to miss the party
that Mary missed the party	was	a pity
missing the party	was	a regretful thing
the party	was	a thing everyone enjoyed

If we introduce an embedded clause, where the domain can only be a single nominal, we get

Mary missed the party =⟦ John gave on his birthday ⟧

to which the analogous relational clause would be

the party   was   the one John gave on his birthday

Notice that while the clause complex structures, paratactic and hypotactic, correspond to an attributive clause, where the 'is' relationship is non-exclusive, the embedded elaboration corresponds to an identifying clause, where the 'is' relationship is exclusive: the party is being identified as the one John gave on his birthday. Thus there is an analogy

identifying process : defining relative
::
attributive process : non-defining relative

2. Extension. The 'extending' relationship, as a relationship between processes, is essentially additive; it is the 'and' relation of co-ordination, as in *John came in and sat down*. As a relationship between things it is a kind of having. The basic meaning is that of adding something, a possession being an addition or increment to its possessor.

The possessive relation can be seen more clearly in co-ordination between nominal groups: *John and his friend* is agnate to *John has a friend*. But the general sense of addition is present in a paratactic clausal relation such as that seen in *Mary came in and sat down*, where the sitting down 'has' (is accompanied by, presupposes) the coming in.

Note in that connection the agnate hypotactic: non-finite clause complex *having come in, Mary sat down*, where the form of the verbal group embodies the *have* of the English secondary past (past in relation to . . .). That *have* likewise embodies the concept of extension: at stage *k*, here the sitting down stage, Mary 'possesses' stage *k-1*, by the addition of one process to which she reaches stage *k*.

3. Enhancing. The 'enhancing' relationship, which as a relationship between processes is one of conditioning or qualifying with some circumstantial feature, as a relationship between things is the process of 'being at (etc.)'; it corresponds in other words to a circumstantial relational clause. For example, if my heart leaps up when I behold a rainbow in the sky, then the

leaping 'is at' the beholding — the one provides the circumstance for the other.

There are large numbers of agnate expressions for relations of the enhancing kind, and in order to give a more detailed illustration of how these logical-semantic relations can be distributed throughout the grammar we shall follow through one particular example. Our text will be Hilaire Belloc's well-known stanza from *The Python*:

> I had an aunt in Yucatan
> Who bought a python from a man
>   And kept it for a pet.
> She died, because she never knew
> These simple little rules, and few; —
>   The Snake is living yet.

From this we shall take the fourth and fifth lines, simplifying them somewhat to save space, so as to read

> She died, because she didn't know the rules.

As a startingpoint, note that in the same way as with the elaborating and extending categories above, we can set up a paradigmatic set such as the following:

(a) paratactic clause complex
 She died; for she didn't know the rules.
(b) hypotactic clause complex
 She died, because she didn't know the rules.
(c) relational process clause: attributive / circumstantial
 Her death was because of her ignorance of the rules.

Again we could add an embedded version, which again would turn out to correspond to an identifying clause; but this time with two kinds, the one related to 'circumstance as participant' (the noun ***consequence***):

(d) embedded clause
 the reason ^{x}⟦ why she died ⟧
(e) relational process: identifying / circumstance as participant
 the consequence was her death

the other related to 'circumstance as process' (the verb *cause*):

(f) embedded clause
 her death ^{x}⟦ resulting from ignorance ⟧
(g) relational process: identifying / circumstance as process
 ignorance caused her death

At this point, let us break off to run more systematically through a set of variations on this causal theme, beginning with a manifestation which is not structural at all but cohesive, in terms of the category of 'conjunction' discussed in Chapter 9, Section 9.5 above.

I Two processes: grammatically unrelated

A. Cohesive

1 She didn't know the rules. Consequently, she died.	$1\ {}^{x}1$
2 She died. But then she didn't know the rules.	$1\ {}^{x}1$

Here the semantic relation of cause has been expressed by cohesion, specifically the conjunctive relation. The typical order is cause ^ effect, as in 1; but, as shown by 2, this can be reversed.

II Two processes: clause complex

B. Paratactic

1 She didn't know the rules; so she died.	$1\ {}^{x}2$
2 She died; for she didn't know the rules.	$1\ {}^{x}2$

Again the typical order is cause ^ effect; but this can be reversed by the use of *for* (in writing; or its spoken equivalent the phonologically weak form of *because* (Chapter 7, Section 7.4.3 above)).

C. Hypotactic

(a) finite

1 She died (,) because she didn't know the rules.	$\alpha\ {}^{x}\beta$
2 Because she didn't know the rules, she died.	${}^{x}\beta\ \alpha$

(b) non-finite

1 She died, through not knowing the rules.	$\alpha\ {}^{x}\beta$
2 Through not knowing the rules, she died.	${}^{x}\beta\ \alpha$

The unmarked order is now effect ^ cause, the cause being combined with the dependent clause. Note that in this α ^ β order, the dying may be either New or Given:

// ‸she / **died** // ‸be/cause she / didn't / know the / **rules** //
'I'm telling you (a) that she died, (b) why she died'

// ‸she / died be/cause she / didn't / know the / **rules** //
'you know she died; I'm telling you why'

Compare the ones under F below.

III One process; clause

D. Transitivity congruent: behavioural process

1 She	died	through ignorance of the rules
Behaver/Theme	Process	Cause

2 Through ignorance of the rules,	she	died.
Cause/Theme	Behaver	Process

Here 'cause = not knowing the rules' has been coded as a circumstantial element in the form of a minor process.

E. Transitivity incongruent: relational process, (i) attributive

(a) circumstantial (circumstance as Attribute)

Her death	was	through ignorance of the rules
Carrier	Process	Attribute/Cause

(b) intensive

Her death	was	due to ignorance of the rules
Carrier	Process	Attribute/Cause

Here the process 'die' has become Carrier of an Attribute expressing cause. In (a) the cause is expressed in a circumstantial prepositional phrase; in (b) it has been lexicalized in the adjective *due* functioning as Head of a nominal group.

F. Transitivity incongruent: relational process, (ii) identifying

(a) circumstantial (circumstance/cause as participant = Value)

1	{ The cause of her death (The reason) why she died }	{ was is given by }	{ her ignorance of the **rules**. (the fact) that she didn't know the **rules**. }
	Identified/Value/Cause		Identifier/Token
2	{ Her ignorance of the **rules** (The fact) that she didn't know the **rules** }	{ was gives }	{ the cause of her death. (the reason) why she died. }
	Identifier/Token		Identified/Value/Cause
3	{ Her ignorance of the rules (The fact) that she didn't know the rules }	{ was gives }	{ the cause of her **death**. (the reason) why she **died**. }
	Identified/Token		Identifier/Value/Cause
4	{ The cause of her **death** (The reason) why she **died** }	{ was is given by }	{ her ignorance of the rules. (the fact) that she didn't know the rules. }
	Identifier/Value/Cause		Identified/Token

For reasons given at the end of Chapter 5, Section 5.4 above, no. 4 is extremely unlikely; it is doubly marked, since it is a passive which has the opposite effect of that which is the typical reason for choosing the passive — it results in a marked, instead of an unmarked, information focus. It also corresponds to a highly unlikely reading of our text sentence:

She **died** because she didn't know the rules.

It was included here for the sake of completeness; but in the three sets below, the corresponding fourth member is omitted.

(b) circumstantial (circumstance/cause as process)

1 Her death / That she died } was caused by { her ignorance of the **rules**. / the fact that she didn't know the **rules**.

Identified/Value	Cause	Identifier/Token

2 Her ignorance of the **rules** / The fact that she didn't know the **rules** } caused her death.

Identifier/Token	Cause	Identified/Value

3 Her ignorance of the rules / The fact that she didn't know the rules } caused her **death**.

	Cause	Identifier/Value

(c) circumstantial (circumstance/effect as participant = Value)

1 The result of her ignorance of the rules was { her **death**. / that she **died**.

Identifier/Value/Result	Identified/Token

2 Her **death** / That she **died** } was the result of her ignorance of the rules.

Identifier/Token		Identified/Value/Result

3 Her death / That she died } was the result of her ignorance of the **rules**.

Identified/Token		Identifier/Value/Result

(d) circumstantial (circumstance/effect as process)

1 Her ignorance of the rules	was resulted in	by her **death**
Identified/Value	Result	Identifier/Token
2 Her **death** / That she **died**	resulted from	her ignorance of the rules.
Identifier/Token	Result	Identified/Value
3 Her death / That she died	resulted from	her ignorance of the **rules**.
Identified/Token	Result	Identifier/Value

Here is the usual rich crop of identifying clauses. Set out as a paradigm, of course, they look absurd. But all of them (and other variants could be added) represent patterns that occur all the time in everyday life. They vary both in their interpretation of the event and in their distribution of the information;

in the context of this particular example, some are more plausible than others, but each one could be derived as the form that would be predicted by a particular configuration of the features of the context of situation.

Not all semantic relations can be combined with such an array of different patterns of interdependency, transitivity, information structure and the like; but it is by no means untypical to find a systematic paradigm of this kind. All of them differ in meaning in some respect, and given a functional grammar we can say what that respect is.

Bibliography

The following is a selective list of works relating directly to the interpretation of English in a systemic-functional framework.

Where a volume of collected papers figures as an entry, articles appearing in that volume are in general not listed separately.

David Abercrombie, *Studies in Phonetics and Linguistics*. London: Oxford University Press (Language and Language Learning 10), 1965

James D. Benson and William S. Greaves (eds.), *Systemic Perspectives on Discourse: selected papers from the Ninth International Systemic Workshop*, Vols. 1 & 2. Norwood, NJ: Ablex, 1984

James D. Benson and William S. Greaves, *You and Your Language*. Oxford: Pergamon Press, 1984

Margaret Berry, *Introduction to Systemic Linguistics*. London: Batsford. Vol. 1: *Structures and systems*, 1975; Vol. 2: *Levels and links*, 1977

Margaret Berry, 'Systemic linguistics and discourse analysis: a multi-layered approach to exchange structure'. In Malcolm Coulthard and Martin Montgomery (eds.), *Studies in Discourse Analysis*, London: Routledge & Kegan Paul, 1981

Christopher S. Butler, *The Directive Function of the English Modals*. University of Nottingham Ph.D. thesis, 1982

Christopher S. Butler, *Systemic Linguistics: theory and applications*. London: Batsford (in press)

Eirian C. Davies, *On the Semantics of Syntax*. London: Croom Helm, 1979

Afaf Elmenoufy, *A Study of the Role of Intonation in the Grammar of English*. University of London Ph.D. thesis, 1969

Robin P. Fawcett, 'Some proposals for systemic syntax' Parts 1, 2 & 3, *MALS* (Midlands Association for Linguistic Study) *Journal*, 1.2, 2.1 & 2.2, 1974/75/76

Robin P. Fawcett, *Cognitive Linguistics and Social Interaction: towards an integrated model of a systemic functional grammar and the other components of a communicating mind*. Heidelberg: Julius Groos Verlag and Exeter: University of Exeter (Exeter Linguistic Studies 3), 1980

Robin P. Fawcett and M.A.K. Halliday (eds.), *New Developments in Systemic Linguistics*. London: Batsford (in press)

Peter H. Fries, 'On the status of theme in English: arguments from discourse'. *Forum Linguisticum* 6.1, August 1981 1–38. Also in János S. Petöfi and Emel Sözer (eds.), *Micro and Macro Connexity of Texts* Hamburg: Helmut Buske Verlag (Papers in Text Linguistics 45), 1983, 116–52

Michael Gregory, *English Patterns: perspectives for a description of English*. Toronto: Glendon College English Department, 1972

M.A.K. Halliday, *Intonation and Grammar in British English*. The Hague: Mouton (Janua Linguarum Series Practica 48), 1967

M.A.K. Halliday, 'Notes on transitivity and theme in English' Parts 1, 2 & 3. *Journal of Linguistics* 3.1, 3.2 & 4.2, 1967/68 37–81, 199–244 & 179–215

M.A.K. Halliday, 'Functional diversity in language, as seen from a consideration of modality and mood in English'. *Foundations of Language* 6, 1970 322–61 Also in Gunther R. Kress (ed.), 1976

M.A.K. Halliday, *Spoken and Written Language*. Geelong, Vic.: Deakin University Press (Language and Learning 5), 1985

M.A.K. Halliday & Ruqaiya Hasan, *Cohesion in English*. London: Longman (English Language Series 9), 1976

M.A.K. Halliday and Ruqaiya Hasan, *Language, Context and Text: a social-semiotic perspective*. Geelong, Vic.: Deakin University Press (Language and Learning 3), 1985

M.A.K. Halliday & J.R. Martin (eds.), *Readings in Systemic Linguistics*. London: Batsford, 1981

Ruqaiya Hasan, *A Linguistic Study of Contrasting Features in the Style of two Contemporary English Prose Writers*. University of Edinburgh Ph.D. thesis, 1964

Ruqaiya Hasan, 'Text in the systemic-functional model'. In Wolfgang U. Dressler (ed.), *Current Trends in Text Linguistics*, Berlin: de Gruyter (Research in Text Theory 2), 1978 228–46

Ruqaiya Hasan, 'Coherence and cohesive harmony'. In James Flood (ed.), *Understanding Reading Comprehension*, Newark, Delaware: International Reading Association, 1983 181–219

Ruqaiya Hasan, *Language, Linguistics and Verbal Art*. Geelong, Vic.: Deakin University Press (Language and Learning 6), 1985

R.D. Huddleston, R.A. Hudson, E.O. Winter and A. Henrici, *Sentence and Clause in Scientific English*. London: University College London, Communication Research Centre (OSTI Programme in the Linguistic Properties of Scientific English, Final Report), 1968

R.A. Hudson, 'Constituency in a systemic description of the English clause'. *Lingua* 18.3, 1967 225–50. Also in M.A.K. Halliday and J.R. Martin (eds.), 1981

R.A. Hudson, *English Complex Sentences: an introduction to systemic grammar*. Amsterdam: North Holland, 1971

Gunther R. Kress (ed.), *System and Function in Language: selected papers by M.A.K. Halliday*. London: Oxford University Press, 1976

William C. Mann and Christian M.I.M. Matthiessen, *Nigel: A Systemic Grammar for Text Generation*. Marina del Rey: University of Southern California Information Sciences Institute (RR-83-105), 1983. Also in James D. Benson and William S. Greaves (eds.), 1984

J.R. Martin, 'Conjunction: the logic of English text'. In Janos S. Petöfi and Emel Sözer (eds.), *Micro and Macro Connexity of Texts*, Hamburg: Helmut Buske Verlag (Papers in Text Linguistics 45), 1983, 1–72

J.R. Martin, *English Text: system and structure*. Oxford: Frances Pinter (forthcoming)

J.R. Martin and P. Peters, 'On the analysis of exposition'. In Ruqaiya Hasan (ed.), *Discourse on Discourse: reports from the Macquarie Workshop in Discourse Analysis*, Applied Linguistics Association of Australia (Occasional Paper 7), 1984

J.R. Martin and Joan Rothery, 'What a functional approach to the writing task can show teachers about "good writing" '. In Barbara Couture (ed.), *Functional Approaches to Writing Research*, London: Frances Pinter (forthcoming)

James Muir, *A Modern Approach to English Grammar: an introduction to systemic grammar*. London: Batsford, 1972

Clare Painter, *Into the Mother Tongue*. Oxford: Frances Pinter (Open Linguistics series), 1984

Joan Rothery, 'The development of genres — primary to junior secondary school'. In Frances Christie (ed.), *Children Writing: study guide*, Geelong, Vic.: Deakin

University Press (ECT 418 Language Studies), 1984, 67–114

John McH. Sinclair, *A Course in Spoken English: Grammar*. London: Oxford University Press (Part 3 of Ronald Mackin, M.A.K. Halliday and John McH. Sinclair, *A Course in Spoken English*), 1972

Jean A. Ure and Jeffrey Ellis, *Patterns and Meanings: an introduction to systemic grammar and its application to the description of registers in contemporary English*. London: Allen & Unwin, 1985

Terry Winograd, *Language as a Cognitive Process: Vol. 1, Syntax*. Reading, Mass.: Addison Wesley, 1983

David J. Young, *The Structure of English Clauses*. London: Hutchinson (Hutchinson University Library), 1980